Handbook of Vocational Psychology

Theory, Research, and Practice

Second Edition

Contemporary Topics in Vocational Psychology
W. Bruce Walsh and Samuel H. Osipow, Series Editors

Handbook of
Vocational Psychology

Theory, Research, and Practice

Second Edition

Edited by

W. Bruce Walsh
Samuel H. Osipow
Ohio State University

LEA LAWRENCE ERLBAUM ASSOCIATES, PUBLISHERS
1995 Mahwah, New Jersey

Lawrence Erlbaum Associates, Inc., Publishers
10 Industrial Avenue
Mahwah, New Jersey 07430

Cover design by Kate Dusza

Library of Congress Cataloging-in-Publication Data

Handbook of vocational psychology : theory, research, and practice /
edited by W. Bruce Walsh and Samuel H. Osipow. — 2nd ed.
p.   cm. — (Contemporary topics in vocational psychology)
Includes bibliographical references and index.
ISBN 0-8058-1374-8
1. Vocational guidance—Psychological aspects. 2. Career
development—Psychological aspects. 3. Occupations—Psychological
aspects. 4. Personality and occupation. I. Walsh, W. Bruce, 1936–
II. Osipow, Samuel H. III. Series.
HF5381.H1335 1995
158.6—dc20   95-12229
                                                            CIP

Books published by Lawrence Erlbaum Associates are printed on acid-free paper,
and their bindings are chosen for strength and durability.

Printed in the United States of America
10 9 8 7 6 5 4 3 2 1

Contents

Preface

The objectives for this second edition of the *Handbook of Vocational Psychology* are very similar to those of the first edition: (a) to make readers aware of the practical and applied aspects of the field and to prepare them to maintain an academically based objectivity about the field; (b) to familiarize readers with a variety of techniques, procedures, and theories available for vocational assessment; (c) to realistically assess the significance of vocational psychology for professional functioning and for societal development; and (d) to stimulate colleagues and students to make a commitment to continued professional growth in theory, practice, and research in the field of vocational psychology.

Here in the second edition of the handbook, as in the first edition, the chapter authors were encouraged, not only to review the salient research and theoretical literature in their chapter topic area, but also to analyze and synthesize the current work. The quality of their contributions is clearly a credit to them and to the field of vocational psychology. We wish to acknowledge and congratulate the authors for their hard work and diligence in approaching the task.

The second edition of the handbook is made up of two parts: Theory and Research and Practice and Other Applications.

Despite similarities to the first edition, this revision departs from its predecessor in some interesting respects. For example, the second edition of the handbook has three chapters focusing on diversity: a chapter examining theoretical issues and cross-cultural career development, a chapter on career counseling with racial/ethnic minorities, and a chapter on international cross-cultural career development. Two chapters focus on assessment: a chapter on research in career assessment and a chapter focusing on integrating career assessment into counseling. Although these two content areas (diversity and assessment) were covered in the first edition of the handbook, the coverage in the second edition is much more comprehensive. New content areas covered in the second edition include an analysis of the interactional perspective in vocational psychology, a discussion of career counseling and psychotherapy, and an examination of current professional issues in vocational psychology. Thus, this second edition of the handbook attempts to keep pace with the field's change, examining key developments since the first edition, but with an eye on the future and potential new directions in the field. Overall, we believe this volume reveals yet again the continuing dynamic growth and vigor in vocational psychology.

—*W. Bruce Walsh*
—*Samuel H. Osipow*

Introduction

W. Bruce Walsh
Samuel H. Osipow
The Ohio State University

Theory

The first part of this handbook consists of five chapters covering current theoretical issues in vocational psychology, the interactional perspective in vocational psychology, theoretical advances in the study of women's career development, a framework for adult career development theory and intervention, and theoretical issues in cross-cultural career development.

The first chapter on current theoretical issues in vocational psychology by Mark Savickas concentrates on two issues that seem to be of overriding importance. Each issue as noted by Savickas involves a substantial intellectual problem to be solved. The first issue deals with convergence, that is, whether or not vocational psychologists should work to unify existing theories of career choice and development. The second issue examined focuses on divergence, namely, the efforts to use postmodern thought to move beyond logical positivism as the philosophy of science for theory and research about vocational behavior. Savickas identifies convergence and divergence as the two fundamental issues in contemporary vocational psychology based on the belief that they structure and maintain the most frequently debated theory and practice questions in vocational psychology. These two theoretical issues give rise to and prompt vocational psychologists' central problems, which separate theory from practice, vocational psychology from basic psychology disciplines, career counseling from psychotherapy, and vocational research agendas from other research agendas. Savickas suggests that much of vocational psychology can be characterized as shaped by or directed at these four theoretical schisms.

The chapter by Judy Chartrand, Stanley Strong, and Lauren Weitzman examines the interactional view of vocational development by reviewing three paradigms that guide interactional research. In the first perspective, traditionally called *person by environment*, person and environment are conceived of as independent entities. This perspective dominates in vocational psychology. Investigators working within this perspective typically seek to describe persons and environments using commensurate dimensions and to demonstrate that the degree of fit between the two sets of measures predicts behavior. In the second perspective, which the authors label *systemic*, person and environment are conceived of as interdependent entities that dynamically interact as reciprocal parts of a unified system. This perspective is apparent in theories of career development. The third perspective, *constructionist*, suggests that divisions between person and environment are artificial distinctions constructed for pragmatic purposes. Investigators emerging from this perspective have focused on the construction and meaning of career narratives. The authors attempt to provide a clear picture of these three paradigms and correspondent philosophical assumptions that guide interactional vocational research. A main purpose of the chapter is to improve translation between the levels of paradigm, theory, and research implementation. The authors suggest that some of the difficulties in current person–environment vocational research stem from a failure to make connections across each level.

The chapter by Louise Fitzgerald, Ruth Fassinger, and Nancy Betz attempts to summarize what is known about women's career development. The chapter provides an overview, not only of the content of knowledge in the area, but also of the way that knowledge has unfolded, developed, and changed across the approximately 25 years that it has been an active field of study. The authors begin with the recognition that the study of women's relationship to work is more complicated than that of men, requiring the identification and study of concepts and variables previously unnecessary and ignored. After a brief review of these developments, which the authors label *pre-theoretical*, they move to a discussion of the initial attempts to theorize about women's vocational behavior. These attempts reflect the early descriptive work and presage the more comprehensive efforts that followed. In the later half of the chapter, the authors examine the major theories of vocational choice and adjustment, focusing on their usefulness and limitations for explaining women's behavior, and conclude with a review of the gender frameworks that arose in the 1980s. Throughout the chapter, the authors examine two themes: First, that women's career development is unique because of the intertwining of work and family in their lives and that, paradoxically, its study can lead to more general insights about vocational behavior.

The chapter by Fred Vondracek and Tomotsugu Kawasaki, focusing on a framework for adult career development theory, suggests that contemporary conceptualizations of adult career development must take into account the increased complexity and interdependency of the world of today. They must reflect the significant advances in theory and research that have been made over the recent decades. Also, in order to have broad applicability, conceptualizations of adult career development must reflect the almost staggering variety of paths that may be chosen and pursued in the course of any individual work life. The authors assume that almost everyone engages in behaviors that can be construed as work during significant portions of the lifespan. These work behaviors may be a coherent, planful pattern of behaviors designed to move the individual from a beginning to an advanced level of work in an organization, or they may be a succession of jobs whose only unifying feature is the fact that they are necessary for the individual's survival. The basic assumption is that as individuals develop throughout their adult lives, their work activities, be they highly organized or not, reflect their ontogeny and may, therefore, be properly studied as career development. In this chapter, the authors endeavor to show how the application of a complex model of human development is essential for understanding adult career development, and that it can be done in a comprehensible and practical way. From this perspective, the chapter may be viewed as an extension of efforts initiated by Vondracek and his colleagues a number of years ago in their presentation of a developmental contextual approach to lifespan career development. The authors rely extensively upon the developmental systems theory proposed by D. Ford and Lerner (1992) as a synthesis of the developmental contextual perspective originally proposed by Lerner and D. Ford's living systems framework. In addition, the authors utilize M. Ford's recent formulations of motivational systems theory, which are derived from the living systems framework, to demonstrate the centrality of motivational factors in adult career development.

The final chapter in this section by Frederick Leong and Michael Brown examines the theoretical issues in cross-cultural career development. The chapter is divided into six sections. The first section is concerned with presenting a brief historical perspective. The next two sections focus on the cultural validity dimension. Initially, the authors provide a critique of majority career theories from a cultural validity perspective. The central problem they note with most, if not all, of the majority career theories is that they lack cultural validity for racial and ethnic minority groups in this country. The authors discuss why these theories lack cultural validity from conceptual and empirical points of view. In the third section, the authors review the current status of tests of the cultural validity of those career choice theories for racial and ethnic minority group individuals. In the fourth section, a transition is made to a focus on cultural specificity. If majority theories lack cultural validity, then what they lack are culture specific considerations. This section is then concerned with culture specific theories and their relation to ethnic minority career development. In addressing the cultural specificity dimension, the section highlights the role of cultural specific constructs such as acculturation among Asian Americans in the vocational behavior of culturally different individuals. The fifth section, also concerned with cultural specificity, takes a comparative view. Here the authors review cultural comparative studies of career development to illustrate how ethnic minorities are different and similar to European Americans. The sixth and final section of the chapter consists of a discussion of the directions for future research and theory development.

Research

This part of the handbook consists of two chapters, one describing research in career assessment prepared by Gail Hackett and Edward Watkins and the other describing the process and outcome of career counseling written by Jane Swanson.

A major goal of the chapter by Gail Hackett and Edward Watkins focusing on research in career assessment is to selectively review the status and trends in career assessment since the publication of the first *Handbook of Vocational Psychology*. More specifically, the authors attempt to update the coverage provided in the Zytowski and Borgen's (1983) chapter of the first handbook. Within this context, the authors followed Betz' (1992) lead in organizing their discussion around the topics of the assessment of (a) individual difference variables (aptitudes, abilities, interests, needs, and values); (b) career process variables (career decision making, career maturity, and adult career adjustment); and (c) career related cognitions (career beliefs and self-efficacy). In each section, some attention is devoted to issues, trends, and new developments as well as the overarching issues of ethnicity and gender in career assessment.

Overall, the authors note that research on career assessment since the publication of the last *Handbook of Vocational Psychology* has continued at a pace consistent with historical trends. The cognitive shift in psychology is one of the most important influences on contemporary vocational research, as evidenced in the career assessment literature by the appearance of several new scales, but also by the increasing attention to career cognitions and cognitive assessment within various theoretical traditions. In any event, research also continues on the mainstays of career assessment: interests, abilities, values, career decision making, and career maturity. The authors are reluctant to prophesize future research trends, but they do make two very broad predictions. They suggest that one wave of the future may be greater movement toward combined assessments of interests, abilities, and various other individual difference dimensions. Secondly, they suggest an increasing emphasis on revising existing instruments and developing new measures to more adequately capture the gender and ethnic diversity of our clientele, the school systems, and workforce. The latter trends, an outcome of shifting demographics and societal pressures, will no doubt continue to exert an important influence on all areas of vocational research in future years.

The chapter by Jane Swanson on the process and outcome of career counseling examines career counseling, but not the larger body of literature defined as *career interventions*. The author notes that the narrower focus was purposely chosen for a number of reasons. First, activities associated specifically with career counseling may be obscured in previous efforts to evaluate the entire body of career intervention literature. Second, career counseling seems to be the core of career intervention, yet we do not have an adequate empirical description of what occurs, either in content or in process, during career counseling. Thus, we need to investigate whether the literature supports the use of career counseling over other less costly interventions. An additional reason to focus specifically on career counseling is that a discussion of process implies the existence of an interaction of a psychological nature. Career interventions is a broad category which includes wide variability in terms of content, methods of delivery, and even whether human interaction occurs at all. On the other hand, career counseling, if clearly defined, entails the kind of psychological interaction that we usually refer to as *process*. If we are to study process and outcome in tandem, a focus on career counseling rather than career intervention is necessary.

Thus, the primary goal of this chapter is to provide an overview of the status of research on process and outcome in career counseling. The chapter is divided into four sections. The introductory section sets the stage with a discussion of the interrelationship of career and personal counseling, how career counseling is viewed by counseling psychologists, and the goals of process and outcome research. The second and third sections review process and outcome research in career counseling, respectively. The final section provides a summary and proposes some directions for future research.

In the final section of the chapter, Swanson proposes three general goals for career counseling research: (a) to evaluate the outcomes specifically of career counseling, (b) to examine the process of career counseling, and (c) to link process and outcome variables in career counseling research. Other recommendations are as follows. First, Swanson recommends that we need to refocus our research to include the human interaction in career counseling. Second, further questions should be addressed regarding outcome of career interventions. For example, why are most career interventions effective? Even brief, almost superficial interventions have positive impact. We need to know for whom and under what conditions career interventions are effective. Third, Swanson believes we need studies that provide true evaluations of the outcome of career counseling. Fourth, it is recommended that we begin to address process issues in career counseling. Swanson believes that process research is one way to refocus attention on the psychological component of career counseling. Finally, process and outcome variables need to be studied in tandem. What is it about individual career counseling that is effective? What role does the counselor/client relationship play in effective career counseling? How do counselors choose interventions to creative an effective treatment experience?

Practice and Other Applications

This part of the handbook consists of six chapters including career assessment, career counseling and psychotherapy, career counseling with racial and ethnic minorities, cross-cultural career development, professional issues, and leading edges of vocational psychology.

The chapter by Linda Subich and Kathleen Billingsley focuses on career assessment issues and techniques relevant to career counseling with specific client populations. Additionally, the authors have emphasized the role of career assessment in the process of career counseling and, when possible, highlighted the integration of assessment results into career counseling. Stated differently, the chapter is an attempt to showcase the treatment utility of career assessment. The authors have chosen a broad view of career assessment, believing that, although objective and quantitative assessment information are clearly valuable, this information should be integrated with clinical and qualitative assessment data to provide a more comprehensive understanding of the individual client. The notion of comprehensive career assessment highlights an underlying assumption of this chapter, that of the critical importance of attending to individual differences. Within this context, the authors have structured their presentation into six sections: women, racial and ethnic minority group members, gay and lesbian career clients, the gifted, adults in transition, and disabled individuals. Each section focuses on the career assessment issues and strategies relevant to the particular client group.

The chapter by David Blustein and Paul Spengler is designed to provide an informed analysis of the complex issues relating to the interface of career and psychotherapeutic interventions. The perspective presented by the authors here is that career counseling and psychotherapy are closely intertwined processes with the most obvious differences existing in the domain of treatment emphasis. Despite the recent extensive calls for the integration of career counseling and psychotherapy, a conceptual framework to guide the integrative treatment and necessary research efforts has not been available. As a means of examining this shortcoming, this chapter: (a) summarizes the current state of knowledge of the relationships among career counseling, psychotherapy, and personal and vocational adjustment, (b) explores new areas of potential theoretical integration, and (c) provides a perspective to direct subsequent inquiry and theoretical developments in this area. Suggestions for practice, research, and training emerge from the analysis and conclude the chapter.

In a discussion of implications for training, Blustein and Spengler suggest that counselors ought to be prepared to work with clients across the array of relevant domains, including career and noncareer contexts. As such, according to the authors, it is important to note that competence in career counseling and psychotherapy require skills in both domains. Thus, they propose that counselors and psychologists who endeavor to integrate these domains be trained in a comprehensive fashion that includes knowledge of personality theory, developmental psychology, assessment, counseling theory and research, career development theory, as well as in occupational sociology, organizational psychology, and related areas. In addition, they believe that supervised experience in delivering career and noncareer services is necessary. Thus, for those psychotherapists interested in career intervention, it is important to employ the rich knowledge base developed by vocational psychologists. At the same time, for those career counselors who wish to broaden their interventions into the noncareer domain, an equally critical task is the development of skills and knowledge in psychotherapy.

The chapter by Nadya Fouad and Rose Bingham focusing on career counseling with racial and ethnic minorities begins by making several assumptions. The first is that effective career counseling takes place within a cultural context. This is true for all clients, regardless of ethnicity. A second assumption is that variables to consider in career counseling across cultures may differ, and the weight placed on those variables may differ across cultures. Thus, it may be that all clients consider family pressures and obligations, but differ in the importance that familial commitments play in their career decisions. A third assumption is that current theoretical models may not adequately explain the career behaviors of racial and ethnic minorities. Fourth, vocational assessment must be culturally sensitive, and that only culturally appropriate tools may be used in vocational assessment. Finally, the authors are approaching cultural differences in career counseling from the perspective of cultural diversity or pluralism rather than cultural deprivation or cultural deficit. By this they mean that cultural differences are acknowledged and valued.

Within the aforementioned context, the authors briefly discuss the changing demographics of the United States, the role of world views and racial identity development in career counseling. Next they examine specific variables that influence ethnic minority clients' career decision making. They then critique the models of career counseling with ethnic minorities for their incorporation of cultural variables. Finally, they propose a model for career counseling with ethnic minorities. This is a seven-step model consisting of the following: (1) Establish rapport and culturally appropriate relationship, (2) Identify career issues, (3) Assess the impact of cultural variables, (4) Structure counseling goals, (5) Develop culturally appropriate counseling interventions, (6) Facilitate the decision-making process, and (7) Implementation and follow-up.

The chapter by Beryl Hesketh and James Rounds examining international cross-cultural approaches to career development focuses on fundamental issues that may facilitate or hinder the generalization of vocational theories, either across cultures within one country, within cultures across countries, or across both cultures and countries. The authors also outline the approaches and criteria that would be needed in order to develop theories that more accurately identify the components that generalize and those that do not, taking into account assumptions associated with absolutism, relativism, and universalism. The discussion is followed by a review of several ideas derived from the cross-cultural literature that provide a potential basis for evaluating which aspects of existing theories of career choice and development are likely to generalize and which are bound by time, country, or culture. This discussion highlights the value of models arising from the cross-cultural literature by presenting examples of core constructs in vocational psychology (self-concept, self-efficacy, interests, and career choice) and by illustrating how these do or do not take on different meanings in different cultures. Finally, the authors provide a set of principles to guide the development of theories able to be more accurate about the extent to which they apply internationally and cross-culturally.

The chapter by John Krumboltz and David Coon identifies and discusses some of the major professional issues facing the profession. The authors organize them under four major headings: (1) Responding to a changing world, (2) Providing greater service to clients, (3) Training and nurturing career professionals, and (4) Evaluating outcomes.

The authors note that the changing nature of work and the workforce and the expanding parameters of our field fuel a variety of professional issues. These factors influence measurement outcomes, the components of effective career counseling, needed training and supervision, the structure of career education program, ethics, and research. In providing greater service to clients, Krumboltz and Coon propose that the number one task of career counselors and educators is to promote learning about skills, interests, beliefs, values, work habits, and personal qualities that are relevant to the creation of a satisfying life. In the area of training and nurturing career professionals, the authors note that we need to demonstrate to clients, employers, and students that, in our own work environments, we can increase respect for individuality and collaboration, enable employees to develop their potential, and manage the diversity of a multicultural work world in a way that enriches our agencies, organizations, and training programs. Finally, in evaluating outcomes, Krumboltz and Coon note that interventions focused on learning require the identification and targeting of needed skills and knowledge, the design and monitoring of learning activities to assist the career development process, and the assessment of changes in peoples' behaviors, self-perception, and views of their environment.

The concluding chapter by Fred Borgen highlights several features of the chapters in the handbook. Borgen comments on his personal reactions to these chapters, most of which focus on a particular set of leading edges of the current field of vocational psychology. His comments were motivated to stimulate the reader and sharpen for readers the differences and similarities among the chapters. From his perspective, they are a diverse set of manuscripts, reflecting the healthy vigor and diversity that characterizes the current field of vocational psychology. Borgen notes that the chapters are particularly diverse in the way that they approach science, from the traditional to the postmodern and from the quantitative to the qualitative ways of knowing. Finally, Borgen generates a list of questions about the discipline of vocational psychology, focusing on its products, its people, and its processes.

REFERENCES

Betz, N. E. (1992). Career assessment: A review or critical issues. In S. D. Brown & R. W. Lent (Eds.), *Handbook of counseling psychology* (2nd ed.) (pp. 453–484). New York: Wiley.

Ford, D. H., & Lerner, R. M. (1992). *Developmental systems theory: An integrative approach.* Newbury Park, CA: Sage.

Zytowsky, D. G., & Borgen, F. (1983). Assessment. In W. B. Walsh & S. H. Osipow, (Eds.), *Handbook of vocational psychology* (Vol. 2, pp. 5–40). Hillsdale, NJ: Lawrence Erlbaum Associates.

PART ONE

THEORY AND RESEARCH

THEORY

Current Theoretical Issues in Vocational Psychology: Convergence, Divergence, and Schism

Mark L. Savickas
Northeastern Ohio Universities College of Medicine

The word *issue* denotes some opposition or differing points of view. Several important theoretical questions or problems in vocational psychology are currently *at issue*, meaning in dispute and to be decided. In this chapter, I concentrate on two issues that seem to be of overriding importance. Each issue involves a substantial intellectual problem to be resolved, and both arouse more than the usual excitement engendered by a scholarly challenge. Because the fundamental direction that the discipline will follow is at issue, each problem elicits strong emotional responses from individuals who are deeply involved in vocational psychology and creates personal tension among colleagues who advocate opposing positions on an issue. I invite the reader to *join issue* in the sense of entering the argument and supporting one of the conflicting beliefs about each topic or even to *take issue* with the existing opinions and to state another conviction about the matter. Eventually, every vocational psychologist will participate in courses of action strongly influenced by his or her views about the two theoretical issues examined herein.

The first issue examined in this chapter deals with *convergence*, that is, whether or not vocational psychologists should work to unify existing theories of career choice and development. The second issue examined addresses *divergence*, namely, the efforts by vocational psychologists to use postmodern thought to move beyond logical positivism as *the* philosophy of science for theory and research about vocational behavior.

I identify convergence and divergence as the two fundamental issues in contemporary vocational psychology because they structure and maintain the most frequently debated questions in vocational psychology. These two underlying theoretical issues give rise to and prompt vocational psychology's central schisms, those splits in beliefs that separate theory from practice, vocational psychology from basic psychology disciplines, career counseling from psychotherapy, and vocational research agendas from others. Much of the material included in this volume can be characterized as shaped by or directed at these four theoretical schisms.

FOUR THEORETICAL SCHISMS IN VOCATIONAL PSYCHOLOGY

The schism between theory and practice has a long history of generating discussion. Currently, these discussions resemble heated debates. Polkinghorne (1992) concluded that counseling psychology now has two sciences: a science of theory and research performed by academicians and a science of practice. Practitioners need knowledge of how to produce beneficial results in clients. They obtain that knowledge, not from theory and research, but from experience with clients, oral tradition, and emerging research on the process of psychotherapy. A series of studies has confirmed the belief that theory is little used by practitioners (Morrow–Bradley & Elliott, 1986; Polkinghorne, 1992). Practitioners accuse theorists and researchers of ignoring their concerns and dismissing the real-world challenges that their clients routinely encounter. Practitioners demand to know if practice will ever inform theory, as they know it must. Theorists counter that they construct theories to deal with selected practical problems. When practitioners apply the correct theory to an amenable problem, they enact counseling psychology's best practices. When theories are misapplied, theory cannot be blamed for the inability to comprehend the problem at hand. Recent publications are evidence of attempts by theorists and practitioners to narrow the schism: theory textbooks that address counseling practice (Brown & Brooks, 1990; Sharf, 1992) and case studies published in the *Career Development Quarterly* (Jepsen, 1986) that demonstrate how master practitioners apply theories to the problems of individual clients.

A second schism separates career theory and research from the other psychological sciences. Vocational psychology remains remarkably isolated from disciplines such as developmental psychology, social psychology, cross-cultural psychology, personality psychology, and gender studies. On the one hand, vocational psychologists continue to lament that their theories and research are undervalued and not discussed in textbooks on adolescent and adult development. On the other hand, they could do more to foster this integration by studying and applying innovations in closely allied specialties of applied psychology. Vondracek, Lerner, and Schulenberg (1986) have been in the forefront of those calling for this integration. They are not alone. For example, Osipow (1993) recently identified two reasons for this isolation and undervaluation. First, vocational psychologists "do not expend sufficient energy in both deriving our concepts and methods from the basic discipline of psychology, and we do not loop back with our findings sufficiently to the basic discipline. . . . A second problem concerns our general inability to extrapolate from our work to larger social problems and issues" (p. 2). The current literature on career self-efficacy exemplifies the benefits that can accrue from the alignment of vocational psychology with related disciplines. Not only has career theory been enriched by Bandura's (1982) construct of self-efficacy, but vocational psychologists who have elaborated the construct in the career development domain find their studies discussed in the personology literature.

A third schism exists between career counseling and psychotherapy. Vocational psychologists have traditionally employed a dichotomy between career counseling and personal counseling to differentiate prevention from remediation and adaptive crises from psychopathology. These dichotomies create a wall of words between two aspects of helping. Some scholars have accepted the dichotomy and have argued about which takes more skill, career counseling or psychotherapy (Crites, 1981). Others have argued that career counseling could be made more attractive to practitioners if it adopted some models and methods from psychotherapy (e.g., Hackett, 1993; Slaney & MacKinnon–Slaney, 1990). Today, many psychologists view career counseling as a subdiscipline of psychotherapy and teach and practice it as such (e.g., Blustein, 1987, 1990). A few counseling psychologists have even claimed to have stopped practicing career counseling as a distinct service. They provide each of their clients with brief psychotherapy, which, in some cases, includes career intervention. A current assessment of the schism between career counseling and psychotherapy can be garnered from journals that have published special issues on this topic, for example, *Journal of Career Development* (Loughead, 1989) and *Career Development Quarterly* (Subich, 1993).

A fourth schism separates research camps from each other. The traditional approach to research in the career domain involves the identification of a construct, the operational definition of that construct, and the implementation of a program of studies that specify the construct's nomological network and sensitivity to intervention. In short, prominence results from distancing oneself from one's colleagues and their research programs. Groups of researchers have coalesced into loosely defined camps, for example, such as those known for taking the developmental, differential, or decisional perspective on vocational behavior. With each individual and camp pursuing distinct agendas, the collection of a critical mass of research studies on many of the important problems in vocational behavior has been difficult. Even a comparison of the results of studies that do address the same problem is difficult because, in investigating the problem, researchers use different operational definitions to characterize the variables involved in the problem. Examples of the problem in research integration are apparent in the meta-analyses and literature reviews concerning the occasional topics that have amassed more than a few studies: career education (Baker & Popowicz, 1983), career counseling (Oliver & Spokane, 1988), congruence (Edwards, 1991), and career indecision (Slaney, 1988).

These four schisms in vocational psychology reflect the underlying theoretical issues of convergence and divergence. The following discussion of these two issues is meant not only to provide information but also to explicate the fundamental differences that prompt and maintain theoretical schisms between and among researchers and practitioners. This chapter concludes with a brief reconsideration of the four schisms in light of this discussion.

CONVERGENCE IN CAREER THEORIES

Alarm about the "crisis of disunity" (Staats, 1983, p. 1) in psychology has prompted vocational psychologists to consider fragmentation, redundancy, diverse philosophical stances, and inconsistency among theories of career choice and development. Advocates for unifying theories in psychology, such as Staats (1991), have argued that science is progressive. Early in the development of a particular science, theorists and researchers typically study different phenomena using different approaches. They seek to produce novel ideas and unique positions that distinguish their theories from other theories. At a later stage in the development of a scientific discipline, some individuals begin to notice relationships among the various theories. This recognition leads them to attempt to integrate the diverse findings into a gestalt rather than to distinguish themselves by establishing unique positions and generating novel ideas. Staats (1991) characterized this late developing endeavor as an effort to stop "artificial diversity" and "untreated redundancy" (p. 905).

Steps Toward Unification

The transition from an early emphasis on uniqueness to a later search for commonality includes the phases of rapprochement, convergence, and unification. Rychlak (1988) believed that the first step in the search for commonality in theories entails widespread agreement throughout a disciplinary community that scientists with disparate views each have something valuable to say.

Rapprochement

Beitman, Goldfried, and Norcross (1989) used the term *rapprochement* to describe the establishment of a state of cordial relations within a particular scientific community. At the start of rapprochement, scholars must deal with what really is at stake—the allocation of resources. Those with long and successful histories of competing for recruits and resources for their theories must adopt new approaches. They must contend with the mistrust engendered by prior efforts to advance conceptual hegemony and with hidden agendas that benefit a particular school. If trust can be instilled and a new spirit of community and collaboration established, then theorists and researchers can feel comfortable looking for common principles and concepts across theories. As rapprochement strengthens, the goal for knowledge production broadens to include not just the discovery of the novel but the interrelation, organization, and simplification of existing knowledge. Rapprochement encourages scholars to view theoretical differences as problems to be resolved, not as errors.

Convergence

Rapprochement and a common language can lead to *convergence*, or growing alike and developing similarities. Beitman et al. (1989) emphasized that "convergence refers, however, to emerging similarities of distinct orientations rather than to their integration per se" (1989, p. 139). According to Staats (1991), "unifying theory analysis" (p. 905) facilitates convergence among theories by establishing a common language by which common constructs can be identified. Different theories incorporate their own technical vocabulary or language to denote the same constructs (e.g., three terms denote person–environment fit: Holland's, 1985, congruence; Dawis & Lofquist's, 1984, correspondence; and Super's, 1963, incorporation). Insiders use their distinctive vocabulary as a shortcut in communication and, in so doing, show that they are informed, that is, an active member of the theory's knowledge–constituent network. Establishing a common language allows for cross-theoretical communication and facilitates the identification of convergence among theoretical concepts and principles. The simple identification of common and unique features across theories produces an agenda of problems to be resolved and offers prospects for cohesive, cross-theoretical projects. Nevertheless, convergence is not really unification.

While theorists consider convergence, practitioners of the discipline engage in their own version of theory convergence, usually under the rubric of *eclecticism*. To meet their needs in applying theories to practice, practitioners construct a technical, atheoretical synthesis of clinical methods (Lazarus, 1967). They use models and methods that work, regardless of which theoretical group generated the materials. In vocational psychology, this approach also means that career counselors select interventions based on client needs, not the counselor's orientation to differential, dynamic, or developmental theories.

Bridging

Following the phases of rapprochement and convergence, the third phase in the transition from a discipline's early search for the novel to its later search for unification involves the application of "interlevel framework theory" (Staats, 1991, p. 908). Unification eventually emerges from studies that bridge theories and reduce redundancy. Obviously, the design of bridging studies requires a cross-theoretical framework that organizes major aspects of the discipline and implicitly prescribes the basic principles that need examination. Specialists in a particular theory cannot be expected to relinquish that theory easily. Thus, the bridging framework must promise advances to specialists who continue to emphasize a particular theory as well as to researchers who investigate theoretical commonalities (Staats, 1981). The movement from the convergence phase into the bridging phase ordinarily starts with modest efforts, such as incorporating two similar theories (e.g., in vocational psychology perhaps Holland's, 1985, theory and Dawis & Lofquist's, 1984, Theory of Work Adjustment) into one internally consistent statement of essential elements; complete unification is unnecessary.

Following the phases of rapprochement, convergence, and bridging, the final step in a discipline's transition from early to late science involves the actual unification of diverse theories into a conceptual synthesis, a synthesis that uses a new "superordinate umbrella, coherent theoretical gestalt, metatheoretical framework or conceptually superior" theory (Beitman et al., 1989, p. 139).

Convergence in Career Theory

Evidence of the efforts toward convergence abounds in the psychotherapy literature and indicates that such efforts are starting to spread throughout most of the subspecialties in psychology, including vocational psychology. Three pivotal publications early in the 1990s highlighted convergence efforts within vocational psychology. The authors of these publications viewed unification from the different phases in the transition from early to late science. A chapter by Super (1992) encouraged rapprochement, an article by Osipow (1990) contributed to convergence, and a chapter by Krumboltz and Nichols (1990) offered a bridging framework.

Super (1969) frequently referred to his theory as *segmental*. He devised separate models around topics such as self-concept, career maturity, life stages, life roles, and work values. In one of his last formal statements regarding career theory, Super (1992) addressed the issue of integrating the segments of his theory into a truly comprehensive theory. He concentrated on integration within his own work, not between his work and that of other theorists. Nevertheless, in the concluding section of his chapter, Super wrote that the understanding of careers requires three theories: one dealing with development, another with matching, and a third with decision making. He viewed unified theory as emerging from some integration of (a) developmental views such as his own (Super, 1980), (b) trait-and-factor views such as those espoused by Holland (1985) and by Dawis and Lofquist (1984), and (c) decision-making models such as the one designed by Mitchell, Jones, and Krumboltz (1979). Super's set of prospects for unification seems essentially the same as the set proposed by Osipow (1990).

Responding to an invitation to write an article celebrating the twentieth anniversary of the *Journal of Vocational Behavior,* Osipow (1990) published an influential article on convergence in theories of career choice and development. Osipow asserted that four major theories had remained influential over the last 40 years and seemed to dominate current thinking about careers because of their empirical base, operational usefulness, or widespread appeal: person–environment typology (Holland, 1985), the theory of work adjustment (Dawis & Lofquist, 1984), social learning theory (Mitchell et al., 1979), and developmental theory (Super, 1980). Osipow described how these theories had come to resemble each other in important ways. Examining these four theories for common constructs and other similarities, he compared them across constructs such as the outcomes that they try to predict, their views of personality, and their descriptions of life stages. Osipow (1990) concluded that each theory included unique elements yet all seemed to be "building on what appears to be a relatively common base of concepts" (p. 129). On the basis of this analysis, Osipow concluded that vocational psychology may be "further along toward the creation of a unified theory of career decision and development than we have thought" (p. 123).

In presenting the case for convergence, Osipow (1990) did note that the theories, despite their similarities, retained important differences. These distinctive features make each theory most appropriate for sets of distinct applications. For example, Holland's (1985) theory is particularly suited for comprehending educational and vocational choices, Krumboltz's (1994) social learning theory conceptualizes the decision-making process, Super's (1980) developmental theory specifies attitudes and competencies that foster adaptation to life-stage tasks, and Dawis and Lofquist's (1984) theory explicates adjustment at the workplace. Osipow directed attention to a convergence idea that is discussed later, namely, that different theories address different problems.

In their chapter about the bridging level of science, Krumboltz and Nichols (1990) contended that the major career theories differed in emphasis and vocabulary yet were not in fundamental disagreement. To make their point, Krumboltz and Nichols likened a theory to a map. A map and a theory both "give us the big picture about a certain area of interest. They both help us understand the most essential characteristics of that area" (Krumboltz & Nichols, 1990, p. 159). They extended the metaphor by explaining that theories and maps both omit nonessential information, distort the reality that they represent, deal with the unobservable, and vary in their purpose. This last point resembles Osipow's reminder that a theory is constructed to serve a specific purpose and thus can be useful for its intended purpose but useless for other purposes.

Krumboltz and Nichols (1990) set for themselves the task of describing how selected theories employ similar concepts and overlap in fundamental principles yet map different terrains. They then suggested that the concept of purpose serve as the superordinate cross-theoretical construct and that the Living Systems Framework (Ford, 1987) serve as the bridging framework with which to organize the structures, processes, and functions involved in vocational behavior. They concluded that the Living Systems Framework could be a heuristic framework if researchers embedded career theories into it.

Given the prodding by Super, Osipow, and Krumboltz and Nichols, the Vocational Behavior and Career Intervention Special Interest Group of the Counseling Psychology Division in the American Psychological Association held a conference in 1992 to debate the merits of a unification agenda for theories of career choice and development (Savickas & Lent, 1994). The group aimed to reinforce evolving rapprochement and disciplinary unity as well as to advance convergence by prompting unifying analyses. Although rapprochement was welcomed, the desirability of convergence and a unification agenda for theories of career choice and development proved to be at issue during the conference—proponents of unification encountered advocates of separation in theory development.

Advantages and Disadvantages of a Unification Project

Advantages. Proponents for unification of career theories asserted three main reasons for examining theoretical convergence and bridging frameworks. First, they highlighted the inadequacy of any single career theory for comprehending the full range of problems and situations that clients bring to career counseling. Lacking a comprehensive theory, counselors have turned to technical eclecticism.

Second, they pointed to the equality of outcomes among career interventions that implement different theories. Most observers have concluded that all treatments have similar effects. The consensus regarding equivalence of outcomes in career counseling suggests that the identification of shared components in theories and interventions may be more fruitful than continued research on differential diagnosis and treatment.

Third, proponents for unification argued that vocational psychology must improve the manner in which it allocates its research resources. With the emphasis on being novel, independent researchers and small research teams focus on identifying new variables and exploring their meaning. Each group uses distinct outcome measures, often author-made measures with little evidence of validity. Because of this diversity in direction, vocational psychology has not accumulated substantial bodies of empirical literature on many important topics. Even in problem domains that have accumulated a critical mass of studies (e.g., career indecision, career exploration, congruence), research integration reviews and meta-analytic studies are thwarted because the measures and operational definitions used in these studies are not the same. Oliver and Spokane (1988) concluded that "we can at this point think of no greater contribution than for a group of researchers to engage in the development of a set of standard measures to be used in career-counseling research" (p. 459). Their conclusion could be extended to include research on vocational behavior. A unification project for vocational psychology could make a major contribution. The central phenomenon and core variables converging from different theories could be identified, and then a standard set of corresponding measures that are useful across all major career theories could be constructed.

Disadvantages. On the other side of the issue, many prominent theorists and researchers think that a unification project is a bad, or at least a premature, idea. They fear that such a project will result in theory construction by committee that could only produce an ungainly theoretical model, which they liken to a camel. Holland (1994) spoke for many who avoid convergence when he argued that theorists espouse divergent beliefs about aims, human development, philosophy of science, political agendas, and career interventions. In strongly opposing a unification agenda, Holland recognized that there may be some convergence, as noted by Krumboltz and Nichols (1990), Osipow (1990), and Super (1992), yet only "a very weak convergence" (p. 45) and only in similarity of background principles assumed by all theories for the last 80 years. Holland (1994) succinctly stated his disagreement with theoretical unification with the title of his chapter, "Separate but Unequal is Better." His main concern involved the allocation of resources and wisely reminded counseling psychologists that vocational research has meager financial resources and relatively few participants. Furthermore, the talents of career researchers and counseling psychology's limited resources must be invested prudently. Investing in an "ill-advised" (p. 45) project such as convergence would not only be futile but worse, it could also siphon off resources from projects with better prospects.

In addition to Holland's articulate presentation of the disadvantages of unification efforts, other theorists and researchers have raised concerns:

1. Unification may discourage creativity of counselors in forming their own theories.
2. Unification efforts may be premature because unification requires a larger empirical base than is now available.
3. Convergence and unification should be empirical questions, not literary projects.
4. Quick integration may lead to ambiguous constructs drawn from different theories.

5. Constructive, piecemeal theory building is better.
6. A unification project may force a political agenda on theorists.
7. Committees cannot construct theories.
8. The most that a unification project could achieve would be convergence in terminology, not in philosophy or theory.
9. Postmodern approaches to science are moving toward pluralism, not unity.
10. In emphasizing convergence, researchers may ignore interesting aspects of each theory.

Clearly the advantages and disadvantages of a unification project are now at issue. The status of this contentious issue can be assessed as follows. Rapprochement is evident yet not universal. Some theorists and researchers suspect proponents of a hidden agenda of advancing a particular theory or of trying to subsume most theories under other theories. Nevertheless, the argumentative dialogue has resulted in a clear recognition that all theories have something important to say. The map metaphor proposed by Krumboltz (1994) has replaced the camel joke (an animal or theory created by committee) in discussions about convergence. Moreover, theorists have become more explicit about the purposes for which they constructed their theories. The theorists and many of their adherents, however, are not ready to address convergence in theories of career choice and development.

Rather than convergence, most scholars seem willing to settle for theory *renovation*, to use a word offered by Holland (1994). Savickas (1994a) organized the major ideas for refurbishing career theories into two groups. The first group consisted of *neglected* topics, such as diversity, salience, context, and ability. The second group consisted of ideas that seem to have been *forgotten*, such as the purpose of career theories and praxis as the goal of theory.

Although most scholars seem to see more disadvantages than advantages in a unification project, several theorists have made serious attempts to examine convergence in that they have been willing to relate their own work to that of other theorists. In doing so, they have identified some potential fulcrums for intertheory analysis.

Six Frameworks for Bridging Career Theories

Those scholars who are willing to examine convergence apparently agree that, to advance the project, attention must turn to selecting and developing a conceptual tool for bridging theories, namely an overarching framework. Six existing frameworks have been proposed: living systems, developmental contextualism, systems theory, learning theory, the person–environment transaction model, and the theory of work adjustment. The suggestion by

Krumboltz and Nichols (1990) that the *Living Systems Framework* (Ford, 1987) serve as the framework with which to organize the structures, processes, and functions that combine to generate vocational behavior has already been described.

Developmental Contextualism. In a major theoretical statement, Vondracek et al. (1986) described a developmental contextualism framework for comprehending vocational behavior. Well suited for bridging theories (Vondracek & Fouad, 1994), this framework emerged from the pioneering work of Lerner (1985). He merged the developmental organic perspective with the environmental contextual perspective to produce a point of view called *developmental contextualism.*

Developmental Systems Theory. Interestingly, these two proposed frameworks, living systems and developmental contextualism, have themselves been integrated. Ford and Lerner (1992) synthesized Lerner's (1985) developmental contextualism perspective with Ford's (1987) living systems framework to produce developmental systems theory. In a subsequent chapter of this volume, Vondracek seeks to reinvigorate the study of adult career development by describing how developmental systems theory can be used to comprehend the processes of vocational behavior in adults.

Systems Theory. A third framework for convergence has been suggested by Blustein (1994) and Bordin (1994). They each offered systems theory as a framework with which scholars could contextualize the vocational behavior of individuals within the proximal setting of family and the distal conditions of the opportunity structure and employment barriers caused by the oppressive triad of racism, sexism, and poverty. With regard to social barriers, Fitzgerald and Betz (1994) concluded that career theories already converge in their ignoring of context and, as a result, are of little use to large segments of the population. They suggested that before attending to convergence, scholars enhance current theories by examining each theory from the perspective of social equality and workplace justice and then by renovating and extending the existing theories to comprehend diverse groups of workers. In the end, the renovation of existing theories to fully comprehend diversity and multiculturalism would itself become a bridging framework.

Learning Theory. A fourth suggested convergence framework is learning theory. Most scholars readily agree that learning theory could serve as a bridging framework. Closer examination, however, indicates that learning theory may address convergence from an interlevel analysis rather than from an intertheory analysis. Learning theory offers a fine-grained level of analysis that complements the coarse-grained concepts in theories such as Holland's and Super's (Dawis, 1994). Thus, in terms of the level of analysis, the use of social learning theory in the examination of theories could prove quite fruitful, although it would not prompt intertheory analysis in the same way that the other proposed frameworks might.

Person–Environment Transaction. A group of distinguished researchers have settled on a fifth potential framework in suggesting that the person–environment (P–E) transaction is a central unifying principle for the converging of theories (Rounds & Hesketh, 1994; Spokane, 1994; Walsh & Chartrand, 1994). They warn, however, that P–E fit means different things in different theories and, therefore, career theorists must sharpen its meaning before attempting to use a P–E model in convergence investigations. Rounds and Hesketh (1994) offered researchers a prospectus for clarifying the latent structure of the variables and moderators in P–E transactions. This prospectus would serve as a precursor to using a P–E model to bridge different concepts of vocational behavior. They suggested five levels of analysis: unit of analysis (i.e., person, environment, or interaction of the two), types of matching variables (e.g., interests, abilities, types), types of criterion variables (e.g., satisfaction, stress, productivity), types of process variables (e.g., activeness, flexibility), and time framework (i.e., repeated measures or longitudinal data).

Theory of Work Adjustment. A sixth framework proposed for convergence is the Theory of Work Adjustment (TWA; Dawis & Lofquist, 1984). Rounds and Hesketh (1994) pointed out, as did Dawis (1994), that TWA has many elements that lend themselves to unified theory because it was constructed as a convergent theory. Dawis (1994) stated that TWA began as an attempt to integrate several concepts: ability from the individual differences tradition, reinforcement from the learning theory tradition, satisfaction from the human relations tradition, and person–environment correspondence from the vocational psychology tradition. Through this integration, TWA bridges the two orientations toward vocational behavior espoused by counseling psychology and industrial–organizational psychology. Dawis showed that TWA converges well with Holland's theory (1985) and concluded that there is not an instance in which these two theories contradict each other. The major distinction between the two theories lies in purpose. Holland (1985) prepared his theory of career choice for counselors to help clients make matching decisions, whereas Dawis and Lofquist (1984) constructed TWA as a means of understanding work adjustment, not career choice. TWA also shares much in common with social learning theories such as Krumboltz's (1994) theory because both rest on learning theory. TWA shares some things in common with Super's (1980) theory, the major differences being that Super's theory is more comprehensive and concentrates on development, whereas TWA concentrates on the work environment and describes development at a coarse-grained level, not a fine-grained level. Dawis believed that TWA can incorporate Bordin's (1994) views about the psychodynamics of motivation, work compulsion, and intrinsic values rather easily because Bordin deals with the source traits that support many TWA constructs. Fitzgerald and Rounds (1994) also viewed TWA as having the potential to deal with context and the vocational behavior of diverse groups.

Summary

Vocational psychologists now face the challenge of formally addressing the artificial diversity and untreated redundancy so obvious in the contemporary theories about and research concerning career choice and development. Their views on the issue of convergence and pursuit of the "holy grail" of science, unified theory, will shape responses to this challenge as well as attempts to reduce the schisms that continue to separate theory from practice, vocational psychology from basic psychology, career counseling from psychotherapy, and research programs from social problems.

Convergence can be separated into two root words. The first is *verge*, meaning to bend or incline toward. The second, *con*, is not defined so simply. *Con* may mean either *with* or *against*. Interestingly, for our purposes this dichotomy makes *con-verge* the perfect word. *Con-verge* can mean coming together or against coming together. *Diverge* has a simpler meaning, mainly to deviate or move away from a direction commonly taken. For our purposes, *divergence* denotes a turning away from, and perhaps even ignoring, the common path taken by vocational psychology, not arguments among or between theorists who still share the common path charted by twentieth century logical positivism. In the following discussion, I examine the issue of turning aside from the common path charted by logical positivism, that is, of divergence in vocational psychology.

DIVERGENCE IN VOCATIONAL PSYCHOLOGY

Debate about the issue of convergence has produced many specific suggestions for making important renovations to existing career theories. These suggestions indicate new directions that would continue to advance the twentieth century project of studying careers. However, some vocational psychologists raise concerns about the future viability of this project. They argue that rather than refurbish career theories, vocational psychologists need to substantially revise or even to replace the construct of career itself. This theoretical issue is most frequently asserted by advocates for a new philosophy of science that is evolving in tandem with the emergence of postindustrial societies. Accordingly, the contemporary scene in vocational psychology, as well as in counseling psychology, fosters an increasing awareness of and discussion about philosophy of science. The resulting greater self-consciousness about philosophy of science prompts escalating debate about the assumptions that structure career theory and research. The central issue under debate can be succinctly formed as a question: Which philosophy of science should structure vocational psychology in the twenty-first century? The issue begs for clarification before the field can progress beyond its current achievements.

Historically, American vocational psychologists have concerned themselves only incidentally with philosophy of science (Morf, 1992). With the early tradition of empiricism vocational psychologists eschewed theory construction and concentrated on measurement and prediction as the premiere methods for establishing the matching model in both career choice and adjustment. Vocational psychologists, with the notable exception of Tiedeman, who did address philosophy of science issues (e.g., Peatling & Tiedeman, 1977; Tiedeman & Miller–Tiedeman, 1984), generally adopted the positivist position that pervaded the first half of the twentieth century psychology. Ultrapositivists of the 1940s and 1950s, exemplified by Skinner (1950), whose now-classic paper "Are Theories of Learning Necessary?" reflected their disposition, found philosophy of science unnecessary for a psychology grounded in operationalism and empiricism. In cumulated contributions spanning the period from 1951 to 1976, however, Marx's (1951, 1963) compendia on theories in contemporary psychology described a swing of the intellectual pendulum toward an increasing emphasis on philosophy of science issues. This zeitgeist was in no little degree created by Kuhn's (1970) landmark treatise, *The Structure of Scientific Revolutions.* Although its evolutionary and paradigmatic interpretations of the history of science have been questioned and criticized (e.g., Marx & Goodson, 1976), a philosophical mood still prevails in psychology. More recently, and closer to home, the special section in the *Journal of Counseling Psychology,* entitled "Philosophy of Science and Counseling Research" (Gelso, 1984), and the issue of *The Counseling Psychologist* entitled "Alternate Research Paradigms" (Fretz, 1989) attest to the currency of philosophical issues.

Now, prompted by the postmodern turn in our culture, vocational psychologists fervently debate issues arising from philosophy of science, that is, "the study of how science works, or should work" (Runes, 1983, p. 191), to arrive at systematic knowledge (Cohen & Nagel, 1934). Today, vocational psychologists realize that they need a philosophy of science to provide a formal schema for constructing theories and conducting research as well as for maintaining a disciplined and public self-consciousness in communicating concepts and conclusions resulting from these efforts.

Growing recognition of the import that philosophy of science holds for theory and research in vocational psychology has highlighted the central issue—Which philosophy of science shall we have? Responses to this question often assume the proportions of irreconcilable ideologies, particularly between those who argue from standpoints in positivist and constructivist grounds. The magnitude of the debate is illustrated by the previously mentioned articles about philosophy of science (Gelso, 1984), in which the received view of science, inherited largely from the positivist tradition, was juxtaposed to revisionist alternatives based on what appear to be qualitatively different cosmic assumptions (Polkinghorne, 1984). Sense too the almost doctrinaire tone of Manicas and Secord's (1983) paper entitled "Implications for Psychology of the New Philosophy of Science," and it becomes increasingly clear that sharp lines have been drawn on which philosophy of science to choose. Lest polarization of viewpoints obscure a simple truth implicit in these articles, it should be noted that they not only express a need for alternatives to established philosophy of science but also signify a far greater freedom of scientists to choose a philosophy. Maslow's (1966) *Psychology of Science*, Bannister's (1970) "Psychology As an Exercise in Paradox," Mahoney's (1976) *Scientist as Subject*, and Grover's (1981) *Toward a Psychology of the Scientist* all conclude, either implicitly or explicitly, that it is the individual who finally chooses which philosophy of science to use. Let us begin to examine the issue of which philosophy of science suits vocational psychology and the construct of career for the twenty-first century by placing the issue in historical context.

Historical Perspectives on Work Ethics and Occupational Choice

The view of career posited in contemporary career theories reflects the spirit of the times in twentieth-century science. During the nineteenth century, feelings dominated the process of knowledge production, so Western society inculcated its members with a vocational ethic that coincided with romanticism. Bruner (1986) noted that romantic conceptualism asserted that meaning resides within the person. According to this view, concepts spring from private encounters with examples of natural states. Because motivation and meaning reside in the person, the path to success and personal fulfillment followed a course shaped by both self-expression and individual effort. On the one hand, the vocational ethic encouraged passion, genius, and creativity in all work. On the other hand, the vocational ethic emphasized independent effort, self-sufficiency, frugality, self-discipline, and humility. This vocational ethic was embraced by the farmers, artisans, and independent business owners who constituted the majority of workers in nineteenth century America. The choice of a particular occupation typically followed family traditions such as staying on the farm or joining the family business.

At the end of the nineteenth century, entrepreneurs organized artisans into companies of workers and built large cities around the resulting industries. These companies and cities changed America from a rural patchwork of farms and small towns to an interconnected network of major cities. With the advent of large organizations that employed modern technology, careers emerged. People who had worked for themselves on farms and in towns then moved to cities to climb the ladder of an organization. To this day, a ladder remains the dominant metaphor for career because it connotes the essential element of a hierarchical view of life in which the adaptive person advances, climbs, and develops.

This concept of career reflects the hallmark characteristics of discourse about modernity: rationality, efficiency, prediction, and control. Borgmann (1992) traced the origins of the modern project of controlling nature and society through rational decision making to three intellectual architects: Bacon, Descartes, and Locke. Bacon provided the idea of domination of nature. Descartes offered methodological universalism in asserting reason as the sole basis of and the scientific method as the sole means of deducing scientific truth. Locke offered the sovereign individual as the fundamental authority, replacing the external authority imposed by kings and the clergy. Comte bound together Bacon's aggressive realism, Descartes' scientific method, and Locke's rugged individualism to create positivism, that is, the empirical philosophy that proposed sensory experience as the path to truth (Champagne, 1992). Comte legitimized truth, not through church or monarchy, but through sensory experience mediated by the value-free application of the objective, scientific method. Positivism shaped the Enlightenment's metanarrative of the gradual yet steady increase of control through reason over nature and ourselves. Positivist scientists emphasized rational action based on knowledge. Thus, in the modern era, reason replaced intuition, religion, and the state as the ultimate authority (Crook, 1992). Culture moved from romantic notions of fate and destiny to modern notions of personal agency empowered by technology.

As twentieth century logical positivism replaced nineteenth century conceptualism, the career ethic replaced the vocational ethic. Unlike conceptualism, which locates meaning in the person, positivism locates meaning in the world. Accordingly, positivism values facts over feelings. Twentieth-century science replaced romantic passion, creativity, and self-expression and emphasized modern reason, observation, and accuracy. American society eventually learned to demand a singular truth and to rely on the objectivity of the scientific method to extract truth from rigorously controlled confrontations with reality.

Modernity organized work and production around mechanical technology in industrial parks located in large cities. Social status was assigned to individuals according to their place in the production system. The processes of urbanization, individualization, secularization, differentiation, commodification, and rationalization, which shaped modernity, also transformed the vocational work ethic (a calling) into a career ethic (what one's neighbors call one). Work as a vocation was comprehensive, self-expressive, and intrinsically meaningful. Work as a career in an organization became restricted and specialized, with a consequent increase in the division of labor.

Career as a Modern Project

Vocational psychology is a product of modernity. It was designed and still functions to help people choose and adjust to the specialized work that dominates their identity, defines their social status, and determines their wages. Placed in this context, career is a viewpoint that emerged in tandem with the bureaucratic form of large twentieth-century organizations. Bureaucratic form provided the structure for organizations, and career provided a core value. At the end of the twentieth century, Western society is again in the process of transforming itself as it moves from the twentieth century industrial age to the twenty-first century information age. As industries downsize, the cities that they supported struggle to survive. Now, the large bureaucratic organizations that supported careers are disappearing. People can no longer expect to spend 40 years at IBM or General Motors, establishing and maintaining their careers through the predictable sequence of stages articulated by Super (1980). As large organizations that support careers disappear, the concept of an occupational career path within a single organization pertains to fewer people.

Therefore, the question arises of whether or not the concept of career has a future. Its critics assert that the concept of career does not further the move from industry to information, from hierarchies to teams, from electromechanical to electronic, and from competition to cooperation. As the millennium turns, the career ethic will seem less and less useful.

Given these circumstances, some scholars proclaim the death of career. At a symposium entitled "The Future of Career: Death or Transfiguration," Collin (1994) noted that current economic, social, and political influences are reshaping organizations. She identified three lines of change as having the potential to fracture the concept of career. According to Collin, organizations are becoming more flexible, adaptive, and elastic. Organizations need flexibility to survive and thrive in fast-changing environments. They need flat structures to adapt quickly to changing environments. And, they need elastic employment contracts that accommodate the use of core and peripheral workers to respond to changing demands with a "reserve army of labor" (p. 7).

Collin (1994) forecast that replacing organizational bureaucracy with flexibility will cause vocational psychologists to revise the metaphor of career as a ladder. She speculated that the new metaphor will be career as a portfolio of skills and accomplishments, with the connecting glue or coherence lying in the story that the individual chooses to tell rather than in the objectively observable organizational pathway of steps up a ladder. Career moves are likely to be lateral rather than vertical. Career planning may be reduced to small, reactive steps, and individual career planning itself may take place within the context of a work team.

Richardson (1993) also speculated about the future of career. She suggested that vocational psychologists demote the concept of career to a peripheral position when theorizing about work in people's lives. A focus on work activities rather than on occupational roles would emphasize "the multiple contexts" of any one individual's life (Richardson, 1993, p. 428). Richardson urged that vocational psychologists take this new direction because simply expanding the "conceptual umbrella of career" (p. 427) (e.g., Super's [1980] life–career rainbow) still equates work with an occupational role. She warned that ignoring work performed outside of the occupational structure perpetuates a bias that validates work accomplished within the occupational structure and devalues work performed in the home and community. Richardson explained that the view of work as individual achievement disconnects work from its fundamental meaning, namely, social contribution. Regardless of the responses to the issues raised by Collin and Richardson (e.g., Savickas, 1994b; Tinsley, 1994), vocational psychologists must recognize that the concept of career has been problematized by their insights and the surrounding dialogue. The concept of career has been besmirched by a postmodern discourse that has demythologized, delegitimated, and deconstructed it.

Postmodern Turn

As the modern career ethic fractures, it may be replaced by a postmodern work ethic rooted in a new perspective on the occupational role, one that emphasizes connectedness and social contribution. Correspondingly, vocational psychologists are being challenged to revise their core philosophy of science and to reform their field into an interpretive discipline. Examples of vocational psychology as an interpretive discipline can be found in the works of Carlson (1988) on career development as meaning making, Cochran (1990, 1991, 1992) on the career project, Collin and Young (1986, 1988) on hermeneutical perspectives in career theory, Csikszentmihalyi and Beattie (1979) on life themes in career development, Neimeyer (1988) on constructivism and career choice, Peavy (1992, 1993) on constructivist career counseling, Ochberg (1988) on narrative construction of career, Osherson (1980) on the private meaning of career choices, Savickas (1989, 1993, 1994c) on career counseling in the postmodern era, Young (1988) on meaning making in career development, and Young and Borgen (1990) on the study of subjective careers.

This postmodern turn from a career ethic to a work ethic springs from a new philosophical stance that is articulated in architecture, physics, literary criticism, gender studies, and critical pedagogy. The posture is generally called *perspectivism, interpretivism,* or *constructivism.* Although there are differences in these terms, I use perspectivism as the general term. Six issues seem to frame the debate between positivists and perspectivists over which philosophy of science vocational psychology should use: epistemic individualism versus collectivism, objectivity versus perspectivity, universality versus particularity, validation versus legitimation, essence versus context, and concepts versus constructs. Each of these issues clearly implicates the postmodern decentering from "them" to "us" and from abstract principles to contextualized practices.

Epistemic Individualism Versus Collectivism. Modern science proposes that individuals use the scientific method to discover knowledge in the world. Subscribing to a Lockean epistemic individualism, adherents of modern science view the individual as the principal agent of knowledge production. In contrast, postmodern thinkers locate knowledge in relationships between people, not in the world. "Emphasis on truth as a relationship suggests seeking meaning contextually in social processes rather than externally in objects" (Jacques, 1992, p. 595). Because knowledge is mediated through discourse and socially constructed subjectivity, communities, not individuals, are the primary agents of knowledge production (Best & Kellner, 1991, p. 83).

This shift from epistemic individualism to epistemic collectivism implies that communities in dialogue provide the basis of truth. Because truth is a matter for decision, not demonstration, communities judge what is knowledge. Although thoughts and personal beliefs must be first expressed by individuals, these thoughts become situated knowledge when communities socially legitimate the thoughts (Harding, 1993). In addition to reason advancing by increasing domination of the object by the subject, reason also increases by search for consensus (Taylor, 1989, p. 509).

Objectivity Versus Perspectivity. Modern positivists seek to discover "the truth" by formulating rational theories and then by using the scientific method to test the theories against reality. According to positivists, the scientific method is the universal method because it controls biases and leads to knowledge as well as to prediction and control. Postmodern scholars assert that positivistic science produces knowledge from one standpoint, not from "the" standpoint. Behind modernity's facade of value-free objectivity stands a commitment to technical rationality. Thus, positivism is one empirical method for knowledge production, not the only method. Postmodern constructivists seek multiperspectival views in the conviction that multiple perspectives on a phenomenon produce richer, deeper, and more complex knowledge.

Perspectivists assault the pretense of value-free science, claiming that objects of knowledge are never separable from the knower. This view argues that meaning and truth depend on one's standpoint, that is, one's assumptions and theoretical groundings. Facts are never independent of the observer who reports them nor of the definitions and categories provided by the observer's culture. "Truth belongs categorically to the world of thought and not to that of perception" (Habermas, 1973, p. 232). This means that vocational psychologists participate in the knowledge that they produce because they frame assumptions, select topics, and conceptualize the data.

Perspectivists argue that, rather than continue to act as if they produce disinterested (value-free) and dislocated (objective) truth, psychologists must now announce their presence in their own research. They must interrogate their biases to reveal how these inclinations conditioned topic selection, conceptual and operational definitions, type of research participants, data analyses, and interpretation of results. In addition to announcing their presence and interrogating their biases, researchers must also explain the intended use of the knowledge. For whom did they produce the knowledge? How is it meaningful for that group? The answers to these questions should include the implications of the knowledge for race, class, and gender.

Universality Versus Particularity.   The search for socially constituted and maintained knowledge shifts research from the generality of testing theoretical principles to the particularity of examining locally situated practices that seem useful in specific circumstances. Postmodern theorists embrace difference and heterogeneity; they reject global and totalizing concepts as well as abstractions that obscure more than they reveal. The move from universality to particularity involves a transition from the search for solutions to the exploration of strategies. Instead of designing experiments, postmodern researchers seek reports of an individual's actual experiences and problem descriptions as well as how she or he eventually responded to and learned from crises, unexpected events, and transitions (Peavy, 1993). The researcher then attempts to extract from groups of these instructive accounts the effective practices that lead to success in daily living.

One flashpoint in the debate about universal versus particular knowledge centers on the issue of generalizability. Positivist vocational psychologists argue that because locally situated knowledge about particulars is not generalizable, it is not scientific knowledge. They dismiss the singular and particular as transitory and insignificant. Perspectivist vocational psychologists counter with the assertion that universal application is not the same as generalizability. They realize that generality is a goal of systematic inquiry. Furthermore, they embrace the goal of generating knowledge that is "lifted up from but not stripped of its particulars" (Doyle, 1990, p. 14) and seek to construct carefully stated generalizations in terms of patterns and themes. These patterns and themes are not scientific laws; they are explanatory propositions that can be applied to the construction of meaning within the domain of vocational behavior. In reference to this issue, Polkinghorne (1992) stated that "a neopragmatic body of knowledge consists of summary generalizations of which type of action has been successful in prior like situations. . . . Neopragmatism does not suppose these generalizations to be predictive of what actions will work in new situations; rather, the generalizations have only heuristic value as indicators of what might be tried in similar situations" (p. 152).

Validation Versus Legitimation. To avoid solipsism, postmodern research requires a new criterion by which knowledge generated from instructive accounts is legitimated. Positivistic science validates knowledge in reference to theory. In effect, postmodern researchers have given up the modern project of seeking universal properties that govern human conduct. Because knowledge is produced in diverse interpretive communities that share a local perspective, there are multiple realities, not singular truths. Thus, with perspectivistic science, knowledge is legitimated by its usefulness when implemented in action rather than validated by its relation to theory. The modern question asks, Is it true? Postmodern questions inquire, Why did she say that? How is it true? For whom is it useful? Could it be otherwise? Thus, the postmodern project reemphasizes the goal of science as a guide to praxis. It engenders a new type of pragmatism (Gavin, 1992) based not on efficiency but rather on developing one's values in the real world.

Essence Versus Context. Rather than impose general concepts on the world, postmodern scholars seek to learn how communities construct and maintain meaning in local sites. Accordingly, they emphasize "decentration" from abstract definitions and essentialized selves toward social context and unique circumstances. They attack the illusion that research participants reflect some universal human nature. Unlike positivists, who view context or culture as a variable, perspectivists view culture as the context of meaning. Perspectivists assert that the complex, contextual nature of vocational behavior limits how far positivism can take career psychology. Vocational behavior is not a pure category; it is always intertwined with race, gender, class, and ethnicity. Vocational psychologists cannot continue the tradition of ignoring social status and context in attempting to homogenize these differences. Simply stated, vocational behavior cannot be understood outside the complex of coherent interrelationships within which it is embedded. Accordingly, vocational psychologists like Vondracek and Fouad (1994) and Spokane (1994) are adopting constructs such as embeddedness and affordances to contextualize vocational behavior instead of continuing to abstract vocational behavior from its context.

This reframing from essence to context enables vocational psychologists to follow anthropology and sociology in concentrating on the ordinary activities of everyday life and, thus, in making the research up close rather than out there. Featherstone (1992) described everyday life as "repetitive, taken-for-granted experiences, beliefs, and practices" (pp. 160–161). The common-sense world of everyday life consists of social action. This perspective raises the question, What social action in the ordinary activities of everyday life falls within the realm of vocational psychology? Richardson (1993) answered this question by asserting that the new location for vocational psychology should be the study of work in the everyday lives of individuals. She argued that vocational psychology, if it is to remain relevant to the real-world concerns of people, needs to make a transition from the study of "careers predominantly located in the occupational structure to a focus on the study of work in people's lives in which work is considered to be a central human activity that is not tied to or solely located in the occupational structure" (p. 427). The contentious issue revolves around the preference for abstract principles or for contextualized particulars.

Concepts Versus Constructs. Postmodern thought emphasizes the power of language to shape reality and to guide action. For example, Gavin (1992) wrote that "there is a sense in which a person creates reality by naming it, by molding it linguistically. This may pose new problems, but it renders inadequate the doctrine that the only purpose of language is the impartial description of events" (p. 72). We now realize that linguistic concepts and their definitions do not mirror reality; they inscribe meaning.

The word *concept* denotes that something in nature was discovered and named. Postmodern vocational psychologists, however, believe that concepts do not reflect reality directly; concepts re-present reality through the filters of self-chosen vocabulary. Postmodern scholars use the term *construct* to denote this personal and cultural component of meaning making. The constructs, as opposed to concepts, that individuals use sensitize them to notice certain things and not to notice other things. Individuals see what they know and do not see what they have not defined. Ideas and feelings not subsumed by constructs remain inexpressible. For example, language limits us in construing the complexities of causation and provokes debates over oppositional dichotomies such as free will and determinism (Mahoney, 1993). Thus, language encapsulates us, words insulate us from experience, and concepts constrain us within a culture.

Adherents of postmodern thought have problemized concepts and definitions that have formed the assumptive structure of vocational psychology by revealing them to be constructs, not concepts. Postmodern thinkers seek to recover the original, and sometimes hidden, meaning of these dichotomous concepts and hierarchical definitions, meaning which is concealed by figurative meanings built on the original, lived experience. This process of hermeneutical recovery of deeper meaning is termed *deconstruction.* Deconstruction subverts the binary oppositions and hierarchies that modernity uses to conceptualize individuality, such as male–female, White–Black, employer–employee, or heterosexual–homosexual. Deconstruction accentuates difference and emphasizes plurality, multiplicity, and decentration. Accordingly, postmodern scholars in different fields deconstruct key concepts that dominate typical discourse within that field.

In vocational psychology words like *career* and definitions of work have mastered us for too long. In her recent social analysis of the definition of work, Richardson (1993) revealed the androcentrism in modern definitions of work. Richardson made the analogy to definitions of moral reasoning that Gilligan (1982) and others revealed as androcentric because the definitions privileged justice and autonomy. Gilligan was able to inscribe an alternative interpretation of moral reasoning from a relationship basis; her definitions privilege caring and connectedness. By analogy, Richardson uncovered something that had been obscured by male biases toward work and its meaning. Work is more than achievement gained through an individual's efforts or a sublimation of aggression in pursuit of future outcomes; it is a relational construct. Richardson has marshaled thinkers who view work as community contribution and social activity that creates interpersonal relationships between people. She defined "caring work," analogous in some ways to relational morality, which does not achieve goals for individuals but maintains the very fabric of society.

Constructs that elaborate the meaning of career, by extension of this logic, are necessarily at issue. For example, the concept of career maturity has come to denote a complex of variables anchored by a future orientation, independence, willingness to compromise, and decisiveness. Vocational psychologists who are sensitive to multicultural diversity have argued that these dimensions of career maturity are not scientific concepts. Instead, they are constructs that reflect the androcentric perspective and individualistic culture of the scholars who have defined career maturity with these dimensions.

Criticisms

Epistemic collectivism, perspectivity, particularity, legitimation, contextualization, and deconstruction of concepts each individually challenge modern theory and research in vocational psychology. Collectively, they assault the fundamental assumptions and methodological imperative that structure the discipline. This invasion of ideas has not gone unnoticed nor uncontested (e.g., Tinsley, 1994). In fact, career theory and research are now at a crossroads. Those who argue about the direction that vocational psychologists should take are engaging in a lively debate about the issue of which philosophy of science to follow: positivism or perspectivism. Those who advocate the benefits of continued adherence to a positivist agenda mourn the loss of science as they know it when contemplating the direction perspectivists seek to pursue. The criticism often raised by positivists against perspectivists centers on complaints that approaches such as constructivism, hermeneutics, and the narrative paradigm are self-centered attempts at meaning making that ignore the iron-clad constraints of reality and that denigrate the accomplishments of modern science and technology. Expressing their anger, they complain that perspectivism is not science. Three major issues of contention deal with perspectivity as an integration of objectivity and subjectivity, as a replacement for objectivity, and as moral relativism.

Integration of Objectivity and Subjectivity

First, perspectivity is not an integration of objectivity and subjectivity. Perspectivists counter the myths of objectivity and value-free science by explaining that the social construction of knowledge affects what counts as science. They also counter the myth of subjectivity (i.e., meaning is personal) by inscribing meaning as relational. However, perspectivists do not seek a solution in combining objectivity and subjectivity, as some would have it. The postmodern turn is "not both but neither." Postmodern scholars use doubt and uncertainty to challenge abstract principles and to make common sense problematic. Instead of pursuing facts, they concentrate on ambiguities and uncertainties.

Replacement for Objectivity

Second, perspectivity is not a replacement for objectivity. Rather, perspectivists seek to reveal the pretense of value-free objectivity. Harding (1991) referred to this stance as *weak objectivity*. Research, recognized as socially situated, can be made more objective although it cannot be made value free. We need this *strong objectivity* to rationally distinguish more partial and less distorted truth. The rigors of empirical knowledge seeking lead to maximal objectivity. Perspectivity does not counter objectivity with "just say no." Rather, perspectivists seek to describe objectivity's limitations.

Relativism

Third, perspectivity is not radical relativism. Positivist scientists argue that perspectivist science amounts to radical relativism: If all knowledge is socially produced, then everyone's view is equal. This charge of epistemic relativism leads quickly to an additional charge: Anything goes, or moral relativism.

A response to charges of radical relativism comes from perspectivists who argue that knowledge is relational, not private, because meaning is between people. A theory of knowledge situated in perspectival social constructionism is by definition a relational theory of knowledge but not necessarily a relativistic theory of knowledge (Grosz, 1988; Luke, 1992). Perspectivity does not mean that everyone's standpoint produces knowledge of equal usefulness. Vocational psychologists can have epistemological relativity (i.e., all views are socially produced) without degenerating to moral relativity if they acknowledge that all views are not equally valid (Bhaskar, 1989). In matters that require action, an interpretive community must make commitments to what works best. In other words, for situations that require action, not all views are equal (Kvale, 1992). For vocational psychologists, this means the rejection of ultrapositivism and of radical relativism in the quest to take the study of context and circumstances as seriously as we have taken the study of vocational behavior itself. The goal is a contextual empiricism that gives rise to situated knowledge.

Proposed Compromises

Koch (1985) accused many contemporary psychologists of substituting program for excellence and inventing a "sacred, inviolable, 'self-corrective' epistemology that renders all inquiry in the field a matter of application of rule which preguarantees success" (p. 77). Rychlak's (1993) stance is relevant to this criticism. He argued to promote tolerance concerning what counts as science. He further reminded us that the subject matter of psychology, human beings, is complex and thus requires diverse approaches to understanding. Unlike the physical sciences, the human sciences focus on purpose and meaning. Rychlak contended that psychologists have relied too long on a singular explanation and have tried to ignore assumptive differences on which knowledge production can be based.

Rychlak (1993) analyzed four theoretical groundings, which he described as predicating paradigms that serve as assumptive influences in framing what psychologists choose to investigate and how they interpret the results. In conducting a study, the psychologist's first choice or action is the selecting of a grounding that will be used to conceptualize the findings. Rychlak contrasted this acknowledgment of assumptive influences that frame topic selection, operational definitions, and conceptual interpretations with "strict positivism, which held that meanings issue exclusively from below, from the preformed substrate of reality" (p. 935).

Rychlak (1993) identified the four major assumptive influences or theoretical grounds as the "Physikos, Bios, Socius, and Logos" (p. 936). These grounds roughly correspond to the grounds of physical science, which explains inanimate events such as gravity; the biological sciences, which base explanation on the physical substance of animate organisms; the social sciences, which explain in terms of group relations and culture; and cognitive sciences, which explain conceptual processes of intelligence and meaning making. Physikos and bios seem to constitute the grounding for the modern science of psychology, and socius and logos are apparently the groundings for a postmodern science of psychology.

Rychlak (1993) asserted that what underlies the current epistemic war between positivists and perspectivists is the propensity on the part of traditional scientists for ranking these theoretical grounds in a knowledge hierarchy from physical to biological to social to cognitive. Or, even more simply put, the tradition ranks "knowing that" above "knowing how." Rychlak wisely urged that the grounds not be ranked; instead, they are to be appreciated as complementary explanations.

Walsh, Craik, and Price (1992) along with Walsh and Chartrand (1994) have taken vocational psychology a step in the direction proposed by Rychlak in explicating the groundings typically used in career theory and research. They used the framework provided by theories of action, which are defined according to the prime mover or locus of action in that theory. The first grounding addresses the individual, such as in trait approaches to conceptualizing career choice. The second general theory of action deals with the external environment, such as in social learning and social cognitive models of vocational behavior. The third general theory of action concentrates on the fit between the individual and the environment, such as in person–environment transaction theories. The final theory of action emphasizes the person and context as coexisting and jointly defining one another, such as in constructivist interpretations of vocational behavior. Therefore, the four grounds of vocational psychology are standpoints in the person, the environment, the person–environment transaction, and developmental contextualism.

The focus of criticism concerning a theory or research study should not be its standpoint in a particular grounding but instead how rigorously the product is given its particular grounding. The validity of a grounding stems from its usefulness to psychologists in solving problems. Researchers must state their ground, and then critics can "examine the internal structure and clarity of this account, its instructiveness and relevance for wider issues, and its consistency with empirical evidence" (Rychlak, 1993, p. 936). A particular grounding does not have to be accepted as useful just because a theorist or researcher selects it as a standpoint. Critics may fairly inquire about how "instructive the ground initially selected proves to be in the theory, collection of data, and analysis that follows from it" (Rychlak, 1993, p. 938). Following Rychlak's advice and the lead of Walsh and Chartrand (1994) would foster a systematic pluralism (Shotter, 1992) and an epistemological eclecticism (Borgen, 1984) that appreciates and incorporates a number of intepretive standpoints for vocational psychology theory and research.

Summary

Postmodern philosophy of science may lead to the "development of theories that are relational, interdependent, and multicausal rather than hierarchical, reductionistic, and dualistic" (Rosser, 1990, p. 50). In vocational psychology, perspectivism already seems to be changing the scientific methodology of researchers and the definition of what counts as knowledge. The newly constructed theories of work life will likely concentrate on context, be elaborated by interdisciplinary research teams, and attract diverse participants. Perspectivism may provide vocational psychology and its consumers major intellectual advances with its focus on relationships, community, social contribution, gender, race, ownership, voice, and power. It may also provide insights into the schisms that separate theory from practice, vocational psychology from basic psychology, career counseling from psychotherapy, and research programs from social problems.

CONCLUSIONS

The theoretical views that psychologists hold about convergence and divergence issues relate to and probably condition their responses to the four central schisms in vocational psychology. First, let us consider the schism between theory and practice. From the convergence perspective, Forsyth and Strong (1986) stated the unificationist view in concluding that practice will be best informed by the "energetic application of the scientific model to generate a theory of biological, social, interpersonal, and psychological relationships that specifies how the dynamics of therapeutic and nontherapeutic settings differ" (p. 118). From the divergence perspective, postmodern psychologists have noted a growing disuse of theory and claim that practice has advanced further than theory. They prefer perspectivist epistemology because it is compatible with practice. They propose that a narrative paradigm, or career as story, offers a metaphor by which a theory of career development can be built, one that is intimately braided with a theory of career counseling. Despite the differences between the convergence and divergence orientations, advocates of both strategies agree that researchers must concentrate on producing knowledge that is useful to practitioners, that realistically addresses the complexities presented by diverse clients in various clinical situations.

With regard to the schism between vocational psychology and the other psychological sciences, convergence adherents argue for more integration with the basic science specialties within psychology. The enormous potential of this integration is starting to be realized in research that merges vocational psychology with personality psychology (e.g., Blustein, 1994; Rounds & Tracey, 1993; Trapnell, 1992), developmental psychology (e.g., Vondracek et al., 1986), and social learning theory (e.g., Betz & Hackett, 1981). Divergence adherents also want an integration with other disciplines, but not with the psychological sciences. Instead, they argue for merger with disciplines such as literary criticism, gender studies, phenomenology, hermeneutics, interpretive sociology, and cultural anthropology. Both advocates for convergence and those for divergence agree that vocational psychology should recognize valuable linkages with other disciplines.

With regard to the schism between career counseling and psychotherapy, convergence advocates emphasize the importance of work as a central life role and strive to convince psychotherapists to include career interventions in their clinical armamentarium. In promoting the integration of career counseling with psychotherapy, convergence adherents suggest that every client receive brief psychotherapy, including relevant career interventions, that increases their sense of agency. Divergence advocates deemphasize work as a central life role and emphasize life design through the use of a panoply of roles. They argue that career counseling should focus on self-definition and self-determination, not on adjustment to the occupational structure. Both sides agree that vocational psychology should emphasize agency and enablement. Moreover, although they start from different positions, they both appear to deemphasize career counseling as a distinct specialty within applied psychology.

With regard to the schism that separates vocational research agendas from each other, convergence advocates are apparently ready to invest in projects that identify unification constructs, that design standard measures, that address important social problems (Fitzgerald & Betz, 1994), and that inform policy (Harmon, 1994; Osipow, 1993). Divergence advocates argue against a value-free and objective vocational psychology. They prefer a vocational psychology that is politically active and that addresses social problems by its focus on the needs of people in the margins, not on the needs of theory. Advocates of convergence and of divergence agree that vocational researchers should do more to address social problems and to influence public policy.

So, as vocational psychology approaches the new millennium, a group of interrelated theoretical issues are rising in prominence. These theoretical issues demand that theorists and researchers in vocational psychology use all available approaches to produce more scholarship and research that rigorously contextualizes vocational behavior; focuses on meaning and interpersonal relationships; emphasizes relationships between work and race, gender, and class; integrates vocational psychology with other disciplines; concentrates on self-definition and self-determination; informs counseling practice; addresses public policy; and deals with social problems.

To deal with such complex issues successfully, vocational psychologists must move quickly beyond epistemic wars. Borgen (1989) wisely counseled that vocational psychology's "research enterprise will prosper if we don't vitiate our energies by joining the debate, but rather openly and nondefensively seek the values of alternate spectacles in research approaches" (p. 93). Multiperspectival theory can coalesce scholars from different standpoints and encourage them to collaborate on their common interests and to consider their individual differences.

Multiperspectival theories avoid the uniperspectival tunnel vision of radical positivism or of extreme constructivism. As they construct multiperspectival theories, vocational psychologists must avoid the confusion inherent in using too many perspectives on a single problem. They must select in advance the standpoints or groundings (Rychlak, 1993: Walsh & Chartrand, 1994) most pertinent to a single problem, not just add a jumble of perspectives that muddle the view. For some problems, a uniperspectival standpoint in positivism or constructivism is appropriate. The positivist tradition, which has furnished the superordinate philosophy of science for vocational psychology, provides a perspective, concepts, and methods that are extremely useful and should not be spurned by constructivists who indeed do offer "alternate spectacles" (Borgen, 1989, p. 93). For their part, positivists must acknowledge that for some problems an array of outlooks rigorously applied could be more useful than the singular perspective to which they are accustomed.

The construction of a sophisticated framework that can map the full complexity of vocational behavior enacted by diverse groups in manifold settings requires the lenses provided by both positivism and perspectivism. The lens of positivism focuses most clearly on macrotheory, whereas the lens of perspectivism focuses sharply on microtheory. With its concentration on particularity, multiplicity, context, difference, and usefulness, perspectivism has the potential to complement positivism by providing a microtheory approach that fills the lacunas in career macrotheory. A combination of modern macrotheory and postmodern microtheory could enrich and deepen vocational psychologists' understanding of work life. The vocational psychologists' first project would be to refurbish modern theories of career choice and development to be more multidimensional and multiperspectival by infusing postmodern microtheory concerning the role of work in everyday life. In this manner, vocational psychology could benefit simultaneously from refinements forged within the distinct career theories, from advances produced by convergence among career macrotheories, and from breakthroughs induced by divergence in work–role microtheory.

REFERENCES

Baker, S. B., & Popowicz, C. L. (1983). Meta-analysis as a strategy for evaluating the effects of career education interventions. *Career Development Quarterly, 31*, 178–186.

Bandura, A. (1982). The self and mechanisms of agency. In J. Suls (Ed.), *Psychological perspectives on the self* (pp. 3–39). Hillsdale, NJ: Lawrence Erlbaum Associates.

Bannister, D. (1970). Psychology as an exercise in paradox. In D. P. Schultz (Ed.), *The science of psychology: Critical reflections* (pp. 4–10). Englewood Cliffs, NJ: Prentice–Hall.

Beitman, B. D., Goldfried, M. R., & Norcross, J. C. (1989). The movement toward integrating the psychotherapies: An overview. *American Journal of Psychiatry, 146*, 138–147.

Best, S., & Kellner, D. (1991). *Postmodern theory: Critical interrogations.* New York: Guilford.

Betz, N. E., & Hackett, G. (1981). A self-efficacy approach to the career development of women. *Journal of Counseling Psychology, 28,* 399–410.

Bhaskar, R. (1989). *Reclaiming reality: A critical introduction to modern philosophy.* London: Verso.

Blustein, D. L. (1987). Integrating career counseling and psychotherapy: A comprehensive treatment strategy. *Psychotherapy, 24,* 794–799.

Blustein, D. L. (1990). An eclectic definition of psychotherapy: A developmental contextual view. In J. K. Zeig & W. M. Munion (Eds.), *What is psychotherapy?: Contemporary perspectives* (pp. 244–248). San Francisco: Jossey–Bass.

Blustein, D. L. (1994). The question of "Who am I?": A cross-theoretical analysis. In M. L. Savickas & R. W. Lent (Eds.), *Convergence in career development theories: Implications for science and practice* (pp. 137–152). Palo Alto, CA: Consulting Psychologists Press.

Bordin, E. S. (1994). Intrinsic motivation and the active self: Convergence from a psychodynamic perspective. In M. L. Savickas & R. W. Lent (Eds.), *Convergence in career development theories: Implications for science and practice* (pp. 53–61). Palo Alto, CA: Consulting Psychologists Press.

Borgen, F. H. (1984). Are there necessary linkages between research practices and the philosophy of science? *Journal of Counseling Psychology, 31,* 457–460.

Borgen, F. H. (1989). Evolution of eclectic epistemology. *The Counseling Psychologist, 17,* 90–97.

Borgmann, A. (1992). *Crossing the postmodern divide.* Chicago: University of Chicago Press.

Brown, D., & Brooks, L. (1990). *Career choice and development: Applying contemporary theories to practice.* San Francisco: Jossey–Bass.

Bruner, J. (1986). *Actual minds, possible worlds.* New York: Plenum.

Carlson, M. (1988). *Meaning-making: Therapeutic process in adult development.* New York: Norton.

Champagne, R. A. (1992). *The structuralists on myth: An introduction.* New York: Garland.

Cochran, L. (1990). *The sense of vocation: A study of career and life development.* Albany: State University of New York Press.

Cochran, L. (1991). *Life-shaping decisions.* New York: Peter Lang.

Cochran, L. (1992). The career project. *Journal of Career Development, 18,* 187–198.

Cohen, M. R., & Nagel, E. (1934). *An introduction to logic and scientific method.* New York: Harcourt, Brace & World.

Collin, A. (1994). Fracture lines for career. *NICEC Bulletin, 42,* 6–11.

Collin, A., & Young, R. (1986). New directions for theories of career. *Human Relations, 19,* 837 853.

Collin, A., & Young, R. (1988). Career development and hermeneutical inquiry: Part II—Undertaking hermeneutical research. *Canadian Journal of Counselling, 22,* 191–201.

Crites, J. O. (1981). *Career counseling: Models, methods, and materials.* New York: McGraw–Hill.

Crook, S. (1992). *Postmodernization: Change in advanced society.* Newbury Park, CA: Sage.

Csikszentmihalyi, M., & Beattie, O. (1979). Life themes: A theoretical and empirical exploration of their origins and effects. *Journal of Humanistic Psychology, 19,* 45–63.

Dawis, R. V. (1994). The theory of work adjustment as convergent theory. In M. L. Savickas & R. W. Lent (Eds.), *Convergence in career development theories: Implications for science and practice* (pp. 33–43). Palo Alto, CA: Consulting Psychologists Press.

Dawis, R., & Lofquist, L. (1984). *A psychological theory of work adjustment.* Minneapolis: University of Minnesota.

Doyle, W. (1990). Themes in teacher education. In R. Houston (Ed.), *Handbook of research on teacher education* (pp. 1–24). New York: Macmillan.

Edwards, J. R. (1991). Person-environment fit: A conceptual integration, literature review, and methological critique. In C. L. Cooper & I. T. Robertson (Eds.), *International review of industrial and organizational psychology* (Vol. 6, pp. 283–356). Chichester, England: John Wiley & Sons Ltd.

Featherstone, M. (1992). Preface—Cultural theory and cultural change. In M. Featherstone (Ed.), *Cultural theory and cultural change* (pp. vii–viii). London: Sage.

Fitzgerald, L., & Betz, N. (1994). Career development in cultural context: The role of gender, race, class, and sexual orientation. In M. L. Savickas & R. W. Lent (Eds.), *Convergence in career development theories: Implications for science and practice* (pp. 103–117). Palo Alto, CA: Consulting Psychologists Press.

Fitzgerald, L., & Rounds, J. (1994). Women and work: Theory encounters reality. In W. B. Walsh & S. H. Osipow (Eds.), *Career counseling for women* (pp. 327–353). Hillsdale, NJ: Lawrence Erlbaum Associates.

Ford, D. H. (1987). *Humans as self constructing living systems: A developmental perspective on personality and behavior.* Hillsdale, NJ: Lawrence Erlbaum Associates.

Ford, D. H., & Lerner, R. M. (1992). *Developmental systems theory: An integrative approach.* Newbury Park, CA: Sage.

Forsyth, D. R., & Strong, S. R. (1986). The scientific study of counseling and psychotherapy: A unificationist view. *American Psychologist, 41,* 113–119.

Fretz, B. R. (Ed.). (1989). Alternate research paradigms: A review and teaching proposal. *The Counseling Psychologist, 17*(1).

Gavin, W. (1992). *William James and the reinstatement of the vague.* Philadelphia: Temple University Press.

Gelso, C. J. (Ed.). (1984). Philosophy of science and counseling research [Special section]. *Journal of Counseling Psychology, 31*(4).

Gilligan, C. (1982). *In a different voice.* Cambridge, MA: Harvard University Press.

Grosz, E. (1988). The in(ter)vention of feminist knowledges. In B. Caine, E. Grosz, & M. deLapervanche (Eds.), *Crossing boundaries* (pp. 92–104). Sydney, Australia: Allen & Unwin.

Grover, S. C. (1981). *Toward a psychology of the scientist: Implications of psychological research for contemporary philosophy of science.* Washington, DC: University Press of America.

Habermas, J. (1973). Theories of truth. In H. Fahrenbach (Ed.), *Reality and perception: A festschrift for Walter Schulz* (pp. 211–265). Frankfurt, Germany: Pfüllingen.

Hackett, G. (1993). Career counseling and psychotherapy: False dichotomies and recommended remedies. *Journal of Career Assessment, 1,* 105–117.

Harding, S. (1991). *Whose science? Whose knowledge: Thinking from women's lives.* Ithaca, NY: Cornell University Press.

Harding, S. (1993). Rethinking standpoint epistemology: What is "strong objectivity"? In L. Alcoff & E. Potter (Eds.), *Feminist epistemologies* (pp. 49–82). New York: Routledge.

Harmon, L. W. (1994). Theoretical convergence: Frustrations, daydreams, and realities. In M. L. Savickas & R. W. Lent (Eds.), *Convergence in career development theories: Implications for science and practice* (pp. 223–232). Palo Alto, CA: Consulting Psychologists Press.

Holland, J. L. (1985). *Making vocational choices* (2nd ed.). Englewood Cliffs, NJ: Prentice–Hall.

Holland, J. L. (1994). Separate but unequal is better. In M. L. Savickas & R. W. Lent (Eds.), *Convergence in career development theories: Implications for science and practice* (pp. 45–51). Palo Alto, CA: Consulting Psychologists Press.

Jacques, R. (1992). Critique and theory building: Producing knowledge "from the kitchen." *Academy of Management Review, 17,* 582–606.

Jepsen, D. A. (1986). Getting down to cases: Editor's introduction. *Career Development Quarterly, 35*(2), 67–68.

Koch, S. (1985). The nature and limits of psychological knowledge: Lessons of a century qua "science." In S. Koch & D. E. Leary (Eds.), *A century of psychology as science* (pp. 75–97). New York: McGraw–Hill.

Krumboltz, J. D. (1994). Improving career development theory from a social learning perspective. In M. L. Savickas & R. W. Lent (Eds.), *Convergence in career development theories: Implications for science and practice* (pp. 9–31). Palo Alto, CA: Consulting Psychologists Press.

Krumboltz, J. D., & Nichols, C. W. (1990). Integrating the social learning theory of career decision making. In W. B. Walsh & S. H. Osipow (Eds.), *Career counseling: Contemporary topics in vocational psychology* (pp. 159–192). Hillsdale, NJ: Lawrence Erlbaum Associates.

Kuhn, T. S. (1970). *The structure of scientific revolutions* (2nd ed.). Chicago: University of Chicago Press.

Kvale, S. (1992). From the archaeology of the psyche to the architecture of cultural landscapes. In S. Kvale (Ed.), *Psychology and postmodernism* (pp. 1–16). London: Sage.

Lazarus, A. A. (1967). In support of technical eclecticism. *Psychological Reports, 21*, 415–416.

Lerner, R. M. (1985). Individual and context in developmental psychology: Conceptual and theoretical issues. In J. R. Nesselroade & A. von Eye (Eds.), *Individual development and social change: Explanatory analysis* (pp. 155–187). New York: Academic Press.

Loughead, T. A. (Ed.). (1989). The integration of career development and mental health counseling [Special issue]. *Journal of Career Development, 16*(1).

Luke, C. (1992). Feminist politics in radical pedagogy. In C. Luke & J. Gore (Eds.), *Feminism and critical pedagogy* (pp. 25–53). New York and London: Routledge.

Mahoney, M. J. (1976). *The scientist as subject: The psychological imperative.* Cambridge, MA: Ballinger.

Mahoney, M. J. (1993). Response to "Steps toward a science of free will": The enduring power of agency and control in theoretical and applied psychology. *Counseling and Values, 38*, 63–66.

Manicas, P. T., & Secord, P. F. (1983). Implications for psychology of the new philosophy of science. *American Psychologist, 38*, 399–413.

Marx, M. H. (Ed.). (1951). *Psychological theory.* New York: Macmillan.

Marx, M. H. (Ed.). (1963). *Theories in contemporary psychology.* New York: Macmillan.

Marx, M. H., & Goodson, F. E. (1976). *Theories in contemporary psychology* (2nd ed.). New York: Macmillan.

Maslow, A. H. (1966). *The psychology of science.* New York: Harper & Row.

Mitchell, A. M., Jones, G. G., & Krumboltz, J. D. (Eds.). (1979). *Social learning theory and career decision making.* Cranston, RI: Carroll.

Morf, M. E. (1992). (Some possible) differences between European and American approaches to the study of work. *European Work and Organizational Psychologist, 2*, 289–302.

Morrow–Bradley, C., & Elliott, R. (1986). Utilization of psychotherapy research by practicing psychotherapists. *American Psychologist, 41*, 188–197.

Neimeyer, G. (1988). Cognitive integration and differentiation in vocational behavior. *The Counseling Psychologist, 16*, 440–475.

Ochberg, R. (1988). Life stories and the psychosocial construction of careers. In D. McAdams & R. Ochberg (Eds.), *Psychobiography and life narratives* (pp. 173–204). Durham, NC: Duke University Press.

Oliver, L. W., & Spokane, A. R. (1988). Career-intervention outcome: What contributes to client gain? *Journal of Counseling Psychology, 35*, 447–462.

Osherson, S. (1980). *Holding on or letting go: Men and career change at midlife.* New York: The Free Press.

Osipow, S. H. (1990). Convergence in theories of career choice and development: Review and prospects. *Journal of Vocational Behavior, 36*, 122–131.

Osipow, S. H. (1993, August). *Toward mainstreaming the study of career psychology: Overcoming the Rodney Dangerfield effect.* Paper presented at the Third International Symposium on Career Development, University of Toronto, Canada.

Peatling, J. H., & Tiedeman, D. V. (1977). *Career development: Designing the Self.* Muncie, IN: Accelerated Development.

Peavy, V. (1992). A constructivist model of training for career counselors. *Journal of Career Development, 18*, 215–229.

Peavy, V. (1993, January). *The counsellor in post-modern society: Dilemmas and transformations.* Paper presented at the National Consultation on Career Development, Ottawa, Canada.

Polkinghorne, D. E. (1984). Further extensions of methodological diversity for counseling psychology. *Journal of Counseling Psychology, 31,* 416–429.

Polkinghorne, D. E. (1992). Postmodern epistemology of practice. In S. Kvale (Ed.), *Psychology and postmodernism* (pp. 146–165). London: Sage.

Richardson, M. S. (1993). Work in people's lives: A location for counseling psychologists. *Journal of Counseling Psychology, 40,* 425–433.

Rosser, S. V. (1990). *Female-friendly science: Applying women's studies methods and theories to attract students.* New York: Pergamon.

Rounds, J., & Hesketh, B. (1994). The theory of work adjustment: Underlying principles and concepts. In M. L. Savickas & R. W. Lent (Eds.), *Convergence in career development theories: Implications for science and practice* (pp. 175–184). Palo Alto, CA: Consulting Psychologists Press.

Rounds, J., & Tracey, T. J. (1993). Prediger's dimensional representations of Holland's RIASEC circumplex. *Journal of Applied Psychology, 78,* 875–890.

Runes, D. D. (Ed.). (1983). *Dictionary of philosophy.* New York: Philosophical Library.

Rychlak, J. F. (1988). Unification through understanding and tolerance of opposition. *International Newsletter of Uninomic Psychology, 5,* 13–15.

Rychlak, J. F. (1993). A suggested principle of complementarity for psychology. *American Psychologist, 48,* 933–942.

Savickas, M. L. (1989). Career-style assessment and counseling. In T. Sweeney (Ed.), *Adlerian counseling: A practical approach for a new decade* (3rd ed., pp. 289–320). Muncie, IN: Accelerated Development Press.

Savickas, M. L. (1993). Career counseling in the postmodern era. *Journal of Cognitive Psychotherapy: An International Quarterly, 7,* 205–215.

Savickas, M. L. (1994a). Convergence prompts theory renovation, research unification, and practice coherence. In M. L. Savickas & R. W. Lent (Eds.), *Convergence in career development theories: Implications for science and practice* (pp. 235–257). Palo Alto, CA: Consulting Psychologists Press.

Savickas, M. L. (1994b). Vocational psychology in the postmodern era: Comments on Richardson (1993). *Journal of Counseling Psychology, 41,* 105–107.

Savickas, M. L. (1994c). Fracture lines in career counselling. *NICEC Bulletin, 42,* 18–21.

Savickas, M. L., & Lent, R. W. (Eds.). (1994). *Convergence in career development theories: Implications for science and practice.* Palo Alto, CA: Consulting Psychologists Press.

Sharf, R. S. (1992). *Applying career development theory to counseling.* Pacific Grove, CA: Brooks/Cole.

Shotter, J. (1992). "Getting in touch": The meta-methodology of a postmodern science of mental life. In S. Kvale (Ed.), *Psychology and postmodernism* (pp. 58–73). London: Sage.

Skinner, B. F. (1950). Are theories of learning necessary? *Psychological Review, 57,* 193–216.

Slaney, R. B. (1988). The assessment of career decision making. In W. B. Walsh & S. Osipow (Eds.), *Career decision making* (pp. 33–76). Hillsdale, NJ: Lawrence Erlbaum Associates.

Slaney, R. B., & MacKinnon–Slaney, F. (1990). The use of vocational card sorts in career counseling. In C. Watkins & V. Campbell (Eds.), *Testing in counseling practice* (pp. 317–372). Hillsdale, NJ: Lawrence Erlbaum Associates.

Spokane, A. R. (1994). The resolution of incongruence and the dynamics of person–enviroment fit. In M. L. Savickas & R. W. Lent (Eds.), *Convergence in career development theories: Implications for science and practice* (pp. 119–136). Palo Alto, CA: Consulting Psychologists Press.

Staats, A. W. (1981). Paradigmatic behaviorism, unified theory, unified theory construction methods, and the zeitgeist of separatism. *American Psychologist, 36,* 239–256.

Staats, A. W. (1983). *Psychology's crisis of disunity: Philosophy and method for unified science.* New York: Praeger.

Staats, A. W. (1991). Unified positivism and unification psychology. *American Psychologist, 46,* 899–912.

Subich, L. M. (Ed.). (1993). How personal is career counseling? [Special issue]. *Career Development Quarterly, 42*(2).

Super, D. E. (1963). *Career development: Self-concept theory.* New York: College Entrance Examination Board.

Super, D. E. (1969). Vocational development theory: Persons, positions, and processes. *Counseling Psychologist, 1,* 2–9.

Super, D. E. (1980). A life-span, life-space approach to career development. *Journal of Vocational Behavior, 16,* 282–298.

Super, D. E. (1992). Toward a comprehensive theory of career development. In D. Montross & C. Shinkman (Eds.), *Career development: Theory and practice* (pp. 35–64). Springfield, IL: Thomas.

Taylor, C. (1989). *Sources of the self: The making of the modern identity.* Cambridge, MA: Harvard University Press.

Tiedeman, D. V., & Miller–Tiedeman, A. (1984, March). *The trend of life in the human career.* Paper presented at the First Congress of School and Vocational Guidance, Madrid, Spain.

Tinsley, H. E. A. (1994). Construct your reality and show us its benefits: Comments on Richardson (1993). *Journal of Counseling Psychology, 41,* 108–111.

Trapnell, P. (1992, August). *Vocational interests and the facet structure of the big five.* Paper presented at the convention of the American Psychological Association, Washington, DC.

Vondracek, F. W., & Fouad, N. A. (1994). Developmental contextualism: An integrative framework for theory and practice. In M. L. Savickas & R. W. Lent (Eds.), *Convergence in career development theories: Implications for science and practice* (pp. 205–212). Palo Alto, CA: Consulting Psychologists Press.

Vondracek, F. W., Lerner, R., & Schulenberg, J. (1986). *Career development: A life-span developmental approach.* Hillsdale, NJ: Lawrence Erlbaum Associates.

Walsh, W. B., & Chartrand, J. M. (1994). Person–environment fit: Emerging directions. In M. L. Savickas & R. W. Lent (Eds.), *Convergence in career development theories: Implications for science and practice* (pp. 185–194). Palo Alto, CA: Consulting Psychologists Press.

Walsh, W. B., Craik, K. H., & Price, R. H. (1992). Person–environment psychology: A summary and commentary. In W. B. Walsh, K. H. Craik, & R. H. Price (Eds.), *Person–environment psychology: Models and perspectives* (pp. 243–268). Hillsdale, NJ: Lawrence Erlbaum Associates.

Young, R. (1988). Ordinary explanations and career theories. *Journal of Counseling and Development, 66,* 336–339.

Young, R., & Borgen, W. (1990). *Methodological approaches to the study of career.* New York: Praeger.

CHAPTER TWO

The Interactional Perspective in Vocational Psychology: Paradigms, Theories, and Research Practices

Judy M. Chartrand
Stanley R. Strong
Lauren M. Weitzman
Virginia Commonwealth University

It is precisely because of the strengths and maturity of our ongoing research community that we are able to consider productive self-renewal of our enterprise. Thus, openness to new thinking in the contexts of both discovery and justification should be our goal, while thoughtfully building on the strengths of the old.

—Borgen (1992, p. 114)

The concept of behavior as a function of person–environment interactions is an indelible equation that crosses the discipline of psychology. In this chapter, we examine the current and potential impact of the person–environment, or interactional, view on vocational psychology. We have organized approaches to the interactional view in terms of a continuum based on the degree to which person and environment are assumed to be independent. Perspectives are described at three points on the continuum—complete independence, dynamic interdependence, and inseparability. These three viewpoints, or perspectives, embody divergent epistemic assumptions and pose distinct conceptual and methodological issues.

With the first perspective, traditionally called *person × environment*, person and environment are conceived as independent entities. This perspective is dominant in vocational psychology. Investigators working from this perspective typically seek to describe persons and environments in terms of commensurate dimensions and to demonstrate that the degree of fit, or congruence, between the two sets of measures predicts behavior. With the

35

second perspective, which we refer to as *systemic*, person and environment are conceived as interdependent entities that dynamically interact as reciprocal parts of a unified system. This perspective is apparent in theories of career development. The third perspective, *constructionism*, asserts that divisions between person and environment are artificial distinctions constructed for pragmatic purposes. Investigations emerging from this perspective have focused on the construction and meaning of career narratives.

In this chapter, we trace and connect epistemological, conceptual, and operational issues in each perspective and, in this way, identify some of the scientific issues and problems that confront those who seek to advance vocational psychology within them. We also reinterpret conceptual problems that plague investigators in one perspective, using the lens of a unified perspective. The three perspectives differ remarkably in the lenses through which one observes events. Both the person x environment and systemic positions are informed by a logical positivist philosophy of science, whereas the constructionist position is informed by a postpositivistic and postmodern philosophy of science. Logical positivism is based on the assumptions that there is a reality beyond our experiencing of it and that we can access this reality directly through objective observation, a view explicitly rejected in postmodern thought. Logical positivism emphasizes the development of systematic statements that identify underlying general laws that account for individual events, and the use of operational definitions in research (Leahey, 1992). Postpositivistic thought recasts the meaning of these efforts, and some adherents of postmodernism reject them as reasonable goals of science. In this chapter, we hope to interrelate and reconcile these contradictory perspectives and thus fulfill Borgen's (1992) eloquent call for communication, consideration, and cooperation across conceptual paradigms.

The interactional perspective in vocational psychology contains streams forged from both venerable and vanguard sources that advance discrepant epistemic assumptions. The literature in vocational psychology flows primarily from investigators working within the received view, although contributions are emerging from those pursuing knowledge based on postpositivist assumptions (e.g., Young & Borgen, 1990). The path ultimately carved by current inquiry is difficult to predict, but we believe that the embracing of multiple paradigms will speed progress. To provide a context for this effort, we begin with a brief history of the interactional view in psychology. We then explore and interrelate the three perspectives.

HISTORICAL OVERVIEW

During the first half of the 20th century, experimental, social, and personality theorists tried to explain behavior in terms of person–environment interactions (Brunswik, 1950; Lewin, 1951; Murray, 1938). At that time, the person x environment perspective began to guide major hypothesis development and interpretation. Dictums that person and context elements needed to be measured in commensurate units (Murray, 1938) and that persons selected and shaped situations (Allport, 1961) were adopted with little fanfare until Mischel (1968) galvanized the person–situation controversy. Suddenly, the feasibility of our trying to predict behavior from the person side of the equation was questioned, and the impact and the fluidity of the context were reemphasized. Persuasive attacks on logical positivism as the guiding philosophy of the social sciences also surfaced in the late 1960s (Leahey, 1992; Polkinghorne, 1983) and contributed to the unrest. The ensuing debates about the merits of logical positivism and the person x environment view led to refined statements about each and paved the way for interpretations from other perspectives.

In the vocational realm, the person–situation controversy also unfolded. Trait–factor conceptions, which evolved from the 1920s, became girders for the stalwart models of career development (Super, 1983). Over a period of years, however, discontent with trait-based formulations, especially within career counseling, grew until the usefulness of the model was questioned (Crites, 1981). This period of doubt remained until articulate retorts were presented (e.g., Rounds & Tracey, 1990). As with the person–situation controversy in other areas of psychology, the exchange between doubters and proponents led to refinements and adaptations of the person x environment perspective. Developmental psychologists (Vondracek, Lerner, & Schulenberg, 1986) also contributed to the evolution of interactionism by using a systemic perspective to describe how person–environment interaction sequences unfold over time. Recently, integrated positions have emerged. If the previous era sparked vociferous discontent, the current era seemingly embraces tolerant discontent. In person–environment psychology, similarities across models are acknowledged (e.g., Walsh, Craik, & Price, 1992) and diverse methodologies encouraged (e.g., Magnusson & Allen, 1983). By identifying points of convergence and developing integrated eclecticism, psychologists within the vocational field have made efforts to expand and improve theories of career counseling and development (Savickas & Lent, 1994), to expand methods of inquiry (Young & Borgen, 1990), and to reconcile epistemic paradigms (Borgen, 1992). This current zeitgeist allows for the juxtaposition of justification and discovery, descriptive and explanatory, nomothetic and idiographic, and molar and molecular. The overarching premise that all psychologists study behavior by taking into account "the situation (S) and the personality (P) of the subject, both interacting to determine the response" (Fraisse, 1987, p. 213) has been accepted.

In the subsequent discussions, we review the person x environment, systemic, and constructionist views, define each perspective, and highlight their central conceptual and operational issues. Examples of research from each perspective are reviewed as illustrations of conceptual points. Finally, we attempt to integrate the philosophical perspectives, using a model of causal pragmatism.

PERSON X ENVIRONMENT PERSPECTIVE

The person x environment view includes both person (trait) and person–environment congruence research. Trait efforts focus on the person, whereas congruence research considers the joint contribution of person and environment components. Both views are consistent with a logical positivist perspective. Criteria for evaluation rest on the quality of operational definitions and testability. The primary scientific goal is the prediction of behavior, and both theory and research designs typically involve linear models by which persons and environments are independently defined and placed as antecedent variables. The basic approach is the identification and description of person and environment characteristics and the study of their independent or interactive effects. An Aristotelian logic pervades, and taxonomic classification of persons and environments is often pursued.

Trait Concepts and Research

Historically, in many fields of psychology, a trait orientation was adopted before person x environment and other interactional conceptions of causality were embraced (Altman & Rogoff, 1987). Because taxonomic development often precedes causal analysis, this strategy served an important function. Consistent with its Aristotelian logic, the trait position is based on the assumption that the causes of a person's behavior are ingrained qualities of the person. The goal of the approach is the characterization of these behavior potentials of the person, typically without direct attention to the context within which the person is embedded (Altman & Rogoff, 1987). This does not mean that environmental context has no influence on behavior. On the contrary, environments or contexts disturb or promote the purity with which the basic personological essences, or traits, manifest themselves. The basic personological essences, or traits, reveal themselves in behavioral stabilities and cross-situational consistencies (Strong, 1991). The heart of trait-based research has been the classification of individual differences in abilities, preferences, and personality; the five-factor model of personality (Costa & McCrae, 1985; Norman, 1963) is a prototypic example of these efforts.

The trait-based perspective characterizes major portions of the vocational psychology literature. For example, identification and quantification of vocational aptitudes, interests, and values has a long, progressive, and impressive history (Dawis, 1992; Super, 1983). Research on the viability and predictive validity of vocational aptitudes is extensive. Empirical support for the structure and intraindividual stability of vocational interests (Swanson & Hansen, 1988) and values (Gay, Weiss, Hendel, Dawis, & Lofquist, 1971; Seaburg, Rounds, Dawis, & Lofquist, 1976) is strong, and the impact of trait-based efforts on vocational theory development and practice is astounding. Several theories of vocational development and adjustment (e.g., Dawis & Lofquist, 1984; Holland, 1985a; Super, 1990) and correspondent career assessment instrumentation incorporate trait concepts. The burgeoning literature on relations between the five-factor model of personality and job performance variables is a relatively new extension of trait research (Barrick & Mount, 1991).

Traits have also been found to serve as moderator variables in congruence research. For example, Tranberg, Slane, and Ekeberg (1993) demonstrated that Holland personality types moderate the congruence–satisfaction relation. They found that the congruence–satisfaction relation was strongest for *social* personalities (mean correlation = .33), and weakest for *realistic* types (mean correlation = .05). Schwartz (1991) reported differences between *investigative* and realistic types in academic achievement—the relation between congruence and achievement disappeared after investigative and realistic scores were controlled. Collectively, these examples demonstrate the importance of trait research, especially for the prediction of salient vocational outcomes such as satisfaction and performance.

Congruence Concepts and Research

The person x environment congruence position brings the context to the foreground because it characterizes environments and people in commensurate terms. Osipow (1987) noted that P x E interaction is what vocational psychology is about, and this perspective is apparent in a number of vocational theories (Dawis & Lofquist, 1984; French, Rodgers, & Cobb, 1974; Holland, 1985a; Schneider, 1987; Vondracek et al., 1986). Reviews of the vocational psychology literature (e.g., annual reviews published in the *Journal of Vocational Behavior*) reveal extensive research devoted to the testing of congruence hypotheses. This prominent status, however, does not imply that the epistemic and empiric issues associated with the person x environment view have been addressed to a point beyond debate. Some of these issues are reviewed here and then related to measurement. Conceptual clarity guides the translation of theoretical constructs to measures of response, and this has been a most arduous path (Nunnally, 1983). Within the person x environment view, major conceptual issues continue to revolve around the defining of the context and the interactional term. With respect to the context, issues include the determination of the level of analysis and of the structure of the context and the distinction between participant and nonparticipant ratings of environments. With respect to the interactional term, the primary issues are the identification of commensurate person and context dimensions and the definition of congruence.

Levels of Analysis. Strong efforts in the trait arena have helped sketch the person side of the equation. Unfortunately, lucid descriptions of the context have proven more elusive. Pervin (1978) reviewed this area and concluded that ambiguous definitions of the context and error and bias in measures have hindered progress in interactional research. He identified three distinct levels of context description—stimulus, situation, and environment—and articulated conceptual differences between them. The appropriate level for any analysis depends on the question being asked. For example, worker productivity may be studied in terms of reactions to a stimulus (e.g., noise level), a situation (e.g., stressful work setting), or environment (e.g., organizational climate). As shown in the following illustrations, each level offers a different component of the context and affords different strengths and limitations.

One of the few studies in vocational psychology in which context was conceptualized at the stimulus level was recently reported by Dawis, Dohm, and Jackson (1993), who studied reinforcement schedules in work settings. According to the theory of work adjustment (TWA; Dawis & Lofquist, 1984), correspondence between worker needs and values and environmental reinforcement predicts satisfaction. Occupational environments are typically profiled in terms of patterns of reinforcement of worker needs, which are called *occupational reinforcer patterns* (ORPs; Borgen, Weiss, Tinsley, Dawis, & Lofquist, 1968). Taking a different approach, Dawis et al. (1993) specified reinforcement in work settings as Skinnerian reinforcement schedules. They translated reinforcement schedules into three dimensions: predictability versus nonpredictability (fixed vs. variable), self versus nonself (ratio vs. interval), and social versus nonsocial (internal vs. external control). Judges then rated 183 occupations according to each dimension. Dawis et al. found that the classification of occupations generated by this method was similar to but far from identical to the classification generated by occupational reinforcer patterns.

Situation has been examined more frequently than stimulus in vocational research, as the following examples indicate. In investigations of sexual harassment, whether or not an incident is viewed as sexually harassing is influenced by situational variables such as gender of victim and harasser, extent of power differential, and type of behavior enacted (Fitzgerald & Shullman, 1993). Situational variables have been identified in measures of occupational stress. For example, Osipow and Spokane's (1984) occupational environment scale includes assessment of situational factors such as exposure to environmental toxins and the amount of daily interpersonal contacts. Tung (1980) developed a scale of job-related stress that measures situational components of task-based work stress, such as interruptions and getting behind in correspondence and report writing. Using a content analysis of supervisor and manager narratives of recent stressful job encounters, Scherer, Owen, Petrick, Brodzinski, and Goyer (1991) classified situational stressors such as work overload, restrictions on behavior, and relations with co-workers.

Most vocational researchers have operationalized context at the environment level by examining characteristics of the work environment in broadly defined terms, such as organizational climate or psychological orientation. In a meta-analysis, Assouline and Meir (1987) reported considerable variability in congruence–satisfaction correlations due to the differences in environmental classification. They categorized the environment into three broad environmental referents (intended occupation, current occupation, educational institution) or into narrower referents (specialty within an occupation, intended major, current major). They found that one of the broad environmental referents, current occupation, yielded a smaller congruence–satisfaction relation (mean correlation = .21) than the more specific specialties within an occupation (mean correlation = .42). In a similar vein, Meir and Yaari (1988) developed a series of within-occupation interest inventories from which specialty congruence scores could be derived. They found median correlations of .41 and .40, using this more specific method. Therefore, although broad-based environmental measures of context apparently offer a common and easily understood language, they may limit the magnitude of predictability (Spokane, 1985) and confine inferences to general statements. Researchers have acknowledged the need for greater specificity at the environmental level, especially when investigating the congruence hypothesis from Holland's theory (Meir, 1989).

Structure of the Environment. The content and structure of the units used for the measurement of context are important considerations (Pervin, 1978). For example, the content of units could be cognitive, affective, or behavioral, and each would yield a different context meaning. This possibility for variations raises the question of whether the identification of universal context dimensions is feasible. At first glance, research like that of Moos (1987) and others suggests an affirmative response to this question. In this program of research, numerous work, school, and health care environments were observed, and three organizational-climate domains were identified: relationship (e.g., co-worker involvement and support), personal growth and goal orientation (e.g., autonomy, task orientation, work pressure), and system maintenance and change (e.g., the amount of clarity, structure, and openness that existed in an occupational setting). Although this program of research is extensive and impressive (see Moos, 1987), the issue of universality remains. For example, cultural differences may lead to qualitatively different perceptions of a given environment. Failure to acknowledge these differences reduces culturally unique perceptions to error variance, which is a precarious practice, given the growing diversity in the work force.

Nonparticipant- Versus Participant-Perceived Work Environments. Another conceptual issue is, Whose perceptions and ratings of context are of interest? The environment may be defined in terms of trained observers' perceptions (*objective*) or in terms of the perceptions of participants in the environment (*subjective*). Various investigators have placed their research at different points along this objective–subjective continuum. For example, Barker (1987) proposed that environments select and shape people, and he focused on the physical and structural properties of situations as rated by trained observers. On the other hand, Magnusson (1988) and his colleagues defined the environment in terms of its occupants' perceptions of it. Rotter (1955) took a two-stage position by suggesting that the context be defined in terms of objective characteristics and then studied in terms of its psychological meaning to its occupants.

Who rates the environment is crucial because the information provided by different observers, although similar, is not identical (Moos, 1974). Most vocational researchers adopt, explicitly or implicitly, an occupant-perceived position. This position, however, is potentially confusing because it is difficult to separate the variable of interest from its effects. Pervin (1978) illustrated this point by asking the question, "If an organization is measured in terms of perceptions of workers, is one measuring the organization or its effects?" (p. 78). Inability to answer this question leads to a tautological loop in which cause and effect are confounded. In general, as the separation between the predictor and criterion variables becomes more distinct, the confusion between the two becomes less problematic.

The difference between conceptualizing and measuring the environment can be illustrated with Holland's (1985a) theory and the TWA (Dawis & Lofquist, 1984). In Holland's theory, the environment is defined by a census of the vocational interest types of persons who inhabit an occupational or educational environment. Characteristics of the environment are inferred from responses of workers in the environment. On the other hand, the TWA relies on supervisor or job-analyst ratings of work environment characteristics. The differences in these methods becomes quite apparent in academic environments, where environmental tasks are often similar across majors but students who comprise the majors vary significantly in their interests and value patterns.

Commensurate Person x Environment Dimensions. The feasibility of generating commensurate person and context dimensions and defining the congruence between them are major conceptual issues. Parallel conceptual domains, structural organization, and units of measurement are prerequisites for some P x E fit indices (Rounds, Lofquist, & Dawis, 1987). Yet, the requirement of parallelism may simply force an anthropomorphic fit on the environment: Person items "can be only metaphorically applied to organizations because items were designed to measure personality" (Chatman, 1989, p. 317). Holland (1985a) side-stepped this issue by defining the environment in terms of the people who compose the environment. This solution, however, is not always satisfactory because the people who compose some environments are highly heterogenous, such as those in basic training in the military (Davis–Blake & Pfeffer, 1989).

The definition of congruence between person and environment variables is crucial because degree of congruence often serves as the primary predictor variable. Often congruence is assumed to be linearly related to beneficial outcomes. The lack of fit between a person and an organization, however, may be a positive force in that it can foster growth and change (Chatman, 1989). Unfortunately, researchers tend to implement a static linear view of congruence (Spokane, 1990); rarely do investigators specify the type of interaction sought and the theory it expresses. Congruence can be conceptualized as moderation, mediation, matching, gestalt, or profile deviation (Venkatraman, 1989), and each of these represents a different theoretical slant and leads to a different research strategy.

Measurement Issues in Person x Environment Research

Issues of measurement extend from the theoretic level to the level of theory-to-data correspondence. The impact of measurement practices on theory is illustrated by how research has shaped Holland's (1985a) theory. The impact of measurement practice on theory-to-data correspondence is demonstrated by the finding that the magnitude of the relation between congruence and vocational outcome depends on how the person, context, and interaction terms are operationalized (Assouline & Meir, 1987; Spokane, 1985; Tranberg et al., 1993).

Measurement of Person Variables. In tests of Holland's theory, the person variable is assessed according to formal scales or people's expressed preferences for occupations. Formal scales are most commonly used and include the Vocational Preference Inventory (VPI; Holland, 1985b), the Self-Directed Search (SDS; Holland, 1978, 1985c), the Strong Interest Inventory (SII; Hansen & Campbell, 1985), the Career Assessment Inventory (Johansson, 1986), the American College Testing Vocational Interest Profile (VIP; American College Testing Program, 1977), and the Unisex Edition of the ACT Interest Inventory (UNIACT; American College Testing Program, 1988). Researchers obtain expressed preferences by classifying a person's stated preferences for an occupation, educational major, or type of vocational training according to the RIASEC code (Holland, 1985a) of that occupation, major, or training. The SDS occupational daydream code is also used as a measure of expressed preference.

Results of comparisons between these methods of predicting choice of training and work experiences have been inconsistent. Gottfredson and Holland (1975) reported that the occupational daydream code was a more efficient predictor of expressed occupational choice over a 1-year interval than was the SDS summary code. However, O'Neill, Magoon, and Tracey (1978) found no differences between one-letter SDS summaries and occupational daydream codes as predictors of present career, graduate major, ideal career, and projected career over a 7-year period. Holland and Gottfredson (1975) found that prediction of expressed occupational choice after 1 year was better when the first letters of SDS occupational daydream codes and SDS summary codes were identical than when the codes were different. Using meta-analysis, Rounds (1988) examined the ability of different interest inventories to predict job satisfaction. He found that the ability of those that contained RIASEC scales were about the same, although studies with effect sizes greater than 0.40 typically incorporated the VPI.

Rounds and Tracey (1993) assessed how well several inventories (SII, UNIACT, SDS, and VPI) conformed to various structural hypotheses of how vocational types relate to one another in psychological space. They found that all of the inventories resulted in structures that conformed to Holland's (1985a) RIASEC model. The instruments differed, however, in how well they conformed to Prediger's (1982) data–ideas and things–people two-factor model and Hogan's (1983) 30-degree rotation of Prediger's (1982) axes. Of the instruments, the SDS had the poorest model fit and the lowest salience ratio, especially when contrasted with results from the UNIACT. Rounds and Tracey (1993) concluded that the SDS was not equivalent to the UNIACT, whereas the UNIACT, SII, and VPI were equivalent to each other.

Measurement of Environmental Variables. The environmental assessment technique (Astin & Holland, 1961), one of the first methods that operationalized the RIASEC environment, is a census-taking approach whereby a particular environmental unit (e.g., business or educational setting) is evaluated in terms of its RIASEC characteristics. Classification is accomplished by (a) the tabulation of either the occupations that exist in the unit or the vocational interests of individuals in the setting, (b) the categorization of the results into the six environmental types, and (c) the translation of the absolute numbers for each type into percentages for the unit (Holland, 1985a). This method has been used predominantly in educational settings (e.g., Astin, 1968), where it has been extended to RIASEC environmental classifications of curricula and faculty (Richards, Seligman, & Jones, 1970). The use of the census-taking method, however, is somewhat unwieldy and time-consuming, characteristics that diminish its use. Alternatively, environments can be coded by Holland (1985a) type according to the *Dictionary of Holland Occupational Codes* (Gottfredson, Holland, & Ogawa, 1982), which provides rationally derived three-letter codes for 12,099 occupations found in the *Dictionary of Occupational Titles* (U.S. Department of Labor, 1977).

In a meta-analysis, Assouline and Meir (1987) found that the method of measuring the environment influenced the magnitude of the congruence–satisfaction relation. When individual personality types were compared to modal personality type in an environment (census-taking method), the mean correlation across 20 congruence–satisfaction correlations was .29. When a rationally derived method of classifying occupations was used, Assouline and Meir obtained a mean correlation across 16 studies of .21. They found additional evidence of the greater utility of the census-taking approach in studies ($N = 3$) of congruence–stability relations.

Measurement of P x E Fit. The greatest measurement challenge for person x environment researchers is to define and scale the person x environment fit term. Usually fit is operationalized as the difference between person and context scores (Rounds et al., 1987). Difference scores, however, pose a host of problems: The reliability of a difference score is less than the average reliability of its component parts, the potential for spurious relations between a fit term and its component parts exists (Venkatraman, 1989); and difference scores do not describe the direction or point on the continuum where differences occur. A difference score of P greater than E is not equivalent to a difference score of E greater than P, even if the magnitude of difference is identical. For example, a person's need for achievement that exceeds available environmental reinforcement is not equivalent to environmental reinforcement for achievement that exceeds a person's desires to achieve. Similarly, not all difference scores are equally meaningful. Discrepancies between person and environment characteristics that are salient for the person may have more influence than differences that are not salient to the person.

In the context of TWA (Dawis & Lofquist, 1984), Rounds et al. (1987) calculated work-value–occupational-reinforcer correspondence and related it to job satisfaction, using 19 different fit indices in two separate vocational samples. They examined conceptually commensurate concepts (relatedness of person and environmental dimensions), commensurate units (equality of person and environment units), and commensurate structures (structural equivalence of person and environment), using agreement, correlational, and various difference-score calculations. The results revealed large differences in the correlations between the different correspondence indices and job satisfaction. Therefore, the degree of support for the correspondence–satisfaction proposition depended on how the fit term was operationalized.

Working in the context of Holland's (1985a) theory, Camp and Chartrand (1992) calculated the relationship of 13 congruence indices to each other and to outcome variables such as academic achievement and adjustment, career indecision, and satisfaction with major. Their results, like those of Rounds et al. (1987), showed variations in the relationships of fit indices to each other and to outcome variables. Tranberg et al. (1993) investigated the influence of the quality of measures (e.g., standardization, reliability) on the congruence–satisfaction relation. Contrary to expectation, studies that used poorer measures had higher mean congruence–satisfaction correlations than studies that used psychometrically better measures. It is apparent from these investigations that how P x E fit is measured greatly affects how congruence relates to outcome measures.

Summary

The person x environment perspective has generated considerable trait and congruence research. This perspective is embodied in several major vocational theories, most notably Holland's (1985a) and the TWA (Dawis & Lofquist, 1984). Some of the shortcomings of these theories (see, e.g., Hackett & Lent, 1992) are not theory-specific but reflect conceptual and measurement issues common to a person x environment perspective. The failure of researchers who test these theories to distinguish level of context, the raters' position in the environment, and assumptions about and the meaning of the fit term lead to conceptually muddled and empirically restricted results. Explicit descriptions of how the person, the context, and the interactional terms are defined and measured is critical from a person x environment view. Not only do investigators need to address specific points within vocational person x environment theories, as articulately discussed by Hackett and Lent (1992), they also need to be sensitive to the assumptions and conceptual issues of the paradigm that drive these theories. This sensitivity may highlight strengths as well as limitations of the person x environment perspective and free investigators to explore alternative paradigms.

SYSTEMIC PERSPECTIVE

In the systemic perspective, an individual's behavior is conceptualized as a product of a dynamic and holistic psychological system in which person and context interact in complex and reciprocal ways (Altman & Rogoff, 1987). From this perspective, the goal of science is the illumination of a core set of principles by which systems function and is achieved through the identification and analysis of patterns in observable events. The primary unit of study is the whole system—this perspective ascribes to the adage that the whole is greater than the sum of its parts. Therefore, although elements can be defined independently, they must be studied in terms of their relations and organization in the system. Similar to the person x environment view, the systemic view ascribes to many canons of traditional scientific inquiry. Objectivity, replicability, testability, and the pursuit of universal laws or principles are valued strategies. The systemic perspective emphasizes reciprocal patterns of relations, whereas the person x environment view studies unidirectional patterns (Altman & Rogoff, 1987).

A marked difference between the person x environment view and the systemic view is the systemic view's incorporation of teleological causality in addition to the more traditional deterministic causal model. Whereas with the deterministic model, researchers identify antecedent events as the causes of consequent behavior, with the teleologic model they identify consequent end-states as the causes of antecedent behaviors. The end-state is a system, goal, or purpose, and the antecedent behavior is a means to that goal or purpose. Teleology underlies systemic principles such as homeostasis and equifinality. In the systemic approach, however, teleological processes are reconceptualized within a deterministic framework on which mechanisms that act in the present are posited and by which the appearance of the future's pulling and causing the present is created. For example, in the Lewinian (1951) tradition, the perception of an end-state in the environment (a goal) that could affect a current state of the person (a need) generates a motive. The motive is a psychological force that acts in the present to energize and direct the person's behavior toward achieving the goal. Homeostasis is conceptualized as a function of detection devices and feedback loops that energize and direct behavior and thereby eliminate deviations from some given state of the system. Equifinality, the notion that the system will achieve the same end-state from diverse beginnings, is conceptualized as the result of deviation–detection–correction mechanisms that operate in the present.

Conceptual Issues

The emphasis on development, change, and continuity makes teleological explanation and the dynamic flow of behavior key concepts in the systemic perspective. To be conceptually consistent, research designs must include a longitudinal component of repeated measures and analyses that take into account autocorrelations among observations. A critical and vexing problem is the measurement of change (Nesselroade & Baltes, 1979). The methodology of studying human change has received considerable attention, although much of this work is ignored in research practice (Nunnally, 1982). Critical developmental issues include intraindividual and interindividual growth rates, the developmental point at which variables of interest are measured, and potentially powerful covariates such as chronological age and physical maturity. The magnitude of relations between measures taken at two or more points in time depends on the intervals between the data points, person's age at first data collection, and stage in the transitional period (Magnusson, 1988). If there is one particular shortcoming of the career development research, it has been the emphasis on career at the expense of development. Empirical efforts lag far behind developmental concepts of career (Crites, 1983).

A thorny issue within the systemic frame is the determination of the appropriate level of complexity at which to study structures and processes. Magnusson (1988) noted that "data appropriate for the elucidation of structure and processes at one level of complexity, can yield meaningless results if applied to problems at other levels" (p. 62). In this research, the level of observation must be that at which the processes of interest operate. For example, data aggregated within situations cannot yield explanations of cross-situational variations. The lack of distinction between levels of analysis leads to mixed results and poor interpretations.

The search for patterns within complex structures or systems also forces a decision of whether the research beam should be directed toward overt covariations or toward mediating processes that drive behavioral manifestations. Consideration of equafinality (varied motives can result in the same behavior), equipotentiality (the same motives can result in varied behaviors), and multideterminism (behavior is an expression of the interaction among multiple motives) forces investigators to ponder different points of research illumination. When these distinctions are coupled with the aforementioned issues of level of complexity, the burden of our simultaneously understanding structure and process within systems is apparent. Reciprocal determinism, another key mechanism in systemic thinking, heightens this intricacy.

Theory and Research

Although there are many imposing directives and few clear directions for optimal research within this view, several research avenues are promising. For example, Pervin (1992) examined goals as motivational forces. He sought to answer the question of why people shifted from situation to situation, emitting different behaviors, and yet retained coherence of personality (Pervin, 1989). In his conceptualization, the environment is composed of affordances in which opportunities are or are not present for the individual to achieve desired goals. Humans are understood in terms of the organization and functioning of their goal systems in various environments. Congruence between person and environment involves relations between multiple goals and environmental affordances. Therefore, person systems, environment systems, and relations between person and environment systems all contribute to the understanding of congruence (Pervin, 1992).

Vondracek et al.'s (1986) life-span approach to vocational development draws from contemporary developmental psychology and is guided by a systemic perspective. The model incorporates interactional processes into a goodness-of-fit model that describes the interplay between individual characteristics and environmental demands. Although Vondracek et al. addressed development across the entire life span, they gave primary attention to adolescence. With the model, individuals are conceptualized as actively contributing to their own development. The organism, via physical characteristics, behavioral styles, and cognitive attributes, is viewed as the meeting place of person and environmental factors. Environments are viewed as multilevel contexts that continue to change interdependently over time. In the model, the environment is composed of four interconnected ecostructures: the microsystem, the context in which the developing person exists directly (e.g., one's family); the mesosystem, which consists of interrelationships among microsystem components (e.g., links between workplace and family); the ecosystem, which represents contexts that do not directly contain, yet still influence, the developing person (e.g., parent's or partner's workplace); and the macrosystem, the set of overarching ideologies and belief systems associated with the developing person's cultural context. Hence, environments are viewed as complex multilayered contexts that incorporate structural aspects (e.g., family size), relationships (e.g., quality of parent–child interactions), and linkages between systems (e.g., intersetting communication and knowledge).

Schulenberg, Vondracek, and Nesselroade (1988) tested Vondracek et al.'s (1986) model by examining intraindividual change in work values. They asked seven college students to complete a work-values inventory every day for 100 consecutive days and to respond to the items according to how they were feeling at that moment. Schulenberg et al. (1988) interpreted the systematic changes in response variability over time as support for their hypothesis that work values have state-like dimensions. In a recent review, Moos (1987) found that the effects of a social environment on an individual depended on the states of the person's other microsystems. For example, the type of learning environment teachers provided for their students was dependent on the teachers' perceptions of co-worker and administrative support and the clarity of role expectations. Task-focused and independence-oriented work environments were associated with teachers' creation of task-focused and highly structured learning environments for their students (Hutcherson, 1982). In the same vein, Nelson (1984) found that students' scholastic self-concepts were enhanced by highly supportive and structured family and classroom environments.

Bidwell, Csikszentmihalyi, Hedges, and Schneider (1992) investigated the contextual effects of relationships with peers, family, and teachers on adolescent career formation. With a diverse sample of adolescents, these investigators collected data using a combination of questionnaires, structured interviews, and the experience sampling method. With the experience sampling method, students were cued with beepers eight times daily over a period of eight days and were asked to report immediately the feelings, thoughts, current actions, and activities they would have preferred to be doing at that moment. The investigators' results indicated that students' ratings of their daily concentration while working and intrinsic motivation for a preferred career accounted for significantly more variance in career clarity and knowledge than age, ascribed characteristics (e.g., gender), or social influences. The longitudinal framework of this study allowed for the examination of change over time. Efforts such as this are essential if researchers are to take theoretically based formulations of systemic processes into the empirical realm.

Measurement and Design Issues

Although some positivist notions, such as reductionism and linear models, are considered limited from a systemic view, the assumption that general principles govern behavior is retained, and quantitative methods are a major part of the research repertoire. A number of authors have presented suggestions for developing longitudinal research (Magnusson, 1988; Nesselroade & Baltes, 1979; Nunnally, 1982; Schaie & Hertzog, 1982; Vondracek et al., 1986). Such research requires measures that are sensitive to change and that have equivalences so that changes over time in person, measure, and error can be identified and separated. Research within the systemic perspective must incorporate multivariate, multidimensional, and multilevel measures of persons and environments.

A statistical method that seems well suited for research within the systemic approach is structural equation modeling (Anderson, 1987). Structural equation models consist of systems of regression equations that describe the relations among sets of observed variables and theoretical constructs. Experimental and nonexperimental and cross-sectional and longitudinal designs can be incorporated in the model. From a systemic perspective, the primary advantage of structural equation modeling methods is the ability it affords investigators to analyze both person and situational systems and to separate measurement error from theoretical relations. Causal and bicausal relations can be specified, and direct, indirect, and autoregression effects can be estimated. Investigators can examine stability of a person or context variable, as well as patterns of reciprocal relations over time, using longitudinal data (Farrell, 1994). Although concerns have been raised about the appropriate use of this methodology, there is notable enthusiasm (Biddle & Marlin, 1987; Connell, 1987; Martin, 1987).

Summary

The systemic perspective is evident in the work of several influential theorists (e.g., Bandura, 1978; Moos, 1987; Pervin, 1992) and in two life-span theories of vocational development (Super, 1990; Vondracek et al., 1986). The systemic perspective incorporates the complex, multilevel nature of environments, and this attribute is both a strength and a weakness. Although it is feasible to conceive of person–environment interactions as dynamic and systemic, the implementation of conceptually consistent research designs has proven difficult. Many investigators who espouse a systemic perspective actually rely on research designs that are more consistent with the assumptions of a person x environment perspective. Regression equations that include person and environment variables for the prediction of a vocational behavior or outcome do not test systemic propositions. Instead, person, environment, and behavior variables must be measured over time so that causal and interactional effects can be determined. Additionally, the interest in both overt covariations and mediating processes suggests that both qualitative and quantitative strategies are necessary in order for the research to meet the assumptions of this perspective.

CONSTRUCTIONISM

The constructionist approach to science differs from approaches that are informed by the received view in one fundamental way: It denies the proposition that people can observe reality independently of their participation in it. The received view is based on the assumptions that there is a reality independent of us (realism) and that we can come to know this reality through objective observation (tabula rasa). From a constructionist point of view, the existence of an external reality can be assumed or not assumed; in any case, it cannot be objectively observed. Constructionists believe that we actively participate in the construction of what we observe. Observations are channeled, limited, and produced by our concepts of how to look and of what we are looking at and by our abilities to sense. Even more, we take for granted many of the concepts that channel our observations: We are not aware of them or of their effects on what we observe (Garfinkel, 1967; Wittgenstein, 1969).

From a constructionist perspective, science is a formative and constructive enterprise, the goal of which is the development of concepts that are pragmatically useful for some purposes. These purposes include both the achievement of desired ends (e.g., putting a rocket on the moon, enhancing P–E fit in the world of work, and influencing people to change) and the promotion of visions of reality that we champion (e.g., androgenous is better, particular people are oppressed, and people act rather than respond). Science is, therefore, a pragmatic and political enterprise.

Theory

Constructionists (Garfinkel, 1967; K. Gergen, 1985; Harre, 1992; Howard, 1992; Shotter, 1984; Taylor, 1985; Von Wright, 1971; Wittgenstein, 1969) conceive of people as products and progenitors of their social environments.

The actions of adult members of society conform to a host of largely unnoticed social practices. These social practices create a background of expected patterns of interaction and expression that render the actors' actions comprehendible to one another. The actions, in turn, embody and perpetuate the social practices. Thus, social reality is socially constructed and socially perpetuated. Through their actions, people generate the realities that they perceive as independent of themselves.

Constructionists conceive of society as a matrix of responsibilities, obligations, and expectations—a moral order—that members of the society maintain and evolve in their ongoing interactions with one another (Muhlhausler & Harre, 1990; Shotter, 1984). Members expect one another to act in ways that are recognizable and accountable within the moral order. They construct and account for their own actions in terms of reasons and understandings that make the actions comprehendible and responsible within the moral order. Thus, constructionists propose that people act in accord with responsibilities, obligations, and expectations (a moral order) that they themselves construct and maintain rather than respond to immutable laws of behavior that exist independently of their acts (a natural order).

Conceptual Issues

Nearly all of the research inspired by constructionism has been discovery oriented. Investigators have used qualitative methods to analyze idiographic data on a case-by-case basis. This choice of methods reflects two rather different issues, one pragmatic and one philosophical. Pragmatically, constructionists believe that how people channel their actions is as yet largely unspecified and unelaborated. Philosophically, constructionists believe that people's actions are, in principle, unpredictable. Although both beliefs recommend the use of qualitative and idiographic methods, they do not necessarily entail one another.

Pragmatically, constructionists assert that much of how people jointly construct and achieve intelligibility and meaning is through the use of social practices that they take for granted and of which they are not aware. Therefore, research necessarily consists of attempts by investigators to penetrate the veil of the taken-for-granted to discover unnoticed regularities. It is difficult to see how a search for new discernments can be anything but qualitative. As phenomena are identified and agreed on, however, qualitative distinctions could be quantified, and concepts and processes could be assessed in the context of verification (Strong, 1991).

Philosophically, constructionists believe that what a person has done can be understood through an analysis of reasons and purposes but that what a person will do cannot be predicted. Future actions are unpredictable because people themselves determine and are responsible for their actions;

their actions are not assignable to some other causal agents or processes (Howard, 1992; Howard & Conway, 1986). Careful analysis of what a person has done can yield constructions of what that person's thinking and goals were but may or may not cast light on what she or he will do next. Further, what is learned about one person may or may not be relevant to another.

The philosophical assertions of constructionists have profound implications for what human sciences are and can be. If, in fact, people choose their actions rather than respond to deterministic principles, then the predictive power of human sciences is necessarily limited: People's actions will always be subject to unpredictable change. If people's actions do not reflect a natural order but rather a moral order that they themselves generate, then what people do cannot be taken as what they *must* do but rather as one expression of what they *could* do. If this is true, then the issue of what they *should* do cannot be avoided. To advance a human practice, discovered through "objective" scientific methods, as a necessary part of human nature is a naive or deliberate attempt by scientists to transform an issue of values into a matter of fact. Debate about the desirability of various human actions is unavoidable and essential. Human sciences must address what people should be as well as what they now are and, consequently, they are moral sciences.

From the constructionist perspective, inquiry in human sciences should focus on the conceptualizing and learning about the moral orders that humans generate or could generate to govern their own actions. To the extent that social practices remain static, this work will generate understandings that researchers could use to predict what people will do and to generate interventions to change what they will do. In such research, scientists would investigate, for example, the roles of reasons and purposes in human action and the moral force that different reasons and purposes exert on human actors.

Granting that qualitative methods are basic to all scientific work (Strong, 1991), constructionists limit themselves unnecessarily by avoiding quantitative developments. Indeed, as qualitative efforts further specify human practices, these discoveries must be systematized into statements of theoretical knowledge, and the implications of these statements must be tested as are any other scientific assertions. In fact, constructionism is a rapidly developing theory about human action, but many of those who are developing the theory deny that they are doing so (cf. Shotter, 1984). This curious state of affairs reflects the political efforts of constructionists to distinguish themselves from "normal science" and to gain acceptance of their propositions, human activities that fall well within their own constructions of what people do.

Research Directions

Research in the constructionist mold requires that investigators penetrate the blinds of the taken-for-granted, notice the unnoticed, reject the assumed, and violate the expected. Garfinkel's (1967) ethnomethodology best illustrates this socially intrusive practice of science. His test of whether he understood a social practice was to violate it and to note how others reacted. He found that when he rejected the assumed and violated the expected, his interactants became disoriented, then angry, and finally depreciatory of his motives, character, and sanity. He interpreted these reactions as validations of the importance of the practices to humans in achieving intelligibility and as demonstrations that members of a moral order are responsible for its maintenance, a responsibility they exercise by monitoring and correcting one another's actions.

Conversation Analysis. With conversation analysis, a derivative of ethnomethodology, researchers use Garfinkel's validation criteria to identify taken-for-granted social practices in conversation (Heritage, 1988). The investigator begins by studying detailed records of interactions in an effort to note regularities; examines instances of the regularities, in minute detail, to identify their normative structure; and, finally, examines instances in which someone failed to conform to the structure to document that others deliberately maintained the structure by monitoring and correcting deviations from it. Through such analyses, investigators have identified regularities in conversations such as how people organize turn-taking (Sach, Schegloff, & Jefferson, 1978), how they manage invitations (Davidson, 1984) and compliments (Pomerantz, 1978), and how they negotiate topic continuance and change (Goldberg, 1978). Recently, Reed, Patton, and Gold (1993) applied conversation-analysis techniques to the analysis of how counselor and client manage turn-taking in career guidance interviews.

Discourse Analysis. Discourse analysis is a method by which investigators discern how people structure their linguistic productions to achieve intelligibility and meaning and identify the meanings they produce. Discourse analysis is applied to texts of all kinds, including published texts, informal narratives, and conversations. Discovering the methods that people use to create meaning and discerning the meanings that they create, together compose for the investigator a highly subjective enterprise. Success depends on the ability of the investigator to understand the context in which the text was created and to discern what the author(s) of the text were trying to achieve, the linguistic tools they employed, and what they did achieve.

Investigators of texts have developed guidelines for conducting discourse analysis (Potter & Wetherell, 1987). Prominent in the guidelines are safeguards against idiosyncratic interpretations, a distinct possibility, given the subjectivity of the method. Investigators are encouraged to attempt to disconfirm the structures and meanings that they identify. They are advised to review emerging conclusions with colleagues to assess intersubjective validity. They are enjoined to seek intersubjective validation from the people who generated the text; that is, interpretations should be intelligible to those who created the text. Reports of research should include samples of the data from which conclusions were derived to help readers assess the validity of claims. Finally, investigators are enjoined to be as explicit as possible about the values and commitments that influenced their choice of texts to be analyzed and that guided their efforts to discern and interpret structure and meaning.

Labov and Fanshel (1977) used discourse analysis to identify the meanings that a counselor and a client constructed in their conversations. Such research on career counseling processes could address how counselors and clients jointly elaborate stories about clients' lives. The process of meaning (story) construction in counseling appears to be hermeneutical: Counselors and clients move back and forth between contexts and elements of experiences in a progressive elaboration of their meanings (Regan & Stewart, 1970). Results of this analysis suggest that counselors foster change, in part, by deliberately channeling the joint process of meaning elaboration to conclusions that, in conjunction with the moral order, have clear implications about who the client is as a person.

Narratives. Narratives are stories people construct to make sense of, account for, and render comprehensible various aspects of their lives (Antaki, 1988). Findings from research on narratives (Gergen, 1988) suggest that people use a small set of patterns to organize their narratives, patterns that give the narratives recognizable thrusts. People anchor narratives in the present as they wish their audience to perceive it to be. They reconstruct the past in ways that make this present sensible; that is, they select and describe past events in ways that make the events reasonable antecedents to the present that they are constructing.

Although individuals use narratives to give the present the meanings they desire, the accounts they give for events are constrained by the accounts of others who participated in the same events. Gergen (1988) proposed that individuals' narratives are joint achievements of the social groups to which the individuals belong. Knudson (1986) and Wenger, Giuliano, and Hertel (1986) proposed that the degree of convergence or divergence between participants' narratives is a barometer of how well the participants are getting along. Coordinated stories are both signs of and contributors to personal closeness; divergent stories are symptoms of and contributors to social disintegration.

Jepson (1993) extended the study of narratives to career. Indeed, if the stories a person tells reflect how she or he wishes to be perceived by the hearers, if the stories are social productions, and if the stories exert a formative force by giving rationale and direction to the person's choices, then narratives about career are an important topic of study in vocational psychology. A person's career narrative is diagnostic of the person's current aspirations, including how the person wants others to view her or him. The narrative not only reflects the person's location in the social–vocational context but also contributes to the definition of that location and to the developmental opportunities it affords. The narrative informs the person's current choices by further elaborating for the person reasons, goals, and purposes. Thus, it exerts a formative force on the trajectory of the person's career development.

Because narratives are social products, a person's career narrative can be influenced by deliberate social interventions. Educational efforts that provide new facts to be accounted for, different ways of interpreting facts, and social groups and audiences that require different coordinations among stories and different self-presentations in the stories seem to be fertile ground for research. Because narratives are social achievements, such interventions are simply intentional and deliberate uses of ongoing social processes.

Summary

The constructionist perspective flows from the proposition that, through our actions, we construct and perpetuate our (social) realities, realities that we, in turn, take to be independent of ourselves. We channel our actions in accord with a moral order of responsibilities, obligations, and expectations that we create through our actions. Therefore, human sciences are moral sciences because what is, is only one expression of what could be, and we ourselves are responsible for creating what is.

Research in the constructionist tradition has been discovery oriented and has relied on qualitative, idiographic, and case-study methods. These characteristics, in part, reflect the belief that much of how people channel their actions is taken for granted and must therefore be discerned and elaborated. To the extent that social practices are stable, this research could lead to quantitative concepts, theory building, and theory testing. Knowledge generated by this effort could be beneficially applied to a number of areas in vocational psychology, including career development, vocational education, and vocational counseling. The most immediately promising arena for research is the career narrative and its effects on career development. Although still in its infancy, the constructionist perspective could be a source of vigorous new ideas and developments in vocational psychology.

RECONCILIATION: CAUSAL PRAGMATISM

From the perspective of investigators working within the person x environment framework, systemic ideas are impossibly complex, and constructionist ideas are relativistic, soft-headed, and impossibly subjective. From the systemic perspective, person x environment ideas are simplistic and inflexible. From the constructionist perspective, person x environment concepts are fatally flawed and misdirected, whereas systemic concepts are overly mechanistic. These perspectives are based on fundamentally different concepts of reality and on different objectives of scientific inquiry. Nevertheless, in a lucid discussion of causality, Von Wright (1971) proposed a way to reconcile these disparate views and to transform them into collaborative and mutually enriching perspectives.

Von Wright (1971) anchored his thesis in the concept that views of causality are themselves human inventions. He noted, as have other philosophers (Ascombe, 1957; Shotter, 1984; Taylor, 1985), that people have available two fundamentally different frameworks for understanding events. One emphasizes Aristotle's final cause or teleology, which accounts for events in terms of the purposes or ends achieved through them. The second framework emphasizes Aristotle's efficient cause, or determinism, which accounts for events in terms of antecedent circumstances that produce them.

Historically, the range of events to which the deterministic framework has been applied has steadily increased, and with astounding practical results. Von Wright (1971) argued that the invention and popularity of the deterministic framework could be understood in terms of how it enhances the effectiveness of people as purposive agents. If people are intentional agents acting to achieve goals and if aspects of the future are indeterminate but determinable, then the invention of the deterministic causal framework was a major contribution to human development. In a world in which the future is emergent, knowledge of how to generate predictable futures greatly enhances the effectiveness of the intentional agent.

On the other hand, we must ask why the teleological framework is making a comeback in psychology and other social sciences after over 50 years of disrepute. Its resurgence may reflect discouragement and disillusionment with the deterministic framework: After a century of our determined efforts to develop thorough, deterministic understandings of human activities, much of what interests us about people remains outside our grasp. The deterministic framework has proved useful for a variety of purposes, but much of what people do remains stubbornly opaque through the deterministic lens. Perhaps the teleological framework will aid our understanding in these areas. We must also acknowledge the zeitgeist. A causal framework that explains events in terms of purpose, or end-states, fits quite well with the increasing popularity of the view that people are proactive and intentional agents (cf. Borgen, 1992).

In Von Wright's (1971) analysis, concepts of teleology and determinism are simply useful human inventions. They are not attributes of reality; they are not right or wrong; they are simply tools that we humans have created to further our understanding of events that are significant to us. The results of this analysis suggest that what scientists should address are the utilities and effects of these applications in different arenas of human interest. They should address two separate issues: utility in generating concepts of pragmatic use and political repercussions of applying the frameworks to the targets of our inquiries (Shotter, 1975). Any human act can be described within both intentional and deterministic frameworks. Descriptions have a formative influence on how the act and actor are perceived. Indeed, human existence is an ongoing struggle between conceiving of ourselves as intentional agents who can be held responsible for our actions and conceiving of ourselves as the intersections of causes that determine our behavior.

From the perspective of Von Wright's (1971) analysis, the person x environment view is a deterministic tour de force intended to generate information that is pragmatically useful in our understanding the world of work and fitting ourselves into it. The person x environment view will surely continue as the major paradigm that guides vocational description and the prediction of work adjustment. The classification of people and environments affords a structure that is useful for our understanding prospective and achieved person–environment situations. Vocational assessment instruments used in career planning epitomize the value of researchers' characterizing prospective person–environment units. These units organize an overwhelming array of information into groupings that can be understood by the career planner. Efforts to integrate various individual-difference models such as personality and interests (e.g., Gottfredson, Jones, & Holland, 1993) will yield elaborated pictures of persons and environments.

The greatest strength of the person x environment view has been the prediction of vocational adjustment. As this area is extended to the study of ongoing adjustive processes (e.g., Dawis & Lofquist, 1984), vignettes of career-development processes emerge. For example, an examination of the flexibility of either person or environment as a moderator of congruence is likely to clarify adjustment and congruence relations. That people seek out and select environments is a given, but mechanisms used to make selections and negotiate within environments is not well understood. The infusion of social–cognitive processes into person x environment models (e.g., Chartrand & Bertok, 1993; Rounds & Tracey, 1990) may shed light on these mechanisms.

A major contribution of those who operate from the systemic view is the explicit acknowledgment that person–environment systems are inherently complex. Super's (1990) and Vondracek et al.'s (1986) life-span models of career development represent the reality of multiple roles and environments within an individual's life space. Most employed adults hold multiple roles, and the growing literature on multiple-role behavior reflects this theme. What occurs at work may be significantly influenced by and, in turn, influence other life roles. A philosophical paradigm that does not encompass this scope or the bicausal direction of influences oversimplifies reality. At a microlevel, Bandura's (1978) model of reciprocal determinism is systemic in that it includes the interaction of person factors (such as beliefs and overt behaviors) and environmental factors (Altman & Rogoff, 1987). At a macrolevel, Moos' (1987) integrative model of person–environment adaptation serves the same conceptual purpose.

The systemic view lends itself to several areas of career development. Occupational stress is a topic of growing interest, and Swindle and Moos (1992) have developed a model that incorporates life domains, stress, and coping. This approach to the study of work adjustment differs from efforts within the person x environment view: It places more emphasis on systemic interactions and less emphasis on commensurate person and environment concepts. As noted, the study of the interplay between multiple life roles is also likely to become more popular. The systemic view also offers a good representation of organizations, which are typically composed of interdependent units.

The constructionist view has not yet had a major influence on the vocational field. Research in this mold, however, holds great promise for deepening understanding, perhaps especially of career development and career counseling. From a constructionist perspective, a person's career and its meanings is an ongoing and evolving achievement of the person and the person's social group. Studies of how people construct narratives (understandings at a specific time slice), how they use information in the constructions, and how various constructions inform future choices may be particularly fruitful. Such studies may provide information that psychologists can use to deliberately affect the careers that people construct. For example, a study of the career narratives of eminent female scientists could generate information of how we can encourage promising young women to pursue such careers (cf. Betz, 1992). Constructionism also offers us ideas and ways to study, interpret, and generate changes in implicit norms and social practices in groups and organizations.

The constructionist model—its research and subsequent applications of research in interventions—draws on both the teleological and deterministic causal models. The constructionist model operates on the assumption that people construct their indeterminate but determinable futures but incorporates deterministic models to guide interventions intended to affect what they construct. Applications of constructionist views to career counseling already exist (Jepsen, 1993; Reed et al., 1993) and are likely to increase.

We hope that these observations illustrate how Von Wright's (1971) integrative framework has the potential to break down the walls between the various interactional approaches, to focus attention on what each approach is especially suited for, and to encourage researchers to use the methods and results of one approach to advance the utility of another. We hope to discourage questions about which approach is right and to encourage questions about what psychologists wish to achieve in scientific work and which approach or combination of approaches will likely help them to accomplish those goals.

SUMMARY

In this chapter we examined the interactional view of vocational development by reviewing three paradigms that guide interactional research. We did not review and critique the strengths and weaknesses of interactional vocational topics and theories. Others (Hackett & Lent, 1992; contributors to *Journal of Vocational Behavior Annual Reviews*) have already done an admirable job of addressing these issues. Instead, we sought to provide a clear picture of the paradigms and correspondent philosophical assumptions that guide interactional vocational research. One of our purposes was to improve translation between the levels of paradigm, theory, and research implementation. Some of the difficulties in current person–environment vocational research stem from a failure to make connections across each level.

Another of our purposes was to forward the notion of causal pragmatism. Vocational development and adjustment, occupational stress and adaptation, organizational functioning, and career counseling, to name just a few, are all complex and very diverse interactional processes. Growing instabilities, complexities, and systematic changes in the social fabric of the world of work and career development necessitate the use of different explanatory frameworks. Investigators who want to study career issues from an interactional perspective will need to distinguish, and we hope be able to comfortably transverse, diverse causal models in the context of both discovery and justification.

REFERENCES

Allport, G. W. (1961). *Patterns and growth in personality.* New York: Holt, Rinehart & Winston.

Altman, I., & Rogoff, B. (1987). World views in psychology: Trait, interactional, organismic, and transactional perspectives. In D. Stokols & I. Altman (Eds.), *Handbook of environmental psychology* (Vol. 1, pp. 7–40). New York: Wiley.

American College Testing Program. (1977). *Handbook for the ACT career planning program.* Iowa City, IA: Author.

American College Testing Program. (1988). *Interim psychometric handbook for the 3rd edition ACT career planning program.* Iowa City, IA: Author.

Anderson, J. G. (1987). Structural equation models in the social and behavioral sciences: Model building. *Child Development, 58,* 49–64.

Antaki, C. (Ed.). (1988). *Analyzing everyday explanation.* London: Sage.

Ascombe, G. E. M. (1957). *Intention.* Ithaca, NY: Cornell University Press.

Assouline, M., & Meir, E. I. (1987). Meta-analysis of the relationship between congruence and well-being measures. *Journal of Vocational Behavior, 31,* 319–332.

Astin, A. W. (1968). *The college environment.* Washington, DC: American Council on Education.

Astin, A. W., & Holland, J. L. (1961). The environmental assessment technique: A way to measure college environments. *Journal of Educational Psychology, 52,* 308–316.

Bandura, A. (1978). The self system in reciprocal determinism. *American Psychologist, 33*, 344–358.

Barker, R. G. (1987). Prospecting in environmental psychology: Oskaloosa revisited. In D. Stokols & I. Altman (Eds.), *Handbook of environmental psychology* (Vol. 2, pp. 1413–1432). New York: Wiley.

Barrick, M. R., & Mount, M. K. (1991). The big five personality dimensions and job performance: A metaanalysis. *Personnel Psychology, 44*, 1–26.

Betz, N. E. (1992). Counseling uses of career self-efficacy theory [Special section: Career self-efficacy]. *Career Development Quarterly, 41*, 22–26.

Biddle, B. J., & Marlin, M. M. (1987). Causality, confirmation, credulity, and structural equation modeling. *Child Development, 58*, 4–17.

Bidwell, C., Csikszentmihalyi, M., Hedges, L., & Schneider, B. (1992). *Studying career choice: Overview and analysis.* Chicago: University of Chicago, Education Studies Group.

Borgen, F. H. (1992). Expanding scientific paradigms in counseling psychology. In S. D. Brown & R. W. Lent (Eds.), *Handbook of counseling psychology* (2nd ed., pp. 111–140). New York: Wiley.

Borgen, F. H., Weiss, D. J., Tinsley, H. E. A., Dawis, R. V., & Lofquist, L. H. (1968). *The measurement of occupational reinforcer patterns.* Minnesota Studies in Vocational Rehabilitation, Vol. 25. Minneapolis: University of Minnesota.

Brunswik, E. (1950). The conceptual framework of psychology. *International encyclopedia of unified science* (Vol. 1). Chicago: University of Chicago Press.

Camp, C. C., & Chartrand, J. M. (1992). A comparison and evaluation of interest congruence indices. *Journal of Vocational Behavior, 41*, 162–182.

Chartrand, J. M., & Bertok, R. L. (1993). The evolution of trait-and-factor career counseling: A person–environment fit approach. *Journal of Career Assessment, 1*, 323–340.

Chatman, J. A. (1989). Improving interactional organizational research: A model of person–organization fit. *Academy of Management Review, 14*, 333–349.

Connell, J. P. (1987). Structural equation modeling and the study of child development: A question of goodness of fit. *Child Development, 58*, 167–175.

Costa, P. T., & McCrae, R. R. (1985). *The NEO Personality Inventory manual.* Odessa, FL: Psychological Assessment Resources.

Crites, J. O. (1981). *Career counseling.* New York: McGraw–Hill.

Crites, J. O. (1983). Research methods in vocational psychology. In W. B. Walsh & S. H. Osipow (Eds.), *Handbook of vocational psychology* (Vol. 1, pp. 305–353). Hillsdale, NJ: Lawrence Erlbaum Associates.

Davidson, J. (1984). Subsequent versions of invitations, offers, requests, and proposals dealing with potential or actual rejection. In J. M. Atkinson & J. Heritage (Eds.), *Structures of social action: Studies in conversation analysis* (pp. 102–128). Cambridge, England: Cambridge University Press.

Davis–Blake, A., & Pfeffer, J. (1989). Just a mirage: The search for dispositional effects in organizational research. *Academy of Management Review, 14*, 385–400.

Dawis, R. V. (1992). The individual differences tradition in counseling psychology. *Journal of Counseling Psychology, 39*, 7–19.

Dawis, R. V., Dohm, T. E., & Jackson, C. R. (1993). Describing work environments as reinforcer systems: Reinforcement schedules versus reinforcer classes. *Journal of Vocational Behavior, 43*, 5–18.

Dawis, R. V., & Lofquist, L. (1984). *A psychological theory of work adjustment.* Minneapolis: University of Minnesota Press.

Farrell, A. D. (1994). Structural equation modeling with longitudinal data: Strategies for assessing group differences and reciprocal relationships. *Journal of Consulting and Clinical Psychology, 62*, 477–487.

Fitzgerald, L. F., & Shullman, S. L. (1993). Sexual harassment: A research analysis and agenda for the 1990s. *Journal of Vocational Behavior, 42,* 5–27.

Fraiss, P. (1987). Unity and diversity in the behavioral and natural sciences. In A. W. Stants & L. P. Mus (Eds.), *Annals of theoretical psychology* (Vol. 5, pp. 213–240). New York: Plenum.

French, J. R. P., Jr., Rodgers, W., & Cobb, S. (1974). Adjustment as person–environment fit. In G. V. Coelho, D. A. Hamburg, & J. E. Adams (Eds.), *Coping and adaptation.* New York: Basic Books.

Garfinkel, H. (1967). *Studies in ethnomethodology.* Englewood Cliffs, NJ: Prentice–Hall.

Gay, E. G., Weiss, D. J., Hendel, D. D., Dawis, R. V., & Lofquist, L. H. (1971). *Manual for the Minnesota Importance Questionnaire.* Minnesota Studies in Vocational Rehabilitation (Vol. 28). Minneapolis: University of Minnesota Press.

Gergen, K. (1985). The social constructionist movement in modern psychology. *American Psychologist, 40,* 266–275.

Gergen, M. M. (1988). Narrative structure in social explanation. In C. Anataki (Ed.), *Analyzing everyday explanation* (pp. 94–112). London: Sage.

Goldberg, J. A. (1978). Amplitude shift: A mechanism for the affiliation of utterances in conversation interaction. In J. Schenkein (Ed.), *Studies in the organization of conversation interaction* (pp. 7–56). New York: Academic Press.

Gottfredson, G. D., & Holland, J. L. (1975). Vocational choices of men and women: A comparison of predictors from the Self-Directed Search. *Journal of Counseling Psychology, 22,* 28–34.

Gottfredson, G. D., Holland, J. L., & Ogawa, D. K. (1982). *Dictionary of Holland occupational codes.* Palo Alto, CA: Consulting Psychologists Press.

Gottfredson, G. D., Jones, E. M., & Holland, J. L. (1993). Personality and vocational interests: The relation of Holland's six interest dimensions to five robust dimensions of personality. *Journal of Counseling Psychology, 40,* 518–524.

Hackett, G., & Lent, R. W. (1992). Theoretical advances and current inquiry in career psychology. In S. D. Brown & R. W. Lent (Eds.), *Handbook of counseling psychology* (2nd ed., pp. 419–451). New York: Wiley.

Hansen, J. C., & Campbell, D. P. (1985). *Manual for the Strong Interest Inventory* (4th ed.). Palo Alto, CA: Consulting Psychologists Press.

Harre, R. (1992). On being taken up by others. In D. Robinson (Ed.), *Social discourse and moral judgement.* San Diego, CA: Academic Press.

Heritage, J. (1988). Explanations as accounts: A conversation analytic perspective. In C. Anataki (Ed.), *Analyzing everyday explanation* (pp. 127–144). London: Sage.

Hogan, R. (1983). A socioanalytic theory of personality. In M. M. Page (Ed.), *Nebraska symposium on motivation, 1982. Personality: Current theory and research* (pp. 55–89). Lincoln: University of Nebraska Press.

Holland, J. L. (1978). *Professional manual for the Self-Directed Search.* Palo Alto, CA: Consulting Psychologists Press.

Holland, J. L. (1985a). *Making vocational choices: A theory of vocational personalities and work environments.* Englewood Cliffs, NJ: Prentice–Hall.

Holland, J. L. (1985b). *Manual for the Vocational Preferences Inventory.* Odessa, FL: Psychological Assessment Resources.

Holland, J. L. (1985c). *The Self-Directed Search: Professional manual.* Odessa, FL: Psychological Assessment Resources.

Holland, J. L., & Gottfredson, G. D. (1975). Predictive value and psychological meaning of vocational aspirations. *Journal of Vocational Behavior, 6,* 349–363.

Howard, G. (1992). Can there be a just and moral social constructionist psychology? In D. Robinson (Ed.), *Social discourse and moral judgement* (pp. 151–165). New York: Academic Press.

Howard, G. S., & Conway, C. G. (1986). Can there be an empirical science of volitional action? *American Psychologist, 41,* 1241–1251.

Hutcherson, S. J. (1982). The relationship of the job satisfaction of classroom teachers to student perceptions of classroom satisfaction (Doctoral dissertation, University of Nebraska, Lincoln, 1981). *Dissertation Abstracts International, 42,* 3826A.

Jepson, D. A. (1993, March). *Career as story: Applications to career counseling practice.* Paper presented at the annual meeting of the American Counseling Association, Atlanta, GA.

Johansson, C. B. (1976). *Manual for the Career Assessment Inventory.* Minneapolis, MN: National Computer Systems.

Johansson, C. B. (1986). *Career Assessment Inventory: The enhanced version.* Minneapolis, MN: National Computer Systems.

Knudson, R. M. (1986). Marital compatibility and mutual identity confirmation. In W. Ickes (Ed.), *Compatible and incompatible relationships* (pp. 233–252). New York: Springer–Verlag.

Labov, W., & Fanshel, D. (1977). *Therapeutic discourse.* New York: Academic Press.

Leahey, T. H. (1992). The mythical revolutions of American psychology. *American Psychologist, 47,* 308–318.

Lewin, K. (1951). *Field theory in social science.* New York: Harper.

Magnusson, D. (1988). *Individual development from an interactional perspective: A longitudinal study.* Hillsdale, NJ: Lawrence Erlbaum Associates.

Magnusson, D., & Allen, V. L. (1983). An interactional perspective for human development. In D. Magnusson & V. L. Allen (Eds.), *Human development: An interactional perspective* (pp. 3–31). New York: Academic Press.

Martin, J. A. (1987). Structural equation modeling: A guide for the perplexed. *Child Development, 58,* 33–37.

Meir, E. I. (1989). Integrative elaboration of the congruence theory. *Journal of Vocational Behavior, 35,* 219–230.

Meir, E. I., & Yaari, Y. (1988). The relationship between congruent specialty choice within occupations and satisfaction. *Journal of Vocational Behavior, 33,* 99–117.

Mischel, W. (1968). *Personality and assessment.* New York: Wiley.

Moos, R. H. (1974). *Evaluating treatment environment: A social ecological approach.* New York: Wiley.

Moos, R. H. (1987). Person–environment congruence in work, school, and health care settings. *Journal of Vocational Behavior, 31,* 231–247.

Muhlhausler, P., & Harre, R. (1990). *Pronouns and people: The linguistic construction of social and personal identity.* Oxford, England: Blackwell.

Murray, H. A. (1938). *Explorations in personality.* New York: Oxford University Press.

Nelson, G. (1984). The relationship between dimensions of classroom and family environments and the self-concept, satisfaction and achievement of grade 7 and 8 students. *Journal of Community Psychology, 12,* 272–287.

Nesselroade, J., & Baltes, P. B. (1979). *Longitudinal research in the study of behavior and development.* New York: Academic Press.

Norman, W. T. (1963). Toward an adequate taxonomy of personality attributes: Replicated factor structure in peer nomination personality ratings. *Journal of Abnormal and Social Psychology, 66,* 574–583.

Nunnally, J. C. (1982). The study of human change: Measurement, research strategies, and methods of analysis. In B. B. Wolman (Ed.), *Handbook of developmental psychology* (pp. 133–148). Englewood Cliffs, NJ: Prentice-Hall.

Nunnally, J. C. (1983). *Psychometric theory.* New York: McGraw–Hill.

O'Neil, J. M., Magoon, T. M., & Tracey, T. J. (1978). Status of Holland's investigative personality types and their consistency levels using the Self-Directed Search. *Journal of Vocational Behavior, 25,* 530–535.

Osipow, S. H. (1987). Applying person–environment theory to vocational behavior. *Journal of Vocational Behavior, 31,* 333–336.

Osipow, S. H., & Spokane, A. R. (1984). Measuring occupational stress, strain, and coping. In S. Oskamp (Ed.), *Applied social psychology annual* (Vol. 5, pp. 67–86). Beverly Hills, CA: Sage.

Pervin, L. A. (1978). Definitions, measurements, and classifications of stimuli, situations, and environments. *Human Ecology, 16,* 71–105.

Pervin, L. A. (1989). Persons, situations, interactions: The history of a controversy and a discussion of theoretical models. *Academy of Management Review, 14,* 350–360.

Pervin, L. A. (1992). Transversing the individual–environment landscape: A personal odyssey. In W. B. Walsh, K. H. Craik, & R. H. Price (Eds.), *Person–environment psychology: Models and perspectives* (pp. 71–88). Hillsdale, NJ: Lawrence Erlbaum Associates.

Polkinghorne, D. (1983). *Methodology for the human sciences: Systems of inquiry.* Albany: State University of New York Press.

Pomerantz, A. (1978). Compliment responses: Notes on the co-operation of multiple constraints. In J. Schenkein (Ed.), *Studies in the organization of conversation interaction* (pp. 79–112). New York: Academic Press.

Potter, J., & Wetherall, M. (1987). *Discourse and social psychology.* London: Sage.

Prediger, D. J. (1982). Dimensions underlying Holland's hexagon: Missing link between interests and occupations? *Journal of Vocational Behavior, 21,* 259–287.

Reed, J. R., Patton, M. J., & Gold, P. B. (1993). Effects of turn-taking sequences in vocational test interpretation interviews. *Journal of Counseling Psychology, 40,* 144–155.

Regan, C. E., & Stewart, D. (Eds.). (1970). *The philosophy of Paul Riceour: An anthology of his work.* Boston: Beacon Press.

Richards, J. M., Seligman, R., & Jones, P. K. (1970). Faculty and curriculum as measures of college environment. *Journal of Educational Psychology, 61,* 324–332.

Rotter, J. B. (1955). The role of the psychological situation in determining the direction of human behavior. In M. R. Jones (Ed.), *Nebraska symposium on motivation* (pp. 245–268). Lincoln: University of Nebraska Press.

Rounds, J. B. (1988, April). *Meta-analysis of research on the relationship of vocational interests and job satisfaction.* Paper presented at the annual meeting of the American Educational Research Association, New Orleans, LA.

Rounds, J. B., Lofquist, L. H., & Dawis, R. V. (1987). Measurement of person–environment fit and prediction of satisfaction in the theory of work adjustment. *Journal of Vocational Behavior, 31,* 297–318.

Rounds, J. B., & Tracey, T. J. (1990). From trait-and-factor to person–environment fit counseling: Theory and process. In W. B. Walsh & S. H. Osipow (Eds.), *Career counseling: Contemporary topics in vocational psychology* (pp. 1–44). Hillsdale, NJ: Lawrence Erlbaum Associates.

Rounds, J. B., & Tracey, T. J. (1993). Prediger's dimensional representation of Holland's RIASEC circumplex. *Journal of Applied Psychology, 78,* 875–890.

Sach, H., Schegloff, E. A., & Jefferson, G. (1978). A simplest systematics for the organization of turn taking for conversation. In J. Schenkein (Ed.), *Studies in the organization of conversation interaction* (pp. 7–56). New York: Academic Press.

Savickas, M. L., & Lent, R. W. (Eds.). (1994). *Convergence in career development theories.* Palo Alto, CA: CPP Books.

Schaie, K. W., & Hertzog, C. (1982). Longitudinal methods. In B. B. Wolman (Ed.), *Handbook of developmental psychology* (pp. 91–115). Englewood Cliffs, NJ: Prentice–Hall.

Scherer, R. F., Owen, C. L., Petrick, J. A., Brodzinski, J. D., & Goyer, K. A. (1991). Initial development of an emic methodology for classification of stressful work situations. *Perceptual and Motor Skills, 73,* 1004–1006.

Schneider, B. (1987). E = f(p,b): The road to a radical approach to person–environment fit. *Journal of Vocational Behavior, 31,* 353–361.

Schulenberg, J. E., Vondracek, F. W., & Nesselroade, J. R. (1988). Patterns of short-term changes in individuals' work values: P-technique factor analysis of intraindividual variability. *Multivariate Behavioral Research, 23,* 377–395.

Schwartz, R. H. (1991). Achievement-orientation of personality type: A variable to consider in tests of Holland's congruence-achievement and other hypotheses. *Journal of Vocational Behavior, 38*, 225–235.

Seaburg, D. J., Rounds, J. B., Dawis, R. V., & Lofquist, L. H. (1976, August). *Values as second order needs.* Paper presented at the 84th annual meeting of the American Psychological Association, Washington, DC.

Shotter, J. (1975). *Images of man in psychological research.* London: Methuen.

Shotter, J. (1984). *Social accountability and selfhood.* Oxford, England: Blackwell.

Spokane, A. R. (1985). A review of research on person–environment congruence in Holland's theory of careers. *Journal of Vocational Behavior, 26*, 306–343.

Spokane, A. R. (1990). Supplementing differential research in vocational psychology using nontraditional methods. In R. A. Young & W. A. Borgen (Eds.), *Methodological approaches to the study of career* (pp. 25–36). New York: Praeger.

Strong, S. R. (1991). Theory driven science and naive empiricism in counseling psychology. *Journal of Counseling Psychology, 38*, 204–210.

Super, D. E. (1983). The history and development of vocational psychology: A personal perspective. In W. B. Walsh & S. H. Osipow (Eds.), *Handbook of vocational psychology* (Vol. 1, pp. 5–38). Hillsdale, NJ: Lawrence Erlbaum Associates.

Super, D. E. (1990). A life-span, life-space approach to career development. In D. Brown & L. Brooks (Eds.), *Career choice and development* (2nd ed., pp. 197–261). San Francisco: Jossey–Bass.

Swanson, J. L., & Hansen, J. C. (1988). Stability of vocational interests over 4-year, 8-year, and 12-year intervals. *Journal of Vocational Behavior, 33*, 185–202.

Swindle, R. W., & Moos, R. H. (1992). Life domains in stressors, coping, and adjustment. In W. B. Walsh, K. H. Craik, & R. H. Price (Eds.), *Person–environment psychology* (pp. 1–34). Hillsdale, NJ: Lawrence Erlbaum Associates.

Taylor, C. (1985). *Human agency and language: Philosophical papers I.* Cambridge, England: Cambridge University Press.

Tranberg, M., Slane, S., & Ekeberg, S. E. (1993). The relation between interest congruence and satisfaction: A metaanalysis. *Journal of Vocational Behavior, 42*, 253–264.

Tung, R. L. (1980). Comparative analysis of the occupational stress profiles of male versus female administrators. *Journal of Vocational Behavior, 17*, 344–355.

U.S. Department of Labor. (1977). *Dictionary of occupational titles* (4th ed.). Washington, DC: U.S. Government Printing Office.

Venkatraman, N. (1989). The concept of fit in strategy research: Toward verbal and statistical correspondence. *Academy of Management Review, 14*, 423–444.

Vondracek, F. W., Lerner, R. M., & Schulenberg, J. E. (1986). *Career development: A life-span developmental approach.* Hillsdale, NJ: Lawrence Erlbaum Associates.

Von Wright, G. H. (1971). *Explanation and understanding.* Ithaca, NY: Cornell University Press.

Walsh, W. B., Craik, K. H., & Price, R. H. (Eds.). (1992). *Person–environment psychology: Models and perspectives.* Hillsdale, NJ: Lawrence Erlbaum Associates.

Wenger, E. M., Giuliano, T., & Hertel, P. T. (1986). Cognitive interdependence in close relationships. In W. Ickes (Ed.), *Compatible and incompatible relationships* (pp. 253–276). New York: Springer–Verlag.

Wittgenstein, L. (1969). *On certainty.* New York: Harper & Row.

Young, R. A., & Borgen, W. A. (1990). *Methodological approaches to the study of career.* New York: Praeger.

CHAPTER THREE

Theoretical Advances in the Study of Women's Career Development

Louise F. Fitzgerald
University of Illinois

Ruth E. Fassinger
University of Maryland

Nancy E. Betz
Ohio State University

INTRODUCTION

Looking back over the history of vocational psychology, Leona Tyler once remarked that it was most appropriately referred to as the "vocational behavior of middle class men" (Tyler, 1978, p. 40). From the earliest discussions of "matching men and jobs" up through Crites' (1969) landmark volume summarizing the field of vocational psychology, researchers and theorists in the area universally and unselfconsciously investigated men's vocational interests, described their career patterns, and sought to explain their vocational behavior— with women representing (sometimes literally) only a footnote to their work.

Almost as Tyler was writing, however, the world of work was undergoing a revolution that would render her description obsolete. Today, the study of women's behavior represents arguably the most active and vibrant area of research and theory in all vocational psychology, with hundreds of references appearing in 1993 alone. From isolated studies and occasional articles, the field has grown to encompass chapters (e.g., Fitzgerald & N. E. Betz, 1983; Fitzgerald & Weitzman, 1992), books (e.g., N. E. Betz & Fitzgerald, 1987; Nieva & Gutek, 1981), edited volumes (Walsh & Osipow, 1994), and empirical articles and programs of research far too numerous to cite, much less enumerate.

This chapter represents our attempt to summarize what is known about women's career development. A far more challenging undertaking than our previous effort over a decade ago (Fitzgerald & N. E. Betz, 1983), the chapter undertakes to provide an overview not only of the content in the area but also of the way that knowledge has unfolded, developed, and changed across the approximately 25 years that it has been an active field of study. We begin where the field itself began, with the recognition that the study of women's relationship to work is more complicated than that of men's, requiring the identification and study of concepts and variables previously unnecessary and ignored. Following a brief review of these developments, which we label *pretheoretical*, we move to a discussion of the initial attempts to theorize about women's vocational behavior, attempts that reflect the early descriptive work and presage the more comprehensive efforts that followed. In the second half of the chapter, we examine the major theories of vocational choice and adjustment, with an eye to their usefulness and limitations for explaining women's behavior, and conclude with a review of the sophisticated gendered frameworks that arose in the 1980s. Throughout the chapter are woven two themes: that women's career development is *unique* because of the intertwining of work and family in their lives and that, paradoxically, its study can lead to more *general* insights about vocational behavior more generally.

PRETHEORETICAL DEVELOPMENTS: CONCEPTS UNIQUE TO WOMEN'S CAREER DEVELOPMENT

> . . . *it is important to point out that woman's role as a childbearer makes her the keystone of the home, and therefore gives homemaking a central place in her career.*
>
> —Super (1957)

The initial and probably most central insight concerning women's career development is that its understanding requires recourse to variables previously unknown to vocational psychology, a discipline that Leona Tyler once referred to as the "vocational behavior of middle class men" (Tyler, 1978, p. 40). Clearly, the factor that has most singularly differentiated women's vocational behavior has been the role of family in their lives. Because women were historically assumed not to pursue careers, the study of their relationship to the world of work began with the development of concepts describing the degree to which they intended to work at all and the importance, if any, of career pursuits in their lives. Thus, the first stage in the study of women's career development focused on the identification and examination of variables such as career (vs. homemaking) orientation, career salience, traditionality of choice, and so forth. This *pretheoretical* stage also saw the description and classification of the various life patterns arising from the interplay of work and family in women's lives. The following discussion provides a brief overview of this research and writing, intended to serve as a historical backdrop and under-pinning to more contemporary formulations.

Homemaking Versus Career Orientation

American society has historically been so completely differentiated on the basis of gender that, until quite recently, men were routinely expected to work and women were expected not to, virtually as a matter of course. Consequently, women who chose to work outside the home became objects of interest to scholars who sought to determine the antecedents and corre-lates of such gender-deviant behavior (e.g., Kriger, 1972). As Betz and Fitzgerald (1987) pointed out, "studies investigating the kinds of vocational choices made by women were less important than were the issues of whether or not and *why* women pursued careers at all" (p. 16). Hence, the early body of research on women and work focused on factors that differentiated career-oriented women from homemakers.

The paradigm for this type of investigation was set by Hoyt and Kennedy (1958), who studied Strong Vocational Interest Blank (SVIB-W; Strong, 1933) scores obtained by women who were classified on the basis of a question-naire as either family or career oriented. They found that career-oriented women were characterized by scores on the higher status occupations tra-ditionally dominated by men, as opposed to the home-oriented group who scored higher on nonprofessional or traditionally female occupations (e.g., secretary, home economics teacher) as well as on the housewife scale. These original findings were replicated many times (e.g., Munley, 1974; Vetter & Lewis, 1964; Wagman, 1966) and proved so stable that subsequent re-searchers began to use such interest patterns as the criterion for identifying women who planned to work outside the home. Once classified, the women could then be studied with respect to a number of variables and correlates (e.g., background factors, ability, achievement orientation) that might bear on the development of this orientation. Studies reporting significant group differences in family background characteristics (e.g., Gysbers, Johnston, & Gust, 1968), in achievement motivation (Oliver, 1974; Rand, 1968; Tyler, 1964), personality characteristics (e.g., Rand, 1968), ability (Rand, 1968; Watley & Kaplan, 1971), and values (Goldsen, Rosenberg, Williams, & Such-man, 1960; R. L. Simpson & I. H. Simpson, 1961; Wagman, 1966) were illustrative (see Betz & Fitzgerald, 1987, for a review).

With the enormous social changes of the past quarter century, working women have become the norm rather than the exception, and the question of why this is so has lost much of its relevance for psychology. It is still true, however, that family continues to play an enormous role in most women's lives and influences their vocational experiences in ways that are still generally not salient for men. Not only are most women motivated to bear and raise children, but society continues to expect them to do so without providing the structural supports (e.g., a national child-care policy) that would assist them in combining family and career responsibilities in a reasonable manner. As it became apparent that most contemporary women planned to pursue both career and family roles (e.g., Levitt, 1972; Oliver, 1974), researchers turned their attention to different concepts to describe these patterns.

Traditional Versus Nontraditional Career Choices

The first major approach to describing the nature (as opposed to merely the fact) of women's career choices involved classifying preferences or choices according to the degree to which they were *traditional* versus *nontraditional* for women. Rossi (1965) was among the first to suggest the utility of differentiating career-oriented women who pursued traditionally female careers (i.e., occupations in which women predominated) from those pursuing *pioneer* careers, that is, occupations in which men have predominated. Women pursuing nontraditional, or pioneer, occupations were also termed *role innovators* (Almquist, 1974; Tangri, 1972). Thus, the terms *pioneer, innovator,* and *nontraditional* have been used interchangeably to differentiate women pursuing male-dominated fields (which were assumed to require stronger and more consistent career commitment and involvement) from *traditionals,* who pursued more traditionally female occupations. Studies of characteristics differentiating pioneers from traditionals dominated research in the early 1970s and documented numerous important differences between the two types of women (e.g., Astin & Myint, 1971; Nagely, 1971; Standley & Soule, 1974; Tangri, 1972).

Related to this concept are the more recent descriptions of the degree to which women choose careers in the sciences and mathematics. Because women have been particularly underrepresented in the sciences, mathematics, and engineering (N. E. Betz, 1991), considerable research has focused on this area of study (Fox, Brody, & Tobin, 1985; Humphreys, 1982; National Science Foundation, 1984; Pfafflin, 1984). Math relatedness and science relatedness have been scaled and used to describe the content of women's choices. For example, Hollinger (1983) combined the ideas of traditionality and math and science relatedness in her study of mathematically talented adolescents. The six resulting categories were nontraditional math careers (e.g., accountant, economist); nontraditional science (e.g., chemist, physician); neutral or traditional math–science (e.g., nurse, bookkeeper); nontraditional nonmath (e.g., lawyer); neutral nonmath (e.g., reporter); and traditional nonmath (e.g., librarian, social worker).

In addition to studies such as these, traditionality has also been used as a moderator of the strength of other relationships. For example, Wolfe and N. E. Betz (1981) found significantly stronger associations between measured interests and field preferences (congruence) for women making nontraditional versus traditional choices. Although this finding was not replicated in a subsequent study (Betz, Heesacker, & Shuttleworth, 1990), there was evidence that women preferring female-dominated occupations were less likely to be using their abilities fully.

Career Salience

At the time this research began, many researchers assumed (erroneously, as it turned out; Osipow, 1973) that traditionality of choice also reflected the strength of a woman's career commitment; others, however, devoted attention to the separate assessment of variables that summarized the importance to the individual of career pursuits and activities, especially in relationship to the relative importance of other life roles (i.e., homemaking). Eyde's (1962) Desire to Work Scale represented the first systematic attempt to assess career orientation as a continuous variable. This scale, which requests respondents to rate their desire to work under varying conditions of marital status, number and ages of children, and perceived adequacy of husband's income, defined stronger career orientation in terms of the extent to which a woman wished to work even if she was also married and a mother.

Almquist and Angrist (1970, 1971; Angrist, 1972) adapted the Desire to Work Scale for the assessment of *career salience*, defined as "aspiration for work as a central feature of adult life, regardless of financial necessity and under conditions of free choice" (Almquist & Angrist, 1971, p. 263). Their Life Style Index contains items pertaining to motivation to work under various family conditions and items concerning adult role aspirations and preferences. Similarly, Richardson (1974) distinguished *work motivation* from *career orientation*. She defined work motivation as a woman's desire to pursue work outside the home although not giving major priority to this role; career orientation, on the other hand, was defined as the desire to pursue work as a primary life focus, with homemaking interests viewed as secondary. A more general, and still widely used, measure is Greenhaus' (1971) Career Salience Scale. This instrument consists of 27 items assessing the importance to the individual of a career (to yield an absolute rating of the importance of career) and a 28th item that requests participants to rank order six life areas, including career and family, in terms of their relative importance in the respondent's life.

Although such scales were originally developed to study unique aspects of the vocational behavior of women, researchers have recently begun to use them to study individual differences among men as well. For example, Neville and Super (1986) developed the Salience Inventory to assess the relative importance of six life roles (including those of work and home) among both men and women. Beere's (1990) *Gender Roles: Handbook of*

Tests and Measures lists 26 scales for the assessment of marital and parental roles (e.g., the Motherhood Inventory and the Eversoll Father Role Opinionaire), 24 for the assessment of gendered work roles (Attitudes Towards Male Nurses; Women in Science Scale), and 30 for the assessment of multiple roles (Home–Career Conflict Measure, Dual-Career Family Scales). Thus, what began as the study 'of gendered role choices among women has since expanded to reflect the fact that both men and women are likely to pursue a variety of life roles and that there are within-gender individual differences in their salience. This is one of the more visible examples of how the study of women as a unique group has enriched the knowledge base of vocational psychology more generally.

Gendered Role Experiences

Early classifications of the effects of gender roles and attitudes on women's career development were those of Sobol (1963) and Psathas (1968). Sobol postulated that the decisions of married women with children to work (or not) outside the home were based on: (a) *enabling conditions,* that is, family characteristics including spouse's salary and satisfaction with the marriage; (b) *facilitating conditions,* for example, educational level and previous work experience; and (c) *precipitating conditions,* including individual characteristics such as self-concept and gender role attitudes. As would be true in subsequent work, Sobol's classification included both situational (e.g., marital) and individual (e.g., attitudinal) factors. Psathas (1968) outlined several factors influencing women's occupational participation. Emphasizing cultural, situational, and chance elements of the environment, he cited intention to marry, time of marriage, the husband's economic situation and attitude toward his wife's working, and the woman's gender role preferences as influential determinants of her decision to work his work; is described more fully below.

Multiple-Role Issues

Although few researchers today invoke the notion of home versus career, the history of women's traditional roles as homemaker and mother continues to influence virtually every aspect of their career choice and adjustment. One critical outcome of this situation is that many women tend to "downscale" their career aspirations to accommodate such factors. The research of Arnold (1987, 1989) and Arnold and Denny (1984, 1985), which followed the lives of Illinois valedictorians, provides a particularly vivid illustration of downscaling in a group of intellectually superior female high-school students. As concluded by Gerson (1986) and discussed further by Eccles (1987), women's choices about work continue to be inextricably linked with their decisions about family and thus set the parameters for their investment in the occupational world. Ironically, family involvement may well serve to increase and facilitate men's career development: not only does it give them a strong rationale for achievement-related behavior, but the role of a wife in managing family responsibilities and providing emotional and practical support also ensures optimal conditions for career development and growth.

By contrast, the situation for (married) women is quite different. Whatever career decision she has made, traditional or otherwise, the assumption remains that a woman is also primarily responsible for maintenance of the home and family, creating serious career obstacles in the form of overload, stress, and role conflict. Research currently shows that 90% of women who pursue careers still expect to have two or more children (Russo & Denmark, 1984). Thus, whereas the family cycle historically superseded the work cycle in women's lives, it now most typically occurs concurrently. The major practical implication of this change is that women are now expected to handle two full-time jobs, simultaneously and successfully—one outside the home and the other as homemaker and mother (Scarr, Phillips, & McCartney, 1989).

Although the overall relationship of marital or familial status to women's vocational behavior has weakened as a result of the tremendous increase in female workforce participation, its relationship to career attainment, commitment, and innovation is still very strong. A vast array of data confirm strong inverse relationships between (a) being married and (b) number of children with every known criterion of career involvement and achievement (see Betz & Fitzgerald, 1987, for a comprehensive review). Once again, this relationship is not true for men—highly achieving men are at least as likely (if not more so) as their less successful counterparts to be married and to have one or more children. Despite considerable discussion in the popular media of changing male gender roles, this continues to be the main difference between women's career development and that of men.

Barriers

Considerations such as these have given rise to the concept of *barriers* to women's career development, a notion that can be extended to provide a useful framework for understanding that development and the design of interventions capable of facilitating it. The original organizational framework was suggested by Farmer (1976), who differentiated six internal, or self-concept, barriers to women (fear of success, gender role orientation, risk-taking behavior, home–career conflict, and low academic self-esteem) and three environmental barriers (discrimination, family socialization, and availability of resources such as child care). Similarly, Harmon (1977) proposed that women's career development was affected by both internal–psychological and external–sociological constraints.

As we elaborated elsewhere (Betz & Fitzgerald, 1987), such barriers to choice include variables or forces related to a woman's tendency to make gender-stereotypic, traditionally female choices, whereas barriers to adjustment are forces acting to limit the employed woman's success or satisfaction. Following Farmer and Harmon, barriers (and facilitators) can be distinguished as either *environmental* or *internal*, the latter generally thought to be the result of gendered role socialization. Internal barriers to choice may include such things as home–career conflict and math anxiety, whereas external ones would include occupational gender stereotypes, gender-restrictive vocational-interest inventories, and gender-biased career counseling. Examples of internal barriers to adjustment include guilt related to home and family and the personalization of discrimination, whereas external adjustment barriers include discrimination itself, sexual harassment, and the effects of being a "token" female in a male-dominated work environment (see Betz & Fitzgerald, 1987; Fitzgerald, 1993; Fitzgerald & Betz, 1994; and Sandler & Hall, 1986, for detailed discussions of these barriers). There now exists an extensive body of research on many of these factors (e.g., math anxiety, sexual harassment, gender bias, and restrictiveness in testing and counseling), which are widely recognized as important from both theoretical and applied intervention perspectives.

EARLY THEORETICAL FORMULATIONS: PATTERNS AND POSTULATES

Even before the resurgence of the Women's Movement focused attention on the changing nature of women's vocational behavior, some writers attempted to describe and explain the ways that women related to the world of work. Although not theories in the formal sense, these formulations provided heuristic concepts and framed important issues in ways that continue to influence the study of women's career development to this day, thus providing a bridge between the atheoretical stage of variable identification, description, and classification and contemporary theoretical statements. The most important of these early efforts are those of Super (1957), Zytowski (1969), and the sociologist George Psathas (1968); their ideas and the research they generated are reviewed briefly in the following sections.

Super's Classification of Women's Career Patterns

The first important writer to devote any attention to women's vocational behavior was Donald Super. In his classic 1957 text, *The Psychology of Careers,* Super noted the two interrelated themes that characterized women's lives. He began by highlighting the central role that homemaking has played in defining women's activities and then cast against this backdrop the accelerating trend of their increasing labor-force participation. From the interplay of these two themes, Super derived seven mutually exclusive categories for describing women's life–career patterns: the *stable homemaking* pattern, describing women who married early and had no significant work experience; the *conventional* career pattern, describing women who entered the workforce after completion of their education and then worked until marriage, at which time they retired from the workplace to engage in full-time homemaking; the *stable* working pattern, characterizing women who did not marry but who worked continuously over their life span; the *double-track* career pattern, describing women who combined work and family roles in a continuous manner; the *interrupted* career pattern, characterized by a return to work later in life, generally after the major duties of childrearing had ended; the *unstable* career pattern, describing an irregular cycle of movement in and out of the workforce; and, finally, the *multiple-trial* career pattern, reflecting essentially an unstable job history.

Early empirical studies supported Super's descriptions. Harmon (1967) examined the career behavior of 98 women 25 years after their graduation from college and found that over 60% of them were either lifelong homemakers (17%) or followed a conventional career pattern (44%) with no significant work involvement after marriage. Slightly over one fourth followed a double-track career pattern (28%), whereas only 6% were stable working, and even fewer (4%) returned to the workforce in midlife. The results of Vetter's (1973) investigation of a national sample of women were similar: Of the sample, 50% were either homemakers or followed a conventional life pattern, although 16% were classified as interrupted, perhaps an early harbinger of the large number of women who returned to the workforce in the wake of the women's movement of the late 1960s. Fourteen percent of her sample followed a double-track pattern, and 16% were classified as unstable. Again, the single working woman was a rarity, with only 3% of the sample fitting the stable working pattern.

In these studies, from 50% to 60% of the women had no significant work experience outside the home; only 20 years later, these numbers are dramatically different, as work has assumed an increasingly visible role in women's lives. Still, Super's categories continue to serve a useful organizing function, albeit with slightly different focus. The interrupted career pattern of the 1950s and 1960s has been replaced by the *returning woman* of the 1970s and 1980s, and the examination of double-track patterns has given way to the study of *multiple-role women*. Only a small percentage of women plan to become full-time homemakers thus shrinking the number of individuals following either a stable homemaking or conventional career pattern. Despite such transformations, Super's description of the central role played by family commitments in structuring the possibilities and limitations of women's vocational behavior remains as viable today as it was over three decades ago.

Psathas' Propositions Concerning Women's Work Motivation

An early attempt to understand the factors that influence women to enter occupational roles was made by the sociologist George Psathas (1968). Psathas began by noting that the upsurge in women's vocational activity focused attention on the relative scarcity of research directed toward the understanding of their occupational behavior. Like many subsequent theorists, he proposed that any general theory of occupational choice requires attention to factors that operate in special ways for women and insisted that the understanding of their career development must begin with the relationship between occupational role and gender role, that is, orientation to marriage and children.

Psathas assumed that all women wished to marry as well as to improve their social position by finding a husband of superior social status. He suggested that occupations that provided proximity to and lessened social distance from potential mates of desirable status would be attractive to women, thus attempting to explain the popularity of occupations such as nurse, flight attendant, secretary, and so forth. In addition, he cited the influence of such factors as the time of marriage, arrival of children, family financial situation and social class, as well as the husband's attitudes as important influences on a woman's vocational involvement.

Psathas questioned the importance of the psychological concept of choice relative to these more societal level variables, remarking, "Our approach to the problem of the factors conditioning entry into occupational roles starts with a questioning of the legitimacy of the concept of 'choice.' Instead of talking about 'choice,' we turned our attention to 'settings,' which in our view engender predictable orientations to the occupational world" (p. 265). Thus, Psathas suggested that individual differences in psychological characteristics, so emphasized by vocational psychologists (e.g., Super, 1949; Super & Crites, 1963), were on the whole less important than differences in social class, perceived opportunity for social mobility, and role influences such as the timing of marriage and children.

Although Psathas' formulations did not generate subsequent empirical work, his insistence that the understanding of women's vocational behavior required variables not salient to the career development of men is reflected in the work of later writers (e.g., Betz & Fitzgerald, 1987; Fitzgerald & Crites, 1980) who have argued that women's work lives are more complex than those of men. Moreover, although few contemporary vocational psychologists would accept his emphasis on the "desire for male association" as an important motivator for women's work behavior, his work was the first attempt to explain (as opposed to merely describe) their relationship to the world of work, and thus represents an early step toward the building of a career psychology of women.

Zytowski's Postulates Concerning Women's Vocational Participation

Appearing at the same time as Psathas' (1968) work but receiving considerably more attention from vocational psychologists and counselors, Zytowski (1969) proposed nine postulates to characterize the pattern and determinants of women's vocational participation. His paper, which was the first to argue that a separate theory of vocational development for women was needed, proposed that although the modal role for women was currently that of homemaker, this role was not static and that social and technological changes would ultimately result in similar roles for men and women. Noting the orderly and developmental sequencing of women's sociobiological behavior (i.e., the timing and sequencing of childbearing and childrearing tasks), he proposed that vocational participation represented a departure from the homemaker role and that homemaking and vocational participation were largely mutually exclusive. He then suggested that women's patterns of vocational participation could be distinguished on the basis of the woman's *age of entry* into the workforce, her *span of participation*, and the traditionality of her occupation, which he labeled *degree of participation*. Combinations of these three variables suggested three distinct career patterns: *mild* (very early or late entry, brief span, traditional occupation); *moderate* (early entry, lengthy span, traditional occupation); and *unusual* (early entry, lengthy span, nontraditional occupation, i.e., high degree of participation). Finally, Zytowski proposed that women's preference for one or another pattern was determined by internal, motivational factors, whereas actual participation in one pattern or another was jointly determined by preferences, environmental considerations, and nonmotivational personal characteristics, such as ability.

Zytowski's (1969) ideas and, particularly, his proposed patterns of vocational participation were investigated in two important studies of women's career development. In the first, Wolfson (1976) conducted a follow-up of 306 women who had received counseling as college students 25 years before. Utilizing an adaptation of Zytowski's system, Wolfson classified her sample into five subgroups: the mild, moderate, and unusual patterns in the original system, a *never worked* group, and a *high moderate* group. This last group was differentiated from the original moderate group by its lengthy and continuous span of participation, that is, 18 or more years of employment out of the 25 years since college. Wolfson reported that these women, who had attended college in the 1930s and were in their 40s and 50s at the time of the study, were most likely to have chosen full-time homemaking or to have worked only until the birth of the first child, or only seasonally or occasionally but not continuously, or not in a career-committed manner. Hence, her findings supported the previous reports of Harmon (1967) and Vetter (1973) that the majority of American (middle- and upper-class) women were not seriously involved with careers.

Betz's (1984) examination of women who graduated in the college class of 1968 documented the dramatic shift in women's career behavior that had been taking place in the years since Wolfson's participants had graduated from college. Betz began by arguing that the Zytowski–Wolfson classification was incomplete, in that there was no way to classify a woman who worked in a nontraditional occupation but whose span of participation was limited. Thus, women who worked in male-dominated occupations such as mechanic, electrician, or scientist but who entered the workforce late, left early, or cycled in and out were essentially unclassifiable. Betz proposed that seven classes, rather than Wolfson's five or Zytowski's three, were needed to accommodate all possible combinations of span and degree of participation. (Betz argued that it was not necessary to consider time of workforce entry, as length of participation subsumed any temporal effects of early or late entry.) She noted further that the designation *unusual* might no longer be an appropriate term for women who were continuously employed in male-dominated occupations, because full-time homemaking was actually more statistically unlikely than continuous, nontraditional employment. She argued that the use of Harmon's (1970) term *commitment* would more accurately reflect the various types of female career involvement in contemporary culture and proposed the following patterns as necessary and sufficient to describe women's work participation: (1) never worked, (2) low commitment–traditional, (3) low commitment–pioneer, (4) moderate commitment–traditional, (5) moderate commitment–pioneer, (6) high commitment–traditional, and (7) high commitment–pioneer. Groups 2, 4, and 7 represented Zytowski's (1969) mild, moderate, and unusual patterns, whereas Group 6 represented Wolfson's (1976) high moderate group; Groups 3 and 5, however, were categories not previously accounted for.

Betz's (1984) results provide dramatic evidence of the change in women's life patterns, a change that has been called the most significant social phenomenon of the twentieth century. The majority of her participants worked continuously outside the home after graduating from college in 1968, and many (28.5%) had entered pioneer occupations. Only 1.4% were full-time homemakers during the decade covered by the study, and the great majority (79%) combined both careers and homemaking. Examination of her new categories supports her attempt to account more carefully for the complexities of women's lives, as she was able to classify a small but significant proportion of women (5%) who would otherwise have been ignored.

In her discussion, Betz (1984) quotes Zytowski's (1969) original hope that "altered social expectations and technological innovation will ultimately result in the obsolescence of this entire scheme" (p. 664), noting that, to some extent, the hope had been realized. Indeed, Zytowski's postulates are rarely invoked today. In particular, the idea that vocational and homemaking participation are mutually exclusive has been swept away by the enormous literature on dual-career couples and multiple-role planning. However, his suggestion that a separate theory for women is needed under current social arrangements is still debated, today, and the important variables coded by the choice of a nontraditional occupation remain elements of every current discussion of women and work. Although less attention has been paid to the motivational aspects of his propositions, it seems reasonable to suggest that Zytowski's was the first serious attempt to construct a theory of women's vocational behavior.

CURRENT THEORETICAL FORMULATIONS

The movement of American women back into the labor market has been called the most significant social phenomenon of the 20th century.
—Weitzman & Fitzgerald (1993)

Following these early theoretical formulations, the decade of the 1970s was marked by a virtual explosion of research on women's vocational behavior. Although no new theoretical statements emerged, the period yielded a wealth of empirical studies examining the nature, antecedents, and correlates of women's career choices as well as the publication of the first book focusing specifically on this topic (Osipow, 1975). The decade closed with the publication of Fitzgerald and Crites' (1980) review "Toward a Career Psychology of Women." In this paper, the authors critiqued the major theories of vocational choice and development (e.g., those of Holland, Super, and others) on the grounds that they were incomplete and inadequate to describe and explain women's work-related behaviors.

In the second half of this chapter, we first revisit the critique of general theoretical frameworks as applied to women and then examine the more recent *gendered* theories that began to appear in the 1980s, that is, those developed with the unique issues facing women explicitly taken into account. We begin with a brief review and critique of the three general theory clusters that have historically dominated vocational research: *developmental approaches* (Super, 1957, 1980, 1990); trait–factor, or *person–environment fit approaches*, including the theory of work adjustment (Dawis & Lofquist, 1984; Lofquist & Dawis, 1984) and Holland's theory (Holland, 1973, 1985; Holland & Gottfredson, 1992); and *social learning approaches* (Krumboltz, Mitchell, & Jones, 1976; Krumboltz & Nichols, 1990; Mitchell & Krumboltz, 1990). We then examine contemporary frameworks that more deliberately incorporate issues relevant to women's career development: *sociopsychological theories* (Astin, 1984; Gottfredson, 1981), *individual differences* models

(Betz & Fitzgerald, 1987; Farmer, 1985; Fitzgerald, Fassinger, & Betz, 1989), and *social cognitive theories* (Betz & Hackett, 1986; Hackett & Betz, 1981; Lent, Brown, & Hackett, 1993).

General Theoretical Frameworks

Developmental Theory

Developmental theory has dominated vocational research for half a century (Borgen, 1991; Hackett & Lent, 1992). This has primarily resulted from the work of Super, who, incorporating concepts from developmental, personality, and individual differences research, and occupational sociology, conceptualized career choice as a *process*, unfolding across time, in which the individual implements the self-concept in the form of a vocational identity (Super, 1957, 1980, 1990). Developmental change processes are assumed to be differentiable into observable *career patterns*, and particular patterns become preeminent at various normative age-graded periods, or stages, of life. At each stage of this process, the person must master particular tasks to move successfully to the next stage; the successful mastery of such developmental tasks is seen as *vocational maturity*. As with all developmental theories, such maturation leads to increasing differentiation and integration with regard to career behavior (e.g., a clearer sense of one's attributes as they relate to occupations, which are, in turn, seen more realistically; Gelso & Fassinger, 1992). Development is seen as contextual and self-constructive, what Fitzgerald and Weitzman (1992) described as "one's dynamic constructions of self-in-the-world" (p. 135). Several expansions in Super's latest (e.g., 1980, 1990) articulations of his theory have been noted as particularly important (Borgen, 1991; Fitzgerald & Weitzman, 1992; Gelso & Fassinger, 1992; Hackett & Lent, 1992). The cyclical process of change has been emphasized as well as the social and economic forces that influence that recycling. Self-concept is now conceptualized in terms of personal constructs, which are seen as products of learning, and the defining and operationalizing of career maturity increasingly emphasized, particularly with respect to readiness to cope with developmental tasks. Perhaps most importantly for women's career development, the interrelated concepts of *life-span* and *life-space* roles (presented as a rainbow, or most recently, an archway; Super, 1980, 1990) and role salience were introduced.

Hackett and Lent (1992) have noted that although few of Super's propositions have been directly subjected to empirical investigation, research on related concepts suggests indirect support for the theory. Moreover, some have suggested that the "wide and multiple-faceted vision" (Borgen, 1991, p. 278) of Super's work may well offer the most comprehensive framework for overall integration of vocational theories (Brown, 1990; Gelso & Fassinger, 1992; Osipow, 1990), as well as for the incorporation of women's unique career issues (Fitzgerald & Weitzman, 1992; Hackett & Lent, 1992). Especially useful in this latter respect are the concepts of personal constructs and role salience, which allow for "more sophisticated representations of the self–environment transaction over time" (Hackett & Lent, 1992, p. 429) and acknowledge the "multidimensional nature of women's (and men's) lives" (Fitzgerald & Weitzman, 1992, p. 135).

However, although Super's later formulations consider biological, social, economic, and learning factors more explicitly than do earlier statements, such factors are still not well integrated into the model (Hackett & Lent, 1992). For example, a great deal of research suggests that women's roles are not as neatly negotiated as implied by Super's rainbow, and, more specifically, that traditional gender role socialization does not prepare them for the complexity of integrating work and family (Fitzgerald & Weitzman, 1992). Moreover, it is likely that for large segments of the population, the concepts of vocational choice and development are simply not relevant, as simple economic survival is a far greater occupational motivator than the implementation of self-concept or some other idea of ego optimization (Bingham & Ward, 1994; Carter & Cook, 1992; Fitzgerald & Betz, 1994). For lower or working-class women and many women of color, developmental concepts may offer little in the way of explanatory power. We should note, however, that because so little research has actually been undertaken on these groups, the potential applicability or inapplicability of most vocational theories is largely unknown (Fitzgerald & Betz, 1994). For developmental theory in particular, much work remains to be done to integrate social and environmental factors more completely into its formulations.

Trait–Factor, or Person–Environment Fit, Theories

The two trait–factor theories commanding the most empirical attention within vocational psychology have been the career choice theory of Holland (1973, 1985; Holland & Gottfredson, 1992) and the Theory of Work Adjustment (Dawis & Lofquist, 1984; Lofquist & Dawis, 1984). Both theories conceptualize career behavior in terms of the fit between persons (e.g., personality traits) and their educational or work environments (e.g., reward structure). Vocational behavior is thus seen as a reflection of the personality, and it is assumed that the most positive outcomes (e.g., satisfaction, performance) occur when educational or occupational environments best allow the expression of personality traits, thus resulting in maximum congruence (Holland, 1973, 1985) or correspondence (Dawis & Lofquist, 1984).

Theory of Work Adjustment. In Dawis and Lofquist's (1984) framework, work adjustment is seen as an ongoing, dynamic process via which the individual work personality achieves correspondence with the work environment. Stronger correspondence leads to tenure in the environment, which is determined by both satisfaction with the environment and success in meeting its demands. Work adjustment theory has generated much empirical activity, a number of measurement tools, and an occupational classification system (Hackett & Lent, 1992). Of the 20 propositions put forth by Dawis and Lofquist (1984), however, only a few have received adequate empirical attention, and consequently, the adequacy of the theory remains largely unknown (Hackett & Lent, 1992).

With respect to its specific applicability to women's vocational behavior, Fitzgerald and Rounds (1994) point to a number of explanatory limitations. For example, the theory predicts that a good match (in terms of ability–job requirements) results in tenure; excess ability (relative to job demands) leads to promotion, whereas inadequate ability results in job failure. As the general distribution of ability is similar for women and men, the theory would predict a similar distribution of occupational level among women and men in the workplace. The reality, of course, is quite different, due to the persistent underutilization of women's abilities and widespread ghettoization in traditionally female, low-level occupations. Such occupational tracking implicates societal factors such as discrimination, sexual harassment, the motherhood mandate, gender role socialization, work–home conflict, and other barriers that limit women's choices and severely compromise optimal fit. With respect to job satisfaction, the second major variable in work adjustment theory, Fitzgerald and Rounds (1994) highlighted the manner in which the stress associated with the home–work interface (exacerbated by nonexistent flextime, family leave, and other organizational policies) compromised job satisfaction for many women. A number of authors (e.g., Bingham & Ward, 1994; Fitzgerald & Betz, 1994; Hackett & Lent, 1992) have called for increased attention to cultural and environmental and structural factors in vocational research concerning women. In their analysis of these factors as related to work adjustment theory, Fitzgerald and Rounds (1994) affirmed its basic soundness but made several suggestions for changes in theory and measurement of variables.

Holland's Theory. The second important trait–factor framework is Holland's (1973, 1985) theory of career choice, recently described as the "most well-researched and probably the most visible conceptual model emanating from vocational/counseling psychology" (Hackett & Lent, 1992, p. 422). Postulating a hexagonal model of individual and workplace personalities (*Realistic, Investigative, Artistic, Social, Enterprising,* and *Conventional*), the theory assumes that a congruent match between the person and the educational or occupational environment will result in more favorable outcomes than will incongruent matches; in addition, the concepts of consistency, differentiation, and identity describe the degree to which individual or occupational personalities are clear and well defined. With respect to empirical support, the predictions that seem to have garnered the most (across both gender and race) are those associated with congruence, that is, that individuals generally prefer environments that match their individual personality types. Additionally, research has tended to yield results supporting the relationship of congruence with achievement and stability, but an even stronger relationship with vocational or educational satisfaction (Hackett & Lent, 1992). Therefore, the theory and its empirical support suggest that the most favorable outcomes (e.g., satisfaction, stability, and achievement) occur when people's occupational preferences can be fully realized.

Despite an impressive body of general support, a number of problems arise when Holland's framework is applied to women. First, the pervasive impact of gender role socialization is reflected in women's continuing concentration in low-level jobs and their (apparent) self-selection out of attractive jobs, particularly those involving math and science; few women, for example, are found in Holland's Realistic or Investigative occupations, whereas an overwhelming majority are found in clerical and service occupations (Fitzgerald & Weitzman, 1992). It is the realism of vocational choice that is at issue here, seldom attained by women because they do not enjoy the same freedom as men in choosing an occupation. Family demands and the lack of structural supports for career plans result in many women making what appear to be unrealistic career choices in terms of congruence vis-à-vis Holland's theory. Such choices, however, may actually represent a level of realism in life planning not accounted for in the theory, which describes but does not explain women's career choices. Fitzgerald and Weitzman (1992) suggested adding the concepts of *satisficing* and *optimization* to explain the behavior of women who choose occupations seemingly inconsistent with ability or interests but that constitute a "good enough" or optimal choice based on other expected roles and demands. Particularly for women of color or working-class women, choices may well be made on the basis of variables other than personal preference. For example, a woman may forgo a risky but interesting job in favor of one that supports her family and provides stability (Carter & Cook, 1992). Indeed, Fitzgerald and Betz (1994) noted that current theoretical statements may well be most useful for (the relatively few) women who have already surmounted the effects of cultural and structural barriers; such frameworks must be enlarged to incorporate explicitly these factors if they are to become comprehensive explanations of the career behavior.

Social Learning Theory

Social learning theory (Krumboltz, Mitchell, & Jones, 1976; Krumboltz & Nichols, 1990; Mitchell & Krumboltz, 1990) is a decision-making theory grounded in the behavioral tradition. It assumes the influence of instrumental, associative, and vicarious learning experiences in interaction with the environment and emphasizes changes in persons regarding preferences for and skills related to various activities and career-related goals. This framework postulates four influences on career decisions: genetic endowment and abilities; environmental events and conditions; and learning experiences, which, in turn, influence the development of task-approach skills. Outcomes salient in this theory (in addition to task-approach skills) include entry behaviors, self-observation generalizations, and world-view generalizations.

Hackett, Lent, and Greenhaus (1991) remarked that social learning theory at its inception had the advantage of being grounded in an already well-developed empirical base from which the propositions were generated and that the hypotheses were clearly laid out for operationalization and testing. They also observed that the theory had become increasingly applied in the last decade and was therefore very practical for designing interventions. It was also noted (Hackett & Lent, 1992), however, that the empirical support for this framework is largely confined to early correlational studies and that it has not evolved significantly in the almost two decades since its original statement. Krumboltz and Nichols' (1990) incorporation of Ford's (1987; cited in Krumboltz & Nichols, 1990) Living Systems Framework was seen as offering new possibilities for updating and expanding the original theory (Hackett & Lent, 1992). Hackett and Lent (1992) also pointed out that social learning theory may benefit from being tied more closely to recent developments in social cognitive theory (Bandura, 1986) and from explicitly including such variables as self-efficacy, triadic reciprocality, outcome expectations, and the like. Finally, Hackett and Lent observed that decision-making theories seem to assume that information about the self and the world of work will be processed objectively, whereas information-processing theory suggests the influence of numerous cognitive distortions. More explicit attention to such issues would seem to be imperative in developing an updated articulation of the theory.

With respect to its applicability to women, Mitchell and Krumboltz (1990) acknowledged the theory's implication that optimal career decision making requires the opportunity to be exposed to the widest possible array of learning experiences; further, the theory assumes that individuals can influence their environments through the nature of some of their learning experiences. For many women, people of color, and working-class individuals, such assumptions are frequently unrealistic (Bingham & Ward, 1994; Carter & Cook, 1992; Fitzgerald & Betz, 1994). As with developmental and person–environment fit theories, the social learning framework must explicitly integrate cultural and structural factors into its theoretical postulates if it is to become a viable *general* explanation of vocational behavior.

Summary

Developmental, trait–factor, and (to a lesser degree) social learning theories have dominated the research in vocational psychology. Those interested in women's career behavior have typically attempted to examine how well or poorly the theories apply to women, most concluding (as do we) that they offer fundamental insights but at the same time suffer from critical limitations. Beginning with Gottfredson (1981), the 1980s saw the appearance of a number of very different types of theoretical efforts, frameworks that incorporated gender and, in fact, placed it at their very center. As we shall see, such efforts, most often developed to explain the behavior of a "special group" (Gottfredson, 1986), have resulted in some of the most comprehensive and sophisticated general explanations of career behavior to date.

Gendered Theoretical Frameworks

Sociopsychological Theories

The initial examples of gendered vocational theory reflected what Astin (1984) termed a *sociopsychological* perspective. Our adoption of the term acknowledges the important ways in which these frameworks attempted to integrate both individual and environmental influences on career behavior; we note, however, the determinative role played by socialization and the power of social forces highlighted in both theories reviewed here.

Astin's Sociopsychological Model of Career Choice and Work Behavior. At the invitation of the Committee on Women of Division 17 of the American Psychological Association, Helen Astin (1984) developed a model of career choice and work behavior that attempted to incorporate both personal (i.e., psychological) characteristics and social forces as well as their interaction. Astin's model, which she explicitly noted was designed to describe the career behavior of both women and men, was based on four major constructs: motivation, expectations, gender role socialization, and the structure of opportunity. Briefly, she proposed that an individual's work behavior is motivated by the need for survival, pleasure, and contribution and that career choices are grounded in expectations concerning the accessibility of alternative types of work and their relative ability to satisfy these three needs. She further proposed that such expectations are based partly on early socialization experiences and partly on the perceived structure of opportunity. Finally, she attempted to account for women's shifting occupational aspirations by proposing that changes in the structure of opportunity altered expectations concerning occupational accessibility and thus modified career choice and work behavior.

Despite its status as the first invited theoretical statement on women's career development, the model has had limited influence on the field to date. In general, it has not proven heuristic, perhaps because the broad generality of its constructs do not lend themselves easily to operationalization, a problem underscored by the one empirical study that attempted to examine it (Poole, Langan–Fox, Ciavarella, & Onedei, 1991). Working with a large three-wave data set collected on Australian youth in 1973, 1976, and 1982, Poole et al. reported support for the importance of three of Astin's basic principles (socialization, structure of opportunity, and work expectations) in predicting professional attainment (in this case, attainment of a professional vs. nonprofessional position). Problems in assessing the theoretical concepts, however, cast doubt on the results as well as highlighting the more general difficulties of testing the model. For example, socialization was assessed by a single item that inquired whether the respondents perceived their parents as wishing them to proceed to postsecondary education, a question that hardly does justice to the concept of gender role socialization. In contrast, the structure of opportunity was operationalized through a heterogeneous set of variables, most of which had little in common with Astin's concept (e.g., reasons for seeking college education, clarity of career plans, and so forth). Finally, the construct of work expectations, which Astin described as a range of career-related issues and questions (e.g., What type of work am I capable of? What options are open and which are closed off?), was equated with a single item that classified the respondents' expected occupation as professional or nonprofessional. Given these extremely weak operationalizations, it is not possible to determine whether the data supported the theory or not.

It is possible, of course, that the model is simply not testable in its present form and is best thought of as a general conceptual framework rather than an articulated theoretical statement. Reconceptualized at this level of generality and freed from the necessity of meeting more formal criteria, the framework directs attention to important factors affecting women's vocational behavior: individual differences in values, beliefs, attitudes, and expectations; socialization factors such as family and education; and what is clearly Astin's most important contribution, the influence of the structure of opportunity.

These three sets of variables, which range from the individual level of analysis through community influences to macro societal level concepts, recall Super and Bachrach's (1957) notion that, in selecting an occupation, the individual is influenced not only by personal psychological characteristics but also by multiple levels of social systems. These systems range from the direct influence of the home, school, and family to community level variables (peer relationships, religious influences, social contacts) to the more general societal influences operating in American culture. Focusing attention on these macroinfluences through her insistence on the importance of the structure of opportunity, Astin reminds us that each woman lives her life within a particular cultural context that shapes not only her opportunities but also her perceptions of those opportunities and, thus, her choices and behavior.

Gottfredson's Theory of Circumscription and Compromise.
Gottfredson (1981) formulated a model of vocational development emphasizing the processes of *circumscription* (narrowing) of career-choice alternatives

and *compromise* between preferences and employment realities. Central to both these processes are perceptions of job–self compatibility along three important dimensions: occupational gender type, prestige, and field of work. Gottfredson suggested that gender type influences choice because, through the process of circumscription, U.S. society functions to limit an individual's perceived options to a reduced range of career alternatives that are gender appropriate. Once this range is set (according to Gottfredson, somewhere between the ages of 6 and 8 years), occupations that fall outside it will not be considered except under unusual circumstances. Hence, Gottfredson's view suggests serious restrictive effects of occupational gender stereotyping on women's aspirations. She further suggested that when compromises between preferences and employment realities must be made, people will most readily sacrifice field of work (i.e., their vocational interests) and will be least willing to compromise the gender-appropriateness dimension of their choice.

Researchers have generally examined the constructs of circumscription and compromise separately. Henderson, Hesketh, and Tuffin (1988) examined the circumscription concept, finding that children exhibited gender-type preferences from an earlier age than the theory would predict and that boys exhibited stronger gender typing than girls. Such findings are consistent with a fairly large body of research showing that children gender stereotyped occupations as early as age 2 and that girls more readily consider "boy" occupations than the reverse (Betz & Fitzgerald, 1987). Henderson et al. also reported that although socioeconomic background (SES) did influence choices after age 9, its influence followed rather than preceded the influence of ability (which Gottfredson postulated to be primary).

For those interested in women's career development, compromise is a particularly important process because of its potential for explaining women's downscaling of their aspirations in college and beyond. Additionally, as discussed by Hesketh, Elmslie, and Kaldor (1990a), the compromise process may also explain why interventions intended to facilitate women's exploration of nontraditional careers are often ineffective. The major difficulty in testing the theory of compromise has been the nonindependence of the dimensions of interest (i.e., gender type, prestige, and interests) when occupational titles are used as the stimuli. For example, as reviewed by Gottfredson (1981), male-gender-typed occupations varied from high to low prestige, but female-gender-typed occupations clustered in the middle-to-low levels with high-prestige female occupations being virtually nonexistent.

Early studies (e.g., Taylor & Pryor, 1985, 1986) employed what Hesketh, Elmslie, and Kaldor (1990a) labeled somewhat artificial methods for comparing the interest code, gender type, and prestige level of students' preferred occupation with their planned compromise and actual job at follow-up. Confounded relationships among the three dimensions and lack of comparability in the methods and scales of measuring the three variables complicated both analysis and interpretation. Recently, Hesketh, Pryor, and Gleitzman (1989) explored the applicability of *fuzzy-set* theory to the conceptualization and measurement of interests, gender type, and prestige. Respondents expressed their preferred ranges of acceptability of prestige levels and gender types on *fuzzy* rating scales which elicited from the participant both a preferred position and a range of acceptability, in this case, the attractiveness of each Holland interest area and a range of attractiveness. This approach to measurement thus yields a *social space*, or zone of acceptable alternatives (Gottfredson, 1981). Hesketh et al. (1989) reported data supporting the reliability and validity of the fuzzy-graphic rating method and consequently used it to explore the compromise process.

Research based on these assessment methods has highlighted the need for modifications in the theory. For example, contrary to Gottfredson's postulate that the range of alternatives is circumscribed with increasing age, Leung and Harmon (1990) reported that the range of acceptable alternatives increased from early childhood through adolescence stabilizing about age 18. In addition, several variables appeared to moderate both the nature and extent of circumscription. Research findings consistently suggest that gender type may limit boys' choices more than girls' choices: Girls are much more likely to prefer and choose male-stereotypic careers than boys are to prefer female-stereotypic careers (Hannah & Kahn, 1989; Henderson et al., 1988; Leung & Harmon, 1990). Leung and Harmon (1990) also found the range of alternatives to vary as a function of gender role orientation, with androgynous respondents most flexible in both gender type and prestige preferences; Henderson et al. (1988) found ability more closely related than social background (SES) to prestige preferences.

Gottfredson's (1981) postulate that, when compromises are necessary, individuals will first sacrifice their interests (field of work), then their desired prestige levels, and only lastly their preferred gender type, has also not been consistently supported (Holt, 1989). If anything, research has suggested that gender type may be the *least*, rather than the most, important factor. The research of Hesketh and her colleagues (Hesketh et al., 1990a; Hesketh, Elmslie, & Kaldor, 1990b) has consistently indicated that individuals of both sexes are more willing to compromise on gender type and prestige than interests, and Leung and Plake (1990) reported that gender type was compromised before prestige except when men were forced to choose between a high-prestige feminine occupation and low-prestige masculine occupation. Holt (1989) found that a tendency among college students to select high-prestige occupations regardless of interest area was more pronounced for engineers than for social-work students, and Leung, Ivey, and Scheel (1991) reported that family approval was more important than prestige, which was, in turn, more important than gender type.

Based on their research, Hesketh et al. (1990b) proposed that interests are the most salient factors in the ultimate career-choice process. They explained this phenomenon by proposing that concepts acquired later (interests) versus earlier (gender type) in development incorporate elements of the earlier concepts and are thus more salient because they are more inclusive. This reformulation of Gottfredson's theory suggests that options can be restored to people who had earlier rejected them, thus supporting the opportunity rather than socialization hypothesis (see Cole & Hansen, 1975). We note that although its validity is questionable, the theory has had considerable heuristic value in highlighting the previously neglected but important process of compromising ideal choices to reality and opportunity. The concepts of circumscription, compromise, and zone of acceptable alternatives help researchers to identify the cognitive processes in career development.

It is also of note that the majority of research on Gottfredson's (1981) theory has been conducted with male as well as female respondents. Some of these studies have yielded gender similarities (e.g., the predominance of interests over gender type in making compromises; Hesketh et al., 1990b), whereas others have highlighted various differences (e.g., greater rigidity in gender-typed preferences among boys than among girls; Henderson et al., 1988; Leung & Harmon, 1990). Thus, once again, conceptual work having particular relevance to women has provided a more comprehensive understanding of career development in general.

Individual Differences Models

In contrast to the sweep of social-psychological theory with its emphasis on broad social forces, traditional work in vocational psychology has highlighted the uniqueness of the individual. In the following section, we discuss two recent individual differences models of career development that explicitly incorporate attention to the unique issues and concerns facing women. What distinguishes these models from their historical forebearers, however, and connects them philosophically to the frameworks discussed previously, is their focus on individual differences in socialization and development as well as in interests and abilities.

Farmer's Model of Career Motivation in Women and Men

The first model considered is that of Farmer (1985), who postulated the importance of *background factors* (gender, race, age, SES, ability), *personal characteristics* (academic self-esteem, independence, values, attributions), and *environmental variables* (parental and teacher support) for predicting career and achievement motivation (specifically, level of aspirations, mastery strivings, and career commitment). She reported support for her theory from path analyses, using data from both men and women as well as from large representative samples of White, Black, Hispanic, and Asian ninth- and twelfth-grade students. Her results suggested that background factors were the strongest predictors of occupational and educational aspirations and that personal variables (particularly independence) were the strongest predictors of mastery strivings. Career motivation was strongly predicted by personal variables, with background and environmental variables adding some predictive power to the model. Overall, background variables were indirectly predictive of achievement and career motivation, and both gender and race differences were found (Hackett & Lent, 1992).

Two recent studies have been reported that further test the concepts of this model. In the latest results from her ongoing, longitudinal study of career motivation and achievement, Farmer and her colleagues (Farmer, Wardrop, Anderson, & Risinger, 1993) reported data from 173 participants (97 women, 76 men) in her 1980 and 1990 phases of data collection who were ninth or twelfth graders in 1980 and aspired to a math, science, or technology career. The results indicated that by 1990, 36% of the women and 46% of the men had persisted in science-related careers. Farmer et al. used causal analyses to obtain fitted models for women and men, with results indicating that the theoretical model fit men considerably better than women, accounting for 97% and 34%, respectively, of the variance in persistence. For women, persistence was best predicted by number of elective science courses taken in high school as well as by current career aspiration and math self-efficacy. More minority women (53%) than White women (33%) who took elective math and science courses and aspired to high-level careers persisted in science-related careers. Home commitment had no relation to persistence in science-related careers for women in this sample but was negatively and significantly related to career commitment. Farmer and her colleagues concluded from these results that the effect of home–career conflict may be similar for both persisters in science careers and those who choose other career fields. They also highlighted the finding that taking math and science courses in high school contributes to persistence in science careers in adulthood (Farmer et al., 1993).

These authors also discussed some of their more detailed findings as related to developmental and trait–factor theoretical predictions. Interestingly, their results indicated that from 1980 to 1990 men increased their support for women working but still scored below women on this variable, whereas women increased the importance they placed on their career roles during this time and increased their career commitment based on the supportiveness of the environment. Taken together, these findings suggest that developmental changes for both women and men include an increasing sense of salience of the work role for women but that conflicts regarding the home–work interface are likely as long as men's and women's expectations remain somewhat at odds. Farmer et al. (1993) suggested that women in the 1990s who are trying to balance home and career may reject science careers as too demanding, a suggestion consonant with Fitzgerald and Weitz-man's (1992) idea of women "satisficing" in their career choices.

Another recent study that partially built on and tested aspects of Farmer's (1985) model is that of McWhirter and Hackett (1993), who tested path models of career commitment and aspirations of Mexican-American high-school girls. Three causal models for predicting career commitment, level of aspirations, and planned schooling were tested with a sample of 280 Mexican-American high-school junior and senior girls. Predictor variables included acculturation, socioeconomic status, academic achievement, gender role characteristics, gender role attitudes, parental support, family commit-ment, teacher support, and perceptions of barriers. Analyses produced plau-sible models of career commitment, planned schooling, and level of aspi-rations; the overall model successfully predicted career commitment but not educational and occupational aspirations. McWhirter and Hackett (1993) also noted the particularly strong influence of acculturation on gender-role atti-tudes and family commitment and of teacher support on career commitment.

These authors concluded that, overall, their results were similar to those in other studies of women's career development in that background vari-ables, gender-related attitudes, support, and career and family commitment seemed to be salient in career aspirations and choices. Additionally, their findings indicated support for acculturation variables as important to the career development of this particular population, a finding that has also appeared in other studies of Latinas (e.g., Gomez & Fassinger, 1994). Al-though the perceived-barriers variable was not a significant predictor in this study (presumably due to psychometric limitations of the instrument used and the naivete of the participants), the fact that this variable was related to other variables suggests the importance of including it in future studies. McWhirter and Hackett (1993) also found that girls from lower socioeco-nomic backgrounds (associated with lower levels of acculturation) perceived their parents as less encouraging of career pursuits, whereas teacher support was important to levels of career commitment; perceptions of barriers were offset by teacher support as well as by liberal gender role attitudes and high commitment to future family. Given the strong family commitment evidenced in this population, the authors suggested increased research and intervention regarding multiple-role demands and conflicts. As with other researchers (Bingham & Ward, 1994; Carter & Cook, 1992; Farmer et al., 1993; Fitzgerald & Betz, 1994), McWhirter and Hackett (1993) suggested that girls may fore-close on desirable careers because of a lack of confidence in balancing family and career. They recommended that in studying career plans, antici-pated as well as actual barriers must be explored, but acknowledge the difficulty of this with young women who have not yet been exposed to the direct effects of sexism and racism or the subtle effects these conditions have on their lives and choices.

Betz–Fitzgerald–Fassinger Model of Career-Choice
Realism in High-Ability Women

Another individual differences model of women's career development, a framework for predicting career choice, was developed by Betz and Fitzgerald (1987; Fitzgerald, Fassinger, & Betz, 1989) and tested by Fassinger (1985, 1990). Their work focused on high-ability college women, for whom individual differences may be assumed to play the most vital role and environmental restraints to be minimal. It is concerned with the underutilization of gifted and talented women and therefore focused on realism of career choice as a major outcome variable, that is, the extent to which a career choice is congruent with the abilities and interests of the individual. The model hypothesized that previous work experience, academic success, role model influence, and perceived encouragement predicted attitudes toward work, self, and gender roles. These, in turn, predicted lifestyle preferences and plans and, ultimately, realism of career choice.

The current status of this model reflects the programmatic research of Fassinger, who first operationalized and tested it with a sample of approximately 300 college women, using structural equation modeling techniques (Fassinger, 1985). Her study yielded a simplified framework in which ability, achievement orientation, and feminist orientation influenced career and family orientation, which, in turn, influenced career choice. In a subsequent study of a larger, more heterogeneous sample of college women, Fassinger (1990) again modified the framework, finding that high ability levels interacted with gender role attitudes (including feminist attitudes) and agentic characteristics to influence career orientation and career choice; other important revisions included the addition of several indicators of mathematics orientation. In the latest extension of this research, O'Brien and Fassinger (1993) tested the revised model with a sample of 409 predominantly college-bound, female high-school seniors and again found general support for the theory. Results indicated that the career orientation and career choice of adolescent women were predicted by ability, agentic characteristics, gender role attitudes, and (in a second hypothesized model) relationship with mother. More specifically, high-ability young women who possessed liberal gender role attitudes were instrumental and efficacious in regard to math and careers, exhibited moderate degrees of attachment to and independence from their mothers, valued their career pursuits, and made nontraditional and prestigious career choices.

In general, the results of this program of research suggest that ability and a sense of personal agency (as manifested in such constructs as instrumentality and self-efficacy; Betz & Hackett, 1987) are critical and to some degree interactive influences on women's career behavior. Another important factor that has consistently emerged in tests of this model is gender-role orientation (especially feminist attitudes), and this variable is related to ability as well.

The overall pattern appears to be one of mutually mediating, interactive influences of ability, agency, and gender role orientation on the development and expression of women's capabilities and achievements. In addition, the variable of career orientation, which presently includes indicators that tap family orientation as well, seems to reflect the current intention of most young women to consider career and family simultaneously.

Problems that remain in the current version of this model include the failure of a number of background variables (role model influences, perceived encouragement, previous work experience) to exert empirical influence, despite a long history of such influence documented in other studies. Fassinger (1985, 1990) cited psychometric limitations in the measurement of these variables, and it may be that their complexity is best tapped by qualitative study. In addition, the operationalization of realism of career choice has proven to be very difficult. Fitzgerald et al. (1989) suggested that simplifying the concept by focusing on ability–level match might produce better results and address the main concern—underutilization of women's talent—more clearly. These authors also noted that the study of employed rather than college women may increase the range of responses in this measure, as not only is there more variability in the demands of occupations than in college majors, but it is also at the level of entry and actual choice that many women (having completed a congruent college major) choose occupations at a level below their capabilities. Finally, the issue of maternal influence, suggested in the O'Brien and Fassinger (1993) study, may prove fruitful for future research. This is consistent with years of empirical findings indicating the importance of mothers to women's career development in terms of attitudes, modeling, and other factors. Moreover, the construct may help to integrate the burgeoning interest in self psychology (Gelso & Fassinger, 1992) into the study of vocational development.

Summary

In their critique of individual differences models, Hackett and Lent (1992) pointed out that these frameworks converge in important ways. Each addresses the important effects of background, intrapsychic, and socialization variables on women's career behavior. Moreover, both frameworks have been tested with large samples and sophisticated modeling strategies. Because each theory addresses a different facet of women's occupational behavior, however, a direct comparison of the findings is difficult. Hackett and Lent (1992) also cautioned against premature conclusions from the results of modeling strategies when alternative models are not postulated for comparison. In addition, much more attention must be given to heterogeneity among women, particularly in regard to the concerns of women of color. Several authors (e.g., Bingham & Ward, 1994; Carter & Cook, 1992; Fitzgerald & Betz, 1994; Gelso & Fassinger, 1992) have called for work in racial identity (e.g., Helms, 1990) to be explicitly incorporated into existing career development theories. Finally, Hackett and Lent (1992) observed that societal shifts lead to constantly changing social roles that, in turn, will have radical impact on the usefulness of what we consider to be current theories, emphasizing the need to remain up to date with social realities when theorizing about women's vocational behavior.

Social Cognitive Frameworks

In this section, we consider two frameworks, self-efficacy theory (Betz & Hackett, 1986; Hackett & Betz, 1981) and an emerging social cognitive theory (Lent et al., 1993; Lent & Hackett, in press), that have developed from the social learning theory of Bandura (1977, 1986). Extending beyond the traditional learning paradigms, these theoretical statements encompass psychosocial phenomena, such as motivational and self-regulatory mechanisms, in a model of triadic reciprocality in which environment, person factors (such as cognition), and behavior mutually influence one another in ongoing interaction. These frameworks represent the most recent, and most sophisticated, theoretical explanation to date of the process of career choice and development. In the landmark paper that first applied Bandura's theory to career development, Hackett and Betz (1981) noted its particular relevance to women's career behavior and it is this on which we focus here; however, its broader applicability to the understanding of vocational behavior more generally make it the premier example of the ways in which the study of women as a unique group has enriched the science of vocational psychology.

Hackett and Betz's Application of Self-Efficacy Theory to Women's Career Behavior

Hackett and Betz (1981) based their work on the assumption that gender role socialization influences cognitive processes that, in turn, influence career decision making and adjustment. In 1981, they proposed that one category of cognitive process, that is, expectations of self-efficacy, was a major mediator of the effects of gender role socialization on gender differences in career choice and adjustment. Briefly, self-efficacy expectations (Bandura, 1977) are expectations or beliefs concerning one's ability to successfully perform a given behavior. Efficacy expectations are postulated to determine whether or not behavior will be initiated, how much effort will be expended, and how long behavior will be sustained in the face of obstacles and aversive experiences. Hence, efficacy expectations are postulated to influence choice, performance, and persistence in career-related domains.

According to Bandura (1977), efficacy expectations are developed (and potentially modified) by four sources of experiential information: performance accomplishments; vicarious learning, or modeling; verbal persuasion, or encouragement from other people to engage in a specific behavior; and the degree of emotional arousal with reference to a domain of behavior, such that the higher the arousal (anxiety), the less self-efficacious the individual will feel. Thus, to the extent that the individual's background experiences in a given behavioral area have been characterized by performance accomplishments, vicarious learning, verbal persuasion and encouragement, and a lack of anxiety associations, the individual would be postulated to develop high self-efficacy expectations with respect to that domain.

Hackett and Betz (1981) postulated that low expectations of self-efficacy with respect to various career areas, particularly those that have historically been male-dominated, are a major mediator of gender differences in vocational choice and subsequent vocational behavior. The evidence they reviewed showed that the background experiences of men and women differ markedly in terms of the sources of efficacy information they provide for subsequent career options, with male socialization providing efficacy information for a considerably broader variety of career options.

In the initial empirical test of the usefulness of this application of self-efficacy theory, Betz and Hackett (1981) examined gender differences in occupational self-efficacy, and tested its utility in predicting the range (number) of occupational alternatives considered by college students. Occupational self-efficacy was assessed by asking participants to respond to questions about their capabilities with regard to the educational requirements and job duties of 10 traditional occupations (defined as occupations in which two thirds or more of the members were women) and 10 nontraditional occupations (i.e., occupations in which men constituted the majority of the membership). Consistent with prediction, significant gender differences were found in occupational self-efficacy expectations when traditionality of the occupation was taken into account. Men's occupational self-efficacy was essentially equivalent for traditionally male-dominated and traditionally female-dominated occupations; women's self-efficacy expectations were lower than men's for nontraditional occupations and significantly higher than men's for traditional occupations. Further, these gender differences in self-efficacy were highly predictive of gender differences in range of traditional and nontraditional occupations considered. The results suggest that perceptions of efficacy with respect to gender-nontraditional careers enhance the likelihood of including them among one's range of options.

The assessment of general occupational self-efficacy as pioneered by Betz and Hackett (1981) has been used in many subsequent studies, with most showing gender differences in occupational self-efficacy (Layton, 1984; Matsui, Ikeda, & Ohnishi, 1989; Mitchell, 1990; Post–Kammer & Smith,. 1985; Williams, 1993; Zilber, 1988). The largest and most robust difference is the higher male self-efficacy with respect to male-dominated occupations. Other studies (e.g., Layton, 1984) have replicated the findings that self-efficacy is related to the range of career options considered. In addition, researchers have found gender differences in efficacy expectations with respect to content domains more closely associated with the background experiences of one gender or the other. For example, there were large and consistent differences in mathematics self-efficacy (Betz & Hackett, 1983; Lent, Brown, & Hackett, 1993; Lent, Lopez, & Bieschke, 1991; Reitman, 1992) and the Realistic and Investigative Holland themes (Lapan, Boggs, & Morrill, 1989).

Intermediate in specificity between general occupational titles and content domains has been the study of self-efficacy with respect to the critical area of scientific and technical careers. Betz and Hackett (1981) included scientific and technical occupations in their measure of self-efficacy (with the striking result that 70% of college men but only 30% of equally able college women believed they could complete the educational requirements of an engineering degree), but subsequent research has examined students actually enrolled in science or engineering schools. Lent, Brown, and Larkin (1984, 1986) investigated the relationship between self-efficacy estimates and the degree of persistence and academic success of students majoring in the sciences and engineering. In their first study, Lent et al. (1984) adapted Betz and Hackett's (1981) assessment procedure to measure self-efficacy with regard to 15 scientific and technical occupations. Using a relatively small sample of students who had declared college majors in engineering, Lent et al. (1984) found significant differences in several measures of academic performance and persistence between participants with high versus low scientific–technical occupational self-efficacy. Generally, students with higher confidence in their abilities relative to the scientific occupations sampled achieved higher grades and persisted longer in their majors. Moderate and significant correlations between technical–scientific self-efficacy and objective measures of mathematics aptitude and high-school achievement were also reported. No gender differences in scientific and technical self-efficacy, however, were found.

In a subsequent study, Lent et al. (1986) conducted a partial replication and extension of their earlier study, with a larger sample. For this study, they developed a second measure of scientific and technical self-efficacy to assess efficacy beliefs with regard to academic milestones, that is, specific accomplishments critical to academic success in science and engineering majors such as completing the mathematics requirements and remaining enrolled in the college of technology. As with the previous study, results from this study indicated an absence of gender differences in efficacy expectations, but scientific–technical self-efficacy was significantly predictive of grades in technical courses, persistence in a major, and range of career options. Thus, although science and engineering self-efficacy was predictive of the postulated outcomes, no gender differences in initial expectations were found. These patterns were likely due to the fact that the young women in this sample had chosen rather than avoided science and engineering majors, and suggest higher science and engineering self-efficacy expectations in comparison to women in general. Similarly, Hackett, Betz, Casas, and Rocha–Singh (1992) reported no gender differences in self-efficacy for science and engineering occupations or the core requirements of the engineering program in a sample of 197 students in a university school of engineering. The strongest predictor of performance (grades) was academic self-efficacy. Because self-efficacy expectations have also been found to be related to the consideration of math–science careers and other career variables (Betz & Hackett, 1983; Hackett, 1985; Post–Kammer & Smith, 1986), they are clearly important considerations in both the understanding and intervention in career decision-making processes.

In accordance with Bandura's (1977) theory of the development of self-efficacy expectations, Matsui, Matsui, and Ohnishi (1990) reported that all four sources of efficacy information (performance accomplishments, modeling, emotional arousal, and verbal persuasion) were related, as predicted, to levels of math self-efficacy. In a similar vein, Lent et al. (1991) reported that past performance accomplishments were the strongest predictors of self-efficacy but failed to provide incremental predictive utility for vicarious learning, social persuasion, or emotional arousal.

An additional construct in the nomological network of math self-efficacy expectations is math–science interests, with several studies showing an important relationship between the two (Lapan et al., 1989; Lent et al., 1991, 1993). Lapan et al.'s findings that math self-efficacy was related to the SII Realistic and Investigative General Occupational Theme (GOT) scores led them to suggest, in fact, that measures of self-efficacy expectations should accompany the interpretation of interest measures, especially for women. On the other hand, Lent et al. (1991) have suggested, on the basis of their findings, that it is the facilitative effect of math self-efficacy on math interests that actually leads to science-related career aspirations. Lapan et al. (1989) suggested, however, that independent roles for preparation and efficacy and gender itself explained scientific and technical interests.

Other researchers have investigated self-efficacy with respect to specific occupational skills (e.g., Ayres, 1980; Zilber, 1988). Rooney and Osipow (1992; Osipow, Temple, & Rooney, 1993) reported the development of the Task-Specific Occupational Self-Efficacy Scale, which contains occupationally relevant skills taken from the 66 occupational groups described in the *Dictionary of Occupational Titles* (U.S. Department of Labor, 1991). The short form (Osipow et al., 1993) contains four interpretable factors: language and interpersonal skills; quantitative, logical, scientific, and business skills; physical strength and agility; and aesthetic skills. Although the authors reported stronger self-efficacy–indecision relationships for men than for women, no gender differences in factor scores were reported.

A still relatively unexplored area of self-efficacy research concerns its applicability to the career adjustment. Theoretically, the postulate that expectations of efficacy influence not only choice but also performance and especially persistence has much relevance to the understanding of retention of women in traditionally male-dominated fields. Survival, when one is a token, when one lacks social support from others like oneself in the work environment, may demand a strong sense of self-efficacy with respect to the demands of the job.

Schoen and Winocur (1988) extended research on self-efficacy to gender differences in achievement in academia. They postulated that women's low self-efficacy with respect to research and administrative tasks was a partial explanation for their overrepresentation in the lower ranks of academia. Completing the Academic Self-Efficacy Scale (Schoen & Winocur, 1988), a measure of self-efficacy with respect to research, teaching, administration, and miscellaneous academic tasks (e.g., journal editing, organizing conferences), women reported higher teaching self-efficacy than research self-efficacy, whereas men reported more equivalent levels of teaching and research self-efficacy. In comparison to men, female participants reported higher teaching self-efficacy and significantly more involvement in teaching and lower research self-efficacy. Differences as a function of rank were also observed, with higher ranks associated with greater self-efficacy.

Landino and Owen (1988) also studied self-efficacy in university faculty members. Men reported significantly higher research and service self-efficacy but equivalent teaching self-efficacy compared to women. Major factors related to research self-efficacy in women included feeling less mentored and feeling undernourished and unrewarded by their departments. Although these studies represent first steps, further investigation into academic and particularly research and writing self-efficacy may broaden the understanding of women's continued underrepresentation in the higher levels of academic careers.

In sum, there is both theoretical and empirical support for the role of perceived self-efficacy as a mediator of gender differences in career-related behaviors. Self-efficacy can influence the degree to which individuals utilize their abilities, develop a range of interests, and consider an expanded rather than restricted range of career options. Self-efficacy may also be related to women's persistence in male-dominated careers. And because of the theoretical linkage of perceived self-efficacy to background experiences, it provides an excellent vehicle both for understanding one of the mechanisms by which gender role socialization influences subsequent career behavior and for designing programs of intervention that have as their objectives ability utilization, interest development, and the widening or restoration of options.

In a review of self-efficacy theory, Hackett and Lent (1992) offered several conclusions based on the research to date: First, self-efficacy beliefs are generally predictive of career entry involving factors such as indecision, choice, and academic persistence; second, self-efficacy relates to work adjustment (e.g., performance); third, directional relationships between self-efficacy and performance are indicated in results of intervention, analogue, and causal modeling studies; fourth, the construct validity of self-efficacy has generally been supported; and finally, gender differences in occupational consideration are frequently explainable by similar differences in self-efficacy.

Hackett and Lent (1992), however, also suggested that the theory has received "vigorous yet uneven empirical attention" (p. 436), with studies focusing primarily on career choice or entry and issues of gender differences. Topics such as occupational adjustment and vocational intervention need far more empirical attention, and research should focus more on how self-efficacy beliefs are developed and modified, as well as how they interact with other critical individual and environmental variables to influence the process of career development. In a related vein, it has been suggested (Lent et al., 1993) that the assumed potency of self-efficacy in predicting behavior is perhaps moderated by outcome expectations; that is, where quality of performance guarantees particular outcomes, self-efficacy is predictive, but where outcomes are only marginally related to performance quality, outcome expectations may make an important independent contribution to behavior. This distinction is especially salient in the vocational behavior of women, for whom self-efficacy may not translate into behavior if the behavior is not expected to be rewarded or if the opportunities to implement behavior are seen as limited. For example, a woman with high self-efficacy expectations regarding math and science careers may reject them because she expects negative outcomes such as lack of support or home–career conflict (Lent et al., 1993). Such considerations have given rise to an attempt by researchers to construct a more integrative framework, which we review in the following section.

Social Cognitive Theory

The emerging social cognitive theory (Lent et al., 1993; Lent & Hackett, 1994) attempts to explain *how* career and academic interests develop, *how* career-relevant choices are made and enacted, and *how* performance outcomes are achieved in terms of the construct of personal agency (see Betz & Hackett, 1987). Built on Bandura's social cognitive theory (1986) and emphasizing triadic reciprocal causality, the theory focuses on self-efficacy, expected outcome, and goal mechanisms, and how they may interrelate with other person or individual factors (such as gender), contextual variables (such as support systems), and experiential and learning factors. Twelve propositions, each with several specific hypotheses (see Lent et al., 1993), are offered to organize existing empirical work and operationalize and guide future research: (1) Occupational interests are reflective of concurrent self-efficacy beliefs and outcome expectations. (2) Occupational interests are also determined by abilities but are mediated by self-efficacy beliefs. (3) Self-efficacy beliefs affect choice goals and actions, directly and indirectly, whereas (4) outcome expectations affect choice goals both directly and indirectly through their influence on occupational interests. (5) People will aspire to enter (i.e., develop choice goals for) occupations consistent with their interests. (6) People will try to enter occupations consonant with their choice goals, provided the goal is clear and close to the point of entry, and they are committed to the goal. (7) Interests affect entry behaviors indirectly through their influence on choice goals. (8) Self-efficacy beliefs influence career performance both directly and indirectly through their effects on performance goals, whereas outcome expectations influence performance only indirectly in their effects on goals. (9) Ability affects career performance both directly and indirectly through its influence on self-efficacy beliefs. (10) Self-efficacy beliefs derive from performance accomplishments, vicarious learning, social persuasion, and physiological reactions in relation to particular occupationally relevant activities. (11) Outcome expectations are generated through direct and vicarious experiences with occupationally relevant activities. (12) Outcome expectations are partly determined by self-efficacy beliefs, especially when outcomes are closely tied to quality of performance. Additional hypotheses for each postulate specifically address contextual determinants (such as gender, race, and class) that affect career behavior and moderate the basic social cognitive model (Lent et al., 1993).

Key points of convergence and divergence relative to existing theories, particularly Krumboltz's (1976, 1990) social learning theory, have been articulated (Hackett & Lent, 1992; Lent et al., 1993). For example, Krumboltz built on Holland's theory by suggesting that the relation between interest and entry behavior is mediated by choice goals and that the relation of goals to actions is moderated by particular social, cultural, and material features of the environment; interests and goals may therefore be less likely to translate into career entry actions in the absence of environmental support. In terms of work adjustment theory, Lent et al. (1993) postulated that the nature and persistence of one's efforts to cope with discorrespondence may depend on one's sense of coping efficacy and outcome expectations, a pattern suggesting that the dispositional factors postulated by Dawis and Lofquist (1984) actually interact with situation- and domain-specific sociocognitive mechanisms. Lent et al. (1993) also claimed that Super's theory lacks precision in its explanation of learning mechanisms and that social cognitive theory "emphasizes specific learning processes and mechanisms that could serve as an adjunct to Super's more macroscopic, trait-oriented view of learning and development" (Lent et al., 1993, p. 59).

In contrasting their social cognitive theory to social learning theory, Lent et al. (1993) offered considerable detail. Some of the more salient differences they noted include the greater emphasis on cognitive processes (particularly self-efficacy) in their model, the specific cognitive constructs included, and their emphasis on the interactive role of cognition in regulating motivation and action rather than on the rationalistic, mechanistic patterns of social learning theory. In the latter, a primary causal role is given to past behavior and learning, whereas social cognitive theory explains the means (e.g., self-efficacy) by which prior experience affects future behavior as well as how the person actively constructs meaning in interaction with environmental events.

Although the social cognitive theory as articulated here is too new for research on its specifics to have appeared, it has the advantage of being formulated from an already rich empirical base. Indeed, Lent et al. (1993) have even presented a meta-analysis of existing research to support their propositions. The detailed hypotheses and operationalization of their model should make it especially amenable to testing and empirical examination.

In terms of applicability to women, the most notable feature of the theory is the deliberate incorporation of the contextual factors which have been highlighted as critical in understanding the career development of women, people of color, working-class people, and others whose vocational behavior does not seem to fit into existing frameworks (Bingham & Ward, 1994; Carter & Cook, 1992; Fitzgerald & Betz, 1994; Hackett & Lent, 1992). Also, because the theory contains very detailed hypotheses, constructs and ideas utilized in other conceptual work can easily be integrated into theoretical postulates and tested. For example, Bingham and Ward (1994) outlined five areas that they believe affect the career development of women of color: information about the work world, familial factors, community influences (including role models and language), impact of socialization, and impact of sexism and racism. Several of the hypotheses derived from Postulates 11 and 12 (concerning the role of outcome expectations in career choice) can be tested with familial factors expressly taken into account, so that the exact nature of the impact of this variable on the career behavior of minority women can be determined. In short, only future research will determine whether this emergent social cognitive theory can fulfill its heuristic promise by making important contributions to the career psychology of women.

BEYOND GENDER? CURRENT STATUS
AND FUTURE DIRECTIONS

In concluding our review of the history and current status of women's career development as a field of study, we come full circle to the themes we noted at the beginning. First, to understand women has required us to examine variables and incorporate concepts previously thought irrelevant to vocational issues (e.g., the role of family, gender role attitudes, and the like) and, second, that studying women has led us, paradoxically, to a better understanding of men as well. We submit that, in addition to characterizing the history of our discipline, these themes also have some important implications for its future.

The study of women's career development began both as the study of a "special" group and as an attempt to integrate knowledge about that group into the more general fabric of vocational psychology. As we have made progress on these goals, it has become increasingly apparent that what we are studying is not only women per se but also *gender* and its differential influences on the career development of both sexes. As the study of women and gender has become more integrated into the study of vocational psychology more generally, it has also become apparent that women are not a homogeneous group and that research needs to begin to take this into account. Thus, from a focus on the ways in which women are different from and similar to men, the question arises, How are we different from—and similar to—one another? And what implications does this have for our relationship to work and family?

Once framed in this fashion, the question becomes a heuristic for a host of other, more specific ones, some of which we have already begun to entertain. Most obviously, how is the career development of women of color similar to that of White women? Or, to frame the question in a more sophisticated manner, What are the effects of race and ethnicity on the career development of women? Similarly, we might ask, What are the effects of sexual orientation? Do family responsibilities have the same effects on career progression when one's partner is a woman, as opposed to a husband? This latter question may well assist us to untangle the effects of heterosexual marriage from those of motherhood, an issue that has been, for the most part, untouched. In learning more about women of color, lesbians, poor women, we will learn more about *all* women, and, if history is any guide, about everyone else (i.e., men) as well.

We suggest that these issues, which we have only begun to explore, are the cutting edge of intellectual progress in our field. And we submit that as we go more deeply into our separateness, our individuality, into that which makes us different, we will learn more about our commonalities as well. We submit that this may well be the lasting legacy of the career psychology of women.

REFERENCES

Almquist, E. M. (1974). Sex stereotypes in occupational choice: The case for college women. *Journal of Vocational Behavior, 5,* 13–21.

Almquist, E. M., & Angrist, S. S. (1970). Career salience and atypicality of occupational choice among college women. *Journal of Marriage and Family, 32,* 242–249.

Almquist, E. M., & Angrist, S. S. (1971). Role model influences on college women's career aspirations. *Merrill–Palmer Quarterly, 17,* 263–279.

Angrist, S. S. (1972). Variations in women's adult aspirations during college. *Journal of Marriage and Family, 34,* 465–468.

Arnold, K. D. (1987). *Values and vocations: The career aspirations of academically gifted females in the first five years after high school.* Paper presented at the annual meeting of the American Educational Research Association, Washington, DC.

Arnold, K. D. (1989). *The Illinois valedictorian project: The careers of academically talented men.* Paper presented at the annual meeting of the American Educational Research Association, San Francisco, CA.

Arnold, K. D., & Denny, T. (1984). *Academic achievement—A view from the top: The lives of high school valedictorians and salutatorians.* Paper presented at the annual meeting of the American Educational Research Association, New Orleans, LA.

Arnold, K. D., & Denny, T. (1985). *The lives of academic achievers: The career aspirations of male and female high school valedictorians and salutatorians* (Rep. No. CE 041 582). (ERIC Document Reproduction Service No. ED 257 951).

Astin, H. S. (1984). The meaning of work in women's lives: A sociopsychological model of career choice and work behavior. *The Counseling Psychologist, 12,* 117–126.

Astin, H. S., & Myint, T. (1971). Career development of young women during the posthigh-school years. *Journal of Counseling Psychology Monograph, 18,* 369–393.

Ayres, A. L. (1980). *Self-efficacy theory: Implications for the career development of women.* Unpublished doctoral dissertation, Ohio State University, Department of Psychology, Columbus.

Bandura, A. (1977). Self-efficacy: Toward a unifying theory of behavioral change. *Psychology Review, 84,* 191–215.

Bandura, A. (1986). *Social foundations of thought and action: A social cognitive theory.* Englewood Cliffs, NJ: Prentice–Hall.

Beere, C. A. (1990). *Gender roles: A handbook of tests and measures.* New York: Greenwood.

Betz, E. L. (1984). A study of career patterns of college graduates. *Journal of Vocational Behavior, 24,* 249–264.

Betz, N. E. (1991). *What stops women and minorities from choosing and completing majors in science and engineering.* Washington, DC: Federation of Behavioral, Psychological, and Cognitive Sciences.

Betz, N. E., & Fitzgerald, L. F. (1987). *The career psychology of women.* New York: Academic Press.

Betz, N. E., & Hackett, G. (1981). The relationship of career-related self-efficacy expectations to perceived career options in college women and men. *Journal of Counseling Psychology, 28,* 399–410.

Betz, N. E., & Hackett, G. (1983). The relationship of mathematics self-efficacy expectations to the selection of science-based college majors. *Journal of Vocational Behavior, 23,* 329–345.

Betz, N. E., & Hackett, G. (1986). Applications of self-efficacy theory to understanding career choice behavior. *Journal of Social and Clinical Psychology, 4,* 279–289.

Betz, N. E., & Hackett, G. (1987). The concept of agency in educational and career development. *Journal of Counseling Psychology, 34,* 311–320.

Betz, N. E., Heesacker, R. S., & Shuttleworth, C. (1990). Moderators of the congruence and realism of major and occupational plans in college students. *Journal of Counseling Psychology, 37.*

Bingham, R. P., & Ward, C. M. (1994). Career counseling with ethnic minority women. In W. B. Walsh & S. H. Osipow (Eds.), *Career counseling for women* (pp. 165–196). Hillsdale, NJ: Lawrence Erlbaum Associates.

Borgen, F. H. (1991). Megatrends and milestones in vocational behavior: A 20-year counseling psychology retrospective. *Journal of Vocational Behavior, 39,* 263–290.

Brown, D. (1990). Summary, comparison, and critique of the major theories. In D. Brown & L. Brooks (Eds.), *Career choice and development* (2nd ed., pp. 338–363). San Francisco: Jossey–Bass.

Carter, R. A., & Cook, D. A. (1992). A culturally relevant perspective for understanding the career paths of visible racial/ethnic group people. In Z. Leibowitz & D. Lea (Eds.), *Adult career development* (2nd ed., pp. 94–110). Alexandria, VA: National Career Development Association.

Cole, N. S., & Hanson, G. R. (1975). Impact of interest inventories on career choice. In E. E. Diamond (Ed.), *Issues of sex bias and sex fairness in career interest measurement.* Washington, DC: National Institute of Education.

Crites, J. O. (1969). *Vocational psychology.* New York: McGraw–Hill.

Dawis, R. V., & Lofquist, L. H. (1984). *A psychological theory of work adjustment.* Minneapolis, MN: University of Minnesota Press.

Eccles, J. (1987). Gender roles and women's achievement-related decisions. *Psychology of Women Quarterly, 11*, 135–172.

Eyde, L. D. (1962). *Work values and background factors as predictors of women's desire to work* (Research Monograph No. 108). Columbus: Ohio State University, Bureau of Business Research.

Farmer, H. S. (1976). What inhibits achievement and career motivation in women? *The Counseling Psychologist, 6*, 12–14.

Farmer, H. S. (1984). Development of a measure of home–career conflict related to career motivation in college women. *Sex Roles, 10*, 663–675.

Farmer, H. S. (1985). Model of career and achievement motivation for women and men. *Journal of Counseling Psychology, 32*, 363–390.

Farmer, H. S., Wardrop, J. S., Anderson, M. Z., & Risinger, F. (1993, August). *Understanding women's career choices: Focus on careers.* Paper presented at the annual meeting of the American Psychological Association, Toronto, Canada.

Fassinger, R. E. (1985). A causal model of career choice in college women. *Journal of Vocational Behavior, 27*, 123–153.

Fassinger, R. E. (1990). Causal models of career choice in two samples of college women. *Journal of Vocational Behavior, 36*, 225–240.

Fitzgerald, L. F. (1993). *The last great open secret: The sexual harassment of women in academia and the workplace.* Washington, DC: Federation of Behavioral, Psychological, and Cognitive Sciences.

Fitzgerald, L. F., & Betz, N. E. (1983). Issues in the vocational psychology of women. In W. B. Walsh & S. H. Osipow (Eds.), *Handbook of vocational psychology.* Hillsdale, NJ: Lawrence Erlbaum Associates.

Fitzgerald, L. F., & Betz, N. E. (1994). Career development in cultural context: The role of gender, race, class, and sexual orientation. In M. L. Savickas & R. W. Lent (Eds.), *Convergence in theories of career choice and development.* Palo Alto, CA: Consulting Psychologists Press.

Fitzgerald, L. F., & Crites, J. O. (1980). Towards a career psychology of women: What do we know? What do we need to know? *Journal of Counseling Psychology, 27*, 44–62.

Fitzgerald, L. F., Fassinger, R. E., & Betz, N. E. (1989, August). *An individual differences model of vocational choice in college women.* Paper presented at the annual meeting of the American Psychological Association, New Orleans, LA.

Fitzgerald, L. F., & Rounds, J. B. (1994). Women and work: Theory encounters reality. In W. B. Walsh & S. H. Osipow (Eds.), *Career counseling for women.* Hillsdale, NJ: Lawrence Erlbaum Associates.

Fitzgerald, L. F., & Weitzman, L. M. (1992). Women's career development: Theory and practice from a feminist perspective. In Z. Leibowitz & D. Lea (Eds.), *Adult career development* (2nd ed., pp. 124–160). Alexandria, VA: National Career Development Association.

Fox, L. H., Brody, L., & Tobin, D. (1985). Women and mathematics: The impact of early intervention programs upon course-taking and attitudes in high schools. In S. F. Chipman, L. R. Brush, & D. M. Wilson (Eds.), *Women and mathematics.* Hillsdale, NJ: Lawrence Erlbaum Associates.

Gelso, C. J., & Fassinger, R. E. (1992). Personality, development, and counseling psychology. *Journal of Counseling Psychology, 39*, 275–298.

Gerson, K. (1986). *Hard choices: How women decide about work, career, and motherhood.* Berkeley: University of California Press.

Goldsen, R. K., Rosenberg, M., Williams, R. M., & Suchman, E. A. (1960). *What college students think.* Princeton, NJ: Van Nostrand.

Gomez, M. J., & Fassinger, R. E. (1994). An initial model of Latina achievement: Acculturation, biculturalism, and achieving styles. *Journal of Counseling Psychology, 41*, 205–215.

Gottfredson, L. S. (1981). Circumscription and compromise: A developmental theory of occupational aspirations. *Journal of Counseling Psychology, 28*, 545–579.

Gottfredson, L. S. (1986). Special groups and the beneficial use of vocational interest inventories. In W. B. Walsh & S. H. Osipow (Eds.), *Advances in vocational psychology: The assessment of interests.* Hillsdale, NJ: Lawrence Erlbaum Associates.

Greenhaus, J. H. (1971). An investigation of the role of career salience in vocational behavior. *Journal of Vocational Behavior, 1*, 209–216.

Gysbers, N. C., Johnston, J. A., & Gust, T. (1968). Characteristics of homemaker and career-oriented women. *Journal of Counseling Psychology, 15*, 541–546.

Hackett, G. (1985). The role of mathematics self-efficacy in the choice of math-related majors of college women and men: A path model. *Journal of Counseling Psychology, 32*, 47–56.

Hackett, G., & Betz, N. E. (1981). A self-efficacy approach to the career development of women. *Journal of Vocational Behavior, 18*, 326–339.

Hackett, G., Betz, N., Casas, J. M., & Rocha-Singh, I. A. (1992). Gender, ethnicity, and social cognitive factors predicting the academic achievement of students in engineering. *Journal of Counseling Psychology, 39*, 527–538.

Hackett, G., & Lent, R. W. (1992). Theoretical advances and current inquiry in career psychology. In S. D. Brown & R. W. Lent (Eds.), *Handbook of counseling psychology* (2nd ed., pp. 419–452). New York: Wiley.

Hackett, G., Lent, R. W., & Greenhaus, J. H. (1991). Advances in vocational theory and research: A 20-year retrospective. *Journal of Vocational Behavior, 38*, 3–38.

Hannah, J. S., & Kahn, S. E. (1989). The relationship of socioeconomic status and gender to the occupational choices of Grade 12 students. *Journal of Vocational Behavior, 34*, 161–178.

Harmon, L. W. (1967). Women's working patterns related to their SVIB housewife and "own" occupational scores. *Journal of Counseling Psychology, 14*, 299–301.

Harmon, L. W. (1970). Anatomy of career commitment in women. *Journal of Counseling Psychology, 17*, 77–80.

Harmon, L. W. (1977). Career counseling for women. In E. Rawlings & D. Carter (Eds.), *Psychotherapy for women* (pp. 197–206). Springfield, IL: Thomas.

Helms, J. E. (Ed.). (1990). *Black and White racial identity: Theory, research, and practice.* New York: Greenwood.

Henderson, S., Hesketh, B., & Tuffin, K. (1988). A test of Gottfredson's theory of circumscription. *Journal of Vocational Behavior, 32*, 37–48.

Hesketh, B., Elmslie, S., & Kaldor, W. (1990a). Career compromise: An alternative account to Gottfredson's 1981 theory. *Journal of Counseling Psychology, 37*, 49–56.

Hesketh, B., Elmslie, S., & Kaldor, W. (1990b). Career compromise: A test of Gottfredson's theory using a policy-capturing procedure. *Journal of Vocational Behavior, 36*, 97–108.

Hesketh, B., Pryor, R., & Gleitzman, M. (1989). Fuzzy logic: Toward measuring Gottfredson's concept of occupational social space. *Journal of Counseling Psychology, 36*, 103–109.

Holland, J. L. (1973). *Making vocational choices: A theory of careers.* Englewood Cliffs, NJ: Prentice–Hall.

Holland, J. L. (1985). *Making vocational choices: A theory of vocational personalities and work environments* (2nd ed.). Englewood Cliffs, NJ: Prentice–Hall.

Holland, J. L., & Gottfredson, G. D. (1992). Studies of the hexagonal model: An evaluation (or, the perils of stacking the perfect hexagonal model). *Journal of Vocational Behavior, 40,* 158–170.

Hollinger, C. L. (1983). Self-perception and the career aspirations of mathematically talented female adolescents. *Journal of Vocational Behavior, 22,* 49–62.

Holt, P. A. (1989). Differential effect of status and interest in the process of compromise. *Journal of Counseling Psychology, 36,* 42–47.

Hoyt, D. P., & Kennedy, C. E. (1958). Interest and personality correlates of career-motivated and homemaking-motivated college women. *Journal of Counseling Psychology, 5,* 44–49.

Humphreys, S. M. (1982). *Women and minorities in science: Strategies for increasing participation.* Boulder, CO: Westview Press.

Kriger, S. F. (1972). Achievement and perceived parental childrearing attitudes of career women and homemakers. *Journal of Vocational Behavior, 2,* 419–432.

Krumboltz, J. D., Mitchell, A. M., & Jones, G. B. (1976). A social learning theory of career selection. *The Counseling Psychologist, 6,* 71–80.

Krumboltz, J. D., & Nichols, C. W. (1990). Integrating the social learning theory of decision-making. In W. B. Walsh & S. H. Osipow (Eds.), *Career counseling: Contemporary topics in vocational psychology* (pp. 159–192). Hillsdale, NJ: Lawrence Erlbaum Associates.

Landino, R. A., & Owen, S. V. (1988). Self-efficacy in university faculty. *Journal of Vocational Behavior, 33,* 1–14.

Lapan, R. T., Boggs, K. R., & Morrill, W. H. (1989). Self-efficacy as a mediator of investigative and realistic general occupational themes on the Strong Interest Inventory. *Journal of Counseling Psychology, 36,* 176–182.

Layton, P. L. (1984). *Self-efficacy, locus of control, career salience, and women's career choice.* Unpublished doctoral dissertation, University of Minnesota, Department of Psychology, Minneapolis.

Lent, R. W., Brown, S. D., & Hackett, G. (1993). *Toward a unified social cognitive theory of career and academic interest, choice, and performance.* Manuscript submitted for publication.

Lent, R. W., Brown, S. D., & Larkin, K. C. (1984). Relation of self-efficacy expectations to academic achievement and persistence. *Journal of Counseling Psychology, 31,* 356–362.

Lent, R. W., Brown, S. D., & Larkin, K. C. (1986). Self-efficacy in the prediction of academic success and perceived career options. *Journal of Counseling Psychology, 33,* 265–269.

Lent, R. W., & Hackett, G. (1987). Career self-efficacy: Empirical status and future directions. *Journal of Vocational Behavior, 30,* 347–382.

Lent, R. W., & Hackett, G. (1994). Sociocognitive mechanisms of personal agency in career development: Pantheoretical prospects. In M. L. Savickas & R. W. Lent (Eds.), *Convergence in theories of career choice and development.* Palo Alto, CA: Consulting Psychologists Press.

Lent, R. W., Lopez, F. G., & Bieschke, K. J. (1991). Mathematics self-efficacy: Sources and relation to science-based career choice. *Journal of Counseling Psychology, 38,* 424–430.

Leung, S. A. (1993). Circumscription and compromise: A replication study with Asian Americans. *Journal of Counseling Psychology, 40,* 188–193.

Leung, S. A., & Harmon, L. W. (1990). Individual and sex differences in the zone of acceptable alternatives. *Journal of Counseling Psychology, 37,* 153–159.

Leung, S. A., Ivey, D., & Scheel, M. (1991, August). *A systematic approach to test Gottfredson's (1981) theory.* Paper presented at the annual convention of the American Psychological Association, San Francisco, CA.

Leung, S. A., & Plake, B. S. (1990). A choice dilemma approach for examining the relative importance of sex type and prestige preferences in the process of career choice compromise. *Journal of Counseling Psychology, 37,* 399–406.

Levitt, E. S. (1972). Vocational development of professional women: A review. *Journal of Vocational Behavior, 1,* 375–385.

Lofquist, L. H., & Dawis, R. V. (1984). Research on work adjustment and satisfaction: Implications for career counseling. In S. D. Brown & R. W. Lent (Eds.), *Handbook of counseling psychology* (pp. 216–237). New York: John Wiley & Sons, Inc.

Matsui, T., Ikeda, H., & Ohnishi, R. (1989). Relations of sex-typed socializations to career self-efficacy expectation of college students. *Journal of Vocational Behavior, 35,* 1–16.

Matsui, T., Matsui, K., & Ohnishi, R. (1990). Mechanisms underlying math self-efficacy learning of college students. *Journal of Vocational Behavior, 37,* 225–238.

McWhirter, E. H., & Hackett, G. (1993, August). *Causal models of the career commitment and aspirations of Mexican-American high-school girls.* Paper presented at the annual meeting of the American Psychological Association, Toronto, Canada.

Mitchell, L. K., & Krumboltz, J. D. (1990). Social learning approach to career decision making: Krumboltz's theory. In D. Brown & L. Brooks (Eds.), *Career choice and development* (2nd ed., pp. 145–196). San Francisco: Jossey–Bass.

Mitchell, S. L. (1990). *The relationship between racial identity attitudes, career self-efficacy, and involvement in campus organizations among black students.* Unpublished doctoral dissertation, Ohio State University, Department of Psychology, Columbus.

Munley, P. H. (1974). Interests of career- and homemaking-oriented women. *Journal of Vocational Behavior, 4,* 43–48.

Nagely, D. (1971). Traditional and pioneer working mothers. *Journal of Vocational Behavior, 1,* 331–341.

National Science Foundation. (1984). *Women and minorities in science and engineering.* Washington, DC: Author.

Neville, D., & Super, D. E. (1986). *The Salience Inventory.* Palo Alto, CA: Consulting Psychologists Press.

Nieva, V. F., & Gutek, B. A. (1981). *Women and work: A psychological perspective.* New York: Praeger.

O'Brien, K. M., & Fassinger, R. E. (1993). A causal model of the career orientation and career choice of adolescent women. *Journal of Counseling Psychology, 40,* 1–14.

Oliver, L. W. (1974). Achievement and affiliation motivation in career-oriented and homemaking-oriented college women. *Journal of Vocational Behavior, 4,* 275–281.

Osipow, S. H. (1973). *Theories of career development* (2nd ed.). Englewood Cliffs, NJ: Prentice–Hall.

Osipow, S. H. (Ed.). (1975). *Emerging women: Career analysis and outlooks.* Columbus, OH: Merrill.

Osipow, S. H. (1990). Convergence in theories of career choice and development: Review and prospect. *Journal of Vocational Behavior, 36,* 122–131.

Osipow, S. H., Temple, R. D., & Rooney, R. A. (1993). The short form of the Task-Specific Self-Efficacy Scale. *Journal of Career Assessment, 1,* 13–20.

Pfafflin, S. M. (1984). Women, science and technology. *American Psychologist, 39,* 1183–1186.

Poole, M. E., Langan–Fox, J., Ciavarella, M., & Onedei, M. (1991). A contextual model of professional attainment: Results of a longitudinal study of career paths of men and women. *Counseling Psychologist, 19,* 603–624.

Post–Kammer, P., & Smith, P. L. (1985). Sex differences in career self-efficacy, consideration, and interests of eighth and ninth graders. *Journal of Counseling Psychology, 32.*

Post–Kammer, P., & Smith, P. L. (1986). Sex differences in math and science career self-efficacy among disadvantaged students. *Journal of Vocational Behavior, 29,* 89–101.

Pryor, R. B., Hesketh, B., & Gleitzman, M. (1989). Making things clearer by making them fuzzy: Counseling illustrations of a fuzzy graphic rating scale. *Career Development Quarterly, 38,* 136–147.

Psathas, G. (1968). Toward a theory of occupational choice for women. *Sociology and Social Research, 52*(2), 253–268.

Rand, L. (1968). Masculinity or femininity: Differentiating career-oriented and homemaking-oriented college freshman women. *Journal of Counseling Psychology, 15,* 444–449.

Rand, L. M., & Miller, A. L. (1972). A developmental cross-sectioning of women's career and marriage attitudes and life plans. *Journal of Vocational Behavior, 2,* 317–331.

Reitman, M. A. (1992). *Gender differences in the development of mathematics self-efficacy expectations in adolescence.* Unpublished Bachelors degree (honors) thesis, College of Liberal Arts and Sciences, University of Illinois.

Richardson, M. S. (1974). The dimensions of career and work orientation in college women. *Journal of Vocational Behavior, 5,* 161–172.

Rooney, R. A., & Osipow, S. H. (1992). Task-specific occupational self-efficacy scale: The development and validation of a prototype. *Journal of Vocational Behavior, 40,* 14–32.

Rossi, A. S. (1965). Women in science: Why so few? *Science, 148,* 1196–1202.

Russo, N. F., & Denmark, F. L. (1984). Women, psychology and public policy: Selected issues. *American Psychologist, 39,* 1161–1165.

Sandler, B. R., & Hall, R. M. (1986). *The campus climate revisited: Chilly, for women faculty, administrators, and graduate students.* Washington, DC: Association of American Colleges, Project on the Status and Education of Women.

Scarr, S., Phillips, D., & McCartney, K. (1989). Working mothers and their families. *American Psychologist, 44,* 1402–1409.

Schoen, L. G., & Winocur, S. (1988). An investigation of the self-efficacy of male and female academics. *Journal of Vocational Behavior, 32,* 307–320.

Simpson, R. L., & Simpson, I. H. (1961). Occupational choice among career-oriented college women. *Marriage and Family Living, 23,* 377–383.

Sobol, M. G. (1963). Commitment to work. In F. I. Nye & L. W. Hoffman (Eds.), *The employed mother in America.* Chicago: Rand McNally.

Standley, K., & Soule, B. (1974). Women in male-dominated professions: Contrasts in their personal and vocational histories. *Journal of Vocational Behavior, 4,* 245–258.

Strong, E. K., Jr. (1933). *Strong Vocational Interest Blank for Women.* Stanford, CA: Stanford University Press.

Super, D. E. (1949). *Appraising vocational fitness.* New York: Harper.

Super, D. E. (1957). *The psychology of careers.* New York: Harper.

Super, D. E. (1980). A life-span, life-space approach to career development. *Journal of Vocational Behavior, 16,* 282–298.

Super, D. E. (1990). A life-span, life-space approach to career development. In D. Brown & L. Brooks (Eds.), *Career choice and development* (2nd ed., pp. 197–261). San Francisco: Jossey–Bass.

Super, D. E., & Bachrach, P. B. (1957). *Scientific careers and vocational development theory.* New York: Teachers College Press.

Super, D. E., & Crites, J. O. (1963). *Appraising vocational fitness* (2nd ed.). New York: Harper.

Tangri, S. S. (1972). Determinants of occupational role innovation among college women. *Journal of Social Issues, 28,* 177–199.

Taylor, N. B., & Pryor, R. G. L. (1985). Exploring the process of compromise in career decision making. *Journal of Vocational Behavior, 27,* 171–190.

Taylor, N. B., & Pryor, R. G. L. (1986). The conceptualization and measurement of vocational and work aspect preferences. *British Journal of Guidance and Counselling, 14,* 66–77.

Tyler, L. E. (1964). The antecedents of two varieties of vocational interests. *Genetic Psychology Monographs, 70,* 177–227.

Tyler, L. E. (1978). *Individuality.* San Francisco: Jossey–Bass.

U.S. Department of Labor. (1991). *Dictionary of occupational titles* (5th ed.). Washington, DC: U.S. Government Printing Office.

Vetter, L. (1973). Career counseling for women. *The Counseling Psychologist, 4,* 54–67.

Vetter, L., & Lewis, E. C. (1964). Some correlates of homemaking versus career preference among college home economics students. *Personnel and Guidance Journal, 42,* 593–598.

Wagman, M. (1966). Interests and values of career- and homemaking-oriented women. *Personnel and Guidance Journal, 44,* 794–801.

Walsh, W. B., & Osipow, S. H. (1994). *Career counseling for women.* Hillsdale, NJ: Lawrence Erlbaum Associates.

Watley, D. J., & Kaplan, R. (1971). Career or marriage? Aspirations and achievements of able young college women. *Journal of Vocational Behavior, 1,* 29–44.

Weitzman, L. M., & Fitzgerald, L. F. (1993). Employed mothers: Labor force profiles and diverse lifestyles. In J. Frankel (Ed.), *Employed mothers and the family context.* New York: Springer.

Williams, T. (1993). *The relationship between career self-efficacy and degree of feminist orientation.* Unpublished doctoral dissertation, Ohio State University, Department of Psychology, Columbus.

Wolfe, L. K., & Betz, N. E. (1981). Traditionality of choice and sex role identification as moderators of the congruence of occupational choice in college women. *Journal of Vocational Behavior, 19,* 61–77.

Wolfson, K. P. (1976). Career development patterns of college women. *Journal of Counseling Psychology, 23,* 119–125.

Zilber, S. M. (1988). *The effects of sex, task performance, and attributional styles on task and career self-efficacy expectations.* Unpublished doctoral dissertation, Ohio State University, Department of Psychology, Columbus.

Zytowski, D. (1969). Toward a theory of career development of women. *Personnel and Guidance Journal, 47,* 660–664.

CHAPTER FOUR

Toward a Comprehensive Framework for Adult Career Development Theory and Intervention

Fred W. Vondracek
Pennsylvania State University

Tomotsugu Kawasaki
Japan Institute of Labour

During the past two decades a great deal has been written about the increasing complexity of the workplace, the relative uncertainty of employment, serial careers, retraining, midlife crises, early retirement, and many other concepts that convey the complexity of the work lives of individuals in our society. Interpersonal relationships, the life cycles of families, and the quality of life are all inextricably intertwined with what people do for a living. The globalization of corporations and of regional and national economies has progressed to the point where the interrelatedness of individuals and their multiple contexts is self-evident. What is also apparent, however, is that the conceptualizations of people's work lives that represent contemporary career development theory were developed at a time when the work lives of most people in Western societies were far simpler and far more predictable than they are today. For the most part, these conceptualizations were developed when the proverbial "40 years and a gold watch" represented a normative pattern of career development that is all but gone in today's world.

Contemporary conceptualizations of adult career development must take account of the increased complexity and interdependency of the world of today. They must also reflect the significant advances in theory and research that have been made in recent decades. In addition, in order to have broad applicability, conceptualizations of adult career development must reflect the almost staggering variety of paths that may be chosen and pursued in the course of any individual work life. Consequently, we use the terms *work life* and *career* interchangeably throughout this chapter. We also assume that the definition of what constitutes work is somewhat arbitrary to start with but that almost everyone engages in behaviors that can be construed as work during significant portions of the life span. These work behaviors may be a coherent, planned pattern of behaviors designed to move the individual from a beginning to an advanced level of work in an organization, or they may be a succession of jobs whose only unifying feature is that they are necessary for the individual's survival. The basic assumption is that as individuals develop throughout their adult lives, their work activities, whether highly organized or not, reflect their ontogeny and may, therefore, be properly studied as career development. To accommodate the great variety in adult career development that is suggested by this definition, researchers must necessarily employ much more complex models than have customarily been used in this area.

The discussion of complex conceptual models—in ways that are meaningful to others—is replete with difficulties of various kinds. On a global level, complex models have appeal because, both intellectually and intuitively, most people know that efforts to understand the course of development of individuals in today's world represent a challenge of utmost complexity for scientists. In other words, life is complicated! When scientists present the results of their efforts to develop detailed models that are capable (at least at a rudimentary level) of accounting for the structures and processes of the human life course, however, many otherwise sensible individuals throw up their hands in despair and exclaim that the conceptualization is simply too complicated to be of any practical utility. In this chapter we endeavor to show that the application of a complex model of human development is essential for the understanding of adult career development and that such a model can be applied in a comprehensible and practical way. In this respect, this chapter may be viewed as an extension of efforts initiated a number of years ago by Vondracek and his colleagues in their presentation of a developmental–contextual approach to life-span career development (e.g., Vondracek, Lerner, & Schulenberg, 1986).

We rely extensively on the developmental systems theory (DST) proposed by D. Ford and Lerner (1992) as a synthesis of the developmental–contextual perspective originally proposed by Lerner (1978, 1989) and of D. Ford's (1987) living systems framework (LSF). In addition, we utilize M. Ford's (1992) recent formulations of motivational systems theory (MST), which were derived from the LSF, to demonstrate the centrality of motivational factors in adult career development.

TOWARD A COMPREHENSIVE THEORY OF ADULT CAREER DEVELOPMENT

There have been disagreements in the literature regarding the necessity for, and wisdom of, proposing what is sometimes disdainfully referred to as "grand theory." Super (1990), for example, has repeatedly proposed that segmental theories are more appropriate in accounting for the complex aspects of life-span career development. Others have argued that our knowledge of human development is simply too limited to permit the development of comprehensive theories and that our methodologies for research cannot handle the complexity imposed by grand theorizing. We disagree with these views and maintain (with M. Ford, 1987) that they are in error because ultimately they inhibit in important ways our capacity to capitalize fully on existing knowledge and ideas. Moreover, comprehensive and integrative theoretical frameworks have specific heuristic utility that is not shared by segmental, or minitheories.

The necessity for such comprehensive and integrative theoretical frameworks has been noted repeatedly by writers in the field of career development. Even Super (1981), although maintaining that segmental theories represent a sensible focus for career researchers in view of the complexity of their problem, stated that "some day global theories of career development will be made up of refined, validated, and well-assembled segments, cemented together by some synthesizing theory to constitute a whole that will be more powerful than the sum of its parts" (p. 39). Osipow (1983) suggested that an emerging

> systems view of career behavior . . . explicitly recognizes that various situational and individual factors operate to influence career behavior in a broad way. With a highly sophisticated systems approach to career development, questions about the role of the biological, social, and situational factors in occupational behavior would become more explicit and . . . understandings of the interactions between these views would be more likely to emerge. (p. 314)

More recently, Vondracek et al. (1986) stated their case for the utility of comprehensive and integrated theoretical frameworks for the study of career development by presenting what they called a developmental–contextual approach to life-span career development.

Some Limitations of Current Theories of Adult Career Development

With our presentation here of a recent refinement of this developmental–contextual approach to career development, namely, a developmental and motivational systems framework (D. Ford & Lerner, 1992; M. Ford, 1992) for the study of adult career development, we are not suggesting that important past work on adult career development be ignored. To the contrary, it is our expectation that this framework may serve to integrate current knowledge of adult development in general and of adult career development in particular. Before presenting the DST and MST frameworks, however, we briefly review some of the more important limitations of current theories of adult career development in order to highlight our rationale for the presentation of a new framework that is comprehensive and integrative.

Other reviewers of the adult vocational literature (e.g., Campbell & Heffernan, 1983) have found it convenient to organize their review of adult career development theory and research into four major phases that characterize the career development cycle: a preparation stage, a stage of demonstrating competence and initial adjustment to work, a maintenance–advancement stage, and a stage characterized by "decline in involvement with the work place" (p. 226). Virtually every major theory of career development that purports to deal with the work lives of adults was shown to rely on some version of such a stage model (e.g., Erikson, 1950; Havighurst, 1952; D. Levinson, Darrow, Klein, M. Levinson, & McKee, 1978; Miller & Form, 1951, 1964; Schein, 1978; Super, 1963; Super & Hall, 1978).

These stage models of adult development regard adult life as a succession of stages, that is, as distinct periods, the intellectual origin of which we can trace as far back as Shakespeare's famous discussion of the seven ages of man (Bromley, 1990). Quite clearly, stage approaches represent normative descriptions of adult life as a progression through successive stages, each associated with particular behaviors and, in most cases, with developmental tasks. The defining feature of stage models of adult development and, by implication, of models of adult career development, is the tendency that they "proceed at a very high level of abstraction and generality, and may neglect the wide range of differences between individuals, the deviant, and the exceptional cases" (Bromley, 1990, p. 31). In other words, Erikson's (1963) stages of ego development or Super's (1957) stages of career development may tell us something about the most likely pattern of development of White middle-class males in the middle of the 20th century who live in industrialized Western countries, but they offer little explanation of the enormous variability and unpredictability in patterns of career development. In fact, the normative patterns proposed as stages may be more a reflection of certain kinds of social and economic patterns that have traditionally channeled career pathways than a reflection of a developmental pattern of individuals (e.g., see Dannefer, 1992).

A number of researchers, both in the field of adult development and in the field of career development, have raised additional questions about the adequacy of stage models in accounting for the complex lives of individuals. For example, in the area of adult development, Thomae and Lehr (1986) documented the great variety of pathways that is possible in the lives of adults, by analyzing the biographies of men and women in terms of important life events. They concluded that it was not adequate to simply examine the nature of the life events experienced by people but that it was essential to place those events within the ecology of individual lives in order to appreciate their specific meaning and significance for each individual. Broad generalizations about phases, stages, or periods in the lives of individuals should therefore be regarded with considerable caution. This premise is central to developmental systems theory and is a major rationale for the adoption of a process-oriented framework such as that offered by DST and MST.

In the field of career development, increasing attention is being given to methodological approaches that depart from the positivistic scientific tradition that has dominated social and behavioral science research, in general, and most of the normative career development research, in particular. These departures include narrative and biography as methods for understanding the career development of individuals (e.g., Bujold, 1990; Cochran, 1990). With these methods, researchers focus on discovering the *meaning* that individuals find in their lives. Proponents of these methods have criticized stage models of career development because stage models require us to reconceive humans as organisms with attributes and result in the loss of the meaning of "careers as lived" (Cochran, 1990, p. 78). They have noted that stage models of career development reduce people to objects, and all one can do about objects is chronicle what happens to them; stage models cannot tell the real story of the work lives of individuals (Cochran, 1990).

There have been some notable longitudinal studies in which researchers followed the lives of individuals for many years in an effort (in part at least) to find patterns and regularities in those individuals' lives. Such studies included Super's career pattern study (Super, 1985; Super & Overstreet, 1960), the Grant study (Vaillant, 1977), and the often cited study by D. Levinson et al. (1978). All made important contributions to our understanding of adult development, but they also have serious limitations. The number of participants in the career pattern study had shrunk to only 142 by the time the participants had reached ninth grade (cf. Osipow, 1983, p. 160); therefore, the generalizability of the findings was seriously limited. Although D. Levinson (1986) concluded that his sequence of eras and periods could be used to describe the lives of both men and women living in different cultures and even in different historical epochs, he also acknowledged "wide variations in the kinds of life structures people build, the developmental work they do in transitional periods, and the concrete sequence of social roles, events, and personality change" (p. 8). He concluded that his theory consequently represented merely a general framework of human development that could be used in the study of differences. Likewise, Vaillant (1977) concluded after the Grant study that the prediction of the course of adult lives was not possible and that "the life cycle is more than an invariant sequence of stages with single predictable outcomes" (p. 373).

An Illustrative Example

In an effort to move beyond abstract conceptualizations, and at the same time, to remain focused on our specific topic, we provide the following illustration as an anchor for subsequent information presented in this chapter.

It is an account of the real-life career development, from adolescence to age 50, of a semifictional character named Will. This account illustrates the complexity of career development and shows how key concepts from DST and MST can be useful not only in the explanation of the processes that are central in adult career development but also in the development of interventions to facilitate career progress.

Will was born in Germany during World War II. He attended a rural school with several grades per classroom and with a single teacher who taught all subjects. When he reached the fourth grade at age 10, his parents decided that he should continue his education in the Volksschule, where he would reach the terminal (eighth) grade at age 14. Then he would go to work with his father as a tile setter's apprentice. After successfully completing his apprenticeship (3 years), Will would pass the examination to be a journeyman tile setter, earn a good living, and have a secure future. Will's parents chose this course based on their own experiences, which included many hardships and a great deal of economic insecurity.

Being a good son, Will became a journeyman tile setter. Even before completing his apprenticeship, however, he attended a special night school that was specifically designed to assist individuals who had pursued a manual, skilled labor occupational role to extend their education beyond eight grades and to qualify them for admission to a college dedicated exclusively to the training of engineers. Although Will did not feel that he wanted to be an engineer, he entered the night school because it represented the only feasible means for him to further his education and to increase his future occupational options. After completing the night school curriculum (four nights a week for three years), Will seemed to be blocked from further educational advancement unless he attended the engineering college.

After exploring various options for overcoming this apparent barrier, Will came to the United States (against his parent's wishes) to continue his education. Being unable to speak more than a few phrases of English, having no money, and lacking an immigration visa, he attempted to join the military service as a means of legalizing his continued stay in the United States and of ensuring the eventual pursuit of his education. Unfortunately, his lack of English proficiency caused him to fail repeatedly the military service entrance examination. In the meantime, he supported himself by working at odd jobs and in some construction-related jobs that permitted him to use his previously learned skills as a tile setter. He gradually acquired a working knowledge of English and, within a few months, discovered a way to obtain an immigrant visa and to enter college.

Due to his still limited knowledge of English, he at first concentrated on science and mathematics but reconfirmed his original view that these did not represent meaningful future career options for him. Within a year of entering college, he decided to major in history. As graduation neared, however, he reviewed job opportunities for historians, discovered that they were few and far between, and quickly decided to change his major to psychology. He applied to graduate schools (it never occurred to him to stop his education until reaching the terminal degree), entered a major university, and obtained a doctorate in psychology, less than 8 years after entering the United States as an immigrant tile setter.

Will (barely 28 years old upon receiving his doctorate) immediately proceeded to assume a postdoctoral internship position with the U.S. Veterans Administration in order to further prepare himself for a career as a clinical psychologist. Halfway through his internship, however, he was contacted by senior administrators at his former university and asked to return as a junior faculty member to teach and do research in a newly formed, professionally oriented college. Because Will felt challenged by this opportunity, he returned after completing his internship. He began to establish himself as a researcher and teacher and earned the respect of his colleagues, who approached him a few years later to assume major administrative positions within the new college. Although Will was successful and admired as an administrator, he relinquished this role after 5 years in order to redirect his career and to enter an entirely new field of research and scholarship.

There is every indication, as judged by Will's colleagues and peers, that he has been quite successful in his career change. Currently in his 25th year at his university, he is considering early retirement options and various opportunities for exploring new career opportunities, opportunities that might permit a better integration of personal and professional goals than his current circumstances afford.

Will's work life (his career) has been presented here without reference to his personal life, his family, his health status, important life events, and other factors that influenced him and helped him determine the progression of his career throughout. Moreover, no specific reference was made to the organizational environment in which he worked, the substantive areas of his research or teaching, the economic conditions of his employment, or the relative degree of satisfaction he experienced in relation to his various work roles. All of these factors, as well as others, however, are important if we want to understand and not just simply describe Will's adult career development. What we need, therefore, is a comprehensive theory that enables us to incorporate all of the important features of adult career development, not just some of them.

It should be apparent from this illustration that stage models cannot help us to understand why Will did what he did and what it was about him that enabled him to do it. For example, the relatively terse story of Will's career development conveyed the direction and drive that energized his career behaviors that would have been lost in a mere listing of milestones, life events, or stages. Moreover, with current stage-oriented theories, even general predictions would have been difficult and intervention would have been ineffective, if not meaningless. In short, although stage models may have some utility for describing population-level patterns, that is, patterns of people in the aggregate, they have little utility for psychologists and other professionals in dealing with the complex career pathways of individuals. Consequently, we must now turn to what kind of theory will enable them to understand the processes that guide and influence adult career development, for it is only through such understanding that facilitative interventions can be designed.

Beyond the Developmental–Contextual Model: An Introduction to Developmental Systems Theory

In 1986, Vondracek and his colleagues introduced the developmental–contextual model for the study of life-span career development (Vondracek et al., 1986). That effort represented a first step toward a comprehensive model and a distinct departure from the dominant normative stage models because it introduced more sophisticated developmental concepts than had been used in previous developmental models of career development (e.g., it specified the precise nature of the developmental concepts that were employed) and it introduced the concept of dynamic interaction between the individual and the various levels of environments in which individual development and behavior are embedded. Nevertheless, the developmental–contextual model was designed as a general conceptual framework, or metamodel, and not, as was concluded erroneously by some writers, as a theory of career development. As a metamodel it is not sufficiently explicit, especially about process, to produce precise and testable hypotheses, although it has been useful as a guide for the design and formulation of overall approaches to career development research.

Since the original presentation of the developmental–contextual metamodel of career development, it has become increasingly apparent that these initial efforts needed to be expanded into a model that not only incorporates the defining features of developmental contextualism but also guides scientists toward understanding the processes underlying career decisions and pathways, the how and why of the behaviors that determine the work lives of individuals. In other words, what is needed is a theoretical perspective that is more explicit about the processes that move someone like Will from being an apprentice tile setter in Germany toward something he could not even know or dream about, namely, to being a professor in a major university in a faraway foreign country. Fortunately, the recent theoretical advances represented by developmental systems theory (D. Ford & Lerner, 1992) and motivational systems theory (M. Ford, 1992) provide a means for the discovery of this perspective.

In introducing DST, D. Ford and Lerner (1992) noted that developmental contextualism is a metamodel that has provided guiding assumptions about development in accord with current knowledge, without, however, deriving a theory that deals with the specific nature of individuals and the processes by which they function and change. They also noted that D. Ford's (1987) living systems framework focuses on just those missing issues and processes.

They concluded that a synthesis of the two could represent "a more comprehensive framework for understanding human development than presently exists" (D. Ford & Lerner, 1992, p. 2). In order to fully appreciate these theoretical advances, we must note that D. Ford's extensive professional history as a counseling psychologist guided his efforts in creating a conceptual framework that could ultimately serve as a practical tool for guiding research *and* intervention.

A summary presentation of a framework as comprehensive and rich as the DST is problematic. Invariably, important concepts will be skimmed over or not discussed at all, and erroneous conclusions about significant issues may be drawn. Consequently, we stress that an adequate understanding of DST can be gained only through careful reading of the original formulation (D. Ford & Lerner, 1992), detailed expositions of developmental contextualism (e.g., Lerner, 1978, 1989), and the living systems framework (e.g., D. Ford, 1987; M. Ford & D. Ford, 1987), which represent the foundation of DST. In our discussion here, we selectively focus on key aspects of the living systems framework and its synthesis with developmental contextualism (i.e., developmental systems theory), particularly those formulations that are salient in adult career development.

In addition to meeting the design criteria required by the developmental–contextual metamodel, DST incorporates from the LSF (D. Ford, 1987) a conceptualization of three basic kinds of phenomena that collectively account for the organized dynamics of human development: "1. the unitary functioning of the whole person-in-context; 2. the functioning of the component parts of the person; and 3. stability and change in the functioning of the component parts of the person and the person-as-a-whole" (M. Ford, 1992, p. 20). Therefore, "the LSF is a comprehensive theory of human functioning and development that integrates scientific and professional knowledge about the characteristics of people in general (nomothetic knowledge) and the organization and operation of these characteristics in individual persons (idiographic knowledge)" (M. Ford, 1992, p. 19). In making the case for such an integrative approach, Nesselroade and D. Ford (1987) argued that useful nomothetic knowledge (i.e., knowledge about characteristic stages of career development) cannot be developed without accurate idiographic knowledge (i.e., information about particular individuals).

It is important to recognize that the LSF represents "at the person-in-context level of analysis, *all* aspects of being human, not just some particular attribute or process" (M. Ford, 1992, p. 19).

> The LSF is composed of a variety of integrated component conceptualizations (e.g., of motor behavior and memory). It describes how the various "pieces" of the person—their goals, emotions, thoughts, actions, and biological processes—functioning both semiautonomously and as part of a larger unit (the person) in coherent "chunks" of context-specific, goal-directed activity (be-

havior episodes). It also describes how these specific experiences "add up" to produce a unique, self-constructed history and personality (i.e., through the construction, differentiation, and elaboration of behavior episode schemata), and how various processes of change (self-organization, self-construction, and disorganization–reorganization) help maintain both stability and developmental flexibility in the organized patterns that result (steady states). Thus, the LSF cannot easily be characterized in terms of traditional theoretical categories. Rather, it is a way of trying to understand persons in all of their complexly organized humanness. (M. Ford & D. Ford, 1987, pp. 1–2)

A basic feature of the LSF (D. Ford, 1987) is it's beginning with an analogy between control systems (which have been the subject of theory and research in the field of cybernetics) on the one hand and humans on the other. A control system model, however, is then transformed into a living system by the addition of special properties of human life not found in classical cybernetic models, namely, capabilities for biological and behavioral self-construction (e.g., self-construction of concepts, goals, and beliefs and biological self-repair). With regard to specific components, the anatomy of the human body corresponds to a control system's physical structure:

> The cognitive functions of humans correspond to the directive, regulatory, and control functions that govern system activity. Humans' sensory–perceptual functions correspond to a control system's information-collection, monitoring, and feedback functions, and their motor capabilities correspond to the action capabilities of control systems. Humans' attentional, consciousness, and emotion-arousal functions correspond to control systems' energizing functions, but they also contribute to the regulatory and control functions. The material and energy-based self-organizing and self-constructing functions correspond to biological processes in humans. The information-based self-organizing and self-constructing functions correspond to information-processing, learning, and action-formation and -execution functions in humans. All of these functions are always occurring in this pattern of organization as long as a person is alive. (M. Ford & D. Ford, 1987, p. 13)

Although behaviors occur in ongoing patterns that are always dependent to some extent on the context within which they are occurring, in the living systems framework model, the person's environment does not *cause* the person's behavioral patterns. Instead, the properties of the individual's environment differentially facilitate and constrain possible developmental pathways. Any particular environment may provide good support for some pathways and moderate support for others but present significant obstructions to still others. Consequently, the isolation of one specific behavior, such as a thought or a movement, from other components of the behavior pattern that is occurring at the time makes no sense. Unfortunately, in many studies of human behavior, researchers have attempted to do precisely that by forcing complex human behavior into a simple, linear cause-and-effect conceptual model. In contrast, the LSF postulates that the study of component responses makes sense only if it occurs within the context of an ongoing behavior–environment pattern. These patterns differ from one person to another and from one occasion to another for the same person

> because people vary in what they want, how they decide to go about producing the desired consequences, what they actually do, the ways they anticipate and evaluate their progress, the emotions that are aroused in relationship to the activity, the conditions of their biological functioning, the kinds of environments in which they interact, and the attributes of those environments upon which they selectively focus their transactions. If any of those functions are ignored, a person's behavior cannot be fully understood. (D. Ford, 1987, p. 145)

To deal with this "unitary functioning of the whole person-in-context" (M. Ford, 1992, p. 29), the LSF incorporates the concepts of behavior episode and behavior episode schemata. The former represents a time-limited pattern of behavior that occurs in a specific context and has several defining attributes. Namely, it is guided by some form of intention or personal goal, it includes a variable pattern of activities that are selectively organized in order for the individual to accomplish the goal, and it occurs within a specific set of environmental conditions that organize the behavior pattern in such a way as to facilitate or constrain progress toward the goal. The behavior episode is terminated when the desired goal is achieved, when some internal or external event preempts continued attention and directs behaviors toward a different goal, or when the evaluation of progress leads to the conclusion that the intended goal cannot be achieved on that occasion (D. Ford & Lerner, 1992). It is clear from this description that "goals and contexts are the anchors that organize and provide coherence to the activities within a behavior episode" (M. Ford, 1992, p. 24).

Behavior episodes are temporary phenomena that, nevertheless, collectively represent a person's past experiences. Because people do not start "from scratch" every time they behave, scientists can assume that people construct a repertoire of relatively enduring, generalized behavioral patterns from the raw material of behavior episodes. In the LSF, the concept of behavior episode schemata (BES) represents the results of this self-construction activity. A BES is an integrated internal representation of a set of similar behavior episode experiences, which may include episodes that have been only imagined or observed. Consequently, "A BES represents the functioning of the whole person-in-context because that is what is involved in any given behavior episode" (M. Ford, 1992, p. 26). The person's overall repertoire of these relatively enduring behavior patterns may be conceptualized as representing the person's personality.

The DST also provides propositions about developmental dynamics that are of basic significance to the understanding of adult career development. It describes specific processes that protect the stability of existing patterns and that can also produce both incremental and transformational change. As a consequence, development is open-ended and somewhat unpredictable. (For a discussion of the probabilistic nature of developmental change in relation to career development, see Vondracek et al., 1986.) Any individual's developmental pathway can lead in directions no one could have predicted, and developmental pathways may change significantly during a person's lifetime. For example, Will's decision to immigrate to the United States in search of a more facilitative environment for the realization of his career goals launched him in a direction that was, by necessity, completely different from the possible outcomes he might have achieved had he remained in Germany. Clearly, specific behaviors on the part of individuals can create drastic discontinuities in some aspects of their development, while maintaining stability and continuity in other aspects.

Our interest in adult career development causes us, at this point, to further qualify the kinds of behavior episodes in which we are particularly interested. Specifically, we are interested in behaviors and behavior patterns that are *effective*, that is, those that accomplish or facilitate progress toward the underlying career-related goal(s). Any person displaying effective behavior in a given behavior episode must have motivation sufficient to continue working toward the goal directing the episode until it is achieved, the person must have the necessary skill to produce the desired results, and the person's biological systems must be capable of supporting the motivation and skill aspects of the behavior episode. Equally important, the person must be in a *responsive environment*, one that permits successful conclusion of the behavior episode. All four of these conditions are prerequisites for effective functioning; if any one of them is missing, effective functioning will not occur. M. Ford (1992) proposed an elegant short-hand way of describing the "processes contributing to effective person-in-context functioning" (p. 69):

$$\text{Achievement/Competence} = \frac{\text{Motivation} \times \text{Skill}}{\text{Biology}} \times \text{Responsive Environment}$$

Obviously, effective functioning of the person is ultimately the most important ingredient in the career development of adults. Adult career development theory and related issues of intervention must therefore incorporate these four prerequisites of effective functioning. The skills dimension has, perhaps, received the greatest amount of attention from employers and educators. After all, if someone is to be hired for a position or job, researchers can relatively easily determine (by means of education or experience) whether or not the candidate has the requisite skills to be an effective worker. Vocational psychologists and career counselors have often used achievement tests to ascertain the skill level that a person has achieved in a given area. On the other hand, they have given relatively little attention to determining if the biological functioning of the person can support the motivational and skill components of effective functioning. An implicit assumption has been that the achievement of a given level of skill represents an indirect assessment of the adequacy of the underlying biological structures and processes.

A responsive environment is also critical if effective career functioning is to occur. In the field of adult career development this issue has been considered at various levels of analysis. Several formulations of career theory (e.g., Dawis & Lofquist, 1984; Holland, 1985; Vondracek et al., 1986) have focused on various aspects of person–environment congruence, or person–environment fit: In each, the presence of a facilitative, responsive, affording environment is important (for a detailed review, see Rounds & Tracey, 1990; Spokane, 1987).

The importance of a responsive environment is further demonstrated in Krumboltz and associates (1980) Social Learning Theory of Career Decision Making (SLTCDM), which proposes that people have learning experiences that are largely determined by the social contexts within which they operate. The learning experiences, in turn, result in the individual's making self-observation generalizations (e.g., "I am good at comforting grieving widows"), which the individual then assesses in terms of the degree to which they may be useful in the outside world (the environment). This process results in task-approach skills (Krumboltz, Mitchell, & Jones, 1980). Of particular interest here is the fact that, in an ingenious and well-conceived effort to place the theory within a broader theoretical framework, Krumboltz and Nichols (1990) chose the same living systems framework (D. Ford, 1987) that represents one of the basic conceptual building blocks of our efforts here to formulate a comprehensive theory of adult career development (Krumboltz & Nichols, 1990).

Finally, the observation that motivation is critically important in the career development of individuals is not a novel insight. Crites (1969) prefaced his description of the career adjustment process by underscoring the fact that it could account for these processes only in *motivated* workers. In effect, motivation was viewed as a necessary condition for career development and adjustment. More recently, Hackett and Betz (1981) proposed that self-efficacy expectations (motivational factors because of their importance in the initiation and persistence of behavior) play a critical role in determining an individual's "perceived range of career options . . . , effective decision making, and . . . effective and persistent pursuit of career plans" (p. 335). They noted elsewhere that "self-efficacy theory has great potential . . . for the understanding and facilitation of career adjustment" (Betz & Hackett, 1986, p. 286). Clearly, their perceptive choice of the self-efficacy construct as a major explanatory factor in career development theory has been prophetic. The ensuing research (for recent reviews, see Hackett & Lent, 1992; Lent & Hackett, 1987) has generated important evidence that, in our view, lends credence to our present efforts to embed the similar but more comprehensive

MST concept of capability and context beliefs (i.e., personal agency beliefs; M. Ford, 1992) in a comprehensive theory of adult career development.

Throughout our discussion we have remained mindful of the task we set for ourselves, namely, to develop an understanding of how and why Will's career development unfolded as it did. It is obvious that Will engaged in a wide range of *effective* behaviors that enabled him to overcome numerous environmental obstacles and skill deficits and that caused him to single-mindedly pursue his quest for a successful and rewarding career. In light of the prerequisites for effective functioning, it is clear that what set Will apart from others in his circumstances was not his level of skill, not any unique biological capacities (although he was considered intellectually bright by his teachers, he shared that distinction with many others who remained in the career tracks chosen for them by their parents), and not a particularly responsive environment that facilitated his career development (indeed, Will actually left it to find one that was more responsive). Instead, what apparently set Will apart from most of his peers was his motivation, his strong desire for a better future and a fundamental belief that his capabilities and opportunities would somehow take him there.

If we accept this preliminary analysis of Will's career development, a more detailed examination of the motivational components of his career functioning is required. As we observed previously, self-efficacy expectations are important motivational factors in career development; as our following discussion demonstrates, other motivational factors also serve important functions in the instigation and maintenance of career-related behaviors. In our view, a comprehensive theory of career development necessitates a comprehensive theory of motivation. Such a theory, when applied to our example of Will, could account for what M. Ford (1992) has called the selective *direction* of Will's behavior patterns (i.e., what he was trying to do at various points in his work life); the selective *energization* of behavior patterns (i.e., how he became excited at being a student and later a teacher and researcher or disinterested in being a tile setter); and the selective *regulation* of his behavioral patterns (i.e., how he decided to give up tile setting, how he decided to try a completely new environment, and how he decided to persevere toward his educational goals "against all odds") (M. Ford, 1992, pp. 2–3). M. Ford (1992) recently presented a penetrating analysis of these key motivational processes, integrating his work with the formulations of both the LSF (D. Ford, 1987) and the DST (D. Ford & Lerner, 1992). The following discussion briefly describes what he calls motivational systems theory.

Motivational Systems Theory: A Brief Overview

"Motivation provides the psychological foundation for the development of human competence in everyday life" (M. Ford, 1992, p. 16). Hence, motivation is a critical ingredient in what he calls "effective person-in-context functioning"

(p. 66). In adult career development, it is clear that its course and outcomes are inextricably linked to effective functioning of the person. Motivational systems theory (MST) defines effective functioning in terms of two concepts that have considerable face validity in career development theory and practice, namely, achievement and competence. At the situational level of analysis, where behavior is described in terms of behavior episodes, effective functioning is defined as achievement, that is, as "the attainment of a personally or socially valued goal in a particular context" (p. 66). At the personality level of analysis, where behavior is described in terms of behavior episode schemata, effective functioning is defined as competence, that is, as "the attainment of relevant goals in specified environments using appropriate means and resulting in positive developmental outcomes" (p. 67).

It is particularly noteworthy that these definitions of competence and achievement, by their inclusion of "particular contexts," "specified environments," "appropriate means," and "relevant goals," permit competence to be discussed in reference to specific circumstances and value systems, without resort to descriptions that treat competence as a generalized trait. Career counselors know that competence and achievement must be anchored in and related to the contexts within which a person functions in order to be of any meaningful help in understanding that person. As we explain in a later section, a theoretical framework that explicitly recognizes this is likely to significantly facilitate the design of interventions that aim to enhance the achievement and competence of individuals.

Before describing in detail some of the key motivational processes in the career development of adults, we need to emphasize that nonmotivational factors are also important. They include not only the previously noted environmental facilitating and constraining factors but also all of the individual's nonmotivational psychological and behavioral processes that are represented by the skill dimension. In order to understand the distinction between motivational and nonmotivational processes, we must recognize that motivation in MST is viewed entirely as residing within the person. Moreover, motivational processes are always future oriented. Specifically,

> motivational processes help people decide whether to try to maintain or restore an existing state or to strive for new or improved outcomes. They are not, however, directly involved in the task of changing the current state into a preferred state. In other words, motivational processes identify and "size up" problems and opportunities, but they are not responsible for solving those problems or turning those opportunities into reality. The biological, skill, and environmental components of the person-in-context system carry that burden. (M. Ford, 1992, p. 73)

Using these criteria for identifying those processes that are motivational and those that are not, M. Ford (1987) identified three motivational components of human functioning: personal goals, personal agency beliefs, and emotions. Because each is critically important in the course of adult career development, we discuss them in some detail. Each of these motivational components is discussed separately only for conceptual and expositional clarity and convenience. In real life, they are typically represented by complex patterns of motivational processes; that is, they operate as a motivational team.

Personal Goals. In MST, personal goals have two major properties: They are thoughts about the consequences one wishes to achieve (or avoid), and they direct or mobilize the various components of the functioning person to try to produce the desired consequences or to prevent the undesired consequences. The relevance of personal goals to career development is suggested by the fact that the content of a person's goals represents what the person wants and what the person is trying to accomplish. Moreover, the content of the person's goals offers clues as to why a person does what he or she does. In effect, then, when a career counselor asks, What are you trying to do? or What are you trying to accomplish? the inquiry is directed at determining the content of the client's goals. Some career theorists have noted that a person's goals, conceptualized in this manner, represent the single most important concept in understanding the career decision-making process (Krumboltz & Nichols, 1990).

Personal goals can be differentiated on the basis of a variety of characteristics (Winell, 1987). They may be short-term, concrete, goal-directed activities such as getting to a meeting with the career counselor on time, or they may be life goals, or guiding visions of desired consequences that are frequently conceptualized as values or core goals (Nichols, 1991). Personal goals can also refer either to desired internal states (e.g., tranquility, enjoyment, excitement) or to desired effects in relation to the external environment (e.g., acquiring a skill, building a house, helping a friend). Personal goals can also be active or dormant. Sometimes people defer pursuit of a goal or temporarily lose interest in pursuing it as other goals take precedence or as expectancies for goal attainment are diminished. Goals are usually consciously pursued consequences of behavior, but sometimes people organize their behavior around the accomplishment of certain objectives without being fully, consciously aware of what they are actually trying to accomplish. Finally, goals may be rational or irrational. They are consequences that are desired, nothing more and nothing less, and, hence, they need not make sense or even be consistent with other goals a person may be pursuing.

Goals are important because they cause people to direct and organize their behavior selectively in order to enhance the likelihood that they can obtain their goals. Behavior that is focused in this manner, that is, around well-conceived goals, is more likely to produce results. Conversely, when there are no specific goals in place or when there is ambiguity or confusion about goals, the ensuing behaviors are likely to be ineffective. When people identify clear goals, however, and achieve them, they obtain positive feedback and are likely to experience emotional satisfaction (Winell, 1987). This satisfaction, in turn, can lead to what D. Ford (1987, p. 40) called "feedforward" information, which leads to the anticipation of positive outcomes as a consequence of such goal-directed behaviors.

The foregoing discussion is intended merely to underscore the fact that personal goals represent an important aspect of the motivational structure of individual functioning. As such, they play an important role in the individual's organizing behavior patterns toward the attainment of desired consequences and the avoidance of undesired ones. The relevance of these processes in adult career development is rather obvious. A number of concepts important to career theory may be reconceptualized as personal goals within the MST framework. For example, some have suggested that vocational or career interests represent the individual's recognition of an opportunity to pursue a desired goal (Krumboltz & Nichols, 1990). Work values, or what Pryor (1981) called Work Aspect Preferences can also be viewed as personal goals, that is, desired consequences. Locke and Latham (1990) have provided theoretical and empirical support for the importance of goals and goal setting in the areas of work performance and work satisfaction.

Most people have multiple goals, and these are usually conceptualized in terms of a goal hierarchy: Some goals are more important to the individual than others, some goals are viewed as more attainable than others, and some goals have greater emotional salience than others. The most highly prioritized goals may be considered *intentions*, and they are likely to produce instrumental action because the person has made a specific commitment to achieving the goal. Once such a commitment to achieve a goal has been made, the motivational burden is likely to shift from personal goals to personal agency beliefs and emotions (M. Ford, 1992).

Personal Agency Beliefs and Emotional Arousal Processes. Personal agency beliefs represent a person's evaluation of whether or not he or she has the ability and opportunity to obtain a goal or achieve a desired result. They involve "a comparison between a desired consequence (i.e., some goal) and an anticipated consequence (i.e., what the person expects to happen if they pursue that goal)" (M. Ford, 1992, p. 125). Personal agency beliefs are important only if a goal is in place and only if that goal is being actively pursued. Such beliefs can, however, facilitate the elaboration of new goals in contexts that are engaged in for other reasons (e.g., Will's change to a psychology major based, in part, on the belief that this would afford more opportunities for future goal attainment).

In MST, personal agency beliefs are conceptualized as consisting of *capability beliefs* and *context beliefs*. The former are judgments concerning whether or not one has the skill needed to function effectively, whereas the latter are judgments pertaining to whether or not one has the kind of responsive environment needed to engage in effective functioning. The concept of capability beliefs is similar to Bandura's (1977, 1982) concept of self-efficacy expectations. M. Ford (1992) has argued, however, that the concept of capability beliefs is preferable because it encompasses different kinds of skills in different circumstances and because it is not "restricted to beliefs about task goals in context-specific behavior episodes" (p. 128), which is characteristic of the way in which the concept of self-efficacy has been used.

Personal agency beliefs and their motivational impact are best understood when they are considered in light of the joint contributions of capability and context beliefs to effective functioning. In most applications of the self-efficacy concept, however, capability beliefs are examined to the virtual exclusion of context, or outcome, beliefs. For example, Hackett and Betz (1981), in their pioneering application of Bandura's (1977) concept of self-efficacy expectations to the career development of women, correctly noted that efficacy beliefs should be differentiated from outcome beliefs. They also implied, however, that outcome beliefs are not nearly as important as efficacy beliefs in accounting for the career development of women. This stance appears to be contrary to Bandura's (Bandura, 1982, 1984) more recent position, in which he indicated that the joint influence of efficacy expectations and outcome expectations should be considered. Even here, however, outcome beliefs are viewed more as a function of self-efficacy expectations than as a powerful motivational process in its own right.

M. Ford (1992) demonstrated the utility of an integrated approach by examining different patterns of personal agency beliefs and proposing a taxonomy consisting of 10 different patterns. The patterns range from a *robust* pattern (consisting of strong capability beliefs and positive context beliefs) to a *hopeless* pattern (consisting of weak capability beliefs and negative context beliefs). The entire taxonomy of personal agency belief patterns is presented in Table 4.1, adapted from M. Ford (1992, p. 134). He suggested that the robust and tenacious patterns are obviously the most motivationally powerful patterns because people with these patterns typically persist in their expectation that they will achieve their goals even when they encounter obstacles, difficulties, and failures. It is also important to understand that personal agency beliefs should not be viewed as trait-like in nature because thoughts about personal and contextual capabilities may vary broadly across situations and over time. Moreover, no single personal agency belief pattern is necessarily best for all circumstances (M. Ford, 1992).

Personal goals and personal agency beliefs are influenced in important ways by emotions. Emotions are capable of performing an energizing function by supporting and facilitating behaviors designed to produce desired consequences. They also serve what D. Ford (1987) called an "affective

TABLE 4.1
MST Taxonomy of Personal Agency Belief Patterns

	Capability Beliefs		
Context Beliefs	Strong	Moderate or Variable	Weak
Positive	R	M	F
	Robust Pattern	Modest Pattern	Fragile Pattern
Neutral or Variable	T	V	S
	Tenacious Pattern	Vulnerable Pattern	Self-Doubting Pattern
Negative	A1 or A2	D	H
	Accepting or Antagonistic Pattern	Discouraged Pattern	Hopeless Pattern

Definitions (adapted from Webster's Seventh New Collegiate Dictionary):

R Pattern	Robust—"strong and firm in purpose or outlook"
M Pattern	Modest—"placing a moderate estimate on one's abilities"
F Pattern	Fragile—"intact but easily broken or damaged"
T Pattern	Tenacious—"suggests strength in dealing with challenges and obstacles"
V Pattern	Vulnerable—"functioning adequately but may be at risk under conditions of stress"
S Pattern	Self-doubting—"having a lack of faith in one's chances for success"
A1 Pattern	Accepting—"to endure difficulties quietly and with courage"
A2 Pattern	Antagonistic—"tending toward actively expressed annoyance or hostility"
D Pattern	Discouraged—"being deprived of but potentially maintaining some confidence or hope"
H Pattern	Hopeless—"having no expectation of success"

Note: From *Motivating Humans: Goals, Emotions, and Personal Agency Beliefs* (p. 134), by M. E. Ford, 1992, Place of Publication: Sage Publications, Inc., Newbury Park, CA. Copyright 1992, Sage Publications. Reprinted by Permission.

regulatory function" (p. 470) by providing evaluative information pertaining to the person's interactions with the environment. In many respects, emotions represent a neglected dimension in many models of behavioral functioning in general and in career development models in particular. This neglect may be due in part to the fact that emotions operate somewhat differently in children than in adults. In adults, emotions tend to be activated by cognitive evaluations regarding one's circumstances. Cognitive evaluations and emotions typically work together in contributing to effective decision making. Whereas personal agency beliefs tend to be particularly important in the individual's making decisions about long-range or overarching goals, emotions tend to exert their effects more readily in relation to short-term goals and more imminent circumstances. Thus, personal agency beliefs may lead to specific decisions (e.g., whether one should go to graduate school or join the business world), whereas emotions mobilize the person and facilitate effective functioning under conditions of an immediate threat or opportunity.

In short, both personal agency beliefs and emotions represent important motivational factors, and both are complex, organized patterns consisting of several interrelated processes.

This conceptualization of the role of emotions in human motivation is more comprehensive than that presented by Hackett and Betz (1981), who focused exclusively on the role of anxiety in influencing efficacy expectations. They concluded that because women tend to experience higher levels of anxiety than men do, they are also less likely to experience high self-efficacy (in MST terms, this is equivalent to the conclusion that women are more likely than men to manifest fragile, vulnerable, or self-doubting patterns of personal agency beliefs). Although there is some empirical support for this viewpoint, a comprehensive conceptualization of personal agency beliefs, such as that proposed by M. Ford (1987), takes account of the full range of human emotionality. Based on D. Ford's (1987) review of different emotional themes reported in the theoretical and research literature on human emotionality, MST incorporates eight different patterns of *instrumental emotions* (emotions that help regulate behavior episodes) and six patterns of *social emotions* (emotions that play a role in facilitating social functioning). For example, the emotional pattern of downheartedness–discouragement–depression facilitates the termination of unsuccessful behavior episodes and is therefore associated with personal failure and incompetence (e.g., discouraged or hopeless personal agency beliefs). This same pattern, however, has a positive impact because it helps the person avoid unproductive activities (e.g., wasting time trying to achieve an unrealistic goal). On the other hand, the emotional pattern of curiosity–interest–excitement is a pattern that promotes explanatory behavior, for example, the investigation of career options (M. Ford, 1992).

TOWARD AN ENHANCED FRAMEWORK FOR INTERVENTION IN ADULT CAREER DEVELOPMENT

Up to this point, we have focused on outlining some basic features of a comprehensive theory of adult career development. We started by pointing out the limitations of current theories, and we criticized the normative and nomothetic emphases within them. We suggested that theoretical advances were necessary, advances that would permit a better understanding of the dynamics of individual careers as they developed through the adult years. As a means to this goal, we introduced some of the basic concepts from developmental systems theory (D. Ford & Lerner, 1992), which represents an advancement over the developmental–contextual model of life-span career development that was proposed by Vondracek et al. (1986). Furthermore, because motivation is at the center of our conceptualization of adult career development, we introduced the motivational systems theory (M. Ford, 1992). The choice of MST was based, in part, on the fact that it is derived from D. Ford's (1987) living systems framework, which is also prominently featured in DST. Thus, the theoretical framework for the study of adult career development, which we have presented in as parsimonious a manner as possible, relies on important theoretical advances in the fields of human development and human motivation.

Our work would be incomplete, however, if we did not also address the question of how psychologists and counselors can intervene in the career development of individuals in order to facilitate work lives that are satisfying and successful. In this connection we agree with Crites (1969, 1976) that satisfaction and success have different meanings at different points in a person's career but that the dynamics involved are essentially the same. Throughout the chapter, we have referred to the career development of Will as a means of demonstrating the need for a comprehensive theory of adult career development capable of accounting for the immense complexity of the work lives of adults. We continue to use Will as an example in our discussion of intervention.

The rationale for our focus on human motivation included the notion that motivation represents the psychological foundation for the development of specific achievements and competence (M. Ford, 1992). It follows that problems in human motivation are at the very core of problems in adult career development, which requires achievement and competence if it is to unfold in the constructive directions desired by most people. In our example of Will, we noted that it was ultimately his *motivation* that made it possible for him to depart from the unsatisfactory course chosen for him by his parents and to travel new and novel roads to his success. A detailed review of the developmental antecedents of his goals and personal agency beliefs is clearly beyond this chapter. We do discuss in the remaining section, however, how interventions can be designed to address the problems of unproductive motivational patterns and demotivating environments in the career development of adults.

According to MST, the problem of motivating humans should be approached as the complex and individualistic task that it is. Making people care about things or forcing them to want to do things ultimately results in failure, especially if long-term consequences are sought. "Facilitation, not control, should be the guiding idea in attempts to motivate humans" (M. Ford, 1992, p. 202). When approached from this perspective, the problem of motivating people can be understood at the level of the behavior episode. That is, the counselor's task would be to facilitate the successful achievement of the goal associated with that particular behavior episode in a specific context. This could also be approached, however, from the perspective of behavior episode schemata, which has been likened to the personality level of analysis. At this level, efforts to motivate people would be expected to result in long-term, enduring change, the kind of change that is considered to be "elaborative change" (D. Ford & Lerner, 1992, p. 35) in DST. M. Ford (1992) suggested that such change may be produced through the facilitation, strengthening, and activation of the behavior episode schemata that contain powerful motivational components. He argued that this kind of change would enhance the person's competence to deal with similar situations in the future. In short, although enhancing the motivation of individuals to obtain *short-term goals* may lead to a greater probability of *achievement* of those goals, facilitating motivation of individuals to make *enduring changes* is much more likely to result in increased *competence*.

Principles of the Motivational Systems Theory for Motivating Humans

M. Ford (1992) summarized 17 principles for motivating humans that are derived directly from MST. Because these principles have been stated at a level of generality that makes them applicable to many different situations and because most of them are based not only on MST but also to some extent on empirical evidence, we briefly summarize them here and illustrate them, when possible, with reference to our example of Will.

The Principle of Unitary Functioning. Anyone wishing to intervene in the motivational functioning of individuals must realize that it is always the whole person with whom one is dealing. Consequently, it is essential that we respect the uniqueness of the individual and of his or her motivational patterns and recognize that changes in some aspects of a person's motivational patterns (e.g., Will's commitment to a new career goal) will produce changes in other aspects of the person-in-context system (e.g., the development of relevant skills and discovery of new environments responsive to that goal).

The Motivational Triumvirate Principle. All three components of motivation—goals, emotions, and personal agency beliefs—must be addressed if we are to significantly facilitate a person's motivation. In Will's case, for example, early statements of his goals alone (e.g., I want to get a doctorate degree) led to replies such as "You must be crazy." The respondents failed to understand that Will's goals were accompanied by strong emotions and positive personal agency beliefs that ultimately made the achievement of such lofty goals possible. Had the goal existed merely as a "wish" (M. Ford, 1992, p. 250), without the deep emotional and evaluative conviction required of Will to develop and maintain a firm commitment to the goal in the face of tremendous obstacles, the incredulous response would have been entirely warranted.

The Responsive Environment Principle. M. Ford (1992) stressed that the interventionist who is attempting to enhance a person's environment immediately becomes part of that environment and consequently a factor in determining the person's ability to engage in effective functioning. It is therefore critically important that the interventionist have the proper relationship with and to that person. This relationship includes the common-sense, but often overlooked, idea that the interventionist's objectives must be congruent with what the person is aiming to accomplish and with the person's various capabilities. Moreover, the interventionist's objectives must be realistic and appropriate, and the interventionist must ensure the presence of an emotional climate that supports and facilitates effective functioning. Motivational interventions frequently fail because one or more of these components of the responsive environment principle are not met.

The Principle of Goal Activation. Goals are a necessary prerequisite for the occurrence of any desired behavior pattern. Although goals, emotions, and personal agency beliefs all participate in motivational patterns, the selection and activation of relevant goals is so important that little else really matters until such selection and activation have been accomplished. Will's goal of obtaining a high level of education and a professional occupational role represented the guiding vision of his behavior for many years. Without the goal, he might have been side-tracked and might have pursued, for example, opportunities that offered greater and more immediate material rewards than the professional occupation he sought.

The Principle of Goal Salience. Activated goals facilitate effective functioning only when the individual clearly understands what the goal means in terms that guide current behavior and that promote commitment to pursue the goal in the future. One way the interventionist can help the individual accomplish this is to link a desired future outcome (high educational attainment) to specific subgoals (being admitted to night school or to college) that signify progress toward the outcome. Those who intervene in efforts to motivate people can help individuals by assisting them to clearly state their goals in terms of both short- and long-term behavioral objectives, by focusing effort and attention on specific actions that can be taken in the present, and by explaining why any given activity may be facilitative of the achievement of personally relevant goals.

The Multiple Goals Principle. The basic idea of this principle is that the most powerful motivational patterns occur in relation to multiple goals that synergistically link a variety of goals that contribute to desired outcomes. Will was powerfully motivated toward educational attainment by a combination of affective goals, for example, experiencing excitement from the discovery of new knowledge; cognitive goals, for example, gaining knowledge, developing interesting ideas, and acquiring self-confidence; task goals, for example, achieving mastery by the passing of examinations; and self-assertive social-relationship goals, for example, feeling unique, experiencing self-determination, and comparing himself favorably to others in terms of success (goal categories are derived from the taxonomy of human goals by M. Ford & Nichols, 1991).

The Principle of Goal Alignment. A clear message in the MST is that clear goals facilitate a person's motivation. If multiple goals are being pursued, however, the interventionist must help the person to align these goals in "win–win" fashion and to avoid goal conflicts that constrain motivation; goal conflicts can often produce a "lose–lose" situation in which neither goal is accomplished. Moreover, in view of the fact that most people pursue their goals within social contexts, it is important that their multiple goals are aligned (i.e., free of conflict) within as well as between people. M. Ford (1992) also pointed out that goal alignment involves the arrangement of proximal and distal goals within a person in such a way as to promote desired future outcomes. For example, Will was able to keep his long-term desired outcomes in view while pursuing immediate goals, such as successfully completing his apprenticeship and continuing his night-school studies. Any efforts designed to facilitate motivation and effective functioning must therefore include helping people to prioritize and organize immediate subgoals in a way that facilitates rather than constrains the ultimate achievement of the long-term outcomes that are most important to them.

The Feedback Principle. To maintain motivation over time, people need feedback information that informs them about the progress they are making toward their goals. They can use this information not only to make necessary modifications in the goal structure but also to reinforce and strengthen the salience of the desired outcomes, thereby strengthening the underlying motivation. Feedback is also the primary source of information that shapes capability and context beliefs, that is, the regulatory "feedforward" cognitions (D. Ford, 1987, p. 92).

The Flexible Standards Principle. Will realized that his ultimate objective was quite distant and required a long-term commitment in order to be realized. Consequently, he adopted flexible standards that allowed him to avoid the demotivating effect of *negative feedback*, that is, feedback indicating that he was not living up to his own standards. For example, on receiving a disappointing grade on a physics examination, he nevertheless maintained his motivation by recognizing that he was making progress, in spite of the disappointing grade, toward attainment of his goals. Thus, making standards flexible helps the person avoid some of the pressures that come with unrealistically high and rigid expectations and ensures that movement toward desired outcomes and the development of competence proceed not only when all the news is good but also when disappointments occur. The person can view disappointments as useful markers of progress rather than as "the end of the world."

The Optimal Challenge Principle.   The optimal challenge principle reflects the well-established notion that motivation is maximized when the attainment of a person's goal is judged to be quite difficult but still attainable, with vigorous and persistent effort. Under such circumstances, representing an optimal challenge, successful goal attainment tends to be unusually satisfying and "highly empowering in terms of personal agency beliefs" (M. Ford, 1992, p. 212).

The Principle of Direct Evidence.   Clear, direct, and compelling evidence of the individual's personal capabilities and of environmental responsiveness is most helpful (and ultimately essential) in facilitating positive personal agency beliefs. Such evidence is best developed through efforts that explicitly focus on those components of the relevant personal agency beliefs that the person judge to be weak or negative. If a person has serious doubts about his or her capabilities for engaging in behaviors that are important for the attainment of a specific goal, the interventionist's demonstrating to that person that he or she in fact has those specific capabilities (for example, by having the person successfully engage in the requisite behaviors) is very likely to boost weak capability beliefs and the motivational power devoted to attaining the desired outcome. Similarly, if an environment is inaccurately judged to be arbitrary or untrustworthy, the interventionist's providing direct, personal evidence of its fairness and responsiveness can be an effective intervention strategy.

The Reality Principle.   There are some limits to motivational interventions. Nonmotivational components of the person-in-context system—skill, biological readiness, and responsive environment—are ultimately essential for the attainment of a goal. Motivation may, in some instances, compensate for deficits in the nonmotivational parts of the system by facilitating the individual's efforts to increase skills or to seek out responsive environments. For example, Will's academic aptitude was clearly essential for his eventual goal attainment. Moreover, when he depleted his facilitating environments, he simply moved to an environment that was facilitative. This example demonstrates the basic notion of the reality principle, namely, that personal agency beliefs eventually require real skills and a truly responsive environment for the person to attain the desired outcomes.

The Principle of Emotional Activation. This principle states that strong emotions are typically associated with strong motivational patterns and that the individual can use these emotions to shape and strengthen motivational patterns that are weakened by goal conflicts or weak personal agency beliefs. Will felt very strongly that his opportunities for experiencing satisfaction and success had been unnecessarily abridged by his parents' choice of his educational course and occupation. He felt that their choice implied a lack of confidence in his abilities, and this perception generated a strong emotional reaction that could be best summarized as "I'll show them!" When interventions are contemplated to help the person strengthen and support motivational patterns, the interventionist must understand that emotions represent essential motivational tools and that to view them as obstacles or distractions is to overlook a potent means of facilitating powerful motivational patterns.

The "Do It" Principle. Sometimes motivation can be weakened by unreasonably negative or conflictual self-evaluations that inhibit effective behavior. According to this principle, if the person is capable of producing the desired behaviors and really wants to do so, just getting the person to do *something* to get him or her going often works to help the person overcome motivational problems. This push can set a direction and provide the person some quick, positive feedback. It thus triggers more positive motivational patterns because the person is able to accomplish or make progress toward what he or she had grave doubts about prior to simply "doing it." Will found himself in a circumstance that involved significant negative self-evaluations when he first entered college in the United States; he found that he was not yet mastering the language skills that were needed. He was persuaded, nevertheless, to just proceed and to write the required essays and term papers, even though they were likely to be relatively unsatisfactory. By persisting in this "do it" mode, Will gradually obtained increasingly positive feedback and eventually the top grade in his advanced English composition class. The repeated application of this particular principle is instrumental in the individual's building exceptionally strong habits (behavior episode schemata) that can serve her or him very well under conditions of stress and anxiety (M. Ford, 1992).

The Principle of Incremental Versus Transformational Change. When motivational patterns are unproductive or unsatisfactory, either for reasons that reside within the person or for reasons that exist in the person's environment, a choice is often required. The person must decide whether incremental or gradual changes will be sufficient to produce the desired results or whether transformational changes are required. Will decided that a number of transformational changes were required in his career development, first, when he decided to give up his secure job as a tile setter in order to pursue his education and, later, when he decided to relinquish his administrative responsibilities as department head in his university in order to pursue teaching and research. In each instance, he judged that incremental change would be unlikely to produce the outcomes that were ultimately desired. Generally, however, it is assumed that incremental change offers a less risky and more reliable means of changing motivational patterns than does transformational change, which typically involves a process of disorganization–reorganization. M. Ford (1992) suggested that transformational changes should be attempted only when strong social support mechanisms or expert professional guidance are available to guide the individual through the process.

The Equifinality Principle. The equifinality principle is based on the recognition that there may be a variety of pathways that can ultimately lead to the desired outcomes. In practice, this means if one approach does not lead to the desired outcomes, another one may. The people and the contexts within which they operate are both so diverse that the idea of one single correct path or solution is highly improbable. Correspondingly, one particular way of motivating a person is unlikely to be the only correct or effective way. This suggests that if one way does not work, another way should be tried, one that may have a better chance of succeeding.

The Principle of Human Respect. This final principle of how to motivate people is based on the ideas that people like to be treated as unique individuals and that they like to believe their performance and behaviors can represent unique contributions, not only to themselves, but also to their organizations or communities. Treating people with respect facilitates goal alignment and enduring goal commitment and, therefore, satisfaction and success, that is, achievement and competence (see, e.g., Deci, 1980; Deci & Ryan, 1985; Maehr & Braskamp, 1986).

Using MST to Facilitate the Career Development of Adults

This presentation of M. Ford's (1992) 17 MST principles for motivating humans and their application to Will's career development suggest some ways in which they might be useful in interventions designed to facilitate adult career development. M. Ford (1992) presented a number of specific examples, showing how MST can be used to increase the individual's motivation for learning and school achievement, how it might be applied to the problem of helping people lead an emotionally healthy life, and how it might be instrumental in counselors' efforts to understand and facilitate the links between job satisfaction and work productivity. In this last aspect, which is most relevant for the topic of this chapter, Ford (1992) explained that the generally low correlation between job satisfaction and work productivity can very likely be the result of a widespread lack of alignment between the personal goals of employees and the goals of their employers that, in turn, results in a violation of the principle of goal alignment. He then noted that jobs can be organized and work environments structured so that such violations are avoided, worker motivation is enhanced, and the relationship between job satisfaction (i.e., helping workers to obtain desired outcomes as a result of their work) and work productivity (i.e., helping companies to obtain their objectives) is increased.

A comprehensive analysis of other ways in which MST can be useful in the design and implementation of interventions in adult career development is beyond our scope here. It should be clear, however, that career counselors who pursue adult career interventions from this perspective will proceed differently from those counselors who are guided by the normative frameworks discussed in the beginning of this chapter. Clearly, a stronger focus on understanding personal goals is in order, independent of the specific life stage that might characterize a person who is seeking intervention. Because work is conceptualized within a broader framework of human development, such goal assessment is not restricted to goals that are directly relevant to work and career; assessment can also focus on the core goals that individuals hold and pursue across different domains of functioning (M. Ford & Nichols, 1991; Nichols, 1991). Mindful of the fact that goals, emotions, and personal agency beliefs work in concert to orchestrate human motivation, as counselors we must also be careful to take into account the relevant capability beliefs, context beliefs, and emotional functioning in our efforts to assess goal content and goal hierarchies.

The specific means by which people are helped to formulate clear and compelling goals that are well aligned with one another and with the goals of important others, depend on the skills, training, and preferences of the interventionist, on the characteristics of those seeking help, and on the circumstances. Moreover, the same is true for efforts designed to help people change their goals, personal agency beliefs, or emotional functioning. The principle of equifinality asserts that there are usually multiple avenues by which we can achieve desired outcomes. It does make a difference, however, whether the intervention efforts are focused around the notion of helping individuals to negotiate stages that they are supposed to be passing through or whether individuals are empowered to choose their own futures based on goals they value and beliefs they can generate about their capabilities and opportunities for obtaining those goals. The latter option seems more appealing, and it is the goal of this chapter to stimulate others to think along these lines and to further develop these notions in the field of adult career development.

ACKNOWLEDGMENTS

The authors are grateful to Donald H. Ford, Martin E. Ford, and Robert B. Slaney for insightful comments on an earlier draft of this chapter.

REFERENCES

Bandura, A. (1977). Self-efficacy: Toward a unifying theory of behavior change. *Psychological Review, 84,* 191–215.

Bandura, A. (1982). Self-efficacy mechanism in human agency. *American Psychologist, 37,* 122–147.

Bandura, A. (1984). Recycling misconceptions of perceived self-efficacy. *Cognitive Therapy and Research, 8,* 231–255.

Betz, N. E., & Hackett, G. (1986). Applications of self-efficacy theory to understanding career choice behavior. *Journal of Social and Clinical Psychology, 4,* 279–289.

Bromley, D. B. (1990). *Behavioural gerontology: Central issues in the psychology of aging.* New York: Wiley.

Bujold, C. (1990). Biographical–hermeneutical approaches to the study of career development. In R. A. Young & W. A. Borgen (Eds.), *Methodological approaches to the study of career* (pp. 57–69). New York: Praeger.

Campbell, R. E., & Heffernan, J. M. (1983). Adult vocational behavior. In W. B. Walsh & S. H. Osipow (Eds.), *Handbook of vocational psychology: Vol. 1. Foundations* (pp. 223–260). Hillsdale, NJ: Lawrence Erlbaum Associates.

Cochran, L. R. (1990). Narrative as a paradigm for career research. In R. A. Young & W. A. Borgen (Eds.), *Methodological approaches to the study of career* (pp. 71–86). New York: Praeger.

Crites, J. O. (1969). *Vocational psychology.* New York: McGraw–Hill.

Crites, J. O. (1976). A comprehensive model of career development in early adulthood. *Journal of Vocational Behavior, 9,* 105–118.

Dannefer, D. (1992). On the conceptualization of context in developmental discourse: Four meanings of context and their implications. In D. V. Featherman, R. M. Lerner, & M. Perlmutter (Eds.), *Life-span development and behavior* (Vol. 2, pp. 83–109). Hillsdale, NJ: Lawrence Erlbaum Associates.

Dawis, R. V., & Lofquist, L. H. (1984). *A psychological theory of work adjustment: An individual differences model and its applications.* Minneapolis: University of Minnesota Press.

Deci, E. L. (1980). *The psychology of self-determination.* Lexington, MA: Lexington.

Deci, E. L., & Ryan, R. M. (1985). *Intrinsic motivation and self-determination in human behavior.* New York: Plenum.

Erikson, E. H. (1950). *Childhood and society.* New York: Norton.

Erikson, E. H. (1963). *Childhood and society* (2nd ed.). New York: Norton.

Ford, D. H. (1987). *Humans as self-constructing living systems: A developmental perspective on personality and behavior.* Hillsdale, NJ: Lawrence Erlbaum Associates.

Ford, D. H., & Lerner, R. M. (1992). *Developmental systems theory: An integrative approach.* Newbury Park, CA: Sage.

Ford, M. E. (1987). Overview of the heuristic utility of the Living Systems Framework for guiding research and professional activities. In M. E. Ford & D. H. Ford (Eds.), *Humans as self-constructing living systems: Putting the framework to work* (pp. 377–393). Hillsdale, NJ: Lawrence Erlbaum Associates.

Ford, M. E. (1992). *Motivating humans: Goals, emotions, and personal agency beliefs.* Newbury Park, CA: Sage.

Ford, M. E., & Ford, D. H. (Eds.). (1987). *Humans as self-constructing living systems: Putting the framework to work.* Hillsdale, NJ: Lawrence Erlbaum Associates.

Ford, M. E., & Nichols, C. W. (1991). Using goal assessments to identify motivational patterns and facilitate behavioral regulation and achievement. In M. L. Maehr & P. R. Pintrich (Eds.), *Advances in motivation and achievement* (Vol. 7, pp. 51–84). Greenwich, CT: JAI.

Hackett, G., & Betz, N. E. (1981). A self-efficacy approach to the career development of women. *Journal of Vocational Behavior, 18,* 326–339.

Hackett, G., & Lent, R. W. (1992). Theoretical advances and current inquiry in career psychology. In S. D. Brown & R. W. Lent (Eds.), *Handbook of counseling psychology* (2nd ed., pp. 419–451). New York: Wiley.

Havighurst, R. J. (1952). *Developmental tasks and education* (2nd ed.). New York: Longmans, Green, & Company.

Holland, J. L. (1985). *Making vocational choices: A theory of vocational personalities and work environments* (2nd ed.). Englewood Cliffs, NJ: Prentice–Hall.

Krumboltz, J. D., Mitchell, A. M., & Jones, G. B. (1980). A social learning theory of career selection. In T. L. Wentling (Ed.), *Annual review of research in vocational education* (Vol. 1, pp. 259–282). Urbana: University of Illinois Press.

Krumboltz, J. D., & Nichols, C. W. (1990). Integrating the social learning theory of career decision making. In W. B. Walsh & S. H. Osipow (Eds.), *Career counseling: Contemporary topics in vocational psychology* (pp. 159–192). Hillsdale, NJ: Lawrence Erlbaum Associates.

Lent, R. W., & Hackett, G. (1987). Career self-efficacy: Empirical status and future directions [Monograph]. *Journal of Vocational Behavior, 30,* 347–382.

Lerner, R. M. (1978). Nature, nurture, and dynamic interactionism. *Human Development, 21,* 1–20.

Lerner, R. M. (1989). Developmental contextualism and the life-span view of person–context interaction. In M. Bornstein & J. S. Bruner (Eds.), *Interaction in human development* (pp. 217–239). Hillsdale, NJ: Lawrence Erlbaum Associates.

Levinson, D. J. (1986). A conception of adult development. *American Psychologist, 41,* 3–13.

Levinson, D. J., Darrow, C. N., Klein, E. B., Levinson, M. H., & McKee, B. (1978). *The seasons of a man's life.* New York: Knopf.

Locke, E. A., & Latham, G. P. (1990). (Eds.). *A theory of goal setting and task performance.* Englewood Cliffs, NJ: Prentice–Hall.

Maehr, M. L., & Braskamp, L. (1986). *The motivation factor: A theory of personal investment.* Lexington, MA: Lexington.

Miller, D. C., & Form, W. H. (1951). *Industrial sociology: An introduction to the sociology of work reactions.* New York: Harper & Row.

Miller, D. C., & Form, W. H. (1964). *Industrial sociology: The sociology of work organizations.* New York: Harper & Row.

Nesselroade, J. R., & Ford, D. H. (1987). Methodological considerations in modeling living systems. In M. E. Ford & D. H. Ford (Eds.), *Humans as self-constructing living systems: Putting the framework to work* (pp. 47–79). Hillsdale, NJ: Lawrence Erlbaum Associates.

Nichols, C. W. (1991). *Manual: Assessment of core goals.* Palo Alto, CA: Consulting Psychologists Press.

Osipow, S. H. (1983). *Theories of career development* (3rd ed.). Englewood Cliffs, NJ: Prentice–Hall.

Pryor, R. G. L. (1981). *Manual for the Work Aspect Preference Scale.* New South Wales: D. West, Government Printer.

Rounds, J. B., & Tracey, T. J. (1990). From trait-and-factor to person–environment fit counseling: Theory and process. In W. B. Walsh & S. H. Osipow (Eds.), *Career counseling* (pp. 1–44). Hillsdale, NJ: Lawrence Erlbaum Associates.

Schein, E. H. (1978). *Career dynamics: Matching individual and organizational needs.* Reading, MA: Addison–Wesley.

Spokane, A. R. (1987). (Ed.). Conceptual and methodological issues in person–environment fit research [Special Issue]. *Journal of Vocational Behavior, 31*, 217–221.

Super, D. E. (1957). *The psychology of careers.* New York: Harper & Row.

Super, D. E. (1963). Vocational development in adolescence and early adulthood: Tasks and behaviors. In D. E. Super, R. Starishevsky, N. Matlin, & J. P. Jordan (Eds.), *Career development: Self-concept theory* (Research Monograph No. 4). New York: College Entrance Examination Board.

Super, D. E. (1981). A developmental theory: Implementing a self-concept. In D. H. Montross & C. J. Shinkman (Eds.), *Career development in the 1980s: Theory and practice* (pp. 28–42). Springfield, IL: Thomas.

Super, D. E. (1985). Coming of age in Middletown: Careers in the making. *American Psychologist, 40*, 405–414.

Super, D. E. (1990). Career and life development. In D. Brown & L. Brooks (Eds.), *Career choice and development* (2nd ed., pp. 197–261). San Francisco: Jossey–Bass.

Super, D. E., & Hall, D. T. (1978). Career development: Exploration and planning. *Annual Review of Psychology, 29*, 333–372.

Super, D. E., & Overstreet, P. L. (1960). *The vocational maturity of ninth grade boys.* New York: Teachers College Press.

Thomae, H., & Lehr, U. (1986). Stages, crises, conflicts, and life-span development. In A. B. Sorensen, F. E. Weinert, & I. R. Sherrod (Eds.), *Human development and the life course: Multidisciplinary perspectives* (pp. 429–444). Hillsdale, NJ: Lawrence Erlbaum Associates.

Vaillant, G. E. (1977). *Adaptation to life.* Boston: Little, Brown.

Vondracek, F. W., Lerner, R. M., & Schulenberg, J. E. (1986). *Career development: A life span developmental approach.* Hillsdale, NJ: Lawrence Erlbaum Associates.

Winell, M. (1987). Personal goals: The key to self-direction in adulthood. In M. E. Ford & D. H. Ford (Eds.), *Humans as self-constructing living systems: Putting the framework to work* (pp. 261–287). Hillsdale, NJ: Lawrence Erlbaum Associates.

CHAPTER FIVE

Theoretical Issues in Cross-Cultural Career Development: Cultural Validity and Cultural Specificity

Frederick T. L. Leong
Ohio State University

Michael T. Brown
University of California, Santa Barbara

HISTORY AND DEVELOPMENT
OF ETHNIC MINORITY PSYCHOLOGY

Within the field of psychology, there have been two parallel approaches with regard to the relevance of our theories and research for culturally different individuals (defined by D. W. Sue and D. Sue, 1990, as Americans who are not of European descent). The earlier approach was strongly influenced by anthropology and is referred to as cross-cultural psychology (Berry, Poortinga, Segall, & Dasen, 1992). This approach is characterized by a concern with the generalizability of laws underlying the behavior of European Americans to persons of other cultures or countries. From the perspective of this approach, European Americans constitute the majority in the United States and, in the framework of Tyler, Brome, and Williams (1991), are the culture-defining group (i.e., their values and beliefs dominate much of American society). The approach further reflects the tendency of anthropologists to use countries as their units of analysis (e.g., Mead's *Coming of Age in Samoa*, 1928). As a result, cross-cultural psychologists have expressed interest, for example, in whether the inverse cuvilinear relationship between anxiety and performance found in the United States exists in another country, like Japan, and what cultural factors in Japan may account for observed differences in the relationship. As the example illustrates, the dual goals of cross-cultural psychologists were and continue to be the discovery of the universal and the culture-specific in human behavior.

The second development, influenced by sociology, has been concerned with racial and ethnic minority issues. It is no accident that much of the sociology practiced in the United States has been concerned with subgroups within this country regardless of whether the subgroups are the effects of social stratification or the antecedents of income inequities. Like sociology, ethnic-minority psychology has tended to use racial and ethnic groups in this country as their primary units of analysis. As such, psychologists who study ethnic minorities have focused on understanding, for example, why racial and ethnic minorities are segregated into certain occupational clusters and the role of race in observed patterns of intergenerational occupational mobility. The approach assumes that race and ethnicity are powerful social-psychological categories and have significant consequences associated with them.

There are similarities and differences between these two approaches. In both approaches, researchers seek to study the nature and scope of culture's influence on the behavior of culturally different individuals, whether those individuals live in different countries or are ethnic minority members in the same country. Furthermore, some of the variables used in both approaches cut across the different levels of analyses. For example, cultural values and intergroup dynamics are central to both approaches. Yet, there are differences in the two approaches. The cross-cultural psychology approach is much more influenced by the *etic* perspective, which focuses on identifying universal laws of behavior across disparate cultural groups (e.g., schizophrenia is universal and found in all cultures). The cross-racial–cross-ethnic approach is much more concerned with an *emic* perspective, which focuses on culturally unique factors in the experiences of persons in each ethnic group that causes them to behave in certain ways.

In order to increase the understanding of the career development of culturally different individuals in this country and elsewhere, it is important that both approaches be pursued and the results integrated. In attempting this integration, we have reviewed the literature in cross-cultural psychology and cross-cultural counseling, particularly as they pertain to the career development and vocational behavior of culturally different individuals in this country. As we reviewed this literature, it became clear to us that cultural validity and cultural specificity are two dimensions that can serve as components of a unifying theoretical framework for cross-cultural career development. Cultural validity is concerned with the construct, concurrent, and predictive validity of theories and models across other cultures, that is, for culturally different individuals. For example, Holland's (1985a) concept of congruence has been found to be predictive of job satisfaction among White Americans. Is it also predictive of job satisfaction for African Americans or Asian Americans? Cultural specificity is concerned with concepts, constructs, and models that are specific to certain cultural groups in terms of its role in explaining and predicting behavior. For example, is colorism, or level of melanin in the skin, of African Americans a variable in vocational behavior?

Before we proceed to a description of these two dimensions, let us clarify our position on the confusing terminology with regard to *multicultural* versus *cross-cultural* career development. Although both terms are often used interchangeably, we believe that the latter, *cross-cultural*, is more appropriate. The former, *multicultural*, has evolved from the recognition that the United States is increasingly becoming multicultural (i.e., a nation of many cultures). When the term *multicultural*, however, is applied to either career development or career counseling, it fails to adequately describe the science. Literally, the study of multicultural career development is concerned with the study of career development in many cultures. The same is true with multicultural career counseling, with the implication being that counselors are concerned with career counseling in many different cultures. Most of the theories and research in vocational psychology, however, are concerned with cross-cultural career development and cross-cultural career counseling. For example, the majority of the studies of the career development of African Americans is concerned with how this racial group behaves and adjusts in a European-American work environment and society; that is, the studies are primarily cross-cultural studies. Moreover, when the study of the career counseling process involves, for example, Hispanic Americans, researchers are trying to understand how a White counselor or an Asian American counselor might interact with that Hispanic American client. We belabor this point because it is important to be clear in the use of our terminology when referring to our knowledge base. Vocational psychologists have been and continue to be concerned with cross-cultural career development (e.g., Why are Asian Americans segregated into the scientific and technical occupations in the United States?) and cross-cultural career counseling (e.g., How should a White counselor approach an African-American client?).

In recognition of the two dimensions of cultural validity and cultural specificity, we have organized this chapter along these theoretical lines. The chapter is further divided into six sections. This first section is concerned with a brief historical perspective. The next two sections are concerned with the cultural validity dimension. In the second section, in keeping with other authors (e.g., E. Smith, 1983), we provide a critique of majority career theories from a cultural-validity perspective. The central problem with most, if not all of the majority career theories is their lack of cultural validity for racial and ethnic minorities in this country. We discuss this lack of cultural validity from conceptual and empirical points of view. In the third section, we review the status of tests of the cultural validity of those career-choice theories for racial and ethnic minority individuals. In the fourth section, we make the transition from the issue of cultural validity to cultural specificity. If majority theories lack cultural validity, then what they lack are culture-specific considerations (e.g., African-American racial identity as it pertains to vocational behavior). The fourth section is concerned with culture-specific theories and their relation to ethnic minority career development. In addressing the cultural specificity dimension, we highlight the role of culture-specific constructs, such as acculturation among Asian Americans, in the vocational behavior of culturally different individuals. The fifth section, also concerned with cultural specificity, provides a comparative perspective. We review comparative culture studies of career development to illustrate how ethnic minorities are different from and similar to European Americans. The sixth and final section is a discussion of the directions for future research and theory development.

ETHNIC MINORITY CRITIQUES
OF MAJORITY CAREER THEORIES

Scholars have observed that current theories of career development are underdeveloped (D. Brown, 1990; Hackett & Lent, 1992). Most scientists recognize that a broad range of career behavior is being exhibited by an increasingly diverse populace but that career development theories currently cover a much narrower band of this behavior (Gottfredson, 1986; Hackett & Lent, 1992; E. Smith, 1983; Warnath, 1975). A better accounting of the career behavior of culturally diverse persons would represent a significant advance in the field.

General Criticisms of Current Theories
From a Cross-Cultural Perspective

Four major and interrelated criticisms have plagued current career-choice theories and have led some scholars either to dismiss the theories as models for understanding the career behavior of diverse groups or to call for rearticulations that would render them more cross-culturally relevant (cf. Brooks, 1991; E. Smith, 1983). (1) The theories are based on a restricted range of persons. (2) The theories are based on assumptions of limited scope. (3) When cross-cultural perspectives are introduced, terms such as *race, ethnicity,* and *minority* are confused or inappropriately defined. (4) The theories tend to ignore or to limitedly address the sociopolitical, socioeconomic, social-psychological, and sociocultural realities of cross-cultural individuals.

The criticism that most theories of career development are based on research conducted on primarily White, middle-class men appears incontestable. Consider Super's (1953) "Middletown" study, Holland's (1959) early theoretical articulation, and Roe's (1951a, 1951b, 1953) study of eminent scientists. Though some researchers (e.g., Carter & Cook, 1992; Cheatham, 1990; E. Smith, 1975, 1983) have therefore concluded that the theories are inapplicable to cross-cultural others, the conclusion may be untimely, given the paucity and inadequacy of the research testing the theories that have used diverse research samples (M. Brown, in press). The conclusion also ignores those findings demonstrating that at least some concepts drawn from extant theories have found demonstrable empirical support when applied to some diverse populations (see, e.g., M. Brown's, in press, review). Nonetheless, the cross-cultural usefulness of most theoretical concepts remains to be demonstrated.

As many critics (e.g., Arbona, in press; Brooks, 1991; M. Brown, in press; Gottfredson, 1986; Osipow, 1983; E. Smith, 1983; Warnath, 1975) have observed, most theories of career choice make five assumptions, the validity of which appears particularly suspect when considered from a cross-cultural perspective: Career development is continuous, uninterrupted, and progressive; decision makers possess the psychological, social, and economic means of affecting their choices; there is dignity in all work; there exists a free and open labor market; and most career choices flow essentially from internal (viz., personality) factors. Although these assumptions have been reviewed in detail elsewhere (e.g., M. Brown, in press; E. Smith, 1983) and have been found not to apply to many diverse ethnic group persons, it is useful to highlight one of them here. The assumption that people possess the means necessary to effect their choices is patently absurd, given the preponderance of data indicating that many diverse groups, including women and ethnic minorities, are poor, uneducated, and often the lone providers for their families (cf. Arbona, 1990, in press; M. Brown, in press; Johnson, Swartz, & Martin, in press; Leong, 1985, in press; Leong & Serafica, in press; Martin, 1991).

In regard to the criticism that scholars have confused the terms *race*, *ethnic*, and *minority*, Axelson (1985) and E. Smith (1983) have pointed out that such a practice can lead to illogical and erroneous conclusions. The term *race* is meant to refer to a group of persons categorized on the basis of distinctive physical characteristics of supposed genetic origin (cf. Axelson, 1985); the validity of such a classification system has yet to be demonstrated (Axelson, 1985). The term *minority* is customarily used to refer to the relative numerical size of a cultural group but has also been used to refer to the relative standing of certain groups with respect to political and economic power. It has been argued that the term, by definition, compares persons in minorities in a diminutive fashion to a European-American standard, the presumed cultural majority in this country, and thus contributes to disempowering them (cf. Cook & Helms, 1988). The term *ethnic* refers to a group of persons who can be identified on the basis of social, cultural, and psychological characteristics such as language, customs, beliefs, and religion (cf. Axelson, 1985; E. Smith, 1983); such groups may include persons of visibly different characteristics. We argue that terms such as *ethnic group* and *cultural group* are preferred.

The fourth criticism, that current theories ignore the sociopolitical, socioeconomic, social-psychological, and sociocultural influences of many diverse groups, has essentially been addressed. We must not forget, however, the fundamental implication of all four criticisms; that is, the mechanisms of career choice among various culturally diverse groups may well operate on the basis of influences not yet addressed by current theories (Cheatham, 1990; Gottfredson, 1986; Leonard, 1985; Leong, 1985; E. Smith, 1983).

The Absence of a Comprehensive Model of Cross-Cultural Career Development

Given the long-standing and serious nature of the criticisms leveled at existing theories of career choice, it is critical that a viable, comprehensive, and culturally pertinent career-choice theory be produced. To be sure, a number of the dominant and contemporary theories have acknowledged the role of ethnicity and socioeconomic status (cf. Gottfredson, 1981; Holland, 1985; Roe & Lunneborg, 1991; Super, 1990). Perhaps more significant, Cheatham (1990) proposed a model of African-American career development. Still, besides the efforts just described and those of a few other scholars (Arbona, 1990, in press; M. Brown, in press; Leonard, 1985; Leong, 1985, in press; Leong & Serafica, in press; Johnson et al., in press; Martin, 1991) who have attempted to identify the salient variables affecting the career development of various ethnic group members, no comprehensive model of the career development of the culturally different currently exists (Hackett & Lent, 1992).

What does exist, though, is a literature, pejoratively termed *special groups literature* (Gottfredson, 1986), that uniformly and unequivocally condemns poverty and unfair discriminatory social practices for observed ethnic group differences in education, occupation, and income. Those joint processes are blamed for unfairly shaping the opportunity structure to the advantage of a few cultural groups and to the disadvantage of many others. As Gottfredson (1986) rightly points out, however, there is yet to appear a detailed description and explanation of how political, social, economic, and cultural conditions affect individuals and their career-choice behavior. Furthermore, the literature can also be criticized for narrowly focusing on one group at a time and ignoring the similar concerns of other diverse groups; assuming or overemphasizing differences between cultural groups and, ironically, reinforcing stereotypes as a result; inappropriately mixing levels of analysis in blaming macrolevel processes, like societal racism, for microlevel individual reactions, like dropping out of school; and falsely assuming that culturally relevant variables, like a group's orientation toward community survival versus rugged individualism, function *only* to the advantage of group members and that society is solely to blame for group members' negative experiences (see Gottfredson, 1986, for a discussion of many of these criticisms). Regarding this last point, Thomas and Sillen (1972) cautioned over two decades ago that recognizing the social circumstances that can impede the fulfillment of an individual's potential is much different from and preferable to concluding that those circumstances have severely and irreparably disabled the person.

Detailed Critique of Current Career Development Theories From a Cross-Cultural Perspective

Given the current omissions in and inaccuracies of the contemporary literature on cross-cultural career development, vocational psychologists are left with the alternative of using what is currently known about the culturally different to examine existing career theories and, thereby, determining the extent to which those theories may apply to those persons. Such an examining follows. Also presented is a conceptual analysis of what is missing from those theories that may render them more relevant to the career behavior of multicultural populations. For the purposes of this discussion, the following theories were selected: trait-and-factor theory (as reviewed by D. Brown, 1991), Holland's (1985) theory, Roe's theory (as revised in Roe & Lunneborg, 1991), Super's (1992) theory, Hackett and Betz's (1981) career self-efficacy theory, Gottfredson's (1981) developmental theory of aspirations, and Cheatham's (1990) model of Africentricity and career development.

Trait-and-Factor Theory. The essence of trait-and-factor theory lies in the following four propositions (D. Brown, 1991): Each individual has a unique set of traits that can be reliably and validly measured; occupations require individuals to possess certain traits in order to be successful in those occupations; it is possible and desirable to match a person's unique set of traits to those required by occupations; the closer the match between personal characteristics and those required by an occupation, the greater the likelihood of satisfaction with productivity and tenure in the occupation. D. Brown stated that the theory is as applicable to the culturally different as it is to European-American men, but no cross-cultural test of these propositions has been uncovered.

Contrary to D. Brown's (1991) opinion, the propositions pose problems that limit the extent to which trait-and-factor theory may be useful in the understanding of cross-cultural career development. M. Brown (in press) has addressed these criticisms in detail elsewhere, but two are discussed for their instructional value. Research regarding the proposition that occupations require a person to possess certain traits in order to be successful in them has not addressed whether all cultural groups are required to have the same sets of traits. Consider the work of Edwards and Polite (1992), who developed a profile of successful African Americans. On the basis of their research, they discovered some elements of success that are likely to be relevant to European Americans, such as faith and personal responsibility, but others that are likely to be relevant only to certain ethnic groups, such as transcendence of a racial-victim perspective and managing others' racial perceptions and reactions.

Similarly, the proposition that the closer the match is between individual traits and those traits required by the occupation, the greater is the likelihood of individual success may not generalize to some ethnic groups. The issue has yet to be explored for most ethnic groups. It is well known, however, that psychological measures account for 36% of the variance in performance ratings, at best (D. Brown, 1991); consequently, 64% of performance-rating variance must be determined by other factors. Could factors like those identified by Edwards and Polite (1992) account for some of this unexplained variance?

The previous discussion notwithstanding, it is premature to dismiss trait-and-factor theory as irrelevant to the career behavior of the culturally different, given the dearth of well-controlled, well-designed research testing the validity of trait–factor notions to the career behavior of such persons. Nonetheless, D. Brown's (1991) conclusion that the theory is likely to apply equally well to ethnically diverse individuals is unwarranted.

Holland's Theory. An extension of trait-and-factor theory, Holland's (1985a) theory asserts that people seek work environments that allow them to express their constellation of six personality types: realistic, investigative, artistic, social, enterprising, and conventional. In addition, Holland argued that a range of "isms" (i.e., ageism, classism, racism, sexism) restrict the range of career options available to people and that if persons are blocked from pursuing the expression of the most dominant aspects of their personalities, they will pursue the next most dominant feature. Holland, however, failed to articulate what the implications of experiencing restricted options for an extended period of time may be for personality development; this is the historic experience of many ethnic groups.

One of the major predictions from Holland's (1985a) theory is that persons in different occupations should also evidence different patterns of interests. A number of studies have demonstrated support for this assertion for African Americans (for a review of this literature, see M. Brown, in press), but the prediction has not been studied sufficiently with respect to other ethnic groups.

Regarding personality orientation research, Osipow (1975) suggested that the occupational environments described by Holland (1985a) may not be equally available to ethnic minorities, with many poor African Americans becoming channeled into low-level, realistic jobs. A number of findings (e.g., Arbona, 1989; Gottfredson, 1978; Miller, Springer, & Wells, 1988) support Osipow's assertion for African Americans, but little corroborated evidence exists for other ethnic groups. In the same vein, Leong and Serafica (in press) have pointed out that Holland's theory does not address the role of culture in creating and sustaining environments.

Another major aspect of Holland's (1985a) theory is the notion of person–environmental fit, or congruence. Empirical support for the congruence concept is plentiful with respect to African-American populations, though some evidence indicates that African Americans and other ethnic groups may experience lower congruence relative to European Americans because of real and perceived employment barriers (for a review, see M. Brown, in press).

The Holland (1985a) concepts of differentiation and consistency have not been well investigated for validity with multicultural populations. On the other hand, there are a few corroborated studies that support the relevance of the hexagonal structure to depict the responses of African Americans, Mexican Americans, and Native Americans in terms of Holland types (Henry, 1988; Lamb, 1976, cited in Leong & Serafica, in press).

Although much more study is needed, apparently some of Holland's (1985a) propositions have been found to generalize to African-American populations. Other ethnic groups, however, have not been sufficiently studied. More research with African Americans and other ethnic groups is needed, particularly with respect to the Holland concepts of congruence, consistency, differentiation, and identity.

Roe's Theory. Roe (Roe, 1956; Roe & Klos, 1972; Roe & Lunneborg, 1991) made two major contributions to the career development literature: a psychologically based classification system of occupations and a theory of the effects of personality development on occupational choice. In her classification system, Roe proposed that the range of occupations can be ordered along a continuum based on the intensity and nature of the interpersonal relationships involved in the occupational activities and hierarchically on the basis of the degree of responsibility, capacity, and skill involved in each occupation. No specific test of Roe's structure of occupations with culturally different populations could be located. Roe and Lunneborg (1991) indicated, however, that the classification system does not address "minority issues" (p. 80). Roe and Lunneborg (1991) did not specify those minority issues, but it is clear that the occupational categories fail to consider the occupational segregation of many ethnic group members (cf. Leong, in press).

As for the effects of personality development, Roe (1956; Roe & Lunneborg, 1991) proposed that genetic endowments combine with family background and childrearing experiences to shape individual need structures that, in turn, affect the level and kind of occupation chosen and pursued. In discussing the impact of cultural diversity on occupational choice and opportunity, Roe suggested that social, rather than physical (genetic), differences may account for ethnic differences in career-choice behavior (see Roe, 1956, pp. 57–58). Recently (see Roe & Klos, 1972; Roe & Lunneborg, 1991), Roe stated that an individual's belonging to a minority group may significantly affect his or her career choices, with the determining issue being the extent to which the an individual's social and experiential background differs from that of the majority. Although no specific test of Roe's assertions could be located, a number of questions surfaced that concern the suitability of her proposal for the understanding of cross-cultural career behavior. For example, is it possible to measure the social and experiential difference between various ethnic groups and the cultural majority? If so, what is the relationship between the social–experiential difference of various ethnic groups and occupational need structure?

Concerning the link between parent–child relations and occupational choice, Roe and Lunneborg (1991) concluded that the available evidence does not support a direct relationship; it is important to note, however, that Roe (1956; Roe & Lunneborg, 1991) never appeared to postulate such a relationship (see M. Brown, in press). Nonetheless, it is generally concluded that occupations are distinguishable on the basis of their need-satisfying properties (cf. Dawis & Lofquist, 1984; Osipow, 1983), just as Roe (1956; Roe & Lunneborg, 1991) posited. Nevertheless, no extensive study of the relationship between needs and occupational choice for multicultural populations exists.

There are some other conceptual issues concerning Roe's (1956; Roe & Lunneborg, 1991) theory that also need exploration. Roe stated that genetic inheritance sets limits on all characteristics, especially intellectual abilities and temperament, and that these characteristics affect level of occupational attainment. The protracted controversy surrounding ability testing (cf. Gottfredson, 1986; Helms, 1992) reveals that ethnic differences that are prevalent in measured abilities are difficult to interpret. It is also unclear whether or not culturally relevant abilities, such as those identified by Edwards and Polite (1992), affect occupational-choice behavior.

Super's Theory. Super (1991) proposed that the self-concept determines occupational choices and that both the self-concept and the manner in which it is implemented vary as a function of stage of development. Many scholars contend, however, that discrimination and poverty are more important determinants of the career choices of many ethnic groups (cf. Carter & Cook, 1992; Leong & Serafica, in press; Osipow, 1975; E. Smith, 1983). Super acknowledged the effects of race and socioeconomic status on career development but failed to elaborate on the manner of their operation (cf. June & Pringle, 1977). Further, Super countered criticisms of his theory by citing the research of Kidd (1984) and Salomone and Slaney (1978), which supports the role of the self-concept in the occupational choices of the economically disadvantaged. Notwithstanding, the relationship between the self-concept and career behavior has yet to be systematically investigated with multicultural populations.

Also, Super (1991) failed to address the manner in which discrimination and poverty may alter the self-concept, though such literature exists in related fields. Ogbu (1992; Ogbu & Matute–Bianchi, 1986), writing in the fields of anthropology and education, suggested that in reaction to discrimination and oppression, which they believe to be inescapable and insurmountable, and in an effort to maintain a positive sense of self, many ethnic group members develop a cultural identity in which the behaviors, events, symbols, and even meanings that are viewed as characteristic of the oppressors (i.e., European Americans) are considered inappropriate for them and are therefore rejected. The possible impact of Ogbu's assertion for the career-choice behavior of certain ethnic group members has yet to be explored. The essential point here is that culturally relevant experiences, not unlike any other personal experience, can introduce factors affecting the nature and development of the self-concept. Leong and Serafica (in press) suggested that the individual's readiness to cope with developmental tasks and the role that self-concept may play in cross-cultural career development can vary, depending on the degree of the person's acculturation. Super (1991), though, did not incorporate these observations into his theory.

Super (1991) argued, however, that socioeconomic status has a two-fold effect on career development: the opening and closing of career opportunities and the shaping of occupational concepts and self-concepts. Similarly, it may be that the experience of ethnic discrimination not only restricts the ranges and types of opportunity, as most authors have commonly asserted, but also shapes occupational concept and self-concept. The role of socioeconomic status and discrimination on occupational concepts and self-concept has yet to be investigated. Super and Bohn observed (1970) that discrimination appears to operate in the same way as socioeconomic handicaps do: motivating some people to overcome them, deterring others from trying, and preventing others who do try from achieving (cf. June & Pringle, 1977). This observation has merit because one of the problems with the literature on career development of ethnic minorities is the assumption that all individuals react to discrimination and poverty in the same way, and always in a way that is detrimental. Super (1991), however, failed to articulate the developmental antecedents that may account for these three patterns of occupational behavior.

Super's (1991) assertions that there exist definable stages of career development and that the implementation of self-concept varies as a function of stage of development are ideas that have not been validated with the various ethnic groups in this country. Also, Super's career-maturity concept has been criticized because it is correlated with socioeconomic status and, because certain ethnic groups occupy the lower socioeconomic strata, the concept is viewed as culturally biased (cf. E. Smith, 1975, 1983). Super (1991), in any case, dismissed the correlations as too low to be of practical significance. E. Smith (1983) also argued that career-maturity researchers erroneously assumed that career-maturity inventories measure vocational tasks common to all ethnic groups. Smith proposed that a person's minority status may add additional tasks not taken into account, such as coming to terms with how ethnic bias can affect their career development or developing discrimination-coping strategies (refer also to the work of Edwards & Polite, 1992). The concept of career maturity, then, may need to be revised and reassessed with respect to different cultural groups.

It is currently unknown if differences in the self-concept of members of various ethnic groups and in the manner of its vocational implementation actually occur over time in the manner posited by Super (1991). Research is much needed in this area. It should be noted that as early as 1975, Osipow (1975) argued that Super's stages did not fit the career reality of poor African-American men (e.g., early labor force entry, series of unrelated jobs, sporadic periods of unemployment) and suggested that occupational entry is a reactive rather than a proactive process as Super assumed. Further, Arbona (in press) argued recently that Super's theory may be relevant, chiefly to those ethnic group individuals who are from the middle class and who are college educated.

TESTING THE CULTURAL VALIDITY OF MAJORITY THEORIES FOR CULTURALLY DIFFERENT GROUPS

This section is concerned with the logical extension of the historical and contemporary critiques of majority career theories, namely, the testing of the cultural validity of the majority theories for ethnic minorities. At this point in theory development and testing, it is too early for a definitive determination as to when the majority theories apply to the career development of various cultural groups. Arbona's (in press) position may be the most tenable: To the extent that ethnic group members are middle-class and college-educated persons, the available theories may likely be relevant. Poignantly, every theorist, whose theory has been reviewed here, has indicated, either explicitly or implicitly, that the defining issue determining the cross-cultural relevance of the theories is the degree to which any individual differs from the cultural majority. Herein lies the major criticism to be leveled at the theories, with the exception of Cheatham's (1990) model (described later): The theories have failed to identify relevant dimensions of cultural difference that may help psychologists gauge an individual's level of difference from the cultural majority and that may enable psychologists to understand the assortment of factors that affect the person's career-choice behavior. Although absent from the models just evaluated, these factors are not absent from the general empirical and theoretical literature. A review of a number of the most salient dimensions follows. Before we begin the review, we must first state that current theories are not likely to be salvageable as models of the career-choice behavior of culturally different persons once culturally relevant dimensions are integrated into those perspectives. Those models will always be limited, by definition, given the limited scope of dimensions that they were crafted to address. For example, if new and culturally relevant personality dimensions were identified and incorporated into Holland's (1985a) theory, what would become of the Holland hexagon?

Empirical study of the cultural validity of most of the majority theories for ethnic minorities is quite limited, but there are two recent majority theories that show some promise in their relevance to ethnic groups' experiences. The first is career self-efficacy theory, which is an extension of Bandura's (1986) theory to career development; the second is Gottfredson's (1981) circumscription and compromise theory.

Career Self-Efficacy

The career self-efficacy construct (Betz & Hackett, 1986) appears to offer substantial promise in furthering the understanding of career development of the diverse groups. Based on the work of Bandura (1977, 1986), the theory states that career self-efficacy expectations are beliefs about one's own ability to successfully perform occupationally relevant behaviors and that these expectations determine one's actions, effort, and persistence in regard to the behaviors. As Bandura (1977) initially proposed, outcome expectations, which are personal beliefs about the results of performance, operate independently from efficacy expectations and are dependent on actual performance, which, in turn, stems from efficacy expectations.

Recently, Lent and Hackett (1987) asserted that the construct of self-efficacy may be useful in explaining the career behavior of ethnic minorities. A few studies have recently tested this assertion, mostly with African-American populations, with generally positive results (e.g., Dawkins, 1981; Hackett, Betz, Casas, & Rocha–Singh, 1992; Post, Stewart, & P. Smith, 1991; Post–Kammer & P. Smith, 1986; cf. Arbona, in press).

Although the role of efficacy expectations has been implicated in the career behavior of African Americans and Mexican Americans, much more research is needed, research that addresses the three key questions posed by Hackett and Betz (1981) with a particular focus on diverse ethnic groups. For example, to what extent do efficacy expectations affect the perceived range of academic and occupational options, the effectiveness of career decision making, and the person's academic achievement? If self-efficacy is found to play a major role in the career behavior of multicultural populations, then another set of important questions concerns whether and to what extent the self-efficacy expectations of various cultural groups are modifiable through career intervention.

Some theoretical refinement of the self-efficacy construct may also be in order for its application to the career behavior of ethnically diverse groups (M. Brown, in press). Bandura (1977, 1986) proposed that the outcomes one can expect to receive for a given behavior are determined solely by the adequacy of that behavior that, in turn, is dependent on one's efficacy expectations. For ethnic minorities, however, as M. Brown (in press) observed, discrimination and other forms of systematic bias determine outcomes or one's expectations of outcomes, independent of the adequacy of one's behavior. The outcome expectations aspect of Bandura's model may help more than the efficacy aspect in the understanding of the mechanisms that underlie the career development of "caste-like minorities" (Ogbu, 1992; Ogbu & Matute–Bianchi, 1986, p. 87). According to Ogbu (1992), the job ceiling and related forms of unfair discrimination have severely weakened people's belief that conventional means of attaining success can work for them. As a result, caste-like minorities pursue unconventional means, and sometimes societally prohibited means, of attaining success, not because of the lack of ability to employ conventional methods or of a lack of efficacy with respect to conventional methods. Consequently, both efficacy and outcome expectations may have joint and independent effects on career behavior for ethnic minorities.

Gottfredson's Theory of Circumscription and Compromise

Gottfredson (1981) proposed a theory that may have some relevance in explaining the career development of various diverse populations (Arbona, in press). According to the circumscription aspect of the theory, people's self-concepts develop as they pass through a series of stages. In the first stage, the self-concept acquires an orientation to size and power whereas, in the second stage, the self-concept acquires an orientation toward prevailing gender roles. Most relevant to the present discussion, in the third stage of development, self-concepts acquire an orientation to social evaluation, including social class and race. In the fourth stage, the self-concept develops an orientation toward one's internal uniqueness. A key aspect of the theory is that, as they progress through the developmental stages, individuals successively reject occupations as unsuitable on the basis of the self-concept and the orientations acquired. Gottfredson further stated that occupational choices are a product of perceived job–self compatibility and perceived accessibility of jobs, the latter being a function of one's perception of discrimination in the workplace. Finally, Gottfredson proposed that because the jobs perceived as suitable to the self are sometimes not perceived to be available, people compromise their choices by sacrificing those aspects of the self-concept most recently developed and move toward those orientations developed the earliest. The model indicates that one's perceptions of accessibility and one's self-concept are developed, in part, as a function of prevailing racial attitudes and discrimination. Further, the theory implies that if one were able to measure perceived accessibility of occupations, this perception would be found to vary as a function of the individual's ethnicity. Further, if one were able to measure the individual's ethnic self-concept (how the individual's sees himself or herself as a member of an ethnic group) as well as the individual's socioeconomic class, then one should be able to document a relationship between these variables and occupational choice. Although many of the needed measures exist, the proposed investigations have yet to appear in the empirical literature.

CULTURE-SPECIFIC THEORIES AND THEIR RELATION TO ETHNIC MINORITY CAREER DEVELOPMENT

In a recent editorial published in the *Journal of Vocational Behavior*, introducing a special issue on racial identity and vocational behavior, Tinsley (1994) stated,

> It seems obvious that a somewhat different configuration of factors influences the career development of persons of different cultural and racial heritage. Despite their individuality, people from the same culture share common experiences which help to shape their attitudes, values, expectations, and aspirations. Individuals from different cultural backgrounds can be expected to differ in the expectations, aspirations, and values they bring to the career development process. As a result, they encounter different problems and barriers which they must resolve, and they differ in their attitudes about the career development process. (p. 115)

It would seem important, then, that researchers delineate as many potentially relevant cultural and racial background variables as possible and to discover their vocational relevance. As mentioned at the beginning of this chapter, although much of the energies in the field of cross-cultural career development has been directed at the evaluation and testing of the cultural validity of majority theories for racial and ethnic minorities, at least some of those energies have also been devoted to the analysis of how various culture-specific constructs can enrich the understanding of the career development of these culturally different individuals. Space limitations require us to provide only a sampling of these models. The first is Cheatham's (1990) Afrocentricity model.

Cheatham's Africentricity-Based Model

Cheatham (1990) argued that African Americans share a sociocultural history and experience based on negative attributions of both ethnicity and physiognomy. The author maintained that enforced isolation and disenfranchisement have engendered systems and relations specific to the needs of African Americans. Further, these systems and relations evolved in the United States from an interaction between African and European-American forms and traditions (see Blassingame, 1979; Nobles, 1980). Accordingly, the dominant feature of the psychology of any African American is the product of the interplay of these two cultural traditions and is defined along the following oppositional dimensions, only some of which are explicitly addressed by Cheatham (see Carter, 1990; Kluckhohn & Strodtbeck, 1961; Nobles, 1980; White, W. Parham, & T. Parham, 1980): harmony versus mastery of nature, experiential versus metric time, cooperation versus competition, community versus individual survival and achievement, oral–auditory versus visual–written information production and processing, and the equality versus the superiority of rational and effective experiences.

Cheatham (1990) proposed that if one could measure these cultural orientations, one would be able to empirically document vocational correlates. For example, the overrepresentation of African Americans in social service occupations may be a manifestation of the Africentric value of cooperation and community survival or achievement. Although no test yet appears in the empirical literature, Cheatham's model appears interesting and testable. It also has implications for the generation of a model of the career development of other ethnic groups, whose social psychology is also a product of the interplay between the cultural traditions of their ethnic group and those of the larger society.

Acculturation Models

According to various scholars (Arbona, 1990; Leong, 1986), acculturation is a highly important variable in the understanding of the behavior of Asian Americans, Hispanic Americans, and Native Americans across different domains. Padilla (1980) defined acculturation "as a complex interactional process in which members of the incoming cultural group and members of the host culture may experience change" (p. 48). The two fundamental components of his model of acculturation are the factors of cultural awareness and ethnic loyalty. Padilla described the basic tenets of his model in the following way:

> Cultural awareness refers to an individual's knowledge of specific cultural material (e.g., language, values, history–art, foods, etc.) of the cultural group of origin and/or the host culture. By loyalty we mean the individual's [preference] of one cultural orientation over the other. . . . Preferences are behavioral indices of both cultural awareness and ethnic identification and convey information about the extent of an individual's acculturation. . . . A final consideration is that the process of acculturation is multidimensional in nature. (p. 48)

Padilla (1980) theorized that acculturative change is influenced by five factors: language familiarity and usage, cultural heritage, ethnicity, ethnic pride and identity, and interethnic interaction and interethnic distance. As is evident in our brief descriptions of these dimensions, each dimension includes the two elements of cultural awareness and ethnic loyalty. Padilla included language preference in addition to language familiarity because individuals who are proficient in different languages may prefer to use the languages in different settings. The dimension of cultural heritage includes knowledge of goods associated with particular cultures and the individual's preference for one culture's materials over the other. The maintenance of ethnic pride and identity is evident in identification with the ethnicity of origin, if only in a limited number of social situations. This ethnicity factor, along with the factors of interethnic interaction and interethnic distance, is theorized to influence a person's degree of acculturation. The effects of interethnic interaction and interethnic distance on the acculturation process are evident in the fact that members of ethnic groups who interact more with the members of the host culture than with their own ethnic groups tend to show a higher rate of acculturative change.

Arbona (in press) pointed out that an understanding of the career development of Hispanic Americans requires the consideration of the impact of acculturation. The term *acculturation* first appeared in the anthropological literature in the 1920s and referred to the process of cultural change fostered by the experience of continuous, first-hand contact between two culturally different groups (Keefe & Padilla, 1987; Olmedo, 1979). As Arbona observed, "theoretically, the process of acculturation may result in cultural changes in one or both groups. However, in the case of groups who differ in terms of power, like Hispanic immigrants in the United States, the dominated group is the one who tends to experience the greatest change as a result of the contact" (p. 15). Arbona also hypothesized that "higher levels of acculturation will facilitate the process of career development among Hispanic Americans . . . that among recent immigrants, acculturation level is directly and positively related to socioeconomic status and level of education" (p. 16). However, she cautioned that researchers need to recognize that acculturation is a complex, multidimensional process that may include both an accommodation to the host culture as well as the retention of traditional cultural traits. She further noted that the loss or adoption of cultural traits may vary from trait to trait and may be related to contextual factors.

Johnson et al. (in press) also highlighted the importance of acculturation in the understanding of the career development of Native Americans. They noted that the degree of adherence to cultural heritage or "degree of Indianness" (p. 8) can best be described as a continuum. Johnson et al. (in press) proposed that Native Americans can belong to one of several categories with regard to their acculturation status: *Traditional* refers to individuals who generally speak in their native language and know little English. They observe old traditions and values. *Transitional* refers to individuals who generally speak both English and their native language in the home. They question basic traditionalism and religion yet cannot fully accept the dominant culture and values. *Marginal* refers to those who may be defensively Native American but who are unable either to live the cultural heritage of their tribal group or to identify with the dominant society. This group tends to have the most difficulty coping with social problems due to their ethnicity. *Assimilated* refers to those people who, for the most part, have been accepted by the dominant society. They have generally embraced the dominant culture and values. *Bicultural* refers to those individuals who are, for the most part, accepted by dominant society. This group, however, also know and accept their tribal traditions and culture. They can thus move in either direction, from traditional society to dominant society, with ease. By implication, the acculturation status of Native Americans is believed to interact with their career development process.

The importance of acculturation models in the understanding of the vocational behavior of racial and ethnic minorities is further supported by the fact that various studies have demonstrated the value of acculturation as a culture-specific variable in predicting the vocational behavior of these ethnic minority members. For example, Leong & Tata (1990) examined the relation between the Chinese-American children's level of acculturation and work values. Gender differences in work values among Chinese-American fifth and sixth graders were studied as well. In this study, 177 Chinese-American fifth and sixth graders in a Los Angeles inner-city elementary school were given the Ohio Work Values Inventory (OWVI; Hales & Fenner, 1975) and the Suinn–Lew Asian Self-Identity Acculturation Scale (SL–ASIA; Suinn, Ricard–Figueroa, Lew, & Vigil, 1987). The OWVI yields scores on 11 scales. The results of this study showed that the two most important values for Chinese-American children were money and task satisfaction. Object orientation and solitude appeared to be of considerably lower importance. Boys valued object orientation, self-realization and ideas–data more than did girls. Girls valued altruism more than did boys. These gender differences may represent non-culture-specific gender differences in work values. The sample of children was also divided into three groups according to their SL–ASIA scores: the low-acculturation group, the medium-acculturation group, and the high-acculturation group. Significant acculturation differences were found for self-realization. Highly acculturated Chinese-American children valued self-realization more than low-acculturation Chinese-American children. According to these results, self-realization seems to be more a part of the European-American than of the Chinese-American culture. The authors concluded that knowledge of this pattern of occupational values among Chinese-American children can serve as advance organizers for counselors who help this group of minority children with their career planning. The challenge lies in the broadening of occupational options for Chinese-American children while still respecting their cultural values, which may underlie their occupational values.

Racial and Ethnic Identity Development

Another culture-specific model that was recently applied to the career development of ethnic minorities is the racial and ethnic identity development model. As pointed out by Helms (1993), racial identity theory as it pertains to African Americans can be traced back to models by Cross (1971) and Jackson (1975) that describe the process by which African Americans came to terms with being Black in a predominantly White society. According to Cross' model (1971), which describes the "Negro-to-Black conversion experience," Blacks are hypothesized to move through preencounter, encounter, immersion, and internalization stages. During the preencounter stage, Blacks are "programmed to view and think of the world as being non-Black, anti-Black, or the opposite of Black" (Hall, Cross, & Freedle, 1972, p. 159). Preencounter Blacks are assumed to hold pro-White and anti-Black sentiments. At the next stage, the encounter stage, the Black individual comes face to face with the racism in our society and becomes aware of what being Black means. He or she begins to validate himself or herself as a Black person. During the immersion stage, the Black person rejects all non-Black values and totally immerses himself or herself in Black culture. Finally, in the internalization stage, the Black person gains a sense of inner security and begins to focus on "things other than himself and his own ethnic or racial group" (Hall et al., 1972, p. 160). Cross (1991) offered an update to his 1971 formulations in a recent book, *Shades of Black: Diversity in African-American Identity.*

For Asian Americans, S. Sue and D. W. Sue (1973) formulated a similar ethnic identity model. According to their model, Chinese American personality development encompasses a threefold typology. The *traditionalist* is someone with strongly internalized Chinese values. Primary allegiance is to the family into which she or he was born. Self-worth is defined by obedience to parents and behaviors that bring honor to the family. Failure to live up to parental values arouses guilt. The individual handles prejudice and discrimination by deferring and minimizing the effects. Traditionalists are not taught how to respond aggressively to racism; they believe they can overcome barriers by simply working hard enough. The traditionalist attributes blame for lack of success to himself or herself and to European American society.

The second personality type, *marginal man*, is unwilling to give unquestioning obedience to traditional parental values. This person's self-worth is defined by the ability to acculturate into European American society. By living between the two cultures, he or she suffers from an identity crisis. To resolve this crisis, this personality type may become over-Westernized. This can have detrimental effects, such as development of self-hatred by his or her turning inward the hostility engendered from denying his or her minority culture. Defiance of parental values arouses guilt. Chinese values are blamed for lack of success, with minimal blame on European American society. Finally, denial and minimalization of the effects are this personality type's way of handling prejudice and discrimination. S. Sue and D. W. Sue (1973) explained, "The Marginal Man finds it difficult to admit widespread racism, since to do so would be to say that he/she aspires to join a racist society" (p. 117). Rather than blaming individuals for their inability to assimilate into European American society, he or she blames the entire Chinese population for perpetrating Chinese values that he or she considers maladaptive.

The third personality type described by S. Sue and D. W. Sue (1973) is the *Asian American*, whose self-worth is defined by the ability to attain self-pride by defining a new identity. The Asian American tries to formulate a new identity because he or she realizes that it is impossible to be completely obedient to his or her parents, because racism is something that cannot be ignored, and because he or she feels a lack of self-pride. This person shares some qualities of each of the other two types. Like the traditionalist, he or she associates with other Chinese without being embarrassed. Like marginal man, he or she experiences some guilt for not being fully accepting of parental authority. Defiance is not a rejection of Chinese ways but an attempt to preserve some Chinese values while forming a new identity. Blame for lack of success goes to European American society. The focus is on raising group esteem and pride. Anger and militancy are the ways the Asian American handles prejudice and discrimination. These methods may bring about valuable feelings of power and pride, but they may also make the Asian American extremely sensitive and suspicious.

Two decisions determine which type the Chinese American falls into. The first decision is whether to conform to or rebel against parental values. Someone who chooses to conform adopts Chinese values and is, therefore, in the traditionalist category. Those who choose to rebel against parental values also must decide whether to adopt Western values (marginal man) or develop Asian American values (Asian American). These choices look similar to factors involved in assimilation or acculturation, but S. Sue and D. W. Sue (1973) conceived of these three typologies in terms of personal striving for respect.

Examples of recent theoretical developments in this area include a special issue of the *Journal of Vocational Behavior* (Tinsley, 1994) that was devoted to exploring the role of racial and ethnic identity in the vocational behaviors of ethnic minorities. We review several of these formulations as illustrations of the type of theoretical work being conducted on this front. Helms and Piper (1994) contended that race has been used in one of three ways in psychological research. With the first use, race is a nominal classification variable whereby individuals are assigned to one of several categories. Researchers using this approach have compared Whites and Blacks on different variables in order to identify possible race effects. The second approach consists of a cultural conceptualization of race in which differences between groups are assumed to exist due to differential socialization patterns within these groups. Helms and Piper (1994) cited Ting–Toomey's (1985) comparison of collectivistic and individualistic cultures as an example of this approach. The third approach consists of the use of a sociopolitical conceptualization of race. According to Helms and Piper (1994), the basic premise of this approach is that "one racial group in U.S. society (Whites) historically has defined and controlled access to work, and all other racial groups (African Americans, Asian Americans) and cultural groups (Latinos and Indigenous Americans) have had to function in a societal work environment which they have had comparatively little control over or influence in shaping" (p. 125).

In view of the sociopolitical approach, M. Brown (in press) and Helms and Piper (1994) contended that racial identity is unlikely to have much of an effect on vocational contents (e.g., interests, needs, choice of majors and occupations, and work values) but instead exerts its influence on the vocational process (i.e., career maturity, perceptions of racial climate, preference for racism-reduction strategies in the work environment, satisfactoriness, work adjustment, work satisfaction), possibly by way of a moderator variable called by Helms and Piper "racial salience" (p. 128). Racial salience is defined by the authors as the extent to which a person conceives of race as a significant definer of one's work options. The effects of racial salience are, in turn, governed by racial identity theories that propose when and for whom race is a salient variable in social interactions. Helms and Piper (1994) reviewed findings that showed that racial identity is not related to certain career-choice variables but was related to vocational identity and stages of vocational development. In the same special issue of the *Journal of Vocational Behavior* (Tinsley, 1994), Parham and Austin (1994) and Leong and Chou (1994) suggested a possible linkage between racial identity, acculturation, and the variables of perception of opportunities, occupational stereotyping, and career decision-making processes.

Leong and Chou (1994) further argued that ethnic identity and acculturation are highly related constructs for Asian Americans. They proposed an integrated framework for combining racial and ethnic identity models and acculturation models. According to Leong and Chou (1994), the question of racial and ethnic identity is essentially a two-dimensional problem; namely, how do racial or ethnic minorities view their own cultures and how do they view their dominant host culture? Although called an acculturation model, Berry's (1980) model deals more directly with cultural identity. The model is comprehensive in that it defines acculturation outcomes in terms of each minority's views about its own culture and the host culture. Based on Berry's (1980) model as the foundation, Figure 5.1 presents an integration of the various racial and ethnic identity models.

Leong and Chou (1994) pointed out that Berry's (1980) model maintains that individuals who hold positive views of both their own culture and the host culture are *integrationists*. These individuals attempt to have the best that both cultures have to offer. This group is similar, if not identical, to S. Sue and D. W. Sue's (1973) Asian American, SL-ASIA Scales (Suinn et al., 1987) medium acculturation persons, and Cross' (1971) internalization group (see Helms, 1993). According to Cross (1971), African Americans who have achieved internalization are those who have come to value their Black culture but who also find things of value in the White culture. All four models view this as the ideal outcome.

Assimilationists, the second possible acculturation outcome, hold a positive view of the host culture but a negative view of their own culture (Berry, 1980). This group parallels S. Sue and D. W. Sue's (1973) marginal man, SL-ASIA Scale's (Suinn et al., 1987) high acculturation group, and Cross' (1971) preencounter individual, who holds pro-White and anti-Black attitudes (Helms, 1993).

Individuals who view their host culture negatively and their own culture positively are *separationists* (Berry, 1980), traditionalists (S. Sue & D. W. Sue, 1973), and the low acculturation group (Suinn et al., 1987). Two of Cross' (1971) Black racial identity groups fall into this category: the encounter

Own Culture

		Positive	Negative
Host Culture	Positive	1a. Integration 2a. Asian American 3a. Medium Acculturation 4a. Internalization	1b. Assimilation 2b. Marginal Man 3b. High Acculturation 4b. Preencounter
	Negative	1c. Separation 2c. Traditionalist 3c. Low Acculturation 4c. Encounter/Immersion	1d. Marginal

FIG. 5.1. Integration of racial-ethnic identity and acculturation models. *Note.* 1 = Berry's Model, 2 = Sue & Sue's Model, 3 = Suinn–Lew's Model, 4 = Cross' Model.

and immersion–emersion groups (Helms, 1993). Both of these groups hold negative views of White culture and increasingly positive views of their own Black culture.

Finally, Berry's model includes a group which is not recognized by the other models. Berry's (1980) *marginal* person holds a negative view of both host and own culture. This integrated model of racial and ethnic identity reveals a considerable amount of convergence in the racial and ethnic identity literature, regardless of whether one studies the acculturation of Cree Indians in Canada (Berry, 1976), Asian-American clients struggling with ethnic identity issues at the University of California's Counseling Center (S. Sue and D. W. Sue, 1973), or African-American college students' racial identity (T. Parham & Helms, 1985a; 1985b). Berry's two-dimensional model of acculturation provides an organizational scheme for examining racial and ethnic identity development, it identifies areas of divergence in need of further research, and it points to areas of confusion that need further clarification.

Although Berry's (1980) model provides more information about these acculturation outcomes (more appropriately, cultural identity statuses) than about the actual process of acculturation itself, the model is silent regarding issues such as why some individuals develop negative views of their own culture whereas others develop negative views of their host culture and the factors that influence the divergent paths that lead to different outcomes (Leong and Chou, 1994). Nevertheless, Berry's labels are most descriptive of the acculturation process, as well as generic, and, hence, are applicable to various racial, cultural, and ethnic groups. To make explicit the link from Berry's acculturation model to ethnic identity models, Leong and Chou (1994) recommended adding the term *identity* to the end of each outcome, that is, integrationist identity (II), assimilationist identity (AI), separationist identity (SI), and marginalist identity (MI).

Leong and Chou (1994) further hypothesized about specific career outcomes for Asian Americans, given their differential ethnic identity statuses. For example, they proposed that Asian Americans with a separationist identity are most at risk for negative career outcomes due to their position on the acculturation continuum and the predominantly European American work environments in most organizations and institutions. Leong and Chou (1994) hypothesized that Asian Americans with a separationist identity, as compared to those with integrationist or assimilationist identities, are more susceptible to occupational segregation, occupational stereotyping, and occupational discrimination. As a result of these processes, they are also more likely to have lower levels of job satisfaction and upward mobility and higher levels of job stress. On the other hand, Asian Americans with integrationist or assimilationist identities are hypothesized to be less susceptible to occupational segregation, occupational stereotyping, and occupational discrimination due to the shorter cultural distance between themselves and the managers and supervisors in organizations. They are also hypothesized to exhibit higher levels of job satisfaction and lower levels of job stress than Asian Americans with a separationist identity. Theoretically, Asian Americans with an assimilationist identity are likely to have a slight advantage over those Asian Americans with integrationist identity in terms of various career outcomes. Such differences, however, must await empirical evidence.

Other Culture-Specific Variables

Another culture-specific variable that has implications for the vocational behavior of ethnic minorities, especially Asian Americans, is the concept of "loss of face." In one study illustrating the importance of this concept, Redding & Ng (1982) used questionnaires and interviews to study Chinese middle-level executives in Hong Kong. They found that "face" was a very salient variable, with mainly short-term effects. Having "face" was found to influence success in business transactions; being given "face" was seen as desirable, and losing face as unfavorable; one gave "face" back if given it, and retaliated when it was taken away. The role of "face" in human interactions has been given a significant role in the work of sociologists like Goffman (1959). More recently, Zane (1993) began research on an empirical scale to measure loss of face as a salient variable in understanding the social behavior of Asian Americans.

This emic, or culture-specific, approach, which is concerned with identifying any culture-specific variables among racial and ethnic minorities that may influence the vocational behavior of these groups, is an extremely important alternative strategy for increasing the understanding of the career development and vocational behavior of racial and ethnic minorities. These variables can be unique to an ethnic group (e.g., *sepuku*, "to maintain honor," among Japanese) or common to several ethnic groups (e.g., acculturation as a moderator of behavior among Asian and Hispanic Americans) or common to most groups but hypothesized to be qualitatively different for a particular ethnic group (e.g., loss of face among Chinese Americans). At present, studies incorporating this approach in the understanding of the career development and vocational behavior among racial and ethnic minorities are much more limited than the dominant approach (i.e., the comparative approach). This situation is due largely to the scarcity of research instruments for assessing culture-specific variables among racial and ethnic minorities. This is an area in need of considerable attention if psychologists are to arrive at a complete understanding of racial and ethnic minorities' vocational behavior. Testing the relevance of Western-based models and instruments to ethnic minorities is an important research agenda, but it will only provide partial answers. The influence of both Western and non-Western constructs on the career development of racial and ethnic minorities needs to be investigated.

CULTURE-COMPARATIVE STUDIES OF CAREER DEVELOPMENT AND VOCATIONAL BEHAVIOR

Culture-comparative studies of the differential career development of racial and ethnic minorities continue to play an important role in vocational psychology research. This approach, however, has been criticized along several dimensions. First, many scholars have rightly noted that many studies of ethnic minorities have been unjustly criticized for the lack of a comparison group. The implications of these criticisms are that such studies should have a European American comparison group in order to be of value. These critics maintain that studies of ethnic minorities should have value in and of themselves without reference to the European American majority group. They further noted the hypocrisy in the inherent "double standard" whereby few if any studies of European American samples are criticized for lacking a minority comparison group. A second set of criticism proposes that such global and nominal group comparisons between racial and ethnic groups are unlikely to yield useful information (e.g., see Helms & Piper, 1994).

Although these criticisms are legitimate, it is also important that psychologists do not "throw the baby out with the bath water." The comparative approach is the central design of cross-cultural psychological studies. It enables researchers to identify that which is culture-general (i.e., common across many cultures) and that which is culture-specific (i.e., unique to certain cultures either in quantity, quality, or manner of expression). It also enables researchers to evaluate the degree of the cross-cultural generalizability of the constructs. Without the culture-comparative approach, researchers would be forever limited to emic studies and a series of principles of vocational behavior that has local utility but limited generalizability.

In this section, we review culture-comparative studies to identify both culture-general and culture-specific findings from studies of racial and ethnic minorities. Space limitations prevent us from providing a comprehensive review (see Leong, in press) and so we have chosen a series of culture-comparative studies to illustrate the value of the approach as well as to provide a sampling of important findings. The comparative approach addresses a whole range of questions regarding the career development and vocational behavior of racial and ethnic minorities relative to European Americans or relative to other ethnic groups. For example, do African Americans have higher or lower levels of occupational aspirations than European Americans? Such aspirations are believed to be important because they are likely to influence later career choices. Frost and Diamond (1979) compared the occupational aspirations of African-, Hispanic-, and European-American fourth-, fifth-, and sixth-grade public school students. They found that Hispanic- and European-American girls were more likely than African-American girls to choose non-traditional and high-status occupations. No racial and ethnic differences were found among the boys. In a later study, Dawkins (1981) examined the effect of social background and educational experiences on the occupational prestige expectations of African Americans and European Americans who were freshmen in 1968. Dawkins found that college experiences were more important than social background and high-school experiences in predicting long-range occupational prestige expectations. Subgroup comparisons indicated that gender and college racial composition may interact with other factors that predict occupational expectations.

A study by Chester (1983) of a sample of African-American male and female ninth- through twelfth-graders sheds some light on such gender difference and disadvantages for African-American female adolescents. Based on a review of the literature regarding institutional and racial differences in attitudes toward career development in women, Chester hypothesized that more gender differences would exist among the African American students at the liberal arts school than among those at the vocational school and that these differences would favor the male students. The hypotheses were confirmed. Chester concluded that female African Americans experience environments differently from male African Americans, due to the combined and independent effects of racism and sexism. We conclude that studies involving the effects of different settings on minority behavior should examine relationships separately by gender.

In a few studies investigators have also examined if racial and ethnic minority members are subjected to occupational stereotyping based on their ethnic background. Such stereotyping usually occurs in a comparative framework whereby ethnic minority members are perceived to have more or less of certain negative (or sometimes positive) attributes relative to European Americans. For example, a series of studies by Fernandez (1975, 1981; cited in Helms & Piper, 1994) showed that "high levels of racial stereotyping may be inherent in White managers' attitudes toward Black workers. He found that White managers in a variety of corporations held the following attitudes about Black people: (a) They are slow, lazy, dumb, and to be discounted regardless of their station, (b) they ask for too much and receive undeserved breaks, and (c) they should not be hired, promoted or viewed as partners in the work group" (Helms & Piper, 1994, p. 11).

In another study, Leong and Hayes (1990) examined occupational stereotyping of Asian Americans among White college students by having them rate profiles that were identical except for race and gender. Relative to the White target student, the Asian American target student with an identical background was seen as less qualified to be in insurance sales but more likely to succeed in engineering, computer science, and math. No race and gender interactions were found.

There has also been a series of studies comparing the cultural validity of various interest inventories for racial and ethnic minorities. More specifically, in several of these studies, investigators examined the structure validity of inventories based on Holland's (1985a) model for racial and ethnic minorities. Using a principal factor analysis, Wakefield, Yom, Doughtie, Chang, and Alston (1975) found that the distances between Holland (1985a) codes on the Vocational Preference Inventory (VPI; Holland, 1985b) for African Americans and Whites were quite similar but that the correspondence was weaker for the former group. Lamb (1976), using data from the ACT interest survey, found the hexagonal model to be valid for African American, White, and Hispanic American high-school students but not for Native Americans. Using a multidimensional scaling analysis of responses to the Strong Interest Inventory (SII; Hansen & Campbell, 1985), Swanson (1992) found support for the structural validity of Holland's model for a sample of African-American college students. On the other hand, Haverkamp (1987) used a multidimensional scaling (MDS) procedure to examine the validity of the Holland (1985a) RIASEC hexagonal configuration in the Strong Interest Inventory for four ethnic groups. The Holland configuration was supported for the Hispanic American and Native-American groups. For Asian–Pacific Islanders, the conventional and enterprising themes were reversed. For African Americans, only three of the six themes were identified. Also using an MDS procedure on the Strong Interest Inventory, but with male engineers in Mexico and the United States, Fouad and Dancer (1992) found that the interest structure among the two groups were similar and that Holland's circular structure did hold across the two cultures. However, the feelings did not support the hypothesis that the interest structure was a equilateral hexagon.

Other researchers have also examined the cultural validity of interest inventories for racial and ethnic minorities, by examining other types of validity. For example, O'Brien and Walsh (1976) found that both the VPI (Holland, 1985b) and the Self-Directed Search (SDS; Holland, 1985c) effectively discriminated among the occupational groups according to Holland's (1985a) model. Although O'Brien and Walsh (1976) used only an African American sample and did not include a White comparison group, the results do illustrate that even a study containing only one ethnic group can be interpreted in a comparative framework given previous studies with other ethnic groups. A similar study with a direct comparative approach was conducted by Whetstone and Hayles (1975) using the Strong Vocational Interest Blank (SVIB; Strong & Campbell, 1972) and concluded that the SVIB appeared similarly effective for the African American and White college students.

Another important topic within the comparative framework is the examination of occupational segregation among racial and ethnic minorities. For example, Hsia (1988) examined occupational distribution among Asian-American and European-American workers and found that Asian Americans were more likely to be in professional, technical, and service occupations and less likely to be in sales, production or craft, and operator or laborer occupations. Using a representation index of degree of segregation, Hsia (1988) examined the pattern of occupational segregation among Asian Americans. She found that the highest representation index for Asian Americans was for physicians, medical scientists, physicists, and astronomers, followed by biological scientists, engineers, architects, and accountants. The lowest representation index for Asian Americans was among lawyers, judges, chief executive officers, and general administrators.

In a related study, D. W. Sue and Kirk (1972) compared Chinese-American and European-American college students, using the Strong Vocational Interest Blank (Strong & Campbell, 1972) and found that male and female first-year Asian Americans differed from European American first-year students in expressing more interest in physical sciences, applied technical fields, and business and less interest in social sciences, aesthetic–cultural fields, and verbal–linguistic vocations. Female students were also more oriented toward domestic occupations.

Occupational segregation is also a major problem for African Americans. E. Smith (1983) examined the 1970 U.S. Census data and observed that "Blacks comprised only 2% of all physicians, 1% of lawyers and judges but 8% of all teachers" (p. 173). Using 1980 U.S. Census data, Gouke (1987) found a continuation of this pattern, with African Americans overrepresented in semiskilled and unskilled occupations and underrepresented in white-collar and skilled professions.

Another area of comparative research is racial and ethnic minority students' use of vocational counseling services (see chapter in this volume by Fouad and Bingham). Tracey, Leong, and Glidden (1986) found that Asian Americans were more likely than European Americans to present vocational problems rather than personal–emotional ones. Academic and career problems were overendorsed by Asian Americans and underendorsed by European American students.

In still other studies, researchers have examined racial and ethnic differences in occupational stress and work adjustment. D. Brown, Minor, and Jepsen (1991) found that Asian Americans were least likely to report that their skills were being used well and that more Asian Americans reported stress on the job than African Americans and Hispanic Americans; African Americans more frequently reported perceiving job discrimination. In another study, Kincaid and Yum (1987) compared socioeconomic consequences of migration among first-generation immigrants from Samoa, Korea, the Philippines and Japanese and European American residents of Hawaii. Mean occupational prestige of all except the Japanese immigrants dropped with the first job in Hawaii. The European Americans regained the most in terms of occupational prestige, and they also had highest incidence of personal achievement. The level of highest dissatisfaction was found among the Koreans, who had highest degree of incongruity in occupational prestige of jobs before and after migration.

In another study, Slaney and M. Brown (1983) found that African-American men were more likely than White men, who were matched and divided into upper and lower socioeconomic groups, to perceive lack of talent as a significant career barrier. Slaney and M. Brown (1983) compared 48 African American and 48 White male undergraduates. There were no group differences found on age or educational level. Race differences were noted in preferences for artistic, realistic, and investigative occupations, respectively. There was also a racial difference on one measure of career indecision.

Bartol, Anderson, and Schneier (1981) found that African Americans were separated from Whites on a discriminant function characterized by a lower orientation toward imposing wishes and standing out from the group as well as by a greater affinity for the assertive role.

Finally, the culture-comparative approach is also an invaluable means for identifying potential gender differences within racial and ethnic minorities. For example, Arbona and Novy (1991), in comparing the occupational aspirations and expectations of African Americans, Hispanic Americans, and European Americans, found more gender differences than racial and ethnic differences. Although space limitations prevent us from examining this issue in depth (see Bingham & Ward, 1994 for a recent review), the comparative approach allows researchers to examine the many ways in which the career development issues for ethnic-minority women diverge from those of ethnic-minority men. The comparative approach used in examining the intersections between gender and ethnicity for different groups informs researchers as to which are gender issues and which are cultural issues in the career development and vocational behavior of racial and ethnic minority members.

DIRECTIONS FOR FUTURE THEORY DEVELOPMENT AND RESEARCH

For the following section, we draw heavily on recently published and integrative reviews of the theoretical and empirical literature concerning African Americans, Asian Americans, Hispanic Americans, and Native Americans (cf. Leong, in press) and on the work of Gottfredson (1986). Consistent with the concerns of Gottfredson, emphasis is placed on cross-culturally relevant dimensions.

Theoretical and Empirical Issues

Most critics of current career-choice theories have argued that those theories have failed to address the experiences of discrimination and poverty encountered by various ethnic groups as well as other dimensions of those groups' cultural experiences. More recently, however, Gottfredson (1986) identified 12 career-choice risk factors that all persons may experience as a result of various forms of discrimination but which persons from certain ethnic groups may experience to a greater or lesser extent than persons from other ethnic groups. Those risk factors represented three main types. The first type, based on a comparison between the career-choosing individual and the general population included the following factors: low mental ability, poor education, poverty, cultural isolation, low self-esteem, and functional limitations. The second type of risk factors involved comparisons of the individual to other persons within the same social circle: nontraditional interests, social isolation, low mental ability relative to family and peers, and high mental ability relative to family and peers. Finally, the third type of risk factors involved family responsibilities and were whether and to what degree a person was the primary caregiver and whether and to what degree a person was the primary economic provider. Although we can reasonably argue that many of the factors identified by Gottfredson (1986) need to be more effectively defined (e.g., poor education, cultural isolation, social isolation), the factors represent many of the components identified by other cross-cultural vocational psychologists and need to be integrated into theories that attempt to describe and explain career-choice behavior.

A number of other cultural-specific, within-group dimensions, both related to and distinct from those identified by Gottfredson (1986), have been identified (cf. Arbona, 1990, in press; M. Brown, in press; Johnson et al., in press; Leong, 1985, in press; Leong & Serafica, in press; Martin, 1991). These dimensions have significant potential for increasing the understanding of the career development of most cultural groups: acculturation, or the degree to which ethnically diverse persons identify with the host culture; ethnic identity, or the degree to which persons identify with their own culture; cultural-values orientation, or degree of adherence to those beliefs and practices that characterize cultural groups; country of origin or nationality; migration history, or how recently the individuals had migrated to the host country; language facility, or the degree to which persons can communicate in the host language; and occupational and educational background in country of origin. The possible conceptual and empirical overlap between these dimensions, both among themselves and with those identified by Gottfredson (1986) has yet to be determined and represents an important line of inquiry. For example, it is vital for psychologists to determine if the significance of country of origin or migration history lies in the cultural values to which a person may adhere or if the significance lies in the cultural buffering qualities that having and maintaining a reference-group identity apart from the oppressive effects that the general cultural has on the identity of culturally different others (refer to Ogbu & Matute–Bianchi's, 1986, discussion of the alternation model of behavior). Another issue is whether language facility is an issue of acculturation, cultural values, or a broader intercultural interaction variable.

A word needs to said about the relevance of the language facility variable for African Americans. Although some scholars have erroneously taken positions to the contrary (e.g., Gottfredson, 1986), other scholars (e.g., Smitherman, 1991; White, 1980) have affirmed that African-American language systems are distinct from those of European Americans and affect an African-American's interaction with persons from non-African-American language cultures. Consequently, to the extent that facility with the host culture's language affects the career development of individuals from other cultural groups, that facility may also affect that of some African-American individuals.

There are a number of other culture-specific variables that are potentially useful in the understanding of the career-choice behavior of a more circumscribed set of cultural groups. For example, the concept of "face," one's assessment of the ascribed or achieved reputation one has, is viewed as highly relevant to the career behavior of Asian Americans (cf. Leong & Serafica, in press).

Arbona (in press) also identified migration status, whether an individual has entered the United States legally or illegally, as significantly influential of the career-choice behaviors of various Hispanic Americans, particularly Mexican Americans. However, the variable may also be vocationally salient for some African Americans (viz., Haitians).

Johnson et al. (in press) identified four variables that they believed affect the career choices of Native Americans: two residential factors, reservation versus nonreservation and urban versus rural; salience of life roles; and tribal identification. Only tribal identification and the residential factor of reservation versus nonreservation appear to be specific to the career lives of Native Americans. The significance of tribal identification may lie in the cultural values to which the individual adheres and in regard to the cultural buffering attributed to his or her reference-group identification. The latter's significance may be in the individual's resources or access to resources that affect career choices and in his or her psychological identification with the land.

With regard to African Americans, M. Brown (in press) reviewed evidence indicating that colorism and geographic region of origin could be significant and singular features of their career-choice behavior. Arbona (in press), though, recently suggested that geographic origin may similarly affect the career behavior of some Hispanic Americans. The significance of geographic origin may lie in the subcultural values attributable to persons growing up in different regions of the country; if so, the variable could be significant to the career behavior of other cultural groups as well.

Additional Empirical Concerns

Most pertinent to the present discussion is that the theories currently dominant in the field of career development have not been tested, or tested adequately, with culturally diverse groups. We hope that the critiques offered previously in this chapter will serve as a guide for future cross-cultural testing of the theories.

The empirical documentation of the cross-cultural career-choice relevance of existing, modified, or new theoretical concepts poses singular challenges that probably account for the slow growth of the empirical literature in the area. The need to control for the major demographic variables identified herein, such as gender and geographic region of origin, along with the often confounding variable of socioeconomic status (cf. M. Brown, in press; Lent & Hackett, 1987; Leong & Serafica, in press) creates logistical problems for researchers in gathering the required sample sizes to perform the needed statistical manipulations. To address the sample size requirement issue, we suggest that researchers form national research teams and collaborate in collecting intranational samples and that they conduct programmatic research and successively and systematically control the relevant variables of interest.

We also call for more between-group studies, with the comparison groups representing the range of identifiable cultural groups; such research will allow researchers to determine the extent to which various cultural dimensions apply to the career behavior of a range of groups. On the other hand, we recommend that increased attention be given to within-group analysis of the career-choice behaviors of various ethnic groups, because the assumption of within-group homogeneity has dominated research and theory development too long.

Additionally, the conduct of developmental studies is critical if psychologists are to understand how the relevant variables interact to shape cross-cultural career-choice behavior over time. Both longitudinal and cross-sectional investigations would be useful because none currently exist for members of different cultural groups.

Finally, we would like for researchers to devote more effort to operationalizing the various dimensions of cultural values and to relating those dimensions to the career development of members of various cultural groups. Useful measures currently exist (e.g., Baldwin & Hopkins, 1990; Ibrahim & Kahn, 1987), but many culturally pertinent value dimensions have been articulated (e.g., Hofstede, 1984; Kluckhorn & Strodbeck, 1961; Nobles, 1991; D. W. Sue, 1978), with limited efforts to measure them and no efforts to document their application to vocational behavior.

CONCLUDING STATEMENT

It is our position that until the career-choice meaningfulness of the variables discussed here are determined, most likely through the employment of the suggested research methodologies, the career behavior of culturally different clients will probably remain an enigma. It is clear that a great deal more needs to be done in the examination of the effects of culture-specific factors and variables on the career development and vocational behavior of racial and ethnic minorities. At the same time, the culture-comparative approach, which allows researchers to examine the cultural validity of majority-group theories and models for ethnic minority members, should not be abandoned either.

REFERENCES

Arbona, C. (1989). Hispanic employment and the Holland typology of work. *Career Development Quarterly, 37*, 257–268.

Arbona, C. (1990). Career counseling research and Hispanics: A review of the literature. *The Counseling Psychologist, 18*, 300–323.

Arbona, C. (in press). Theory and research on racial and ethnic minorities: Hispanic Americans. In F. T. L. Leong (Ed.), *Career development and vocational behavior of racial and ethnic minorities.* Hillsdale, NJ: Lawrence Erlbaum Associates.

Arbona, C., & Novy, D. M. (1991). Career aspirations of Black, Mexican American, and White students. *Career Development Quarterly, 39*, 231–239.

Axelson, J. A. (1985). *Counseling and development in a multicultural society.* Monterey, CA: Brooks/Cole.

Baldwin, J. A., & Hopkins, R. (1990). African-American and European-American cultural differences as assessed by the worldview paradigm: An empirical analysis. *Western Journal of Black Studies, 14*, 38–52.

Bandura, A. (1977). Self-efficacy: Toward a unifying theory of behavior change. *Psychological Review, 84*, 191–215.

Bandura, A. (1986). *Social foundations of thought and action: A social cognitive theory.* Englewood Cliffs, NJ: Prentice–Hall.

Bartol, K. M., Anderson, C. R., & Schneier, C. E. (1981). Sex and ethnic effects on motivation to manage among college business students. *Journal of Applied Psychology, 66*, 40–44.

Berry, J. W. (1976). *Human ecology and cognitive style: Comparative studies in cultural and psychological adaptation.* New York: Sage/Halsted.

Berry, J. W. (1980). Acculturation as varieties of adaptation. In A. M. Padilla (Ed.), *Acculturation: Theory, models and some new findings* (pp. 9–25). Boulder, CO: Westview.

Berry, J. W., Poortinga, Y. H., Segall, M. H., & Dasen, P. R. (1992). *Cross-cultural psychology: Research and applications.* New York: Cambridge University Press.

Betz, N. E., & Hackett, G. (1986). Applications of self-efficacy theory to understanding career choice behavior. *Journal of Social and Clinical Psychology, 4*, 279–289.

Bingham, R. P., & Ward, C. M. (1994). Career counseling with ethnic minority women. In W. B. Walsh & S. H. Osipow (Eds.), *Career counseling for women* (pp. 165–195). Hillsdale, NJ: Lawrence Erlbaum Associates.

Blassingame, J. (1979). The slave community: Plantation life in the antebellum south. New York: Oxford University Press.

Brooks, L. (1991). Recent developments in theory building. In D. Brown, L. Brooks, & Associates (Eds.), *Career choice and development* (2nd ed., pp. 364–394). San Francisco: Jossey–Bass.

Brown, D. (1991). Summary, comparison, and critique of major theories. In D. Brown, L. Brooks, & Associates (Eds.), *Career choice and development* (2nd ed., pp. 338–363). San Francisco: Jossey–Bass.

Brown, D. (1991). Trait and factor theory. In D. Brown, L. Brooks, & Associates (Eds.), *Career choice and development: Applying contemporary theories to practice* (2nd ed., pp. 13–36). San Francisco: Jossey–Bass.

Brown, D., Minor, C. W., & Jepsen, D. A. (1991). The opinions of minorities about preparing for work: Report of the second NCDA national survey. *Career Development Quarterly, 40,* 5–19.

Brown, M. T. (in press). The career development of African Americans: Theoretical and empirical issues. In F. T. L. Leong (Ed.), *Career development and vocational behavior of racial and ethnic minorities.* Hillsdale, NJ: Lawrence Erlbaum Associates.

Carter, R. T. (1990). Cultural value differences between African Americans and White Americans. *Journal of College Student Development, 31,* 71–79.

Carter, R. T., & Cook, D. A. (1992). A culturally relevant perspective for understanding the career paths of visible racial/ethnic group people. In H. D. Lea & Z. B. Leibowitz (Eds.), *Adult career development: Concepts, issues, and practices* (pp. 192–217). Alexandria, VA: National Career Development Association.

Cheatham, H. E. (1990). Africentricity and career development of African Americans. *Career Development Quarterly, 38,* 334–346.

Chester, N. L. (1983). Sex differentiation in two high school environments: Implications for career development among Black adolescent females. *Journal of Social Issues, 39,* 29–40.

Cook, D. A., & Helms, J. E. (1988). Visible racial/ethnic group supervisees' satisfaction with cross-cultural supervision as predicted by relationship characteristics. *Journal of Counseling Psychology, 33,* 268–274.

Cross, W. E., Jr. (1971). Negro-to-Black conversion experience: Toward a psychology of Black liberation. *Black World, 20,* 13–27.

Cross, W. E., Jr. (1991). *Shades of black: Diversity in African-American identity.* Philadelphia, PA: Temple University Press.

Dawis, R. V., & Lofquist, L. H. (1984). *A psychological theory of work adjustment.* Minneapolis, MN: University of Minnesota Press.

Dawkins, M. P. (1981). Mobility aspirations of Black adolescents: A comparison of males and females. *Adolescence, 16,* 701–710.

Edwards, A., & Polite, C. (1992). *Children of the dream: The psychology of Black success.* New York: Bantam.

Fouad, N. A., & Dancer, S. L. (1992). Cross-cultural structure of interests: Mexico and the United States. *Journal of Vocational Behavior, 40,* 129–143.

Frost, F., & Diamond, E. E. (1979). Ethnic and sex differences in occupational stereotyping by elementary school children. *Journal of Vocational Behavior, 15,* 43–54.

Goffman, E. (1959). *The presentation of self in everyday life.* New York: Doubleday.

Gottfredson, L. S. (1978). An analytical description of employment according to race, sex, prestige, and Holland type of work. *Journal of Vocational Behavior, 13,* 210–221.

Gottfredson, L. S. (1981). Circumscription and compromise: A developmental theory of occupational aspirations [Monograph]. *Journal of Counseling Psychology, 28,* 545–579.

Gottfredson, L. S. (1986). Special groups and the beneficial use of vocational interest inventories. In W. B. Walsh & S. H. Osipow (Eds.), *Advances in vocational psychology: Vol. 1. Assessment of interests* (pp. 127–198). Hillsdale, NJ: Lawrence Erlbaum Associates.

Gouke, C. C. (1987). *Blacks in the American economy.* Lexington, MA: Ginn.

Hackett, G., & Betz, N. E. (1981). A self-efficacy approach to the career development of women. *Journal of Vocational Behavior, 18,* 326–339.

Hackett, G., Betz, N. E., Casas, J. M., & Rocha–Singh, I. A. (1992). Gender, ethnicity, and social cognitive factors predicting the academic achievement of students in engineering. *Journal of Counseling Psychology, 39,* 527–538.

Hackett, G., & Lent, R. W. (1992). Theoretical advances in career psychology. In S. D. Brown & R. W. Lent (Eds.), *Handbook of counseling psychology* (2nd ed., pp. 419–452). New York: Wiley.

Hales, L. W., & Fenner, B. J. (1975). Measuring the work values of children: The Ohio Work Values Inventory. *Measurement and Evaluation in Guidance, 8,* 20–25.

Hall, W. S., Cross, W. E., Jr., & Freedle, R. (1972). Stages in the development of Black awareness: An exploratory investigation. In R. Jones (Ed.), *Black psychology* (pp. 156–165). New York: Harper & Row.

Hansen, J.-I. C., & Campbell, D. P. (1985). *Manual of the SVIB-SCII.* Palo Alto, CA: Consulting Psychologists Press.

Havercamp, B. E. (1987, August). Structure of interests in U.S. racial-ethnic minority sample. In J. C. Hansen (Chair), *Interest measurement: New perspectives.* Symposium presented at the 95th annual meeting of the American Psychological Association, New York.

Helms, J. E. (1992). Why is there no study of cultural equivalence in standardized cognitive ability testing? *American Psychologist, 47,* 1083–1101.

Helms, J. E. (1993). *Black and White racial identity: Theory, research and practice.* Westport, CT: Praeger.

Helms, J. E., & Piper, R. E. (1994). Implications of racial identity theory for vocational psychology. *Journal of Vocational Behavior, 44,* 124–138.

Henry, P. (1988). Holland's hexagonal model applied to nontraditional premedical students. *Psychological Reports, 62,* 399–404.

Hofstede, G. (1984). The cultural relativity of the quality of life concept. *Academy of Management Review, 9,* 389–398.

Holland, J. L. (1959). A theory of vocational choice. *Journal of Counseling Psychology, 6,* 35–45.

Holland, J. L. (1985a). *Making vocational choices: A theory of vocational personalities and work environments* (2nd ed.). Englewood Cliffs, NJ: Prentice–Hall.

Holland, J. L. (1985b). *Manual for the Vocational Preference Inventory.* Odessa, FL: Psychological Assessment Resources.

Holland, J. L. (1985c). *The Self-Directed Search professional manual.* Odessa, FL: Psychological Assessment Resources.

Hsia, J. (1988). *Asian Americans in higher education and at work.* Hillsdale, NJ: Lawrence Erlbaum Associates.

Ibrahim, F. A., & Kahn, H. (1987). Assessment of world views. *Psychological Reports, 60,* 163–176.

Jackson, B. (1975). Black identity development. In L. Golubschick and B. Persky (Eds.), *Urban social and educational issues* (pp. 158–164). Dubuque, IA: Kendall/Hunt.

Johnson, M. J., Swartz, J. L., & Martin, W. E., Jr. (in press). Applications of psychological theories for career development with Native Americans. In F. T. L. Leong (Ed.), *Career development and vocational behavior of racial and ethnic minorities.* Hillsdale, NJ: Lawrence Erlbaum Associates.

June, L. N., & Pringle, G. D. (1977). The concept of race in the career development theories of Roe, Super, and Holland. *Journal of Non-White Concerns in Personnel and Guidance, 6,* 17–24.

Keefe, S. E., & Padilla, A. M. (1987). *Chicano ethnicity.* Albuquerque: University of New Mexico Press.

Kidd, J. M. (1984). The relationship of self- and occupational concepts to the occupational preferences of adolescents. *Journal of Vocational Behavior, 24,* 48–65.

Kincaid, D. L., & Yum, J. O. (1987). A comparative study of Korean, Filipino, and Somoan immigrants to Hawaii: Socioeconomic consequences. *Human Organization, 46,* 70–77.

Kluckhohn, F. R., & Strodtbeck, F. L. (1961). *Variations in value-orientations.* Evanston, IL: Row, Peterson.

Lamb, R. R. (1976). *Validity of the ACT Interest Inventory for minority group members* (ACT Research Report No. 72). Iowa City, IA: American College Testing Program.

Lent, R. W., & Hackett, G. (1987). Career self-efficacy: Empirical status and future directions. *Journal of Vocational Behavior, 30,* 347–382.

Leonard, P. Y. (1985). Vocational theory and the vocational behavior of Black males: An analysis. The Black male: Critical counseling, developmental, and therapeutic issues: 2. [Special issue]. *Journal of Multicultural Development and Counseling, 13*, 91–105.

Leong, F. T. L. (1985). Career development of Asian Americans. *Journal of College Student Personnel, 26*, 539–546.

Leong, F. T. L. (1986). Counseling and psychotherapy with Asian-Indians: Review of the literature. *Journal of Counseling Psychology, 33*, 196–206.

Leong, F. T. L. (in press). Career development and vocational behaviors of Asian Americans. In L. C. Lee & N. W. S. Zane (Eds.), *Handbook of Asian American psychology.* Hillsdale, NJ: Lawrence Erlbaum Associates.

Leong, F. T. L., & Chou, E. L. (1994). The role of ethnic identity and acculturation in the vocational behavior of Asian Americans: An integrative review. *Journal of Vocational Behavior, 44*, 155–172.

Leong, F. T. L., & Hayes, T. (1990). Occupational stereotyping of Asian Americans. *Career Development Quarterly, 39*, 143–154.

Leong, F. T. L., & Serafica, F. C. (in press). Career development of Asian Americans: A research area in need of a good theory. In F. T. L. Leong (Ed.), *Career development and vocational behavior of racial and ethnic minorities.* Hillsdale, NJ: Lawrence Erlbaum Associates.

Leong, F. T. L., & Tata, S. P. (1990). Sex and acculturation differences in occupational values among Chinese American children. *Journal of Counseling Psychology, 37*, 208–212.

Martin, W. E., Jr. (1991). Career development and American Indians living on reservations: Cross-cultural factors to consider. *The Career Development Quarterly, 39*, 273–283.

Mead, M. (1928). *Coming of age in Samoa.* New York: William Morrow.

Miller, M. J., Springer, T., & Wells, D. (1988). Which occupational environments do Black youths prefer? Extending Holland's typology. *School Counselor, 36*, 103–106.

Nobles, W. W. (1980). African philosophy: Foundations for black psychology. In R. L. Jones (Ed.), *Black psychology* (2nd ed.). New York: Harper & Row.

Nobles, W. W. (1991). African philosophy: Foundations for black psychology. In R. L. Jones (Ed.), *Black psychology* (3rd ed.). Berkeley, CA: Cobb & Henry.

O'Brien, W. F., & Walsh, W. B. (1976). Concurrent validity of Holland's theory for non-college degreed Black working men. *Journal of Vocational Behavior, 8*, 239–246.

Ogbu, J. U. (1992). Understanding cultural diversity and learning. *Educational Researcher, 21*, 5–14.

Ogbu, J. U., & Matute–Bianchi, M. E. (1986). Understanding sociocultural factors: Knowledge, identity, and school adjustment. In Bilingual Education Office, California State Department of Education (Ed.), *Beyond Language: Social and cultural factors in schooling language minority students* (pp. 73–142). Los Angeles: California State University Evaluation, Dissemination and Assessment Center.

Olmedo, E. L. (1979). Acculturation: A psychometric perspective. *American Psychologist, 34*, 1061–1070.

Osipow, S. H. (1975). The relevance of theories of career development to special groups: Problems, needed data, and implications. In J. S. Picou & R. E. Campbell (Eds.), *Career behavior of special groups: Theory, research, and practice* (pp. 9–22). Columbus, OH: Merrill.

Osipow, S. H. (1983). *Theories of career development* (3rd ed.). Englewood Cliffs, NJ: Prentice–Hall.

Padilla, A. M. (Ed.). (1980). *Acculturation: Theory, models, and some new findings.* Boulder, CO: Westview.

Parham, T. A., & Austin, N. L. (1994). Career development and African Americans: A contextual reappraisal using the Nigrescence construct. *Journal of Vocational Behavior, 44*, 139–154.

Parham, T. A., & Helms, J. E. (1985a). Attitudes of racial identity and self-esteem in Black students: An exploratory investigation. *Journal of College Student Personnel, 26*, 143–147.

Parham, T. A., & Helms, J. E. (1985b). The relationship of racial identity attitudes to self-actualization of Black students and affective states. *Journal of Counseling Psychology, 32,* 431–440.

Post, P., Stewart, M. A., & Smith, P. L. (1991). Self-efficacy, interest, and consideration of math/science and non-math/science occupations among Black freshmen. *Journal of Vocational Behavior, 38,* 179–186.

Post-Kammer, P., & Smith, P. L. (1986). Sex differences in math and science career self-efficacy among disadvantaged students. *Journal of Vocational Behavior, 29,* 89–101.

Redding, S. G., & Ng, M. (1982). The role of "face" in the organizational perceptions of Chinese managers. *Organization Studies, 3*(3), 201–219.

Roe, A. (1951a). A psychological study of eminent biologists. *Psychological Monographs, 65*(14, Whole No. 331).

Roe, A. (1951b). A psychological study of eminent physical scientists. *Genetic Psychology Monograph, 43,* 121–239.

Roe, A. (1953). A psychological study of eminent psychologists and anthropologists and a comparison with biological and physical scientists. *Psychological Monographs, 67*(2, Whole No. 352).

Roe, A. (1956). *The psychology of occupations.* New York: Wiley.

Roe, A., & Klos, D. (1972). Classification of occupations. In J. M. Whiteley & A. Resnikoff (Eds.), *Perspectives on vocational development* (pp. 199–221). Washington, DC: American Personnel and Guidance Association.

Roe, A., & Lunneborg, P. W. (1991). Personality development and career choice. In D. Brown, L. Brooks, and Associates, *Career choice and development: Applying theories to practice* (2nd ed., pp. 68–101). San Francisco: Jossey–Bass.

Salomone, P. R., & Slaney, R. B. (1978). The applicability of Holland's theory to nonprofessional workers. *Journal of Vocational Behavior, 13,* 63–74.

Slaney, R. B., & Brown, M. T. (1983). Effects of race and socioeconomic status on career choice variables among college men. *Journal of Vocational Behavior, 23,* 257–269.

Smith, E. J. (1975). Profile of the Black individual in vocational literature. *Journal of Vocational Behavior, 6,* 41–59.

Smith, E. J. (1983). Issues in racial minorities' career behavior. In W. B. Walsh & S. H. Osipow (Eds.), *Handbook of vocational psychology: Vol. 1. Foundations* (pp. 161–222). Hillsdale, NJ: Lawrence Erlbaum Associates.

Smitherman, G. (1991). Talking and testifyin: Black English and the Black experience. In R. L. Jones (Ed.), *Black psychology* (3rd ed., pp. 249–267). Berkeley, CA: Cobb & Henry.

Strong, E. K., & Campbell, D. P. (1972). *Strong Vocational Interest Blank.* Palo Alto, CA: Consulting Psychologist Press.

Sue, D. W. (1978). World views and counseling. *Personnel and Guidance Journal, 56,* 458–462.

Sue, D. W., & Kirk, B. A. (1972). Psychological characteristics of Chinese-American students. *Journal of Counseling Psychology, 19,* 471–478.

Sue, D. W., & Sue, D. (1990). *Counseling the culturally different: Theory and practice.* New York: Wiley.

Sue, S., & Sue, D. W. (1973). Chinese-American personality and mental health. In S. Sue & N. N. Wagner (Eds.), *Asian Americans: Psychological perspectives* (pp. 111–124). Palo Alto, CA: Science and Behavior Books.

Suinn, R. M., Ricard–Figueroa, K., Lew, S., & Vigil, P. (1987). Suinn–Lew Asian Self-Identity Acculturation Scale: An initial report. *Educational and Psychological Measurement, 7,* 401–407.

Super, D. E. (1953). A theory of vocational development. *American Psychologist, 8,* 185–190.

Super, D. E. (1990). A life span, life-space approach to career development. In D. Brown & L. Brooks (Eds.), *Career choice and development* (pp. 197–261). San Francisco: Jossey–Bass.

Super, D. E. (1991). A life-span, life-space approach to career development. In D. Brown, L. Brooks, and Associates, *Career choice and development: Applying contemporary theories to practice* (2nd ed., pp. 197–261). San Francisco: Jossey–Bass.

Super, D. E. (1992, April). Developmental theory. Paper presented at the Conference on Convergence of Theories on Career Choice and Development, Michigan State University, East Lansing.

Super, D. E., & Bohn, M. J., Jr. (1970). *Occupational psychology.* Belmont, CA: Wadsworth.

Swanson, J. L. (1992). The structure of vocational interests for African-American college students. *Journal of Vocational Behavior, 40,* 144–157.

Thomas, A., Sillen, S. (1972). *Racism and psychiatry.* Secaucus, NJ: The Citadel Press.

Tinsley, H. E. A. (1994). Racial identity and vocational behavior. *Journal of Vocational Behavior, 44,* 115–117.

Tinsley, H. E. A. (Editor) (1994). Special issue on racial identity and vocational behavior. *Journal of Vocational Behavior, 44,* 115–234.

Tracey, T. J., Leong, F. T. L., & Glidden, C. (1986). Help seeking and problem perception among Asian-Americans. *Journal of Counseling Psychology, 33,* 331–336.

Tyler, F. B., Brome, D. R., & Williams, J. E. (1991). *Ethnic validity, ecology, and psychotherapy: A psychosocial competence model.* New York: Plenum.

Wakefield, J. A., Jr., Yom, B. L., Doughtie, E. B., Chang, W. C., & Alston, H. L. (1975). The geometric relationship between Holland's personality typology and the Vocational Preference Inventory for Blacks. *Journal of Counseling Psychology, 22,* 58–60.

Warnath, C. F. (1975). Vocational theories: Direction to nowhere. *Personnel and Guidance Journal, 53,* 422–428.

Whetstone, R. D., & Hayles, V. R. (1975). The SVIB and Black college men. *Measurement and Evaluation in Guidance, 8,* 105–109.

White, J. L. (1980). Toward a Black psychology. In R. L. Jones (Ed.), *Black psychology* (2nd ed., pp. 5–12). New York: Harper & Row.

White, J. L., Parham, W. D., & Parham, T. A. (1980). Black psychology: The Afro-American tradition as a unifying force for traditional psychology. In R. L. Jones (Ed.), *Black psychology* (2nd ed., pp. 56–66). New York: Harper & Row.

Zane, N. W. S. (1993). An empirical examination of loss of face among Asian Americans. In R. Carter (Ed.), *Ninth annual cross-cultural Winter roundtable proceedings.* New York: Columbia University.

RESEARCH

Research in Career Assessment: Abilities, Interests, Decision Making, and Career Development

Gail Hackett
Arizona State University

C. Edward Watkins, Jr.
University of North Texas

Career assessment historically has been and remains a rich and fertile area of inquiry for vocational psychologists. Extensive research attention continues to be devoted to the well-established career instruments, new versions of the major career measures have appeared, and new career instruments have been developed in response to theoretical and applied concerns and needs. It is obviously beyond the scope of this chapter for us to address all of the research and developments in the area of career assessment, and it is equally obvious that our coverage must be limited in terms of depth as well as breadth.

Our major goal for this chapter was to selectively review the status and trends in career assessment since the publication of the last *Handbook of Vocational Psychology* (Walsh & Osipow, 1983). Specifically, we have attempted to update the coverage provided in Zytowski and Borgen's (1983) chapter in the first *Handbook* (Walsh & Osipow, 1983). We have followed Betz's (1992) lead in organizing our discussion around the topics of the assessment of individual-difference variables (aptitudes and abilities, interests, needs, and values); career-process variables (career decision making, career maturity, and adult career adjustment); and career-related cognitions (career beliefs and self-efficacy). Within each section some attention is devoted to issues, trends, and new developments as well as to the overarching issues of ethnicity and gender in career assessment. The reader is referred to several contemporary treatments of career assessment for more extensive coverage of the instruments and issues addressed herein (Hackett & Lonborg,

1994; Kapes & Mastie, 1988; Spokane, 1991; Walsh & Betz, 1990; Watkins & V. Campbell, 1990).

ASSESSMENT OF INDIVIDUAL-DIFFERENCES VARIABLES

In career assessment, the study of individual differences has a long and rich history (Dawis, 1992). The individual-differences tradition is steeped in the belief that people differ, that individuals' differences need to be identified, and that their differences ought to be considered in career planning and career exploration efforts. As Betz (1992) pointed out, "The important individual differences variables that need to be taken into consideration include abilities and aptitudes . . . , vocational interests . . . , and needs and values . . ." She continued, "Career counselors and researchers should also take into account two of the most basic individual differences variables—gender and ethnic/racial group—because these variables have had massive influence on perceived career options and adjustment through such mechanisms as gender and race segregation, stereotyping, and gender and racial biases in the work world" (p. 454). In keeping with Betz's statements, we consider the career assessment of individual differences by examining the variables of abilities and aptitudes, vocational interests, needs and values, and gender and ethnic and racial group.

Aptitudes and Abilities

Current Status.   Several measures for the assessment of aptitudes and abilities deserve mention. In the area of college and graduate school admissions, there are the Scholastic Aptitude Test (SAT; College Entrance Examination Board, 1986), American College Testing (ACT, 1989) Assessment Program, and Graduate Record Exam (GRE; Conrad, Trismen, & Miller, 1977). Each of these tests has been around for decades now, and research continues to be conducted to improve them. But what do these tests actually measure? "In general, both the ACT and SAT assess knowledge and skills [e.g., verbal and mathematical skills] acquired in and out of school over a period of years" (Aiken, 1985, p. 31). The GRE, according to Cohn (1985), "is designed to offer a global measure of the verbal, quantitative, and analytical reasoning abilities acquired by an applicant for graduate study over a long period of time and not related to any specific field of study" (p. 623).

Psychometrically, the SAT, ACT, and GRE have much to recommend them. Their internal-consistency reliability coefficients, for example, are uniformly high—in the .80s and .90s. Validity coefficients generally range from moderate to high. Perhaps for these reasons, the SAT and ACT remain the most widely used college admissions tests (Aiken, 1985), and the GRE remains the most common examination for graduate admissions (Jaeger, 1985). Despite the psychometric soundness of these measures, there are some serious limitations to their use, particularly for women and men and women of color (Betz, 1992). Scores from the GRE, SAT, or ACT should never be used as the sole criterion for school admission but rather as one of many criteria on which admission or selection decisions are based.

Three other aptitude tests, the Differential Aptitude Test (DAT, 1990), General Aptitude Test Battery (GATB; U.S. Department of Labor, Employment, & Training Administration, 1980), and Armed Services Vocational Aptitude Battery (ASVAB; U.S. Department of Defense, 1993) also deserve mention here. These three batteries are some of the most, if not *the* most, frequently used batteries for the assessment of multiple abilities now available. The DAT, which is primarily intended for use with students in eighth through twelfth grades is for the assessment of such areas as verbal reasoning, numerical ability, and clerical speed and accuracy; administration takes about 3 hours. First published in 1947, the DAT's most recent revision appeared in the early 1980s. The DAT "is technically very sound" (Pennock–Roman, 1988, p. 66). Reliability estimates are in the .80s or .90s, and extensive validity data exist (Anastasi, 1988; Pennock–Roman, 1985). However, the need for more attention directed towards differential and predictive validity for postsecondary work is necessary (Hambleton, 1985; Sander, 1985). Still, with its limitations recognized, the DAT is considered to be "a very fine multi-factor battery" (Sander, 1985, p. 506) whose "popularity is well-deserved" (Pennock–Roman, 1985, p. 240).

The Armed Services Vocational Aptitude Battery, which is intended for students in eleventh and twelfth grades and in two-year colleges, is for the assessment of such areas as mechanical comprehension, word knowledge, and general science; administration takes about 3 hours. First published in 1966, the battery was revised in 1980 and in the last few years as well. Recently, the Self-Directed Search, Holland's (1985b) self-directed career assessment interest test, has been included as a part of the ASVAB. ASVAB reliability estimates are in the .80s and .90s, and validity estimates are also high (Jensen, 1985, 1988; Weitzman, 1985). According to Jensen (1988), the ASVAB can be viewed "as an exemplar of the state of the art for norm-referenced, group-administered paper-and-pencil tests of mental abilities" (p. 60). As efforts to improve the battery continue to be made, we suspect that that statement will remain true in the near and distant future (e.g., Wise, 1993).

The General Aptitude Test Battery, which is intended for use with students in ninth through twelfth grades and with adults, is for the assessment of such areas as finger dexterity, motor coordination, and verbal and numerical aptitude; it takes about 2½ hours to administer. First published in 1947, the GATB "evaluates an applicant's ability to perform successfully in a wide variety of occupations" (Kirnan & Geisinger, 1987, p. 162); it was most recently revised in the early 1980s. Reliability coefficients for the GATB typically are in the .80s and .90s, and there is also evidence for its validity.

The battery, however, has not been without its critics. Problems with normative sampling, use of a multiple cutoff technique, and high intercorrelations among the measured aptitudes are some of the long-standing criticisms that have been put forth about this battery (Keesling, 1985; Keesling & Healy, 1988; Kirnan & Geisinger, 1987; Zytowski & Borgen, 1983). If the GATB is to be viable, these problems require attention.

In addition to the tests just reviewed, there are many other ability and aptitude measures that have relevance for career assessment purposes (e.g., see Lowman, 1991, pp. 305–307). From our observations, however, the tests mentioned here dominate the field and are likely to continue to be the most commonly used measures of abilities and aptitudes.

New Directions and Research Trends. In the areas of ability measurement, one issue that has received increasing attention is the accuracy of individuals' self-assessments of their abilities. Some research has shown that when measured abilities are compared to self-assessment of one's abilities, considerable variability results (e.g., Westbrook, Sanford, Gilleland, Fleenor, & Mervin, 1988). Because of this, Betz (1992) recommended that career assessors employ caution when using and interpreting clients' ability self-estimates. Specifically, self-assessments of ability can be confounded with efficacy beliefs, particularly among women and minority clients. Individuals who routinely underestimate their abilities require assistance in developing a more robust sense of educational and career efficacy (Betz, 1992; Hackett & Lonborg, 1994).

Swanson (1993) conducted a recent and interesting study on the relationship between self-rated skills and abilities and measured vocational interests. Participants completed the Strong Interest Inventory (Hansen & Campbell, 1985) and a self-rating instrument. "Results . . . suggest that (a) interests, abilities, and skills are sufficiently distinct to be considered separate constructs worthy of independent assessment, yet (b) interests, abilities, and skills within the same Holland type show predictable relations to the other" (Swanson, 1993, p. 63). As for the practice of career assessment itself, Swanson stated that "skills and abilities clearly are distinct constructs from interests and deserve equal attention" (p. 65). In some respects, her data offer support for an interdomain model of career assessment (Lowman, 1991, 1993). Further exploration of the use of self-estimates and measured estimates of ability in career assessment is warranted. This fruitful research area has received all too little attention in the career literature.

Another recent development that seemingly has important implications for the assessment of abilities (as well as for the assessment of interests and job- and community-related variables) is the Campbell Interest and Skill Survey (CISS; D. Campbell, Hyne, & Nilsen, 1992). The CISS is for the assessment of self-reported skills and interests; it is a well-constructed measure that appears to be a valuable career assessment tool. Nevertheless, D.

Campbell (1993b) cautions that "individual's responses to the skill items can best be interpreted as measures of self-confidence rather than as objective measures of skill level" (p. 578).

The CISS is but one component of the Campbell Development Surveys, which is an integrated battery of five psychological surveys. Along with the CISS, the battery includes the Organizational Survey (D. Campbell, 1990) for the assessment of job satisfaction and employee attitudes; the Campbell Leadership Index (D. Campbell, 1991), which yields a measure of leadership characteristics; the Campbell–Hallam Team Development Survey (D. Campbell & Hallam, 1993); and the Campbell Community Survey (D. Campbell, 1993a), for the assessment of residents' feelings about their community. A particularly good, concise summary description of the Campbell Development Surveys has been provided by D. Campbell (1993b). Although it is premature for us to draw strong conclusions about the usefulness of this battery, recent reviews indicate that it may eventually be widely used by career practitioners (Campbell, 1993b; Fuqua, in press).

Gender and Cultural Issues in Ability/Aptitude Assessment. Although the tests mentioned thus far possess good technical properties, effective test use involves far more than good psychometrics. We have come to see that if tests are to be used most appropriately, then the variables of gender, culture, and ethnicity must be taken into account. Test bias can arise through various means, and vocational researchers and practitioners are increasingly cognizant of issues of test fairness (Betz, 1992). Betz (1990) nicely captured some of the major concerns surrounding the issues of test fairness and potential bias when career instruments are used with racial and ethnic minorities:

> At the most fundamental level is the fact that tests are, at least to some extent, culture-bound. It is difficult, if not impossible, to construct a test independently of a cultural context. For example, a test of verbal aptitude is constructed in a given language and is based on what may well be culture-specific item content. Even though test constructors may not purposely favor a given culture, it's difficult to avoid this. Most intelligence and aptitude tests in use were constructed in the context of a White, middle-class value system. Thus, non-White or lower-class examinees would possibly be less familiar with the test content than would examinees representing the White middle class. (pp. 428–429)

Because racial and ethnic minorities often have not had the social and educational advantages of the majority, their ability and aptitude scores can be negatively affected. That possibility must be considered when minorities' ability and aptitude test scores are interpreted (Betz, 1992).

Test fairness in the ability and aptitude assessment of women has also been an issue of concern. Betz and Fitzgerald (1987) provided a number of examples that illustrate sexist language, gender-biased content, and primary use of male characters in the word problems of aptitude tests. Illustrations of gender bias can be found in the GATB:

> Examples of sex-biased content may be drawn . . . from the General Aptitude Test Battery . . . "Tool Matching" Test, which is a measure of the ability of Form Perception. In the GATB Numerical Reasoning Test, male characters and objects predominate—the word problems focus on amounts of lumber and electrical wire rather than on fabric or recipe ingredients. Tools, lumber, and electric wire are far more common in the background experiences of boys than girls growing up in our society. (Betz, 1990, p. 444)

Because the socialization experiences of boys and girls have differed and continue to differ, girls may not have opportunities to experience some of that which is assessed on certain ability and aptitude tests. The previous examples suggest how girls' scores on the GATB may be unfairly affected. Lack of exposure, however, should not be equated with lack of ability. Ability and aptitude tests that do not take different socialization experiences into account can unfairly penalize the test taker. Therefore, it is imperative that counselors be knowledgeable about gender bias—how it can be contained in test materials and how it can be reflected in test results. Furthermore, it is imperative that test developers continue to make ability and aptitude tests fair for both genders (Betz, 1990; Hackett & Lonborg, 1994).

Interests

In the area of career assessment, the measurement of interests has dominated the literature. Since the publication of Zytowski and Borgen's (1983) discussion, much activity has taken place in interest assessment. We consider here some of the recent developments.

Status of the Major Interest Measures. According to a recent survey, the Strong Interest Inventory (SII; Hansen, 1991), Self-Directed Search (SDS; Holland, 1985b), and Kuder Occupational Interest Survey (KOIS; Kuder & Zytowski, 1991) are the three interest measures that counseling psychologists most frequently use (Watkins, V. Campbell, & Nieberding, in press). Since 1983, all three of these measures have been revised, and efforts to further improve them continue.

The Strong Interest Inventory (Hansen & Campbell, 1985) is a 325-item, paper-and-pencil test that asks participants about their preferences for various occupations, school subjects, activities, types of people, and characteristics. It also provides Holland-type information, basic interest information, and specific information about the individual's similarity and dissimilarity to numerous occupations. In addition to the test manual, other good sources of information about the SII can be found in discussions by Hansen (1986,

1990) and in the recently revised *User's Guide for the SII* (Hansen, 1991). In the field of interest assessment, the SII is dominant, apparently in terms of actual test usage (compared to other inventories), in terms of inventories recommended for graduate students to study, and in terms of graduate-school training opportunities (Watkins, 1990, 1993a, 1993b; Watkins, V. Campbell, & Manus, 1991; Watkins et al., in press).

The SII is psychometrically very sound. The test–retest reliability for all of its scales is in the .80s and .90s, and extensive validity data have been reported (e.g., intercorrelations among the general occupational themes are in the expected directions). However, research on the predictive validity of the recent revision of the inventory is still in progress (Borgen, 1988; V. Campbell, 1987).

Layton (1985) noted that "the chief attempts in the . . . 1985 [revision] have been to renorm the occupational samples, to increase the number of occupational scales, and to make the inventory less restrictive from the standpoint of sex and occupational level (i.e., to increase the number of occupational scales for women and nonprofessional/technical occupations)" (p. 1480). From our observations, the most recent revision of the SII has been successful on all counts. Although some past debate centered on the gender restrictiveness of the survey, the current revision meets the National Institute of Education guidelines on gender bias (Layton, 1985), and the inventory's continued use of single-gender occupational scales has decided advantages (Hackett & Lonborg, 1994). It does indeed appear that the SII "offers a breadth and depth in the measurement of occupational interests that is unmatched by any other single instrument" (V. Campbell, 1987, p. 56).

The Kuder Occupational Interest Survey is a 100-triad-item, paper-and-pencil inventory, requiring respondents to indicate their most and least preferred activities in each item triad. The item triads are composed almost entirely of activities; no occupational titles are included. The inventory, whose construction and scoring differ from that of the SII, provides information about the individual's similarity to various occupational groups and college majors. In addition to the manual (Kuder & Zytowski, 1991), other good sources of information can be found in discussions by Diamond (1990), Zytowski (1992), and Zytowski and Kuder (1986).

Modest to good reliability and validity data for the KOIS have been reported. It has, however, also been criticized for the following limitations: limited studies of the inventory's predictive validity, particularly with regard to job satisfaction; concurrent validity data provided for only 30 criterion groups; unknown effect that the KOIS forced-choice format has on test results; and its inclusion of more male-dominated (65) than female-dominated (44) occupational scales (Hackett & Lonborg, 1994; Herr, 1989; Jepsen, 1988; Tenopyr, 1989). Although these criticisms were directed at the 1985 revision of the KOIS, they appear to be largely unaddressed in the 1991 manual revision. The KOIS is certainly a well-constructed instrument that is useful in counseling. However, some important measurement issues require attention if it is to be used most effectively in career assessment.

The Self-Directed Search, unlike the KOIS and SII, is not a normed, standardized interest inventory. Rather, it is "designed to be a self-administered, self-scored, and self-interpreted guide for high school students and adults desiring career planning assistance" (V. Campbell, 1988, p. 117). This assessment tool, based on Holland's (1985a) vocational theory, asks respondents about their occupational daydreams, preferred activities, abilities, and occupational likes and dislikes. After completing the SDS, respondents may refer to useful, easy-to-understand, interpretive materials that can assist them in further thinking about career exploration and career planning, such as *The Occupations Finder* (Holland, 1977). In addition to the manual (Holland, 1985b), some other good sources of information about the SDS can be found in discussions by Holland and Rayman (1986) and Spokane (1990).

Research data suggest that the SDS is generally sound psychometrically (Bodden, 1987; Krieshok, 1987; Manuele–Adkins, 1989). However, predictive validity (which typically is a problem with interest measures) has been cited as one area in need of more attention (Daniels, 1989). Other concerns have been expressed about the measure: the prevalence of scoring errors by test takers; the inconsistent use of Holland's typology across sections of the measure; and questions about test fairness because of the use of raw rather than normed scores (N. Campbell, 1988; Daniels, 1989; Krieshok, 1987; Manuele–Adkins, 1989). Aware of these concerns, Holland (1985b) attempted to address them in the manual. Because of the seriousness of these issues and their potential to affect test takers negatively, continued attention to them can and should be expected from both researchers and practitioners. Still, with the limitations of the SDS recognized, we emphasize that this tool can be of great value in career assessment and career counseling (e.g., Hackett & Lonborg, 1994; Spokane, 1990). As Krieshok (1987) stated, "When compared to other interventions on cost, reactions of test takers, time, research support, and usefulness, the SDS . . . is in a class by itself" (p. 514).

Other Interest Measures. Along with the SII, SDS and KOIS—what Borgen (1986) referred to as the "big three" (p. 83) in interest assessment—several other important interest measures deserve mention: the Career Assessment Inventory–Enhanced Version (CAI–EV; Johansson, 1986), the Jackson Vocational Interest Survey (JVIS; Jackson, 1977), the Vocational Interest Inventory (VII; Lunneborg, 1981), and the Unisex Edition of the ACT Interest Inventory (UNIACT; American College Testing, 1984). The CAI–EV was initially designed to assess the vocational interests of individuals who were not planning to pursue a college degree (e.g., individuals who instead were planning to pursue occupations consistent with a technical school, business school, or subprofessional training background). Although that objective continues to be the focus of its most recent revision, the inventory has also been expanded to include some professional level interests. The CAI–EV consists of 370 items, takes respondents about 30–40 minutes to complete, and is in many respects a "clone" (Borgen, 1986, p. 92) of the SII. As such, it is grounded in Holland's (1985a) model; provides information about occupational themes, basic interests, and occupational scales; and uses a somewhat similar test booklet. Recent reviews of the measure, some quite critical, have been provided by Bauernfiend (1989), McCabe (1988), Rounds (1989), and Wegner (1992). Wegner (1992) stated that the instrument "appears to remain one of the most useful and better developed inventories for measuring the interests of nonprofessionally oriented clients and will probably continue as such. Its potential for use with professionally oriented clients remains in question until more validating information comes available" (p. 46).

Jackson developed the Jackson Vocational Interest Survey in 1977. It consists of 289 item pairs; provides work-style preference, work-role preference, and general-interest pattern information; is designed to help students (high school and college) and adults in their career-planning efforts; and takes about 1 hour for respondents to complete. Borgen (1986) referred to the JVIS as "a psychometric tour de force" (p. 94). Still, the JVIS has received its share of criticism, too. For example, Jepsen (1992) identified several major limitations of the measure: "(a) sparse theoretical background for the work style scales; (b) awkward items that create serious problems for test-takers and interpreters; (c) limited norm group descriptions and data; (d) lack of longitudinal predictive validity; and (e) the lengthy time required for taking and interpreting the test" (pp. 315). Other reviews of the survey, all of which have echoed one or more of these concerns, have been provided by D. Brown (1989), Davidshofer (1985, 1988), and Thomas (1985). Perhaps the most serious limitation, however, was best summarized by Shephard (1989): "A major problem with the JVIS is its inadequate, geographically narrow normative data. The test norms and contents are at least 10 years old" (p. 404). And these comments were made over 5 years ago. Jepsen (1992) recently reported that Jackson and the JVIS test publishers were "committed to starting a revision in 1991" (pp. 315). We hope that this revision is forthcoming.

Lunneborg first published the Vocational Interest Inventory in 1981; it has not been revised since. The VII is composed of 112 forced-choice items, is grounded in A. Roe's (1956) psychology of occupations, is primarily designed to help high-school students in educational and career planning, and provides college major and occupational-type information. In contrast to many other interest inventories, the VII was "designed to minimize sex differences at the *item* level" (Borgen, 1986, p. 98). The extent to which the measure has achieved its goals has been questioned (Hansen, 1985b). Reviewers have also criticized the VII for its limited sample of respondents (all from Washington state) and its lack of predictive validity (Johnson, 1985; Krumboltz, 1985, 1988).

The Unisex Edition of the ACT Interest Inventory is a product of the work of Lamb and Prediger (1981). Consisting of 90 items (work activities), the UNIACT is grounded in Holland's (1985) hexagonal model, is designed to assist students and adults in career planning, and provides interest information via a world of work map (e.g., Prediger, Swaney, & Mau, 1993). Like the VII, the UNIACT strives to minimize gender differences at the item level. Kifer (1985) reviewed the UNIACT, stating that "there is a sufficient amount of technical evidence about UNIACT to make me believe that it is as good as its principal competitors" (p. 35). However, he also cautioned us that the measure "is meant to be a basis for helping persons who are undecided about a career to begin an exploration of various options. From my point of view any other use would be a misuse" (p. 35).

Interestingly enough, although the CAI-EI, JVIS, VII, and UNIACT all have their strengths and unique features, they ultimately have been compared to one or more of the "big three" (e.g., Johnson, 1985; Shepard, 1989; Wegner, 1992). Perhaps such comparisons are inevitable, but they tend to emphasize only further the reasons that the SII, SDS, and KOIS continue to dominate the field.

Alternative Approaches to Interest Assessment. Qualitative assessment has received increasing attention in the assessment literature. Qualitative assessment includes nonnormed procedures and exercises that counselors can use to help clients explore their interests and values. The vocational card sort is a prime example; it requires clients to sort cards (with occupational titles on them) into three stacks—*like*, *dislike*, and *no opinion*. These opinion stacks can then be discussed and explored with the help of a counselor. Currently available card sorts include the Non-Sexist Vocational Card Sort, Missouri Occupational Card Sort, Occ-U-Sort, Vocational Exploration and Insight Kit's card sort, and Missouri Occupational Preference Inventory (Hackett & Lonborg, 1994; Slaney & MacKinnon–Slaney, 1990). Slaney's (1981) card sort, though not commercially available, has been used in a number of card-sort research studies (Slaney & MacKinnon–Slaney, 1990). Such card sorts can involve the client more actively in the assessment process and make assessment more directly relevant and integral to the counseling process (Goldman, 1990). Card sorts have considerable appeal for counselors interested in gender-fair counseling, due to the problems with gender restrictiveness within the standard interest inventories. However, cautious use is advised in that even the Non-Sexist Vocational Card Sort (Dewey, 1974), which was specifically designed to promote gender-fair interest exploration, can be used in a gender-restrictive manner (Hackett & Lonborg, 1993; 1994). Slaney and MacKinnon–Slaney (1990) provided an excellent, comprehensive review about card sort procedures and their assessment, counseling, and research possibilities.

Some other qualitative assessment exercises or procedures include the Life Line, Kidney Machine Game, worksample method, in-basket technique, role plays and simulations, and even homemade assessment methods (Goldman, 1992). All of these have the potential for the facilitation of self-exploration and can be useful in individual or group situations; their value has been recognized by various assessment experts (e.g., Anastasi, 1990). From our observations, however, training in the effective use of qualitative assessment procedures tends to be limited. If qualitative assessment procedures are to become an integral part of the counselor's assessment repertoire, more extensive training in their use is imperative.

Finally, novel work is currently being conducted on the diversity of interests. Although vocational researchers have always acknowledged the importance of breadth of interests as an influence on career choice, there is currently no instrumentation designed specifically for the assessment of the construct. Development of such an instrument would not only be helpful in the understanding of career-development processes but might also contribute significantly to career counseling. Gaeddert and Hansen (1993) reported on seven different ways of assessing the breadth and diversity of interests, six of which were based on data derived from standardized interest and personality inventories such as the SII and the Jackson Personality Inventory. Gender differences were reported, as were different patterns in interest diversity across occupational groups. Although this research program is in a very early stage, preliminary results suggest the potential development of a useful career assessment tool.

Gender and Cultural Issues in Interest Assessment. Many of the same gender and cultural issues mentioned in our discussion of ability and aptitude assessment also apply to interest assessment (Betz, 1992; Hackett & Lonborg, 1994). A primary concern raised with regard to the major interest inventories, however, has been their potential gender restrictiveness. "Vocational interest inventories have, at least until recently, unintentionally emphasized socialized sex differences and, consequently, have perpetuated occupational segregation and limited the options of individual men and women" (Betz, 1990, p. 440). To counter such restrictiveness, several important steps have been taken (e.g., discussing gender role socialization in interpretive materials). Nevertheless, gender restrictiveness remains an issue of critical concern in the assessment literature (Betz & Fitzgerald, 1987; Gottfredson, 1986). For now, the best way of addressing this issue was framed by Betz (1992):

> Until the gender-role socialization of males and females changes to allow both genders unrestricted access to the full range of experiences relevant to the development of vocational interests (including, for example, science and shop for girls and social skills and home economics for boys), same-sex norms and/or sex-balanced inventory scales should be used to minimize the over-

determining effects of stereotypic socialization practices on subsequent career options. (pp. 460–461; cf. Hackett & Lonborg, 1994)

With minorities and cross-cultural groups, the effect of culture on test taking and on test results is likewise important. To what extent does culture affect a client's interpretation of certain test items and how does that interpretation affect the results obtained? This and other related questions must be entertained when interest inventories are used with minority individuals. Although researchers are now conducting some interesting work to make interest inventories more culturally relevant (e.g., Fouad & Hansen, 1987), the work in this area has only just begun (cf. Carter & Swanson, 1990).

Other Developments and Needs. Almost a decade ago, Borgen (1986) identified several research needs in interest assessment: the need for theory-based research on interests; the need for further study of the link between personality and interests; and the need for closer scrutiny of the relationships between expressed and measured interests. Some limited efforts have been devoted to investigations in each of these areas (e.g., Barak, Librowsky, & Shiloh, 1989; S. Brown & Watkins, in press; Costa, McCrae, & Holland, 1984). Continued attention is clearly warranted.

The structure and dimensionality of interests (i.e., the number of interest dimensions and the interrelatedness of these dimensions) have been the subject of increasing conceptual and research inquiry in the vocational literature (Betz, 1992). Roe's (1956) circular model, Holland's (1985a) hexagonal model, and Gati's (1979) hierarchical model have all been the objects of study and debate. Major reviews on this topic have recently been provided by both Gati (1991) and Tracey and Rounds (1993); these reviews all reflect the importance of and unresolved issues in this area. Continuing research on the structure and dimensionality of interests is important and will no doubt continue to be a rich, fertile topic for study.

Work Values and Needs and Career Salience

Values and Needs. In the career literature, the terms *values, needs,* and *preferences* are often defined quite differently, yet the empirical literature indicates that the various work values, needs, and worker preference inventories measure much the same thing (Betz, 1992). Essentially, the scales described in this section all tap into "the kinds of things people look for in satisfying work" (Betz, 1992, p. 464). Unlike some of the other career assessment techniques, work-values scales often have direct roots in theory; both the individual-differences and developmental perspectives emphasize the role of needs and values in career assessment.

The Work Values Inventory (WVI; Super, 1970) is most appropriate as a career exploration tool for high-school and college students, although it has been used with adult workers as well. Scores are reported for 15 work values, with items tapping both intrinsic and extrinsic values. Norms for both genders are available, but because the norm groups have predominantly been high-school students, the usefulness of the inventory with adult workers is limited. Nonetheless, the WVI, along with the Minnesota Importance Questionnaire (MIQ, described below), are the most psychometrically sound of the work values and needs measures (Bolton, 1985). The WVI is somewhat preferred over the MIQ because of its ease of administration and interpretation.

Nevill and Super's (1989) fairly recent measure, the Values Scale (VS), has potential for career assessment and counseling. The VS contains 21 scales for the measurement of both work-related and general values. Compared to the other work values and needs measures, the VS is advantageous for work with female clients because it taps multiple ways in which values may be met, that is, through work as well as through other life roles. It appears to have cross-cultural applicability and does not appear to be gender biased; no significant gender differences have been found on any of the subscales (Harmon, 1988). There are two major drawbacks of the VS: It is still under development, and considerable psychometric sophistication is required for adequate interpretation (Harmon, 1988).

The Minnesota Importance Questionnaire (MIQ; Rounds, Henly, Dawis, Lofquist, & Weiss, 1981), developed in the context of research on the theory of work adjustment, has been widely used in research. Its major advantage, aside from psychometric adequacy, is its specific design for use with adult workers. In addition to scores for 20 worker needs, the measure also provides measures of correlation between the test-taker's needs profile and the profile of needs satisfied in occupational settings. It is therefore useful not only in assessment of career choice but also in counseling for career adjustment. A disadvantage in its use for assessing women's work-related needs is the absence of specific attention to gender issues, but extensive norms on both male and female workers are available.

Career and Work Salience. People vary not only in the what they look for in satisfactory work but also in the degree to which work is important to the individual. The issue of career salience is a neglected dimension in career assessment, but researchers have increasingly acknowledged its importance to all clients and its special importance to women (Betz & Fitzgerald, 1987). Greenhaus' (1971) Career Salience Inventory is the most visible measure of work-role salience in the research literature, but it has not been widely used in career counseling. More recently, Nevill and Super (1986) introduced the Salience Inventory (SI), a measure of the "participation, commitment, and values expectations for five roles: studying, working, community service, home and family, and leisure" (Zytowski, 1988, p. 151). The SI reflects Super's (1980, 1990) theoretical statements about life roles. The SI is available only in a research edition, so the limitations of the VS hold for the SI, although interpretational guidelines are provided for career counselors (Zytowski, 1988). Given the importance of the issues of role salience and role conflict in women's career development, we predict an increased use of the SI and similar measures.

ASSESSMENT OF CAREER PROCESS VARIABLES

Traditionally, counselors have relied on measures of individual differences to assist clients in making career choices, and researchers have done so to predict and understand the *content* of career choices. In the following sections, we discuss the major career assessment instruments designed to measure various aspects of the career decision-making *process*, or how people go about making work-related choices and adjusting to jobs and careers.

Career Decision Making

Measures of career decision making have been developed to help psychologists better understand both career decisions and career indecision, or indecisiveness. Career indecision is clearly a multidimensional construct, but the literature remains unclear about the specific nature and number of the dimensions or antecedents of indecision (Betz, 1992). Total scores on career-indecision scales may reflect aspects of the decision-making process, such as clarity and certainty, as well as indecision (Betz, 1992). Distinctions have also been made between individuals who experience developmentally normal undecidedness (or simple indecision) and those who are indecisive, or chronically undecided (Betz, 1992); determinations of developmental versus chronic undecidedness have important implications for intervention.

Psychologists have found several measures to be useful in understanding the career-decision status of clients and in identifying sources of career indecision. Originally designed as a diagnostic tool for use in counseling, the Career Decision Scale (CDS, Osipow, 1987) is not only the oldest of the decision scales but is also the most widely used; it has also stimulated a large body of research (Osipow, 1991). The CDS is a 19-item scale that requires only about 10 minutes for respondents to complete. Sixteen of the items address antecedents of career or educational indecision, 2 items address overall decisional status, and 1 item is written in a free-response format. The CDS provides both a measure of undecidedness and information about the sources of indecision (Osipow, 1987). Typically a total score for the 16 indecision items is obtained, although users may also choose to obtain subscale scores across four factors: lack of structure and confidence, barriers, approach–approach problems, and personal conflict.

The consensus in the field indicates that the CDS is a very good instrument, with a large amount of support for its reliability and validity (Slaney, 1988). Nevertheless, debates have raged over the factor structure of the CDS. Osipow (1991) prefers the use of the total indecision score because of the small number of items per subscale and the instability of the factor structure. Others have argued for the use of subscale scores to clarify the various antecedents of career indecision (Vondracek, 1991), basing their argument on factor analyses that confirm a fairly stable four-factor solution (Schulenberg, Shimizu, Vondracek, & Hostetler, 1988; Shimizu, Vondracek, Schulenberg, & Hostetler, 1988). The debates seem to revolve around the question of whether the instrument ought to be revised or whether it adequately achieves its original purpose. Currently the CDS does a very good job for what it was designed to do, namely, to provide an overall measure of indecision. It is perhaps unfair, in response to the increasing pressure for a measure more precisely targeting the multidimensionality of career indecision (Betz, 1992), to hold the CDS to a standard it was not designed to address.

Holland, Daiger, and Power's (1980) My Vocational Situation Scale (MVS) was also designed for the assessment of career indecision, but it provides, as well, information about specific types of vocational assistance the client may need. The MVS includes three subscales: the Vocational Identity scale, an 18-item measure of clarity and stability of one's career-related attributes; a 4-item Occupational Information scale; and a 4-item Barriers scale (Holland, Johnston, & Asama, 1993; Slaney, 1988). High subscale scores indicate the respondent's need for assistance in clarifying goals, interests, personality, and talents (Vocational Identity); obtaining occupational information; or overcoming obstacles to career goals (Barriers). Scores on the Vocational Identity scale correlate highly with scores on the CDS and are also related to subsequent job satisfaction (Holland, Johnston, & Asama, 1993).

There is now adequate evidence of the reliability and validity of the MVS (Holland, 1993; Slaney, 1988). The Vocational Identity scale, in particular, has become widely used by counselors as a quick method of assessing the level of career assistance required and as an outcome measure of the effectiveness of career interventions (Holland, 1993). Additionally, there is some evidence that the Vocational Identity scale taps into some of the types of beliefs measured by Krumboltz's (1991) Career Beliefs Scale. In addition to its usefulness as a measure of career-decision status, the MVS has the potential to assist clients in exploring perceptions of environmental obstacles and barriers. On the other hand, although the MVS has been presented as a diagnostic scheme, the research support for its validity as a diagnostic tool is still anecdotal (Westbrook, 1988).

Finally, some researchers have worked on measures of constructs related to career decidedness. For example, Swanson and Tokar (1991) developed a measure of perceptions of barriers to career development, including barriers of unique concern to women. This instrument may ultimately prove to be useful for the identification of factors that contribute to women's (and men's) career indecision, but it is still in the developmental phase. Blustein, Ellis, and Devenis (1989) conducted research on scales to measure commitment to career choice, specifically, the Vocational Exploration and Commitment (VEC) and the Tendency to Foreclose (TTF) scales. Another new scale was designed to help counselors distinguish undecided from chronically indecisive clients. Preliminary data on the reliability and construct validity of Serling and Betz's (1990) Fear of Commitment Scale (FOCS) strongly indicate that this scale has great potential as a tool for the identification and understanding of indecisiveness (Betz & Serling, 1993).

Career Maturity

Westbrook (1983) argued that the concept of career maturity does not have a universal meaning or definition and that it may even be an endangered species. Still, progress toward better understanding and conceptualizing of career maturity has been made in recent years, and we strongly suspect that such work will continue. Although career maturity may not have universal meaning, some researchers have made general, useful attempts to define it. For example, Betz (1988) stated that "career maturity can be generally defined as the extent to which the individual has mastered the vocational development tasks, including both knowledge and attitudinal components, appropriate to his or her stage of career development" (p. 80). That definition nicely captures much of how career maturity has been and is typically being considered by career maturity theorists.

Currently, the Career Maturity Inventory (CMI) and the Career Development Inventory (CDI; Super, Thompson, Lindeman, Jordaan, & Myers, 1988b) are the two mainstays of career maturity measurement. The CMI emerged from a model of career maturity earlier proposed by Crites (1978a, 1978b). The CMI–Attitude Scale (CMI–AS) yields an assessment of five variables related to the career-decision process: decisiveness in career decision making, involvement in career decision making, independence in career decision making, orientation to career decision making, and compromise in career decision making (Crites, 1978c). The scale is designed for use by students in sixth through twelfth grades. Although acceptable reliability and validity data have been reported for the CMI–AS, "after hundreds of studies, four questions about the Attitude Scale's validity remain unanswered" (Savickas, 1990, p. 403). These pertain to concerns about construct validity, criterion-related validity, convergent and discriminant validity, and validity for use. In addition to these concerns, other problems with the CMI–AS have been identified. As Savickas (1990) stated, "The most pressing research need relative to the Attitude Scale is a literature review. The last literature review appeared in the *Theory and Research Handbook* (Crites, 1978c)" (p. 404). "The most pressing empirical research need is for studies of the validity of the five subscales. In order for these subscales to be helpful to counselors, their validity for use must be formally established" (Savickas, 1990, p. 404). To our knowledge, nothing has yet been done in response to these CMI–AS concerns. Reviews and descriptions of the CMI–AS (which has not been revised since the 1970s) have been written by Betz (1988), Katz (1978, 1982), Savickas (1990), and Zytowski (1978).

The CDI was first published in the early 1970s, was later modified, and now exists in its 1988 published form (Super, Thompson, Lindeman, Jordaan, & Myers, 1988b). It takes about 40–60 minutes for respondents to complete, it is designed for use by high-school and college students, and it provides information about such areas as career planning, career exploration, career decision making, world of work, and knowledge about one's preferred occupational group. Favorable validity data have been reported for the CDI, but reliability and stability are not as good for some of the CDI scales as users may wish. Reviews of the CDI have been written by Betz (1988), Hansen (1985a), Locke (1988), Pinkney (1985), and Savickas (1990). As with the CMI–AS, Savickas (1990) also identified some of the most pressing research needs for the CDI: "The CDI needs criterion-related research to firmly establish its validity and nomological network. . . . Practitioners would also benefit from research on the interpretative hypotheses suggested for each CDI scale. . . . Some revision of the CDI itself to increase scale reliabilities would support work on scale and profile interpretation" (p. 393). The CDI has a prominent role in the career development assessment and counseling model (Super, Osborne, Walsh, S. Brown, & Niles, 1992). The CDI surely fills a void and has its uses, but further work in the areas mentioned here are clearly needed if the CDI is to overcome its current limitations.

In addition to the CMI–AS and CDI, other measures of career maturity have been developed, for example, Cognitive Vocational Maturity Test (Westbrook & Mastie, 1974). The models and measures developed by Super and Crites, however, have long received and will likely continue to receive primary attention in the career maturity area.

In recent years, reports of some interesting conceptual work on the topic of career maturity have appeared. Betz (1988), for example, proposed a path model for the maturity construct, identifying antecedents (intelligence, acceptance of middle-class values, and extent of career-related experiences) as well as consequents (interests, abilities, and consistency over time) of career maturity. Savickas (1984, 1993) proposed a classification scheme—stimulus (S), organism (O), response (R), and adjustment (A)—for thinking about career maturity. In the S–O–R–A scheme, *S* refers to vocational development tasks, *R* refers to coping behaviors (e.g., decision making, planning) that the individual uses to deal with vocational development tasks, O refers to those organism or person characteristics (e.g., attitudes) that facilitate the person's coping, and A refers to the outcomes of one's coping behaviors. Betz's model and Savickas' scheme both have potential for advancing research and practice.

Adult Career Adjustment

Although career development is a process that extends throughout the life span, all too little work has focused on adult career development. However, two recently developed assessment tools, the Adult Career Concerns Inventory (ACCI) and the Career Mastery Inventory (CMAS), are excellent measures of adult career development. The ACCI, developed by Super, Thompson, Lindeman, Jordaan, & Myers (1988a), is a 61-item inventory that is grounded in Super's (1980) model of career development. It takes about 30 minutes for the respondent to complete, provides information about career development tasks of concern to adults, and is intended for use by those 18 years of age and older. In addition to the test manual, useful descriptions and reviews of the ACCI have been provided by Betz (1988), S. Brown and Rounds (1988), Herr and Niles (1988), Savickas (1992), and Whiston (1990). Reviewers tend to agree that the ACCI is a valuable tool and meets a real need in career assessment. A number of concerns, however, have been consistently voiced about the ACCI, for example, limited validation studies and norming problems (Betz, 1988, 1992; S. Brown & Rounds, 1988; Whiston, 1990). Because of these concerns, cautious use of the ACCI for counseling purposes has been recommended.

The CMAS, developed by Crites (1990), is a two-part, 110-item inventory that is grounded in Crites' model of career adjustment. It provides information about the person's degree of coping in terms of six career-development tasks (organizational adaptability, position performance, work habits and attitudes, coworker relationships, advancement, and career choice and plans) and types of strategies (integrative, adjustive, nonadjustive) the individual uses to solve work problems. The CMAS, like the ACCI, appears to have much potential for use in assessment, counseling, and research. A particularly good description of the CMAS has been provided by Savickas (1992). On the other hand, Betz (1992) has pointed out that "widespread use [of the CMAS] should await the appearance of its forthcoming *Theory and Research Handbook*" (p. 468).

ASSESSMENT OF CAREER-RELATED COGNITIONS

The most dramatic shift in research on career assessment in recent years, prompted by the cognitive revolution in psychology, is the increased attention devoted to career-related cognitions. Systematic coverage of the assessment of career cognitions was notably absent in Zytowski and Borgen's 1983 review. On one hand, vocational researchers have always acknowledged the importance of cognitive processes in career development. For example, in 1978 Tyler remarked that "individuals create themselves . . . it is development we must study, but the development of the shaper rather than the shaped (quoted in Zytowski & Borgen, 1983, pp. 34–35). On the other hand, cognitive trends in career assessment and research represent a distinct new approach in vocational psychology (Lent & Hackett, 1994). What clearly differentiates this new area of inquiry from past trends is the systematic theoretical and research attention devoted to the central role of cognitions in career choice and adjustment and the concurrent emphasis on personal agency in career pursuits. "Vocational researchers of all theoretical persuasions are exhibiting a greater tendency to include cognitive variables in their research, and to view people as active agents in their own career development, as opposed to passive reactors to intrapsychic or external determinants" (Lent & Hackett, 1994, p. 81).

As a result of more intense research scrutiny devoted to the role of cognitions in vocational behavior, many writers have also argued for the importance of the assessment of career-related cognitions in counseling (Betz, 1992). D. Brown and Brooks (1991) devoted considerable attention to the assessment of cognitive clarity; Spokane (1991) spoke to the need for a cognitive structure for the evaluation of career alternatives; Rounds and Tracey (1990) argued for an information-processing approach to career assessment and counseling; Neimeyer (1988) proposed that cognitive vocational schema are important; and Brown and Brooks (1990) showed that cognitive problem-solving and decision-making abilities have long been considered crucial to career development. Two major types of career cognitions have received enough research attention to warrant counselors' routine consideration in career assessment: career beliefs and career-related self-efficacy (Betz, 1992).

Career Beliefs

Several measures of irrational beliefs have been developed, but Krumboltz's (1991) Career Beliefs Inventory (CBI) is the one measure specifically created for use in career counseling. "For many years counselors have observed that a person's beliefs about potential vocational alternatives can either foster or interfere with his or her decision-making, but until the development of the Career Beliefs Inventory . . . there has been no formal tool for assessing career beliefs" (Holland, Johnston, Asama, & Polys, 1993). Specifically, "the Career Beliefs Inventory is a counseling tool designed to help people identify career beliefs that may be preventing them from achieving their career goals" (Krumboltz, 1991, p. 1).

Influenced by earlier work on the role of irrational beliefs in human functioning by Ellis and others and by research on myths and preconceptions about careers, Krumboltz (1991) based his work on the premise that

> the way in which people make career decisions, search for jobs, and seek promotions depends on what they believe about themselves and the world of work. If their beliefs are accurate and constructive, they will act in ways that are likely to foster the achievement of their goals. If their beliefs are inaccurate and self-defeating, they will act in ways that make sense to them but may hinder accomplishment of their goals. (p. 1)

Based logically on these premises, a measure designed to assist counselor and client alike to better understand these underlying career beliefs and assumptions should improve assessment and enhance the effectiveness of career interventions.

The CBI consists of 96 items that form 25 subscales, comes with computerized scoring sheets, and takes about 25 minutes for the user to administer (Krumboltz, 1991, 1994a). The subscales are organized under five headings designed to provide the counselor guidance in understanding CBI subscale scores: My current career situation, What seems to be necessary for my happiness, Factors that influence my decisions, Changes I am willing to make, and Effort I am willing to initiate. The test–retest reliability of the scale is "acceptable but nothing to rave about" (Walsh, 1994, p. 432). One-month reliabilities range from .35 to .74, and 3-month test–retest reliabilities for the CBI range from .27 to .68. One problem with the reliability of the measure appears to be the overabundance of very short subscales. On the other hand, Krumboltz (1994b) has argued that, theoretically, the reliabilities ought to be moderate because the measure is for assessing changeable cognitions.

Some interesting validity data for the CBI have been collected. Evidence for concurrent validity is suggested by the modest correlation between CBI scores and job satisfaction. Career beliefs appear to be conceptually distinct from interests and personality; CBI scores are unrelated to scores on various interest and personality measures. CBI scores indicative of continuing career decision making are also inversely correlated with MVS career commitment scores. Further evidence of the construct validity of the CBI has been provided by research conducted by Holland and his associates. For example, Holland, Johnston, Asama, and Polys (1993) reported that the CBI correlates in expected directions with several inventories and scales, including the NEO Personality Inventory (Costa & McCrae, 1985), the SDS, and the Vocational Identity Scale (Holland et al., 1980).

The CBI does not appear to contain any overtly gender-biased items, and no significant gender differences have been found for the various subscales

(Krumboltz, 1991). On the other hand, the inventory also contains no items specifically addressing gender role beliefs, a common problem for women seeking career counseling (Hackett & Lonborg, 1993). Although preliminary studies have also found no racial or ethnic differences across the subscales of the CBI, the appropriateness of cross-cultural applicability awaits further research.

Reviewers have raised concerns about the psychometric properties of the CBI and about some of the theoretical assumptions underlying the scale, in particular, the clarity with which the construct of beliefs has been defined, and have called for a reexamination of the factor structure of the scale (Fuqua & Newman, 1994; Walsh, 1994). Nevertheless, reviewers also noted that the CBI holds promise for clinical and diagnostic usage: "Consistent with its intended purpose, the CBI is an excellent practical tool for career counseling" (Fuqua & Newman, 1994, p. 429). The manual for the CBI contains suggestions for its use in career counseling and Holland, Johnston, Asama, and Polys (1993) reported that the inventory is helpful in promoting client discussion and interaction in career counseling. We envision increased research attention to this new instrument, with concomitant revisions and improvements.

Another new instrument that contains subscales for the assessment of career beliefs and attitudes is Holland and Gottfredson's (1993) Career Attitudes and Strategies Inventory (CASI). Developed out of Holland's ongoing research program, the CASI "attempts to assess a person's attitudes, beliefs, and strategies about careers including both the work and non-work environments that impinge on career-changing, work performance, and job satisfaction" (Holland, 1993, p. 8). The CASI is a 130-item measure that yields subscale scores on 9 dimensions: job satisfaction, work involvement, skill development, dominant style, career worries, interpersonal abuse, family commitment, risk-taking style, and geographical barriers. Preliminary research suggests that the scale may effectively supplement other career measures, especially those based on Holland's (1985) theory, to further the understanding of important processes such as career stability, career change, and job satisfaction (Holland, 1993). The CASI obviously requires further psychometric study, but we believe that we will see much more use of the scale in the future.

Career Self-Efficacy

As a consequence of the expanding literature on the applications of Bandura's (1977, 1986) self-efficacy theory to the career domain, measures of career-related self-efficacy have proliferated. Explicit applications of self-efficacy theory to career development originated with Hackett and Betz's (1981) initial statement detailing the role of efficacy beliefs in the career development of women. Hackett and Betz (1981) argued that self-efficacy theory provides a heuristic framework for the understanding of the cognitive and affective mediators of women's gender role socialization experiences and the resulting gender differences in career-choice patterns that can still be observed in the work force. In most of the early studies in this area, researchers therefore investigated gender differences in perceived self-efficacy for occupations and the links between occupational or, more broadly, career self-efficacy and the consideration of traditional (for women) and nontraditional (for women) career pursuits. The research quickly expanded, however, to examinations of self-efficacy with respect to a wide range of career-related pursuits and to explorations of the career self-efficacy of men as well as of women (Hackett, in press; Hackett & Betz, 1992).

Considerable evidence now exists to support Hackett and Betz's (1981) original contention that career-efficacy beliefs are predictive of gender differences in educational and career choice. More generally, support has been found for the central mediating role of self-efficacy in career choice and adjustment (Hackett & Betz, 1992). For example, evidence of the direct and indirect contribution of perceived efficacy to both academic and career choice exists as does evidence of the role of efficacy beliefs in the development of interests (Lent, S. Brown, & Hackett, 1994). Results of studies that have compared self-efficacy theory to alternate theoretical models also convincingly demonstrate that self-efficacy is a powerful predictor of career choice and other career-related variables. The research literature on career self-efficacy is also exerting an influence on career counseling. For example, career counselors have been advised to assess self-efficacy beliefs hand-in-hand with measured aptitudes and abilities (Betz, 1992). Work has also begun on the formulation of an explicit set of theoretical propositions, derived from social cognitive theory, to clarify the interrelationships among career self-efficacy and other career-relevant variables, including social contextual factors (Lent et al., in press). This work may well guide future research and assessment efforts.

Research instruments have been developed for the assessment of self-efficacy with respect to a wide range of career behaviors, for example, occupational choices, mathematics and science achievement, academic performance in high school and college, career decision making, and multiple-role conflict (Hackett, in press; Hackett & Betz, in press). Although there are a number of unresolved methodological issues in the measurement of career self-efficacy, the internal consistency and predictive validity data are generally adequate for most measures (Hackett & Lent, 1992; Lent & Hackett, 1987). Aside from their nascent state of development, career self-efficacy measures have a distinct disadvantage, one that causes confusion for many. Self-efficacy must be assessed with reference to some specific set of behaviors or tasks. Self-efficacy is *not*, conceptually, a stable personality trait. It is more accurately defined as a cognitive appraisal of one's capabilities (Hackett & Lent, 1992). There is no one self-efficacy measure, but rather multiple measures of multiple areas. Counselors and researchers must therefore select the measure most appropriate for a particular client's concerns or targeted domain of inquiry. As anticipated by theory, self-efficacy assessments tailored to particular domains of functioning yield more predictive utility than broad, generic measures (e.g., Betz & Hackett, 1983; Lent et al., 1994). For example, occupational self-efficacy is strongly predictive of the career fields students choose, whereas academic self-efficacy is a better predictor of academic persistence and achievement in college (Hackett, in press). The following represents a highly selective overview of the instruments that have been developed for the assessment of various forms of career self-efficacy.

Occupational Self-Efficacy. Many studies of occupational self-efficacy have incorporated Betz and Hackett's (1981; 1993b) Occupational Self-Efficacy Scale (OSES). The OSES is a 20-item scale for assessing the individual's confidence in succeeding in various occupations. Occupations from six fields are represented; half of the occupations are female-dominated (67% or more women in the occupation) and half have traditionally been dominated by men. Either an overall score or the subscale scores for the male- and female-dominated occupational subscales can be used. The subscale scores can be useful indicators of gender restrictions in career choice. Internal-consistency reliabilities for the overall scale and the two subscales are high, ranging from .89 to .95 over various studies (Betz & Hackett, 1993b). A one-week test–retest reliability of .70 for the confidence scores was reported in one study (Hackett & O'Halloran, 1985). The validity of the instrument has been documented in numerous investigations (Betz & Hackett, 1993b, Hackett, in press; Lent & Hackett, 1987).

There are several drawbacks of the OSES. One is the lack of extensive psychometric analyses. Also, the instrument is not published, although a manual is available from the authors. Because of societal changes since the instrument was first developed, another problem is whether or not the original designations of occupations as male- and female-dominated remain valid. An expansion of the range of occupations included on the OSES may also be desirable for more adequate representation of potential career choices. Research is currently underway to update and revise the original OSES (Hackett, Chen, & Byars, 1994).

Several other measures have been used for the assessment of overall efficacy with regard to occupations. Most are modeled after the OSES, albeit with differences such as variations in the list of occupations included or by the provision of occupational information with the list of occupational titles (Hackett, in press). The effects of including occupational information within a measure of efficacy beliefs has not been directly examined. However, providing career information is surely an intervention and may produce misleading estimates of career self-efficacy, given that most individuals make career decisions based on occupational stereotypes rather than on reliable information. Clearly, investigations of the various formats now used for the measurement of career efficacy beliefs are necessary.

Of the many career self-efficacy instruments available, only Rooney and Osipow's (1992) Task-Specific Occupational Self-Efficacy Scale (TSOSS) was developed with a counseling use in mind. The original TSOSS required respondents to estimate their confidence in performing 230 job tasks. The test–retest reliability of the scale was .77, and support for the validity of the scale has been forthcoming (Rooney & Osipow, 1992). A shorter, 60-item version of the TSOSS has been developed (Osipow, Temple, & Rooney, 1993). The short TSOSS consists of four factors: language and interpersonal skills; quantitative, logical, scientific, and business skills; physical strength and agility; and aesthetic skills. Internal consistency and test–retest reliabilities for the short form are high, and preliminary validity data are promising (Osipow et al., 1993; Temple & Osipow, 1994).

The TSOSS certainly has much to recommend it, and we predict that it will receive increasing research scrutiny. Nevertheless, there are some potential problems when counselors attempt to assess career efficacy beliefs via job or work tasks. The extent to which people make judgments about their ability to successfully pursue different lines of work by examining the discrete task subskills related to particular occupations is unclear; efficacy beliefs across clusters of work tasks are not believed to be equivalent to overall occupational self-efficacy. For example, perceived efficacy for job tasks and efficacy for occupational roles are only modestly interrelated (Rooney & Osipow, 1992). On the other hand, we think that the TSOSS might be very useful in counseling, particularly in identifying the sources of low overall self-efficacy, for example, in cases in which there is a disparity between general occupational self-efficacy and efficacy for clusters of occupationally relevant tasks. The careful work that researchers have performed to create and validate the TSOSS is very likely to result in a strong and psychometrically valid instrument for counseling as well as for research purposes, but the resolution of some of these conceptual issues awaits further research.

Other Career Self-Efficacy Measures.   Two other measures have received enough research attention to warrant mention. First, the Mathematics Self-Efficacy Scale (MSES; Betz & Hackett, 1983, 1993a) has been used in a number of studies of academic achievement in mathematics and science as well as the choice of science- and math-related college majors and careers. The original MSES is a 75-item scale for the assessment of the individual's confidence in three domains related to mathematics performance: everyday math tasks, college courses, and math problems. Validity data are strong, and reliabilities for the MSES are high, with internal-consistency estimates ranging from .92 to .96 and the test–retest reliabilities in the .90s (Betz & Hackett, 1993a). The MSES was not designed for counseling usage, but ongoing development work may yield a scale useful to counselors in enhancing career exploration and addressing barriers to career choice. The introduction of a shorter, 34-item form of the MSES consisting of the college courses and math tasks subscales, is especially promising (cf. Betz & Hackett, 1993a).

The Career Decision-Making Self-efficacy Scale (CDMSE; Betz & Taylor, 1993; Taylor & Betz, 1983) has also generated much empirical attention. Designed for the assessment of the individual's confidence in successfully negotiating the tasks prerequisite to effective decision making, the CDMSE Scale consists of 50 career decision-making tasks organized into five subscales: accurate self-appraisal, gathering occupational information, goal selection, making plans for the future, and problem solving. Support for the reliability of the CDMSE Scale is strong, and evidence for the content, concurrent, discriminant, and predictive validity of the scale has been reported (Betz & Taylor, 1993). One of the key questions about the CDMSE Scale concerns its factor structure, that is, whether the CDMSE scale should be used as a general measure of career decision-making self-efficacy or whether the subscale scores yield valid estimates of efficacy with respect to discrete domains (Robbins, 1985; Taylor & Popma, 1990). Nevertheless, research findings have largely supported the usefulness of the CDMSE Scale in predicting career indecision, and the scale may prove quite useful in counseling.

Future Directions. A new direction in research on career self-efficacy is represented by a few recent studies of efficacy for the individual's coping with multiple roles. Because women who work outside the home remain responsible for the majority of household and child-care responsibilities within families, the impact of multiple roles on women's work behavior and career development has received increasing attention (Hackett & Lonborg, 1993). Although most of the research has focused on the multiple-role conflicts of adult workers, the focus has recently shifted to investigations of the influence of girls' anticipation of multiple-role conflicts on their career choices. Girls and women often adopt "satisficing" (Fitzgerald & Weitzman, 1992, p. 131) strategies, choosing traditionally female occupations that are perceived to be easier to combine with home and family responsibilities rather than optimally translating their interests and abilities into career pursuits. Multiple-role efficacy may therefore play an important role in governing whether girls and women lower their aspirations and settle for a career that is "good enough" or attempt to pursue more challenging careers.

Two measures of multiple-role efficacy have appeared, one developed by Stickel and Bonett (1991; Bonett & Stickel, 1992), the other by Lefcourt and Harmon (1993). Stickel and Bonett's (1991) scale is an adaptation of

Betz and Hackett's (1981) instrument but includes occupational information and a different set of instructions. Respondents are asked to indicate their confidence in handling each of 18 occupations. They are also asked to indicate their perceived ability to combine home and family responsibilities while pursuing each career. This latter set of questions serves as the measure of multiple-role efficacy. Reliability for this scale is adequate, but the extent to which this approach (i.e., simply tacking questions about multiple roles onto an occupational self-efficacy scale) is valid must be verified empirically.

Conversely, Lefcourt and Harmon's (1993) Self-efficacy for Role Management Measure (SEERM) was developed as an assessment of efficacy with respect to a variety of specific multiple-role issues. Strong internal consistency and test–retest reliabilities have been reported for this 150-item scale, and preliminary factor analyses are encouraging. Although it is much too early to anticipate the course of the research on the SEERM, this type of scale is important to inquiry in the area of women's career development and holds promise for career counseling with women.

FINAL COMMENTS

Overall, research on career assessment since the publication of the last *Handbook of Vocational Psychology* (Walsh & Osipow, 1983) has continued at a pace consistent with historical trends. The cognitive shift in psychology is one of the most important influences on contemporary vocational research, as evidenced not only by the appearance of several new scales in the career assessment literature but also by the increasing attention to career cognitions and cognitive assessment within various theoretical traditions (Lent & Hackett, 1994). Yet research also continues on the mainstays of career assessment: interests, abilities, values, career decision making, and career maturity.

We are reluctant to prophesy the future trends in this complex and vital research area, but it does appear safe to venture two very broad predictions: There will likely be greater movement toward combined assessments of interests, abilities, and various other individual-difference dimensions, and there will likely be an increased emphasis on the revision of existing instruments and development of new measures that more adequately capture the gender and ethnic diversity of our clientele, the school systems, and the work force. These latter trends, a result of shifting demographics and societal pressures, will no doubt continue to exert an important influence on all areas of vocational research in future years.

REFERENCES

Aiken, L. R. (1985). Review of ACT Assessment Program. In J. V. Mitchell, Jr. (Ed.), *The ninth mental measurements yearbook* (Vol. 1, pp. 29–31). Lincoln, NE: Buros Institute of Mental Measurements.

American College Testing. (1984). *Vocational interest, experience, and skill assessment user's manual.* Iowa City, IA: Author.

American College Testing. (1989). *Preliminary manual for the Enhanced ACT Assessment.* Iowa City, IA: Author.

Anastasi, A. (1988). *Psychological testing* (6th ed.). New York: Macmillan.

Anastasi, A. (1990). Diversity and flexibility. *The Counseling Psychologist, 18*, 258–261.

Bandura, A. (1977). Self-efficacy: Toward a unifying theory of behavioral change. *Psychological Review, 84*, 191–214.

Bandura, A. (1986). *Social foundations of thought and action: A social cognitive theory.* Englewood Cliffs, NJ: Prentice-Hall.

Barak, A., Librowsky, I., & Shiloh, S. (1989). Cognitive determinants of interests: An extension of a theoretical model and initial empirical examinations. *Journal of Vocational Behavior, 34*, 318–334.

Bauernfiend, R. H. (Ed.). (1989). Review of the Career Assessment Inventory–Enhanced Version. *AMECD Newsnotes, 25*, 1.

Betz, N. E. (1988). The assessment of career development and maturity. In W. B. Walsh & S. H. Osipow (Eds.), *Career decision making* (pp. 77–136). Hillsdale, NJ: Lawrence Erlbaum Associates.

Betz, N. E. (1990). Contemporary issues in testing use. In C. E. Watkins, Jr. & V. L. Campbell (Eds.), *Testing in counseling practice* (pp. 419–450). Hillsdale, NJ: Lawrence Erlbaum Associates.

Betz, N. E. (1992). Career assessment: A review of critical issues. In S. D. Brown & R. W. Lent (Eds.), *Handbook of counseling psychology* (2nd ed., pp. 453–484). New York: Wiley.

Betz, N. E., & Fitzgerald, L. F. (1987). *The career psychology of women.* New York: Academic Press.

Betz, N. E., & Hackett, G. (1981). The relationship of career-related self-efficacy expectations to perceived career options in college women and men. *Journal of Counseling Psychology, 28*, 399–410.

Betz, N. E., & Hackett, G. (1983). The relationship of mathematics self-efficacy expectations to the selection of science-based college majors. *Journal of Counseling Psychology, 23*, 329–345.

Betz, N. E., & Hackett, G. (1993a). *Manual for the mathematics self-efficacy scale: Forms A and B.* Unpublished manuscript, Ohio State University, Columbus.

Betz, N. E., & Hackett, G. (1993b). *Manual for the occupational self-efficacy scale.* Unpublished manuscript, Ohio State University, Columbus.

Betz, N. E., & Serling, D. A. (1993). Construct validity of fear of commitment as an indicator of career indecisiveness. *Journal of Career Assessment, 1*, 21–34.

Betz, N. E., & Taylor, K. M. (1993). *Manual for the Career Decision Making Self-Efficacy Scale.* Unpublished manuscript, Ohio State University, Columbus.

Blustein, D. L., Ellis, M. V., & Devenis, L. E. (1989). The development and validation of a two-dimensional model of the commitment to career choices process. *Journal of Vocational Behavior, 35*, 342–378.

Bodden, J. L. (1987). The Self-Directed Search. In D. J. Keyser & R. C. Sweetland (Eds.), *Test critiques compendium* (pp. 422–427). Kansas City, MO: Test Corporation of America.

Bolton, B. (1985). Work values inventory. In D. J. Keyser & R. C. Sweetland (Eds.), *Test Critiques* (Vol. 2, pp. 835–843). Kansas City, MO: Test Corporation of America.

Bonett, R. M., & Stickel, S. A. (1992). A psychometric analysis of the Career Attitude Scale. *Measurement and Evaluation in Counseling and Development, 25*, 14.

Borgen, F. H. (1986). New approaches to the assessment of interests. In W. B. Walsh & S. H. Osipow (Eds.), *Advances in vocational psychology: Vol. 1. The assessment of interests* (pp. 83–125). Hillsdale, NJ: Lawrence Erlbaum Associates.

Borgen, F. H. (1988). Strong–Campbell Interest Inventory. In J. T. Kapes & M. M. Mastie (Eds.), *A counselor's guide to career assessment instruments* (2nd ed., pp. 121–126). Alexandria, VA: National Career Development Association.

Brown, D. T. (1989). Review of the Jackson Vocational Interest Survey. In J. C. Conoley & J. J. Kramer (Eds.), *The tenth mental measurements yearbook* (Vol. 1, pp. 401–403). Lincoln, NE: Buros Institute of Mental Measurements.

Brown, D., & Brooks, L. (1991). *Career counseling techniques.* Boston: Allyn & Bacon.

Brown, S. D., & Rounds, J. B., Jr. (1988). Adult Career Concerns Inventory. In D. J. Keyser & R. C. Sweetland (Eds.), *Test critiques* (Vol. 7, pp. 20–26). Kansas City, MO: Test Corporation of America.

Brown, S. D., & Watkins, C. E., Jr. (1994). Psychodynamic career theory: Emergent issues, problems, and concerns. In M. L. Savickas & R. W. Lent (Eds.), *Convergence in career theories* (pp. 197–206). Palo Alto, CA: Consulting Psychologists Press.

Campbell, D. P. (1990). *Manual for the Campbell Organizational Survey.* Minneapolis, MN: National Computer Systems.

Campbell, D. P. (1991). *Manual for the Campbell Leadership Index.* Minneapolis, MN: National Computer Systems.

Campbell, D. P. (1993a). *Manual for the Campbell Community Survey.* Minneapolis, MN: National Computer Systems.

Campbell, D. P. (1993b). A new integrated battery of psychological surveys. *Journal of Counseling and Development, 71,* 575–587.

Campbell, D. P., & Hallam, M. (1993). *Manual for Campbell–Hallam Team Development Survey.* Minneapolis, MN: National Computer Systems.

Campbell, D. P., Hyne, S. A., & Nilsen, D. L. (1992). *Manual for Campbell Interest and Skill Survey.* Minneapolis, MN: National Computer Systems.

Campbell, N. J. (1988). The Self-Directed Search. In J. T. Kapes & M. M. Mastie (Eds.), *A counselor's guide to career assessment instruments* (2nd ed., pp. 116–120). Alexandria, VA: National Career Development Association.

Campbell, V. L. (1987). Strong–Campbell Interest Inventory (4th ed.). *Journal of Counseling and Development, 66,* 53–56.

Carter, R. T., & Swanson, J. L. (1990). The validity of the Strong Interest Inventory with Black Americans: A review of the literature. *Journal of Vocational Behavior, 36,* 195–209.

Cohn, S. J. (1985). Review of Graduate Record Examination–General Test. In J. V. Mitchell, Jr. (Ed.), *The ninth mental measurements yearbook* (Vol. 1, pp. 622–624). Lincoln, NE: Buros Institute of Mental Measurements.

College Entrance Examination Board (1986). *Manual for the Scholastic Aptitude Test.* Princeton, NJ: Educational Testing Service.

Conrad, I., Trismen, D., & Miller, R. (Eds.). (1977). *Graduate Record Examinations Technical Manual.* Princeton, NJ: Educational Testing Service.

Costa, P. T., Jr., & McCrae, R. R. (1985). *The NEO Personality Inventory.* Odessa, FL: Psychological Assessment Resources.

Costa, P. T., Jr., McCrae, R. R., & Holland, J. L. (1984). Personality and vocational interests in an adult sample. *Journal of Applied Psychology, 69,* 390–400.

Crites, J. O. (1978a). *Administration and use manual for the Career Maturity Inventory* (2nd ed.). Monterey, CA: CTB/McGraw–Hill.

Crites, J. O. (1978b). *The Career Maturity Inventory.* Monterey, CA: CTB/McGraw–Hill.

Crites, J. O. (1978c). *Theory and research handbook for the Career Maturity Inventory* (2nd ed.). Monterey, CA: CTB/McGraw–Hill.

Crites, J. O. (1990). *Career Mastery Inventory.* Boulder, CO: Crites Career Consultants.

Daniels, M. H. (1989). Review of the Self-Directed Search. In J. C. Conoley & J. J. Kramer (Eds.), *The tenth mental measurements yearbook* (Vol. 1, pp. 735–738). Lincoln, NE: Buros Institute of Mental Measurements.

Davidshofer, C. (1985). Review of Jackson Vocational Interest Survey. In J. V. Mitchell, Jr. (Ed.), *The ninth mental measurements yearbook* (Vol. 1, pp. 739–740). Lincoln, NE: Buros Institute of Mental Measurements.

Davidshofer, C. O. (1988). Jackson Vocational Interest Survey. In J. T. Kapes & M. M. Mastie (Eds.), *A counselor's guide to career assessment instruments* (2nd ed., pp. 95–99). Alexandria, VA: National Career Development Association.

Dawis, R. V. (1992). The individual differences tradition in counseling psychology. *Journal of Counseling Psychology, 39*, 7–19.

Dewey, C. R. (1974). Exploring interests: A non-sexist method. *Personnel and Guidance Journal, 52*, 311–315.

Diamond, E. E. (1990). The Kuder occupational interest survey. In C. E. Watkins, Jr., & V. L. Campbell (Eds.), *Testing in counseling practice* (pp. 211–278). Hillsdale, NJ: Lawrence Erlbaum Associates.

Fitzgerald, L. F., & Weitzman, L. M. (1992). Women's career development: Theory and practice from a feminist perspective. In H. D. Lea & Z. B. Leibowitz (Eds.), *Adult career development: Concepts, issues and practices* (2nd ed., pp. 124–160). Alexandria, VA: National Career Development Association.

Fouad, N. A., & Hansen, J. C. (1987). Cross-cultural predictive accuracy of the Strong–Campbell Interest Inventory. *Measurement and Evaluation in Counseling and Development, 20*, 3–10.

Fuqua, D. R. (in press). Campbell's psychological surveys. In J. T. Kapes & M. M. Mastie (Eds.), *A counselor's guide to career assessment instruments* (3rd ed.). Alexandria, VA: National Career Development Association.

Fuqua, D. R., & Newman, J. L. (1994). An evaluation of the Career Beliefs Inventory. *Journal of Counseling and Development, 72*, 429–430.

Gaeddert, D., & Hansen, J. C. (1993). Development of a measure of interest diversity. *Journal of Career Assessment, 1*, 294–308.

Gati, I. (1979). A hierarchical model for the structure of vocational interests. *Journal of Vocational Behavior, 15*, 90–106.

Gati, I. (1991). The structure of vocational interests. *Psychological Bulletin, 109*, 309–324.

Goldman, L. (1990). Qualitative assessment. *The Counseling Psychologist, 18*, 205–213.

Goldman, L. (1992). Qualitative assessment: An approach for counselors. *Journal of Counseling and Development, 70*, 616–621.

Gottfredson, L. S. (1986). Special groups and the beneficial use of vocational interest inventories. In W. B. Walsh & S. H. Osipow (Eds.), *Advances in vocational psychology: Vol. 1. The assessment of interests* (pp. 127–198). Hillsdale, NJ: Lawrence Erlbaum Associates.

Greenhaus, J. H. (1971). An investigation of the role of career salience in vocational behavior. *Journal of Vocational Behavior, 1*, 209–216.

Hackett, G. (in press). Self-efficacy in career choice and development. In A. Bandura (Ed.), *Self-efficacy in adaptation of youth to changing societies.* Cambridge, England: Cambridge University Press.

Hackett, G., & Betz, N. E. (1981). A self-efficacy approach to the career development of women. *Journal of Vocational Behavior, 18*, 326–336.

Hackett, G., & Betz, N. E. (1992). Self-efficacy perceptions and the career-related choices of college students. In D. H. Schunk & J. L. Meece (Eds.), *Student perceptions in the classroom: Causes and consequences* (pp. 229–246). Hillsdale, NJ: Lawrence Erlbaum Associates.

Hackett, G., & Betz, N. E. (in press). Career choice and development. In J. E. Maddux (Ed.), *Self-efficacy, adaptation, and adjustment: Theory, research, and application.* New York: Plenum.

Hackett, G., Chen, C., & Byars, A. (1994). [Examination of the psychometric properties of two versions of the occupational self-efficacy scale]. Unpublished raw data.

Hackett, G., & Lent, R. W. (1992). Theoretical advances and current inquiry in career psychology. In S. D. Brown & R. W. Lent (Eds.), *Handbook of Counseling Psychology* (2nd ed., pp. 419–451). New York: Wiley.

Hackett, G., & Lonborg, S. D. (1993). Career assessment for women: Trends and issues. *Journal of Career Assessment, 3,* 197–216.

Hackett, G., & Lonborg, S. D. (1994). Career assessment and counseling for women. In W. B. Walsh & S. H. Osipow (Eds.), *Career counseling for women* (pp. 43–86). Hillsdale, NJ: Lawrence Erlbaum Associates.

Hackett, G., & O'Halloran, S. (1985). *Test–retest reliabilities of career self-efficacy measures.* Unpublished manuscript.

Hambleton, R. K. (1985). Review of Differential Aptitude Tests (Forms V and W). In J. V. Mitchell, Jr. (Ed.), *The ninth mental measurements yearbook* (Vol. 1, pp. 504–505). Lincoln, NE: Buros Institute of Mental Measurements.

Hansen, J. C. (1985a). Career Development Inventory. *Measurement and Evaluation in Counseling and Development, 18,* 220–224.

Hansen, J. C. (1985b). Review of Vocational Interest Inventory. In J. V. Mitchell, Jr. (Ed.), *The ninth mental measurements yearbook* (Vol. 2, pp. 1677–1679). Lincoln, NE: Buros Institute of Mental Measurements.

Hansen, J. C. (1986). Strong Vocational Interest Blank/Strong–Campbell Interest Inventory. In W. B. Walsh & S. H. Osipow (Eds.), *Advances in vocational psychology: Vol. 1. The assessment of interests* (pp. 1–29). Hillsdale, NJ: Lawrence Erlbaum Associates.

Hansen, J. C. (1990). Interpretation of the Strong Interest Inventory. In C. E. Watkins, Jr. & V. L. Campbell (Eds.), *Testing in counseling practice* (pp. 177–209). Hillsdale, NJ: Lawrence Erlbaum Associates.

Hansen, J. C. (1991). *User's guide for the SII* (2nd ed.). Stanford, CA: Stanford University Press.

Hansen, J. C., & Campbell, D. P. (1985). *Manual for the SVIB-SCII* (4th ed.). Stanford, CA: Stanford University Press.

Harmon, L. W. (1988). Review of the Values Scale. In J. T. Kapes & M. M. Mastie (Eds.), *A counselor's guide to career assessment instruments* (2nd ed., pp. 156–158). Alexandria, VA: National Career Development Association.

Herr, E. L. (1989). Review of the Kuder Occupational Interest Survey, Revised. In J. C. Conoley & J. J. Kramer (Eds.), *The tenth mental measurements yearbook* (Vol. 1, pp. 425–427). Lincoln, NE: Buros Institute of Mental Measurements.

Herr, E. L., & Niles, S. G. (1988). Adult Career Concerns Inventory. In J. T. Kapes & M. M. Mastie (Eds.), *A counselor's guide to career assessment instruments* (2nd ed., pp. 160–164). Alexandria, VA: National Career Development Association.

Holland, J. L. (1977). *The occupations finder.* Palo Alto, CA: Consulting Psychologists Press.

Holland, J. L. (1985a). *Making vocational choices: A theory of vocational personalities and work environments* (2nd ed.). Englewood Cliffs, NJ: Prentice-Hall.

Holland, J. L. (1985b). *The Self-Directed Search: Professional manual–1985 edition.* Odessa, FL: Psychological Assessment Resources.

Holland, J. L. (1993, August). *P–E Psychology: Models and perspectives using a career theory to explain person–environment encounters.* Paper presented at the American Psychological Association Annual Meeting, Toronto, Canada.

Holland, J. L., Daiger, D. C., & Power, P. G. (1980). *My vocational situation.* Palo Alto, CA: Consulting Psychologists Press.

Holland, J. L., & Gottfredson, G. D. (1993). *The Career Attitudes and Strategies Inventory.* Unpublished manuscript.

Holland, J. L., Johnston, J. A., & Asama, N. F. (1993). The Vocational Identity Scale: A diagnostic and treatment tool. *Journal of Career Assessment, 1,* 12.

Holland, J. L., Johnston, J. A., Asama, N. F., & Polys, S. M. (1993). Validating and using the Career Beliefs Inventory. *Journal of Career Development, 19,* 233–244.

Holland, J. L., & Rayman, J. R. (1986). The Self-Directed Search. In W. B. Walsh & S. H. Osipow (Eds.), *Advances in vocational psychology: Vol. 1. Assessment of interests* (pp. 55–82). Hillsdale, NJ: Lawrence Erlbaum Associates.

Jackson, D. N. (1977). *Manual for the Jackson Vocational Interest Survey.* Port Huron, MI: Research Psychologists Press.

Jaeger, R. M. (1985). Review of Graduate Record Examination–General Test. In J. V. Mitchell, Jr. (Ed.), *The ninth mental measurements yearbook* (Vol. 1, pp. 624–626). Lincoln, NE: Buros Institute of Mental Measurements.

Jensen, A. R. (1985). Armed Services Vocational Aptitude Battery. *Measurement and Evaluation in Counseling and Development, 18,* 32–37.

Jensen, A. R. (1988). Armed Services Vocational Aptitude Battery. In J. T. Kapes & M. M. Mastie (Eds.), *A counselor's guide to career assessment instruments* (2nd ed., pp. 58–62). Alexandria, VA: National Career Development Association.

Jepsen, D. A. (1988). Kuder Occupational Interest Survey, Form DD. In J. T. Kapes & M. M. Mastie (Eds.), *A counselor's guide to career assessment instruments* (2nd ed., pp. 105–109). Alexandria, VA: National Career Development Association.

Jepsen, D. A. (1992). Jackson Vocational Interest Survey. In D. J. Keyser & R. C. Sweetland (Eds.), *Test critiques* (Vol. 9, pp. 308–318). Kansas City, MO: Test Corporation of America.

Johansson, C. B. (1986). *Career Assessment Inventory: The enhanced version.* Minneapolis, MN: National Computer Systems Interpretive Scoring System.

Johnson, R. W. (1985). Review of Vocational Interest Inventory. In J. V. Mitchell, Jr. (Ed.), *The ninth mental measurements yearbook* (Vol. 2, pp. 1678–1679). Lincoln, NE: Buros Institute of Mental Measurements.

Kapes, J. T., & Mastie, M. M. (Eds.). (1988). *A counselor's guide to career assessment instruments* (2nd ed.). Alexandria, VA: National Career Development Association.

Katz, M. R. (1978). Review of the Career Maturity Inventory. In O. K. Buros (Ed.), *The eighth mental measurements yearbook* (Vol. 1, pp. 1562–1565). Highland Park, NJ: Gryphon Press.

Katz, M. R. (1982). Career Maturity Inventory. In J. T. Kapes & M. M. Mastie (Eds.), *A counselor's guide to vocational guidance instruments* (pp. 122–125). Falls Church, VA: National Vocational Guidance Association.

Keesling, J. W. (1985). Review of General Aptitude Test Battery. In J. V. Mitchell, Jr. (Ed.), *The ninth mental measurements yearbook* (Vol. 2, pp. 1645–1647). Lincoln, NE: Buros Institute of Mental Measurements.

Keesling, J. W., & Healy, C. C. (1988). USES General Aptitude Test Battery. In J. T. Kapes & M. M. Mastie (Eds.), *A counselor's guide to career assessment instruments* (2nd ed., pp. 69–74). Alexandria, VA: National Career Development Association.

Kifer, E. (1985). Review of ACT Assessment Program. In J. V. Mitchell, Jr. (Ed.), *The ninth mental measurements yearbook* (Vol. 1, pp. 31–36). Lincoln, NE: Buros Institute of Mental Measurements.

Kirnan, J. P., & Geisinger, K. F. (1987). General Aptitude Test Battery. In D. J. Keyser & R. J. Sweetland (Eds.), *Test critiques compendium* (pp. 162 180). Kansas City, MO: Test Corporation of America.

Krieshok, T. S. (1987). Review of the Self-Directed Search. *Journal of Counseling and Development, 65,* 512–514.

Krumboltz, J. D. (1985). Review of Vocational Interest Inventory. *Measurement and Evaluation in Counseling and Development, 18,* 38–41.

Krumboltz, J. D. (1988). Vocational Interest Inventory. In J. T. Kapes & M. M. Mastie (Eds.), *A counselor's guide to career assessment instruments* (2nd ed., pp. 137–142). Alexandria, VA: National Career Development Association.

Krumboltz, J. D. (1991). *Manual for the Career Beliefs Inventory.* Palo Alto, CA: Consulting Psychologists Press.

Krumboltz, J. D. (1994a). The Career Beliefs Inventory. *Journal of Counseling and Development, 72,* 424–428.

Krumboltz, J. D. (1994b). Potential value of the Career Beliefs Inventory. *Journal of Counseling and Development, 72,* 432–433.

Kuder, F., & Zytowski, D. G. (1991). *Kuder Occupational Interest Survey Form DD general manual* (3rd ed.). Monterey, CA: CTB Macmillan/McGraw–Hill.

Lamb, R. R., & Prediger, D. J. (1981). *Technical report for the unisex edition of the ACT Interest Inventory* (UNIACT). Iowa City, IA: American College Testing Program.

Layton, W. L. (1985). Review of Strong–Campbell Interest Inventory. In J. V. Mitchell, Jr. (Ed.), *The ninth mental measurements yearbook* (Vol. 2, pp. 1480–1481). Lincoln, NE: Buros Institute of Mental Measurements.

Lefcourt, L. A., & Harmon, L. W. (1993, August). *Self-efficacy expectations for role management (SEERM): Measure development.* Paper presented at the Annual convention of the American Psychological Association, Toronto, Ontario, Canada.

Lent, R. W., Brown, S. D., & Hackett, G. (1994). Toward a unifying social cognitive theory of career and academic interest, choice, and performance. *Journal of Vocational Behavior, 45,* 79–122.

Lent, R. W., & Hackett, G. (1987). Career self-efficacy: Empirical status and future directions [Monograph]. *Journal of Vocational Behavior, 30,* 347–382.

Lent, R. W., & Hackett, G. (1994). Sociocognitive mechanisms of personal agency in career development: Pantheoretical prospects. In M. L. Savickas & R. W. Lent (Eds.), *Convergence in career development theories* (pp. 77–101). Palo Alto, CA: CPP Books.

Locke, D. C. (1988). Career Development Inventory. In J. T. Kapes & M. M. Mastie (Eds.), *A counselor's guide to career assessment instruments* (2nd ed., pp. 175–179). Alexandria, VA: National Career Development Association.

Lowman, R. L. (1991). *The clinical practice of career assessment: Interests, abilities, and personality.* Washington, DC: American Psychological Association.

Lowman, R. L. (1993). The inter-domain model of career assessment and counseling. *Journal of Counseling and Development, 71,* 549–554.

Lunneborg, P. W. (1981). *The Vocational Interest Inventory manual.* Los Angeles: Western Psychological Services.

Manuele–Adkins, C. (1989). Review of the Self-Directed Search: A guide to educational and vocational planning–1985 revision. In J. C. Conoley & J. J. Kramer (Eds.), *The tenth mental measurements yearbook* (Vol. 1, pp. 738–740). Lincoln, NE: Buros Institute of Mental Measurements.

McCabe, S. P. (1988). Career Assessment Inventory–The Enhanced Version. In J. T. Kapes & M. M. Mastie (Eds.), *A counselor's guide to career assessment instruments* (2nd ed., pp. 76–80). Alexandria, VA: National Career Development Association.

Neimeyer, G. J. (1988). Cognitive integration and differentiation in vocational behavior. *The Counseling Psychologist, 16,* 440–475.

Nevill, D. D., & Super, D. E. (1986). *Manual for the salience inventory: Theory, application, and research.* Palo Alto, CA: Consulting Psychologists Press.

Nevill, D. D., & Super, D. E. (1989). *Manual for the Values Scale* (2nd ed.). Palo Alto, CA: Consulting Psychologists Press.

Osipow, S. H. (1987). *Career decision scale: Manual.* Odessa, FL: Psychological Assessment Resources.

Osipow, S. H. (1991). Developing instruments for use in counseling. *Journal of Counseling and Development, 70,* 322–326.

Osipow, S. H., Temple, R. D., & Rooney, R. A. (1993). The short form of the task-specific occupational self-efficacy scale. *Journal of Career Assessment, 1,* 13–20.

Pennock–Roman, M. (1985). Differential Aptitude Tests. In D. J. Keyser & R. J. Sweetland (Eds.), *Test critiques* (Vol. 3, pp. 226–245). Kansas City, MO: Test Corporation of America.

Pennock–Roman, M. (1988). Differential Aptitude Tests. In J. T. Kapes & M. M. Mastie (Eds.), *A counselor's guide to career assessment instruments* (2nd ed., pp. 63–68). Alexandria, VA: National Career Development Association.

Pinkney, J. W. (1985). Review of Career Development Inventory. In J. V. Mitchell, Jr. (Ed.), *The ninth mental measurements yearbook* (Vol. 2, pp. 1210–1212). Lincoln, NE: Buros Institute of Mental Measurements.

Prediger, D., Swaney, K., & Mau, W. (1993). Extending Holland's hexagon: Procedures, counseling applications, and research. *Journal of Counseling and Development, 39,* 7–19.

Psychological Corporation. (1990). *Differential Aptitude Test* (5th ed.). New York, NY: Author.

Robbins, S. B. (1985). Validity estimates for the career decision making self-efficacy scale. *Measurement and Evaluation in Counseling and Development, 18,* 64–71.

Roe, A. (1956). *The psychology of occupations.* New York: Wiley.

Rooney, R. A., & Osipow, S. H. (1992). Task-specific occupational self-efficacy scale. *Journal of Vocational Behavior, 40,* 14–32.

Rounds, J. B. (1989). Review of the Career Assessment Inventory–The Enhanced Version. In J. C. Conoley & J. J. Kramer (Eds.), *The tenth mental measurements yearbook* (Vol. 1, pp. 139–141). Lincoln, NE: Buros Institute of Mental Measurements.

Rounds, J. B., Henly, G. A., Dawis, R. V., Lofquist, L. H., & Weiss, D. J. (1981). *Manual for the Minnesota Importance Questionnaire.* Minneapolis: University of Minnesota, Vocational Psychology Research.

Rounds, J. B., & Tracey, T. J. (1990). From trait-and-factor to person–environment fit counseling: Theory and process. In W. B. Walsh & S. H. Osipow (Eds.), *Career counseling: Contemporary topics in vocational psychology* (pp. 1–44). Hillsdale, NJ: Lawrence Erlbaum Associates.

Sander, D. (1985). Review of Differential Aptitude Tests (Forms V and W). In J. V. Mitchell, Jr. (Ed.), *The ninth mental measurements yearbook* (Vol. 1, pp. 505–507). Lincoln, NE: Buros Institute of Mental Measurements.

Savickas, M. L. (1984). Career maturity: The construct and its measurement. *Vocational Guidance Quarterly, 32,* 222–231.

Savickas, M. L. (1990). The use of career choice process scales in counseling practice. In C. E. Watkins, Jr. & V. L. Campbell (Eds.), *Testing in counseling practice* (pp. 373–417). Hillsdale, NJ: Lawrence Erlbaum Associates.

Savickas, M. L. (1992). New directions in career assessment. In D. H. Montross & C. J. Shinkman (Eds.), *Career development: Theory and practice* (pp. 336–355). Springfield, IL: Thomas.

Savickas, M. L. (1993). Predictive validity criteria for career development measures. *Journal of Career Assessment, 1,* 93–104.

Schulenberg, J. E., Shimizu, K., Vondracek, F. W., & Hostetler, M. (1988). The factor structure of career indecision in junior and senior high school students. *Journal of Vocational Behavior, 33,* 63–81.

Serling, D. A., & Betz, N. E. (1990). Development and validation of a measure of fear of commitment. *Journal of Counseling Psychology, 37,* 91–97.

Shephard, J. W. (1989). Review of the Jackson Vocational Interest Survey. In J. C. Conoley & J. J. Kramer (Eds.), *The tenth mental measurements yearbook* (Vol. 1, pp. 403–404). Lincoln, NE: Buros Institute of Mental Measurements.

Shimizu, K., Vondracek, F. W., Schulenberg, J. E., & Hostetler, M. (1988). The factor structure of the career decision scale: Similarities across selected studies. *Journal of Vocational Behavior, 32,* 213–225.

Slaney, R. B. (1981). *The Vocational Card Sort—Understanding your results.* Unpublished manuscript, The Pennsylvania State University, University Park, PA.

Slaney, R. B. (1988). The assessment of career decision making. In W. B. Walsh & S. H. Osipow (Eds.), *Career decision making* (pp. 33–76). Hillsdale, NJ: Lawrence Erlbaum Associates.

Slaney, R. B., & MacKinnon–Slaney, F. (1990). The use of vocational card sorts in career counseling. In C. E. Watkins, Jr. & V. L. Campbell (Eds.), *Testing in counseling practice* (pp. 317–371). Hillsdale, NJ: Lawrence Erlbaum Associates.

Spokane, A. R. (1990). Self-guided interest inventories as career interventions: The Self-Directed Search. In C. E. Watkins, Jr. & V. L. Campbell (Eds.), *Testing in counseling practice* (pp. 285–316). Hillsdale, NJ: Lawrence Erlbaum Associates.

Spokane, A. R. (1991). *Career intervention.* Englewood Cliffs, NJ: Prentice–Hall.

Stickel, S. A., & Bonett, R. M. (1991). Gender differences in career self-efficacy: Combining a career with home and family. *Journal of College Student Development, 32,* 297–301.

Super, D. E. (1970). *Work Values Inventory Manual.* Chicago: Riverside.

Super, D. E. (1980). A life span, life-space approach to career development. *Journal of Vocational Behavior, 16,* 282–298.

Super, D. E. (1990). A life span, life-space approach to career development. In D. Brown, L. Brooks, and Associates, *Career choice and development* (pp. 197–261). San Francisco: Jossey-Bass.

Super, D. E., Osborne, W. L., Walsh, D. J., Brown, S. D., & Niles, S. G. (1992). Developmental career assessment and counseling: The C–DAC model. *Journal of Counseling and Development, 71,* 74–80.

Super, D. E., Thompson, A. S., Lindeman, R. H., Jordaan, J. P., & Myers, R. A. (1988a). *Manual for the Adult Career Concerns Inventory.* Palo Alto, CA: Consulting Psychologists Press.

Super, D. E., Thompson, A. S., Lindeman, R. H., Jordaan, J. P., & Myers, R. A. (1988b). *Manual for the Career Development Inventory.* Palo Alto, CA: Consulting Psychologists Press.

Swanson, J. L. (1993). Integrated assessment of vocational interests and self-rated skills and abilities. *Journal of Career Assessment, 1,* 50–65.

Swanson, J. L., & Tokar, D. M. (1991). College student's perceptions of barriers to career development. *Journal of Vocational Behavior, 38,* 92–106.

Taylor, K. M., & Betz, N. E. (1983). Applications of self-efficacy theory to the understanding and treatment of career indecision. *Journal of Vocational Behavior, 22,* 63–81.

Taylor, K. M., & Popma, J. (1990). Construct validity of the career decision-making self-efficacy scale and the relationship of CDMSE to vocational indecision. *Journal of Vocational Behavior, 37,* 17–31.

Temple, R. D., & Osipow, S. H. (1994). The relationship between task-specific self-efficacy egalitarianism and career indecision for females. *Journal of Career Assessment, 2,* 82–90.

Tenopyr, M. L. (1989). Review of the Kuder Occupational Interest Survey, Revised (Form DD). In J. C. Conoley & J. J. Kramer (Eds.), *The tenth mental measurements yearbook* (Vol. 1, pp. 427–429). Lincoln, NE: Buros Institute of Mental Measurements.

Thomas, R. B. (1985). Review of Jackson Vocational Interest Survey. In J. V. Mitchell, Jr. (Ed.), *The ninth mental measurements yearbook* (Vol. 1, pp. 740–742). Lincoln, NE: Buros Institute of Mental Measurements.

Tracey, T. J., & Rounds, J. (1993). Evaluating Holland's and Gati's vocational-interest models: A structural meta-analysis. *Psychological Bulletin, 113,* 229–246.

U.S. Department of Defense. (1993). *ASVAB 18/19 Technical Manual.* North Chicago, IL: U.S. Military Entrance Processing Command.

U.S. Department of Labor, Employment, & Training Administration. (1980). *Manual for the USES General Aptitude Tests Battery section II: Occupational aptitude patterns structure.* Washington, DC: U.S. Government Printing Office.

Vondracek, F. W. (1991). Osipow on the Career Decision Scale: Some comments. *Journal of Counseling and Development, 70,* 327.

Walsh, W. B. (1994). The Career Beliefs Inventory: Reactions to Krumboltz. *Journal of Counseling and Development, 72,* 431–432.

Walsh, W. B., & Betz, N. E. (1990). *Tests and assessment* (2nd ed.). Englewood Cliffs, NJ: Prentice–Hall.

Walsh, W. B., & Osipow, S. H. (1983). *Handbook of Vocational Psychology.* Hillsdale, NJ: Lawrence Erlbaum Associates.

Watkins, C. E., Jr. (1990). Further reflections on the Strong Vocational Interest Blank, Form M and SII. *Journal of Personality Assessment, 55,* 818–819.

Watkins, C. E., Jr. (1993a). Vocational assessment training in terminal master's-level counseling psychology programs: Follow-up to a previous study. *Journal of Career Assessment, 1,* 193–196.

Watkins, C. E., Jr. (1993b). What have surveys taught us about the teaching and practice of vocational assessment? *The Counseling Psychologist, 21,* 109–117.

Watkins, C. E., Jr., Campbell, V. L., & Manus, M. (1991). Is vocational assessment training in counseling psychology programs too restricted? *Counselling Psychology Quarterly, 3,* 295–298.

Watkins, C. E., Jr., Campbell, V. L., & Nieberding, R. (in press). The practice of vocational assessment by counseling psychologists. *The Counseling Psychologist.*

Wegner, K. W. (1992). Career Assessment Inventory–The Enhanced Version. In D. J. Keyser & R. J. Sweetland (Eds.), *Test critiques* (Vol. 9, pp. 36–47). Kansas City, MO: Test Corporation of America.

Weitzman, R. A. (1985). Review of Armed Services Vocational Aptitude Battery. In J. V. Mitchell, Jr. (Ed.), *The ninth mental measurements yearbook* (Vol. 1, pp. 83–84). Lincoln, NE: Buros Institute of Mental Measurements.

Westbrook, B. W. (1983). Career maturity: The concept, the instrument, and the research. In W. B. Walsh & S. H. Osipow (Eds.), *Handbook of vocational psychology* (Vol. 1, pp. 263–303). Hillsdale, NJ: Lawrence Erlbaum Associates.

Westbrook, B. W. (1988). My vocational situation. In J. T. Kapes & M. M. Mastie (Eds.), *A counselor's guide to career assessment instruments* (2nd ed., pp. 187–190). Alexandria, VA: National Career Development Association.

Westbrook, B. W., & Mastie, M. M. (1974). The Cognitive Vocational Maturity Test. In D. E. Super (Ed.), *Measuring vocational maturity for counseling and evaluation* (pp. 41–50). Washington, DC. American Personnel and Guidance Association.

Westbrook, B. W., Sanford, E. E., Gilleland, J., Fleenor, J., & Mervin, G. (1988). Career maturity in grade 9: The relationship between accuracy of self-appraisal and ability to appraise the career-relevant abilities of others. *Journal of Vocational Behavior, 32,* 269–283.

Whiston, S. C. (1990). Evaluation of the Adult Career Concerns Inventory. *Journal of Counseling and Development, 69,* 78–80.

Wise, L. L. (Chair). (1993, August). *The new ASVAB.* Symposium conducted at the annual meeting of the American Psychological Association, Toronto, Canada.

Zytowski, D. G. (1978). Review of Career Maturity Inventory. In O. K. Buros (Ed.), *The eighth mental measurements yearbook* (Vol. 2, pp. 1565–1567). Highland Park, NJ: Gryphon Press.

Zytowski, D. G. (1988). Review of the Salience Inventory. In J. T. Kapes & M. M. Mastie (Eds.), *A counselor's guide to career assessment instruments* (2nd ed., pp. 151–154). Alexandria, VA: National Career Development Association.

Zytowski, D. G. (1992). Three generations: The continuing evolution of Frederic Kuder's interest inventories. *Journal of Counseling and Development, 71,* 245–248.

Zytowski, D. G., & Borgen, F. (1983). Assessment. In W. B. Walsh & S. H. Osipow (Eds.), *Handbook of vocational psychology* (Vol. 2, pp. 5–40). Hillsdale, NJ: Lawrence Erlbaum Associates.

Zytowski, D. G., & Kuder, F. (1986). Advances in the Kuder Occupational Interest Survey. In W. B. Walsh & S. H. Osipow (Eds.), *Advances in vocational psychology: Vol. 1. The assessment of interests* (pp. 31–53). Hillsdale, NJ: Lawrence Erlbaum Associates.

CHAPTER SEVEN

The Process and Outcome
of Career Counseling

Jane L. Swanson
Southern Illinois University at Carbondale

The activity of career counseling is intimately tied to the establishment of counseling psychology as a specialty (Osipow, 1982; Whiteley, 1984), and continues to be a part of our unique identity (Gelso & Fretz, 1992). Although the view of career counseling has changed throughout the years from Parsons' (1909) initial formulations to more recent conceptualizations (cf. Walsh & Osipow, 1990), assisting individuals in making career choices is an important part of what we do. Yet in spite of the central nature of this activity, empirical evaluation of what occurs in career counseling and how individuals benefit from career counseling has not been as thoroughly investigated as one might expect.

Examination of the extant literature regarding process and outcome in career counseling suggests an interesting paradox: Although we know a great deal about the effectiveness of career *interventions* in general, we know considerably less about career *counseling* specifically, and further, we know almost nothing about career counseling *process* (Meier, 1991; Oliver & Spokane, 1988; Rounds & Tinsley, 1984; Spokane, 1991). Within this paradox lie two disparities in our knowledge: between what we know about career counseling *process* and career counseling *outcome* and between what we know about the process of *career* counseling and the process of *personal* counseling. Spokane (1991) noted, "Although extensive theory and research have been generated on the process of personal counseling, there is only the beginning of such a literature in career counseling" (p. 23). This view was echoed by Meier (1991): "Surprisingly, process factors studied in personal–emotional counseling research are not commonly investigated in career studies. . . . A greater focus on what takes place in career counseling sessions would appear to be a necessary, and potentially fruitful, avenue for future investigations" (p. 154).

In this chapter I examine *career counseling*, not the larger body of literature defined as *career interventions*. This narrower focus was purposely chosen for several reasons. First, activities associated specifically with career counseling may be obscured in previous efforts to evaluate the entire body of career intervention literature. Second, career counseling seems to be the "heart and soul" of career intervention, despite some earlier predictions that it would become obsolete (Holland, 1974), and yet, we do not have an adequate empirical description of what occurs, either in content or in process, during career counseling. Moreover, because previous writers (Fretz, 1981; Holland, 1974; Krivatsy & Magoon, 1976; Oliver & Spokane, 1988) have raised concerns about the relative inefficiency and expense of individual career counseling, we need to investigate whether the literature supports the use of career counseling over other less costly interventions. A related issue is that the need for career interventions appears to be increasing at the same time that career-related issues seem to be becoming more complex (Blustein, 1992; Flamer, 1986), creating a conflicting set of demands: More people need access to career services, a demand that argues for the cost effectiveness of group or course interventions, yet the greater complexity of career issues argues for more individually tailored integrative work.

A final reason that I focus specifically on career counseling is that a discussion of process implies the existence of an interaction of a psychological nature. Career interventions is a broad category which includes wide variability in terms of content, methods of delivery, and even whether human interaction occurs at all. Career counseling, on the other hand, if clearly defined, entails the kind of psychological interaction that we commonly refer to as "process." Further, a focus on career counseling rather than on career intervention is necessary if we are to study process and outcome in tandem (Hill, 1991).

Thus, my goal in this chapter is to provide an overview of the status of research on process and outcome in career counseling. The chapter is divided into four sections. The introductory section sets the stage with a discussion of the interrelationship of career and personal counseling, how career counseling is viewed by counseling psychologists, and the goals of process and outcome research. The second and third sections review process and outcome research in career counseling, respectively. The final section provides a summary and proposes some directions for future research.

INTRODUCTION

Defining Career Counseling

Career interventions typically are defined quite broadly, for example, as "any activity or program intended to facilitate career development" (Fretz, 1981, p. 78) or as "any treatment or effort intended to enhance an individual's career development or to enable the person to make better career-related decisions" (Spokane & Oliver, 1983, p. 100). The proliferation of such diverse activities or treatments prompted Osipow (1982) to conclude that "it is almost impossible to identify clearly what is meant by career counseling," a problem which he cited as one reason that research in career counseling has been "so diffuse." (p. 29).

In contrast, for the purpose of this chapter, career counseling is defined as an ongoing, face-to-face interaction between counselor and client, with career- or work-related issues as the primary focus. Career counseling is therefore a subset of career interventions. This definition excludes other interventions such as computer-based guidance systems, didactic experiences such as ongoing courses or single-session workshops, and self-guided career instruments. Furthermore, this definition is consistent with ones offered previously (Crites, 1981; Spokane & Oliver, 1983). For example, Crites (1981) viewed career counseling as an "interpersonal process focused upon assisting an individual to make an appropriate career decision" (p. 11). Further, Crites (1981) defined career counseling not only as giving and interpreting tests but also as involving a relationship between counselor and client, a relationship requiring the client to be an active participant in the decisional process, not simply a passive recipient of information.

An important assumption of this definition is that the interaction is psychological in nature. In other words, although career counseling may include activities such as information giving and computer-based exploration, it is not limited to these activities. More important, these activities take place in the context of a relationship between counselor and client. For example, as part of career counseling, the counselor may challenge the client to examine underlying reasons for career decisions, interpret the client's reported or in-session behavior, give the client feedback about his or her presentation and his or her interaction with the counselor, and explore conflicts the client is experiencing with family or between work and nonwork areas of life. In general, career counseling requires the counselor to use the same kinds of therapeutic skills that are used in other counseling settings.

Excluding more broadly defined career interventions does not imply, however, that that literature is irrelevant to a consideration of career counseling. On the contrary, the activities that occur in other interventions, such as gathering of occupational information, skill rehearsal, social learning, and modeling, also occur in career counseling. Reviews of previous literature regarding career interventions (Fretz, 1981; Oliver & Spokane, 1988; Phillips, 1992; Spokane & Oliver, 1983) are therefore directly relevant to career counseling: We know that these activities are helpful. Individual career counseling differs, however, in that the interventions can be tailored in presentation, timing, sequence, and format to match the client's style and needs.

Viewing career counseling as a subset of career interventions emphasizes the commonalities underlying effective treatments (Holland, Magoon, & Spokane, 1981). A further connection, discussed in the next section, is to view career counseling as intersecting with personal counseling. Thus, as shown in Fig. 7.1, career counseling represents the intersection between career interventions, on the one hand, which involves a diversity of content delivered by a diversity of methods, and personal counseling, on the other hand, with a focus on interpersonal process and counselor–client interaction.

The Relation Between Career Counseling and Personal Counseling

> Given the relationship between work and mental health, it is perplexing that there has been an artificial distinction between career counseling and mental health counseling on the part of many clients and counselors. Career counseling and personal counseling are often referred to as if they were completely separate entities. In fact, there are few things more personal than a career choice. (Niles & Pate, 1989, p. 64)

In spite of the central role of career counseling in the establishment and identity of counseling psychology, we often seem to view career counseling and personal counseling as independent activities. Further, career counseling often suffers from decreased status when compared to personal counseling. This pattern presents another interesting paradox: We value career counseling as a unique part of our specialty's niche in applied and theoretical

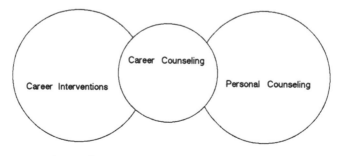

FIG. 7.1. Relation of career counseling to career interventions and personal counseling.

psychology, yet apparently we do not think very highly of it. Because these conflicting attitudes have implications for research regarding process and outcome in career counseling, this section summarizes the literature regarding the intersection of career and personal counseling. The next section reviews the evidence of how counseling psychologists view career counseling activities.

Although the issue of how career counseling and personal counseling intersect has been debated for quite some time, the issue is being revisited with renewed vigor due to recent evidence suggesting that counseling psychologists are decreasing their involvement in career counseling and vocational psychology (Fitzgerald & Osipow, 1986, 1988; Watkins, Lopez, Campbell, & Himmell, 1986). Several overlapping themes emerge from the literature addressing the relation of career counseling and personal counseling: (a) defining whether career counseling and personal counseling are identical, subsets of one another, or distinct activities; (b) integrating a client's career and personal issues within counseling; (c) extending the application of career counseling from young adults dealing with initial career choice to employed adults dealing with work–nonwork interactions, with particular attention to the mental health consequences of adverse work situations; and (d) debating whether career counseling should precede, coincide with, or follow personal counseling.

Career Counseling "Versus" Personal Counseling

Consensus has not been reached regarding the extent of the overlap between career counseling and personal counseling (Hackett, 1993; Subich, 1993; Super, 1993). One point of view is that career counseling and personal counseling are, if not identical, then quite similar. This view is most explicitly stated by Rounds and Tinsley (1984), who argued that career intervention is "a form of *psychotherapy* and should be viewed as a method of behavior change and tied to psychotherapy theory" (p. 138). They believed that such a view would provide a broader framework for practicing and evaluating career interventions.

On the other hand, a number of authors (Crites, 1981; Hackett, 1993; Spokane, 1989, 1991) have argued for a distinction between career counseling and personal counseling. Hackett (1993) argued that "career counseling is *not* simply the application of counseling theory to vocational issues" (p. 110). Spokane (1991), too, warned against the overapplication of psychotherapy theories to career counseling. Crites (1981) argued that career counseling is

> both more and less than personal adjustment counseling or psychotherapy. The assumption that all vocational problems are personal problems is specious and untenable. Vocational and personal problems are different, but they do

interact. Thus, career counseling often embraces personal counseling but it goes beyond this to explore and explicate the client's role in the main arena of life—the world of work. (p. 11)

In addition to considering career and personal counseling as separate activities, these views include the belief that career counseling is more difficult than personal counseling and that it requires more training because expertise is necessary in a broader range of domains (Crites, 1981; Hackett, 1993).

Integrating Career Counseling and Psychotherapy

In contrast to the first theme, the second theme focuses on how personal and career *issues* intersect within counseling. For example, despite Hackett's (1993) distinction between career and personal counseling, she encouraged the integration of career and personal issues in counseling: "We are undoubtedly doing our clients a disservice by any attempt to neatly compartmentalize their lives" (p. 110). Betz and Corning (1993) also argued for the inseparability of career and personal issues in counseling, using the variables of gender and race to illustrate the need for a holistic approach.

Spokane (1989) offered a model in which the two domains of work and mental health issues "coexist but do not intersect except in times of stress or transition" (p. 20). The model includes risk factors and coping strategies that influence and are influenced by difficult career decisions; it proposes that the two domains are independent before a difficult career decision, converge during such a decision, then separate once again after the decision.

The distinction between career and personal issues (and career and personal counseling) may be reinforced by perceptions of career counseling. Manuele–Adkins (1992) described elements of a stereotypic view of career counseling that discredit its psychological component and affect the quality and delivery of career counseling services. In this stereotypic view, career counseling is a rational process, with an emphasis on information-giving, testing, and computer-based systems; it is short-term, thus limiting the range of possible intervention strategies and obscuring psychological processes such as indecision; and it is different from personal counseling, thus lowering the perceived value of career counseling and increasing a false separation between work and nonwork. Haverkamp and Moore (1993) discussed the perceptual dichotomy existing in the profession in which career counseling and personal counseling appear to function as distinct cognitive schemas. They argued that the implicit definition of personal counseling is too broad, consisting of anything that is not directly related to career; the implicit definition of career counseling, on the other hand, is too narrow, consisting primarily of initial career choices of young adults and neglecting adult work adjustment.

The distinction between career and personal counseling is also maintained by the way that agencies serving these concerns are organized on many college and university campuses (Krumboltz, 1993; Pinkerton, Etzel, Rockwell, Talley, & Moorman, 1990). When agencies for career and personal counseling are separated administratively and geographically, presenting issues are unnecessarily differentiated. Counseling often proceeds in one realm (personal or career) without recognition of potential issues in the other realm, and a client might seek both types of services simultaneously. Several studies, however, have suggested that it is unwise for us to view clients with career issues as different from clients with personal issues. Lucas (1992) reported that students who sought help for career issues or for personal issues were not fundamentally different from one another. J. M. Gold and Scanlon (1993) also reported that students with noncareer issues were not more psychologically distressed than students with career issues, yet the former received twice as many counseling sessions. Osipow and J. A. Gold (1968) found that students who requested personal counseling also had career development difficulties, as compared to a control group.

Several authors have offered suggestions for integrating career and personal issues. Corbishley and Yost (1989) discussed four specific aspects of career counseling that require a psychological approach: identifying and clarifying client expectations for career counseling; using a holistic approach to counseling that recognizes the interactions of work and nonwork; understanding how client characteristics relate to the counseling process and how they might be expressed in a work situation; and understanding process variables by borrowing concepts from psychotherapy, such as attention to nonverbal material, client–counselor relationship, and client resistance. In addition, researchers have used case studies to illustrate explicitly the integration of career and personal issues in counseling, addressing concerns related to dual-career relationships (Tolsma, 1993), to substance abuse (Blustein, 1987), to sexual orientation (Croteau & Thiel, 1993; Tolsma, 1993), to adult work adjustment (Haverkamp & Moore, 1993), and to developmental maladjustment (Lucas, 1993). Finally, Niles and Pate (1989) discussed counselor competencies necessary to deliver both career and mental health services, and particularly, competencies required to integrate the two.

The first two themes address quite different questions: Are career counseling and personal counseling the same? Should career and personal issues be integrated? In spite of the distinctiveness of the questions, they often are intertwined in the literature. The blurring of these two issues makes resolution of either quite difficult. For example, an answer to the question Is career counseling the same as personal counseling? might be, It depends. The answer depends primarily on how the question is asked. Should career counseling focus only on career issues (or personal counseling on "personal" issues)? Few would answer yes. Are career and personal counseling indistinguishable from one another? Again, few would answer yes.

Perhaps a moderate position would be the argument that career counseling can be very similar to personal counseling, but it also can be very different. Career counseling requires the counselor to use many of the same skills as personal counseling requires, and, therefore, the process, at least at times, can be quite similar. At times, career counseling probably requires more process-oriented skills than does personal counseling, such as negotiating counselor–client roles and responsibilities, integrating disparate material, and engaging the client in sharing personal information and experiences. The definition of career counseling used in this chapter includes a psychological component. The more that career counseling is psychological in nature, the more it is likely to resemble personal counseling.

Career Counseling and Mental Health Issues With Adult Clients

The third theme highlights the connections between career counseling and mental health outcomes. This perspective stems from the recognition that counseling psychology has been too focused on the initial career choices of young adults: "Career counseling includes work adjustment as well as occupational choice problems in its purview and is just as relevant for adults as it is for young people" (Brown & Brooks, 1985, p. 861).

There is increasing recognition that work and mental health are interwoven and that adult vocational needs are complex (Davidson & Gilbert, 1993; Flamer, 1986; Hackett, 1993; Haverkamp & Moore, 1993; Herr, 1989). For example, Herr (1989) described work-related problems as intrapsychic, environmental, or interactive in nature. He then concluded, "If one considers work and mental health to be linked, and career counseling to be an effective process in helping persons choose work wisely and improve their adjustment to it, then, logic would argue for career counseling to be a useful process in the service of improved mental health, where questions of work satisfaction and purpose are involved." (Herr, 1989, p. 13).

Brown and Brooks (1985), holding a similar view, argued that career counseling with adults may be a viable alternative to stress management and even to personal counseling. Further, they argued that psychologists have overlooked the potential of career counseling, due to its oversimplification and misunderstanding. Brown and Brooks (1985) encouraged practitioners to recognize that the source of psychological symptoms may be in the work situation rather than intrapsychic. They also proposed that although all practitioners cannot be skilled career counselors, all should become skilled in recognizing situations in which career counseling is an appropriate intervention and that warrant referral.

Which Comes First?

The fourth and final theme in the literature regarding career and personal counseling is whether career counseling should precede, coincide with, or follow psychotherapy. For example, Brown and Brooks (1985) voiced their concern about the view that career counseling should follow psychotherapy.

Is a certain level of mental health required before a client can proceed with career counseling? Brown (1985) challenged this idea, arguing that an unsuitable work environment can produce symptoms that appear to indicate severe psychological disorders. Moreover, even if the central issue is not career related, work may be affected to the point that career counseling is needed. Brown further argued that "career counseling is a viable intervention with clients that have rather severe emotional problems" (p. 197) and suggested that the decision of whether personal or career counseling is warranted should be based on assessment of chronicity, sources of social support, role of the work environment in experienced distress, and the individual's opportunity and motivation for a job change.

Crites (1981) is often cited by others as advocating that psychotherapy should precede career counseling. A reading of his original text, however, suggests that his premise was that *if* psychotherapy occurred, *then* career counseling should follow, due to the disruption likely to occur in the work realm as a result of change in one's personal life. Further, Crites argued that career counseling not only facilitates career development but also enhances personal adjustment.

Writing from the perspective of a psychoanalytically oriented psychotherapist, Kleinberg (1988) discussed clients who initially presented with a work-related crisis but actually needed more intensive psychotherapy. He focused on how to use the presenting issue to help the client prepare for and overcome his or her resistance to psychotherapy. "Vocational counseling methods are offered to individuals who are able to use data, make reasonably sound decisions, and implement them with proficiency," whereas more intensive therapy is indicated for people with "troubled work relationships, unsound vocational decisions, disturbances of motivation and self-esteem" (p. 246).

One curious aspect of most of the literature regarding the relation between career and personal counseling is its theoretical or anecdotal nature; until quite recently, researchers have exerted little effort to examine these issues empirically. Some comparisons have been made between effectiveness rates for career counseling and personal counseling; however, little is known about the similarities or differences between the process of career counseling and that of personal counseling.

Perceptions of Career Counseling

A related area of research examines how counselors feel about conducting career counseling. If, these studies reason, counselors prefer to perform activities other than career counseling, then how does this attitude affect what occurs in career counseling? As Hackett (1993) noted, "Counselors' perceptions of the importance and role of career counseling not only determine whether they actively engage in career counseling, but also meaningfully influence their work with all clients" (p. 107).

Research in this area can be divided into studies that have examined perceptions of counseling psychologists toward career- and personal-counseling activities (Pinkney & Jacobs, 1985; Schneider & Gelso, 1972) and studies that examine the effects those perceptions may have on counseling performance (Gelso et al., 1985; Spengler, Blustein, & Strohmer, 1990).

Counseling Psychologists' Attitudes Toward Career Counseling

In a study of graduate training programs 25 years ago, Schneider and Gelso (1972) reported that directors of 20 counseling psychology training programs viewed students as being significantly more prepared to conduct personal than career counseling and as having significantly greater comprehension of personality theory than of vocational theory. However, a distinction was not made between ratings of students' preparation and what the programs emphasized, and perceptions were gathered only from program directors and not from the trainees themselves. Pinkney and Jacobs (1985) addressed the question, "What if many counselors have little intrinsic interest in career counseling?" (p. 454). They asked a small sample of trainees and new professionals to respond to a four-item survey about working as a counselor. Job titles reflecting personal–emotional counseling were ranked more highly than those reflecting career counseling. Participants also indicated less interest and willingness to work with clients with specified career issues than with clients with personal–emotional issues. Moreover, narratives written by participants to describe a rewarding but typical day at work were much less likely to contain any reference to career counseling activities than to personal–emotional counseling activities. Pinkney and Jacobs (1985) speculated that the relative disinterest in career counseling might be reflected in task performance and urged more attention to professional socialization to view career counseling as part of the specialty.

Impact of Attitudes on Performance

Gelso et al. (1985) questioned whether the negative attitude expressed by counseling psychologists for career counseling might be transmitted to clients early in the counseling process. They examined actual intake reports written over a 5-year period by 15 doctoral-level counselors for 113 clients. Reports for career clients were shorter, judged as less useful, and addressed fewer of the dimensions that the agency defined as critical to a good intake report; however, these results were related to degree of client dysfunction. Counselors' ratings of client dysfunction were lower for clients with career issues than for clients either with personal issues or a combination of career and personal issues. Interest in conducting career counseling was unrelated to quality of reports for clients with career issues but was related to length and judged usefulness of reports for clients with personal issues. Reports for clients with career issues were less likely to address family dynamics, personality characteristics, client motivation for counseling, and case-management issues than were reports for clients with personal issues; in fact, these criteria were rarely included.

In a study of clinical bias, Spengler et al. (1990) examined "diagnostic overshadowing" of career issues. Vignettes describing a 25-year-old, married, college-educated White male were constructed according to a well-designed multistep procedure, resulting in three personal-problem vignettes of varying severity relative to a career-problem vignette. Vocational overshadowing occurred only for participants who indicated a preference for personal counseling over career counseling: When the personal issue was equal to or twice as severe as the career issue, these participants were less likely to diagnose the career problem; to recommend provision of career counseling, job search skills, or occupational information; or to suggest use of interest inventories. The fact that only a subgroup of the sample demonstrated overshadowing illustrates the importance of including counselor variables, in this case, preference for counseling activities.

Gelso et al. (1985) and Spengler et al. (1990) raised similar issues regarding the acceptability of personal issues taking precedence over career issues and of differential attention to clients with greater dysfunction. These studies also raised a methodological issue that may be difficult to circumvent. Although both studies included ratings of severity, the accuracy of these ratings could be compromised by ingrained attitudes that undervalue career counseling. That is, career issues may be judged as less severe simply because they are career issues. Gelso et al. (1985) questioned whether the lower dysfunction ratings assigned to career clients in their study truly reflected less client dysfunction or reflected counselor bias to perceive career issues as less serious than personal issues. As noted earlier, clients with career issues are not necessarily less distressed than clients with personal issues (J. M. Gold & Scanlon, 1993; Lucas, 1992; Osipow & J. A. Gold, 1968).

Other studies have provided additional evidence of how counselor characteristics influence judgments that they make about clients with career issues. Bishop and Richards (1984) examined the relation between the theoretical orientation of 12 counselors and the judgments they made during 1443 intake interviews. Humanistic counselors judged clients to have more severe educational problems, and to have more anxiety about talking to a counselor. Moreover, humanistic counselors tended to judge vocational problems as more severe and client-defined goals as less realistic than did cognitive counselors. Hill, Tanney, Leonard, and Reiss (1977) reported that vignettes portraying two personal issues were rated as more serious than those portraying career issues, and Melnick (1975) found that responses of counselor trainees were rated as more genuine, affective, and exploratory for personal than for career problem vignettes. Two studies (Borresen, 1965; Sharp & Marra, 1971) examined whether use of a specific diagnostic category system over others differed by client or by counselor. Emotional problems were more likely to be presented by women, and vocational problems by men, and clusters of counselors were identified based on their differential use of the categories of emotional, career, or educational problems, and their attributions of causal factors. Eells and Guppy (1963) reported that some counseling staff placed academic or career issues higher in agency importance than in personal preference; in other words, they believed the agency should serve clients with career issues, but they preferred not to do it themselves.

In summary, the literature suggests that some counseling psychologists hold negative attitudes toward career counseling and that these attitudes may be communicated to clients and reflected in the quality of counseling. Suggestions have been made to increase enthusiasm for career counseling as part of socialization into the profession (Blustein, 1992; Niles & Pate, 1989; Pinkney & Jacobs, 1985; Warnke et al., 1993). Dorn (1986) suggested some interesting research directions stemming from these studies, such as investigating how counseling psychologists' commitment to career counseling is "developed, transmitted, or retained" (p. 217).

Goals of Process and Outcome Research

Generally, *process* refers to what happens during counseling sessions, either overtly or covertly, in terms of therapist behaviors, client behaviors, and the interaction between therapists and clients. Process researchers therefore analyze the counseling interaction to determine *how* changes occur in counseling. On the other hand, *outcome* refers to the changes that occur as a *result* of counseling; outcome research is focused on questions of efficacy, with the emphasis on whether or what changes occur. Typical research design and methodology also vary, depending on whether the primary focus is on process or on outcome: Outcome researchers frequently use designs to compare several treatment groups or a treatment group to a control group and examine changes in pre- and posttherapy measures. Because process research focuses on what occurs during counseling, a number of different designs are often used, including intensive single-subject, within-subjects, and between-subjects designs (Heppner, Kivlighan, & Wampold, 1992; Hill & Corbett, 1993).

In spite of a definitional distinction, however, the boundaries between process and outcome can easily become blurred, such as when within-session changes are considered a form of outcome; when continuous assessment is used; or when a variable is defined as process in one study and as outcome in another, for example, client satisfaction (Hill, 1982). Moreover, counseling process and outcome should be conceptually and empirically linked. "Without process, outcome tells us little about how change comes about. Without outcome, we have no context for giving meaning to process events" (Hill, 1991, p. 88).

The dichotomous division of counseling research into process and outcome has been criticized as logically indefensible (Krumboltz, Becker–Haven, & Burnett, 1979). For the sake of clarity, however, I review process and outcome separately in the next two sections, recognizing that this is an artificial dichotomy: Although not all outcome studies deal with process, almost all process studies deal with outcome.

CAREER COUNSELING PROCESS

Overview

Process in career counseling has been virtually ignored until recently, yet an understanding of process variables should be of interest to researchers and therapists alike. Hill's (1991) statement regarding the reason for process research in personal counseling applies equally to career counseling: "We want to know what makes counseling work. We want to know how to help clients change and how we can be better counselors and therapists" (p. 86).

Recently, there has been a resurgence of writing about what happens in career counseling, which, in turn, has expanded the view of career counseling and rekindled interest in process variables. For example, Spokane's (1991) text on career interventions and Walsh and Osipow's (1990, 1994) edited volumes of career counseling theories and techniques and career counseling for women provide a state-of-the-art perspective of how career counseling might be conducted. Other writings include Corbishley and Yost's (1989) consideration of psychological factors in career counseling and Borders and Archadel's (1987) discussion of the role of core self-beliefs in career counseling and decision making.

Because little research has focused on process in career counseling, this section draws from process research in personal counseling. Whether the process of career counseling is similar to process of personal counseling is as yet untested. Based on the literature reviewed previously regarding career versus personal counseling, one could build an argument for why process should be the same or why process should differ. Some evidence, to be reviewed in this section, suggests that more similarities than differences exist between process in career counseling and process in personal counseling. Regardless of the similarity of process in career and in personal counseling, the available methods of study should be similar.

In the realm of personal counseling, research began with a focus on process (Hill & Corbett, 1993). Process research enjoyed a great deal of activity until Eysenck's (1952) report against the efficacy of therapy undermined the momentum of researchers. One consequence of Eysenck's conclusion was the shift in the focus of research from process to outcome (Hill & Corbett, 1993). In contrast to the historical development of research in personal counseling, the evolution of research in career counseling is reversed: Outcome research took precedence, with process research still currently in its infancy. Even outcome research in career counseling is relatively recent (Holland et al., 1981), perhaps because the immediate outcomes of career counseling are more evident and accessible to participants and to interested observers and may be more behavioral or action-oriented in nature (e.g., a decision was made regarding college or job choice).

Relationship to Process Research
in Personal Counseling

Two issues are important for investigators to consider with regard to process research in career counseling vis-a-vis process research in personal counseling. First, given the disparity between process and outcome research within career counseling and between process in career counseling and process in personal counseling, it seems prudent for process research in career counseling to be informed by other lines of research. In other words, it would be inefficient for investigators to reinvent the wheel in pursuing process research within career counseling.

Second, it is imperative that we not sequester career counseling process research as special or different (that is, of interest to only a few); stated differently, the study of process should be a natural venue for a meeting of career and personal counseling. If the study of career counseling process is segregated, the implication is that it has nothing to offer counseling in general. On the contrary, because career counseling is "both more and less" than personal counseling (Crites, 1981), knowledge of career counseling process should inform personal counseling, and vice versa. For example, how does process differ between a session devoted to exploring career options and a session of test interpretation? How does the counselor facilitate the transition from exploration to information-giving and back again? What happens when the client expects to be given information but receives open-ended questions? These research questions are of interest not solely to career counselors, but are applicable across the range of counseling settings. Questions asked by other researchers need also to be asked about process within career counseling. For example, Hill and Corbett (1993) defined career counseling process as a separate direction for process research in general, yet their other questions, such as those regarding quality of and competence in counseling, also should be asked about career counseling.

Methodological Issues in Process Research

A full discussion of methods and strategies in process research is beyond the scope of this chapter. My intent here is to provide a brief overview, then review the literature regarding process in career counseling. Abundant information is available in the ample resources regarding what we know about counseling process or about conducting process research (cf. Greenberg, 1986; Greenberg & Pinsof, 1986; Heppner et al., 1992; Hill, 1982, 1991, 1992; Mahrer, 1988; J. Martin, 1984, 1992; Watkins & Schneider, 1991).

Heppner et al. (1992) provided a useful summary of critical measurement issues in process research. They outlined four questions that researchers must address in designing a process study: What to measure? From whose perspective? How much to measure? How to analyze these data?

The first question of what to measure addresses the aspect of process that the researcher wants to examine, for example, participants' behaviors or the developing relationship. The question further encompasses two subquestions: (1) What particular focus is desired, such as content (what is said), action (what is done), style (how), quality (how well), intention (why), and reaction (internal effect)? (2) At what level will these aspects be measured, from micro (speech acts) to macro (relationship)? Heppner et al. (1992) categorized representative measures of process variables by focus and level of measurement. They cited Hill's (1982) observation that counselor process variables attract more attention than do client process variables. Heppner et al. (1992) called this a "critical omission that hampers our understanding of the counseling process . . . we strongly recommend that the client be conceptualized not as a passive agent to whom interventions are administered, but rather as an *active processor* of information in the change process" (Heppner et al., 1992, p. 338).

The second question, from whose perspective? is based on evidence suggesting that counselor, client, and observer may have discrepant views of what occurs and that these views probably vary depending on what aspect of process is being measured. According to Heppner et al. (1992), the question of whose perspective is overstated, as there really is only one perspective, that of the researcher, who chooses the coding system and interprets the results. For this reason, Hill (1982) emphasized the selection and training of raters as the most important part of measurement considerations.

How much to measure? refers to how much of each session and how many sessions are necessary to ensure a representative sampling of therapy events. Heppner et al. (1992) noted that the final question, How to analyze the data? stems from the trend of researchers explicitly examining links between process and outcome. Traditionally, analyses have been correlational in nature, but researchers have begun to use sequential analyses to examine the mutual influence of counselor and client; such analyses allow a greater degree of causal interpretations.

Review of Research Regarding Process
in Career Counseling

In spite of the paucity of research on career counseling process (Meier, 1991; Osipow, 1982; Rounds & Tinsley, 1984; Spokane, 1991), the research that does exist offers a diversity of methods and hints at the wealth of interesting questions yet to be examined. These studies are reviewed in the following two sections and are divided into naturalistic and analogue studies.

Naturalistic Studies

In several studies on process variables, researchers used actual clients in naturalistic settings. These studies included conversational analysis of interest inventory interpretations (Reed, Patton, & P. Gold, 1993), case studies of career counseling (Dorn, 1988; Kirschner, 1989; Kirschner, Hoffman, & Hill, 1994; Spokane & Fretz, 1993), examinations of expectations of career counseling (Galassi, Crace, G. Martin, James, & Wallace, 1992; Robbins, Mullison, Boggs, Riedesel, & Jacobson, 1985), and analyses of facilitative factors in group career counseling or career exploration classes (P. Gold, Kivlighan, Kerr, & Kramer, 1993; Kivlighan, Johnsen, & Fretz, 1987).

Case Studies. In three studies researchers used a case-study format to provide an intensive examination of process variables in career counseling: (1) therapist intentions, client reactions, session impact, and critical incidents (Kirschner, 1989; Kirschner et al., 1994); (2) links between process variables and mental health outcomes (Spokane & Fretz, 1993); and (3) use of a social-influence framework (Dorn, 1988).

Kirschner and her colleagues (Kirschner, 1989; Kirschner et al., 1994) examined the covert cognitive processes of counselor intentions and client reactions and the links between process and outcome variables, in seven 50-minute sessions of career counseling. The client was a 43-year-old White woman, who was currently employed as a speech therapist, and the counselor was a 34-year-old female White counseling psychologist with 7 years postdoctoral experience.

Results of analysis of process measures obtained after each session indicated that the most frequent counselor intentions (Hill & O'Grady, 1985) across the seven sessions were change, insight, feelings, and information giving. The most frequent client reactions (Hill, Helms, Spiegel, & Tichenor, 1988) were supported, challenged, and understood. The seven sessions were divided into three stages based on their content: establishing rapport and obtaining information (Session 1), test interpretation (Sessions 2–4), and consolidating career choices (Sessions 5–7). Counselor intentions in the first stage differed substantially from those in the remaining two stages. Stage 1 intentions were characterized by the counselor's providing structure and support and assessing the client's issue, and in Stages 2 and 3 they were characterized by the counselor's focus on feelings, insight, and challenge. Client reactions related to "therapeutic work" (Kirschner et al., 1994) steadily increased through the three stages. Sequential analyses indicated which client reactions were most likely to follow specific counselor intentions; for example, the counselor intention to give information was most often followed by the client reactions of supported and educated. Analysis of the deepest session, as rated by counselor and client, indicated more counselor intentions to give information and change and fewer intentions to set limits, clarify, and self-control, as compared to the most shallow session.

Analysis of critical events indicated a 75% rate of agreement between client and counselor (Kirschner et al., 1994). Specific positive events were a guided career fantasy; repeated feedback about client's skills, abilities, and interests; exploration of self-concept; and discussion of the therapeutic relationship and of termination issues. The negative events were related to time constraints and to avoidance of more extensive discussion of client's feelings about the counseling relationship. The counselor also listed as negative some of her own interventions, or instances in which she wished she had responded. The client often listed her own in-session feelings as positive or negative critical events (Kirschner, 1989).

Analysis of the outcome measures administered one week after termination of counseling indicated that the client had completed more exploration (of self and environment), experienced more stress related to exploration, and was more satisfied with the information she obtained. Results also indicated a slight increase in vocational identity, a decrease in need for occupational information, and a decrease in perceived barriers. Ratings by counselor and client indicated that the client had made gains on all three of her self-defined goals. At an 18-month follow-up, exploration and stress both had decreased. Vocational identity had increased, and there was no perceived need for occupational information, although there was an increase in perceived barriers. The client had reduced her list of occupational alternatives from three to one, had maintained gains on two of her three goals, and had increased substantially on attainment of her third goal. In a telephone interview 5 years after counseling, the client reported that she had changed jobs, was highly satisfied with her job, and had remarried. She indicated that counseling had increased her level of self-understanding and had been a very significant influence; she was able to vividly recall specific events that had occurred in counseling.

The results of this study were compared to those from previous research on personal counseling (Fuller & Hill, 1985; Hill, Carter, & O'Farrell, 1983; Hill & O'Grady, 1985; O'Farrell, Hill, & Patton, 1986). Although there were some differences, the "similarities between the two were quite striking . . .

most of the predominant counselor intentions and client reactions experienced were the same as those found in several cases of psychotherapy" (Kirschner, 1989, p. 258). The primary difference was that more emphasis was placed on giving information in career counseling, in addition to the other intentions. The intentions of the particular counselor in the career counseling study also were compared to her intentions in four single sessions of personal counseling conducted at least 5 years earlier. This comparison indicated a few differences: The counselor reported more intentions to set limits and give information and fewer intentions of cognitions and self-control in career counseling than in personal counseling (Kirschner et al., 1994).

Kirschner's (Kirschner, 1989; Kirschner et al., 1994) study offers a glimpse of what can be uncovered with a discovery-oriented examination (Mahrer, 1988) of the process of career counseling. The study was well designed: Multiple measures of process and outcome were administered at frequent intervals, judges verified the career-related content of sessions and the similarity of counselor- and client-identified critical events, and process variables were linked to outcome variables. These results suggest a parallel in what occurs in career counseling with what occurs in personal counseling. Based on their results, Kirschner et al. (1994) suggested that career counseling be considered a form of brief, focused counseling.

Spokane and Fretz (1993) reported on work in progress, a research project designed to examine how career counseling affects career and personal adjustment. Forty people were selected, based on demonstrating moderate levels of career indecision and psychological distress, to receive eight sessions of individual career counseling; the sessions were conducted by 14 experienced career counselors. Three sets of variables were measured, each consisting of multiple measures at repeated occasions: (a) career adjustment (measures of indecision, interests, beliefs, behavior, options under consideration, and work history), (b) personal adjustment (problem checklists), and (c) counseling process (measures of anxiety, information-seeking behavior, goal attainment, perceptions of the counselor, and session impact).

Results of this project have the potential to provide us a great deal of insight into the process and outcome of career counseling, connections between process and outcome, and the relation of career counseling to personal and mental health outcomes. Planned analyses include examination of pre- and postcounseling scores on all variables to determine whether career counseling affects mental health status and whether career counseling differentially affects different presenting issues; an examination of whether person–environment congruence is related to mental health variables; a study of most and least helpful events in counseling; and, the relation of anxiety across sessions. Further, these data will be available for a substantial number of clients and will therefore provide the richness of a case study with the additional benefit of increased generalizability.

In the third case study, Dorn (1988) used the social-influence model as a framework for a client in career counseling. The client was a college sophomore majoring in pre-medicine; her presenting issues were poor study skills and a low grade point average. An additional central concern, uncovered in counseling, was that the client lacked an interest in medicine but felt she needed to pursue this career to please her parents. She received five sessions of career counseling from Dorn, who employed a social-influence intervention (Dorn, 1988, 1990). The counselor's focus of the sessions was to change the client's negative message of "I'm not good enough" for medicine to a positive attribution that she had other talents and interests and to offer emotional support to the client.

The client completed the Counselor Rating Form (CRF; Barak & LaCrosse, 1975) and the Career Decision Scale (CDS; Osipow, Carney, Winer, Yanico, & Koschier, 1976) after the first, third, and fifth sessions. Visual inspection of CRF scores suggested that Trustworthiness and Expertness scores remained constant (and high) across sessions; Attractiveness scores, on the other hand, were high after the first session, dropped after the third session, and increased slightly after the fifth session. Career indecision increased from Session 1 to Session 3, then decreased by Session 5.

Dorn (1988) concluded that social influence fluctuated during the course of counseling. Such fluctuation is contrary to what might be predicted by Strong (1968), who conceptualized counseling as a two stage process in which the counselor's social power is established first, then the counselor can use his or her power to influence the client. Dorn (1988) speculated that the decrease in Attractiveness scores might be due to his discussion in Session 3 of a conflict that the client was experiencing. He also noted that different patterns were observed on the three scales of the CRF, suggesting that three separate dimensions may exist, contrary to some previous evidence of the unidimensional nature of the CRF.

Dorn's (1988) study represents the application of an established counseling-process model to career counseling. An interesting direction for future researchers using the social influence model is the examination of what actually occurs in counseling sessions through analysis of the counselor–client interaction.

Conversational Analysis. Reed et al. (1993) used a qualitative, conversational analysis methodology to examine the process of interpreting vocational interest inventories: They focused on the "commonsense speaking practices with which counselors attempt to give test results practical significance for clients through the sequential, interactive talk that constitutes their social occasion" (p. 144). Rather than use a verbal coding or classification system, they maintained the contextual, sequential nature of counselor and client interactions and focused on turn-taking as an element of conversational structure. They analyzed interviews of five counselors and five clients, in which results of interest inventories were interpreted.

Reed et al. (1993) reported a regular, ongoing sequence of conversational turn-taking that was used to link inventory scores with information about the client; this sequence was accomplished by an *adjacency pair*, in which the first speaker constructed a turn that strongly shaped the content of the second speaker's next turn. This pair "exerts a powerful influence or constraint on the talk because the speaker of the first part allocates a turn to the second speaker, but one that normatively requires the second speaker to provide an utterance selected from a certain class of utterances" (Reed et al., 1993, p. 149).

Reed et al. (1993) identified two types of adjacency pairs, each serving a different function, that were linked together in a four-turn structure. The first adjacency-pair type often began with the counselor's introducing a specific interest inventory score and inviting the client to provide a description of his or her own experiences to confirm the score. The client then responded in a way that "confirms the test scores by locating the origin of their scores in their own biographies" (Reed et al., 1993, p. 150). The second adjacency-pair type constitutes the third (counselor) and fourth (client) turn of the four-turn sequence; in this second pair, counselors "transform the sense of clients' talk by recasting it into reportable . . . and putative evidence of preexisting attributes of clients that have presumably been there all along" (p. 150). These attributes then were used by counselors to categorize clients as "typical kinds of people with typical vocational alternatives available to them" (p. 150). The client response (fourth turn) confirmed the counselor's assessment. This last response could be viewed as evidence that counselors have influenced clients to accept their views. Reed et al. (1993) suggested that the "counselors exercised social influence over their clients through their tacit and skillful management of the turn-taking system in their conversations with clients" (p. 153).

This study represents a fascinating approach to the analysis of counseling interactions, and the findings make intuitive sense. Questions of generalizability include whether similar results would be observed in other interpretation interviews (these were part of a career workshop), in other career counseling interviews, or with other investigators.

Expectations About Career Counseling. In two studies researchers examined an aspect of what Hill (1991) categorized as input or pretherapy variables. Galassi et al. (1992) asked clients what they preferred and what they anticipated in career counseling, through 15 open-ended questions given prior to the first counseling session. Analysis of 1,546 unitized responses suggested that what clients preferred and what they anticipated were not always the same.

Galassi et al. (1992) concluded that clients had a clear idea about their preferences: career counseling should take about three sessions, it should result in a clearer sense of direction or in confirmation of choice, and testing would have an important role. Further, clients preferred counseling that focused on specific career plans and decision making; exploring both self and careers, with an active counselor who gave advice; and, researching careers between counseling sessions. In contrast, clients were less clear about what they anticipated would actually occur in career counseling, and discrepancies occurred between preferences and anticipations, suggesting that clients anticipated accomplishing less than they desired.

Results of this study suggest the importance of the separation of preferences from anticipations, both in research and in practice. The study raises a set of intriguing questions regarding how clients develop preferences about career counseling, what leads to the observed discrepancies between what clients prefer and what they anticipate, why they believe that counseling will not address their preferences, how counselors react to client preferences, and how the discrepancies affect the outcome of career counseling.

A study reported by Robbins et al. (1985) provides a second example of the assessment of pretherapy characteristics, in this case a comparison of attendees of career development workshops to those who registered but did not attend. Reasons for nonattendance were elicited in interviews and were categorized by two judges: of the nonattendees, 45% gave internal reasons (forgotten or felt discouraged), 38% gave environmental reasons (problems with scheduling or transportation), and 17% felt they already had met their goals. Compared to attendees, participants with internal reasons had lower self-esteem and participated in fewer information-seeking activities; those with environmental reasons were more decided; and those who had met their goals were more decided, reported more information-seeking behaviors, and had higher self-esteem and comfort with the academic environment. No differences between attendees and nonattendees as a group were found on any variables; these differences only emerged when the nonattendees were categorized by their reasons for nonattendance.

Group Career Counseling. The final two studies of career counseling process within a naturalistic paradigm focus on group counseling and career classes. Kivlighan et al. (1987) examined how participants of career groups rated the importance of Yalom's (1985) 11 therapeutic factors. The most highly ranked factors were expressing feelings, a sense of universality, taking responsibility for one's decision, and the cohesiveness of being involved as a group member. The least valued aspects were seeing the group as a recapitulation of family experience, feedback on one's impact, revelation of sensitive issues, and instillation of hope. Comparison of the career groups according to rankings made by an encounter group indicated little overlap in how participants in the two groups viewed the change process. A further analysis identified the four groups with greatest and the smallest pretreatment-to-posttreatment changes according to vocational-identity scores. The two groups with the greatest change had higher means on advice or suggestions, instillation of hope, experimenting, revealing, and understanding.

Using participant-guided methodology, P. Gold et al. (1993) examined what students perceived as helpful events in career exploration classes. Perceptions were assessed by means of written narratives and coded according to a scheme of therapeutic impact. Factor analysis of codings indicated three dimensions: Affective Factors, Identifying and Coping with Problems, and Insight Gained. Affective Factors was the best predictor of change in vocational identity. No differences were found by pretreatment levels of vocational identity.

Analogue Studies

In analogue studies of career counseling process, researchers typically have examined how varying aspects of counselor behavior influenced how counselors are perceived, including counselor verbal responses (Lillard, 1991; Watkins, Savickas, Brizzi, & Manus, 1990) and other in-session behavior (Bacorn & Dixon, 1984; Miller, 1992). In addition, in one study process in an initial interview was examined (Hampl, Lonborg, Lassiter, Williams, & Schmidt, 1984, cited in Kirschner, 1989). In general, these studies have the potential of adding to our knowledge of process-related variables because more control is exerted over the setting; they have, however, the disadvantage of limited generalizability to actual career counseling.

Counselor Verbal Responses.

Watkins et al. (1990) compared the effects of four types of counselor responses (self-disclosing, self-involving, empathic, and open-question statements) on college students' perceptions of a counselor. Participants viewed a videotape containing five occurrences of one of the four types of counselor responses and indicated their perceptions of the counselor and their confidence in the counselor's ability to help resolve 10 career issues.

A significant three-way interaction occurred in ratings of the counselor: The male counselor was rated as more expert and trustworthy when using self-involving rather than self-disclosing statements with a female client, and as more expert and trustworthy when using empathic statements with a male client than self-disclosing statements with a female client. No significant differences emerged from the measure of confidence in the counselor.

Watkins et al. (1990) were surprised by the lack of a main effect due to type of counselor response and questioned whether perceptions of counselor responses varied between career and personal counseling. However, there were several limitations to the study, mostly related to its analogue design:

The manipulation was based on a short videotape of an initial counseling session, and the client response immediately following the manipulated counselor response was identical across conditions.

Lillard (1991) used the social-influence perspective to examine how differences in interpretation style (tentative vs. absolute) were perceived. Participants viewed one of two 8-minute videotapes of a counseling vignette. The videotapes depicted a female client and a male counselor discussing various career myths and ways of overcoming them. In the tentative-style vignette, the counselor used interrogative statements, whereas in the absolute-style vignette, the counselor used declarative statements. No differences were observed between the interpretation-style conditions in perceptions of the counselor. Endorsement of career myths was reduced in both conditions.

Counselor In-Session Behavior. In an investigation of the effects of touch in counseling, Bacorn and Dixon (1984) screened female volunteer participants for two types of issues, depression and career indecision, and assigned the participants to a touch or no-touch condition. Five male counselors conducted a single 30-minute counseling session with each participant. In the touch condition, four occurrences of touch were included in the interview. No differences were observed by presenting problem or by touch or no-touch in relationship characteristics nor in willingness to return for a second interview. Of particular interest to the present discussion is that comfort with counselor touch varied by presenting problem: Participants who discussed a career concern were significantly more comfortable with touch than those who discussed depression. However, the higher level of comfort apparently was not reflected in higher ratings of perceptions of counselor nor in willingness to return for a future session.

Although Bacorn and Dixon (1984) used an analogue design, their study allows for greater generalizability because their participants actually received a session of counseling, rather than merely watching a session. One issue that may be important with regard to touch is gender of client and counselor; Bacorn and Dixon (1984) used male counselors and female clients.

Miller (1992) also used a social-influence perspective in a study of the effects of note-taking during a career counseling interview. Two 14-minute videotapes, varying only by presence or absence of brief note-taking five times during the session, were viewed by participants. No differences were observed in ratings of perceived counselor expertness, attractiveness, or trustworthiness, as measured by the CRF (Barak & LaCrosse, 1975). Participants, however, did indicate a greater willingness to see the counselor in the non-note-taking condition.

Process in Initial Interviews. A study by Hampl et al. (1984, cited in Kirschner, 1989) represents one of the first attempts to examine the process of career counseling; they examined process and outcome in initial career counseling analogue sessions as well as the mediating role of client conceptual level. Participants were 20 career-undecided volunteers selected according to their high or low conceptual level scores; the five counselors were counseling psychology doctoral students. Counselors and participants were matched in same-gender pairs and participated in a 40-minute initial career counseling interview.

The most frequent counselor responses, as rated by judges, were minimal encouragers, requests for information, supplying of information, and interpretations; empathic responses, direct guidance, and requests for clarification were rarely used. Analysis of three overarching categories (requests, directives, complex responses) indicated no effects due to conceptual level but did indicate a significant increase in use of directives from beginning to end of the session. Nearly half of the client responses were classified as cognitive and behavioral self-descriptions; no differences were found by conceptual level or across the session. Measures of relationship characteristics and perceptions of counselors did not vary by conceptual level.

Thus, client conceptual level did not contribute significantly to process and outcome in this career counseling analogue. Hampl et al. (1984, cited in Kirschner, 1989) noted that much of the verbal interaction between counselor and client was of a cognitive, rather than an emotional nature. They interpreted this pattern as being consistent with the stereotypical nature of career counseling. However, Kirschner reported quite different results; the counselor–client interaction in her case study clearly corresponded more closely to what occurs in personal counseling than what occurred in the Hampl et al. study (Kirschner, 1989; Kirschner et al., 1994).

Generalizability of the Hampl et al. (1984, cited in Kirschner, 1989) study is limited by its use of a small sample of volunteer "clients," who were counseled by trainees, in a single, brief session. Further, although the study examined career counseling, the outcome measures were not relevant to career counseling, and no attempt was made to link process to outcome (Kirschner, 1989).

Summary of Process Research

Dorn (1988) noted that the actual interaction occurring between counselor and client was "a virtually unexplored territory in career counseling" (p. 278). The studies reviewed here suggest that it also is a very rich territory. Process in career counseling seems to share a great deal with process in personal counseling (Kirschner, 1989; Kirschner et al., 1994), yet there are aspects of career counseling, such as initial interviews and test interpretations, that might be structured in unique ways (Hampl et al., 1984, cited in Kirschner, 1989; Reed et al., 1993). Clients seem to have clear preferences about career counseling, yet they also seem to realize that these preferences may not be met (Galassi et al., 1992). A picture is emerging of what clients find helpful in career groups and classes (P. Gold et al., 1993; Kivlighan et al., 1987), as well as why they do not attend such activities (Robbins et al., 1985). Varying counselors' verbal responses apparently does not affect clients' perceptions, at least not in analogue settings (Lillard, 1991; Watkins et al., 1990). Other counselor behaviors, however, such as note-taking and touch, may have some impact on clients' perceptions (Bacorn & Dixon, 1984; Miller, 1992).

The diverse methodology reflected in these studies represents another way in which career counseling process is a rich territory. As discussed previously, the borrowing of established methodology is an efficient approach to process research in career counseling; clearly, such borrowing, in addition to some innovative methods, is occurring. Further, to reiterate a point made earlier, I believe that these results are relevant to researchers interested in the process of personal counseling as well as to those interested in career counseling.

CAREER COUNSELING OUTCOME

Overview

The primary question of whether career interventions are effective has been answered in the affirmative (Oliver & Spokane, 1988; Rounds & Tinsley, 1984). As Phillips (1992) noted, "Regardless of the difficulty in defining what career counseling is, there is considerable evidence that it works. The evidence accumulated over many decades, with many different intervention strategies, and for many different populations, is reassuring: what career counselors do, helps" (p. 513).

This section includes a summary of previous reviews and recommendations regarding research methodology and is followed by a review of studies related specifically to career counseling. As I noted previously, because the outcome of career interventions has received sufficient attention from reviewers, in this section I focus on the outcome of career counseling.

Summary of Previous Reviews of Outcome Research

Previous reviewers have provided a comprehensive perspective of the literature related to the effectiveness of career interventions (Fretz, 1981; Lunneborg, 1983; Oliver & Spokane, 1988; Phillips, 1992; Spokane & Oliver, 1983). A few points are summarized here; interested readers are referred to the reviews for more detailed information.

Phillips (1992) organized her review to correspond to five components of an ideal, "problem-free" career-choice process (self-definition, readiness to choose, decision making, choice and commitment, and implementation), and reviewed the theoretical and empirical literature related to each component. Although she reached the conclusion that "what career counselors do, helps" (p. 513), she also raised a further question in noting that "there has been less attention to the question of whether what we are able to do is what needs to be done" (p. 513). She concluded that the majority of career intervention research has focused only on problems related to readiness, decision making, and choice. The topic of self-definition has received recent attention, but implementation seems to "have been largely abandoned by counseling psychologists" (p. 539).

Fretz (1981) evaluated the literature regarding effectiveness of career interventions and speculated that the findings of small gains due to career interventions might obscure aptitude-by-treatment interactions (ATI): Outcome studies typically were evaluations of only one treatment, were often without a comparison or control group, and did not account for individual differences among clients. Fretz outlined ATI dimensions relevant to the study of career intervention outcomes: client attributes (classified as demographic, psychological, or career related), treatment parameters (content domain, interpersonal context, and degree of structure), and outcome variables (career knowledge and skills, career behavior, sentiments, and effective role functioning).

The aptitude-by-treatment interaction approach advocated by Fretz (1981) has been useful in illuminating what occurs in career interventions. For example, in Kivlighan's (1990) review of studies examining career group process, he observed that important results were found when client differences were taken into account. Fretz and Leong (1982) evaluated the effectiveness of diagnostic scales that measure career indecision, vocational identity, and career maturity as a means of predicting variables typically defined as outcomes of career interventions. They found fewer predictable results for men than for women, and further, the pattern of results for women varied for a subgroup classified as *social* in Holland's (1985a) typology. Another example of the application of Fretz's (1981) ATI suggestions is a study by Robbins and Tucker (1986). Participants in interactional career workshops fared better than those in the self-directed workshops; those with higher goal instability had better outcomes in the interactional rather than in the self-directed workshops, whereas those with lower goal instability had similar outcomes in either workshop.

Spokane and Oliver (Oliver & Spokane, 1988; Spokane & Oliver, 1983) conducted the most comprehensive reviews of career intervention outcome research published to date. In each review, they used meta-analytic procedures (Smith & Glass, 1977) to examine effect sizes for differences between treatment and control groups. In their initial review (Spokane & Oliver, 1983), they included 52 studies published during the period 1950–1980 and examined individual versus group/class interventions. In the second review (Oliver & Spokane, 1988), they extended the number of studies to 58, divided the studies into eight categories (individual counseling, group counseling, individual test interpretation, group test interpretation, workshop/structured group, class, computer, and counselor-free), and examined characteristics of the studies.

Their results demonstrated that career interventions are effective: The mean effect size for all treatment groups versus all control groups was 0.85 (Spokane & Oliver, 1983), which they considered a large difference; in comparison, Smith and Glass (1977) reported a mean effect size of 0.68 for psychotherapy studies. Further, Spokane and Oliver (1983) reported that the mean effect size for group and class interventions was larger (1.11) than the effect size for individual interventions (0.87). The category of group or class interventions encompassed a wide variety of treatments that differed in length and intensity and that might "teach to the test." Further, the results for individual interventions were based on fewer studies.

In their second review, Oliver and Spokane (1988) examined specific characteristics of the studies. Their analyses included 58 studies published between 1950 and 1982, with a total of 7,311 participants, and allowed 240 comparisons between treatment and control groups. Given the effects demonstrated in the first review, Oliver and Spokane (1988) asked more specific questions. They examined relations between characteristics of the studies and their outcomes, hypothesizing that sample characteristics, design characteristics, type of treatment, type of outcome measure, dropout rate, and counselor experience would be related to outcome.

Of the treatment modalities they examined, the most effective as measured by effect sizes were classes (2.05), group test interpretations (0.76), workshops/structured groups (0.75), and individual counseling (0.74). However, because the number of hours and number of sessions varied considerably over these types of interventions, they calculated four additional indices of effect size to account for intensity of intervention: effect per hour, effect per session, effect per hour per counselor, and cost per session. Based on these indices, individual counseling was the most effective in terms of number of hours or number of sessions but also was the most expensive. A regression analysis indicated that the only study characteristic that significantly predicted effect size was treatment intensity (number of hours plus number of sessions entered as a block).

One of the most intriguing aspects of the initial, unweighted effect sizes is the high effect size (0.75) of individual counseling, given that the average duration of treatment was only 1.4 hours. These figures can be compared to those for group counseling, with an effect size of 0.62 and 7.7 hours of treatment. Career classes clearly had the largest effect size (2.05) but also were considerably longer in duration (20.9) hours. Surprisingly, almost half of the studies involved only one or two sessions.

Oliver and Spokane (1988) concluded:

> We feel that we can assert with a reasonable degree of confidence that individual counseling and workshops or structured groups seem slightly superior to group interventions, except for classes, which had the largest ES, 2.05, of any treatment. However, the class interventions required more hours to achieve this larger effect. Thus type of treatment is confounded with intensity of treatment . . . individual career counseling emerged as the most effective intervention per unit of time involved. (p. 458)

As these statements imply, Oliver and Spokane's (1988) review seemed to be an initial step in addressing Fretz's (1981) concern that we "need to clarify what, if any, unique gains can be achieved by the experience of the face-to-face individual counseling" (p. 84). Our next step is to examine what it is about career counseling that contributes to client gain.

Summary of Research Recommendations

Previous reviewers have offered a number of recommendations regarding choice of criteria, research methodology, instrumentation, and sampling.

Outcome Criteria. Oliver (1979) recommended the use of multiple criteria and of specific and global measures, an emphasis on measurement of short-term effects, and careful definition of constructs. Her discussion was echoed by Rounds and Tinsley (1984), who observed that "one of the most fundamental issues in career interventions is determining what to measure and at which point in time it is appropriate to do so" (p. 162). Further, they argued that the issue of what to measure "is contingent on the diagnosis and classification of vocational problems. Until a classification system is agreed on, this perennial issue will not be resolved." (Rounds & Tinsley, 1984, p. 163). A similar argument was made by Oliver and Spokane (1988), who promoted the need to connect outcome criteria to the reasons clients seek counseling: "Researchers will do well to determine why clients seek career counseling and what their goals are for that counseling. . . . Studies using diagnostic procedures are badly needed" (p. 458–459).

Other issues related to outcome criteria are the difficulty in defining what constitutes a "good" career choice (Krumboltz et al., 1979), the need to include follow-up as well as posttreatment measurement of outcome (Fretz, 1981), and the utility of developing a set of standard measures to be used in research (Oliver & Spokane, 1988).

Instruments. How variables are measured has received much attention. Authors have commented on the lack of reliability and validity information, particularly with researcher-designed measures, the reactivity of measuring devices, and lack of clear, operational definitions (Oliver, 1979; Oliver & Spokane, 1988).

Design and Analysis. Oliver (1979) reminded researchers to pay attention to internal and external validity, spontaneous remission and deterioration effects, types of experimental design, and adequacy of data analytic strategies. Of particular concern are random assignment of participants to treatments and inclusion of control or comparison groups (Gottfredson, 1978; Oliver, 1979; Rounds & Tinsley, 1984). In addition, Rounds and Tinsley (1984) discussed some alternative research strategies that would allow answers to questions of relative efficacy of treatment components. These included a dismantling strategy, by which components are systematically removed to isolate critical components, and a constructive strategy, by which components are systematically added to build a "maximally effective treatment package" (Rounds & Tinsley, 1984, p. 169).

It has also been recommended that researchers increase the number of studies using aptitude-by-treatment interaction designs (Phillips, 1992); use actual clients as well as comparisons between true clients and solicited clients (Oliver & Spokane, 1988); report such vital information as descriptive data, attrition rates, counselor experience, and reliability and validity information (Oliver & Spokane, 1988); and provide additional information such as treatment costs for each intervention (Fretz, 1981).

Review of Research Regarding Outcome of Career Counseling

This review focuses on outcomes of career counseling. As a point of clarification, other authors use the terms *career counseling* and *career intervention* interchangeably; however, career counseling is defined here as an ongoing, face-to-face interaction between counselor and client, with the primary focus on work- or career-related issues; the interaction is psychological in nature, with the relationship between counselor and client serving an important function.

The distinction between career counseling and career intervention is not always easy to uphold when the relevant literature is examined, primarily because some studies, particularly earlier ones, contain little description of what the treatment entailed. Further, the determination of when an intervention becomes counseling is difficult. For example, if an experimental treatment includes a single individual session, is this individual counseling? What is the distinction between group counseling and other group activities such as workshops and structured groups? Many of these studies are described as examinations of "counseling," although at times the terminology seems inaccurate. Studies were chosen for inclusion if the intervention seemed to be (or resembled) actual counseling.

Studies are organized by modality of counseling: individual counseling, group counseling, and comparisons of individual versus group counseling. In addition, readers are reminded that several studies reviewed previously, in the section on career counseling process, also contained outcome variables (Kirschner, 1989; Kirschner et al., 1994; Spokane & Fretz, 1983).

Individual Career Counseling

Quite a few studies are described as evaluations of individual career counseling. Some of what was termed "counseling" were single-session test interpretations or interventions that were quite structured or didactic, and are not included in the present review. In the studies reviewed here, researchers examined the relation between the content of counseling sessions and outcome (Phillips, Friedlander, Kost, Specterman, & Robbins, 1988); the effects of brief career counseling on vocational identity (Buescher, Johnston, Lucas, & Hughey, 1989); career maturity (Flake, Roach, & Stenning, 1975); and realism or appropriateness of career plans (Gonyea, 1963; Pool, 1965).

In a retrospective study, Phillips et al. (1988) examined the relationship between topical focus in career counseling and counseling outcome. Topical focus was rated by clients and by judges who reviewed counselors' progress notes. The three outcome measures were client satisfaction with occupational status, client satisfaction with counseling, and judges' ratings of whether counseling goals were achieved (determined by a review of counselors' termination reports). The client variables of gender, age, and previous counseling experience did not predict any of the outcome variables; however, the addition of counselor experience predicted client satisfaction with counseling, and the addition of the treatment variables of topical focus and counseling duration predicted goal achievement. Counseling that was more career-related in focus and longer in duration was related to greater goal achievement.

The retrospective nature of clients' responses places limits on the generalizability of these results. Further, the possibility of selective reporting by counselors of topical focus seems likely, in light of the evidence that some counselors prefer personal over career content and that personal content might be overrepresented in progress notes because of its greater interest or novelty.

In several studies, researchers examined the effects of brief interventions, which often were semistructured in nature. Buescher et al. (1989) examined whether a 1½-hour individual session influenced the vocational identity of undecided college freshmen. The intervention included the participants completing a 90-item card sort, discussing career options, and touring a career center. Compared to a no-treatment control group, participants in the treatment group had higher vocational identity scores at a 6-month follow-up but not immediately following treatment or 3 months later. The lack of differences at the earlier intervals underscores the importance of assessment at multiple times. Flake et al. (1975) selected tenth-grade students based on low career-maturity scores; the intervention consisted of three individual sessions provided by three separate people. Career-maturity scores for participants in the treatment group increased from pre- to postintervention and decreased for those in the control group.

Pool (1965) investigated the impact of three sessions of counseling on realism of career choice among hospitalized Veterans Administration patients. Those who were counseled did show greater realism of career choices than did a control group. Further analyses of the scores for the counseled group indicated differences in needs for those who became more realistic and those who did not; the latter had lower scores on measures of endurance and intraception and higher scores on measures of autonomy and need for help and support.

Finally, Gonyea (1963) examined appropriateness of career plans for students who had received career counseling. Precounseling career plans had been assessed when students entered as college freshmen, and post-counseling plans were assessed 4–6 years later for students who had received counseling in the intervening time. Half of the male clients were judged as having inappropriate career plans at the follow-up, compared to 20% for noncounseled group; however, the client sample also had less appropriate plans as freshmen. No information was given about the counseling, such as when it occurred, duration, or how much time had elapsed since termination; follow-up apparently occurred at widely varying times, from immediately to 6 years later.

Group Career Counseling

In studies of the outcome of group career counseling, researchers examined the variables of perceptions of self (Catron, 1966; Healy, Bailey, & Anderson, 1973) and career maturity (Powers, 1978; Swails & Herr, 1976). In two studies, aptitude-by-treatment interactions, such as personality types and treatment types (Kivlighan, Hageseth, Tipton, & McGovern, 1981) and level of motivation (Dorn, 1989), were examined.

How does congruence between personality types and treatment types affect the outcome of group career counseling? Kivlighan et al. (1981) examined this aptitude-by-treatment interaction question by designing treatments to match people-oriented or task-oriented Holland (1985a) types. Participants in groups that matched their type had higher career-maturity scores after treatment: *realistic* or *investigative* types in groups that emphasized self-exploration and *social* and *enterprising* types in groups that emphasized interaction among group members. Further, matching also resulted in higher evaluative ratings of the groups as well as in greater information-seeking behavior. It is important to note that there were no significant main effects, so clearly the ATI was a critical feature.

In another investigation of ATIs, Dorn (1989) used the social-influence paradigm to examine the connection between client motivation and counseling outcome. College students who sought career counseling were assigned to high- or low-motivation counseling groups according to their scores on the Motivation scale of the Expectations About Counseling instrument (EAC; Tinsley, Workman, & Kass, 1980). After two 2-hour group meetings, no differences were observed in perceived counselor characteristics or in career indecision due to motivation level; however, scores for the total sample did increase significantly on the career-indecision scale measuring certainty of college major and decreased on the scale measuring lack of structure for making a career decision.

Swails and Herr (1976) found no differences in career maturity for ninth-grade students in three types of career counseling groups (consisting of eight 50-minute sessions) and a control group. Catron (1966) reported that high school students showed positive changes in Q-sort perceptions of self after participating in 14 sessions of group counseling conducted over a 5-week period.

Finally, two studies addressed group counseling with specialized populations. Powers (1978) evaluated the use of structured, small-group counseling with former drug-abuse patients in Veterans Administration hospitals. Participants in the treatment groups had significantly higher career maturity scores and rated their occupational plans as clearer, compared to participants in control groups. Healy et al. (1973) examined whether career counseling affected the ability to differentiate oneself with respect to a variety of occupations. Participants were male Vietnam War veterans enrolled in a college transition program to address academic-skill deficiencies. Those with higher self-esteem (defined as the difference between ratings for self and ideal self) showed more differentiation than those with lower self-esteem; those who were counseled tended to show more differentiation than the noncounseled.

Group Versus Individual Counseling

Several studies have examined the differential effectiveness of group versus individual career counseling. These studies tend to be problematic because of the difficulty in controlling variations in the content, duration, and other factors, across different types of treatments. Fretz (1981) observed that the amount of interpersonal contact and of structure in individual counseling differ substantially from other interventions, which are confounding factors in empirical comparisons of individual counseling to other treatments. In these studies, researchers examined the differential impact of individual and group counseling on realism (Hanson & Sander, 1973), career indecision (Barak & Friedkes, 1981; Cooper, 1986; Davis & Horne, 1986), and vocational development (Babcock & Kaufman, 1976; Smith & Evans, 1973). Career counseling also was compared to a self-administered instrument (Krivatsy & Magoon, 1976).

In a well-designed study, Hanson and Sander (1973) compared the effectiveness of group and individual career counseling on vocational realism in a sample of eleventh- and twelfth-grade boys who had been identified as highly unrealistic; the boys had been further classified as "overshooters" or "undershooters." Individual counseling consisted of a median of 3.3 sessions per student. The group counseling sessions (4–6 sessions) incorporated a case-study format in which each participant presented information and received feedback related to his career decision. Three weeks after treatment, results indicated a significant interaction between type of unrealism and type of treatment: The greatest gains in realism of choice were found for the overshooters in group counseling and the undershooters in individual counseling. This study included clearly described and well-controlled procedures, and the definition of two subtypes of unrealism was an important aptitude-by-treatment interaction.

Barak and Friedkes (1981) examined whether participants with different types of career indecision benefited from different modes (direct vs. indirect and individual vs. group) of test interpretation. Level of posttreatment decidedness differed by indecision subtype but not due to mode of counseling or method of test interpretation. Participants classified as indecisive due to lack of structure gained the most from counseling (but also had the most to gain), and those classified as indecisive due to external barriers and personal conflicts gained the least.

Cooper (1986) compared the impact of individual and group career counseling on career and personal indecision; the two treatments consisted of similar duration and content. Personal indecision was lower for both conditions after treatment, but career indecision was unchanged. Cooper concluded that career and personal indecision are independent constructs; however, no reliability or validity information was provided for the measure of personal indecision.

Smith and Evans (1973) recruited participants (volunteers and actual clients) who scored below the midpoint on a scale designed to measure crystallization. An experimental group intervention consisted of 5 weeks of individual learning activities via audiotapes, large-group meetings, and 1-hour small-group sessions; individual counseling consisted of 2–4 sessions per person. Both intervention groups scored higher than the control group on three scales that indicate more advanced stages of vocational development, with the experimental group outscoring the individual-counseling group. No differences were found on client evaluations of counseling. The two treatments differed substantially from one another in duration, structure, and content.

Babcock and Kaufman (1976) examined the effectiveness of a career course versus individual career counseling in a sample of upperclass women. Participants in the career course demonstrated greater gain than did the other two groups on self-knowledge and participated in more planning activities to become informed about careers. Participants in the two interventions had greater gains than the control group in changes in expressed occupational choice. Participants in individual counseling reported receiving more assistance in job-search skills, and those in the course reported more assistance in comprehensive self-appraisal. A possible contamination could have occurred because the senior author taught the career course and provided half of the individual counseling; further, the course met for 14 hours, whereas the mean number of individual counseling sessions was 1.3.

Davis and Horne (1986) compared the relative effectiveness of group career counseling and a career course. Recruited participants were randomly assigned to either a 40-hour course delivered over a 16-week period or a 12-hour group of 12 students. Although both groups exhibited significant pretreatment-to-posttreatment differences in career indecision and career maturity, no differences were observed between the two treatment groups; the lack of group differences is surprising given the differences in duration and intensity of the treatments.

Krivatsy and Magoon (1976) compared traditional counseling to two methods that incorporated the Self-Directed Search (Holland, 1985b): a standard administration and an adaptation that consisted of structuring the use of the SDS and the summary codes. Similar pretreatment-to-posttreatment changes were reported for all three groups on a variety of outcome measures, such as satisfaction with career plans and frequency of information-seeking behavior. Krivatsy and Magoon (1976) concluded that the three treatments were equally effective but differentially costly. Strengths of the study included the use of multiple outcome measures and the approximately equivalent duration of interventions.

Summary of Outcome Studies

Oliver and Spokane's (1988) general conclusions about the effectiveness of career interventions and career counseling clearly are borne out when specific studies are considered. Individual career counseling seems to be effective, as measured by commonly used outcome variables such as career maturity, vocational identity, and realism of choice. Group career counseling also appears to be effective, as measured by the same types of outcome variables. Further, group and individual counseling may be differentially effective for different types of clients, and different types of clients may benefit from different types of groups.

The most surprising feature about the career outcome literature was the brevity of many of the interventions and the frequent use of recruited or no-choice participants rather than actual clients. In fact, researchers really have not yet adequately evaluated career *counseling*. Although Oliver and Spokane (1988) gave the highest marks to individual counseling, the question of whether these results are generalizable to actual career counseling remains. Studies that appear to be evaluations of career counseling often consist of a single session, are structured or didactic in nature, and focus on test interpretation or information-giving. In short, they do not seem to resemble career counseling.

Finally, Williamson and Bordin's (1941) question still seems pertinent: "What counseling techniques (and conditions) will produce what types of results with what types of students?" (p. 5). Although we have made gains in addressing this question, there still are a multitude of questions yet unanswered. As Holland et al. (1981) noted, "More rigorous evaluations of all forms of vocational intervention are still required. It is surprising that we have come so far with so little" (p. 299).

SUMMARY AND CONCLUSIONS

If all goes well, vocational counseling will eventually be used only for a few unusual clients. . . . A few psychologists will give demonstrations at conventions to illustrate how vocational counseling used to be done, but eventually they will be shunted off to hobby fairs along with bookbinding and calligraphy. (Holland, 1974, p. 26)

We have witnessed explosive growth in the number and diversity of career interventions in the last two decades. Moreover, the demand for career interventions continues to grow, and career concerns are becoming more complex across the life span, particularly with acknowledgment of the reciprocal influence of work and nonwork in adult life (Swanson, 1992). Yet, in spite of the growth in alternative interventions and the increased demand for cost-effective services, career counseling remains a vital activity that we continue to practice and teach. Given that career counseling appears to be an entrenched activity of counseling psychologists despite warnings to the contrary, it is time for researchers to devote more serious attention to it. This final section includes some observations about the career counseling literature and recommendations for future research.

Some Observations About the Literature Regarding Career Counseling

It seems ironic that in spite of a recent interest and writing about career counseling theory (cf. Walsh & Osipow, 1990), the majority of empirical work has focused, not on career counseling, but rather on other types of interventions, such as workshops or structured groups. We act as though we know the critical components of career counseling, yet there has not been nearly enough empirical verification (Holland et al., 1981). On the other hand, the literature documenting the effectiveness of career interventions provides a foundation that is informative and that we can apply to career counseling.

Other authors have called for more rigorous evaluation of career interventions as a whole. Although this is important, we have established that these interventions generally are efficacious (Oliver & Spokane, 1988; Spokane & Oliver, 1983), and so we are led to the next level of specificity in research questions about interventions: What are the most crucial components of interventions? How and by whom are they most effectively delivered? Equally pressing is the need for us to focus considerably more attention on career counseling to obtain empirical evaluation of what occurs in career counseling and how individuals benefit from career counseling. As Fretz (1981) observed, we "need to clarify what, if any, unique gains can be achieved by the experience of the face-to-face individual counseling" (p. 84).

Comparative studies still may be useful in answering questions such as what type of client benefits most from what type of intervention, but the methodology needs to be more sophisticated. For example, we must examine aptitude-by-treatment interactions and be more attentive in matching important treatment-related variables such as sheer amount of time. Nonequivalence of treatments becomes even more problematic when one of the treatments is individual counseling: If the duration, content, or structure of counseling is specified so that it matches another treatment, then it becomes less like counseling. As one approach in solving this problem, investigators could use methodological strategies that allow the disentanglement of treatment components, such as the dismantling and constructive techniques discussed by Rounds and Tinsley (1984).

Recommendations for Career Counseling Research

There are three general goals for career counseling research: the evaluation of the outcomes, specifically those of career counseling; the examination of the process of career counseling; and the linking of process and outcome variables in career counseling research. There are five additional recommendations.

First, research needs to be refocused to include the human interaction in career counseling. The body of outcome research, in particular, has not focused on the interactive, psychological component of career counseling; much of the research, particularly earlier studies, seemed to treat counselors primarily as instructional or information-delivery systems. However, career counseling clearly is more than instruction and information. Our not addressing the psychological interaction in career counseling has contributed to the image that process is not important in career counseling.

Second, further questions should be addressed regarding outcome of career interventions. Why are most career interventions effective? Even brief, almost superficial interventions have positive impact. The broader career intervention literature tells us that there are numerous types of interventions that are effective; now we need to know for whom and under what conditions (Williamson & Bordin, 1941). Further, when are interventions not effective, and why and for whom are they ineffective?

Third, studies that provide true evaluations of the outcome of career *counseling* are needed. What happens during career counseling? This is an extremely broad question that we truly are just beginning to consider. The case study by Kirschner and colleagues (Kirschner, 1989; Kirschner et al., 1994) gave us a glimpse of what may occur, and Spokane and Fretz's (1993) ongoing project promises further insight.

Fourth, researchers must begin to address process issues in career counseling. Until they do, career counseling will continue to be perceived as qualitatively different from personal counseling (Blustein, 1992; Osipow, 1982) in ways that may be inaccurate. Process research is one way to refocus attention on the psychological component of career counseling.

Process in career counseling still is "a virtually unexplored territory" (Dorn, 1988, p. 278), but we are not without a road map. There are many methods available and certainly no shortage of questions. Hill and Corbett (1993) recently described steps toward improving process research, such as the use of case-study methodology (Galassi & Gersh, 1993); sequential analysis; the study of significant events (Greenberg, 1986); discovery-oriented, or exploratory, approaches; and a blend of qualitative and quantitative approaches.

One of Blustein's (1992) suggestions for reinvigorating vocational psychology was for us to understand more about the process of working with clients with career-related concerns. He suggested several possible implications of this line of study: It might tell us how clients respond to career-related interventions; it also may tell us how counselors respond to various career-related problems; and it may demonstrate that career counseling is more complex than its stereotype suggests.

Osipow's (1982) comments, although written over a decade ago, still hold true:

> The reader will note an absence of any serious discussion of process research in career counseling. . . . In addition, career counselors have rarely talked about the process aspect of career counseling in terms special to careers. Where interest in processes involved in career counseling exists, the same dynamics and concepts applied to other types of counseling relationships would seem to hold true. . . . The absence of process emphasis in career counseling has made career counseling very different from other kinds of counseling modalities. (pp. 32–33)

Finally, process and outcome variables need to be studied in tandem. What is it about individual career counseling that is effective? What role does the counselor–client relationship play in effective career counseling? How do counselors choose interventions to create a "maximally effective treatment package" (Rounds & Tinsley, 1984, p. 169) for clients?

Clearly, many unanswered questions exist regarding the process and outcome of career counseling and are worthy of continued research attention. Answers to these questions have the potential to benefit both counselors and clients and could offer insight into the intersection of career and personal counseling.

ACKNOWLEDGMENTS

I wish to thank Kim Daniels, Kathy Hope, Macy Lai, Kim Stark–Wroblewski, Leslie Strategier, and Denise Wallis for stimulating thought about process and outcome in career counseling, and Kathleen Chwalisz for feedback on an earlier version of the chapter.

REFERENCES

Babcock, R. J., & Kaufman, M. A. (1976). Effectiveness of a career course. *Vocational Guidance Quarterly, 24*, 261–266.

Bacorn, C. N., & Dixon, D. N. (1984). The effects of touch on depressed and vocationally undecided clients. *Journal of Counseling Psychology, 31*, 488–496.

Barak, A., & Friedkes, R. (1981). The mediating effects of career indecision subtypes on career-counseling effectiveness. *Journal of Vocational Behavior, 20*, 120–128.

Barak, A., & LaCrosse, M. B. (1975). Multidimensional perception of counselor behavior. *Journal of Counseling Psychology, 22*, 471–476.

Betz, N. E., & Corning, A. F. (1993). The inseparability of "career" and "personal" counseling. *Career Development Quarterly, 42*, 137–142.

Bishop, J. B., & Richards, T. F. (1984). Counselor theoretical orientation as related to intake judgments. *Journal of Counseling Psychology, 31*, 398–401.

Blustein, D. L. (1987). Integrating career counseling and psychotherapy: A comprehensive treatment strategy. *Psychotherapy, 24*, 794–799.

Blustein, D. L. (1992). Toward the reinvigoration of the vocational realm of counseling psychology. *The Counseling Psychologist, 20*, 712–723.

Borders, L. D., & Archadel, K. A. (1987). Self-beliefs and career counseling. *Journal of Career Development, 14*(2), 69–79.

Borresen, A. M. (1965). Counselor influence on diagnostic classification of client problems. *Journal of Counseling Psychology, 12*, 252–258.

Brown, D. (1985). Career counseling: Before, after, or instead of personal counseling? *Vocational Guidance Quarterly, 33*, 197–201.

Brown, D., & Brooks, L. (1985). Career counseling as a mental health intervention. *Professional Psychology: Research and Practice, 16*, 860–867.

Buescher, K. L., Johnston, J. A., Lucas, E. B., & Hughey, K. F. (1989). Early intervention with undecided college students. *Journal of College Student Development, 30*, 375–376.

Catron, D. W. (1966). Educational–vocational group counseling: The effects on perception of self and others. *Journal of Counseling Psychology, 13*, 202–207.

Cooper, S. E. (1986). The effects of group and individual vocational counseling on career indecision and personal indecisiveness. *Journal of College Student Personnel, 27*, 39–42.

Corbishley, M. A., & Yost, E. B. (1989). Psychological aspects of career counseling. *Journal of Career Development, 16*, 43–51.

Crites, J. O. (1981). *Career counseling: Models, methods, and materials.* New York: McGraw–Hill.

Croteau, J. M., & Thiel, M. J. (1993). Integrating sexual orientation in career counseling: Acting to end a form of the personal–career dichotomy. *Career Development Quarterly, 42*, 174–179.

Davidson, S. L., & Gilbert, L. A. (1993). Career counseling is a personal matter. *Career Development Quarterly, 42*, 149–153.

Davis, R. C., & Horne, A. M. (1986). The effect of small-group counseling and a career course on career decidedness and maturity. *Vocational Guidance Quarterly, 34*, 255–262.

Dorn, F. J. (1986). Needed: Competent, confident and committed career counselors. *Journal of Counseling and Development, 65*, 216–217.

Dorn, F. J. (1988). Utilizing social influence in career counseling: A case study. *Career Development Quarterly, 36*, 269–280.

Dorn, F. J. (1989). An examination of client motivation and career certainty. *Journal of College Student Development, 30*, 237–241.

Dorn, F. J. (1990). The social influence process in career counseling. In W. B. Walsh & S. H. Osipow (Eds.), *Career counseling: Contemporary topics in vocational psychology* (pp. 193–203). Hillsdale, NJ: Lawrence Erlbaum Associates.

Eells, K., & Guppy, W. (1963). Counselors' valuations of and preference for different types of counseling problems. *Journal of Counseling Psychology, 10*, 146–155.

Eysenck, H. J. (1952). The effects of psychotherapy: An evaluation. *Journal of Consulting Psychology, 16*, 319–324.

Fitzgerald, L. F., & Osipow, S. H. (1986). An occupational analysis of counseling psychology. *American Psychologist, 41*, 535–544.

Fitzgerald, L. F., & Osipow, S. H. (1988). We have seen the future, but is it us? The vocational aspirations of graduate students in counseling psychology. *Professional Psychology: Research and Practice, 19*, 575–583.

Flake, M. H., Roach, A. J., Jr., & Stenning, W. F. (1975). Effects of short-term counseling on career maturity of tenth-grade students. *Journal of Vocational Behavior, 6*, 73–80.

Flamer, S. (1986). Clinical-career intervention with adults: Low visibility, high need? *Journal of Community Psychology, 14*, 224–227.

Fretz, B. R. (1981). Evaluating the effectiveness of career interventions. *Journal of Counseling Psychology, 28*, 77–90.

Fretz, B. R., & Leong, F. T. L. (1982). Career development status as a predictor of career intervention outcomes. *Journal of Counseling Psychology, 29*, 388–393.

Fuller, F., & Hill, C. E. (1985). Counselor and helpee perceptions of counselor intentions in relation to outcome in a single counseling session. *Journal of Counseling Psychology, 32*, 329–338.

Galassi, J. P., Crace, R. K., Martin, G. A., James, R. M., Jr., & Wallace, R. L. (1992). Client preferences and anticipations in career counseling: A preliminary investigation. *Journal of Counseling Psychology, 39*, 46–55.

Galassi, J. P., & Gersh, T. L. (1993). Myths, misconceptions, and missed opportunity: Single-case designs and counseling psychology. *Journal of Counseling Psychology, 40*, 525–531.

Gelso, C. J., & Fretz, B. R. (1992). *Counseling psychology.* New York: Harcourt Brace Jovanovich.

Gelso, C. J., Prince, J., Cornfeld, J. L., Payne, A. B., Royalty, G., & Wiley, M. O. (1985). Quality of counselors' intake evaluations for clients with problems that are primarily vocational versus personal. *Journal of Counseling Psychology, 32*, 339–347.

Gold, P. B., Kivlighan, D. M., Jr., Kerr, A. E., & Kramer, L. A. (1993). The structure of students' perceptions of impactful, helpful events in career exploration classes. *Journal of Career Assessment, 1*, 145–161.

Gold, J. M., & Scanlon, C. R. (1993). Psychological distress and counseling duration of career and noncareer clients. *Career Development Quarterly, 42*, 186–191.

Gonyea, G. G. (1963). Appropriateness of vocational choices of counseled and uncounseled college students. *Journal of Counseling Psychology, 10*, 269–275.

Gottfredson, G. D. (1978). Evaluating vocational interventions. *Journal of Vocational Behavior, 13*, 252–254.

Greenberg, L. S. (1986). Change process research. *Journal of Consulting and Clinical Psychology, 54*, 4–9.

Greenberg, L. S., & Pinsof, W. (Eds.). (1986). *The psychotherapeutic process: A research handbook*. New York: Guilford.

Hackett, G. (1993). Career counseling and psychotherapy: False dichotomies and recommended remedies. *Journal of Career Assessment, 1*, 105–117.

Hanson, J. T., & Sander, D. L. (1973). Differential effects of individual and group counseling on realism of vocational choice. *Journal of Counseling Psychology, 20*, 541–544.

Haverkamp, B. E., & Moore, D. (1993). The career–personal dichotomy: Perceptual reality, practical illusion, and workplace integration. *Career Development Quarterly, 42*, 154–160.

Healy, C. C., Bailey, M. L., & Anderson, E. C. (1973). The relation of esteem and vocational counseling to range of incorporation scores. *Journal of Vocational Behavior, 3*, 69–74.

Heppner, P. P., Kivlighan, D. M., Jr., & Wampold, B. E. (1992). *Research design in counseling*. Belmont, CA: Brooks/Cole.

Herr, E. L. (1989). Career development and mental health. *Journal of Career Development, 16*, 5–18.

Hill, C. E. (1982). Counseling process research: Philosophical and methodological dilemmas. *The Counseling Psychologist, 10*(4), 7–19.

Hill, C. E. (1991). Almost everything you ever wanted to know about how to do process research on counseling and psychotherapy but didn't know who to ask. In C. E. Watkins, Jr. & L. J. Schneider (Eds.), *Research in counseling* (pp. 85–118). Hillsdale, NJ: Lawrence Erlbaum Associates.

Hill, C. E. (1992). An overview of four measures developed to test the Hill process model: Therapist intentions, therapist response modes, client reactions, and client behaviors. *Journal of Counseling and Development, 70*, 728–737.

Hill, C. E., Carter, J. A., & O'Farrell, M. K. (1983). A case study of the process and outcome of time-limited counseling. *Journal of Counseling Psychology, 30*, 3–18.

Hill, C. E., & Corbett, M. M. (1993). A perspective of the history of process and outcome research in counseling psychology. *Journal of Counseling Psychology, 40*, 3–24.

Hill, C. E., Helms, J. E., Spiegel, S. B., & Tichenor, V. (1988). Development of a system for categorizing client reactions to therapist interventions. *Journal of Counseling Psychology, 35*, 27–36.

Hill, C. E., & O'Grady, K. E. (1985). A list of therapist intentions illustrated in a case study and with therapists of varying theoretical orientations. *Journal of Counseling Psychology, 32*, 3–22.

Hill, C. E., Tanney, M. F., Leonard, M. M., & Reiss, J. A. (1977). Counselors' reactions to female clients: Type of problem, age of client, and sex of counselors. *Journal of Counseling Psychology, 24*, 60–65.

Holland, J. L. (1974). Career counseling: Then, now, and what's next. *The Counseling Psychologist, 4*(3), 24–26.

Holland, J. L. (1985a). *Making vocational choices* (2nd ed.). Englewood Cliffs, NJ: Prentice–Hall.

Holland, J. L. (1985b). *Manual for the Self-Directed Search.* Odessa, FL: Psychological Assessment Resources.

Holland, J. L., Magoon, T. M., & Spokane, A. R. (1981). Counseling psychology: Career interventions, research, and theory. *Annual Review of Psychology, 32,* 279–305.

Kirschner, T. (1989). *A case study of the process and outcome of career counseling.* Unpublished doctoral dissertation, University of Maryland, College Park.

Kirschner, T., Hoffman, M. A., & Hill, C. E. (1994). Case study of the process and outcome of career counseling. *Journal of Counseling Psychology, 41,* 216–226.

Kivlighan, D. M., Jr. (1990). Career group therapy. *The Counseling Psychologist, 18*(1), 64–79.

Kivlighan, D. M., Jr., Hageseth, J. A., Tipton, R. M., & McGovern, T. V. (1981). Effects of matching treatment approaches and personality types in group vocational counseling. *Journal of Counseling Psychology, 28,* 315–320.

Kivlighan, D. M., Jr., Johnsen, B., & Fretz, B. (1987). Participants' perception of change mechanisms in career counseling groups: The role of emotional components in career problem solving. *Journal of Career Development, 14,* 35–44.

Kleinberg, J. L. (1988). Utilizing career crises to prepare patients for intensive psychotherapy. *Journal of Contemporary Psychotherapy, 18,* 240–248.

Krivatsy, S. E., & Magoon, T. M. (1976). Differential effects of three vocational counseling treatments. *Journal of Counseling Psychology, 23,* 112–118.

Krumboltz, J. D. (1993). Integrating career and personal counseling. *Career Development Quarterly, 42,* 143–148.

Krumboltz, J. D., Becker–Haven, J. F., & Burnett, K. F. (1979). Counseling psychology. *Annual Review of Psychology, 30,* 555–602.

Lillard, M. N. (1991). *Career counseling from a social influence perspective: Effects of interpretation style with career indecisive clients.* Unpublished doctoral dissertation, Memphis State University.

Lucas, M. S. (1992). Problems expressed by career and non-career help seekers: A comparison. *Journal of Counseling and Development, 70,* 417–420.

Lucas, M. S. (1993). Personal aspects of career counseling: Three examples. *Career Development Quarterly, 42,* 161–166.

Lunneborg, P. W. (1983). Career counseling techniques. In W. B. Walsh & S. H. Osipow (Eds.), *Handbook of vocational psychology* (pp. 41–76). Hillsdale, NJ: Lawrence Erlbaum Associates.

Mahrer, A. H. (1988). Discovery-oriented psychotherapy research: Rationale, aims, and methods. *American Psychologist, 43,* 694–702.

Manuele–Adkins, C. (1992). Career counseling is personal counseling. *Career Development Quarterly, 40,* 313–323.

Martin, J. (1984). The cognitive mediational paradigm for research on counseling. *Journal of Counseling Psychology, 31,* 558–571.

Martin, J. (1992). Intentions, responses, and private reactions: Methodological, ontological, and epistemological reflections on process research. *Journal of Counseling and Development, 70,* 742–743.

Meier, S. T. (1991). Vocational behavior, 1988–1990: Vocational choice, decision-making, career development interventions, and assessment. *Journal of Vocational Behavior, 39,* 131–181.

Melnick, R. R. (1975). Counseling response as a function of problem presentation and type of problem. *Journal of Counseling Psychology, 22,* 108–112.

Miller, M. J. (1992). Effects of note-taking on perceived counselor social influence during a career counseling session. *Journal of Counseling Psychology, 39,* 317–320.

Niles, S. G., & Pate, R. H., Jr. (1989). Competency and training issues related to the integration of career counseling and mental health counseling. *Journal of Career Development, 16*(1), 63–71.

O'Farrell, M. K., Hill, C. E., & Patton, S. (1986). Comparison of two cases of time-limited counseling with the same counselor. *Journal of Counseling and Development, 65,* 141–145.

Oliver, L. W. (1979). Outcome measurement in career counseling research. *Journal of Counseling Psychology, 26,* 217–226.

Oliver, L. W., & Spokane, A. R. (1988). Career-intervention outcome: What contributes to client gain? *Journal of Counseling Psychology, 35,* 447–462.

Osipow, S. H. (1982). Research in career counseling: An analysis of issues and problems. *The Counseling Psychologist, 10*(4), 27–34.

Osipow, S. H., Carney, C., Winer, J., Yanico, B., & Koschier, M. (1976). *The Career Decision Scale.* Odessa, FL: Psychological Assessment Resources.

Osipow, S. H., & Gold, J. A. (1968). Personal adjustment and career development. *Journal of Counseling Psychology, 15,* 439–443.

Parsons, F. (1909). *Choosing a vocation.* Boston: Houghton Mifflin.

Phillips, S. D. (1992). Career counseling: Choice and implementation. In S. D. Brown & R. W. Lent (Eds.), *Handbook of counseling psychology* (2nd ed., pp. 513–547). New York: Wiley.

Phillips, S. D., Friedlander, M. L., Kost, P. P., Specterman, R. V., & Robbins, E. S. (1988). Personal versus vocational focus in career counseling: A retrospective outcome study. *Journal of Counseling and Development, 67,* 169–173.

Pinkerton, R. S., Etzel, E. F., Rockwell, J. K., Talley, J. E., & Moorman, J. C. (1990). Psychotherapy and career counseling: Toward an integration for use with college students. *College Health, 39,* 129–136.

Pinkney, J. W., & Jacobs, D. (1985). New counselors and personal interest in the task of career counseling. *Journal of Counseling Psychology, 32,* 454–457.

Pool, D. A. (1965). The relation of personality needs to vocational counseling outcome. *Journal of Counseling Psychology, 12,* 23–27.

Powers, R. J. (1978). Enhancement of former drug abusers' career development through structured group counseling. *Journal of Counseling Psychology, 25,* 585–587.

Reed, J. R., Patton, M. J., & Gold, P. B. (1993). Effects of turn-taking sequences in vocational test interpretation interviews. *Journal of Counseling Psychology, 40,* 144–155.

Robbins, S. B., Mullison, D., Boggs, K., Riedesel, B., & Jacobson, B. (1985). Attrition behavior before career development workshops. *Journal of Counseling Psychology, 32,* 232–238.

Robbins, S. B., & Tucker, K. R. (1986). Relation of goal instability in self-directed and interactional career counseling workshops. *Journal of Counseling Psychology, 33,* 418–424.

Rounds, J. B., Jr., & Tinsley, H. E. A. (1984). Diagnosis and treatment of vocational problems. In S. D. Brown & R. W. Lent (Eds.), *Handbook of counseling psychology* (pp. 137–177). New York: Wiley.

Schneider, L., & Gelso, C. (1972). Vocational versus personal emphases in counseling psychology training programs. *The Counseling Psychologist, 3*(3), 90–93.

Sharp, W. H., & Marra, H. A. (1971). Factors related to classification of client problem, number of counseling sessions, and trends of client problems. *Journal of Counseling Psychology, 18,* 117–122.

Smith, M. L., & Glass, G. V. (1977). Meta-analysis of psychotherapy outcome studies. *American Psychologist, 32,* 752–760.

Smith, R. D., & Evans, J. R. (1973). Comparison of experimental group guidance and individual counseling as facilitators of vocational development. *Journal of Counseling Psychology, 20,* 202–208.

Spengler, P. M., Blustein, D. L., & Strohmer, D. C. (1990). Diagnostic and treatment overshadowing of vocational problems by personal problems. *Journal of Counseling Psychology, 37,* 372–381.

Spokane, A. R. (1989). Are there psychological and mental health consequences of difficult career decisions? *Journal of Career Development, 16*(1), 19–23.

Spokane, A. R. (1991). *Career intervention.* Englewood Cliffs, NJ: Allyn & Bacon.

Spokane, A. R., & Fretz, B. R. (1993). Forty cases: A framework for studying the effects of career counseling on career and personal adjustment. *Journal of Career Assessment, 1,* 118–129.

Spokane, A. R., & Oliver, L. (1983). The outcomes of vocational intervention. In W. B. Walsh & S. H. Osipow (Eds.), *Handbook of vocational psychology* (pp. 99–16). Hillsdale, NJ: Lawrence Erlbaum Associates.

Strong, S. (1968). Counseling: An interpersonal influence process. *Journal of Counseling Psychology, 15,* 215–224.

Subich, L. M. (1993). How personal is career counseling? *Career Development Quarterly, 42,* 129–131.

Super, D. E. (1993). The two faces of counseling: Or is it three? *Career Development Quarterly, 42,* 132–136.

Swails, R. G., & Herr, E. L. (1976). Vocational development groups for ninth grade students. *Vocational Guidance Quarterly, 24,* 256–260.

Swanson, J. L. (1992). Vocational behavior, 1989–1991: Life-span career development and reciprocal interaction of work and nonwork. *Journal of Vocational Behavior, 41,* 101–161.

Tinsley, H. E. A., Workman, K., & Kass, R. (1980). Factor analysis of the domain of client expectations about counseling. *Journal of Counseling Psychology, 27,* 561–570.

Tolsma, R. (1993). "Career or noncareer?" That is the issue: Case examples. *Career Development Quarterly, 42,* 167–173.

Walsh, W. B., & Osipow, S. H. (Eds.). (1990). *Career counseling: Contemporary topics in vocational psychology.* Hillsdale, NJ: Lawrence Erlbaum Associates.

Walsh, W. B., & Osipow, S. H. (Eds.). (1994). *Career counseling for women.* Hillsdale, NJ: Lawrence Erlbaum Associates.

Warnke, M. A., Kim, J., Koeltzow–Milster, D., Terrell, S., Dauser, P. J., Dial, S., Howie, J., & Thiel, M. J. (1993). Career counseling practicum: Transformations in conceptualizing career issues. *Career Development Quarterly, 42,* 180–185.

Watkins, C. E., Lopez, F. G., Campbell, V. L., & Himmell, C. D. (1986). Contemporary counseling psychology: Results of a national survey. *Journal of Counseling Psychology, 33,* 301–309.

Watkins, C. E., Savickas, M. L., Brizzi, J., & Manus, M. (1990). Effects of counselor response behavior on clients' impressions during vocational counseling. *Journal of Counseling Psychology, 37,* 138–142.

Watkins, C. E., & Schneider, L. J. (Eds.). (1991). *Research in counseling.* Hillsdale, NJ: Lawrence Erlbaum Associates.

Whiteley, J. M. (1984). A historical perspective on the development of counseling psychology as a profession. In S. D. Brown & R. W. Lent (Eds.), *Handbook of counseling psychology* (pp. 3–55). New York: Wiley.

Williamson, E. G., & Bordin, E. S. (1941). The evaluation of educational and vocational counseling: A critique of methodology of experiments. *Educational and Psychological Measurement, 1,* 5–25.

PART TWO

PRACTICE AND OTHER APPLICATIONS

CHAPTER EIGHT

Integrating Career Assessment Into Counseling

Linda Mezydlo Subich
Kathleen D. Billingsley
The University of Akron

There is a vast recent literature on the topic of career assessment in which are thoroughly documented the various assessment tools available to the career counselor (e.g., D. Brown & Brooks, 1991; Gysbers & Moore, 1987; Isaacson & D. Brown, 1993; Kapes & Mastie, 1988; Lowman, 1991; Wise, 1989; Zunker, 1990) as well as the usefulness of these tools within traditional models of career counseling (e.g., Jepsen, 1993; Krumboltz & Jackson, 1993; Walsh & Osipow, 1990; Watkins, 1993). We, therefore, have chosen not to duplicate others' efforts but rather to focus on career assessment issues and techniques relevant to career counseling with specific client populations.

Additionally, we have focused on the role of career assessment in the *process* of career counseling and, when possible, have highlighted the integration of assessment results into career counseling. Wise (1989) noted that assessment techniques facilitate career counseling in various ways, including opening topics for conversation, providing direction, suggesting new career options and alternative strategies, and evaluating the client's progress. A few years earlier, and from a more general perspective, Hayes, Nelson, and Jarrett (1987) suggested a focus in psychology on the "treatment utility of assessment" (p. 963); they noted that at times the process of assessment may contribute as much, or more, to treatment outcome than the results obtained from the assessment. This chapter is our attempt to showcase the "treatment utility" of career assessment.

Career assessment has been defined by some to mean, almost exclusively, objective data. Dawis (1992), for instance, stressed the value of quantitative information, stating that "to describe a person in numerical terms is not to demean the person," but rather "to make even more explicit the character of the person's individuality" (p. 12). Others, although recognizing the value of objectively derived information, have cautioned against the exclusive use of this type of data. Wrenn (1988) noted the fractional nature of the information obtained from tests and inventories and advocated a more holistic approach. Still others have recommended that the counselor assess the client through both quantitative and qualitative means, stressing that sole reliance on quantitative and objectively derived information encourages clients to remain in a dependent role and denies the influence of environmental and contextual variables (Chartrand, 1991; Healy, 1990; Isaacson & D. Brown, 1993). We have chosen to take a broad view of career assessment in this presentation, believing that although objective and quantitative assessment information are clearly valuable, this information should be integrated with clinical and qualitative assessment data to provide a more comprehensive understanding of the individual client.

The notion of comprehensive career assessment illustrates an underlying assumption of this chapter—the critical importance of the counselor's attending to individual differences. We also recognize, however, the commonalities of people who share certain conditions or characteristics. Dawis (1992) pointed out that in the past few decades, various minorities, including women, members of racial and ethnic groups, older individuals, and those with disabilities, have been growing at a faster rate in the labor force than has the majority. This increasing diversity of the workforce, then, suggests the need for counselors to pay particular attention to the special career assessment needs of members of these groups and others. We, therefore, have structured our presentation into six sections: women, racial and ethnic minority group members, gay and lesbian clients, the gifted, adults in transition, and disabled individuals. In each section we focus on the career assessment issues and strategies relevant to the particular client group.

CAREER ASSESSMENT WITH WOMEN

Much has been written in recent years on the career development of women and issues salient to career counseling, including assessment, with women. Betz and Fitzgerald's (1987) comprehensive text overviewed the extant literature in this area and served to direct the attention of researchers and practitioners to important topics in the career psychology of women, and more recently Betz (1992) reviewed a number of gender issues in career assessment. Most recently, almost the entire Summer 1993 issue of the *Journal of Career Assessment* (Walsh, 1993) was devoted to career assessment issues for women. There clearly has been tremendous interest in this topic.

General Issues in Career Assessment With Women

In the *Journal of Career Assessment* issue, Hackett and Lonborg (1993) overviewed both general and specific issues of concern in career assessment with women. They stressed the importance of the counselor's being sensitive to gender issues in assessment, as well as to the potential for assessment procedures to raise new issues for clients; for example, answering questions about one's interests or abilities may spark conflict, self-doubt, or anxiety for some clients and necessitate a change of focus in counseling. Hackett and Lonborg's comments with regard to this latter issue, and similar ones made by authors such as Fee–Fulkerson (1988) and Ward and Bingham (1993), reinforce the perspective taken in this chapter that assessment must be viewed as part of the overall fabric of counseling, not as separate from it. Career assessment *is* an intervention in its own right.

In discussing specific career assessment strategies and their application to women, Hackett and Lonborg (1993) noted the potential for gender bias in the assessment interview if the counselor differentially attends to the various life issues relevant to career development (e.g., the counselor notes the importance of a lack of occupational information to career indecision but overlooks the relation of role conflict to it). They also suggested that how the assessment interview is conducted may be important; both the overall counseling process as well as the kind of information elicited can be influenced by the counselor's adoption of a dominant role that pulls for traditional, subordinate responses from the woman.

If testing is used, Hackett and Lonborg (1993) noted that counselors need to be informed as to the gender fairness of the test selected. They recommended, among others, the following tests for use with women career clients: Nevill and Super's (1989) Values Scale; the Minnesota Importance Questionnaire (Rounds, Henly, Dawis, Lofquist, & Weiss, 1981); Greenhaus' (1971) Career Salience Inventory; Nevill and Super's (1986) Salience Inventory; the Career Decision Scale (Osipow, 1987); and measures of career self-efficacy, role conflict, and gender role traditionality. Behavioral assessment is yet another suggested option but requires attention to the context of the behavior; for example, women's interests or abilities may be differentially expressed in traditional and nontraditional contexts. Also, consideration of environmental barriers to career development is critical to the counselor's getting a well-rounded picture of a woman's career issues; in addition to the assessment interview, Swanson and Tokar's (1991) career barriers measure may offer counselors a way of assessing this area.

Finally, Hackett and Lonborg (1993) discussed the utility of qualitative assessment methods. Use of card sorts, life lines, fantasy exercises, autobiographies, genograms, and values-clarification exercises are promoted as ways of assessing issues especially salient to women's career development and, at the same time, sidestepping the cultural bias inherent in many traditional assessment instruments. These measures do require, however, that the counselor or assessor be skilled and sensitive in the processing of the technique. As an added benefit of these methods, they provide an assessment of salient issues and serve to begin the intervention process.

Cognitive Assessment

Perhaps the most exciting developments relevant to career assessment with women are those that explicitly recognize the importance of cognition to the vocational development and vocational counseling processes. Borgen (1991) noted the tremendous growth of interest in cognitive constructs in career counseling over a 20-year period and described this as a megatrend. We can trace the special implications of this focus for women's career development to the landmark article by Betz and Hackett (1981) in which they applied self-efficacy theory to vocational choice processes and found significant gender differences. Their findings generated much subsequent research on how cognition, often operationalized in terms of self-efficacy, affects women's career development.

The importance of assessing women's cognitions regarding careers was highlighted by Betz (1989) in her discussion of the "null environment" (p. 136) hypothesis. Women's perceptions of their abilities and opportunities may constrain their vocational exploration and choice. Science and math careers may be especially likely to be compromised. In order to restore options a counselor needs to know the level of the woman's self-efficacy for various courses of study or occupations as well as what beliefs she holds about the appropriate choices for her.

Self-efficacy cognitions may be assessed with items constructed along the lines of those used by Betz and Hackett (1981) and Lent, S. Brown, and Larkin (1987), or modeled after those presented by Isaacson and D. Brown (1993). For a more standardized and comprehensive approach, however, Rooney and Osipow (1992) developed the Task Specific Scale of Occupational Self-Efficacy, for which Osipow (1991) reported some preliminary reliability and validity information. This scale shows promise for the counselor seeking a way to explore more broadly a client's occupational self-efficacy.

Gender role orientation, which can affect perceptions of what occupational choices are socially appropriate for oneself, can be assessed in the clinical interview or with any of a number of inventories. Hackett and Lonborg (1993) identified the Bem Sex-Role Inventory (Bem, 1981) and the Personal Attributes Questionnaire (Spence, Helmreich, & Stapp, 1974) as two possibilities but preferred the overall positive focus of the latter. In addition, one may want to consider measures of feminist orientation, such as the Attitudes Toward Women Scale (Spence & Helmreich, 1972).

The value of attending to both self-efficacy cognitions and gender role orientation is supported by data from O'Brien and Fassinger's (1993) test of Fassinger's (1990) model of women's career orientation and choice. They found that ability, agency, gender role attitudes, and relationship with mother predicted career orientation and choice. Their results suggest that it may be relevant for counselors to assess and process in counseling a woman's gender role attitudes, math and science self-efficacy, and attachment and independence from mother in order to better understand and facilitate her career-related behavior.

In an article not specifically targeting, but relevant to, women career clients, Borders and Archadel (1987) discussed the importance for career counseling of what they termed "self-beliefs" (p. 69). Standard clinical interview or paper-and-pencil methods (e.g., self-efficacy measures, Krumboltz's, 1991, Career Beliefs Inventory) could be useful for such assessments. Less widely considered approaches including Rational Emotive Therapy, paradox, and two-chair techniques are also discussed in this article.

Especially relevant to the consideration of career assessment for women, however, is Borders and Archadel's (1987) discussion of how a client's self-worth and self-esteem are likely to be at least indirectly relevant to vocational behavior and thus to merit the counselor's attention. To the extent that such beliefs are especially salient to women due to their socialization experiences, it seems important that the counselor examine and reality-test them.

Use of the Rational Emotive Therapy framework for assessing and intervening in women's career belief systems was handled in more depth by Richman (1988). She suggested counselors assess rational and irrational career beliefs relevant to a woman's particular developmental stage and then use Rational Emotive Therapy techniques to challenge those that are maladaptive for the woman. A number of examples are provided to aid the counselor is identifying and assessing career beliefs at specific life stages.

Assessment of Interests and Abilities

In addition to assessing cognitions regarding agency and gender role, the career counselor working with a woman client also needs information more traditionally associated with the career counseling process. Abilities, interests and personality variables must be examined. In an article featured in the *Journal of Career Assessment,* Betz (1993) focused on ability and interest assessment and the issues to be considered when working with women. She recommended that ability tests be used cautiously and that the counselor be vigilant regarding their potential for adverse impact. Such tools should be screened carefully by the counselor for bias in item content, test structure, and norms or selection predictions and then should be presented to the client with a full disclosure of any limitations. Women must clearly understand a test's capabilities. They must also be aware that a low score in an ability area does not mean that the area cannot be developed, but rather that it had not been developed at the time of the testing. Counselors, too, must approach low scores cautiously and be certain to consider alternative explanations for results; perhaps mediating variables, such as math anxiety or low self-efficacy, have artificially deflated a woman's scores.

Interest assessment for women may be most problematic in its potential to restrict women's options. Betz (1993) noted that women's socialization experiences may be the root of this restriction and that interest inventories differ in how they handle such socialization differences. The counselor looking for a measurement tool that restores options to women may want to consider the Strong Interest Inventory (SII; Strong, Hansen, & Campbell, 1985), the Unisex Edition of the ACT Interest Inventory (UNIACT; American College Testing Program, 1981), or the Vocational Interest Inventory (Lunneborg, 1981), rather than the Self-Directed Search (Holland, 1985b) or the Kuder Occupational Interest Survey (Kuder, 1985). Same-gender norms, equivalent numbers and types of occupational alternatives offered for men and women, unbiased language, and gender-balanced items are some of the advantages of the former assessment tools.

Even when using the best interest measure, however, counselors must be sensitive to the effects of self-efficacy on interests and cognizant that interests can be developed. Additionally, the relation of gender role orientation to interests is highlighted for counselors in work by Douce and Hansen (1988, 1990). In general, Betz (1993) stressed the wisdom of counselors' viewing interest inventories as exploratory, rather than as confirmatory, tools in career counseling.

Feminist Assessment Approaches

Another approach to career assessment with women involves the application of feminist theory. Kahn (1988) suggested the value of this integration and identified client attitudes and characteristics relevant for the counselor who undertakes such an integration. From Kahn's perspective, assessment of a woman's self-esteem, socialization history, social context, and experience with sexism are some of the important issues a counselor may want to incorporate into a feminist approach to career counseling. In particular, gender role analysis may be useful in helping a woman determine how she wants to plan her life.

Forrest and Brooks (1993) expanded on the idea of integrating feminist theory and career counseling for women by focusing specifically on the career assessment process. They pointed to the necessity for the assessment process to be egalitarian, with counselor and client working as collaborators from the point of test choice to interpretation. They also recommended gender role analysis as a useful technique in raising a woman's consciousness regarding the effects of socialization. This technique is another example of an assessment strategy's integral role in the overall counseling process.

Environmental assessments and some innovative sentence completions (e.g., "As a woman I am required to ___," p. 238) also are suggested by Forrest and Brooks (1993) as ways for the counselor to determine how social forces affect career development. Also relevant to the effects of social forces may be an assessment of home–career conflict, such as that proposed by Tipping and Farmer (1991). Their projective measure allows the assessment of affect related to the interplay of these two life arenas, and it provides scores that correlate with gender role orientation and the dissonance between one's own and others' expectations.

Assessment With Minority Women

When a woman is a member of a racial or ethnic minority, special issues in assessment may arise. Two recent articles (Gainor & Forrest, 1991; Ward & Bingham, 1993) addressed some of these issues. Gainor and Forrest (1991) focused on the role of self-concept in career decisions, and their discussion of career counseling with African-American women highlighted the importance of counselors' identifying and understanding the multiple self-referents used by these women. The extent to which an African-American woman's group, sociopolitical, female, Eurocentric, possible, and unique selves each influence her occupational behavior is important for the counselor to determine; no two persons will likely have the same self-referent mix, and the dominant referent may illuminate much about the woman's career direction. The career counselor may want to use the clinical interview, standard psychological instrumentation (e.g., identity scales, gender role inventories, measures of possible selves) or perhaps experiential techniques (e.g., multiple chairs in which different selves sit) to assess the nature and strength of these various self-referents.

In related work, Ward and Bingham (1993) focused on the broad effect of culture on career counseling. They noted that culture affects both client and counselor and all aspects of the counseling process. They proposed that the career counselor's first important assessment must be one of what the ethnic minority woman needs from counseling; the results can determine whether or not traditional career counseling methods are appropriate. Ward and Bingham stated that ethnic minority women may ask for career counseling because they are uncomfortable with requesting psychological assistance for other matters; the alert counselor must not overlook this possibility.

If career counseling is most appropriate, the effect of culture on the client's career development and planning is next assessed. This information may be obtained by interview methods, but Ward and Bingham (1993) also described a career checklist by which the counselor can assess, among other things, how a client's perceptions of diversity issues affect her career development. Their checklist includes some items specific to diversity (e.g., "My ethnicity may influence my career choice"), others that address issues noted to be especially salient for the career development of ethnic minority women (e.g., family responsibilities, religious values, efficacy concerns, environmental barriers), and still others that address areas traditionally included in career assessment (e.g., indecision, occupational information). One advantage of such a checklist, according to the authors, is that it provides the counselor an opportunity to discuss openly with the client how all of the areas included in it may relate to career development and why those issues may need to be addressed in career counseling. Ward and Bingham's approach to career assessment is another example of how assessment can be woven through the entire counseling process.

Assessment of Other Subgroups of Women

Career issues relevant to more limited subgroups of women have been addressed in other recent publications. Often the issues that are highlighted are similar to those already mentioned, but in some cases additional foci for career assessment are suggested. For example, Ibrahim and Herr (1987) discussed a life–career counseling program for battered women and noted the importance of the counselor's identifying the level of the woman's self-esteem and her gender role orientation, two areas already mentioned as important in working with women; but they also emphasized the importance of the counselor's assessing career decision-making and implementation skills in light of the dependency issues that are of special concern for battered women. It seems that Taylor and Popma's (1990) findings with regard to Taylor and Betz's (1983) Career Decision-Making Self-Efficacy Scale may have special utility for career counseling with battered women, as scores on it are related to both career indecision and locus of control, two very salient characteristics of this population.

Similarly, Melcher (1987) not only noted the role that self-esteem and family issues play in the career counseling process with Evangelical Christian women, but also highlighted the importance of addressing these women's feelings of guilt and their religious beliefs. The career counselor working with such women may want to add the assessment of guilt feelings and religious conviction to her or his counseling agenda and incorporate this information into the counseling process.

Finally, assessment issues relevant to women already in the workforce were discussed by Russell and Eby (1993). With their focus on career counseling and assessment with working managerial women, they provided a very comprehensive listing and description of the assessment tools, and the issues for which each is applicable, relevant to these women. Some issues (e.g., self-efficacy, self-esteem, values clarification, gender role stereotyping, career barriers) and the associated assessment strategies have already been mentioned in this discussion of career assessment with women. Others (e.g., coping styles, political skills, role conflict, dual-career concerns, social isolation), however, serve to broaden further the scope of areas, issues, and strategies a counselor may want to consider in career assessment with women. Russell and Eby's article provides the career counselor with a tremendous resource for working with the managerial woman; they have identified and documented the means of accessing information relevant to almost any concern that might bring such women to counseling.

Summary

Overall, then, although career assessment with women encompasses a very broad range of issues, strategies, and problems, some repetitive themes in the literature can be ascertained. In addition to the cautious use of traditional assessment strategies and tools, the literature stresses the importance of assessing the influence of socialization processes and the effects of environmental barriers. Cognitions, in particular maladaptive ones, are another important area for the counselor to examine. Finally, approaching the assessment process in an open and collaborative fashion is stressed by most authors; such an approach may not only enhance the counseling relationship but also may result in the acquisition of better assessment data.

RACE AND ETHNICITY IN CAREER ASSESSMENT

A client's racial and ethnic background is also an important consideration in career assessment and counseling, a fact recognized with increasing frequency in the vocational literature (Betz, 1992). Often racial and ethnic minority clients experience a special set of risk factors (Spokane & Hawks, 1990) that may complicate their career development process. These factors warrant careful assessment and consideration by the career counselor. Fouad (1993) recently summarized a number of issues that are especially relevant to career assessment with racial or ethnic minority clients.

Perhaps most important, the vocational counselor must understand that his or her world view is only one of many possible world views and that the same can be said of the world views that underlie many of our standard assessment practices (Fouad, 1993). For example, the definition of career maturity that serves as the underpinning of the Career Maturity Inventory (Crites, 1978) may not be the only or the best definition for the counselor to use when working with a given client. The culturally sensitive career counselor is aware of and open to alternative definitions of constructs and alternative strategies for assessing those constructs in her or his practice of career assessment.

Fouad (1993) also noted the importance of ensuring that the assessment process is culturally appropriate for a client who is a member of a racial or ethnic minority. In the assessment interview and during testing, for example, information may be disclosed hesitantly, selectively, or not at all, depending on the level of trust established by the counselor and on the client's cultural norms. To the extent that this occurs, the counselor should be cautious about the conclusions she or he draws and the subsequent actions she or he takes.

Important cross-cultural issues related to assessment tools were also raised by Fouad (1993). The reliability and validity of frequently used instruments are often unknown or are tentative for ethnic and racial minority clients. Also, appropriate norms are often unavailable for these clients. Language may be another barrier to the extent that an assessment tool assumes proficiency in standard English.

Cunningham and Tidwell (1990) highlighted still another general issue in career assessment with racial and ethnic minority clients. They pointed out that socioeconomic status (SES) can and often does interact with minority status. They emphasized the salience of a client's SES and implied the value of the counselor's assessing it along with other environmental factors such as limited educational opportunities and stressors associated with adapting to the majority culture.

These general concerns and other more specific ones are evident in the growing literature about career assessment with members of particular racial and ethnic minorities. Following is a selection of this literature for African Americans, Hispanic Americans, Native Americans, and Asian Americans. Although we recognize that the diversity of individuals within each of these groups is great, we focus on those career assessment and counseling issues noted to be common to group members.

Career Assessment With African Americans

It is clearly important for counselors to assess African Americans' interests, abilities, and values (Lee, 1987; Lee & Simmons, 1988), but Lee (1987) also suggested the salience of carefully examining external constraints (e.g., finances and support systems). In addition, Cheatham (1990) stressed the different values inherent in Africentric and Eurocentric perspectives. In career counseling and assessment, counselors need to be aware of some African Americans' greater valuing of affiliation, family, collectivism, deference to authority, and affect expression, as well as the ramifications of these values in the counseling and career-development process. Cheatham also remarked on the deficiencies inherent in many of our assessment tools and strategies and suggested that counselors beware of instrumentation or techniques that do not recognize the existence of cultural differences in clients' definitions of work, experience with structural biases, or differential opportunities for employment.

Perhaps most valuable, however, is Cheatham's (1990) model of African Americans' career development. It implies the need for counselors to assess African Americans' history of economic deprivation and discrimination, experiences with both Africentric and Eurocentric social orders, and perceptions of and experience with labor market realities, as well as other personal and career variables judged to be culturally relevant. All of this information can then be utilized in the counseling process. Cheatham offered this model as a way of including the Africentric perspective in the typically Eurocentric models of career counseling.

Issues of Africentricity and Eurocentricity relevant to career counseling were also discussed by Todisco and Salomone (1991). They echoed Cheatham's (1990) focus on values issues, the cultural biases inherent in many of our tests, and the role of environmental barriers in career counseling with African-American clients. As such, they endorsed a focus during assessment on the client's cultural identity and "multisource, multilevel, and multimethod strategies" (p. 153). In this way, test and assessment biases can be attenuated through examination of multiple data sources.

One assessment strategy that may be especially problematic for use with African Americans is the ability test. Ability tests often are used for selection purposes and for prediction of occupational success, yet many routinely differentiate between African Americans and White Americans. Spokane and Hawks (1990) reported that African Americans' scores are generally one standard deviation below those of White Americans on these tests and that this score pattern often leads to adverse career-related consequences. This use of ability test scores occurs despite research that suggests that ability test scores and occupational performance typically correlate on the order of only .3–.5.

Interest assessment with African Americans was the topic of a review article by Carter and Swanson (1990). They examined the literature on the validity of the Strong Interest Inventory (SII; Strong et al., 1985) with African Americans. Not only is there a relative paucity of research on this topic, but that which is available suggests a number of problems. For example, there is a lack of information on the racial characteristics of SII criterion groups, despite early work that suggested African Americans tend to score lower than White Americans. Carter and Swanson noted that the verity of this problem is demonstrated by the equivocal research findings currently available on the validity of the SII with African Americans.

Further, the SII is organized from the perspective of Holland's (1985a) vocational choice theory. Swanson (1992) found that although Holland's model may be appropriate for use with African Americans, not all of his assumptions regarding the model are borne out with this population. The interpretation and counseling application of assessment results derived from Holland-based instruments, such as the SII, should therefore be done cautiously.

Carter and Swanson (1990) also highlighted the fact that most literature indicates that African Americans have interest patterns different from White Americans. African Americans often express stronger interests in social and business areas and weaker interests in scientific, technical, and trade areas than do White Americans. These interest patterns may be a function of culture or opportunity and, thus, a full exploration and assessment of the client's cultural background and environment and their possible effects on SII responses seem warranted. In all, the limited nature of available literature on the SII suggests that counselors can use it with caution. Carter and Swanson suggested that the collection of local normative data on the SII for African Americans would enhance its use.

More recently, Tomlinson and Evans–Hughes (1991) also examined the relation of race to SII results. They found no main effects for race but did note an interaction between race and gender for some SII scores. Specifically, African-American women scored lower on the Artistic scale than did African-American men, they scored higher on the Academic Comfort scale than did African-American men, and they were more introverted than were African-American men. These findings support the recommendation by Carter and Swanson (1990) that gender patterns of African Americans' interests be further investigated.

Finally, the validity of the Career Maturity Inventory (CMI; Crites, 1978) for African Americans and White Americans has also been examined (Westbrook & Sanford, 1991). Westbrook and Sanford found that although White high-school students obtained higher scores than did African-American students on the Attitudes scale of the CMI, the test had limited reliability for members of either racial group. Further, there was little relation for either group of students between the CMI scores and a vocational choice criterion measure. In addition to the basic validity issues raised by these findings, the findings clearly imply that race must be a factor in the development of norms for this test; as it is, the CMI may indicate that White students in general are more career mature than African-American students. As with the ability test data previously reviewed, there is potential for harm to clients if counselors and evaluators are not informed and not cautious in how they interpret and apply CMI results.

Career Assessment With Hispanic Americans

Arbona's (1990) review summarized much of the available literature on career counseling and assessment with Hispanic-American clients. The salience in career counseling and assessment of the Hispanic-American client's cultural background and level of acculturation is a pervasive theme in her article. Assessment of a client's cultural identity and level of acculturation may provide useful information for the counselor to consider later, in conjunction with other background, interest, ability, and values data.

Although she recognized the important role of culture and culturally specific values in career counseling, Arbona (1990) also cautioned that Hispanic-American clients' perceptions of the availability of occupational choices should be given due emphasis because such perceptions may be most predictive of career behavior. This observation and the often observed mismatch between Hispanic Americans' career aspirations and expectations strongly support the need for counselors to examine these clients' perceptions regarding environmental and social barriers to their career development. Swanson and Tokar's (1991) career barriers scale may be used effectively with this population.

Many traditional areas for career assessment are also likely to be relevant and useful in career counseling with Hispanic Americans. For example, Arbona (1990) suggested assessment from the perspective of Holland's (1985a) theory is appropriate with these clients, and Fouad (1993) reported similarly promising data in this regard. Arbona advised, however, that SES and education may affect clients' interest profiles as well as their value profiles. Further, as with gender and interest profiles for African Americans, Arbona warned that gender patterns in interests among Hispanic Americans may not parallel those found with White Americans. Career counselors are cautioned to leave stereotypical notions regarding men's and women's interest patterns outside the counseling session.

Other areas relevant to assessment with Hispanic-American clients include culturally endorsed gender roles, language skills, and self-efficacy (Arbona, 1990; Lauver & Jones, 1991). Gender roles and their effect on career choice and development have been discussed previously, but language skills deserve further mention. Arbona (1990) pointed out that if English is a client's second language, the validity of many standard assessment tools may be compromised. Career counselors should therefore ascertain a client's proficiency with standard English early in the counseling process.

Lauver and Jones' (1991) work supports the relevance of self-efficacy to career assessment with Hispanic Americans. Self-efficacy of Hispanic-American high-school students, however, was found to be related to their SES, a finding that supports the important role of environment in their career development. Consequently, the authors recommended that researchers consider self-efficacy expectations in a cultural and social context; this recommendation seems relevant to the career counselor as well. Ability assessment that aims to emphasize strengths may be one way the counselor can strengthen the client's self-efficacy, but this type of assessment should be done cautiously, as Spokane and Hawks (1990) reported test scores 1 *SD* below the mean for Hispanic Americans as well as for African Americans.

Career Assessment With Native Americans

Darou (1987) reviewed a number of issues relevant to career assessment with Native Americans. Darou suggested that cultural background is an important moderator of the counseling process and, given that assessment is embedded within the overall counseling process, cultural background likely also affects the career assessment process. Specifically, interpersonal relationship differences between Native Americans and White Americans may affect the kind and amount of information obtained during cross-cultural assessment. Thus, cultural identity and level of acculturation are once again highlighted as aspects that should be evaluated in formal or informal assessment, and counselors are enjoined to use this information in evaluating all aspects of the career counseling process.

Depending on the results of such assessment, the counselor may want to focus attention on the Native-American client's time perspective and values (Darou, 1987). These characteristics are also important aspects for the counselor to consider in conjunction with any assessment of the Native-American client's career maturity. In addition, Darou pointed out that the way in which the Native-American client defines career success may differ from definitions held by White American clients; counselors must be certain to determine the client's frame of reference for such career-related constructs and proceed accordingly in counseling.

Darou (1987) further emphasized that counselors should be aware of environmental barriers (e.g., finances, geographic area, economic conditions, prejudice) faced by Native-American clients, a sentiment echoed by Herring (1990). Such barriers to career development may result, over time, in clients' unduly restricting their perceived options. Finally, as was noted for other racial and ethnic minority group members, the role of significant others from the family and community in the client's career development processes should be examined, and, when appropriate, these individuals should be included in the counseling process.

The Native-American client's educational background and occupational information base are additional important aspects for the counselor to assess (Herring, 1990). Both can relate significantly to vocational behavior and can limit the client's exploratory behavior and opportunities. Herring also reported that internal barriers, such as client anxiety and decision-making difficulties, are salient. Self-efficacy is yet another internal barrier meriting attention with Native-American clients. Additional data from research by Lauver and Jones (1991) indicated that Native Americans' self-efficacy was lower than that of White Americans, but the career counselor is again cautioned to interpret clients' self-efficacy in a cultural context.

Assessment of interests will likely be useful in career counseling with Native-American clients, but cautious use of instrumentation again seems justified. Hansen's (1987) review of the literature on cross-cultural vocational interests suggested interest-pattern differences for Native Americans and White Americans; Native-American women and men scored higher than their White counterparts on realistic and conventional interests, respectively. These differences may relate to cultural background or perhaps were affected by education level of the individuals sampled. It is up to the counselor to explore fully what factors might have influenced the client's responses.

Finally, Native Americans living on reservations may have special life circumstances, such as limited occupational opportunities or inadequate occupational information, to which the career counselor should attend during assessment and counseling (Martin, 1991). Martin additionally highlighted the effects of level of acculturation, the influence of family and community members on an individual's career behavior, and the inadequacies and biases of our assessment tools. With regard to our assessment tools, a lack of normative data and language problems are but two of the specific issues to be considered. Martin recommended that counselors consider, in some cases, oral administration of career assessment instruments or use interview strategies to avoid evident language barriers. Examination of item responses is another strategy the counselor can use to better understand the effects of language and culture on client responses.

Career Assessment With Asian Americans

Traditional interest-, ability-, and values-assessment tools can be quite helpful to the career counselor working with an Asian-American client. Again, however, results must be interpreted cautiously. Fouad (1993) noted complex patterns of interest differences for Asian Americans and White Americans. Specifically, investigative and conventional interest scores were higher for Asian Americans than for White Americans. Scores such as these should be interpreted in the context of the client's cultural background and environmental conditions.

Differences in cultural values relevant to career counseling and assessment with Asian Americans were noted by Leong (1993). He suggested that Asian Americans may emphasize collectivism and respect for authority to a greater extent than do White Americans. It is important for career counselors to recognize that these values can affect the range of vocational choices considered by the client, the way in which the client makes career decisions, and the nature of the counseling process.

Obviously cultural background plays an important role in the career development processes of Asian Americans, just as it does for members of other racial and ethnic minorities. Thus, once again, counselors are advised to assess level of acculturation of Asian-American clients (Leong, 1993). In the context of a case study of a social learning approach to career counseling with a Chinese-American woman, Krumboltz and Jackson (1993) discussed this issue as well as the importance of examining the Asian-American client's career beliefs and self-efficacy expectations. These cognitions may be associated with or a function of the client's cultural background and level of acculturation.

In another discussion of career counseling with Asian-American women, the importance of gender role issues in the career development of these women was a central focus (Yang, 1991). Counselors are advised to assess the extent to which such roles restrict a woman's choices, although cultural context must also be considered.

Finally, Asian immigrants were the focus of an article by Westwood and Ishiyama (1991). They proposed the critical importance of language in career assessment and counseling with these clients. Regardless of whether one uses tests, interviews, or behavior samples, language is an important moderator variable. In addition, even if language is not an assessment issue, the appropriateness of our assessment tools is still questionable. Most have not been normed on immigrant populations, and reliability and validity are uncertain.

Asian immigrants also may lack relevant occupational information and be especially subject to environmental barriers (Westwood & Ishiyama, 1991). Both areas warrant the attention of the career counselor during assessment and counseling as they may limit clients' career choices and development. Loss of identity, autonomy, and family and social support systems are additional issues that the counselor should examine in career counseling with these clients; such multiple and pervasive losses may complicate both the counseling and career development processes.

Summary

Some common themes are evident across authors and literature with regard to specific racial and ethnic minority group members. Although authors typically support the relevance and value of traditional career assessment strategies and topics, they also highlight additional ones. Acculturation and cultural identity are important regardless of the client's cultural background. As in the literature on women, the importance of environmental barriers is stressed by most, if not all, authors; poverty may be the most commonly noted barrier in this regard. Finally, the deficiencies in our assessment tools when used with clients other than White Americans are repeatedly pointed out; normative data and reliability and validity information are all lacking. These issues must be considered carefully in career assessment and counseling with racial and ethnic minority clients; they will influence the interpretations made and interventions undertaken by the culturally sensitive career counselor.

SEXUAL ORIENTATION AND CAREER ASSESSMENT

Similarities exist between many of the issues relevant to the career assessment of women and ethnic and racial minority clients and those relevant to the career assessment of gay male and lesbian clients. For example, as in career counseling with women and members of ethnic and racial minorities, assessment of the following factors is also important in career counseling with gay male and lesbian clients: experienced and perceived discrimination as well as other environmental barriers (Croteau & Hedstrom, 1993; Elliott, 1993; Hetherington, Hillerbrand, & Etringer, 1989; Hetherington & Orzek, 1989; Morgan & L. Brown, 1991), individual and occupational stereotyping (Hetherington et al., 1989; Hetherington & Orzek, 1989; Morgan & L. Brown, 1991), identity development (Croteau & Hedstrom, 1993; Hetherington & Orzek, 1989; Morgan & L. Brown, 1991), and the availability of role models (Hetherington et al., 1989). Notwithstanding such similarities, important differences also exist in issues relevant to career assessment with gay male and lesbian clients.

In their discussion of training and practice issues for counseling psychologists who work with lesbian women and gay men, Buhrke and Douce (1991) noted that examination of assessment tools for heterosexist bias is important. At worst, test items that assume a heterosexual orientation can distress or alienate the lesbian or gay male client; at best, they can result in invalid test results for that client. Similarly, certain interest and personality measures include scales for masculinity and femininity, and these scales and their underlying assumptions of heterosexual orientation may be distressing or offensive to the lesbian or gay male client. Also, few tests have been examined specifically for use with or normed explicitly on gay male and lesbian individuals; the validity of results for these clients is thereby compromised.

Morgan and L. Brown (1991) noted that values of lesbian women may differ from those of heterosexual women; for example, lesbian women may hold stronger feminist and nontraditional values. In turn, these values may be important influences on their career and life choices. This finding underscores the concern raised previously as to the lack of normative data on lesbian and gay male individuals for many assessment instruments. It also supports the potential value of a feminist approach to career counseling with some lesbian clients.

Internalized homophobia also may play a role in lesbian women's career development (Morgan & L. Brown, 1991). Self-esteem and self-worth, both vital to the career-development process, may be compromised because of internalized homophobia. When the counselor is aware that her or his client is lesbian or gay, she or he may want to assess explicitly for internalized homophobia and later address this issue in counseling.

Croteau and Hedstrom (1993), Elliott (1993), Hetherington et al. (1989), and Hetherington and Orzek (1989) highlighted other specific areas the counselor may want to assess when working with gay male and lesbian clients. Lifestyle preferences, including the degree to which the client chooses to disclose or not disclose her or his sexual orientation at school or at work, is one such area. A counseling focus on the implications of the client's choice is an important follow-up to such an assessment. Hetherington and Orzek (1989), writing specifically about lesbian career clients, suggested that a counselor ask the client to what extent she believes sexual orientation is relevant to the careers she is considering, to what extent workers in these occupations are likely to accept a lesbian colleague, and to what extent she wishes to disclose her sexual orientation prior to entering her first job.

Further, dual-career issues may be more complicated for gay male and lesbian clients, and career counselors may want to assess and process to what extent the client has considered these issues (Hetherington & Orzek, 1989). Dual-career issues may be particularly salient for lesbian women, as data suggest that most adult lesbian women are likely to be living with partners (Hetherington & Orzek, 1989) and employed (Morgan & L. Brown, 1991). Therefore, career counseling with the couple may be helpful in working through some of these issues.

Finally, Morgan and L. Brown (1991) recommended that career counselors routinely make one other "assessment" (and perhaps the most critical one), that of the client's sexual orientation. Unlike many other personal characteristics, Morgan and Brown reminded counselors that sexual orientation is easily, and often adaptively, hidden. In order to avoid complete placement of the risk and responsibility for disclosure of sexual orientation on the client, the counselor is enjoined by Morgan and Brown never to assume a heterosexual orientation and always to be open to information from the client that may suggest that she is lesbian or that he is gay. Elliott (1993) went further, recommending that the career counselor routinely include questions that address sexual orientation in the initial assessment interview. Whether the assessment of a client's sexual orientation is made directly or indirectly, though, it is perhaps the one assessment that can have the most effect on the nature and quality of subsequent career counseling.

CAREER ASSESSMENT WITH THE GIFTED

Many of the issues relevant to the career assessment of gifted and talented clients are unique due to the interaction of their personal characteristics with the impact of messages from family, peers, and society. Noble (1987) pointed out that historically the American culture has had an ambivalent attitude toward the special needs of the gifted and that psychologists and counselors who work with this population therefore need to examine their own attitudes and beliefs. One common belief is that the recognition of the potential of the gifted individual places undue pressure on that person that will negatively affect her or his development. Various authors, in countering this belief, forcefully have argued that without intervention, many gifted individuals (particularly gifted women) will never reach their full potential (Garrison, Stronge, & Smith, 1986; Hollinger, 1988; Kerr, 1993; Noble, 1987; Roper & Berry, 1986).

Another belief, even more strongly held according to Noble (1987), is that special attention to the gifted is not needed, as these individuals will develop satisfactorily on their own. The belief that the gifted and talented will succeed despite all odds ignores the special problems these clients have in planning their careers.

An additional misconception, also commonly held, is that individuals identified as gifted are generally similar in their career assessment needs (Noble, 1987; Roper & Berry, 1986). These clients are often viewed simplistically as a homogeneous group of persons who possess superior abilities, yet, gifted individuals are often more different than alike. According to Noble (1987), the types of abilities in which the gifted may be superior include intelligence, academic aptitude, creativity, rate of growth or development of a socially desirable variable, and talent. In addition, the personal characteristics, needs, and potential problems of gifted clients apparently cluster into categories determined by their unique abilities. It follows, then, that the career counselor must first assess the type and pattern of abilities that characterize a particular client. Roper and Berry (1986) suggested a categorization of gifted subgroups that may be useful in this regard.

The first subgroup discussed by Roper and Berry (1986), the *multipotentialed*, have been described by various authors as having a wide range of interests and aptitudes that results in confusion and indecisiveness as to career choice (D. Brown & Brooks, 1991; Garrison et al., 1986; Kerr, 1993). In addition, these clients may want to make the one, perfect choice of career so as to please others (Garrison et al., 1986; Roper & Berry, 1986). The *early emergers*, the second category discussed by Roper and Berry, express firm career interests at an early age, often in the fields of science, math, or music. Because from an early age they have spent much of their time alone in their interest area, early emergers may have few friends and lack self-confidence in areas outside their chosen field. Though unhappy, they fear expanding their career interests for fear of failing. *Creatively gifted* individuals compose the third subgroup described by Roper and Berry. These individuals are characterized as independent, as nonconformists, and as frequent rule breakers. They are not necessarily interested in the basic academic classes that may be required of them, seeing them as a waste of time. Also, they may lack the perseverance necessary to complete the assignments in their chosen fine arts field. The final subgroup classification discussed by Roper and Berry is *academically gifted*. These individuals are characterized as having high verbal reasoning skills, a history of academic excellence, and a tendency to conform to societal expectations and as being dependent on others' approval for their major source of self-esteem. Their need for approval may influence them to take courses in which they are assured of a superior grade rather than taking ones that more closely fit their own interests and values.

Awareness of the various gifted subgroups alerts the career counselor to potential issues that might arise with a gifted client. One way counselors can identify the subgroup to which a particular client belongs is through combining the information gathered through the interview process with the information gained from various other assessment techniques used during counseling. For instance, a client who obtains high scores on numerous ability and interest measures, who states that he or she is confused, and who appears indecisive regarding a career choice is most likely a multipotentialed career client. One way the counselor can help the multipotentialed client become more focused is by increasing self-awareness through an emphasis on values and needs rather than on abilities and interests (D. Brown & Brooks, 1991; Garrison et al., 1986; Kerr & Ghrist–Priebe, 1988). After the client completes a values inventory, the counselor can use the values found to be important to the client both to eliminate some careers and to highlight others, and thereby narrow the range of options for the individual.

Irrational beliefs and unrealistic expectations may also differentiate these subgroups. For instance, multipotentialed clients may believe that their work should satisfy *all* of their interests and abilities, whereas the creatively gifted may believe that rules were made to be broken and be unaware of long-range consequences. The counselor can assess irrational or unrealistic beliefs throughout the counseling process, using the clinical interview or various inventories, such as Krumboltz's (1991) Career Beliefs Inventory. Additionally, the counselor can use qualitative assessment methods to identify irrational or unrealistic beliefs. For instance, Kerr and Grist–Priebe (1988) discussed the method of presenting clients with an exercise in which they were asked to choose a future goal and to describe the immediate and further steps necessary to attain the goal. Oleksy–Ojikutu (1986) also described a future-oriented exercise in which clients completed a career time line from current age to some specified age in the future. They were asked to indicate any major events regarding their career choice as well as personal events that they expected to occur. Once identified, unrealistic or irrational beliefs can be discussed and countered through the use of cognitive restructuring (Borders & Archadel, 1987; D. Brown & Brooks, 1991; Mitchell & Krumboltz, 1987) or Gestalt exercises (Borders & Archadel, 1987) in which the rational self dialogues with the irrational self.

In addition to the issues of the various groups just discussed, the career counselor should be aware of the special needs of the gifted woman. As gifted girls reach the teen years, they typically begin to face problems unique to women in American society (Garrison et al., 1986; Kerr, 1993; Noble, 1987; Roper & Berry, 1986). The decisions made in adolescence and beyond as a result of these problems often have a negative effect on the career development of the gifted woman.

One challenge faced by gifted women relates to the conflicting societal expectations placed on them (Garrison et al., 1986; Kerr, 1993; Noble, 1987; Roper & Berry, 1986). As gifted individuals, they are expected to excel and to develop their potential to the utmost; as women they are expected to be responsible for home and family. The result of this perceived role conflict is often a lowering of career aspirations. Additionally, these conflicting demands may delay career plans until lifestyle plans regarding marriage or relocation are decided (Garrison et al., 1986).

Others have made suggestions for the assessment of beliefs regarding career aspirations and beliefs regarding lifestyle and career integration. For instance, gender role orientation inventories such as the Bem Sex-Role Inventory (Bem, 1981) and the Personal Attributes Questionnaire (Spence et al., 1974) may provide information helpful in the assessment of social role stereotypes held by the gifted female client. The career time line (Oleksy–Ojikutu, 1986), discussed previously, would be a useful tool for determining not only what the client plans for her future but also whether those plans are realistic and rational. Finally, imagery techniques can provide access to information not attainable through other means (Skovholt, Morgan, & Negron–Cunningham, 1989). Kerr (1993) provided an example of such an imagery technique; she suggested that counselors use the Perfect Future Day Fantasy to determine the client's beliefs and expectations regarding her future.

Other beliefs held by gifted women also present challenges to their career development and should be examined in counseling. Low self-efficacy expectations, particularly for math and science, and low self-esteem (Garrison et al., 1986; Kerr, 1993) as well as the belief that one's attractiveness to men is more important than the development of one's talents and abilities (Kerr, 1993) can all impede career planning. Both informal questioning during the counseling interview and objective self-esteem and self-efficacy measures can help the counselor assess these beliefs.

Once maladaptive beliefs and attitudes are identified, the counselor can employ a variety of techniques to help gifted women overcome these barriers to their career development. All of the following techniques are effective: teaching life-planning skills that allow for planned interruptions in one's career (Garrison et al., 1986; Kerr, 1993; Noble, 1987); countering low self-efficacy beliefs with objective evidence of abilities, such as achievement test data and school grades (Kerr, 1993); and employing feminist-oriented psychotherapy (Noble, 1987). In addition, Kerr (1993) suggested that the assessment of values and an emphasis on the importance of integrating them into a meaningful life can help the client counter the culture of romance encountered by young women.

In summary, a review of the recent literature regarding the career development of gifted individuals highlights the need for careful assessment of the individual client. Rather than forming a homogeneous group, the gifted cluster into several subgroups, each with its own unique concerns. Furthermore, gifted female clients may face additional barriers, both external and internal, that overlay the unique concerns of the gifted subgroups. Counselors can use career assessment techniques both as a means of identifying the individual client's concerns and as an intervention tool to help solve the problems presented.

CAREER ASSESSMENT FOR ADULTS IN TRANSITION

Recent changes in the U.S. economy have given rise to shifting labor-force demographics (Cahill & Salomone, 1987; Herr, 1990; Pedersen, Goldberg, & Papalia, 1991). Many individuals have experienced involuntary job loss, and many older Americans are remaining in the work force past the traditional retirement age. The number of voluntary midlife career changers seeking counseling added to the number of affected by recent demographic trends highlights the need for counselors to address career assessment for adults in transition.

Involuntary Job Loss and Career Assessment

As the number of unemployed individuals in our post-cold war society increases so does the number of issues relevant to this population. One issue unique to clients who have suffered involuntary job loss is the emotional reaction they experience, described as similar to the grief cycle triggered by the death of a loved one (Liptak, 1991; Neinas, 1987; Pedersen et al., 1991). In addition to the anger and depression that often accompanies grief, the unemployed client may also experience anxiety (Neinas, 1987) and a loss of self-esteem (Gordus, 1986). The career counselor, then, must first assess the emotional state of the client, either during the interview or with appropriate inventories, and deal with these emotions before beginning the career exploration process.

Once career counseling begins, it is important for the counselor to assess the unemployed client's assumptions and beliefs about careers and career counseling. Liptak (1991) identified five irrational beliefs commonly held by these clients that must be assessed and challenged: the belief that one must have the *perfect* job-search plan in order to find a job; the belief that it is unnecessary to learn job-search skills as they will not be needed again; the belief that the career counselor is the expert and will find a job for the client; the belief that rejection after a job interview is catastrophic; and the belief that one must preoccupy oneself with and make oneself nervous about the job-search process. Gordus (1986) added to this list the client's belief that he or she is to blame for his or her job loss and the unrealistic expectations many unemployed clients have regarding the starting wages of a new job. These irrational and unrealistic beliefs can be identified with standardized measures, such as Krumboltz's (1991) Career Beliefs Inventory, or through interview techniques. Liptak (1989) suggested that counselors use guidelines such as those developed by Mitchell and Krumboltz (1984) and then challenge maladaptive beliefs through the use of Rational Emotive Therapy techniques. Gordus (1986) also emphasized the importance of cognitive restructuring but warned that, to be effective, this process takes time.

Unemployed clients' self-knowledge should also be assessed, as it may be the first time that such clients have ever explicitly considered their values, interests, and abilities in terms of work preferences (Gordus, 1986; Neinas, 1987; Pedersen et al., 1991; Roessler & Hastings, 1987). Neinas (1987), writing about unemployed blue-collar workers, cited the General Aptitude Test Battery (U.S. Employment Service, 1982), Myers–Briggs Type Indicator (I. Myers & Briggs, 1977), Strong Interest Inventory (Strong et al., 1985), and Career Assessment Inventory (Johansson, 1986) as most useful with this population. In addition, Manzi (1987) found that skills assessment with the Skills Sort (Hampl, 1983) could be particularly helpful in that it encourages the client's self-awareness and helps him or her identify skill competencies as well as skill deficits, information that can be indicative of the need for further training. Counselors also may want to assess unemployed clients' job-seeking, resume-writing, and interview skills as they may all be inadequate (Gordus, 1986; Pedersen et al., 1991; Roessler & Hastings, 1987).

Career Assessment and Midlife Career Changers

Though many of the issues concerning the unemployed (e.g., lack of self-knowledge and job-search skills) also arise with voluntary midlife career changers, voluntary changers face some unique assessment issues that should be addressed. Fee–Fulkerson (1988), in a discussion that focused on women but is relevant to men as well, suggested that for individuals who are unhappy in their career choice despite being successful, the assessment process should be structured around three areas. These three areas are client dislikes regarding present career, factors contributing to success despite client dislike of career, and reasons the client remains in the disliked career. Fee–Fulkerson maintained that the exploration of these areas can help the counselor identify both realistic and unrealistic barriers to change. Discussion of these issues can then help the client determine whether her or his goal is to remove the barriers and to change careers or to moderate the present conditions and to remain in the present career. In addition, Whiston (1990) found that the integration of information obtained from the Adult Career Concerns Inventory (Super, Thompson, Lindeman, R. Myers, & Jordaan, 1985) with that obtained through other types of assessment aided in determining the goal of counseling with individuals unhappy in their current job.

Burr (1986) described one way that the midcareer changer can translate future goals into reality. The client is asked to write a minimum of three different life-style scenarios, and, after completing the scenarios, to prepare an exhaustive list of strengths and weaknesses, likes and dislikes. The self-knowledge gained from the assessment of skills, values, interests, and personality can be particularly helpful in enabling the client to prepare this list. Finally, the scenarios are assessed in terms of the one that takes advantage of the greatest number of client strengths and likes, and contains the fewest client limitations and dislikes.

Finally, because there may be very real, practical constraints to career change, Burlew (1989) and Liptak (1990, 1991) stressed the importance of exploring the role of leisure. The assessment of client skills, values, and interests can provide data about alternative outlets for meeting the client's needs if the career-planning process integrates work and leisure into a life plan.

Career Assessment and Older Adults

Issues relevant to the career assessment needs of older adults are becoming increasingly salient due to the trend of older people extending their work lives. Factors influencing the reconsideration of traditional retirement practices include increasing longevity, population demographics, and financial necessity, as well as a heightened awareness of the detrimental effects of forced retirement on the health and life satisfaction of older adults (Cahill & Salomone, 1987; Kouri, 1986).

Due to the ageist biases so prevalent in American society, Cahill and Salomone (1987) emphasized the need for counselors to assess the client's own beliefs regarding aging and to refute them with facts, if necessary. They noted, for instance, that older workers are often more responsible, loyal, and accurate than are younger workers and have less absenteeism and fewer accidents. Although Cahill and Salomone recognized the many assets of older workers, they also recognized the real losses experienced by older adults in physical strength, hearing and vision acuity, and reaction time. They stressed the need for counselors to assess the client's beliefs regarding these losses and suggested that counselors help older clients structure accommodation and flexibility (e.g., part-time work and job sharing) into their career and life plans. Leisure counseling, as discussed in the section on midlife career changers, would also be appropriate.

The appropriateness for older adults of our career assessment tools is another important issue (Sommerstein, 1986). Most career inventories have inadequate norms as well as problems with test reliability and validity with regard to this population. Additionally, physical factors (e.g., visual and auditory deficits) as well as emotional factors (e.g., fear of failure, lack of self-confidence) may affect client performance. Finally, Sommerstein noted that many careers suggested by the results of interest inventories are not relevant to older adults for reasons such as length of training or physical demands. Career counselors must be sensitive to test limitations as well as forthright with clients regarding these limitations in order to prevent premature termination.

Last, in a discussion aimed at career clients in general, but especially appropriate to older clients, Wrenn (1988) urged career counselors to recognize the limitations of objective-test information. He stressed that counselors should view clients holistically and should incorporate test information with information gathered through other means. For instance, he suggested one way to gather more information from the client is for the counselor to encourage the individual to talk about her or his life from childhood to the present, concentrating on events that were positive, successful, and satisfying. This strategy may increase client self-esteem as well as provide useful information to the counselor. Such information, combined with that obtained through fantasy, imagery, and other nonobjective means may be particularly helpful with older adult clients.

CAREER ASSESSMENT WITH ADULTS WITH DISABILITIES

Another distinct client group that deserves special mention with regard to career assessment issues and strategies is that of individuals with disabilities. Persons with disabilities are defined by Zunker (1990) as those persons with "an impairment or functional limitation in one or more bodily systems" (p. 448). Although the career counseling literature has at times addressed this population, people with disabilities are more commonly a focus in the rehabilitation counseling literature.

In two recent career counseling texts (Isaacson & D. Brown, 1993; Zunker, 1990), however, issues relevant to career counseling and assessment with individuals with disabilities have been addressed relatively extensively. Both texts stress the important role of assessment and the utility of many traditional career assessment practices (e.g., interest inventories, values scales, ability tests) in work with this population. Both also suggest, however, that at times the counselor may find it especially useful to choose nontest options for assessing such persons; work samples or data from realistic job previews may be as informative as or more informative than results of ability tests in some cases. To this end, Zunker's (1990) chapter on career counseling for persons with disabilities includes informative descriptions of two ability tests (Micro-Tower and Valpar Component Work Sample System) that allow for the assessment of work samples for evaluating the client's skills. Further, Isaacson and D. Brown (1993) noted that the counselor's obtaining information from third parties, such as a client's physician, may be appropriate at times in order to understand fully the vocational ramifications of the person's disability.

Behavioral assessment with clients with disabilities was discussed by Dickens (1986). In describing a career intervention aimed at a number of college-student clients with special needs, including individuals with disabilities, she stressed the importance of a personal assessment. Included in this assessment were the examination of work samples, a skills assessment, and an assessment of the amount of occupational information the individual possessed. The assessment results then served as the foundation for facilitating the client's career exploration process, the other piece of the intervention. Exit interviews indicated that students did feel that they had obtained important information and had increased their vocational exploration as a result of the counseling.

A somewhat discordant note regarding the value of vocational assessment with clients with disabilities, however, was sounded by Caston and Watson (1990). They found that the recommendations derived from vocational evaluations for such clients were often disregarded or, if followed, resulted in unsuccessful outcomes. In discussing their findings, Caston and Watson speculated that their sample might have included a disproportionate number of difficult cases, which, in turn, might have increased the probability of negative outcomes. Despite this sampling issue, these data are important in that they raise the potential issue of the differential value of vocational assessment for certain individuals with disabilities.

In general, however, there is relatively strong agreement on the importance of some type of career assessment with clients with disabilities, and it is the question of what areas to assess that remains to be answered. Interest, ability, values, personality, and career decision-making tests are traditional vocational assessment tools also regarded as relevant to career counseling with individuals with disabilities (Isaacson & D. Brown, 1993; Roessler & Hastings, 1987; Schriner & Roessler, 1987; Zunker, 1990). The career counselor should carefully consider, though, whether a test's lack of norms for such persons compromises its results (Isaacson & D. Brown, 1993; Zunker, 1990); for example, psychologists with physical disabilities may have different patterns of interests or personality characteristics than do psychologists without such disabilities. Also, Schriner and Roessler (1987) noted that discrepancies between interests and abilities may be more likely to occur for clients with disabilities than for others, a likelihood further complicating the interpretation and application of career assessment results in counseling.

The importance of assessing environmental conditions was noted by Grisson, Eldridge, and Nelson (1990); their focus was on vocational rehabilitation processes for substance abusers, but environmental assessment seems applicable to clients with a variety of disabilities. Other authors have suggested the value of examining specific environmental conditions such as support networks (Grisson et al., 1990; Schriner & Roessler, 1987), the availability of occupational role models (Zunker, 1990), and the client's family system (Fohs, 1991). These factors have all been noted to have the potential to affect a client's career development, and they thereby warrant attention during the assessment process. Counselors can use interview strategies to gather this information, and Fohs (1991) additionally suggested use of the genogram as a way for counselors to examine the family systems issues impinging on the career development of clients with disabilities.

Other areas that may be relevant to assessment for adults with disabilities include the client's independent living skills (Zunker, 1990), self-concept (Schriner & Roessler, 1987; Zunker, 1990), and the circumstances surrounding onset of the disability (Zunker, 1990). Zunker (1990) and Schriner and Roessler (1987) pointed out that the social stigma associated with a client's being different and the related, increased likelihood of her or his experiencing rejection due to this difference may result in an impoverished self-concept; a history of the onset of the client's disability and its functional repercussions for him or her may provide information about the extent of such efforts. To determine whether self-concept issues are affecting the client's career development, the counselor may find measures of self-esteem, self-concept, or self-efficacy useful in an assessment battery. Markus and Nurius' (1986) concept of "possible selves" (p. 954), what the individual believes he or she *could* be, may be another aspect of self for the career counselor to assess with the client with disabilities.

Fohs (1991) and Zunker (1990) also discussed the need for the career counselor to assess for the presence of other problems often associated with disability—pain, depression, and substance abuse. These issues may have serious consequences for both career counseling and the client's career development. All three may impede the counseling process due to a client's diminished energy available for counseling. They also may compromise career development in that the client may be unable or unwilling to carry out the work behaviors required to obtain or maintain a position.

Finally, Isaacson and D. Brown (1993) emphasized the special importance of the counselor's highlighting such a client's strengths, when utilizing assessment results in career counseling. A client with disabilities may be more likely than a nondisabled client to have focused intensively on her or his limitations in the past, and the career counselor may greatly assist her or him by charting positive strengths and possibilities rather than emphasizing the negative implications of the disability. Isaacson and D. Brown (1993) go so far as to state that a focus on the client's strengths "is even more important than accurate identification of what she cannot do" (p. 312).

SUMMARY

In this chapter we presented a portion of the voluminous recent literature on career assessment. As we noted in our introduction, other authors have done masterful work in documenting the assessment tools available to the new career counselor and in presenting the fit of such tools with traditional models of career intervention. For our part, we have tried to synthesize findings from the growing literature on assessment issues and practices relevant to some specific client populations and to suggest counseling applications for these findings.

Our presentation covered a wide range of topics due to our broad definition of career assessment. Some consistent themes, however, are evident. First, most authors endorsed the *cautious* use of current interest, ability, values, maturity, and career decision-making instruments. When used, the psychometric and cultural limitations of these tools should be considered by the counselor, and results should be appraised with an eye to other client information. Second, the importance of the assessment of cognitive variables was discussed by many authors. Self-efficacy, self-esteem, level of acculturation, perceived barriers, gender role stereotypes, role conflicts, and irrational beliefs are only a few of the many cognitions that seem to have implications for career development and career counseling.

The value of the assessment interview and qualitative approaches to career assessment also were underscored in many articles. Certain clients may be more comfortable with these types of assessment, and certain types of information may be most easily accessed with these strategies. Finally, the role of environmental constraints in career development featured prominently in the literature we reviewed. No longer are person variables the sole or primary consideration in career assessment; changing attitudes, social conditions, and theoretical models have led to explicit recognition that career development is often profoundly affected by factors outside the person's control.

REFERENCES

American College Testing Program. (1981). *Technical report for the Unisex Edition of the ACT Interest Inventory (UNIACT)*. Iowa City, IA: Author.

Arbona, C. (1990). Career counseling research and Hispanics: A review of the literature. *The Counseling Psychologist, 18*, 300–323.

Bem, S. L. (1981). *Bem Sex-Role Inventory: Professional manual.* Palo Alto, CA: Consulting Psychologists Press.

Betz, N. E. (1989). Implications of the null environment hypothesis for women's career development and for counseling psychology. *The Counseling Psychologist, 17,* 136–144.

Betz, N. E. (1992). Career assessment: A review of critical issues. In S. D. Brown & R. W. Lent (Eds.), *The Handbook of Counseling Psychology* (2nd ed., pp. 453–484). New York: Wiley.

Betz, N. E. (1993). Issues in the use of ability and interest measures with women. *Journal of Career Assessment, 1,* 217–232.

Betz, N. E., & Fitzgerald, L. F. (1987). *The career psychology of women.* Orlando, FL: Academic Press.

Betz, N. E., & Hackett, G. (1981). The relationship of career-related self-efficacy expectations to perceived career options in college women and men. *Journal of Counseling Psychology, 28,* 399–410.

Borders, L. D., & Archadel, K. A. (1987). Self-beliefs and career counseling. *Journal of Career Development, 14,* 69–79.

Borgen, F. H. (1991). Megatrends and milestones in vocational behavior: A 20-year counseling psychology retrospective. *Journal of Vocational Behavior, 39,* 263–290.

Brown, D., & Brooks, L. (1991). *Career counseling techniques.* Boston: Allyn & Bacon.

Buhrke, R. A., & Douce, L. A. (1991). Training issues for counseling psychologists in working with lesbian women and gay men. *The Counseling Psychologist, 19,* 216–234.

Burlew, L. D. (1989). The life-long leisure graph: A tool for leisure counseling. *Journal of Career Development, 15,* 164–173.

Burr, E. W. (1986). What next after fifty? *Journal of Career Development, 13,* 23–29.

Cahill, M., & Salomone, P. R. (1987). Career counseling for work life extension: Integrating the older worker into the labor force. *Career Development Quarterly, 35,* 188–196.

Carter, R. T., & Swanson, J. L. (1990). The validity of the Strong Interest Inventory with Black Americans: A review of the literature. *Journal of Vocational Behavior, 36,* 195–209.

Caston, H. L., & Watson, A. L. (1990). Vocational assessment and rehabilitation outcomes. *Rehabilitation Counseling Bulletin, 34,* 61–66.

Chartrand, J. M. (1991). The evolution of trait-and-factor career counseling: A person × environment fit approach. *Journal of Counseling and Development, 69,* 518–524.

Cheatham, H. E. (1990). Africentricity and career development of African Americans. *Career Development Quarterly, 38,* 334–346.

Crites, J. O. (1978). *Career Maturity Inventory.* Monterey, CA: CTB/McGraw–Hill.

Croteau, J. M., & Hedstrom, S. M. (1993). Integrating commonality and difference: The key to career counseling with lesbian women and gay men. *Career Development Quarterly, 41,* 201–209.

Cunningham, J. V., & Tidwell, R. (1990). Cognitive–developmental counseling: Preparing low-income students for college. *The School Counselor, 37,* 225–232.

Darou, W. G. (1987). Counseling and the northern Native. *Canadian Journal of Counselling, 21,* 33–41.

Dawis, R. V. (1992). The individual differences tradition in counseling psychology. *Journal of Counseling Psychology, 39,* 7–19.

Dickens, P. R. (1986). Vocational assessment and exploration for students with special needs in a community college. *Journal of College Student Personnel, 27,* 181–182.

Douce, L. A., & Hansen, J. C. (1988). Examination of the construct validity of the SVIB–SCII Adventure scale for college women. *Measurement and Evaluation in Counseling and Development, 20,* 171–174.

Douce, L. A., & Hansen, J. C. (1990). Willingness to take risks and college women's career choice. *Journal of Vocational Behavior, 36,* 258–273.

Elliott, J. E. (1993). Career development with lesbian and gay clients. *Career Development Quarterly, 41,* 210–226.

Fassinger, R. E. (1990). Causal models of career choice in two samples of college women. *Journal of Vocational Behavior, 36,* 225–248.

Fee–Fulkerson, K. (1988). Changing canoes in white water: Counseling women successful in careers they dislike. *Journal of Career Development, 14,* 249–258.

Fohs, M. W. (1991). Family systems assessment: Intervention with individuals having a chronic disability. *Career Development Quarterly, 39,* 304–311.

Forrest, L., & Brooks, L. (1993). Feminism and career assessment. *Journal of Career Assessment, 1,* 233–245.

Fouad, N. A. (1993). Cross-cultural vocational assessment. *Career Development Quarterly, 42,* 4–13.

Gainor, K. A., & Forrest, L. (1991). African American women's self-concept: Implications for career decisions and career counseling. *Career Development Quarterly, 39,* 261–272.

Garrison, V. S., Stronge, J. H., & Smith, C. R. (1986). Are gifted girls encouraged to achieve their occupational potential? *Roeper Review, 9,* 101–104.

Gordus, J. P. (1986). Coping with involuntary job loss and building a new career: Workers' problems and career professionals' challenges. *Journal of Career Development, 12,* 316–326.

Greenhaus, J. H. (1971). An investigation of the role of career salience in vocational behavior. *Journal of Vocational Behavior, 1,* 209–216.

Grisson, J. K., Eldridge, G. M., & Nelson, R. E. (1990). Adapting the vocational evaluation process for clients with a substance abuse history. *Journal of Applied Rehabilitation Counseling, 21,* 30–32.

Gysbers, N. C., & Moore, E. J. (1987). *Career Counseling.* Englewood Cliffs, NJ: Prentice–Hall.

Hackett, G., & Lonborg, S. D. (1993). Career assessment for women: Trends and issues. *Journal of Career Assessment, 1,* 197–216.

Hampl, S. P. (1983). The Skills Sort: A career planning tool. *Journal of College Student Personnel, 24,* 463–464.

Hansen, J. C. (1987). Cross-cultural research on vocational interests. *Measurement and Evaluation in Counseling and Development, 19,* 163–176.

Hayes, S. C., Nelson, R. O., & Jarrett, R. B. (1987). The treatment utility of assessment: A functional approach to evaluating assessment quality. *The American Psychologist, 42,* 963–974.

Healy, C. C. (1990). Reforming career appraisals to meet the needs of clients in the 1990s. *The Counseling Psychologist, 18,* 214–226.

Herr, E. L. (1990). Employment counseling in a global economy. *Journal of Employment Counseling, 27,* 147–159.

Herring, R. D. (1990). Attacking career myths among Native Americans: Implications for counseling. *The School Counselor, 38,* 13–18.

Hetherington, C., Hillerbrand, E., & Etringer, B. D. (1989). Career counseling with gay men: Issues and recommendations for research. *Journal of Counseling and Development, 67,* 452–454.

Hetherington, C., & Orzek, A. (1989). Career counseling and life planning with lesbian women. *Journal of Counseling and Development, 68,* 52–57.

Holland, J. L. (1985a). *Making vocational choices: A theory of vocational personalities and work environments* (2nd ed.). Englewood Cliffs, NJ: Prentice–Hall.

Holland, J. L. (1985b). *Self-Directed Search.* Odessa, FL: Psychological Assessment Resources.

Hollinger, C. L. (1988). Toward an understanding of career development among g/t female adolescents. *Journal for the Education of the Gifted, 12,* 62–79.

Ibrahim, F., & Herr, E. L. (1987). Battered women: A developmental life-career counseling perspective. *Journal of Counseling and Development, 65,* 244–248.

Isaacson, L. E., & Brown, D. (1993). *Career information, career counseling, & career development* (5th ed.). Boston: Allyn & Bacon.

Jepsen, D. A. (1993). Appraisal in developmental career counseling. *Journal of Career Assessment, 1,* 375–392.

Johansson, C. B. (1986). *Career Assessment Inventory.* Minneapolis, MN: NCS Professional Assessment Services.

Kahn, S. E. (1988). Feminism and career counseling with women. *Journal of Career Development, 14,* 242–248.

Kapes, J. T., & Mastie, M. M. (1988). *A counselor's guide to career assessment instruments* (2nd ed.). Alexandria, VA: National Career Development Association.

Kerr, B. (1993). Career assessment for gifted girls and women. *Journal of Career Assessment, 1,* 258–266.

Kerr, B. A., & Ghrist–Priebe, S. L. (1988). Intervention for multipotentiality: Effects of a career counseling laboratory for gifted high school students. *Journal of Counseling and Development, 66,* 366–369.

Kouri, M. K. (1986). A life design process for older adults. *Journal of Career Development, 13,* 6–13.

Krumboltz, J. D. (1991). *Career Beliefs Inventory.* Palo Alto, CA: Consulting Psychologists Press.

Krumboltz, J. D., & Jackson, M. A. (1993). Career assessment as a learning tool. *Journal of Career Assessment, 1,* 393–409.

Kuder, G. F. (1985). *Kuder Occupational Interest Survey, Form DD* Chicago: Science Research Associates.

Lauver, P. J., & Jones, R. M. (1991). Factors associated with perceived career options in American Indian, White, and Hispanic rural high school students. *Journal of Counseling Psychology, 38,* 159–166.

Lee, C. C. (1987). The case of Felisha: Response. *Career Development Quarterly, 36,* 6–8.

Lee, C. C., & Simmons, S. (1988). A comprehensive life-planning model for Black adolescents. *The School Counselor, 36,* 5–10.

Lent, R. W., Brown, S. D., & Larkin, K. C. (1987). Comparison of three theoretically derived variables in predicting career and academic behavior: Self-efficacy, interest congruence, and consequence thinking. *Journal of Counseling Psychology, 34,* 293–298.

Leong, F. T. L. (1993). The career counseling process with racial–ethnic minorities: The case of Asian Americans. *Career Development Quarterly, 42,* 26–40.

Liptak, J. J. (1989). Irrational expectations in the job search process. *Journal of Employment Counseling, 26,* 35–40.

Liptak, J. J. (1990). Preretirement counseling: Integrating the leisure planning component. *Career Development Quarterly, 38,* 360–367.

Liptak, J. J. (1991). Leisure counseling: An antidote for "the living death." *Journal of Employment Counseling, 28,* 115–120.

Lowman, R. L. (1991). *The clinical practice of career assessment: Interests, abilities, and personality.* Washington, DC: American Psychological Association.

Lunneborg, P. W. (1981). *The Vocational Interest Inventory.* Los Angeles: Western Psychological Services.

Manzi, P. A. (1987). Skills assessment in career counseling: A developmental approach. *Career Development Quarterly, 36,* 45–54.

Markus, H., & Nurius, P. (1986). Possible selves. *American Psychologist, 41,* 954–969.

Martin, W. E. (1991). Career development and American Indians living on reservations: Cross-cultural factors to consider. *Career Development Quarterly, 39,* 273–283.

Melcher, C. R. (1987). Career counseling tailored to the Evangelical Christian woman at mid-life. *Journal of Psychology and Theology, 15,* 113–123.

Mitchell, L. K., & Krumboltz, J. D. (1984). Social learning approach to career decision making: Krumboltz's theory. In D. Brown & L. Brooks (Eds.), *Career choice and development: Applying contemporary theories to practice* (pp. 235–280). San Francisco: Jossey-Bass.

Mitchell, L. K., & Krumboltz, J. D. (1987). The effects of cognitive restructuring and decision-making training on career indecision. *Journal of Counseling and Development, 66,* 171–174.

Morgan, K. S., & Brown, L. S. (1991). Lesbian career development, work behavior, and vocational counseling. *The Counseling Psychologist, 19,* 273–291.

Myers, I. B., & Briggs, K. C. (1977). *Myers–Briggs Type Indicator.* Palo Alto, CA: Consulting Psychologists Press.

Neinas, C. C. (1987). Outplacement services for the blue-collar worker. *Journal of Career Development, 14,* 80–89.

Nevill, D. D., & Super, D. E. (1986). *Manual for the Salience Inventory: Theory, application, and research.* Palo Alto, CA: Consulting Psychologists Press.

Nevill, D. D., & Super, D. E. (1989). *Manual for the Values Scale* (2nd ed.). Palo Alto, CA: Consulting Psychologists Press.

Noble, K. D. (1987). The dilemma of the gifted woman. *Psychology of Women Quarterly, 11,* 367–378.

O'Brien, K. M., & Fassinger, R. E. (1993). A causal model of the career orientation and career choice of adolescent women. *Journal of Counseling Psychology, 40,* 456–469.

Oleksy–Ojikutu, A. E. (1986). The career time-line: A vocational counseling tool. *Career Development Quarterly, 35,* 47–52.

Osipow, S. H. (1987). *Career Decision Scale: Manual.* Odessa, FL: Psychological Assessment Resources.

Osipow, S. H. (1991). Developing instruments for use in counseling. *Journal of Counseling and Development, 70,* 322–326.

Pedersen, P., Goldberg, A. D., & Papalia, T. (1991). A model for planning career continuation and change through increased awareness, knowledge, and skill. *Journal of Employment Counseling, 28,* 74–79.

Richman, D. R. (1988). Cognitive career counseling for women. *Journal of Rational–Emotive and Cognitive–Behavior Therapy, 6,* 50–65.

Roessler, R. T., & Hastings, L. O. (1987). Employability counseling: Who, what, where, when, & how. *Journal of Applied Rehabilitation Counseling, 18,* 9–11.

Rooney, R. A., & Osipow, S. H. (1992). Task-Specific Occupational Self-Efficacy Scale: The development and validation of a prototype. *Journal of Vocational Behavior, 40,* 14–32.

Roper, C. J., & Berry, K. (1986). College career centers: Reaching out to the gifted and talented. *Journal of Career Development, 13,* 49–60.

Rounds, J. B., Henly, G. A., Dawis, R. V., Lofquist, L. H., & Weiss, D. J. (1981). *Manual for the Minnesota Importance Questionnaire.* Minneapolis: University of Minnesota, Vocational Psychology Research.

Russell, J. E. A., & Eby, L. T. (1993). Career assessment strategies for women in management. *Journal of Career Assessment, 1,* 267–293.

Schriner, K. F., & Roessler, R. T. (1987). An occupational choice strategy for disabled individuals in field and facility settings. *Journal of Applied Rehabilitation Counseling, 18,* 6–10.

Skovholt, T. M., Morgan, J. I., & Negron–Cunningham, H. (1989). Mental imagery in career counseling and life planning: A review of research and intervention methods. *Journal of Counseling and Development, 67,* 287–292.

Sommerstein, J. C. (1986). Assessing the older worker: The career counselor's dilemma. *Journal of Career Development, 13,* 52–56.

Spence, J. T., & Helmreich, R. L. (1972). The Attitudes Toward Women Scale: An objective instrument to measure attitudes toward the rights and roles of women in contemporary society. *JSAS Catalog of Selected Documents in Psychology, 2,* 66 (Ms. NO. 153).

Spence, J. T., Helmreich, R. L., & Stapp, J. (1974). The Personal Attributes Questionnaire: A measure of sex role stereotypes and masculinity–femininity. *JSAS Catalog of Selected Documents in Psychology, 4,* 43 (Ms. NO. 617).

Spokane, A. R., & Hawks, B. K. (1990). Annual review: Practice and research in career counseling and development, 1989. *Career Development Quarterly, 39*, 98–128.

Strong, E. K., Hansen, J. C., & Campbell, D. P. (1985). *Strong Interest Inventory.* Palo Alto, CA: Consulting Psychologists Press.

Super, D. E., Thompson, A. S., Lindeman, R. H., Myers, R. A., & Jordaan, J. P. (1985). *Adult Career Concerns Inventory.* Palo Alto, CA: Consulting Psychologists Press.

Swanson, J. L. (1992). The structure of vocational interests for African-American college students. *Journal of Vocational Behavior, 40*, 144–157.

Swanson, J. L., & Tokar, D. M. (1991). College students' perceptions of barriers to career development. *Journal of Vocational Behavior, 38*, 92–106.

Taylor, K. M., & Betz, N. E. (1983). Applications of self-efficacy theory to the understanding and treatment of career indecision. *Journal of Vocational Behavior, 22*, 63–81.

Taylor, K. M., & Popma, J. (1990). An examination of the relationships among career decision-making self-efficacy, career salience, locus of control, and vocational indecision. *Journal of Vocational Behavior, 37*, 17–31.

Tipping, L. M., & Farmer, H. S. (1991). A home-career conflict measure: Career counseling implications. *Measurement and Evaluation in Counseling and Development, 24*, 111–118.

Todisco, M., & Salomone, P. R. (1991). Facilitating effective cross-cultural relationships: The White counselor and the Black client. *Journal of Multicultural Counseling and Development, 19*, 146–157.

Tomlinson, S. M., & Evans–Hughes, G. (1991). Gender, ethnicity and college students' responses to the Strong Campbell Interest Inventory. *Journal of Counseling and Development, 70*, 151–155.

U.S. Employment Service. (1982). *USES General Aptitude Test Battery.* Washington, DC: Author.

Walsh, W. B. (Ed.). (1993). Career assessment for women [Special feature]. *Journal of Career Assessment, 1*, 197–293.

Walsh, W. B., & Osipow, S. H. (Eds.). (1990). *Advances in vocational psychology: Vol. 3. Career counseling.* Hillsdale, NJ: Lawrence Erlbaum Associates.

Ward, C. M., & Bingham, R. P. (1993). Career assessment of ethnic minority women. *Journal of Career Assessment, 1*, 246–257.

Watkins, C. E. (1993). Psychodynamic career assessment: An Adlerian perspective. *Journal of Career Assessment, 1*, 355–374.

Westbrook, B. W., & Sanford, E. E. (1991). The validity of career maturity attitude measures among Black and White high school students. *Career Development Quarterly, 39*, 199–208.

Westwood, M. J., & Ishiyama, F. I. (1991). Challenges in counseling immigrant clients: Understanding intercultural barriers to career adjustment. *Journal of Employment Counseling, 28*, 130–143.

Whiston, S. C. (1990). Evaluation of the Adult Career Concerns Inventory. *Journal of Counseling and Development, 69*, 78–80.

Wise, P. S. (1989). *The use of assessment techniques by applied psychologists.* Belmont, CA: Wadsworth.

Wrenn, C. G. (1988). The person in career counseling. *Career Development Quarterly, 36*, 337–342.

Yang, J. (1991). Career counseling of Chinese American women: Are they in limbo? *Career Development Quarterly, 39*, 350–359.

Zunker, V. G. (1990). *Career counseling: Applied concepts of life planning* (3rd ed.). Pacific Grove, CA: Brooks/Cole.

CHAPTER NINE

Personal Adjustment: Career Counseling and Psychotherapy

David L. Blustein
University at Albany
State University of New York

Paul M. Spengler
Ball State University

An often cited maxim within psychology and the helping professions is that one of the hallmarks of mental health is the capacity to work and love (e.g., Erikson, 1963; Freud, 1930; Savickas, 1991). Although this statement presents work and love together, these domains have generally been treated discretely via the relatively circumscribed modalities of career counseling and psychotherapy (Herr, 1989; Subich, 1993). To redress the "false dichotomy" (Hackett, 1993, p. 105) between career counseling and psychotherapy, we have designed the present chapter to provide an informed analysis of the complex array of issues relating to the interface of career and psychotherapeutic interventions.

The perspective that we develop here is that career counseling and psychotherapy are closely intertwined processes with the most obvious differences existing in the *domain* of treatment emphasis. Despite the recent plethora of articulate calls for the integration of career counseling and psychotherapy (e.g., Betz & Corning, 1993; Dorn, 1992; Krumboltz, 1993; Pinkerton, Etzel, Rockwell, Talley, & Moorman, 1990; Rounds & Tracey, 1990), a conceptual framework to guide integrative treatment and necessary research efforts has not been available. To address this shortcoming, we summarize the current state of knowledge of the relationships among career counseling, psychotherapy, and personal and vocational adjustment; explore new areas of potential theoretical integration; and provide a perspective to guide subsequent inquiry and theoretical developments in this area. Suggestions for practice, research, and training emerging from our analysis conclude the chapter.

DEFINITIONAL DISTINCTIONS

An examination of the definitions of career counseling and psychotherapy reveals the general lack of integration between these two treatment modalities. Naturally, it is difficult to develop a definition of psychotherapy that would encompass the theoretical diversity that is inherent in the field. In a project by Zeig and Munion (1990), 90 authors from various theoretical perspectives were asked to provide their definition of psychotherapy. In integrating these definitions, Zeig and Munion (1990) advanced the following theory-nonspecific definition: "Psychotherapy is a change-oriented process that occurs in the context of a contractual, empowering, and empathic professional relationship. Its rationale explicitly or implicitly focuses on the personality of the client(s), the technique of psychotherapy, or both" (p. 14).

In the career counseling realm, considerable diversity of positions along theoretical lines also exists, although the sheer number of approaches pales in comparison to the psychotherapy field. A selected review of many texts (e.g., Brown & Brooks, 1991; Crites, 1981; Spokane, 1991; Walsh & Osipow, 1990) reveals a number of common themes, which can be captured by the definition provided by Spokane (1992). For Spokane, career intervention represented "any attempt to assist an individual in making improved career decisions through such means as workshops, classes, consultation, prevention, etc." (p. 44). He then noted that "it is possible to view career intervention on a continuum from the most counselor and client intensive dyadic interventions to the least intensive alternative treatments, such as brief inventories and informational interventions" (p. 44). Given the objectives of this chapter, we focus on the more intensive individual and group interventions.

A closer look at the various definitions of career counseling and psychotherapy tends to underscore the relative discreteness of these definitions. For example, of the 90 contributions in the Zeig and Munion (1990) book, only one (i.e., Blustein, 1990) included any reference to work or career in its definition of psychotherapy. A similar review of definitions of career counseling in recent textbooks and other publications reveals a consistent focus on the work or career domain of human functioning (e.g., Spokane, 1991, 1992), although more integrative definitions are also available (e.g., Brown & Brooks, 1991). Thus, a cursory review of the definitional bases of career counseling and psychotherapy portray relatively distinct treatment modalities.

Despite these evident differences, a growing number of writers are attempting to recast the traditional distinctions between these treatment modalities, using a variety of conceptual and methodological vantage points. In the review of this literature that follows, we have selected a particular semantic perspective with respect to domains of psychological treatment. We have elected not to use the personal-versus-career distinction because we endorse the view that career issues are by their very nature personal issues (cf. Davidson & Gilbert,

1993; Manuele–Adkins, 1992). As such, we refer to counseling or intervention as occurring in career and noncareer domains.

We begin the chapter by first reviewing the relationship between career counseling and psychotherapy from the vantage point of the major career-development theories and follow with a review of the relevant empirical research on various aspects of the career counseling–psychotherapy debate. In order to understand the interplay between the career and noncareer domains, we next examine the degree to which career interventions influence noncareer outcomes and the degree to which noncareer interventions influence career outcomes. We then introduce new directions of inquiry that are directly related to the relationship between career counseling and psychotherapy. The chapter concludes with the description of a domain-sensitive approach to counseling along with suggestions for research and training.

THE VIEW FROM THE MAJOR
CAREER COUNSELING THEORIES

In turning to the specific theories of career counseling, we examine how four major schools of career counseling (i.e., person–environment fit, social learning, life-span developmental, and psychoanalytic) have grappled with the relationship between career counseling and psychotherapy.

Person–Environment Fit Theories

In the traditional person–environment fit (P–E fit) theories (e.g., Holland, 1985), career counseling has generally been presented in a relatively circumscribed fashion. Although there has been considerable attention devoted to the role of personality factors in career counseling (e.g., Holland, 1985), little explicit attention has been devoted to the integrating of treatment modalities. However, recent advances in P–E fit theory (e.g., Lofquist & Dawis, 1991; Rounds & Tracey, 1990) have addressed career counseling with greater attention to the broad range of problems that clients present. For example, Lofquist and Dawis (1991) applied the use of their P–E fit model to a wide array of client problems, including career-related issues, marital counseling, and addiction counseling.

In an innovative analysis of P–E fit theory, Rounds and Tracey (1990) proposed that career counseling is actually a subset of psychotherapy. Specifically, Rounds and Tracey argued that viewing career counseling as a form of psychotherapy would allow for a better understanding of the change processes in the career domain. In relation to the counseling process, Rounds and Tracey used a problem-solving framework that integrated components of decision-making, information processing, and general problem-solving models derived from both career and noncareer theories. In the Rounds and Tracey perspective, the range of issues addressed by an intervention would vary in accordance with information-processing level; as such, interventions conceivably could encompass noncareer issues, depending on the clients' presenting issues and their capacity to engage in adequate problem solving.

Social Learning and Cognitive Theories

Because the theoretical framework for the social learning approach to career counseling is similar to existing models of cognitive therapy (e.g., Meichenbaum, 1977), the potential exists for an integrative analysis of client concerns. Although this potential was not fully developed in earlier social learning contributions (e.g., Krumboltz, 1979), Krumboltz (1993) recently outlined a rationale for considering career problems in conjunction with personal problems. Krumboltz also proposed that the view of career problems as representing deficits in cognitive or instrumental skills needs to be supplemented by an awareness of the anxiety that can be associated with career concerns.

From a somewhat different perspective, Richman (1988) presented a rational–emotive approach that is designed to enhance the personal adjustment of individuals within the work setting. Using a life-span perspective to present career issues, Richman described a number of integrative treatment strategies for clients, based on her in-depth understanding of the rational–emotive and career development literatures. One asset of the cognitive approach outlined by Richman and the social learning model of Krumboltz (1979) is its explicit focus on the environment and the work setting. For example, Richman highlighted the need for counselors to address the irrational expectations and beliefs of recruiters and managers. In sum, the contributions of Krumboltz (1993) and Richman (1988) provide a viable, cognitively oriented perspective for integrating career and noncareer interventions.

Life-Span Developmental Theories

Like the cognitive theories, the life-span developmental models were primarily derived from general theories of human behavior; as such, these theories offer a useful framework for integrating counseling efforts. Super (1955) initially addressed this issue by arguing that vocational counseling has the potential of enhancing personal adjustment. In developing his argument, Super (1955) presented an extensive case vignette in which a client with difficulties in the career and noncareer realms was assisted by a vocationally focused treatment plan. More recently, Super (1993) addressed the career counseling–psychotherapy debate by arguing that there are, in fact, two fields: situational counseling which has subspecialties which focus on differing types of situations (career, family, etc.), and personal counseling, in which the focus on individuals whose problems are based primarily in their own approach to and coping with situations, not on factors in the situations they encounter. (p. 135)

Super (1993) concluded his thoughtful analysis by cautioning that these two types of counseling ought not be treated as discrete interventions, but that they be considered along a continuum. In addition, Super's (1980) life-space, life-span model, which incorporates a full array of life roles, provides a conceptual framework with which we can view career and non-career issues together in counseling.

Other prominent developmentally oriented theorists also have attempted to discern the relationship between career counseling and psychotherapy. Building on current advances in developmental theory, Jepsen (1990) provided a theoretically expansive view of career intervention. Although Jepsen did not address the career counseling–psychotherapy question directly, his integration of general developmental theory and Super's (1980) life-roles construct in particular may be useful in an integrative approach to treatment. In addition, Jepsen's inclusion of the work by Vondracek, Lerner, and Schulenberg (1986) sets the stage for a view of career intervention that incorporates important elements of the developmental context. The Vondracek et al. contribution provided a powerful theoretical rationale for considering career intervention as a subset of human development intervention. Their approach is built on the need for counselors to understand the broader landscape of career development, which naturally would encompass attention to other developmental domains.

As this brief overview of the life-span developmental perspective has suggested, we can perhaps understand the career counseling–psychotherapy issue best by examining the nature of a client's developmental context. As suggested by the major developmental theorists (e.g., Super, 1957; Vondracek et al., 1986), career development occurs within a framework that includes both proximal and distal factors (such as family, historical and social influences, economic factors, and developmental progress in other domains of psychosocial functioning). Consequently, the context-rich developmental perspective necessitates the counselor's attention to the client's overall status, thereby promoting the potential for integrative interventions, when such interventions are indicated.

Psychoanalytic Theories

Emerging directly from theories that focused on mental health concerns, the psychoanalytic approaches have addressed the career counseling–psychotherapy question, within a number of specific theoretical frameworks. Initially, the work of Bordin and his colleagues (e.g., Bordin, Nachmann, & Segal, 1963) used an orthodox, drive-oriented perspective to understand career-choice behavior, without a clear focus on career intervention. More recently, Bordin (1990) incorporated advances in object relations and ego psychology theories in his examination of career choice and development. Bordin (1990) also described an approach to career counseling that addresses noncareer issues within the scope of the overall treatment (e.g., family issues).

Watkins and Savickas (1990) employed perspectives derived from the work of Adler (e.g., 1956) and Erikson (e.g., 1963) in their approach to psychodynamic career counseling. Although not explicitly addressing the integration of psychotherapy and career counseling, Watkins and Savickas presented a comprehensive conceptualization of career counseling that attends to such issues as ego identity, life themes, and social interest. Adopting the Watkins and Savickas perspective would allow for attention to a broad array of contextual factors that influence career behavior and, therefore, may promote an optimal level of focus on the full texture of a client's life. A number of new innovations in psychoanalytic theory falling under the rubric of relational models also have been applied to the career domain and are reviewed later in this chapter.

Conclusion

This selected review highlights a number of recent statements emerging from the major career counseling theories that, when taken together, present a rationale for our considering career counseling and psychotherapy as closely related treatment strategies. As this review has indicated, the rationale that is emerging from some quarters of the major theories suggests that there are meaningful relationships among various life roles across settings and that an examination of these relationships can enhance the quality and impact of career interventions. This assumption provides the basis of a conceptual framework for integrative interventions or interventions that are sensitive to the relationships among various domains of life.

AN EMERGING DEBATE: SUBSTANTIVE DISTINCTIONS OR SUBTLE DIFFERENCES BETWEEN CAREER COUNSELING AND PSYCHOTHERAPY

As reflected by the perspectives emerging from the major career counseling theories, few would deny that career and noncareer domains interact. However, differences in opinion exist as to the appropriateness of theorists' blurring of distinctions between these two approaches to intervention. For example, Herr (1989) argued in favor of the integration of career development and mental health counseling, whereas others (e.g., Crites, 1981; Spokane, 1989) have taken a more moderate view by maintaining that unique aspects of career interventions also exist. The crux of this debate rests on two fundamental points: (a) evidence in support of and against the interplay between career and noncareer domains of functioning and (b) observations of shared and unique change processes in career counseling and psychotherapy.

Interplay of Career and Noncareer Domains

Most career development researchers would agree that compelling evidence exists in support of an interrelationship between work and mental health. Studies abound on the reciprocal nature of relationships between unemployment (e.g., Osipow & Fitzgerald, 1993), job stress (e.g., Osipow, 1979), and undesirable mental health sequelae of work-related problems (see Herr, 1989). Similar links are found between career satisfaction and factors such as anxiety, depression, somatic complaints, and self-esteem (Lofquist & Dawis, 1984). Research also has identified the moderating effect of personal attributes on the relationships between career and noncareer variables. For example, early family experiences may be related to work dysfunction and stress (Firth–Cozens, 1992). Staw and Ross (1985) found that job attitudes reflect personality dimensions more than do objective environmental factors.

In response to these observations, several perspectives have been proposed for integrating career counseling into various aspects of noncareer functioning, with attention given to issues such as family functioning (O'Neil, Fishman, & Kinsella–Shaw, 1987), sexual orientation (Tolsma, 1993), and interpersonal relationships (Haverkamp & Moore, 1993). The consensus underlying these models is that effective counseling treats the whole person (Betz & Corning, 1993) as opposed to maintaining overt distinctions between career and noncareer domains.

Yet do problems with career development and adjustment *always* interact in a symbiotic relationship with mental health or personal adjustment problems? As our review has indicated, the answer appears to be, probably not. For example, research on vocational rehabilitation shows that improvements in personal adjustment do not necessarily lead to improvements in work performance (e.g., Neff, 1985). In a scholarly review of the treatment of depression and the functional capacity to work, J. Mintz, L. Mintz, Arruda, and Hwang (1992) observed that depressive symptoms resolve far earlier than do returns to gainful and satisfactory employment. Clearly, occasions arise when problems exist only in the career domain. For example, there are identifiable subgroups of college students who experience career indecision (Lucas & Epperson, 1988), some of whose problems are confounded by personal attributes (e.g., anxiety) and others who need focused help only in career decision making. In discussing these issues, Spokane (1989) proposed that some interdependence exists between career and personal adjustment, particularly at times of developmental transition or periods of stress, but that the two domains do not necessarily function in unison *at all times*. It would be fair to conclude that there is probably considerable overlap between career and noncareer domains of functioning, yet it is also clear that unique areas of functioning exist that will require domain-focused interventions.

Shared and Unique Change Processes

One potentially useful means of our understanding the similarities and differences between career counseling and psychotherapy may be a comparison and contrast of the change processes that are shared by and unique to both intervention domains. Recent interest in this topic has led to a number of scholarly discussions (Betz & Corning, 1993; Hackett, 1993; Spokane, 1991; Super, 1993) and related empirical studies (Clarke & Greenberg, 1986; Galassi, Crace, Martin, James, & Wallace, 1992; Gold, Kivlighan, Kerr, & Kramer, 1993; Kivlighan, Johnson, & Fretz, 1987; Phillips, Friedlander, Kost, Specterman, & Robbins, 1988; Watkins, Savickas, Brizzi, & Manus, 1990). In relation to the questions posed here, the small number of career-oriented process studies may be particularly useful in generating insights about the similarities and differences between career counseling and psychotherapy (Heppner & Hendricks, in press; Kirschner, Hoffman, & Hill, 1994; Spokane et al., 1993).

A common focus in psychotherapy research is the study of process and outcome, either as separate or as interactive elements of the change process (see Marmar, 1990). In this line of inquiry, theorists and researchers are beginning to identify commonalities or common sources of gain shared by various approaches to psychotherapy (Mahoney, 1991). For example, research incorporating the Working Alliance Inventory (Horvath & Greenberg, 1986) suggests that elements of the therapeutic relationship—identified as task, bond, and goal—account for up to 47% of final outcome variance (see Horvath & Symonds, 1991).

Career development researchers have recently proposed the importance of examining the application of these and other process components to effective career counseling (e.g., Betz & Corning, 1993; Corbishley & Yost, 1989; Hackett, 1993). Although this line of work represents the exception rather than the rule, process questions are beginning to be investigated, such as When is the optimal time to support and when is the optimal time to provide information? (see Kirschner et al., 1993). This form of questioning moves our discourse beyond issues regarding differences in the *domain* of intervention to some interesting speculations about shared *processes*.

Our review of common sources of gain in psychotherapy (see J. Frank, 1982; Mahoney, 1991) leads us to propose that a comparison of career and noncareer interventions may yield a number of important shared process dimensions as opposed to absolute qualitative differences. For example, group counseling research has suggested that affective and relationship factors are inherently important to any change process, regardless of whether the individual seeks help for a career or a noncareer problem (e.g., Kivlighan et al., 1987; Lieberman, Yalom, & Miles, 1973). Furthermore, in a particularly well-conceived study on individual counseling, Kirschner et al. (1994) identified a biphasic process in a seven-session intervention that was initiated by rapport building, information seeking, and test interpretation. This initial phase was followed by a synthetic phase, which focused on values, barriers, implementation, and termination. Kirschner et al. utilized Hill and O'Grady's (1985) psychotherapy debriefing procedure to evaluate the counselor's intentions and the client's reactions after each session. The primary counselor intentions were insight, feelings, and change, whereas the primary client reactions were feeling supported, understood, and challenged. The only major difference between these results and those of some illustrative psychotherapy process studies (e.g., Fuller & Hill, 1985) was that in the career counseling case, the counselor provided more information.

Another study by Heppner and Hendricks (in press) presented an in-depth investigation of the process elements of two career counseling cases involving a career-undecided and indecisive client. Using methodological advances culled from psychotherapy process research, Heppner and Hendricks sought to identify the role of specific counseling events, the role of the relationship, and counselor intentions in the sessions judged best and worst. Their results indicated that the counseling process differed in ways that were consistent with the specific presenting problems of these two clients. Moreover, Heppner and Hendricks observed that both clients attributed significant importance to the therapeutic relationship.

Related investigations have tended to support the findings of Kirschner et al. (1994) and Heppner and Hendricks (in press) regarding the utility of relationally oriented factors in career interventions. In a study of helpful events reported by college students in career exploration courses, Gold et al. (1993) found that affective components (such as experiencing support or encouragement) accounted for the most change in vocational identity, followed by tasks requiring behavior implementation and then changes in insight. Kivlighan et al. (1987) found that affective and relational factors (catharsis and cohesion) were, respectively, the first and third most important mechanisms of change (in career-exploration groups) that also targeted changes in participants' vocational identity. In contrast, Watkins et al. (1990) observed that verbal responses that promote the relationship, such as empathy or self-involving counselor responses, may be less necessary in career than in noncareer counseling. Despite the absence of completely uniform results, the majority of the aforementioned findings, in conjunction with other studies (e.g., Clarke & Greenberg, 1986; Robbins & Tucker, 1986), point to the potential importance of the therapeutic relationship and emotional experiencing as sources of gain in career counseling.

A related issue is the lack of attention to client resistance in the career counseling literature (Hampl, 1990), in contrast to the considerable attention this factor has received in the psychotherapy literature (e.g., Wachtel, 1982). This disparity creates the impression that career counseling is inevitably a logical and cooperative process between the counselor and client. In psychotherapy, counselors give much attention to helping people make changes they can imagine but have not yet been able to invoke due to internal conflicts, anxiety, cognitive distortions, family restrictions, and the like. In actuality, career counseling may be no different. In fact, research on personal and mental health correlates of career functioning has suggested that emotional and cognitive blocks often represent the core of adult career clients' problems (Hampl, 1990; Herr, 1989).

In comparing the change processes in career and noncareer counseling, Holland, Magoon, and Spokane (1981) provided a useful integrative perspective. Holland et al. concluded that there were four sources of gain in successful career interventions: cognitive rehearsal, information about self and the world of work, the provision of a framework, and social support. With the exception of the imparting of information about the world of work, each of these process components are analogous to change components in psychotherapy. That affective components were omitted is probably more a reflection of the sorts of questions being asked by career researchers rather than a lack of importance attached to emotional experiencing in career counseling (see Gold et al., 1993). Other sources of gain identified by psychotherapy researchers also may be relevant in career counseling (e.g., hope, Spokane, 1991; social influence, Dorn, 1988). In sum, it appears that the elements of the change processes in career counseling and psychotherapy may be very similar, although the degree of similarity may be a function of factors (e.g., degree of interplay between domains) not yet addressed by researchers.

SCOPE OF INTERVENTION
AND TREATMENT OUTCOMES

As reflected in the literature reviewed thus far, questions pertaining to the relationship between career counseling and psychotherapy have been posed from various perspectives. The career counseling–psychotherapy debate may be illuminated further by our examining the effect of career and noncareer interventions in collateral domains of functioning. Therefore, in this next section, we review the degree to which career interventions influence noncareer variables and the degree to which psychotherapy influences career functioning.

Noncareer Outcomes of Career Interventions

Meta-analyses of career counseling outcomes have indicated that career counseling is effective and may even produce overall effects that are larger than those reported in meta-analyses of psychotherapy outcome studies (see Oliver & Spokane, 1988; Spokane & Oliver, 1983). Many of the career studies reviewed in the two contributions by Oliver and Spokane included noncareer outcomes such as changes in self-concept (self-esteem, self-adjustment, interpersonal competence), personal attitudes, locus of control, cognitive complexity, and levels of anxiety. Attention by career researchers to noncareer outcomes is not uncommon and is reflected in other reviews of career counseling research (e.g., Holland et al., 1981), in recommendations for career outcome measures (Oliver, 1979), and in diagnostic systems for career problems (R. Campbell & Cellini, 1981).

Herr (1989) stated that

> if one considers work and mental health to be linked, and career counseling to be an effective process in helping persons choose work wisely and improve their adjustment to it, then, logic would argue for career counseling to be a useful process in the service of improved mental health, where questions of work satisfaction and purpose are involved. (p. 13)

In fact, the empirical literature appears to support Herr's assumption. Of the 58 studies identified in the meta-analysis by Oliver and Spokane (1988), 17 were examinations of noncareer outcomes. To determine the impact of career interventions on noncareer outcomes, we summed Oliver and Spokane's reported mean effects for the noncareer outcomes and then divided that sum by the total number of comparisons. This simple reanalysis of their data resulted in an overall effect size of 0.58 for noncareer outcomes. Although smaller than the reported overall career intervention effect size of 0.85 (Spokane & Oliver, 1983), this effect size supports the position that career interventions positively affect noncareer domains of functioning.

Some issues, however, limit our ability to comment on the extent to which career counseling can serve as a mental health intervention. First, the research in this area is somewhat inconclusive. As early as 1940, Williamson and Bordin studied the effect of brief career counseling with college students on measures of general life and personal satisfaction, as well as on measures of career adjustment and development. A 25-year follow-up study demonstrated small but sustained effects of the career counseling intervention (D. Campbell, 1965). However, the follow-up revealed significantly higher levels of distress in the counseled group ($n = 367$) than in the noncounseled group ($n = 250$). More immediate negative mental health outcomes following career counseling have also been noted, including the aggravation of psychopathology levels that subsequently evoked referrals for psychotherapy

(Spokane et al., 1991). However, another interpretation of this finding is that the career intervention engendered an interest in further self-exploration and personal growth.

A second challenge to our assessing the relationship between career counseling and mental health is the sparse number of career studies in which psychopathologically oriented outcomes have been investigated. In one study, Conklin (1985) reported that 2 months of career counseling was an effective treatment for women with agoraphobia. In another study, Massimo and Shore (1963) utilized a vocationally oriented psychotherapeutic program to treat 20 male adolescents with antisocial behaviors. The first phase consisted of relationship building and was followed by job-skills training, job-readiness preparation, and assistance with the implementation of a career choice. After placement, the third phase of therapy moved to problems encountered at work. Positive changes in vocational and nonvocational adjustment, including a reduction of acting out antisocial behaviors, were achieved and remained evident up to 10 years later (see Shore & Massimo, 1973).

In contrast to these examples, the vast majority of career studies with non-career outcomes have been examinations of variables that might be more appropriately labeled *personal adjustment*. Very few investigators have studied the effects of career interventions as a treatment for more significant problems in noncareer functioning, such as affective or anxiety disorders. We find this fact surprising given the high base rates of these psychological problems and the psychological and economic costs of impaired vocational functioning.

In conclusion, we find some modest support for Herr's (1989) assumption that career interventions can be helpful in noncareer domains; however, it is difficult for us to ascertain to what extent career decision-making and work-adjustment interventions, alone, will improve indices of mental health. We expect that under certain conditions they probably do. Overall effect sizes, however, such as the one we crudely calculated, mask finer relationships, outliers, and negative effects. Additional research is needed, especially longitudinal and attribute-by-treatment designs, for determining the specific conditions and client populations for which career counseling may positively affect selected domains of mental health functioning.

Career Outcomes of Psychotherapy

Although the general domain of vocational functioning remains one of the most neglected topics in psychotherapy outcome assessment (see Lambert, Ogles, & Masters, 1992), attention to career outcomes by psychotherapy researchers may be on the rise. Recommendations for standard batteries for the assessment of psychotherapy outcome are now beginning to include vocational functioning. Lambert et al. (1992) identified three broad domains for measurement; one of these is "social-role performance" (p. 529) and includes work-related activities as a major portion. Elliot (1992) expanded on the Lambert et al. (1992) framework by delineating both occupational and academic functioning. Although the enlarged scope of these frameworks is welcomed, they have not specified which aspects of work adjustment, or for that matter which aspects of the broader domain of career development and adjustment, may be affected by psychotherapy.

In contrast to the general lack of attention to these issues, members of the Sheffield Psychotherapy Project are engaged in a systematic program of research on the utility of psychotherapy for treatment of occupational stress (Firth & Shapiro, 1986), work-related depression (Barkham & Shapiro, 1990), and improvement of job perceptions and career satisfaction (Firth–Cozens & Hardy, 1992). A unique contribution of this work is their emphasis on psychodynamic approaches. Labeled *exploratory therapy*, this approach has been compared with a combination of cognitive–behavioral and behavioral interventions (called *prescriptive therapy*) in a number of vocationally oriented studies (Barkham & Shapiro, 1990; Firth & Shapiro, 1986; Firth–Cozens & Hardy, 1992).

In a prototypical investigation, Firth and Shapiro (1986) found that eight sessions of prescriptive therapy were superior to eight sessions of exploratory therapy for treatment of occupational stress but that the sessions were equivalent in reducing job-related problems. In this study, variations in vocational functioning included measures of time off, performance loss, overt friction, and lack of interest. In a larger study of the psychological treatment of white-collar workers with depression, Firth–Cozens and Hardy (1992) found that 16 sessions of exploratory therapy resulted in alleviation of depression and corresponding improvement in job satisfaction and attitudes toward work (i.e., control, skill use, feeling valued, and interpersonal contact). Finally, Barkham and Shapiro (1990) found that job-related depression could be effectively treated in 55%–73% of cases by either brief (three sessions) exploratory or prescriptive vocationally oriented psychotherapy. Barkham and Shapiro concluded that personal distress can be expressed as work stress and that brief vocationally oriented treatment can be effective in these cases.

Results of analyses by J. Mintz et al. (1992) lend modest support to the assumption about the responsiveness of vocational functioning to psychotherapy. Mintz et al. conducted a review of 4,000 psychiatric studies and identified only 10 that were investigations of the effect of treatment for depression on the functional capacity to work. Their sophisticated reanalysis of raw data from 827 patients indicated that changes in work satisfaction and interest preceded serious depressive disorders in approximately 50% of patients. This finding suggests the importance of vocational interventions for the prevention of affective disorders. Another important finding of the Mintz et al. report was that the client's return to work functioning took longer to achieve than affective symptom relief. Of the 10 studies, only 3 were investigations of the effect of psychotherapy, whereas the remainder were psychopharmacological investigations (Elkins et al., 1989; Frank, Kupfer, & Perel, 1989; Rehm, Kaslow, & Rabin, 1987). In all three of these investigations, assessment of work functioning was secondary to the primary analyses.

This selective review supports the importance of the inclusion of vocational outcome measures in psychotherapy research. If we accept that an interplay exists between career and noncareer functioning, then vocational outcomes logically should be assessed by psychotherapy researchers. Lambert, Shapiro, and Bergin's (1986) comment on outcome measurement summarizes this position: "Clearly, one of the most important conclusions to be drawn from past psychotherapy outcome research is that the results can be easily misunderstood and even misrepresented through failure to appreciate the multidimensionality of the change process" (p. 191).

Conclusion

When considered collectively, the literature reviewed in this section points to the tendency for a given intervention to foster a modest, yet discernible, positive effect (or spillover) on collateral domains of functioning. Of course, the spillover of outcomes from an intervention in one domain to another is not always uniform or consistent. Yet the prevalent findings in this review suggest that interventions in both the career and noncareer domains as well as integrative interventions have the potential for a relatively broad scope of influence. The fact that the scope tends to embrace both career and noncareer domains in generally predictable ways supports the assumption of meaningful interconnections between these aspects of psychological functioning.

NEW DIRECTIONS FOR INQUIRY

For the most part, the theories and research reviewed thus far have provided compelling support for the position that career counseling and psychotherapy are related, but not identical, processes. Given the logic of the conceptual arguments and the empirical relationships between various process and outcome elements of career counseling and psychotherapy, it seems clear that the potential exists for important new advances in theory development, research, and practice. To establish an expanded conceptual foundation and research agenda for this work, we point to a number of new developments in theory and research that, when taken together, provide a foundation for the development of an integrative intervention framework.

The Role of the Context in Career Development

From a number of directions, researchers and practitioners in career development are becoming increasingly aware of contextual issues in understanding career behavior. Interest in contextual variables can be found in a number of early theoretical statements in career development (e.g., Super, 1957). However, changes in scientific thought (e.g., Vondracek et al., 1986; Young & Collin, 1992) coupled with significant changes in the workforce (e.g., Betz & Fitzgerald, 1987; Marshall & Tucker, 1992) have underscored the importance of the historical, intellectual, and social landscape in career development theory and practice. In this section, we review a number of relevant contextual factors that are increasingly pertinent in career development and that engender a' strong press for integrative interventions.

The Changing Nature of Work. That the workforce is undergoing rapid and complex changes at the present time is becoming obvious to public policy officials (e.g., Marshall & Tucker, 1992; Reich, 1991) and to career development scholars (e.g., Herr, 1990). In relation to the issues addressed in this chapter, the changes in the nature of work are creating far more uncertainty in the career lives of all individuals throughout Western society (cf. Gelatt, 1989). While the need to shift career directions represents one important aspect of the changing labor market, other more ominous trends are emerging. In short, the expectation of a relatively stable array of vocational options for workers in the Western world is rapidly changing; the environment that is emerging is one with increasingly circumscribed occupational options for workers across the spectrum of educational and economic levels (see Marshall & Tucker, 1992, and Reich, 1991, for summaries of these changes).

Our view is that the structural changes in the workforce are evoking a degree of uncertainty that is likely to influence a number of domains of psychosocial functioning. Although the work environment has been relatively consistent for some (but clearly not all) citizens in the Western world, the dramatic shifts in the economy are likely to evoke a complex set of responses in individuals, depending on a host of factors (e.g., access to the opportunity structure, personal and social resources). For example, research has documented the considerable psychological toll that is associated with unemployment, which is manifested by increases in suicide rates and other indices of mental health problems (e.g., Osipow & Fitzgerald, 1993). One observation that can be inferred from the increasingly unpredictable labor market is that career concerns may have a greater influence on an individual's life than before and may evoke problems in various noncareer domains (e.g., family discord, anxiety, adjustment disorders). The changes in the structure of the workforce are even more pronounced for individuals from diverse racial and ethnic groups and for women. These effects are summarized in the following sections.

Visible Racial and Ethnic Groups. Two excellent literature reviews (i.e., Carter & Cook, 1992; Smith, 1983) present cogent analyses of the context that encompasses the vocational lives of visible racial and ethnic groups.

The close interaction between career and noncareer aspects of life for visible racial and ethnic groups are particularly evident when one considers the notion of self-concept implementation, which is central in many prominent career development theories. In contrast to the idealized perspective found in many career theories is the stark reality that the work experiences of many minority individuals detract from their self-concepts (Smith, 1983). Carter and Cook used terms such as "psychological trauma" (1992, p. 200) to describe the process whereby members of visible racial and ethnic groups internalize blame for their own career struggle. Taken together, these views present an articulate case for the way in which noncareer processes interact with the career development of visible racial and ethnic groups.

The context of the career development of visible racial and ethnic groups is beset with implicit and explicit racism (Carter & Cook, 1992). The consistent exposure to racism and to inadequate educational and career resources has the pervasive and pernicious effect of detracting from one's sense of hopefulness and connectedness to society (Carter & Cook, 1992; Richardson, 1993; Smith, 1983). Given this view, it is difficult for us to imagine that the career issues of racial and ethnic group members would be easily circumscribed into an exclusively career or noncareer focus. Carter and Cook (1992) recommended a systems perspective in working with visible racial and ethnic groups. The context of the systems view for Carter and Cook, which includes family, racial and cultural identity, socioeconomic status, and educational background, presents a framework for career intervention that acknowledges and utilizes the complex network of pertinent psychosocial influences.

Gender and Career Development. As Betz and Corning (1993) so aptly noted, the interrelationships between career and noncareer issues are clearly evident when one considers the career development of women. The entire enterprise of selecting, implementing, and adjusting to a work role for women is characterized by close interactions among related aspects of psychosocial functioning. In a recent review of the literature on women's career development, Fitzgerald and Weitzman (1992) presented a variety of arguments that, when considered collectively, point to the interrelatedness of career and noncareer domains. The prevalence of such issues as role conflict, role overload, and sexual harassment all serve to reinforce the complex web of psychological and social factors that influences women's career lives.

Although the social consequences of gender are not nearly as destructive in the career development of men, O'Neil and Fishman (1992) observed that men struggle with a variety of emotional experiences as a result of gender role conflict during normative and nonnormative career transitions. The increased awareness of the psychological impact of gender on career development that has been detailed in recent years serves to highlight the complex linkages between career and noncareer issues for both men and women.

Disability and Career Development. The integration of career and noncareer issues perhaps has been most evident historically in the vocational rehabilitation literature (see, e.g., Neff, 1985). Because a given disability can affect both career and noncareer domains, the conceptual frameworks and treatment strategies employed in this area have been far more integrated than the counseling interventions for nondisabled clients (e.g., Black, 1988; Neff, 1985). For example, one of the guiding principles for counselors working with clients with disabilities is the need to attend to the clients' adjustment to the disabling condition. In addressing issues of adjustment, counselors generally need to examine feelings of loss and the potential for emotional support within the client's current life in conjunction with career issues (Neff, 1985). In addition, Neff's work provided an insightful analysis of the psychological meanings of work, which foreshadows much of the current discourse in this area (cf. Lowman, 1993).

Career Development and Collateral Lines of Development. Beginning with Super's (1957) important contributions, career development has been viewed as taking place within a framework of broader human development. From a theoretical perspective, Cytrynbaum and Crites (1989) and Vondracek et al. (1986) presented excellent integrative reviews culminating in the perspective that career development is closely intertwined with developmental progress in other domains.

The similarities between career development and overall developmental progress are evident in those studies that have related career development in late adolescence to the identity-formation process (e.g., Blustein, Devenis, & Kidney, 1989). Further support for this position can be inferred from theory (e.g., Lopez & Andrews, 1987) and from research (e.g., Blustein, Walbridge, Friedlander, & Palladino, 1991; Lopez, 1989) that has identified the relationships between career development and developmental transitions relating to family interactions. It is important to note that because the magnitude of the relations identified in these studies is modest, we should not infer that career development is completely analogous to or subsumed by other lines of development.

Conclusion. Although this discussion did not address all possible contextual factors emerging from the person and environment, our intention has been to stimulate the sort of context-rich perspective that is necessary to provide effective interventions to an increasingly complex array of client problems. The relevance of the context becomes even more evident in the following sections, which address selected theoretical advances.

Relevant Theoretical Advances

As our previous discussion of the major career counseling theories revealed, issues pertaining to the career counseling–psychotherapy debate have been most effectively addressed via new theoretical advances in a given school of thought. The expansion of theoretical perspectives, beyond the traditional models of career development, offers the possibility for an even greater understanding of the relationships between interventions in the career and noncareer domains.

Social Constructionist Theory. The social constructionist movement, which has introduced far-reaching ramifications in relation to career development theory (Richardson, 1993; Savickas, 1993), is highly relevant to the development of a framework for integrative interventions. Cushman (1991) cogently summarized the social constructionist position with respect to psychological theory: "Humans cannot be studied outside of their lived context. . . . It is not possible to develop universal, transhistorical laws because humans are not separated from their culture and history: they are fundamentally and inextricably intertwined" (p. 207). In effect, the social constructionist movement is attempting to contextualize psychology within a social, historical, and political framework that seeks to understand how theory is constructed and employed (Cushman, 1991; Gergen, 1991).

One of the major research tools of the constructionist movement has been the use of narratives from those who are the objects of our inquiry. A narrative consists of an individual's own story that attempts to capture the richness and subjectivity that is inherent in human experience (Gergen, 1991; Ochberg, 1988). One criticism of traditional career development research that is informed by social constructionism is that our empirical paradigms set up an artificial perspective that tends to decontextualize career from its natural historical, political, and psychological settings (Young & Collin, 1992). A review of some of the narratives that have been published in recent years in the career realm reveals a context that embraces noncareer issues (e.g., Ochberg, 1988; Young & Collin, 1992). Thus, when clients and research participants are asked openly about their career lives, they tend to describe a context-rich experience wherein their career and noncareer experiences are closely interrelated.

Savickas (1993) argued that career counseling is undergoing a conceptual transformation as social constructionist and other postmodern ideas are incorporated in theory and practice. In relation to counseling practice, Savickas noted that "when the work role is no longer artificially isolated from other life roles, counselors view the distinction between personal and career counseling as a wall created by words" (p. 212). A similar view was proposed by Richardson (1993), who used a social constructionist analysis to propose a focus on the role of work in people's lives as opposed to the notion of career, which is viewed as containing a middle-class bias. In Richardson's analysis, a focus on work encourages an integrative view of human functioning that fosters greater sensitivity to the way in which various lines of development intersect. Carlsen (1988) also used a social constructionist argument in providing a means of integrating career and noncareer issues. In Carlsen's approach, clients are encouraged to make meaning of their lives in the career and noncareer domains via the use of autobiographical exercises, along with interviewing, counseling, and testing.

Systems Theories. As in social constructionist thought, systems theories provide an epistemological lens with which to view a given phenomenon. In general, a systems perspective refers to the interplay and interdependence of human behavior (Bowen, 1978). Typically, researchers have used the systems perspective to understand families in which "a change in one part of the system is followed by compensatory change in other parts of the system" (Bowen, 1978, p. 155).

Using the family systems literature, a number of authors have argued that career indecision may serve to maintain a family's equilibrium (e.g., Lopez & Andrews, 1987). Other relevant examinations of family systems and the workplace have been contributed by Ulrich and Dunne (1986) and Piotr-kowski (1979). These authors have developed cogent arguments detailing the degree and nature of interaction between family functioning and work life. Ulrich and Dunne described a number of family processes that function to inhibit career development. For example, in the process of designation, family members establish roles for their children that continue to be enacted in the career decision-making process and within the work setting. Both the Ulrich and Dunne and Piotrkowski volumes developed cogent cases for considering the reciprocal nature of work and family life.

A family systems perspective also has been adopted by Cochran and his colleagues (e.g., Chusid & Cochran, 1989; Zimmerman & Cochran, 1993) in their innovative conceptualization of work as a place wherein individuals enact family dramas. According to these authors, some family-of-origin strug-gles are thought to be recapitulated within the work site. In the Cochran line of work, as well as in the other theoretical perspectives cited herein, family and career issues are seen as interrelated, such that functioning within one domain will have a predictable, although not necessarily uniform, in-fluence on functioning in the other domain.

Problem-Focused Treatments. In recent years, those in the field of psychotherapy have witnessed the emergence of short-term models (see Wells & Giannetti, 1990). Although many differences exist among the various short-term approaches, one common theme among some of the models is their focus on specific client problem areas (e.g., Wells & Phelps, 1990). Adherents of the focused, or problem-based, treatments maintain that client issues can be conceived of as personal problems and that treatment provides a means for solving these problems (O'Hanlon & Weiner–Davis, 1989). The range of these problems varies depending on the client's personal history and current life experiences; however, work-related issues can certainly be considered a focus of brief intervention efforts (Lowman, 1993).

Although not emerging directly from the short-term psychotherapy perspectives, Lowman's (1993) recent contribution can be viewed as a problem-focused model. Lowman argued in favor of the development of psychotherapeutic interventions for work-related problems. Beginning with a description of how psychotherapists have generally ignored the workplace, Lowman offered a framework for the consideration of various work dysfunctions, such as work inhibition, patterns of undercommitment and overcommitment, and work-related anxiety and depression. Although Lowman's extensive literature review did not address many important aspects of career development (e.g., the role of life stages and gender issues in vocational behavior), his contribution provides a foundation for a more integrative perspective toward treatment.

Relational Models of Human Behavior. Emerging from such diverse areas as object relations theory (e.g., Fairbairn, 1952), self psychology (e.g., Kohut, 1977), feminist thought (e.g., Gilligan, 1982), and developmental theory (e.g., Bowlby, 1982) is a perspective that falls under the rubric of relational theory. Although differences exist among each of these specific theories, they are linked by a set of assumptions regarding the centrality of human relationships in development and behavior. In brief, proponents of the relational models maintain that the human striving for connectedness lies at the core of human motivation, development, and personality expression. (For more extensive summaries of this literature, see Jordan, Kaplan, Miller, Stiver, & Surrey, 1991; Josselson, 1992; Mitchell, 1988.)

Recent efforts by theorists to cast a relational perspective on selected aspects of vocational behavior have attempted to do so via theoretical considerations (e.g., Blustein, 1994; Forrest & Mikolaitis, 1986) and empirical research (Blustein et al., 1991; Hazan & Shaver, 1990). Researchers have used relational models, such as attachment theory (e.g., Bowlby, 1982) and self psychology (Kohut, 1977), to identify those factors that foster progress in career decision making (e.g., Blustein et al., 1991) and that promote vocational adjustment (e.g., job satisfaction; Hazan & Shaver, 1990).

The amount of research and theory addressing the overlap between relational models and career behavior is still quite modest; however, this literature suggests that strivings for connectedness seem related to career experiences. When we consider the relational perspective in conjunction with the career development literature, it seems plausible that counseling approaches can be designed that integrate attention to our mutual needs for achievement and relatedness.

Conclusion. As the preceding review indicates, the social construction-ist, systems, and relational models each underscore the centrality of selected contextual features in human experience. With their focus on these contextual factors, these perspectives offer the promise of more broad-reaching intervention theories and models. Oné potential liability of these perspectives, however, is that counselors may overlook the validity of career concerns, which often form the core of presenting problems (Lucas, 1992), in an effort to find a broader or deeper meaning for a given issue. For example, a systemic-oriented counselor may possibly view a career issue simply as a manifestation of family dynamics when the actual etiology of the client's problem may be an abusive supervisor or incongruent career choice. However, this concern can be mitigated by the development of intervention models that clearly validate career concerns and by the training of counselors to appreciate the multiple meanings and complexity of presenting issues.

The problem-focused approaches offer possibilities for both more integrative and more discrete treatments than previously available. On the integrative side, contributions such as the book by Lowman (1993) present work-related problems at the forefront of consideration for psychological intervention; this emphasis highlights the centrality of work in human behavior. Alternatively, the problem-focused treatments may encourage the counselor's attention to circumscribed domains of a client's presenting issues; this approach may lead the counselor to the sort of distinct treatments of career and noncareer issues that currently exist for many clients. These caveats notwithstanding, the theoretical innovations described in this section have the potential for informing the design of interventions that address both career and noncareer domains.

New Directions in Counselor Judgment

Although the theoretical and contextual issues reviewed thus far provide an emerging conceptual framework for integrative interventions, recent observations of counselor bias against career counseling suggest some potential obstacles to the achievement of this goal. In a study by Spengler, Blustein, and Strohmer (1990), 165 counseling psychologists were provided with one of four clinical vignettes, each of which described the same client problem with career dissatisfaction. Three of these vignettes also included coexisting problems in the noncareer domain, ranging from mild insomnia to a severe panic attack. The respondents who had indicated a stronger preference for working with noncareer rather than career problems were less likely to recognize, assess, or treat the client's dissatisfaction, even when the two problems were rated as similar in clinical severity.

Results of the few studies on counselor judgments with respect to career and noncareer issues (e.g., Melnick, 1975; Spengler et al., 1990) suggest that the counselor's decision to provide integrative counseling may be challenged by his or her relative interests in noncareer and career counseling. An informative perspective on counselor judgment is found in the social cognition literature (e.g., Nisbett & Ross, 1980); according to this work, the perceived saliency or vividness of career and noncareer issues may be influenced by a variety of other characteristics, such as counselors' preferences, desires, motives, and values. We recognize that the assessment of multiple client problems and the integration of interventions involve cognitive operations that may be inherently difficult (Spengler, Strohmer, Dixon, & Shivy, in press). However, even when counselors choose to provide integrated interventions, subtle and overt biases against career issues may interfere with their achieving this goal.

One clear implication of the work on counselor judgments is the need for more extensive research to further our understanding of how counselor biases are formed and how they can best be treated. A second implication is the need for further efforts by researchers to define ways for counselors to value the career-oriented experiences of their clients and to relate these experiences in a meaningful way to other aspects of psychological functioning. Thus, as the theoretical framework guiding interventions expands to embrace the career domain, a similar expansion is needed in our understanding of how counselors can work effectively with career and noncareer issues. As such, one useful initiative would be a conceptual framework for counselors who wish to maintain sensitivity to both career and noncareer issues. Although such a framework would not necessarily eliminate all sources of cognitive and attitudinal biases, it could provide a means for counselors to consider career and noncareer issues as interrelated aspects of their clients' experiences.

Conclusion

This review of the various new theoretical advances in conjunction with the rapid changes in the landscape of career development reveals a number of converging trends. First, it seems likely that the challenges of a rapidly shifting labor market will continue to influence various aspects of individuals' functioning in both career and noncareer domains. Second, the context-rich views of the social constructionist, systems, problem-solving, and relationally oriented models provide a theoretical framework for a view of career development that does not make arbitrary distinctions among domains of functioning. When considering these trends in relation to the growing knowledge base about counselor judgment biases, it seems clear that we need to move beyond comparisons of treatment modalities to the development of an intervention framework that encompasses the full texture of life experiences that clients present.

TOWARD A DOMAIN-SENSITIVE APPROACH
TO INTERVENTION

The picture that emerges from the diverse literature reviewed thus far points to a growing awareness of meaningful interactions between behavior in the career and noncareer domains. The awareness of such predictable relationships between the domains is further enhanced by the literature that has identified considerable overlap between treatment methods, scope of intervention, and conceptual assumptions, particularly among some of the new theoretical perspectives. To address the need for an intervention approach that attends effectively to both career and noncareer domains, we offer a domain-sensitive approach to counseling. In this section, we identify the general characteristics of this approach and specific implications for counselors, clients, and the therapeutic relationship.

Characteristics of a Domain-Sensitive Approach

A domain-sensitive approach refers to a way of intervening with clients such that the full array of human experiences is encompassed. The goals of such an intervention are to improve adjustment and facilitate developmental progress in both the career and noncareer domains. The term *domain* pertains to the scope of the client's psychological experiences, encompassing both career and noncareer settings. By following *domain* with the term *sensitive*, we are attempting to capture counselors' inherent openness, empathy, and interest with respect to both the career and noncareer domains and their ability to shift between these content domains effectively. In effect, a domain-sensitive approach is characterized by the counselor's concerted interest in and awareness of all possible ramifications of a client's psychological experience and its behavioral expression. In this approach, the counselor clearly values the client's experiences in both the career and noncareer domains. The counselor bases a decision about where to intervene on informed judgments about where the problem originated and where it is most accessible for intervention.

Although the specific theoretical orientation and goals of counseling naturally will vary depending on the client and counselor, one defining feature of a domain-sensitive approach is the emphasis on the role of the context, broadly conceived. *Context* refers to "that group of settings that influence developmental progress, encompassing contemporary and distal familial, social, and economic circumstances" (Blustein, 1994, p. 140). In our view, interventions that are context-rich naturally demand a broad scope of attention that fosters an integration across the career and noncareer domains.

Another defining characteristic of a domain-sensitive approach is the counselor's freedom to move between the career and noncareer domains, thereby providing integrative treatments, when such interventions are indicated. Thus, counselors are able to intervene in both domains and to use the interrelationship between these domains as a means of further understanding and helping a client. A domain-sensitive approach, however, does not mean that all career counseling cases would be automatically converted to in-depth psychotherapy cases. For example, a domain-sensitive counselor who determines that a client's problems are circumscribed within the career domain would naturally deliver an equally delineated intervention (cf. Spokane, 1991). The underlying asset of a domain-sensitive approach is that interventions are not based on discrete or arbitrary distinctions between treatment modalities but are determined by the unique attributes of each client's history and presenting problem.

Counselor's Experience.   Prior to our describing the specific counselor characteristics of a domain-sensitive approach, we should state that all treatment decisions, including those to expand or to narrow the domain of intervention, need to be made in conjunction with the client. Given a client's commitment to an integrative intervention, the counselor can then engage in a systematic assessment of the client's problem status, with an attempt to understand how both contextual and psychological factors have influenced the client's development.

If a given case conceptualization suggests an integrative focus, one of the counselor's initial steps is to understand parallels and distinctions between client behavior in the career and noncareer domains. For each client, the differences and similarities between her or his behavior in the various domains of life experience are likely to be unique; therefore, the determination of the individual meaning of these patterns of behavior is an important part of any psychological intervention. For example, if an individual wishes to shift careers primarily due to interpersonal conflict at work, the revelation of a conflictual history with parents and other authority figures may become a central element in the counseling process. When the desire for a career shift, however, is not confounded by interpersonal conflict (Lowman, 1993) or reenactments of family dramas (Chusid & Cochran, 1989) or the like, a more circumscribed intervention is indicated. Thus, for those counselors trained to intervene in both career and noncareer domains, a domain-sensitive approach may offer a level of flexibility with respect to their work, a flexibility that may enhance their creativity while also benefiting their clients.

Client's Experience. In general, a domain-sensitive approach offers clients a means of validating their various experiences in both the career and noncareer domains. Thus, rather than learning about their career and noncareer issues through circumscribed conceptual perspectives or different counseling experiences, clients have a valuable opportunity to integrate their life experiences in a manner that can promote important gains. In a domain-sensitive approach, clients can learn about the meaning or consequences of their behavior in the domain that is more open to exploration and emotional depth. Thus, if a client is defending against psychological distress relating to a given issue within the career domain, similar manifestations may be observed in a noncareer domain, thereby offering the counselor an opportunity for intervention. Then, a sensitive shift to other domains where this issue is also manifested can be initiated.

Another characteristic of a domain-sensitive approach for clients is the development of new coping strategies and behaviors in the domain that is most supportive of such changes. Once a client has received some positive consequences from such initiatives, he or she may possibly be able to apply these new behaviors to the domain that represents the greater challenge. For example, a client whose career indecision is related to fears of commitment may find it somewhat easier to begin implementing important new decisions in the social realm; success in this area can enhance her or his confidence in facing the complex tasks of career decision making. Similarly, for a client who is struggling with self-esteem issues in one domain, the counselor's helping the client to internalize his or her accomplishments in another domain may help to solidify a fragile sense of self. Therefore, a domain-sensitive approach opens up a wider range of life experiences for a client and thereby enhances the growth-promoting properties of all interventions.

The Counselor–Client Relationship Within a Domain-Sensitive Approach

The potential effects of the integration of career and noncareer interventions on the counselor–client relationship requires careful consideration, particularly given the importance of the therapeutic alliance in psychological treatments in general (Horvath & Symonds, 1991). Perhaps the thorniest issue involves the effect of the introduction of vocational appraisal into an integrative treatment (cf. Betz & Corning, 1993). Vocational appraisal, like a number of aspects of career counseling, involves relatively active modes of intervention. For those counselors who wish to employ interventions based on careful examination of the therapeutic relationship (e.g., transference), the idea of using tests or of suggesting specific career-exploration activities may seem undesirable. However, among those perspectives that rely on psychodynamic interpretation and learning directly from the therapeutic relationship, a number of perspectives have been described wherein a more active mode of intervention is indicated (e.g., Wachtel, 1993). In short-term, action-oriented psychodynamic and nonpsychodynamic approaches, the use of more active career interventions may be employed, providing that the shifts within the therapeutic relationship are carefully discussed and understood. In cases for which vocational assessment is indicated, counselors need to consider how such an active intervention will fit in with their overall approach with a particular client and their sense of the evolving alliance.

Yet many cases that call for integrative treatment may not require the use of tests or other forms of active career intervention. In such cases, the exploration of the therapeutic relationship (or transference, depending on one's theoretical orientation) may continue to unfold whether the content focuses on career or on noncareer issues. We acknowledge that there may be other times when the best decision may be the postponement of an integrative approach or the referral of the client to a colleague who can offer a particular intervention conjointly. For example, in cases in which there is clear or imminent danger (e.g., suicide or assaultive risk) or in which a client is actively abusing psychoactive substances, the counselor first needs to focus on reducing the risk situation. In addition, for those counselors without skills in both domains of treatment, appropriate referrals are indicated.

With the domain-sensitive approach, we also acknowledge that counselors broach each situation with inherent cognitive and emotional issues that affect judgments and treatment decisions. This approach is based on the fact that a counseling relationship consists of two individuals, each of whom contributes a particular history and set of beliefs and values that affect the course of treatment. Thus, the literature on counselor judgment would seem to be a critical factor in the determination of the nature of counselor biases (e.g., Spengler et al., 1993). Similarly, counselors need to be aware of their own issues relating to work and career. In dignifying the importance of career in human experience, we believe that counselor feelings (e.g., countertransference) relating to work as well as to relationships and family issues can be evoked. Because counselors have their own histories in the career domain, it is conceivable that client issues may engender envy, competition, admiration, and other such feelings that can influence the course of a counseling relationship.

Conclusion

In sum, with a domain-sensitive approach we are not attempting to replace existing theories of counseling and psychotherapy or seeking to address questions regarding the timing of career and noncareer interventions. Instead, through this approach counselors can become sensitized to the complexities and subtle nuances of intervention, a sensitivity that ideally can help clients develop in their various life roles.

IMPLICATIONS FOR FUTURE RESEARCH

Although the amount of literature devoted to the career counseling–psychotherapy issue has grown in recent years, little empirical research, with some notable exceptions (e.g., Phillips et al., 1988; Spengler et al., 1990), has been conducted in this area. Based on this review, a number of promising research directions can be identified. One such direction is the need for psychologists to understand more about counseling processes (cf. Hackett, 1993; Hill & Corbett, 1993). For example, the effects of who (i.e., counselor or client) shifts the content domain and when this shift occurs would be a useful avenue of inquiry in explicating integrative counseling interventions. Also, the effect of vocational appraisal or other active career interventions on various aspects of the therapeutic relationship and on transference represents a fruitful area of inquiry. If the factors that promote progress in career intervention are essentially similar to those processes that promote growth in psychotherapy, the distinctions between these areas may become less critical in subsequent theory development and research efforts.

Another direction that merits inquiry involves counselor judgment. The existing literature suggests the existence of some counselor biases against career issues (e.g., Spengler et al., 1990). For example, is it possible that the existence of counselor biases in favor of noncareer issues sends a subtle message to clients that detracts from the validity of their career concerns? Questions such as this can be addressed through the use of the social cognition and judgmental heuristics literatures (Nisbett & Ross, 1980) in addition to the use of extensive process research paradigms that have been developed in recent years (e.g., Hill & O'Grady, 1985).

Our review also suggests a host of research questions with regard to the explication of the interrelationships between vocational functioning and psychological functioning. Thus, research on the mutual linkages between family systems and career development, which is emerging as an important area of inquiry, may yield informative results. In addition, further research is needed on the coexistence of career and noncareer issues from an epidemiological perspective.

Our review of the reciprocal influence of treatment on career and noncareer domains has revealed a relatively circumscribed literature. It is clear that additional research is needed in this area, particularly investigations that integrate process and outcome elements simultaneously. In addition, a context-rich perspective offers important suggestions for counselors and researchers in their attending carefully to the broader social, historical, political, and cultural aspects of clients and of research questions (Gergen, 1991).

Finally, our review suggests that theoretical developments in the intervention domain need to encompass a more integrative focus. In fact, the general insulation that exists in theory development, particularly in the noncareer domain, is disconcerting. That work and career issues are central to human functioning is increasingly apparent. We hope that discussions such as this and others (e.g., Blustein, 1987; Hackett, 1993) will underscore the theory development efforts that are needed in order for counselors to serve clients in an increasingly complicated environment.

IMPLICATIONS FOR TRAINING

The approach that has emerged from our review suggests that counselors ought to be prepared to work with clients across the array of relevant domains, including career and noncareer contexts. Prior to our detailing suggestions for training and supervision, we must note that competence in career counseling and psychotherapy requires skills in both domains (cf. Crites, 1981; Niles & Pate, 1989). Therefore, we propose that counselors and psychologists who endeavor to integrate these domains be trained in a comprehensive fashion that includes knowledge in personality theory, developmental psychology, assessment, counseling theory and research, and career development theory, as well as in occupational, sociological, and organizational psychology and related areas. Moreover, we believe that supervised experience in delivering career and noncareer services is necessary. Thus, for those psychotherapists interested in career intervention, it is critical that they employ the rich knowledge base developed by vocational psychologists (cf. Hackett, 1993). Similarly, for those career counselors who wish to broaden their interventions into the noncareer domain, an equally critical task for them is the development of skills and knowledge in psychotherapy.

More specific recommendations can be culled from the work of Niles and Pate (1989), who urged that counselor educators and supervisors provide students with integrative training experiences. Niles and Pate argued on behalf of systematic training in both the career and noncareer domains of intervention, an argument consistent with our position. Moreover, they recommended that faculty offer practica experiences that combine these domains. To integrate these suggestions with the literature reviewed herein, we suggest that educators encourage domain-sensitive approaches to treatment by offering practica and courses that integrate career and noncareer issues in a systematic fashion. In relation to supervision, we encourage a similar sort of synthesis, in which treatment planning and case conceptualization encompass the career and noncareer domains, as indicated by the client's concerns. Furthermore, we believe that educators should address trainee biases about career and noncareer issues early in supervision so that such issues can be discussed in a safe and supportive learning environment. Finally, one of the most important yet overlooked aspects of the training of counselors in career intervention has to do with *how* the material is presented to students and trainees. We propose that educators and supervisors share their excitement about career development with their students by emphasizing the highly personal nature of career issues (Betz & Corning, 1993).

CONCLUSION

In this chapter, we have attempted to provide a focused review of the complex relationships between career counseling and psychotherapy. In addition to reviewing the existing literature, we identified relevant new directions emanating from advances in theory development and empirical research. This emerging literature provided a compelling rationale for the consideration of integrative interventions for clients who present with collateral concerns in both the career and noncareer domains. However, as others have suggested (e.g., Hackett, 1993; Spokane, 1991), the delivery of integrative interventions should not function to reduce the importance of the critical knowledge base of vocational psychology or of the necessity of skills in career counseling. In fact, our interpretation of the shifting context in the social and occupational environment suggests that career issues will become increasingly more prevalent in the lives of most individuals in our society. To address the needs of clients whose problems will not fall into neat categories of career or noncareer issues, we proposed a domain-sensitive approach through which client experiences across contexts are dignified. Our hope is that the literature reviewed herein will foster the needed practice, research, and training efforts necessary for a fully integrated knowledge base about interpersonal relationships and work, the two major domains of contemporary human experience.

ACKNOWLEDGMENTS

We would like to express our gratitude to Belkeis Alawadi, Sharon Bowman, Lawrence Gerstein, Debra A. Noumair, and Susan D. Phillips for their helpful comments on an earlier draft of this chapter.

REFERENCES

Adler, A. (1956). *The individual psychology of Alfred Adler* (H. L. Ansbacher & R. R. Ansbacher, Eds.). New York: Basic Books.

Barkham, M., & Shapiro, D. A. (1990). Brief psychotherapeutic interventions for job-related distress: A pilot study of prescriptive and exploratory therapy. *Counselling Psychology Quarterly, 3,* 133–147.

Betz, N. E., & Corning, A. F. (1993). The inseparability of "career" and "personal" counseling. *Career Development Quarterly, 42,* 137–142.

Betz, N. E., & Fitzgerald, L. F. (1987). *The career psychology of women.* Orlando, FL: Academic Press.

Black, B. J. (1988). *Work and mental health: Transitions to employment.* Baltimore: Johns Hopkins University Press.

Blustein, D. L. (1987). Integrating career counseling and psychotherapy: A comprehensive treatment strategy. *Psychotherapy, 24,* 794–799.

Blustein, D. L. (1990). An eclectic definition of psychotherapy: A developmental contextual view. In J. K. Zeig & W. M. Munion (Eds.), *What is psychotherapy: Contemporary perspectives* (pp. 244–248). San Francisco: Jossey–Bass.

Blustein, D. L. (1994). "Who am I?": The question of self and identity in career development. In M. L. Savickas & R. W. Lent (Eds.), *Convergence in career development theories: Implications for science and practice* (pp. 139–154). Palo Alto, CA: Consulting Psychologists Press.

Blustein, D. L., Devenis, L. E., & Kidney, B. A. (1989). Relationship between the identity formation process and career development. *Journal of Counseling Psychology, 36,* 196–202.

Blustein, D. L., Walbridge, M. M., Friedlander, M. L., & Palladino, D. E. (1991). Contributions of psychological separation and parental attachment to the career development process. *Journal of Counseling Psychology, 38,* 39–50.

Bordin, E. S. (1990). Psychodynamic models of career choice and satisfaction. In D. Brown & L. Brooks (Eds.), *Career choice and development: Applying contemporary theories to practice* (2nd ed., pp. 102–144). San Francisco: Jossey–Bass.

Bordin, E. S., Nachmann, B., & Segal, S. J. (1963). An articulated framework for vocational development. *Journal of Counseling Psychology, 10,* 107–116.

Bowen, M. (1978). *Family therapy in clinical practice.* New York: Aronson.

Bowlby, J. (1982). *Attachment and loss: Vol. 1. Attachment* (2nd ed.). New York: Basic Books.

Brown, D., & Brooks, L. (1991). *Career counseling techniques.* Boston: Allyn & Bacon.

Campbell, D. P. (1965). *The results of counseling: Twenty-five years later.* Philadelphia: Saunders.

Campbell, R. E., & Cellini, J. V. (1981). A diagnostic taxonomy of adult career problems. *Journal of Vocational Behavior, 19,* 175–190.

Carlsen, M. B. (1988). *Meaning making: Therapeutic processes in adult development.* New York: Norton.

Carter, R. T., & Cook, D. A. (1992). A culturally relevant perspective for understanding the career paths of visible racial/ethnic group people. In H. D. Lea & Z. B. Leibowitz (Eds.), *Adult career development* (pp. 192–217). Alexandria, VA: National Career Development Association.

Chusid, H., & Cochran, L. (1989). Meaning of career change from the perspective of family roles and dramas. *Journal of Counseling Psychology, 36,* 34–41.

Clarke, K. M., & Greenberg, L. S. (1986). Differential effects of the Gestalt two-chair intervention and problem-solving in resolving decisional conflict. *Journal of Counseling Psychology, 33,* 11–15.

Conklin, R. C. (1985). Career counselling agoraphobic clients. *Canadian Counsellor, 19,* 190–198.

Corbishley, M. A., & Yost, E. B. (1989). Psychological aspects of career counseling. *Journal of Career Development, 16,* 43–51.

Crites, J. (1981). *Career counseling.* New York: McGraw–Hill.

Cushman, P. (1991). Ideology obscured: Political uses of the self in Daniel Stern's infant. *American Psychologist, 46,* 206–219.

Cytrynbaum, S., & Crites, J. O. (1989). The utility of adult development theory in understanding career adjustment process. In M. B. Arthur, D. T. Hall, & B. S. Lawrence (Eds.), *Handbook of career theory* (pp. 66–88). New York: Cambridge University Press.

Davidson, S. L., & Gilbert, L. A. (1993). Career counseling is a personal matter. *Career Development Quarterly, 42*, 149–153.

Dorn, F. J. (1988). Utilizing social influence in career counseling: A case study. *Career Development Quarterly, 36*, 269–280.

Dorn, F. J. (1992). Occupational wellness: The integration of career identity and personal identity. *Journal of Counseling and Development, 71*, 176–178.

Elkins, I., Shea, M. T., Watkins, J. T., Imber, S. D., Sotsky, S. M., Collins, J. F., Glass, D. R., Pilkonis, P. A., Leber, W. R., Docherty, J. P., Fiester, S. J., & Parloff, M. B. (1989). National Institute of Mental Health Treatment of Depression Collaborative Research Program: General effectiveness of treatments. *Archives of General Psychiatry, 46*, 971–982.

Elliot, R. (1992). Conceptual analysis of Lambert, Ogles, and Master's conceptual scheme for outcome assessment. *Journal of Counseling and Development, 70*, 535–537.

Erikson, E. H. (1963). *Childhood and society* (2nd ed.). New York: Norton.

Fairbairn, W. R. D. (1952). *An object relations theory to the personality.* NY: Basic Books.

Firth, J., & Shapiro, D. A. (1986). An evaluation of psychotherapy for job-related distress. *Journal of Occupational Psychology, 59*, 11–119.

Firth–Cozens, J. (1992). The role of early family experiences in the perception of organizational stress: Fusing clinical and organizational perspectives. *Journal of Occupational and Organizational Psychology, 65*, 61–75.

Firth–Cozens, J., & Hardy, G. E. (1992). Occupational stress, clinical treatment and changes in job perceptions. *Journal of Occupational and Organizational Psychology, 65*, 81–88.

Fitzgerald, L. F., & Weitzman, L. M. (1992). Women's career development: Theory and practice from a feminist perspective. In H. D. Lea & Z. B. Leibowitz (Eds.), *Adult career development* (pp. 124–160). Alexandria, VA: National Career Development Association.

Forrest, L. & Mikolaitis, N. (1986). The relationship component of identity: An expansion of career development theory. *Career Development Quarterly, 35*, 76–88.

Frank, E., Kupfer, D. J., & Perel, J. M. (1989). Early recurrence in unipolar depression. *Archives of General Psychiatry, 46*, 397–400.

Frank, J. D. (1982). Therapeutic components shared by all psychotherapies. In J. H. Harvey & M. M. Parks (Eds.), *Psychotherapy research and behavior change* (pp. 5–37). Washington, DC: American Psychological Association.

Freud, S. (1930). *Civilization and its discontents.* London: Hogarth.

Fuller, F., & Hill, C. E. (1985). Counselor and helpee perceptions of counselors' intentions in relation to outcome in a single counseling session. *Journal of Counseling Psychology, 32*, 329–338.

Galassi, J. P., Crace, R. K., Martin, G. A., James, R. M., Jr., & Wallace, R. L. (1992). Client preferences and anticipations in career counseling: A preliminary investigation. *Journal of Counseling Psychology, 39*, 46–55.

Gelatt, H. B. (1989). Positive uncertainty: A conceptual framework for counseling. *Journal of Counseling Psychology, 36*, 252–256.

Gergen, K. J. (1991). *The saturated self: Dilemmas of identity in contemporary life.* NY: Basic Books.

Gilligan, C. (1982). *In a different voice.* Cambridge, MA: Harvard University Press.

Gold, P. B., Kivlighan, D. M., Jr., Kerr, A. E., & Kramer, L. A. (1993). The structure of students' perceptions of impactful, helpful events in career exploration classes. *Journal of Career Assessment, 1*, 145–161.

Hackett, G. (1993). Career counseling and psychotherapy: False dichotomies and recommended remedies. *Journal of Career Assessment, 1*, 105–117.

Hampl, S. P. (1990, August). *Adult career counseling is not a trivial activity.* Paper presented at the meeting of the American Psychological Association, Boston, MA.

Haverkamp, B. E., & Moore, D. (1993). The career–personal dichotomy: Perceptual reality, practical illusion and workplace integration. *Career Development Quarterly, 42*, 154–160.

Hazan, C., & Shaver, P. R. (1990). Love and work: An attachment–theoretical perspective. *Journal of Personality and Social Psychology, 59*, 270–280.

Heppner, M. J., & Hendricks, F. (in press). A process and outcome study examining career indecision and indecisiveness. *Journal of Counseling and Development.*

Herr, E. L. (1989). Career development and mental health. *Journal of Career Development, 16*, 5–18.

Herr, E. L. (1990). Employment counseling in a global economy. *Journal of Employment Counseling, 27*, 147–159.

Hill, C. E., & Corbett, M. (1993). A perspective on the history of process and outcome research in counseling psychology. *Journal of Counseling Psychology, 40*, 3–27.

Hill, C. E., & O'Grady, K. E. (1985). List of therapist intentions illustrated in a case study and with therapists of varying theoretical orientations. *Journal of Counseling Psychology, 32*, 3–22.

Holland, J. L. (1985). *Making vocational choices: A theory of vocational personalities and work environments* (2nd ed.). Englewood Cliffs, NJ: Prentice–Hall.

Holland, J. L., Magoon, T. M., & Spokane, A. R. (1981). Counseling psychology: Career interventions, research, and theory. *Annual Review of Psychology, 32*, 279–305.

Horvath, A. O., & Greenberg, L. S. (1986). The development of the Working Alliance Inventory. In L. S. Greenberg & W. M. Pinsof (Eds.), *The psychotherapeutic process: A research handbook* (pp. 529–556). New York: Guilford.

Horvath, A. O., & Symonds, B. D. (1991). Relation between working alliance and outcome in psychotherapy: A meta-analysis. *Journal of Counseling Psychology, 38*, 139–149.

Jepsen, D. A. (1990). Developmental career counseling. In W. B. Walsh & S. H. Osipow (Eds.), *Career counseling: Contemporary topics in vocational psychology* (pp. 117–157). Hillsdale, NJ: Lawrence Erlbaum Associates.

Jordan, J. V., Kaplan, A. G., Miller, J. B., Stiver, I. P., & Surrey, J. L. (1991). *Women's growth in connection: Writings from the Stone Center.* New York: Guilford.

Josselson, R. (1992). *The space between us: Exploring the dimensions of human relationships.* San Francisco: Jossey–Bass.

Kirschner, T., Hoffman, M. A., & Hill, C. E. (1994). A case study of the process and outcome of career counseling. *Journal of Counseling Psychology.*

Kivlighan, D. M., Jr., Johnson, B., & Fretz, B. (1987). Participants' perception of change mechanisms in career counseling groups: The role of emotional components in career problem solving. *Journal of Career Development, 14*, 35 44.

Kohut, H. (1977). *The restoration of the self.* New York: International Universities Press.

Krumboltz, J. D. (1979). A social learning theory of career decision making. In A. M. Mitchell, G. B. Jones, & J. D. Krumboltz (Eds.), *Social learning and career decision making* (pp. 19–49). Cranston, RI: Carroll.

Krumboltz, J. D. (1993). Integrating career and personal counseling. *Career Development Quarterly, 42*, 143–148.

Lambert, M. J., Ogles, B. M., & Masters, K. S. (1992). Choosing outcome assessment devices: An organizational and conceptual theme. *Journal of Counseling and Development, 70*, 527–532.

Lambert, M. J., Shapiro, D. A., & Bergin, A. E. (1986). The effectiveness of psychotherapy. In S. L. Garfield & A. E. Bergin (Eds.), *Handbook of psychotherapy and behavior change* (3rd ed., pp. 157–212). NY: Wiley.

Leiberman, M. A., Yalom, I. D., & Miles, M. B. (1973). *Encounter groups: First facts.* New York: Basic Books.

Lofquist, L. H., & Dawis, R. V. (1984). Research on work adjustment and satisfaction: Implications for career counseling. In S. D. Brown & R. W. Lent (Eds.), *Handbook of counseling psychology* (pp. 216–237). New York: Wiley.

Lofquist, L. H., & Dawis, R. V. (1991). *Essentials of person–environment correspondence counseling.* Minneapolis: University of Minnesota Press.

Lopez, F. G. (1989). Current family dynamics, trait anxiety, and academic adjustment: Test of a family-based model of vocational identity. *Journal of Vocational Behavior, 35,* 76–87.

Lopez, F. G., & Andrews, S. (1987). Career indecision: A family systems perspective. *Journal of Counseling and Development, 65,* 304–307.

Lowman, R. L. (1993). *Counseling and psychotherapy of work dysfunctions.* Washington, DC: American Psychological Association.

Lucas, M. S. (1992). Problems expressed by career and noncareer help seekers: A comparison. *Journal of Counseling and Development, 70,* 417–420.

Lucas, M. S., & Epperson, D. L. (1988). Personality types in vocationally undecided students. *Journal of College Student Development, 29,* 460–466.

Mahoney, M. J. (1991). *Human change processes: The scientific foundations of psychotherapy.* New York: Basic Books.

Manuele–Adkins, C. (1992). Career counseling is personal counseling. *Career Development Quarterly, 40,* 313–323.

Marmar, L. R. (1990). Psychotherapy process research: Progress, dilemmas, and future directions. *Journal of Consulting and Clinical Psychology, 58,* 265–272.

Marshall, R., & Tucker, M. (1992). *Thinking for a living: Education and the wealth of nations.* New York: Basic Books.

Massimo, J. L., & Shore, M. F. (1963). The effectiveness of a comprehensive vocationally oriented psychotherapeutic program for adolescent delinquent boys. *American Journal of Orthopsychiatry, 33,* 634–642.

Meichenbaum, D. (1977). *Cognitive-behavior modification.* New York: Plenum.

Melnick, R. R. (1975) Counseling responses as a function of problem presentation and problem type. *Journal of Counseling Psychology, 22,* 108–112.

Mintz, J., Mintz, L. I., Arruda, J. A., & Hwang, S. S. (1992). Treatments of depression and the functional capacity to work. *Archives of General Psychiatry, 49,* 761–768.

Mitchell, S. A. (1988). *Relational concepts in psychoanalysis.* Cambridge, MA: Harvard University Press.

Neff, W. S. (1985). *Work and human behavior* (3rd ed.). New York: Atherton.

Niles, S. G., & Pate, R. N. (1989). Competency and training issues related to the integration of career counseling and mental health counseling. *Journal of Career Development, 16,* 63–72.

Nisbett, R., & Ross, L. (1980). *Human inference: Strategies and shortcomings of human judgment.* Englewood Cliffs, NJ: Prentice–Hall.

Ochberg, R. L. (1988). Life stories and the psychosocial construction of careers. *Journal of Personality, 56,* 173–204.

O'Hanlon, W. H., & Weiner–Davis, M. (1989). *In search of solutions: A new direction in psychotherapy.* New York: Norton.

Oliver, L. W. (1979). Outcome measurement in career counseling research. *Journal of Counseling Psychology, 26,* 217–226.

Oliver, L. W., & Spokane, A. R. (1988). Career intervention outcome: What contributes to client gain. *Journal of Counseling Psychology, 35,* 447–463.

O'Neil, J. M., & Fishman, D. M. (1992). Adult men's career transitions and gender-role themes. In H. D. Lea & Z. B. Leibowitz (Eds.), *Adult career development* (pp. 161–191). Alexandria, VA: National Career Development Association.

O'Neil, J. M., Fishman, D. M., & Kinsella–Shaw, M. (1987). Dual-career couples' career transitions and normative dilemmas: A preliminary assessment model. *The Counseling Psychologist, 15,* 50–95.

Osipow, S. H. (1979). Occupational mental health: Another role for counseling psychologists. *The Counseling Psychologist, 8,* 65–70.

Osipow, S. H., & Fitzgerald, L. F. (1993). Unemployment and mental health: A neglected relationship. *Applied and Preventive Psychology, 2,* 59–63.

Phillips, S. D., Friedlander, M. L., Kost, P. P., Specterman, R. V., & Robbins, E. S. (1988). Personal versus vocational focus in career counseling: A retrospective outcome study. *Journal of Counseling and Development, 67,* 169–173.

Pinkerton, R. S., Etzel, E. F., Rockwell, K., Talley, J. E., & Moorman, J. C. (1990). Psychotherapy and career counseling: Toward an integration for use with college students. *Journal of American College Health, 39,* 129–136.

Piotrkowski, C. S. (1979). *Work and the family system: A naturalistic study of working-class and lower middle-class families.* New York: The Free Press.

Rehm, L. P., Kaslow, N. J., & Rabin, A. S. (1987). Cognitive and behavioral targets in a self-control therapy program for depression. *Journal of Consulting and Clinical Psychology, 55,* 60–67.

Reich, R. B. (1991). *The work of nations.* New York: Vintage Books.

Richardson, M. S. (1993). Work in people's lives. *Journal of Counseling Psychology, 40,* 425–433.

Richman, D. R. (1988). Cognitive psychotherapy through the career cycle. In W. Dryden & P. Trower (Eds.), *Developments in cognitive psychotherapy* (pp. 190–217). London: Sage.

Robbins, S. B., & Tucker, K. R., Jr. (1986). Relation of goal instability to self-directed and interactional career counseling workshops. *Journal of Counseling Psychology, 33,* 346–355.

Rounds, J. B., & Tracey, T. J. (1990). From trait-and-factor to person–environment fit counseling: Theory and process. In W. B. Walsh & S. H. Osipow (Eds.), *Career counseling: Contemporary topics in vocational psychology* (pp. 1–44). Hillsdale, NJ: Lawrence Erlbaum Associates.

Savickas, M. L. (1991). The meaning of work and love: Career issues and interventions. *Career Development Quarterly, 39,* 315–324.

Savickas, M. L. (1993). Career counseling in the postmodern era. *Journal of Cognitive Psychotherapy: An International Quarterly, 7,* 205–215.

Shore, M. F., & Massimo, J. L. (1973). After ten years: A follow-up study of comprehensive vocationally oriented psychotherapy. *American Journal of Orthopsychiatry, 43,* 128–132.

Smith, E. J. (1983). Issues in racial minorities' career behavior. In W. B. Walsh & S. H. Osipow (Eds.), *Handbook of vocational psychology* (Vol. 1, pp. 161–222). Hillsdale, NJ: Lawrence Erlbaum Associates.

Spengler, P. M., Blustein, D. L., & Strohmer, D. C. (1990). Diagnostic and treatment overshadowing of vocational problems by personal problems. *Journal of Counseling Psychology, 37,* 372–381.

Spengler, P. M., Strohmer, D. C., Dixon, D. N., & Shivy, V. C. (in press). A scientist-professional model of psychological assessment: Implications for training and practice. *The Counseling Psychologist.*

Spokane, A. R. (1989). Are there psychological and mental health consequences of difficult career decisions?: A reaction to Herr. *Journal of Career Development, 16,* 19–24.

Spokane, A. R. (1991). *Career intervention.* Englewood Cliffs, NJ: Prentice–Hall.

Spokane, A. R. (1992). Career intervention and counseling theory for adults: Toward a consensus model. In H. D. Lea & Z. B. Leibowitz (Eds.), *Adult career development* (pp. 42–54). Alexandria, VA: National Career Development Association.

Spokane, A. R., Fretz, B. R., Hoffman, M. A., Nagel, D., Davison, R., & Jaschik, M. (1991, April). *Progress toward a clinical science of career intervention.* Paper presented at the meeting of the American Educational Research Association, Chicago, IL.

Spokane, A. R., Fretz, B. R., Hoffman, M. A., Nagel, D., Davison, R., & Jaschik, M. (1993). Forty cases: A framework for studying the effects of career counseling on career and personal adjustment. *Journal of Career Assessment, 1,* 118–129.

Spokane, A. R., & Oliver, L. W. (1983). The outcomes of vocational intervention. In W. B. Walsh & S. H. Osipow (Eds.), *Handbook of vocational psychology* (Vol. 1., pp. 99–136). Hillsdale, NJ: Lawrence Erlbaum Associates.

Staw, B. M., & Ross, J. (1985). Stability in the midst of change: A dispositional approach to job attitudes. *Journal of Applied Psychology, 70,* 469–480.

Subich, L. M. (1993). How personal is career counseling? *Career Development Quarterly, 42,* 129–131.

Super, D. E. (1955). Personality integration through vocational counseling. *Journal of Counseling Psychology, 2,* 217–226.

Super, D. E. (1957). *The psychology of careers.* New York: Harper & Row.

Super, D. E. (1980). A life-span, life-space approach to career development. *Journal of Vocational Behavior, 16,* 282–298.

Super, D. E. (1993). The two faces of counseling: Or is it three? *Career Development Quarterly, 42,* 132–136.

Tolsma, R. (1993). "Career or non-career?" That is the issue: Case examples. *Career Development Quarterly, 42,* 167–173.

Ulrich, D. N., & Dunne, H. P. (1986). *To love and work: A systemic interlocking of family, workplace, and career.* New York: Brunner/Mazel.

Vondracek, F. W., Lerner, R. M., & Schulenberg, J. E. (1986). *Career development: A life-span developmental model.* Hillsdale, NJ: Lawrence Erlbaum Associates.

Wachtel, P. L. (Ed.). (1982). *Resistance: Psychodynamic and behavioral approaches.* New York: Plenum.

Wachtel, P. L. (1993). *Therapeutic communication.* New York: Guilford.

Walsh, W. B., & Osipow, S. H. (Eds.). (1990). *Career counseling: Contemporary topics in vocational psychology.* Hillsdale, NJ: Lawrence Erlbaum Associates.

Watkins, C. E., & Savickas, M. L. (1990). Psychodynamic career counseling. In W. B. Walsh & S. H. Osipow (Eds.), *Career counseling: Contemporary topics in vocational psychology* (pp. 79–116). Hillsdale, NJ: Lawrence Erlbaum Associates.

Watkins, C. E., Savickas, M. L., Brizzi, L., & Manus, M. (1990). Effects of counselor response behavior on clients' impressions during vocational counseling. *Journal of Counseling Psychology, 37,* 138a–142.

Wells, R. A., & Giannetti, V. J. (Eds.). (1990). *Handbook of the brief psychotherapies.* New York: Plenum.

Wells, R. A., & Phelps, P. A. (1990). The brief psychotherapies: A selective overview. In R. A. Wells & V. J. Giannetti (Eds.), *Handbook of the brief psychotherapies* (pp. 3–26). New York: Plenum.

Williamson, E. G., & Bordin, E. S. (1940). Evaluating counseling by means of a control-group experiment. *School and Society, 52,* 434–440.

Young, R. A., & Collin, A. (Eds.). (1992). *Interpreting career: Hermeneutical studies of lives in context.* Westport, CT: Praeger.

Zeig, J. K., & Munion, W. M. (Eds.). (1990). *What is psychotherapy?: Contemporary perspectives.* San Francisco: Jossey–Bass.

Zimmerman, J., & Cochran, L. (1993). Alignment of family and work roles. *Career Development Quarterly, 41,* 344–349.

CHAPTER TEN

Career Counseling With Racial and Ethnic Minorities

Nadya A. Fouad
Rose Phillips Bingham
University of Memphis

The population of the United States is more racially and ethnically diverse than it has ever been and is predicted to become even more culturally diverse in the next 10 years. The U.S. workforce is reflective of those changes in ethnic and cultural diversity. Since Parsons (1909) began his attempt to match people with careers, counselors have been attempting to help individuals decide which career or job is the right one for them. Most often when counselors were trained to provide vocational services, they were trained with models that were operationalized on White samples. Now, with the changes in the proportion of ethnic representation in the United States and recognition of the varying needs of racial and ethnic minority members, authors have generally agreed that counselors must be competent to work with a diverse population. Because of the changing complexion of the workplace, it is critically important that career counselors effectively deliver vocational counseling services to racial and ethnic minorities.

In this chapter we briefly discuss the changing demographics of the United States and the roles of world views and of racial-identity development in career counseling. Next, we examine specific variables that influence ethnic minority clients' career decision making. Then we critique the models of career counseling with ethnic minorities for their incorporation of cultural variables. Finally, we propose a model for career counseling with ethnic minorities.

CHANGING DEMOGRAPHICS

Changes in racial and ethnic demographics in the United States are due both to increased immigration and to differences in birth rates between dominant culture groups (declining) and minority members (increasing). The implications of population changes are evident in elementary and secondary school systems, higher education, and the workforce. The workforce is expected to grow more slowly than it has in the past six decades, and minority participation in the workforce will grow faster than White participation. It is also expected to become more gender balanced (Saveri, 1991). Women and minority members are expected to compose nearly three fourths of new entrants into the workforce. Although the entire workforce will still be primarily White, the increase in White participation is predicted to grow by only 17% contrasted with a 27% growth rate for all minority members by 2005. African-American growth is expected to be nearly 32%, and growth for Hispanic Americans and Asian Americans is predicted to be 75% for each group.

Students in higher education are more representative of the cultural diversity in the population than 20 years ago, although minority members in colleges are still underrepresented at all levels. In 1976, 15.6% of Whites had completed a bachelor's degree program, whereas 7.8% of African Americans, 3.1% of Hispanics, 29.2% of Asian Americans, and 5.8% of Native Americans had completed a bachelor's degree program. In 1986, the latest date for these figures, rates of completion of college had increased for all groups, with 29.4% of Whites, 19.2% of African Americans, 10.9% of Hispanics, 56.1% of Asian Americans, and 18.5% of Native Americans completing college (Department of Labor, 1992). From 1980 to 1988, college enrollment increased for Whites by 4.6%, 2.1% for African Americans, 44.2% for Hispanics, 10.3% for Native Americans, and 73.4% for Asian Americans. Contrasting with these figures is the higher attrition rate for minority members at all educational levels. In 1990, 9% of Whites, 13.2% of African Americans, and 32.4% of Hispanics had dropped out of high school (figures were not available for other minority members).

Many writers have expounded in depth on these changes (e.g., Herr, 1989; Ponterotto & Casas, 1991), and we will not replicate their discussions. Suffice it to say that the changes in the ethnic and racial makeup in schools and in the workforce make it imperative that counselors learn more about cultural diversity in vocational counseling and assessment. Counselors must be conversant with how cultural diversity affects vocational issues at all points in the career development (Fouad, 1993).

ASSUMPTIONS

We are making several assumptions in this chapter. The first is that effective career counseling takes place within a cultural context. This is true for all clients, regardless of ethnicity. White clients bring their culture to career counseling, just as racial and ethnic minority clients do. However, because traditional career counseling has been formed by White counselors and researchers, the cultural encapsulation of that counseling is often difficult for counselors to see (Wrenn, 1962). We believe it is imperative that the cultural context of career counseling be at the forefront of the counseling process. Ultimately, counseling within a cultural context will be more effective for all clients, because considerable cultural diversity exists within the dominant culture as well as between cultures.

Our second assumption is that the variables to be considered in career counseling across cultures may differ, and the weight placed on those variables may differ across cultures. Thus, all clients may consider family pressures and obligations, but the importance that familial commitments play in their career decisions may differ.

A third assumption is that current theoretical models may not adequately explain the career behavior of racial and ethnic minorities, a possibility discussed by Leong and M. Brown (in press). Fourth, vocational assessment must be culturally sensitive, and only culturally appropriate tools should be used in vocational assessment (Fouad, 1993).

Finally, in our discussion we approach cultural differences in career counseling from the perspective of cultural diversity, or pluralism, rather than from a perspective of cultural deprivation or cultural deficit (D. W. Sue & D. Sue, 1990). By this we mean that cultural differences are acknowledged and valued. We do not compare all cultural groups to a White standard. A central implication in this assumption is that differences among cultural groups will not disappear if opportunity structures are equal or if minority members are exposed to an intervention. The goal of career counseling is not to have all clients make the same choices but to help clients make career choices that are culturally appropriate.

CAREER COUNSELING WITH RACIAL AND ETHNIC MINORITIES: OVERVIEW

Career counseling or career intervention has been defined in various ways, but most agree that career counseling is a process, one occurring between two (or more) individuals and designed to help clients reach a career decision (e.g., Brown & Brooks, 1991; Herr & Cramer, 1992). The decision may be focused on the client's entering a career, adjusting to a career, or leaving a career. Specific processes and techniques used in career counseling will depend on the counselor's theoretical orientation. Almost all theories, however, have some aspect of matching the individual to the environment (Spokane, 1991).

Individual variables assessed in career counseling typically include interests, needs, values, abilities, personality variables, skills, decision-making style, self-concept, and self-efficacy. Environmental variables may include parental and societal influences, racism, acculturation, cultural values, and political and economic systems. The role that environmental influences plays in the career decisions of minority clients differs from that of many White clients. This difference is typically not anticipated by career counselors and is therefore not adequately integrated into their career counseling. It is critical for career counselors to be áware that all existing theories underexplain the role of environmental influences in the career behavior of minority clients.

We believe that in order to be effective as a career counselor with racial and ethnic minority clients the counselor must first become skilled in cross-cultural counseling. D. W. Sue, Arrendondo, and McDavis (1992) delineated several competencies for cross-cultural counseling. Their framework consists of a three-by-three matrix, with three characteristics of the multiculturally competent counselor each having three dimensions. The three characteristics are awareness of own cultural values, understanding the world view of culturally different clients, and developing appropriate intervention strategies. Three dimensions of these characteristics are attitudes, knowledge, and skills. The matrix therefore yields nine competencies. Thus, for example, a multiculturally competent counselor is aware of his or her own biases and attitudes, has knowledge about different cultures, and has developed specific intervention strategies to work with culturally diverse clients. Consistent with D. W. Sue et al.'s (1992) competencies, the career counseling competencies delineated by the National Career Development Association (NCDA, 1992) include knowledge and skills in the counselor's relating to special populations. These competencies are an important step forward in our realization that career counseling must be culturally sensitive.

The need for counselor knowledge and training in how cultural issues affect career decisions and adjustment becomes even greater when we consider the lack of minority clients' willingness to enter counseling and poor retention of minority populations in traditional counseling services (D. W. Sue & D. Sue, 1990) and the need expressed by minority adults for more and better career services (Brown, Minor, & Jepsen, 1991). Brown et al. found that African Americans, in particular, were more likely than others to report needing help with career decisions and occupational information and to believe that career development activities in school systems needed improvement. Thus, we appear not to fully meet the career guidance and information needs of racial and ethnic minorities. Counselors must help clients make career decisions, using culturally appropriate interventions and goals. One avenue to cross-cultural understanding is a sensitivity to the client's world view and his or her stage of racial-identity development.

CULTURAL VARIABLES IN CAREER DECISION MAKING

Many authors are beginning to call for multiculturally competent career counseling (e.g., Arbona, in press; Bingham & Ward, 1994; Bowman, 1993; Fouad, 1993, in press; Leong, 1993; Leong & Serafica, in press; Richardson,

1993; Swanson, 1993; Ward & Bingham, 1993). These articles lead the reader to discern or hypothesize that minority members must have some special needs that differ from those of the majority. Indeed, if these authors, as well as D. W. Sue and D. Sue (1990), Pedersen (1976), Leong (1985), and Helms (1990), are right, then ethnic minority clients are likely to have experiences in the majority society that will lead to identity development processes that differ from those of most European Americans. D. W. Sue and D. Sue (1990) and Nobles (1976) also believe that racial and ethnic minorities have world views different from those of many European Americans in this society. A world view, more fully discussed later, encompasses all of the cultural norms, mores, and folkways that are passed on to successive generations in an identifiable group. Values, interests, and familial and interpersonal relationships are greatly determined by those world views, which, in turn, are hypothesized to influence career choice. Thus, minority clients' world views will affect their career decisions in ways that may differ from those of the majority.

Katz discussed the sociopolitical nature of counseling in her seminal (1985) article, noting that counseling occurs in both a social and a political context. Individuals with differing interests and abilities may be influenced by the conditions of the social, political, and economic milieu in which they were reared. It behooves the career counselor to be knowledgeable about these factors when an individual seeks services so that the counselor is aware of moderating variables and the weight accorded to each, as interests and possible careers are explored.

Career counselors need a context or frame of reference in which to place cultural variables so that counseling can be conducted in a consistent and reasonable fashion regardless of the race or ethnicity of the individual who presents for services. We propose that counselors need to be familiar with theories of world views and theories of racial and ethnic identity development.

Role of World Views on Career Choice

A world view can be thought of as the frame of reference through which one experiences life. It is the foundation for values, beliefs, attitudes, relations, and so forth. Among the first writers in the counseling field to delineate features of varying world views was Nobles. Nobles (1976) described an African world view and a European world view. In the African world view, there is a focus on the group or tribe, its survival, and harmony with nature. On the other hand, the European world view emphasizes the individual survival of the fittest and control of nature. (The European world view is assumed to predominate for individuals in the U.S. dominant culture.) Individuals brought up within the diametrically opposed frames of reference (European vs. African) are likely to express their interests, values, and attitudes in quite different ways. For example, a client with an African world view may be more inclined to subordinate individual goals to the goals of the group. If this client seeks vocational counseling he or she may find it very difficult to make a career choice without considering the effect of the choice on his or her ethnic or racial group. A traditional therapist may diagnose separation and individuation problems because the client is unwilling to focus just on the implications of career choices for herself or himself. In this case, however, the career counselor is working with a client who has a world view that mandates a consideration of the group above that of the person's unique desires. The counselor's consideration of the client's world view and the influence of that world view on her or his career decision is an important component in career counseling and will help the client to make the most culturally appropriate career choice. On the other hand, for clients with an European world view, it would be perfectly reasonable for the counselor to encourage a client to focus on his or her individual choices. Moreover, if the client seemed too dependent on the approval of family and others for making a career choice, a diagnosis of separation and individuation problems would be quite appropriate.

Interestingly, many of the career guidance instruments seem to be designed from a European world view perspective. For example the Discover Computer-Assisted Career Choice program (DISCOVER, 1977) has numerous categories with questions about individuals' interests, attitudes, and abilities. However, there is not a section on the role of the family or cultural group. An effective career counselor will need to interview the client for that information. The same can be said of other instruments, such as the Strong Interest Inventory (Hansen, 1992) or the Self-Directed Search (Holland, 1985b). If such instruments are used with racial and ethnic minorities, the counselor must likely do more in-person interviewing to determine the client's world view and its relevance to career choice.

D. W. Sue and D. Sue's (1990) description of world views appears to be more politically defined than other descriptions. They define world view as "how a person perceives his/her relationship to the world (nature, institutions, other people, things, etc.)" (p. 137). They focused on internal versus external locus of control and internal versus external locus of responsibility, maintaining that in the United States, Whites tend to have a sense of internal locus of control (IC) and internal locus of responsibility (IR). This notion is apparent in White societal appreciation for people who "pull themselves up by their own bootstraps." The individual is believed to be in control of his or her life and is responsible for what happens in life. This world view seems very similar to that of the European world view proposed by Nobles (1976). On the other hand, in D. W. Sue and D. Sue's world view, model minority individuals hold some combination of different kinds of perceptions of their worlds. They may believe that they are responsible for what happens to their career (IR) and yet feel no sense of control (external locus of control) over what happens to them. Sue and Sue maintain that such individuals are likely to ascribe their failure in a career to their own laziness or stupidity. Also, these individuals likely aspire to be like those in the majority yet maintain a sense of inferiority. Sue and Sue further described people who have no sense of control of self or of the environment. These individuals may most easily be described as having given up or as having developed the phenomenon of learned helplessness. The fourth group in Sue and Sue's model is much more like the African world view proposed by Nobles. These people have a sense of internal responsibility for themselves; however they are cognizant of barriers such as racism and sexism that may be before them. Although they may feel free to select a career, they know that there are environmental barriers, such as sexism and racism, that may influence their ability to function and advance in a chosen career. The reader is referred to Carter (1990) for an in-depth discussion of cultural values.

A culturally competent career counselor needs to be aware of the possibility that a client may hold any of these psychological orientations, or world views, or others as described by Pedersen, Draguns, Lonner, and Trimbles (1989) The important points here are that the concept of world views does exist and that the career counselor must be familiar with his or her own as well as that of the counselee. Bingham and Ward (1994) asserted that counseling may not be effective if the counselor does not understand the concept of world views yet seeks to conduct career counseling with someone who holds a different world view. For example, a counselor may hold a European world view, whereas the client has an African world view. The counselor may select the Discover program (DISCOVER, 1977) as the intervention, without determining the client's need for exploration of family and ethnic group concerns. The client is likely to leave counseling without answers to his or her questions and possibly with a view that counseling is a useless process. The counselor may never know what went wrong, if, indeed, he or she is aware that something was not right. Of course the client and counselor may have a similar miscommunication if they are in conflictual stages of racial-identity development.

Racial Ethnic Identity Development

In 1971, Cross proposed that African Americans go through a four-stage, racial-identity development process that evolves from the first stage of a pro-White–anti-Black frame of reference to a fourth stage that is internally determined and appreciative of all ethnic and racial groups. In the first stage of the model, *preencounter*, the individual does not want to be described in racial terms but rather prefers being seen as a human being. He or she tends to be very pro-White and anti-Black. During the second stage, *encounter*, the individual begins to question the previous belief system of Stage 1. In the *immersion–emersion* stage, the person becomes quite hostile to Whites and is adamantly pro-Black. As the individual's life situation changes, he or she will begin to question such unequivocal stands and will become more internally secure, more pluralistic, and more appreciative of all ethnic groups. Helms (1990) and Atkinson, Morten, and D. W. Sue (1992) provide support for the model. In fact, Atkinson and his colleagues proposed a model that is reflective of all oppressed minorities. Minority members go through a process very similar to that described by Cross in the Negro-to-Black conversion model. Individuals move from being very depreciative of their own group and appreciative of the majority to questioning, to being immersed in their own culture, and finally to being appreciative of their group and other ethnic groups as well as of the majority. Bingham and Ward (1994) proposed that career counselors need to give strong consideration to the minority client's stage of racial-identity development because it has implications for the relationship that will be established with the counselor.

The client's stage of development may have implications for his or her career aspirations and expectations. For example, if an ethnic minority client is in Stage 3 of Cross' (1971) model, the immersion–emersion phase, he or she may not want to consider careers that would take him or her into the typical White corporate structure of most companies. On the other hand, a client who is in the preencounter stage may want to be a social worker, but if too much work is needed with his or her own ethnic group, then social work may be seen as a less desirable career choice. It is important for the career counselor to assess the stage development of each racial or ethnic minority client in order to have a greater understanding of how that factor may be influencing the vocational decision-making process.

Bingham and Ward (1994) maintained that although counselors must have information about the client's racial-identity development, it is equally important that they understand their own racial-identity development. This applies to White counselors as well as to minority counselors. We have already discussed identity development for minorities. More recently, theorists have begun to propose a White racial-identity development process. Sabnani, Ponterotto, and Borodovsky (1991) summarized three similar models (those proposed by Hardiman, 1982; Helms, 1984; and Ponterotto, 1988a) that delineate the stages of development. Each of these theorists maintained that Whites go through a process somewhat similar to that of racial and ethnic minorities. In the first stage, Whites have no sense of themselves as racial beings. In the second stage, White individuals may experience a conflict in which they become aware of their whiteness and of a perceived difference from other racial and ethnic groups. Sabnani et al. (1991) maintained that Whites experience a conflict between wanting to maintain majority status quo and wanting to be more nonracial in their beliefs and behaviors. In the third stage, Whites sometimes feel guilt, anger, or depression because of this conflict. Some Whites become very prominority to alleviate the guilt. At the other end of the spectrum, some Whites react to the second stage (awareness of differences) with fourth-stage behavior, which is angry and withdrawn. They retreat into a totally White culture. The last stages of the model (fifth stage for some of the models, sixth for others) are marked by more internal security and a more culturally transcendent view of all ethnic groups.

Bingham and Ward (1994) indicated that the White counselor's stage of development could pose special problems for the racial or ethnic minority client if the counselor does not understand his or her own stage of racial-identity development. For example, a White counselor who is in the fourth stage (angry and withdrawn) may not even want to see a Black client. If an African-American client is in Cross' (1971) Stage 3, immersion–emersion, she or he is likely to feel very hostile toward Whites. If these two individuals are in an agency that offers them no choice except to see each other, then a counseling failure is probable. Similarly, an African-American counselor who is in Cross' Stage 2 (beginning awareness of racial differences and questioning of dominant culture beliefs) and who encounters a White client who is in the first stage (has no sense of self as a racial being) may find herself or himself pushing the client to become aware of racial differences. This situation, too, may be end as a counseling failure.

The very hallmark of a successful counseling interaction is the rapport that the counselor is able to establish with the client. It is, therefore, incumbent on the counselor to understand theories of racial-identity development and his or her own stage in order to effectively serve the racial or ethnic minority client. Additionally, Parham (1989) maintained that the stage developments herein described may not be linear. He suggested that individuals may loop back through stages depending on life circumstances. Thus, counselors must continuously assess their own development as well as that of their clientele.

Aspirations and Expectations

There apparently is some consensus among authors that aspirations and expectations do influence career choice. The literature consistently reveals that racial and ethnic minority individuals have high career aspirations and that the level of aspiration does not differ significantly among groups (Arbona, 1990; Arbona & Novy, 1991; Leong, 1993; Spokane & Richardson, 1992). In fact, Arbona and Novy (1991) found more gender differences than ethnic or racial differences in aspiration and expectations. Further, an examination of the distribution of jobs in the United States indicates that ethnic group members expect to enter the job market at about the same rate that jobs are available. Indeed, Arbona and Novy (1991) noted that although Gottfredson (1981) reported that men and women aspired to enter *enter-*

prising occupations (based on Holland's typology) in far lower numbers than available jobs, they found that the expectation levels for men and women were closely aligned with the job market in those categories.

In spite of high levels of expectation, ethnic groups are over- and under-represented in various career groupings. For example, African Americans are overrepresented in *realistic* and *social* occupations, whereas Asians are overrepresented in the sciences and engineering. What accounts for these differences between aspirations and occupational attainment? Spokane and Richardson (1992) purported that the career-choice process can be described in two ways, as search or as compromise. The search method is most accurately reflected by the trait–factor career model and in the work of theorists like Holland (1985a), who contended that a career decision is an expression of personality. These theorists hold that personality is relatively stable over time and that people seek careers that fit their personalities. On the other hand the compromise method is reflected in Super's (1957) work. Super and theorists with similar views maintained that a career decision is the result of a series of compromises the individual makes as a result of life circumstances.

Perhaps the compromise theory accurately reflects what happens to racial and ethnic minorities in this society. Moreover, theorists have hypothesized that the compromise method accounts for gender differences in occupational attainment. Gainor and Forrest (1991) suggested that African-American women may limit their career choices because of their perceptions about the amount of sexism and racism they may encounter in the profession. Hackett and Betz (1981) hypothesized that women's vocational choices may be influenced by their self-efficacy and that women feel more confident in their ability to compete and to succeed in traditionally female jobs. Arbona and Novy (1991) supported this hypothesis, finding that Hispanic women were more likely to expect to enter traditionally female jobs.

Racial and ethnic minority members' occupational attainment may be a result of a combination of societal barriers and within-group socialization. For example, Leong (1993) found that Asian Americans reported a more Dependent decision-making style than did their White counterparts. He suggested that the result might be explained by an Asian world view that is more group than individually oriented. An Asian American may feel greater need to give consideration to the family's expectation, whereas a White American family may think it more important that each person makes a separate and individual vocational decision. Socialization, however, does not account for all of the variance in occupational attainment. We cannot reasonably hypothesize that a group would expect its members to enter the lowest paying jobs, a pattern is found in African-American representation in the relatively low-wage realistic occupational categories (Holland, 1985a). It is more likely that environmental barriers have more influence than socialization in these instances.

Spokane and Richardson (1992) found that many women and minority members felt they would be unable to implement some of their career aspirations because of environmental barriers. A woman who is also a member of a minority may be a victim of both racism and sexism. For example, in a study of occupational profiles of African Americans in management, McRae and Carter (1992) found that men were paid higher salaries than were women.

Career counselors face the delicate task of helping racial and ethnic minority clients to explore their aspirations and to identify possible realistic obstacles in their paths. Further, an effective career counselor must help the client become aware of any self-efficacy issues that may be restricting career choices. Within the context of D. W. Sue and D. Sue's, (1990) model of internal and external locus of control and locus of responsibility, the counselor must help the client find the combination of internal and external assignment of control and responsibility that will maximize the client's chances for a satisfying career. This assistance may include identification of variables within the client's control, as well as identification of external barriers and possible solutions for overcoming those barriers. Similarly, the counselor will increase his or her opportunities for success if he or she sufficiently understands the roles of world views and racial-identity development in the career decision-making process.

CAREER COUNSELING MODELS

We have examined several overarching cultural variables that affect the career decision making and counseling of minority members. We now turn our attention to how cultural variables are incorporated into various career counseling models. A variety of career counseling models are reviewed by Swanson (this volume). We therefore limit our focus to more recently developed proposals.

It may be useful for us to first examine how the broad career counseling literature addresses cultural variables. Herr and Cramer (1992) have written one of the most comprehensive career development and career guidance texts available, currently in its fourth edition. They do not specifically propose a model of career counseling but compiled literature on several counseling models and their applications to career counseling. Herr and Cramer defined career counseling as a verbal interaction between client and counselor that helps "bring about self-understanding and . . . decision-making in the counselee, who has responsibility for his or her own actions" (p. 583). The authors then described a counseling cycle that includes self-exploration, exploration of the world of work, and career decision making. Although Herr and Cramer mentioned that their discussion pertained primarily to Western culture, very little consideration was given to cultural variables within counseling. Herr and Cramer did, however, devote several sections of their text to a review of the literature relevant to cultural variables and noted, in their last section, the need for more research on the effects of cultural and economic factors.

In Walsh and Osipow's (1990) edited book on career counseling, several authors discussed how they implemented their own theoretical orientation in counseling. Trait–factor (Rounds & Tracey, 1990), person-centered (Bozarth & Fisher, 1990), psychodynamic (Watkins & Savickas, 1990), developmental (Jepsen, 1990), social learning (Krumboltz & Nichols, 1990), social-psychological (Dorn, 1990) theories and computers in career counseling (Rayman, 1990) were summarized and integrated by Walsh (1990). Cultural variables were not mentioned by any of the authors, a glaring omission.

We must conclude that writers who take a broad-brush approach to career counseling are not incorporating culture as a set of variables critical to the career counseling process. This pattern is consistent with Subich's (1993) conclusion that the least well developed area in career counseling is what she termed "diverse person variables" (p. 8) and with Richardson's (1993) concern that vocational psychology is too oriented to the White middle class.

We now turn to authors who have recently created models of career counseling, each designed to fill a gap in current literature. Yost and Corbishley (1987) proposed an eight-stage model of career counseling that is imbedded in a broad psychological context. Yost and Corbishley noted that the distinction between career and personal issues is unclear and that they often are intertwined. Their introductory chapter includes a section on working with minority populations. They noted that some minority members may experience internal and external constraints and cautioned counselors to individualize their approach for minority clients as they would for all clients. They encouraged counselors to develop an adequate knowledge base and to be sensitive to cultural differences. They also pointed out that not all cultural group members need to focus on their minority status. They did not specifically incorporate cultural variables into their model and did not indicate how a counselor could go about being sensitive to clients of other cultural groups.

Spokane's model (1991) is one of the most comprehensive career counseling systems that incorporates personal and career issues. He outlined three major phases (*beginning, activation, completion*), each with two or three subphases. As comprehensive as this model is, however, Spokane did not address its specific application to minority members or to women.

Peterson, Sampson, and Reardon (1991) approached career counseling from a cognitive-information processing perspective. They delineated three domains of information processing relevant to career decision making: knowledge (consisting of self-knowledge and occupational knowledge), decision making, and executive processing. Peterson et al. briefly discussed ethnicity and culture, noting that culture directly influences identity development and that although no theory specifically links culture to career development they "can use the C[ognitive] I[nformation] P[rocessing] paradigm to demonstrate how the emergence of these perspectives influences career problem solving and decision making" (p. 79). Their paradigm includes four assumptions and propositions: (1) Culture is a determinant of meaning, (2) cultural differences in communication are meaningful, (3) no cultural group is superior to another (cultural relativity), and (4) effective cross-cultural counseling is important. They then briefly described two models of ethnic awareness, discussed the effects of culture on each of the domains of the information processing hierarchy, and reviewed cultural values inherent in White-dominated counseling models, first described by Katz (1985). Although their discussion of the possible significance of culture in the different domains is interesting, it is also quite cursory, and little effort appears to have been made for a thorough review of the literature in the area. For example, as previously discussed in the section on racial-identity development, several authors have developed Black racial-identity and White racial-identity models (e.g., Atkinson, Morten, & D. W. Sue, 1993; Cross, 1971; Helms, 1990; Parham, 1989; Ponterotto, 1988b). The only models that Peterson et al. (1991) reviewed were those proposed by D. W. Sue (1981), which was extensively updated (D. W. Sue & D. Sue, 1990) and by Christensen (1989). Peterson et al. also neglected to review any of the literature that has been conducted on cultural influence on career development, and they did not specifically incorporate cultural variables into their model. They did extensively describe a case study of a Hispanic high-school girl who was struggling to make a career decision, but no specific cultural issues were discussed as a part of this example.

Brown and Brooks (1991) also took a cognitive approach to career counseling, advocating the initial assessment of a client's cognitive clarity prior to the initiation of career counseling. If a client has cognitive clarity, then career counseling can proceed; otherwise a client is referred for personal counseling. Brown and Brooks' (1991) work is the most extensive discussion of the impact of cultural variables of any current discussion on career counseling. An entire chapter is devoted to a discussion of ethnicity and race in career counseling; another chapter focuses on gender as a variable in career counseling. Also included are an overview of occupational stereotypes of minority members, a critique of current career development and career counseling literature, and a review of the cross-cultural competencies proposed by D. W. Sue et al. (1982). The discussion of attitude bases includes the need for counselor self-awareness and a review of the Katz (1985) cultural values of counseling. The chapter also gives a brief overview of some of the cultural values and mores of each major U.S. minority (Asian Americans, Hispanics, African Americans, and Native Americans). A discussion of general cross-cultural counseling is given, and a brief discussion of career counseling across cultures ensues. The authors ended the chapter with specific recommendations for counselors' learning to be a skilled in cross-cultural counseling and noted that we need more information about effective practices in this area.

Interestingly, Brown appears to have taken a different approach in another text (Isaacson & Brown, 1993), predicting a "convergence of thinking about the career counseling practices for whites and . . . ethnic minorities" (p. 499). This prediction is based on an assumption that experiences of individuals living in the same country are overwhelmingly similar because "we speak the same language, go to the same schools, watch the same television programs, and generally live in the same culture" (p. 499). Isaacson and Brown concluded that previous literature had not indicated a need for different strategies based on culturally different clients.

CULTURALLY APPROPRIATE CAREER COUNSELING MODEL

We take strong issue with Isaacson and Brown's (1993) statements and believe it is imperative that we devise different strategies for culturally diverse clients. We find their remarks ethnocentric and assume that they are unaware of the large body of literature that indicates that racial or ethnic identity is an important determinant of behavior and perception (cf., Atkinson & Thompson, 1992; Hale–Benson, 1986, 1990; Helms, 1990; Ogbu, 1990). As we noted earlier, world views and racial identities differ across groups and are based on cultural values and sociopolitical environments. Isaacson and Brown's remarks also discount and devalue the enormous effect of racism and discrimination in this country (Ponterotto & Pedersen, 1993; D. W. Sue & D. Sue, 1990).

We propose that culture is a critical variable in career counseling, should enter into every part of the counseling process, and may modify counseling. We also propose that the assessment of the effect of cultural variables is a very specific step. We incorporate these factors in a culturally appropriate career counseling model, depicted in Figure 10.1.

The model illustrated in Figure 10.1 is an extension of that described by Ward and Bingham (1993; Bingham & Ward, 1994) and is predicated on the assumptions discussed earlier in this chapter. The seven steps of the model include the counselor's establishing a culturally appropriate relationship (Step 1), identifying career issues that the client brings to counseling (Step 2), assessing the impact of cultural variables on those career issues (Step 3), setting culturally appropriate processes and goals (Step 4), determining and implementing a culturally appropriate intervention (Step 5), and helping the client make a culturally appropriate decision (Step 6). Step 7 includes the implementation of the client's plans and follow-up. Clients may

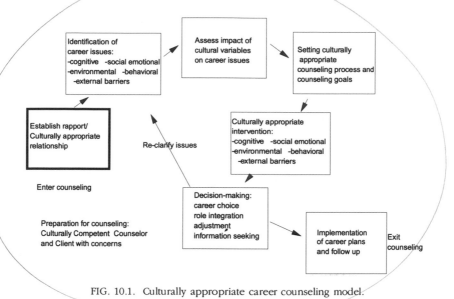

FIG. 10.1. Culturally appropriate career counseling model.

choose to cycle back through this model to clarify their career issues, reentering at Step 2 (identification of career issues). Each step in the model is more fully described later.

It is not within the scope of this chapter for us to fully describe career counseling strategies or to replicate the discussion of career counseling interventions and strategies by Swanson (this volume) in general or those for specific minority groups (e.g., Bowman, 1993; Fouad, in press; Leong & Gim, in press; Martin, in press). Rather, our intent is to propose an initial model of incorporating cultural variables into career counseling. We fully hope and expect that this model will be modified and extended as research is conducted on the model by us and by others to see if, in fact, it helps to make career counseling more culturally relevant for culturally diverse clients.

Preparation for Counseling

Before any effective counseling occurs, both the client and counselor must be prepared for counseling. The client comes to counseling with some concerns to clarify or with goals to set and accomplish. The counselor comes to counseling ready to suspend judgment and to be available to listen to the client. In multiculturally counseling, we presuppose a culturally competent counselor. Following the three-by-three model proposed by D. W. Sue et al. (1992) discussed earlier, we believe a counselor should have awareness, knowledge, and skills about his or her own culture, others' cultures, and a variety of counseling techniques.

Bingham and Ward (1994) delineated several components in counselor preparation for cross-cultural counseling. The first is cultural sensitivity, or an openness to and enjoyment of clients' experiences. This means the counselor lets clients know that their experiences are valued and respected. It also means the counselor does not interpret all clients' experiences through his or her own perspective. For example, a White counselor who says in response to a concern about family pressures "Oh, I just told my parents to go jump off a roof when they told me to be a doctor!" has very little empathy for the real struggle between individual choice and family obligations for many minority clients.

The second component outlined by Bingham and Ward (1994) is the counselor's being knowledgeable about cultural groups. It is important that she or he is familiar with some information about all ethnic groups and to have some knowledge on which to base initial work with clients. All training programs in counseling psychology and counselor education are expected to provide students with a minimal level of cross-cultural knowledge, and counselors are encouraged to continue to increase their familiarity with cultural groups through workshops, readings, and lectures. This effort notwithstanding, familiarity with all the behavioral and attitudinal norms particular to each cultural group in the United States is very difficult. Bingham and Ward suggested that the counselor try to become quite familiar with one group different from her or his own or familiar with the ethnic groups in a specific geographic region. They also suggested that familiarity involve more than intellectual knowledge but also include personal interaction with the group, including participation in festivals and religious ceremonies (where appropriate) and keeping track of political issues pertinent to the group.

A third issue advocated by Bingham and Ward (1994) is knowledge of the cultural strengths that clients bring to counseling. Rather than viewing a client as weak and a victim of his or her cultural group, it is important for the counselor to acknowledge the strengths that clients have and for counseling to proceed from those strengths.

Openness to clients as cultural teachers is another competence that counselors should have before they see culturally different clients. Even if one has much knowledge about a client's cultural group, the counselor can still learn about that culture from the client. Beginning counselors often ask What if I don't know anything about Hispanics (or African Americans or Asian Americans or Native Americans)? How can I be effective? Clients can teach counselors what that culture is like for them. The ability of the counselor to learn from the client rests on the counselor's ability to suspend judgment and stereotyping, the capacity to approach every client as an individual, and the skill to encourage the client to communicate what is meaningful about being a Hispanic (African American, etc.).

Two additional areas of preparation for counselors is knowledge of their own world view and knowledge of their own racial identity. Counselors must be aware of their own culture and the impact of that culture on their attitudes and behavior. It is important for counselors to have a sense of their racial-identity stage and how that may affect their relationships with clients of different cultures. They should have a knowledge of the impact of their socioeconomic status on their counseling, as well as the impact of their political views, and know what assumptions they make about work and the role of work in their clients' lives (Bingham & Ward, 1994). A counselor who has a strong bias toward achieving the highest prestige job possible, or working up to potential, has a strong possibility of biasing clients' choices. We maintain that adequate preparation for career counseling means knowing oneself, knowing one's biases, and viewing the client from *the client's* perspective (Cheatham, 1990).

As their seventh and final component, Bingham and Ward (1994) recommended that in preparing for cross-cultural counseling counselors become comfortable with clients of diverse backgrounds. It is critical that counselors examine their own biases and become comfortable with challenging their own culturally based assumptions about work and life roles (Bingham & Ward, 1994; D. W. Sue & D. Sue, 1990; Ward & Bingham, 1993).

Ward and Bingham (1993) developed a checklist with 13 items relevant to counselor preparation. The items are designed to jog a counselor's memory when entering a relationship with a culturally different client and include items such as, "I am familiar with the minimum cross-cultural competencies"; "I am aware of my own world and how it was shaped"; "I have information about this client's ethnic group's history and local sociopolitical issues and the client's attitude toward seeking help"; "I am aware of the importance that the interaction of gender and race or ethnicity has in my client's life." (pp. 250–251). A counselor may use these items to determine gaps and essential information that would be useful as she or he prepares for the client. After such preparation, the counselor is ready for the first step in the proposed model.

Case Example

To illustrate the use of the model in career counseling, we use the following case of Sharon. Sharon, an African-American woman, lived in a southern state. She came from a middle-class background that seemed to emphasize a European world view with material success in prestigious occupations. She had declared business as her major and was currently in her third year in college. Sharon, however, was failing academically. She had sought traditional career counseling to help her understand why she was doing so poorly. She decided career counseling was not working because she continued to fail her courses and was referred to another counselor for psychological counseling. The second counselor, Janelle, realized, however, that career issues were still an important area for Sharon to explore but that

Sharon's race and world view were also playing a part in her decision making. Janelle felt comfortable working with an African-American client, was herself working through the fifth Stage of White racial-identity development (introspection and respect for other cultural groups), had a Eurocentric world view, and had recently taken a workshop on the strengths of the African-American family in therapy.

Step 1. Establishment of Rapport (Culturally Appropriate Relationship).
Janelle and Sharon began their counseling relationship by discussing Sharon's previous counseling, her expectations for her counseling with Janelle, and the possible effects of the differences between their two races on counseling. They briefly discussed what being African American meant to Sharon, and Janelle answered some questions about being White. Although Janelle did not think that she and Sharon had had an in-depth discussion about race, she did believe that their openness about racial differences helped to prepare the way toward their establishing a relationship. She also thought that Sharon's world view appeared to be Africentric rather than European and hypothesized that Sharon was possibly feeling in conflict with her family's Eurocentric world view.

Sharon and Janelle had established a counseling relationship. It is relevant for us to note, whether the discussions are centered on world views or on stage development, that relationships seem to be central with many racial and ethnic minority people. Sometimes the emphasis is on family, and other times it is on the entire group or people. In either case, because relationships are so important, counselors may find it essential to give considerable attention to the rapport they are able to establish with their clientele. Establishing rapport and developing a firm relationship may be more important than any of the assessment instruments the counselor may use.

As shown in Figure 10.1, Step 1 in career counseling is the establishment of a relationship. It is critical for the counselor to establish a culturally appropriate relationship with the client, which as the term applies, may differ across cultures. For example, Hispanic clients may be interested in personal information about the counselor.

The core conditions that help in the establishment of a relationship and that constitute empathy in generic counseling also apply to career counseling: positive regard, respect and warmth, concreteness, genuineness, and immediacy. Ivey, Ivey, & Simek-Morgan (1993) outlined a three-stage model of multicultural empathy in which counselors listen to and observe clients' comments, learning how they wish to be related to; respond to client's main words and construct, using basic attending skills; and check out statements with the client. Culturally appropriate relationships set the context for a working consensus (Bingham & Ward, 1994) and diffuse mistrust of the counselor with which a client may approach counseling.

As we noted earlier, differential skills are needed for clients of different cultural groups. For example, Asian Americans may prefer directive and structured counseling, with the counselor in an authoritative and expert role (Leong, 1985). D. W. Sue and D. Sue (1990) reviewed several studies that indicate that many minority members prefer active and directive counseling rather than passive and nondirective reflection of feelings and insight-oriented therapy. The most critical aspects of the establishing of a relationship with a client are flexibility, suspension of stereotypes and assumptions, and attention to the counselor role the client wants.

Step 2. Identification of Career Issues. After completing the career checklist (Ward & Bingham, 1993), Sharon realized that she had never wanted to major in business and that she needed help in making a different career choice. She wanted a new career in which she could help others, especially other African Americans. Janelle and Sharon identified the career issues relevant to counseling, choosing a different college major and career, which is Step 2 in the model. Sharon further disclosed that she was sure that her family would be upset because she did not want to go into business (and perhaps into law, as her father hoped). She and Janelle also discovered that her study skills were deficient and that she needed to work on time management. Janelle referred her for help in these areas.

It is important for career counselors to take a broad approach to career issues. What is troubling the client? What is she or he identifying as areas of concern? These may be cognitive issues, social or emotional issues, behavioral concerns, environment issues, or they may be external issues that the client needs help in identifying and remediating. The career issues may also, of course, be any combination of all of these. Brown and Brook's (1991) problem areas of cognitive clarity is an excellent set of diagnostic categories to help career counselors with cognitive issues. Several authors have described emotional concerns and behavioral concerns in career counseling (Gysbers & Moore, 1987; Brown & Brooks, 1991; Spokane, 1991; Yost & Corbishley, 1987). An example of an emotional issue is a client's sudden onset of panic attacks at work and his or her decision to change jobs to eliminate the panic attacks. Behavioral concerns may include a client's chronic tardiness at work. Environmental issues are those related to any factors of concern to the client because of the working environment. These may include working conditions, coworkers, or supervisors. In our model, environment issues are distinct from external barriers, which may include discrimination, oppression, racism, sexism, financial concerns, or any constraint that a client may experience outside his or her control.

Critical to the model is the explicit definition of external barriers because, for many minority clients, career choice is a matter of balancing those factors within their control with those outside their control. As we briefly discussed earlier, D. W. Sue and D. Sue (1990) proposed a four-component model in which individuals may identify with internal locus of control–internal locus of responsibility (IC–IR), external locus of control–internal locus of responsibility (EC–IR), internal locus of control–external locus of responsibility (IC–ER), or external locus of control–external locus of responsibility (EC–ER). Most traditional counseling follows the predominant White pattern of IC–IR, in which the individual can affect the outcome of their actions and are responsible for their own success (or lack thereof). However, many minority clients may realistically feel that the system operates against them, having experienced racism or prejudice. It is important for counselors to accept and appreciate the world view of the client and not to impose their own identity on their clients. The reader is referred to Sue and Sue for an in-depth discussion of each of these four patterns.

Step 3. Assessment of Effects of Cultural Variables. In the third step of the model, counselors must fully assess the effects of cultural variables on career issues. Janelle helped Sharon assess how her race and Africentric world view helped to shape her career choice. They discussed the effects that her decision to leave business would have on her family and the consequences for Sharon if she disappointed her parents. One of the reasons Sharon did not want to enter the corporate world was her not wanting to deal with her perception of the glass ceiling African-American women faced in business. Sharon was afraid that her desire to help others would be perceived by her parents as lacking in ambition and risking her financial security just to "help others."

With Step 3 of the model, we raise the central question: How do cultural variables influence career decisions? If we accept Holland's (1985a) contention that a career choice is an expression of personality, then we can look at those things that influence personality.

Although one can argue that all behavior is biologically determined, the theories and evidence seem to support the notion that at least a portion of personality is shaped by one's interactions in families, in racial or ethnic cultures and in the mainstream culture.

Figure 10.2 is a graphic illustrating how each of these variables may influence an individual. The core unit is the individual. It is difficult for us to know how much behavior is already determined at birth, but we do know that fully functioning babies come with an intact brain that guides much of what they do. The person is born with a genetic stamp that will influence and shape behavior. We call this the core, which is represented by the innermost sphere. The core of the individual is the self and represents the essence of that individual. The self is shaped by all of the sociocultural forces around the individual, but we are depicting a model in which each individual has an immutable set of characteristics unique to that individual.

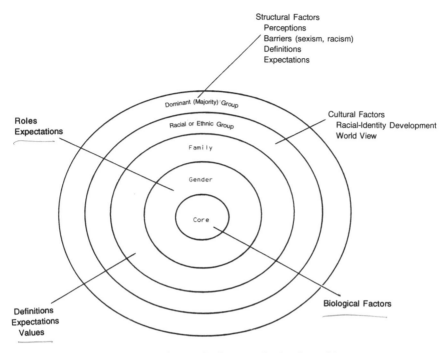

FIG. 10.2. Spheres of influence of cultural variables.

In this society we begin shaping children's behavior based on gender almost from the moment of birth. Therefore, the next sphere is gender. There is an entire body of literature on women's career development, as evidenced by annual reviews for the last 10 years in the *Journal of Vocational Behavior* and the *Career Development Quarterly* and, more recently, in the *Journal of Career Assessment.* Forrest and Mikolaitis (1986) provided a brief summary of the application and expansion of career development theory to women.

Especially important in our model is the work of Cook (1993). She maintained that "the gender-based differentiation of our society is as robust as ever" (p. 227). Cook further stated that as a result of the socialization process men and women "tend to develop different orientation with respect to occupational achievement" (p. 229). We maintain that gendered context and orientation is thoroughly woven into the fabric of this society and begins at birth.

We continue to see evidence of color designation based on gender, that is, pink for girls, blue for boys (Bridges, 1993). Early on, male and female children begin to receive messages about careers that may be appropriate for each gender, even while they are yet babies. According to Bridges, the congratulatory messages on baby cards differentiate between the sexes.

Gender clearly continues to shape the individual's sense of self and perception of appropriate career choices. The effect of gender on career choices differs across cultural groups. For example, traditional Hispanic men are expected to behave differently from Hispanic women, who are expected to be subservient to men and to follow a patriarchal hierarchy (Fouad, in press).

Hackett and Betz (1981) have written extensively on self-efficacy in women. The literature suggests that women's career decisions are influenced by their perceptions of how well they can perform in particular occupations. Gainor and Forrest (1991) hypothesized that African American women restrict their career choices when they perceive that sexism will be problematic. It is clear, therefore, that gender affects career decisions.

Next, we maintain that families begin to shape the career expectations of the daughters and sons. Akbar (1981), Comas–Diaz and Jacobsen (1987), Evansoki and Wu Tse (1989), and Wehrly (1988) have documented the importance of families in counseling and even in the career process. The role of the family as a vital determinant of human behavior has been well presented in the extensive volume by McGoldrick, Pearce, and Giordano (1982). All of these authors highlighted the role of family in various ethnic groups in matters that ranged from marriage to career choice. Very important in the consideration of the family sphere in the model are values around a wide variety of issues such as silence, authority, family-member roles, and so forth.

Spiegel (1982) indicated that it is essential for the counselor to know who is the head of the family in many ethnic groups. For example, the father is often the main figure in Puerto Rican families, and it would be wise for the counselor to determine early in the counseling intervention what influence he may have on his son's or daughter's career decision. On the other hand, Attneave (1982) reported that in many Native-American families, silence is valued. In the career counseling encounter, the client may need to be silent and to assess the counselor before the real intervention can begin. Denga (1988) reported that in Nigerian families women are expected to subordinate their career needs to those of the men in the family. In other ethnic minority families, children are expected to enter the career that the family has selected for them. Asian-American children, for example, are taught the strong cultural value that family obligations supersede individual desires, a lesson that may lead them to choose a career congruent with family expectations. Native Americans have a strong cultural value of cooperation and noncompetition, and this may have an influence on career choice that deemphasizes competition. In some instances, if children do not follow the expected path they are ostracized from the family. Families therefore play a significant role in defining and shaping the expectations of its members. It is important that we also remember that those definitions and expectations are shaped by the world views of the families.

The fourth sphere in the model depicts the racial or ethnic group as the next most significant influence. Included in this circle are cultural factors, such as world views and racial identity (Fitzgerald & Betz, 1992). World views of families are shaped by their racial or ethnic cultures. In the section on world views and racial-identity development, we discussed the effects of these variables on career decision making. We again stress that an effective career counselor must understand his or her own world view and racial-identity stage as well as those of her or his clients. Clients may receive messages from the racial or ethnic group about which careers are acceptable for its members. Those messages may influence the client's choices in very subtle ways. The counselor must be aware of that possibility as career assessment is concluded.

Finally, we hypothesize that the dominant culture is a major influence in career decision making. Information and understanding about the client's cultural group is especially important when that group is not the dominant or majority group and yet counseling is couched in the majority culture. One can expect that an ethnic minority individual will receive messages from the majority about who the racial and ethnic individuals are and what their roles and careers are expected to be in the larger society. Racial and ethnic minority individuals may accept those definitions and expectations, depending on their stages of racial-identity development and their world views.

In reality, the achievement of a career goal may be related to the structural factors imposed by the dominant group and those perceived by the racial or ethnic minority person. Fitzgerald and Betz (1992) defined structural factors as those elements of the society that limit participation in careers and career opportunities. For example, in addition to sexism, Gainor and Forrest (1991) maintained that African-American women restricted their career choices because of their perceptions of racism. It is a fact that the majority of inner-city elementary and high-school populations are composed of racial and ethnic minority individuals (Locke & Parker, 1991). Those schools tend to be underfunded and to have poorer equipment, and students have fewer opportunities to gain exposure to a wide variety of career role models. All of these realities can have a detrimental effect on career aspirations, expectations, and subsequent career decisions.

The spheres in this model are not equal for all racial and ethnic minority groups and individuals and may expand or shrink depending on ethnicity. Martin (in press), for example, outlined the moderating cultural variables for Native Americans, including language, cultural orientation (traditional, transitional, marginal, assimilated, or bicultural), home community (off or on reservation or both), family system (extended or nuclear), and communication style (client's responsiveness to attending, influencing, or focusing skills). Some groups may be more greatly influenced than others by family. Even if a group exists in a society in which their cultural group is a minority, that group may live a very isolated existence and have very limited contact with outsiders (see Figure 10.3). Also, the values of the group or family may be so deeply ingrained that no dominant-group values can penetrate the smaller group. Other racial and ethnic groups want their children to assimilate; very little of their ethnicity is encouraged within the group, and the dominant or majority group may therefore be the more significant factor (see Figure 10.4). The counselor will do well to keep the model in mind and then assess the strength of each of the dimensions.

The model also has implications for within-group and individual differences. A client from a culture in which the family sphere occupies a large portion of the model may seek career counseling. As the counselor assesses the situation, he or she may find that in the client's mind the family is nearly all encompassing and that the client feels unable to make a decision because of what that decision will mean to the family. The counselor may need to help the client reduce the size of the family sphere and, perhaps, to increase the size of other spheres in the model. The counselor may use the size of the sphere to determine the intervention that will most effectively help the client and still leave the sphere intact.

Sharon's career issues can be depicted by those in Figure 10.3. Although Janelle did not try to change the size of the spheres, an assessment was made from an ethnic perspective, and the intervention flowed from that assessment. This example may clarify how the counselor can use the spheres to conduct assessments and to help set goals in treatment. It is important

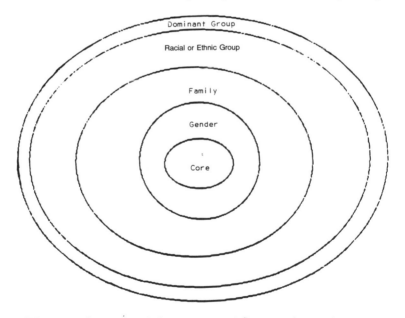

FIG. 10.3. Spheres of weak dominant-group influence and strong family and ethnic- or racial-group influence.

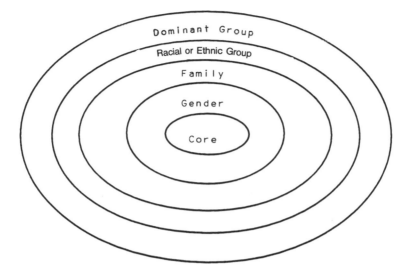

FIG. 10.4. Spheres of strong dominant-group influence and weak ethnic- or racial-group influence.

that the counselor consider the cultural-variables spheres when making a culturally relevant intervention. Culturally relevant interventions may involve psychological counseling or the teaching of a decision-making strategy to the client. In any event, we can easily see that the spheres can be used to help set goals in treatment.

Step 4. Setting of Counseling Goals. Step 4 is the point at which client and counselor may set goals. Janelle and Sharon established the following goals: clarifying interests, making a career decision, and discussing the change in her plans with her mother. family members

D. W. Sue and D. Sue (1990) described a four-condition model of counseling to which a culturally different client may be exposed: appropriate process–appropriate goals (AP–AG), appropriate process–inappropriate goals (AP–IG), inappropriate process–appropriate goals (IP–AG), and inappropriate process–inappropriate goals (IP–IG). Leong (1993) applied this model to cross-cultural career counseling, labeling the AP–AG quadrant as *on-target counselor,* the AP–IG quadrant as *good-hearted bumbler,* the IP–AG quadrant as *barking up the wrong tree,* and the IP–IG quadrant as *miss-by-a-mile counselor.* He discussed several concerns specific to Asian Americans. Inappropriate processes for this minority include direct confrontation, verbal assertiveness, direct negative comments, self-exploration, and the counselor's not acknowledging the hierarchical structure within the family. Inappropriate goals may include career choices based on self-actualization rather than on a pragmatism.

Step 5. Culturally Appropriate Counseling Interventions. As we noted in Step 2, Sharon completed the career counseling checklist (Ward & Bingham, 1993), and Janelle assessed her responses as described by those two authors. The assessment indicated that Sharon needed a career that allowed her to affect more directly the lives of her ethnic group. She completed the Strong Interest Inventory (Harmon, Hansen, Borgen, & Hammer, 1994), a values clarification exercise, and decided she would indeed like to leave her business major and to enter the education field. Her mother was brought into the counseling session and was very supportive of her daughter's career change.

After goals have been agreed on, the counselor, with the client's trust, determines culturally appropriate interventions. Bowman (1993) noted the paucity of literature on career interventions with minority clients. She concluded her review with several recommendations to counselors: Use group interventions with those minority members who operate in a framework that is more collectivistic than individualistic. Involve the family in career decision making. Use race- and gender-appropriate role models to expand awareness of opportunities. Present interventions in native languages when appropriate and possible. Also, depending on the racial identity of the client, the most effective counseling will be conducted by a counselor of the same race or ethnicity.

Many of Bowman's (1993) recommendations are consistent with those by Cheatham, A. Ivey, M. Ivey, and Simek–Morgan (1993) in their discussion of multicultural counseling and therapy (MCT). Among the major components of this approach, those relevant to career counseling are the use of community resources, information giving, personal validation of experiences, and the development of *conscientizacao*. Conscientizacao, a concept originally discussed by Freire (1972), is the "process of learning a balance of individual and societal responsibility and acting on that knowledge" (Cheatham et al., 1993, p. 95). Multicultural counseling and therapy promotes conscientizacao and the development of critical consciousness. Within the context of career counseling, it may be important for the counselor to use interventions that help a client become responsible for his or her own actions but to temper such interventions with a realistic appraisal of external barriers. Counseling may also involve the client's network of communities. These may be the family, extended family, community, and so forth.

Traditionally, the process of career counseling involves assessment. Cross-cultural vocational assessment has unique issues and concerns. Fouad (1993) outlined several issues specific to the use of standard assessment tools with a culturally diverse clientele. These included issues of cultural values, functional and linguistic equivalence, translation, test bias, and norms. Cultural values may come into play, as mentioned previously, when a client has a collective, or group-oriented, world view, with most assessment tools very individually oriented. It is important that counselors augment their use of traditional assessment instruments with other tools to help them identify the variables important for clients in their career decision making. One example of an alternative instrument is found in Ward and Bingham's (1993) career counseling checklist," which helps women identify various factors that influence their decision making, including ethnicity and family variables.

Functional and conceptual equivalence are related to cultural values and world views (Fouad, 1993). Functional equivalence refers to the role that behavior plays across cultures. It is important for counselors to determine, for example, the role that interests play across cultures or that individual decision-making styles play. Knowledge that these play different functions may affect the test-taker's responses and will affect the interpretation of the information to the client. Conceptual equivalence is related and refers to how similar the meaning of various items is across cultures. Fouad described the item Churchworker on the Strong Interest Inventory. In their work on the Spanish translation of the inventory, Hansen and Fouad (1984) found that this item elicited different perceptions in Mexico and the United States.

Fouad (1993) described the appropriate procedures for translation of instruments, pointing out that it is important for clients to compute an assessment instrument in the language with which they are familiar. Triandis (1993) noted, however, that the procedure she described of using bilingual field-testing may be particularly susceptible to social desirability and encouraged both the creation of instruments for use with a specific population and the collection of local norms. The appropriate use of norms is a critical component of competent cross-cultural assessment, and counselors must take the norming group into account.

The interventions used in career counseling may range from traditional "test and tell" trait–factor approaches to fantasy exercises (Spokane, 1991), to genograms (Brown & Brooks, 1991), to informational interviewing (Yost & Corbishley, 1987). It is very important that cross-culturally competent career counselors link their interventions to the career issues defined by the client, with an incorporation of cultural variables. Thus, their interventions are tailored to meet their client's needs, rather than limited by the counselor's comfort with a particular technique, strategy, or instrument.

Step 6. Decision Making. Sharon decided to learn additional study skills and to apply herself to finishing the semester with better grades. She decided to become an elementary school teacher, with an early childhood emphasis, and hoped to become a Head Start teacher. She believed that the Head Start certification would increase her marketability, a reason that pleased her father.

As clients move toward decision making and the realization of counseling goals, Step 6 in the model, they may be making career choices, deciding to adjust their work roles or work salience, or deciding they need more information to make a choice. Those clients may make plans, and counseling tapers off as they begin to implement their plans and exit the process. Some clients, for whom counseling has clarified issues, may choose to cycle back through career counseling to work on different goals. Counselors should be open to that process, particularly for minority clients who do not see career counseling in a linear, rational decision-making mode. Hispanic clients, for example, are more likely to see counseling as more circular than linear and may need to circle several times through the process (Fouad, in press). Counselors who are impatient with this process are imposing their own world view on the client.

Step 7. Implementation and Follow-Up. Sharon was successful in completing the semester with As and Bs and was satisfied with her choice of major. She felt that counseling had met her needs, had helped her to clarify her goals, and had helped her to deal successfully with her family, an aspect that was extremely important to her.

A minority client may conclude the career counseling process by implementing the career plans worked out with the counselor. A client may have decided on a career or a major area of study leading to a career, as Sharon did. The counselor must be sure that the plan satisfies the requirements of the client's world view or that the client understands that his or her plan will be in opposition to some traditional family values. Also useful is the counselor's helping the client predict some of the possible consequences of the decisions made in Step 6.

Finally, it may be important for the counselor to encourage the client to return to counseling if the need arises. Some ethnic minority clients may have ascribed a familial or expert role to the counselor. In such a case, the client may find a return to counseling difficult because he or she interprets the need to return as a failure. Moreover, a failure may result in loss of face for the client. If a counselor can reinforce the work that has taken place and normalize the possibility of returning for help, a client may feel more generally satisfied with the career counseling process.

CONCLUSION

Traditional career counseling was not effective for Sharon because it did not acknowledge the cultural variables that influenced her career decisions. When she entered counseling with a multiculturally competent counselor, she made and began to implement a career decision. The difference between this outcome and that with the first counselor stemmed from Janelle's discussion, from the outset, of race and how Sharon's culture and world view affected her career decisions.

The seven-step model we have proposed incorporates cultural variables in every step. We believe that this incorporation is critical in counselors' effectively helping minority clients and that failure to incorporate them may result in counseling failure. In our case example, Sharon was not counseled to proceed and to fight the discrimination she perceived in a corporate environment, but it was acknowledged that her perception affected her decision. The model includes recognition of external barriers that affect racial and ethnic minority clients. This recognition is vitally important to any counseling model for racial and ethnic minority clients because they are disproportionately affected by external barriers of discrimination and prejudice. Not only are minority clients affected by the overt experience of discrimination, but those experiences may also have a cumulative affect. Consequently, these clients may make decisions to avoid such experiences, or the experiences erode their self-confidence and self-efficacy. A multiculturally competent career counselor will acknowledge and validate those experiences and will be prepared to help his or her client learn advocacy skills but will not push clients to overcome external barriers if they are not ready and prepared to do so.

The effects of cultural variables on career decisions (Step 3) were more fully discussed than the other steps in the model because counselors must overtly address those areas with clients and because from that step a culturally appropriate intervention follows. The case may be that effective career counseling of *all* clients will incorporate the influences of family, gender, and culture. If it did, clients could explore what role they want work to play in their lives, what balance they want between work and family, or what messages from their culture and family they want to accept, discard, or change. In this way, the "gendered context of work" (Cook, 1993, p. 229) may be addressed with both men and women of all races and ethnicities.

RECOMMENDATIONS FOR FUTURE RESEARCH

This model is just a beginning proposal for the incorporation of cultural variables into career counseling. We fully anticipate and, frankly, hope that research into the effectiveness of the model will modify and clarify it. We have some recommendations for future research.

First, we are assuming that this model of career counseling is more effective than those of traditional career counseling. This assumption should be empirically tested with racial and ethnic minority clients. Analogue studies of minority clients who receive traditional career counseling or multicultural career counseling would be informative. Traditional career counseling could be defined in a variety of ways: trait–factor, developmental, social learning, and so forth. We should also investigate whether group interventions are more effective delivery models (as Bowman, 1993, advocates) than individual counseling.

Second, we lack empirical information about the career behavior of racial and ethnic minority members. Much work is still needed in this area. Fruitful areas already identified for cross-cultural investigation include assessment (Arbona, in press; Fouad, 1993; Leong & Serafica, in press), identity development (Fouad & Arbona, in press), counseling expectations and goals (Leong & Gim, in press), collectivism (Fouad, in press; Leong & Gim, in press), value conflicts (Leong & Gim, in press), career maturity (Fouad & Arbona, in press; Leong & Serafica, in press), developmental tasks (Fouad & Arbona, in press; Leong & Serafica, in press; Martin, in press), social network (Martin, in press), and learning styles (Bowman, 1993). This is by no means an exhaustive list of areas for investigation. Such a small amount of empirical bases exists for us to make conclusions about the career behavior of racial and ethnic minority clients that almost all areas of vocational behavior are open to researchers.

Third, the discussion of cultural variables is too easily interpreted as overgeneralizing about members of various racial and ethnic groups. Just as it is important to investigate differences among minority groups, it is equally, if not more, important to investigate within-group differences. All Asian Americans are not the same, neither are Hispanics, nor Native Americans, nor African Americans. Much work needs to be undertaken so we can determine the moderating variables that explain within-group behavior. These variables may include generational status, acculturation and assimilation, SES, racial identity, or language proficiency.

Fourth, we are proponents of a developmental model. Cross-cultural differences in the process of managing developmental tasks or in the nature of the tasks themselves are a major area of future research. Is the pattern of acquisition of tasks the same? Does career maturity have the same construct validity across cultural groups? Do we need to add developmental tasks that include racial identity? Family? Social roles?

Fifth, we have not included sexual orientation in our model. We are sensitive to the cultural influence that sexual orientation may have on the career decision-making process for individuals at various developmental stages, but we are unaware of how to include that in the model. We look to colleagues to initiate this research and modify the model appropriately.

Sixth, we advocate qualitative research in addition to quantitative research. Although empirical quantitative studies are needed and will help us further our understanding of minority career behavior, our knowledge will be complete only if we understand the process variables that may affect vocational choices. These variables are best understood by our asking individuals to talk about their experiences and do not lend themselves well to quantitative analysis.

Finally, we add our voices to those of many others (e.g., Arbona, in press; Bingham & Ward, 1994; Bowman, 1993; Fouad, in press; Leong & Serafica, in press; Martin, in press) who say that we must begin to build theoretical models that explain and predict the career behavior of minority members. Such models must be the ultimate goal if we are to help racial and ethnic group members make the best career decisions possible.

REFERENCES

Akbar, N. (1981). Mental disorder among African Americans. *Black Books Bulletin, 7*, 18–25.

Arbona, C. (1990). Career counseling research with Hispanics: A review of the literature. *The Counseling Psychologist, 18*, 300–323.

Arbona, C. (in press). Theory and research on racial and ethnic minorities: Hispanic Americans. In F. T. L. Leong (Ed.), *Career development and vocational behavior of racial and ethnic minorities*. Hillsdale, NJ: Lawrence Erlbaum Associates.

Arbona, C., & Novy, D. (1991). Career aspiration and expectations of Black, Mexican-American, and White students. *The Career Development Quarterly, 39*, 231–239.

Atkinson, D. R., Morten, G., & Sue, D. W. (1983). *Counseling American minorities: A cross-cultural perspective* (2nd ed.). Dubuque, IA: Brown.

Atkinson, D. R., Morten, G., & Sue, D. W. (1993). *Counseling American minorities* (4th ed.). Madison, WI: Brown.

Atkinson, D. R., & Thompson, C. E. (1992). Racial, ethnic and cultural variables in counseling. In S. D. Brown & R. W. Lent (Eds.), *Handbook of counseling psychology* (2nd ed., pp. 349–382). New York: Wiley.

Attneave, C. (1982). American Indians and Alaska native families: Emigrants in their own homeland. In M. McGoldrick, J. K. Pearce, & J. Giordano (Eds.), *Ethnicity and family therapy* (pp. 55–83). New York: Guilford.

Bingham, R. P., & Ward, C. M. (1994). Career counseling with ethnic minority women. In W. B. Walsh & S. Osipow (Eds.), *Career counseling with women* (pp. 165–195). Hillsdale, NJ: Lawrence Erlbaum Associates.

Bowman, S. L. (1993). Career intervention strategies for ethnic minorities. *Career Development Quarterly, 42*, 14–25.

Bozarth, J. D., & Fisher, R. (1990). Person-centered career counseling. In W. B. Walsh & S. Osipow (Eds.), *Career counseling: Contemporary topics in vocational psychology* (pp. 45–78). Hillsdale, NJ: Lawrence Erlbaum Associates.

Bridges, J. S. (1993). Pink or blue: Gender-stereotypic perceptions of infants as conveyed by birth congratulations cards. *Psychology of Women Quarterly, 17*, 193–205.

Brown, D., & Brooks, L. (1991). *Career counseling techniques*. Boston: Allyn & Bacon.

Brown, D., Minor, C. W., & Jepsen, D. A. (1991). The opinions of minorities preparing for work: Report of the second NCDA National Survey. *Career Development Quarterly, 40*, 5–19.

Carter, R. T. (1990). Cultural values: A review of empirical research and implications for counseling. *Journal of Counseling and Development, 70*, 164–173.

Cheatham, H. (1990). Africentricity and career development of African Americans. *The Career Development Quarterly, 38*, 334–346.

Cheatham, H. E., Ivey, A. E., Ivey, M. B., & Simek–Morgan, L. (1993). Multicultural counseling and therapy: Changing the foundations of the field. In A. E. Ivey, M. B. Ivey, & L. Simek–Morgan (Eds.), *Counseling and psychotherapy: A multicultural perspective* (3rd ed., pp. 93–123). Boston: Allyn & Bacon.

Christensen, C. P. (1989). Cross-cultural awareness development: A conceptual model. *Counselor Education and Supervision, 28*, 270–287.

Comas–Diaz, L., & Jacobsen, F. M. (1987). Ethnocultural identification in psychotherapy. *Psychiatry, 50*, 232–241.

Cook, P. E. (1993). The gendered context of life: Implications for women's and men's career-life plans. *The Career Development Quarterly, 41*, 227–237.

Cross, W. E. (1971). Negro-to-Black conversion experience: Toward a psychology of Black liberation. *Black World, 20*, 13–27.

Denga, D. I. (1988). Influence of traditional factors on career choice among Nigerian secondary school youth. *Journal of Multicultural Counseling and Development, 16*, 1–15.

Department of Labor. (1992). *Statistical abstracts.* Washington, DC: Author.

DISCOVER Foundation (1977). *Discover: A computer based career development and counselor support system.* Westminster, MD: Author.

Dorn, F. (1990). Career counseling and the social influence model. In W. B. Walsh & S. Osipow (Eds.), *Career counseling: Contemporary topics in vocational psychology* (pp. 193–223). Hillsdale, NJ: Lawrence Erlbaum Associates.

Evansoki, P. D., & Wu Tse, F. (1989). Career awareness program for Chinese and Korean American parents. *Journal of Counseling and Development, 67*, 472–474.

Fitzgerald, L., & Betz, N. E. (1992, April). *Career development in cultural context: The role of gender, race, class, and sexual orientation.* Paper presented at the Conference on Theories Convergence in Vocational Psychology, East Lansing, MI.

Forrest, L., & Mikolaitis, N. (1986). The relational component of identity: An expansion of career development theory. *Career Development Quarterly, 35*, 76–88.

Fouad, N. A. (1993). Cross-cultural vocational assessment. *Career Development Quarterly, 42*, 4–13.

Fouad, N. A. (in press). Career assessment and intervention with Hispanic Americans. In F. T. L. Leong (Ed.), *Career development and vocational behavior of racial and ethnic minorities.* Hillsdale, NJ: Lawrence Erlbaum Associates.

Fouad, N. A., & Arbona, C. (1994). Careers in a cultural context. *Career Development Quarterly, 43*, 96–104.

Freire, P. (1972). *Pedagogy of the oppressed.* New York: Herder & Herder.

Gainor, K., & Forrest, L. (1991). African American women's self-concept: Implications for career decisions and career counseling. *Career Development Quarterly, 39*, 261–272.

Gottfredson, L. S. (1981). Circumscription and compromise: A developmental theory of occupational aspiration. *Journal of Counseling Psychology, 28*, 545–579.

Gysbers, N. C., & Moore, E. J. (1987). *Career counseling: Skills and techniques for practitioners.* Englewood Cliffs, NJ: Prentice–Hall.

Hackett, N. E., & Betz, N. (1981). A self-efficacy approach to the career development of women. *Journal of Vocational Behavior, 18*, 326–339.

Hale–Benson, J. (1986). *Black children: Their roots, culture and learning style.* Baltimore: Johns Hopkins University Press.

Hale–Benson, J. (1990). Visions for children: Educating Black children in the context of their culture. In K. Lomotey (Ed.), *Going to school: The African-American experience* (pp. 113–134). State University of New York Press.

Hansen, J. (1992). *User's guide: Strong Interest Inventory.* Palo Alto, CA: Consulting Psychology Press.

Hansen, J. C., & Fouad, N. A. (1984). Validation of the Spanish translation of the Strong-Campbell Interest Inventory. *Measurement and Evaluation in Guidance, 16*, 192–197.

Hardiman, R. (1982). White identity development: A process-oriented model for describing the racial consciousness of White Americans. *Dissertations Abstracts International, 43*, 104A. (University Microfilms No. 82–10330)

Helms, J. E. (Ed.). (1990). *Black and white racial identity: Theory, research, and practice.* Eastport, CT: Greenwood.

Helms, J. E. (1984). Toward a theoretical explanation of the effects of race on counseling: A Black/White interactional model. *The Counseling Psychologist, 12,* 153–165.

Herr, E. L. (1989). *Counseling in a dynamic society: Opportunities and challenges.* Alexandria, VA: American Association of Counseling and Development.

Herr, E. L., & Cramer, S. H. (1992). *Career guidance and counseling through the life span: Systematic approaches* (4th ed.). New York: HarperCollins.

Holland, J. L. (1985a). *Making vocational choices.* Englewood Cliffs, NJ: Prentice–Hall.

Holland, J. L. (1985b). *The self-directed search: Professional manual.* Odessa, FL: Psychological Assessment Resources.

Isaacson, L. E., & Brown, D. (1993). *Career information, career counseling and career development* (5th ed.). Boston: Allyn & Bacon.

Ivey, A. E., Ivey, M. B., & Simek–Morgan, L. (1993). *Counseling and psychotherapy: A multicultural perspective.* Boston: Allyn & Bacon.

Jepsen, D. A. (1990). Developmental career counseling. In W. B. Walsh & S. H. Osipow (Eds.), *Career counseling: Contemporary topics in vocational psychology* (pp. 117–157). Hillsdale, NJ: Lawrence Erlbaum Associates.

Katz, J. H. (1985). The sociopolitical nature of counseling. *The Counseling Psychologist, 13,* 615–624.

Krumboltz, J. D., & Nichols, C. W. (1990). Integrating the social learning theory of career decision making. In W. B. Walsh & S. H. Osipow (Eds.), *Career counseling: Contemporary topics in vocational psychology* (pp. 159–192). Hillsdale, NJ: Lawrence Erlbaum Associates.

Leong, F. T. L. (1985). Career development of Asian Americans. *Journal of College Student Personnel, 26,* 539–546.

Leong, F. T. L. (1993). The career counseling process with racial–ethnic minorities: The case of Asian Americans. *Career Development Quarterly, 42,* 26–40.

Leong, F. T. L., & Gim, R. H. C. (in press). Career assessment and intervention for Asian Americans. In F. T. L. Leong (Ed.), *Career development and vocational behavior of racial and ethnic minorities.* Hillsdale, NJ: Lawrence Erlbaum Associates.

Leong, F. T. L., & Brown, M. (in press). Vocational theory and research. In W. B. Walsh & S. H. Osipow (Eds.), *Handbook of vocational psychology* (2nd ed.).

Leong, F. T. L., & Serafica, F. C. (in press). Career development of Asian Americans: A research area in need of a good theory. In F. T. L. Leong (Ed.), *Career development and vocational behavior of racial and ethnic minorities.* Hillsdale, NJ: Lawrence Erlbaum Associates.

Locke, D. C., & Parker, L. D. (1991). A multicultural focus on career education (Doc. No. 071). Columbus, OH: The ERIC Clearing House on Adult, Career, and Vocational Education. (ERIC Document Reproduction Service No. ED341877).

Martin, W. E., Jr. (in press). Career development assessment and intervention strategies with American Indians. In F. T. L. Leong (Ed.), *Career development and vocational behavior of racial and ethnic minorities.* Hillsdale, NJ: Lawrence Erlbaum Associates.

McGoldrick, M., Pearce, J. K., & Giordano, J. (Eds.). (1982). *Ethnicity and family therapy.* New York: Guilford.

McRae, M. B., & Carter, R. T. (1992). *Journal of Employment Counseling, 29,* 2–4.

National Career Development Association. (1992). Career counseling competencies. *Career Development Quarterly, 40,* 378–386.

Nobles, W. W. (1976). Extended self: Rethinking the Negro self-concept. *Journal of Black Psychology, 2,* 15–24.

Ogbu, J. U. (1990). Literacy and schooling in subordinate cultures: The case of Black Americans. In K. Lomotey (Ed.), *Going to school: The African-American experience* (pp. 113–134). State University of New York Press.

Parham, T. (1989). Cycles of psychological nigrescence. *The Counseling Psychologist, 17*, 187–226.

Parsons, F. B. (1909). *Choosing a vocation.* Boston: Houghton Mifflin.

Pedersen, P. B. (1976). The field of intercultural counseling. In P. Pedersen, W. J. Lonner, & J. G. Draguns (Eds.), *Counseling across cultures* (pp. 17–41). Honolulu: University of Hawaii Press.

Pedersen, P., Draguns, J., Lonner, W., & Trimbles, J. (1989). *Counseling across cultures.* Honolulu: University of Hawaii Press.

Peterson, G. W., Sampson, J. P., & Reardon, R. C. (1991). *Career development and services: A cognitive approach.* Pacific Grove, CA: Brooks/Cole.

Ponterotto, J. G. (1988a). Racial consciousness development among white counselor trainees: A stage model. *Journal of Multicultural Counseling and Development, 16*, 146–156.

Ponterotto, J. G. (1988b). Racial/ethnic minority research in the *Journal of Counseling Psychology:* A content analysis and methodological critique. *Journal of Counseling Psychology, 35*, 410–418.

Ponterotto, J. G., & Casas, J. M. (1991). *Handbook of racial/ethnic minority counseling research.* Springfield, IL: Thomas.

Ponterotto, J. G., & Pedersen, P. B. (1993). *Preventing prejudice: A guide for counselors and educators.* Newbury Park, CA: Sage.

Rayman, J. R. (1990). Computers and career counseling. In W. B. Walsh & S. H. Osipow (Eds.), *Career counseling: Contemporary topics in vocational psychology* (pp. 225–262). Hillsdale, NJ: Lawrence Erlbaum Associates.

Richardson, M. S. (1993). Work in people's lives: A location for counseling psychologists. *Journal of Counseling Psychology, 40*, 425–433.

Rounds, J. B., & Tracy, T. J. (1990). From trait-and-factor–person–environment fit counseling: Theory and process. In W. B. Walsh & S. H. Osipow (Eds.), *Career counseling: Contemporary topics in vocational psychology* (pp. 1–44). Hillsdale, NJ: Lawrence Erlbaum Associates.

Sabnani, H. B., Ponterotto, J. G., & Borodovsky, L. G. (1991). White racial identity development and cross-cultural training: A stage model. *The Counseling Psychologist, 19*, 76–102.

Saveri, A. (1991). The realignment of workers and work in the 1990s. In J. M. Kummerow (Ed.), *New directions in career planning and the workplace: Practical strategies for counselors* (pp. 117–154). Palo Alto, CA: Consulting Psychologists Press.

Spiegel, J. (1982). An ecological model of ethnic families. In M. McGoldrick, J. K. Pearce, & J. Giordano (Eds.), *Ethnicity and family therapy* (pp. 31–54). New York: Guilford.

Spokane, A. R. (1991). *Career intervention.* Englewood Cliffs, NJ: Prentice–Hall.

Spokane, A. R., & Richardson, T. Q. (1992). Everything you need to know about career development you already know. *NACADA Journal, 12*, 42–48.

Subich, L. M. (1993, August). Teaching and training perspective. In M. L. Savickas (Chair), *Career counseling theory—Problems and prospects.* Symposium conducted at the annual meeting of the American Psychological Association, Toronto, Canada.

Sue, D. W. (1981). *Counseling the culturally different: Theory and practice.* New York: Wiley.

Sue, D. W., Arrendondo, P., & McDavis, R. J. (1992). Multicultural counseling competencies and standards: A call to the profession. *Journal of Multicultural Counseling and Development, 20*, 64–88.

Sue, D. W., Bernier, J. E., Durran, A., Feinbert, L., Pedersen, P., Smith, E., & Vasquez–Nuttal, E. (1992). Position paper: Cross-cultural counseling competencies. *The Counseling Psychologist, 10*, 45–52.

Sue, D. W., & Sue, D. (1990). *Counseling the culturally different: Theory and practice* (2nd ed.). New York: Wiley.

Super, D. E. (1957). *The psychology of careers.* New York: Harper & Row.

Swanson, J. L. (1993). Integrated assessment of vocational interest and self-rated skills and abilities. *Journal of Career Assessment, 1*, 50–65.

Triandis, H. C. (1993). Comments on multicultural counseling. *Career Development Quarterly, 42,* 50–52.

Walsh, W. B. (1990). A summary and integration of career counseling approaches. In W. B. Walsh & S. H. Osipow (Eds.), *Career counseling: Contemporary topics in vocational psychology* (pp. 263–282). Hillsdale, NJ: Lawrence Erlbaum Associates.

Walsh, W. B., & Osipow, S. H. (Eds.). (1990). *Career counseling: Contemporary topics in vocational psychology.* Hillsdale, NJ: Lawrence Erlbaum Associates.

Ward, C. M., & Bingham, R. P. (1993). Career assessment of ethnic minority women. *Journal of Career Assessment, 1,* 246–257.

Watkins, C. E., & Savickas, M. L. (1990). Psychodynamic career counseling. In W. B. Walsh & S. H. Osipow (Eds.), *Career counseling: Contemporary topics in vocational psychology* (pp. 79–116). Hillsdale, NJ: Lawrence Erlbaum Associates.

Wehrly, B. (1988). Influence of traditional factors on career choice among Nigerian secondary school youth. *Journal of Multicultural Counseling and Development, 16,* 3–5.

Wrenn, G. (1962). The culturally encapsulated counselor. *Howard Education Review, 32,* 444–449.

Yost, E. B., & Corbishley, M. A. (1987). *Career counseling: A psychological approach.* San Francisco: Jossey–Bass.

CHAPTER ELEVEN

International Cross-Cultural Approaches to Career Development

Beryl Hesketh
Macquarie University

James Rounds
University of Illinois at Champaign

At least two other chapters in this handbook address cross-cultural issues relevant to the theory and practice of vocational psychology. In the present chapter, we have chosen to focus on fundamental issues that may facilitate or hinder the generalization of vocational theories, across cultures within one country, within cultures across countries, or across both cultures and countries. We also hope to outline the approaches and criteria that would be needed in order for researchers to develop theories that not only identify more accurately the components that generalize and those that do not but also take into account assumptions associated with absolutism, relativism, and universalism (Adamopoulos & Lonner, 1994).

Several advantages arise out of a focus on fundamental cross-cultural issues. First, the approach highlights important implicit and often unstated assumptions underlying the major theories developed predominantly in the United States. These assumptions may relate to typical patterns of education, geographic and economic factors affecting the opportunity structure, and the prevailing value system, all of which provide important boundary conditions for the theories and related practical approaches (Boyacigiller & Adler, 1991). Associated with this, a second advantage lies in the improved science and practice that is likely to arise from the perspective gained through a view of theories outside of the cultural paradigm of their origin. Philosophy of science points to the value of an external perspective from which researchers can evaluate approaches developed within a particular paradigm or framework.

A third advantage of focusing on fundamental issues from an international perspective lies in the early warning that this may provide about the danger of "used by dates" for current vocational theory and practice in Western countries. The pace of change in society, particularly as it relates to work organization, is immense (Hesketh & Bochner, 1993; Offermann & Gowing, 1990). Theory and practice developed for the 20th Century may not be appropriate for the twenth-first century. An international cross-cultural perspective may highlight those aspects of the current theory and practice that are dependent on the way Western society is and has functioned in the past and, hence, may help researchers identify the features that may not generalize to societies of the 21st Century. The fourth advantage is related and is the identification of ETIC, or universal, features of career theory and practice and the EMIC features that are specific to careers in a particular culture or time (Berry, 1979). A clear differentiation of the ETIC and EMIC aspects of career theory and practice can help to ensure that approaches are tailored to the situation and to particular client needs.

A fifth point relates to the possibility of researchers' evaluating the potential role of relevant factors (gender, ethnicity, country, and culture) in traditional theories of career choice and development. Rounds and Hesketh (1994) noted the importance of researchers' testing whether or not demographic factors within one country or culture affect the validity of predictions arising from the Minnesota Theory of Work Adjustment (Dawis & Lofquist, 1984) and other theories. An international cross-cultural perspective on career development permits a more detailed exploration of these issues.

A final advantage arising from an international and cross-cultural perspective is the spotlight that it places on the different relationships of vocational psychology to other disciplines (Fitzgerald & Rounds, 1989). In the United States, vocational psychology is a small but specialized area of research and practice. In most other countries, it forms part of a larger field of industrial and organizational psychology, or occupational psychology. In Europe, work psychology covers traditional industrial and organizational psychology as well as career development. The orientations and approaches arising from an integrated perspective differ markedly from those dominating the U.S. scene. The international perspective permits an assessment of the advantages and disadvantages of the specialization in vocational psychology, which appears to be a feature in the United States.

We can place the previous discussion in the context of fundamental assumptions with respect to philosophical positions of absolutism, relativism, and universalism. Absolutism, which forms the basis of many of the approaches taken in psychology, assumes that there is an underlying "true" nature in all human beings that is waiting to be discovered. Within this view, culture is a nuisance variable that interferes with the search for true universals (Adamopoulos & Lonner, 1994). By contrast, a relativist argues that it is possible to describe human behavior only in the context of its sociocultural environment. Gergen's (1991) social constructionism is, in part, a form of relativism. The universalist position is less extreme, permitting a search for universals although also arguing that such universals are sensitive to culture (Adamopoulos & Lonner, 1994). Within the universalist position, it would be necessary for vocational theories to contain statements clarifying which components of the theory constitute common absolutes applicable across all cultures and countries (the ETIC features) and which are subject to relativistic arguments (the EMIC features).

In the next section we review several ideas derived from the cross-cultural literature that provide a potential basis for the evaluation of those aspects of existing theories of career choice and development that are likely to generalize and those that are bound by time, country, or culture. To illustrate the value of models arising from the cross-cultural literature, we discuss examples of core constructs in vocational psychology (self-concept, self-efficacy, interests, and career choice) and illustrate how these do or do not take on different meanings in different cultures. Finally, we provide a set of principles for the development of theories so that such theories more accurately delineate the extent to which they apply internationally and cross-culturally.

Cross-Cultural Typologies

Several systems for comparing countries and cultures have been identified by cross-cultural researchers (Hofstede, 1980, 1991; Ronen & Shenkar, 1985; S. Schwartz & Bilsky, 1987; Triandis, Bontempo, Vilareal, Masaaki, & Lucca, 1988). Ronen and Shenkar (1985) reviewed the results of several studies by which investigators clustered countries on work-attitude measures. A synthesis of these clusters suggested the following groupings: Anglo (United States, Canada, Australia, New Zealand, United Kingdom, Ireland, and South Africa), Latin European (France, Belgium, Italy, Portugal, and Spain), Latin American (Argentina, Venezuela, Chile, Mexico, Peru, and Colombia), Far Eastern (Malaysia, Singapore, Hong Kong, Philippines, South Vietnam, Indonesia, and Thailand), Arab (Bahrain, Kuwait, United Arab Emirates, and Oman), Near East (Turkey, Iran, and Greece), Nordic (Finland, Norway, Denmark, and Sweden), and Germanic (Austria, Germany, and Switzerland). Countries such as Brazil, Japan, India, and Israel remained comparatively independent, although Israel was grouped with the Anglo countries in some studies. The relevance of these groupings becomes more apparent when the ideas such as those derived from Hofstede (1980, 1991) are examined.

Although not without limitations, Hofstede's (1991) approach is widely used in industrial and organizational psychology. Hofstede outlined the results of research carried out in IBM companies in 40 countries, in which local employees were asked to respond to a series of work-organization and work-value questions. Four dimensions that appeared to differentiate the countries emerged. The most commonly known, and the most relevant to notions of vocational development, is the *individualism–collectivism* dimension. Cross-cultural psychologists other than Hofstede have drawn attention to the centrality of individualism–collectivism to the understanding of differences in cultural values and practices (Bond, 1994; S. Schwartz, 1992; Triandis, 1990, 1993). Bond (1994) provided descriptive illustrations of how the Chinese in Hong Kong place greater significance on the successes and failures of their group than do persons in individualistic countries, such as Canada, where personal success or failure is paramount (see also Bond, 1991). Others have used the Schwartz Value Survey (S. Schwartz, 1992) to show the extent to which the values held by people in different countries serve individualistic interests of power, achievement, stimulation, and self-direction or collectivist interests, such as benevolence, tradition, and conformity.

People in countries in Ronen and Shenkar's (1985) Anglo cluster (e.g., Australia, Canada, and the United States) scored high on individualism, whereas those in many of the Far Eastern countries (e.g., the Philippines, Hong King, and Thailand), with their different religious and philosophical orientations, scored high on collectivism. Scores by individuals in Israel fell between these two groups, with moderate levels of individualism. As we show later in this chapter, this distinction has important implications for the development of the self-concept (Erez, 1993; Erez & Earley, 1993), and has been researched extensively (see Kagitcibasi & Berry, 1989, for a review).

The next most frequently cited dimension in the Hofstede (1991) model is *power–distance*. High power–distance cultures (such as Malaysia, India, and Yugoslavia) place considerable emphasis on respect for authority and traditional institutions; in contrast, low power–distance cultures (e.g., New Zealand, Israel, Australia, and the United States) tend toward less respect for authority and demonstrate a greater questioning of tradition. Although conceptually distinct, in practice individualism–collectivism and power–distance are highly correlated (Bochner & Hesketh, 1994). For example, a country that is high on power–distance also tends to be collectivist. The remaining two dimensions in the Hofstede model are high or low *uncertainty–avoidance* and *masculinity–femininity*, both of which are cited less frequently in discussions of Hofstede's model.

Cautions for the Use of Cross-Cultural Models

In the application of cross-cultural models and constructs such as individualism and collectivism, investigators must acknowledge the danger of inappropriate stereotyping. Cultural change is occurring rapidly, and many individuals who have adopted a different country soon take on the values of their new home. Australia is a typical example, having been populated with comparatively recent waves of immigrants from Europe, southeastern Mediterranean countries, the Middle East, and more recently all parts of Asia. There is considerable variation in the degree to which immigrants have retained an identity with their countries of origin. Assumptions about cultural identity cannot be based simply on the country of origin of a person, yet the assumption that traditional individualistic Western values predominate is also false.

In exploring cross-cultural issues, investigators must also be particularly aware of the possible confounding of social class with cultural differences. For example, Cashmore and Goodnow (1986) discovered that differences between Anglo-Australian and Italian parents in Australia decreased when several indicators of socioeconomic status were taken into account. Furthermore, differences emerge between countries like the United States and Australia with respect to the recognition of achievement, even though both countries are Anglo-Celtic and people in both score high on individualism. Feather and McKee (1993) drew attention to the tendency by persons in Australia to cut down "tall poppies," in that conspicuous success is not considered good, in part because it leads to inequalities and differences in status. In the United States, persons have less tendency to devalue individual achievements, possibly because there is less concern about inequalities.

The cautionary statement about cultural change occurring as the result of immigration is also needed because of an increasing influence that indigenous peoples have on countries such as New Zealand and Australia, previously considered exclusively Anglo-Celtic. Hesketh and Kennedy (1991) commented on the influence of the increasing biculturalism in New Zealand on economic and cultural developments and on the delivery of vocational guidance. Within the last 10 years, Maori has been accepted as an official language, and all government agencies are required by law to include a Maori perspective. B. Jamieson (personal communication, 1993) described the value differences that exist between the Maori and Anglo-Celtic groups in New Zealand and illustrated the effects through the process of selection interviewing. The Maori, like Hispanic Americans (Marin, 1994), rely on their families rather than on themselves for advocacy. The Maori are also respectful of authority and tradition and, in the presence of elders, tend to look down and keep comparatively quiet. These characteristics created problems in the context of selection interviewing, during which applicants are typically expected to "sell" themselves. To overcome the cultural difficulty, the New Zealand public service has, in fact, introduced *whanau* interviewing, in which a small group or the family may support and speak on behalf of the applicant. In a context such as this, any measures of self-concept and self-efficacy, constructs discussed more fully later, would need to include the whanau or family.

Bond (1994) provided an example from Hong Kong that also illustrates the differences in ways in which achievements are presented. Bond described how a potential job candidate devalued his achievements rather than advocating himself for a position. To a Westerner, the applicant's behavior seemed strange, but the process of self-deprecation was understood well by the Chinese involved in the selection. These examples are illustrative only, but they do serve to highlight that career-related behaviors and approaches considered acceptable and desirable in one culture may be viewed very differently in others. Differences in the roles of the individual and the group and ways of valuing success and failure underlie some of these illustrations.

In summary, our central concern in this chapter is to explore the core constructs and theories in vocational psychology in order to determine the extent to which they will generalize across cultures and time. To this end, we use the cross-cultural typologies, particularly the main Hofstede (1991) dimension of individualism–collectivism. On the basis of the discussion, we provide a set of general guidelines for the development of theory that identifies more accurately those components that are culture or country specific and those that can be applied internationally.

CORE CONSTRUCTS

Self-Concept

Self-concept has been a key construct in several theories of career development, notably that of Super (1957, 1990) and the social learning theory (Krumboltz, 1979). The self consists of all statements made by a person, overtly or covertly, that include the words "I," "me," "mine," and "myself" (Triandis, 1989, p. 506). Super (1957) referred to this as "psychtalk" and noted the importance of commensurate "occtalk," consisting of work-relevant statements that the person made. Erez (1993) referred to the self as consisting of schemas, prototypes, goals, and images. Schemas can be thought of in terms of self-observation generalizations (SOGs) described in social learning theory (Krumboltz, 1979; Krumboltz, Mitchell, & G. Jones, 1978).

Erez (1993) argued that several self-regulatory processes are used to sustain the self: self-enhancement, as reflected in the individual's seeking and maintaining a positive cognitive and affective state about the self; self-efficacy, reflected in the desire to perceive oneself as competent and self-efficacious; and self-consistency, which is the individual's desire to sense and experience coherence and continuity.

The self and its evaluation are embedded in the rich context of cultural and family influences. More important for the argument developed in this chapter, Erez (1993) suggested that self-evaluation is gained from several possible sources: from others (public evaluation), from personal or internal standards (self-evaluation), or from the contribution that one makes to the collective or reference group (social identity; Tajfel, 1978). Tajfel argued that part of the individual's self-concept arises out of the knowledge that he or she belongs to a social group that holds common values. Emotional significance is attached to such membership. The relative importance of the criteria used to evaluate the self vary from culture to culture. Individualistic cultures tend to result in an emphasis on the use of private self-evaluations. Autonomy and independence are reinforced in the development of the self. By contrast, in collectivist cultures, self-evaluation and identity are fostered through group membership, where private or individual goals are subordinated for those of the collective. The differences in the emphasis placed on various sources of self-evaluation across cultures may have implications for the generality of the vocational theories developed and tested in an individualistic culture.

Self-Efficacy

One component of the self-concept identified by Erez (1993) is the feeling of self-efficacy. The term self-efficacy, first coined by Bandura (1977) within the context of social learning theory, refers to the person's feelings of confidence in the ability to perform particular behaviors or tasks and takes into account both level and generality. As a construct, self-efficacy has received considerable attention in recent vocational literature (Betz & Hackett, 1987; Lent & Hackett, 1987) and has become established as an important component of the career-choice process. Self-efficacy continues to be the subject of considerable research (e.g., Betz & Hackett, 1987; Hackett, Betz, O'Halloran, & Romac, 1990; Lauver & P. Jones, 1991; Luzzo, 1993; Vasil, 1992). In some of this research, investigators examined cultural or ethnic differences (e.g., Bores–Rangel, Church, Szendre, & Reeves, 1990; Church, Teresa, Rosebrook, & Szendre, 1992; Zanc, Sue, Hu, & Kwon, 1991).

Vasil (1992), whose research is typical of general self-efficacy studies in vocational psychology, found that self-efficacy accounted for a significant proportion of the variance in the productivity of academic faculty. Vasil also examined attributions and found that the person's attributing successful outcomes to his or her ability increased perceptions of self-efficacy.

In an experimental study, Hackett et al. (1990) found that performance enhanced self-efficacy and interest in the task, whereas failure had the opposite effects. As was appropriate to the U.S. context, the Vasil (1992) and Hackett et al. (1990) studies were based on the assumption of an individualistic perspective of both self-efficacy and attributions, with an emphasis on individual success and failure. In line with the arguments forwarded by Bond (1994), investigations of the differential effects of individual and group success and failure on self-efficacy for people with collectivist or individualist cultural backgrounds would be instructive. It would also be useful if such research were to provide information on attributional processes.

Church et al. (1992), in a study of cultural minorities within the United States, found no differences between Native-American, English-instructed

Hispanics, and Spanish-speaking Hispanic participants in terms of their self-efficacy. Interestingly, no correlation was obtained between generality of self-efficacy and measured aptitudes among the minorities. The authors suggested that for ethnic minorities, self-efficacy may relate to resources and opportunities rather than to abilities or that the information this group received about their school performance may not have reflected their real ability. Note that this study related to minorities within an American culture, and the differences may have more to do with disadvantage and social class than with cultural differences per se.

Bandura's (1977) original ideas on self-efficacy and anxiety have been studied and applied in many different countries and cultures. The core ideas do generalize, but specific applications can be influenced by cultural considerations. Such influences were illustrated in a study by Zanc et al. (1991) in relation to assertive behavior, a behavior that is more relevant to individualistic cultures than to collectivist cultures. Zanc et al. (1991) found a significant ethnic effect, in that Asian Americans expected to be significantly less effective than White Americans when performing an assertive response in interactions with strangers. In situations involving acquaintances or inmates, there were no ethnic differences in self-efficacy. The authors argued that cultural differences in assertiveness are not a matter of different social-learning processes. Rather, ethnic differences in assertion are situational, with Asian Americans reporting less assertion and feeling less self-efficacious than White Americans but only in situations involving strangers. These findings point to one possible way of determining the universal and specific aspects of career theory. It would seem likely that those aspects of theory that deal with processes (e.g., social learning theory) are more likely to generalize than are theories that emphasize normatively appropriate behaviors, an emphasis often typical of developmental theories, which designate specific stages of career development.

Findings from research undertaken by Luzzo (1993) point to different results for self-efficacy for attitudes and self-efficacy for skills. In general one would anticipate more cultural differences in attitudes than in skills. In light of the Luzzo (1993) findings, it would seem important for theorists to be quite specific about which content aspects of self-efficacy are likely to have universal application and which are likely to be time and culture bound, although it is probable that the learning processes involved are universal. For example, in collectivist countries, some aspects of self-efficacy may possibly develop from and be embedded in a sense of confidence in what the group or family can do. Even in a traditionally individualist country like Australia, the collectivist influence is currently being felt in Australian industry.

Hesketh, Feiler, and Kanavaros (1993) developed a short six-item measure of self-efficacy for learning skills related to each of the Holland (1985) themes. Respondents in a large Australian manufacturing organization completed this measure as well as one that profiled their jobs in terms of the Holland themes. Interestingly, the results reflected a disproportionate strength in the *social* component of work, even in a manufacturing environment. The finding reflects changes that have occurred within the Australian work- and industrial-relations context, where there has been a major shift away from an individualistic approach toward the increased use of semiautonomous and self-managing work teams (James, 1992). In this context, all members of the group take responsibility for skill development and training, the group shares successes and failures, and members of the group must have increased social competencies (Hesketh, Feiler, & Kanavaros, 1994). In Australia, typically considered an individualistic country, changes in the work structures have increased the social nature and group-based context of work, even in jobs traditionally defined as *realistic*. The pattern of self-efficacy estimates for learning these skills also reflect the changes that have occurred, in that confidence in capacity to acquire social skills were related to perceptions of future progress within the organization.

These examples highlight a principle that may help researchers determine what components of constructs or theories generalize. When a process is described, such as how self-efficacy develops, the findings are likely to generalize. However, the content or specific application of the construct or theory, such as the value attached to a self-efficacy for different types of behavior or areas of work, is likely to differ across cultures and to vary over time.

Career Choice

Career choice is probably the most frequently researched dependent variable in vocational psychology. Many theories and much research have been aimed at the identification of those factors that can predict level and area of career choice. Career choice is also studied as an independent or predictor variable in investigations of the outcomes of choice, such as satisfaction, stability, or productivity of people in their chosen fields of work. Despite the widespread use of the concept of career choice, its meaning differs across countries, as do the factors predicting it and possibly even the outcomes arising from it.

In the United States, an individualistic and moderately low power–distance country in Hofstede's (1980, 1991) terms, choice is the responsibility of the individual. Not surprisingly, individual choice and responsibility are implicit in much of the theory and practice of vocational psychology literature published in the United States. Perhaps because of the nature of their society and political systems, Americans tend to see themselves as capable of controlling their own environment and, as such, as able to change themselves (Boyacigiller & Adler, 1991). This belief accords with a belief in free will. In other Western countries, such as New Zealand, Australia, and the United

Kingdom, countries also comparatively individualistic and low on power–distance, there has been some debate about the extent to which individuals do have choice in the individualistic sense. The debate in these countries, however, relates mainly to the factors that limit the implementation of choices such as opportunity, education, bias, and other critical filters. In collectivist and high power–distance countries, choice is unlikely to have the individualistic overtones present in current theory. In many of these countries, causality may be seen as determined by factors beyond the control of the individual, a view that has implications for the concept of career choice. In collectivist countries, preferences may also reflect much more strongly the goals and aspirations of significant reference groups and of the society as a whole, rather than the particular interests of the individual.

The different emphases on the role of the individual in choice have implications for the types of issues researched and the measures used for research and practice. Much cross-cultural research is carried out with translations of instruments developed in another country, usually the United States. Whether translated research instruments are sufficiently sensitive to cultural nuances to detect them is the source of considerable debate. Few researchers have used instruments that have met the various criteria outlined by Lonner (1985) for establishing the cultural equivalence of the measures. Kagitcibasi and Berry (1989) draw attention to the importance of researchers' no longer simply comparing mean scores across countries or cultures but rather gaining a conceptual understanding of the items, tests, contexts, and behaviors measured by instruments within the context of the culture.

In relation to the call for vocational theorists to address the issue of diversity in the United States, Dawis (1994) argued that cultural differences are merely reflected in different responses to the typical measures used. If one could assume that existing measures are sufficiently sensitive to capture differences, the Dawis (1994) argument has merit. On the other hand, if cultural equivalence has not been established, as is usually the case, the picture is less clear. Instruments developed within a particular culture will differentiate most clearly those attributes relevant to that culture. If culture were used as a moderating variable, it would be surprising if substantive differences emerged. In contrast, if the instruments were developed within the context of multiple cultures, constructs important to all cultures would probably be included, and the moderating influence of culture on the relative importance of these constructs could well emerge. Erez (1993) pointed to the more elaborated constructs that collectivist cultures develop for appraising and evaluating others compared to the elaborate constructs evolved in individualistic countries for evaluating the self. We have chosen to illustrate the implications of an international and cross-cultural perspective for measurement of vocational constructs through a discussion of vocational interests.

Vocational Interests

An Operant Perspective. Surprisingly little attention has been given to the definition of interests. Pryor (1991) defined vocational interests as work *activity* preferences, whereas work values were defined as work *aspect* preferences. Pryor's (1991) definition does little more than identify interests with preferences. As such, however, interests can be viewed within an operant perspective such as the Premack principle (Premack, 1965), which may provide a richer and more universal understanding of the concept. Premack (1965) argued that the attractiveness of an activity can be determined by observing what happens when people are faced with an unconstrained choice involving that activity. The outcome of the choice can predict whether or not an activity is functioning as a reward. If a person prefers one activity over another, the opportunity to engage in the preferred activity can be used as a reward for the less preferred activity (Hesketh & Westbrook, 1991). According to B. Schwartz (1984), the implication of the Premack principle and various subsequent modifications is that the motivating potential (capacity to reinforce) of various actions is relative. The Premack principle offers a behavioral basis for determining preference. All things being equal, the relative frequency with which different behaviors or activities are chosen provides an indication of the relative preference for these activities. The idea is referred to as *revealed preference* in the behavioral economics literature (Rachlin, 1980).

Interest measures provide a mechanism for the identification of the hierarchy of orientations toward (or away from) particular activities. An individual's hierarchy of orientations toward different types of activities provides information about the probability of choice. Therefore, interests are considered good indicators of motives, and they relate quite easily to career choice, occupational membership, occupational change, and job and career satisfaction (Dawis, 1991). We must note, however, that the link between a stated interest and behavioral actions is dependent on an assumption of unconstrained choice.

Interests in the Cross-Cultural Literature. Vocational interests have been central in many theories of career development and in the practice of career counseling. Despite this emphasis, a perusal of major cross-cultural texts, reviews, and books of readings (e.g., Adamopoulos & Lonner, 1994; Berry, Poortinga, Segall, & Dawen, 1992; Marsella, Tharp, & Ciborowski, 1979; Shweder & Sullivan, 1993) shows that the topic of vocational interests has been ignored. There are possible practical and theoretical reasons for the lack of attention to interests in the cross-cultural literature.

Practically, the heavy emphasis on interest measurement may be limited to Anglo-Celtic countries, where individuals experience comparatively unconstrained choice and where the emphasis is on individual choice. In these countries where, at least in previous years, individuals have had some chance of implementing choices, the practical value of assessing vocational interests in order to obtain a hierarchy of orientations toward and away from activities is obvious. The assumption that career choice is based on the types of work individuals like and dislike, however, may not be valid in many cultures. Consequently, it is not surprising that less attention has been given to interest measurement in countries where family and other group influences are considered more important than individual preferences and where career and work opportunities are comparatively limited.

The lack of theoretical attention given to interests in the mainstream cross-cultural literature may also follow from the atheoretical nature of much interest research. Vocational interest research has been guided by operational definitions and the actual measurement of interests rather than by conceptual definitions. Dawis (1991) noted that the field of vocational interest research has yet to develop a well-articulated theoretical foundation. The operant basis for interests outlined earlier has the potential to provide a theoretical basis, but its focus is on process rather than on content. The advantage of the operant approach is its greater likelihood of applying universally, whereas any theory that emphasizes the content of interests may need to be modified to accommodate cultural relativity. In order to examine the extent to which structural models of interests generalize across cultures, we have chosen to focus on Holland's (1985) theory of careers.

Holland's Theory. Holland (1985) viewed vocational interests as an expression of personality. Holland asserted that there are six personality types and six occupational environments: *realistic* (R), *investigative* (I), *artistic* (A), *social* (S), *enterprising* (E), and *conventional* (C). These are collectively referred to as RIASEC. Holland further asserted that the structural relations among the personality types (and the environments) are best represented by a circular order of R–I–A–S–E–C (often called the hexagonal model). The personality types (and the occupational environments) that are adjacent on the hexagon are more similar than types that are located one removed or on the opposite side of the hexagon. The posited hexagonal structure of interests has both theoretical and applied implications. Theoretically, predictions of stability, satisfaction, and other outcomes are derived from the application of the hexagon to the match between individuals and work environments. The internal relations among the RIASEC types, represented by the hexagon, are the cornerstone for Holland's (1985) behavioral descriptions of each personality type. The meaning of each personality type is derived from the nomological network of relations among other types. An example of the practical application of the hexagon can be found in the latest revision of the Strong Interest Inventory (Hansen & Campbell, 1985), which incorporates the structure as an organizing framework for feedback on the inventory. In general, as discussed by Borgen (1986), Holland's theory and research has had far-reaching effects on how vocational interests are conceptualized and measured.

Internationalizing Holland's Theory. With such widespread acceptance of Holland's (1985) RIASEC model in the United States, it is not surprising that researchers and practitioners have adopted his model and measures internationally. Holland and Gottfredson (1992) reported that the Vocational Preference Inventory and the Self-Directed Search have been translated into 20 languages and that the various versions of the Strong Interest Inventory have been translated into 17 languages. The Career Decision-Making Interest Survey (Harrington, 1986; Harrington & O'Shea, 1993), a measure of RIASEC types, has recently been marketed in French and Spanish editions. Instead of translating or adapting U.S. RIASEC inventories, researchers in Australia (Athanasou, 1986), France (Dupont, 1979), and Canada (Tetreau & Trahan, 1986, 1989, 1992) have developed new measures based on Holland's RIASEC model.

There has been some debate about the structure of interests. Gati (1991) argued for a hierarchical model whereas others have argued in favor of the hexagon (Rounds, Tracey, & Hubert, 1992; Tracey & Rounds, 1993). Reviews of cross-cultural studies of Holland's model have usually concluded that the relations among RIASEC types support the hexagon. For example, Holland (1985), summarizing the literature, stated, "The ordering (RIASEC) of types or occupational categories is similar even when the data, sexes, and cultures vary" (p. 119). Likewise, Hansen (1987) has taken an absolutist position, stating, "Generally, the structure of interests of international and cross-ethnic populations seems to correspond to Holland's model almost as well as does the structure of interests of Whites" (p. 173). Nevertheless, as evident in a special issue of the *Journal of Vocational Behavior* (Tinsley, 1992) devoted primarily to a cross-national and cross-ethnic study of the structure of RIASEC types, Holland's and Hansen's conclusions may be premature. The Fouad and Dancer (1992) study of engineering students and professional engineers from Mexico and Swanson's (1992) study of African-American college students both provide mixed support for Holland's structural assertions. Hansen (1992), reacting to Fouad and Dancer's and Swanson's research, has become more cautious, stating that "the construct of interests appears to have a broad pattern of structural similarity across cultures in concert with specific sample differences that reflect the individual differences of cultures" (p. 188).

Two major problems with previous reviews of the cross-cultural literature are evident: The reviews are based on a few selected studies and leave unexamined many potential sources of data, and researchers used inappropriate methods to examine the hexagon (Tracey & Rounds, 1993). To remedy these methodological problems, Rounds and Tracey (1994) conducted a metastructural analysis to evaluate the fit of Holland's and Gati's models on 20 U.S. ethnic RIASEC correlation matrices and 76 international matrices (representing 18 countries). Using U.S. majority data as a benchmark, they found for both the U.S. ethnic groups and the international samples that Holland's model did not fit well. Only 2 of the 18 countries (i.e., Iceland and Israel) showed an adequate hexagonal pattern. Gati's model, however, showed a reasonable fit to the international samples but poor fit to the U.S. ethnic samples. Rounds and Tracey's study raises serious concerns about the cross-cultural applicability of Holland's model. Certainly, some caution is in order when researchers apply Holland's constructs cross-culturally.

ISSUES ASSOCIATED WITH GENERALIZING THEORIES ACROSS TIME AND CULTURE

Theories and related concepts differ in terms of the emphasis placed on the process or content of vocational behavior. Social learning theory (Krumboltz, 1979; Krumboltz et al., 1978) has a major emphasis on process. The theory does not, for example, outline the content or structure of self-observation generalizations, whereas the associative and instrumental learning experiences that derive from fundamental behavioral principles are universal. In contrast, developmental theories that specify particular stages of development (e.g., Levinson, 1978, 1986) and particular vocational tasks that must be mastered at each stage (Super, 1990), without detailing the mechanisms of how development occurs, are more likely to be time and culture bound. Appropriate career behaviors for particular stages are a function the school and tertiary education systems in different countries and are normative expectations for age-related behavior. However, it is possible that with the advent of a global village, these expectations may increasingly converge across cultures.

One theory that has the potential to generalize across time and cultures is the Minnesota Theory of Work Adjustment (TWA; Dawis & Lofquist, 1984). Like social learning theory, the systems aspect of the TWA, which deals with the dynamic components of the adjustment process, is sufficiently general to apply to any culture and, indeed, to any situation in which two parties interact. At an abstract level, the notion of person–environment fit implicit in the TWA is content free and thus has a high level of generality. The factors on which the matching, or fit, should occur, however, may differ across both culture and time. So that cultural differences as well as changes within a particular culture are accommodated, a much broader range of matching factors than those traditionally incorporated in the TWA may be required. For example, to ensure the relevance of theories to adult career development in the current context of change (Hesketh & Bochner, 1993) theorists may need to include additional matching factors such as career path concepts and types of contracts. These are issues that we raise again in the final section of the chapter.

As we discussed earlier, Holland's (1985) theory has been used widely in countries other than the United States, a use pointing to the practical value of simplicity for practical purposes. As with the TWA, the notion of congruence underlying Holland's theory is sufficiently general for its application in many countries. Doubt exists, however, about the cross-cultural generality of a key theoretical component of Holland's theory, namely the hexagonal structure of the RIASEC types (Rounds & Tracey, 1994). Furthermore, the emphasis on individual interests or preferences for activities, which forms the major component of Holland's theory, is less likely to be the basis of choice in countries with a collectivist orientation or where choice is more constrained. Because Holland's (1985) theory does not address the process of an individual's achieving adjustment if a choice cannot be implemented or if congruence is low, it is less likely than the TWA to generalize across time and culture.

Gottfredson's (1981) theory of career circumscription and compromise is a comparatively new theory and one of the few that acknowledges the effects of social factors on choice. Consequently, it has the potential to apply to less individualistic cultures. Gottfredson (1981) argued that careers are circumscribed initially in terms of sex-type at a comparatively early age (approximately 6 years), whereas prestige affects choice at a later stage (approximately 9 years of age), with interests and values influencing choice only during the teen years. Although many aspects of Gottfredson's theory remain in doubt (Hesketh, Elmslie, & Kaldor, 1990; Leung & Harmon, 1990), the acknowledged importance of sex-type and prestige as constructs that influence choice is valuable.

With respect to gender and a cross-cultural perspective, interesting issues warrant examination. Kagitcibasi and Berry (1989) drew on the work of Papanek (1973) and L. Fallers and M. Fallers (1976) in Pakistan and Turkey, respectively, to suggest, somewhat provocatively, that women experience more psychological freedom in gender-segregated societies than women in those societies where integration has occurred. Moreover, this freedom helps them to separate their gender and professional identities. Clearly the influence of sex-type on preferences will be related to societal attitudes toward the role of women, although theoretically, the cognitive basis underlying Gottfredson's (1981) theory would predict universal early circumscription of choice on the basis of gender.

As a construct, prestige (Chartrand, Dohm, Dawis, & Lofquist, 1987; Daniel, 1983), the other social variable in Gottfredson's (1981) theory, is also likely to influence preference and choice universally, although cultural differences may emerge in terms of the content of what is considered prestigious. For example, in many Asian countries, the mathematics requirements for an area of work are an indication of prestige. This attitude results in higher prestige being attached to engineering than is often the case in countries such as the United Kingdom, the United States, and Australia.

Having evaluated several core constructs in psychology from an international and cross-cultural context and having discussed the implications for the generality of theories, we return to the broader issue of the relation of vocational psychology to other disciplines. Our reason for attention to this broader issue is our concern that the focused specialization of the field of vocational psychology in the United States, a feature that is not evident in other countries, may have resulted in a failure by theorists and practitioners to recognize threats to several assumptions underlying vocational theory and practice.

THREATS TO THE ASSUMPTIONS UNDERLYING VOCATIONAL PSYCHOLOGY

A major aim of vocational psychologists is to describe, understand, and predict work and career-related behavior and attitudes and to use this knowledge to improve the quality of working life. An impressive body of vocational theory and research has developed in the United States, although many of the ideas were based on work as it was organized and defined between 1950 and the early 1980s. Some aspects of this theory and research will generalize to work settings in the United States in the 1990s and to other cultures, but other aspects may need updating as several assumptions about the nature of work have changed. Savickas (1993) identified a similar concern in addressing the needs of career counseling in the postmodern era.

We argue that one of the reasons that threats to underlying assumptions have not been identified in the vocational literature and research is the existence of a group of specialist vocational psychology researchers in the United States. Vocational psychology has always drawn on several related disciplines for its theory development, research, and practice. In light of this, it is not surprising that the discipline is taught variously as part of education, psychology, management, or even labor economics. Countries differ in terms of which disciplines overlap most with vocational psychology. In the United States, vocational psychologists overlap most with counseling psychologists, and much of the research is undertaken in schools of education. In the United Kingdom, the field is covered by educationalists and organizational psychologists, whereas in Europe, vocational psychology is an integral component of work psychology.

Specialization of vocational psychology in the United States has engendered a vigorous group of researchers and a substantive body of theory with practical applications. Nevertheless, the specialist area of vocational psychology appears uninfluenced to a degree by highly relevant research carried out under the broader context of industrial and organizational psychology (Murphy, 1993). There is also no apparent awareness of the radical changes that have occurred in the nature of work and in the employment contract. This lack of influence is surprising in light of the excellent reviews of recent research in industrial and organizational psychology provided in the *Journal of Vocational Psychology* (e.g., Blau, Linnehan, Brooks, & Hoover, 1993; Fitzgerald & Rounds, 1989; Morrow, Mullen, & McElroy, 1990). A review by Fitzgerald and Rounds (1989) provides some insight into this issue. They identified 14 clusters of topics covered in the *Journal of Vocational Behavior* and located these on two dimensions: (1) counseling psychology or industrial and organizational psychology and (2) studies that emphasized preentry (into an organization) or postentry adjustment. The nonuse of the industrial and organizational psychology literature by most vocational psychologists in the United States is also probably due to the primary emphasis by the majority of the researchers on the preoccupational entry stage (Fitzgerald & Rounds, 1989), a function of most research arising from departments of education and from counseling units in colleges. Thus, despite the broad coverage of topics in the *Journal of Vocational Behavior*, little integrative perspective is taken in vocational research in the United States and surprisingly little cross-fertilization occurs between cluster areas.

Integrative research is perhaps more evident in European psychology as illustrated in the work of Frese, which spans occupational socialization (Frese, 1982) as well as traditional topics dealing with training, such as the role of errors in learning (Frese & Altmann, 1989), and other forms of computer-based training. Interestingly, European work psychologists tend to use assessment centers, traditionally employed for selection, as a major tool in career development. It appears that a concern about conflicts between individual and institutional goals in the European context does not prevent an integration of ideas from careers and organizational psychology. Furthermore, the theories and approaches used by researchers have a closer link with mainstream theoretical developments in psychology than occurs in the United States. An interesting example of this integration is found in the work of Frese and Zapf (1993), who showed how the concept of action, derived originally from Miller, Galanter, and Pribram's (1960) discussion on goals, forms a core of work psychology. The preentry emphasis of much of the vocational theory and research in the United States and the lack of integration with industrial and organizational psychology are somewhat limiting factors. Arguably, with the changes occurring in the nature of work, changes that point to recurrent decision making throughout life (Hesketh & Bochner, 1993; Rounds & Hesketh, 1994), researchers will need to pay more attention to adult career development (Nicholson & West, 1988).

Work now offers much less security, more short-term contracts, far fewer opportunities for traditional linear career paths, and increasingly a requirement to work abroad for a period of time (Herriot, 1992; Hesketh & Bochner, 1993; Hesketh, Gardner, & Lissner, 1992; Rousseau, 1990). The individual's flexibility and a capacity to cope with change are key requirements in employees. In this climate, individuals with set ideas about their interests and expectations that they will find outlets for these may be disappointed. Furthermore, from an employer perspective, individuals with clearly crystallized interests may not be the most desirable employees. These changes threaten many assumptions underlying traditional approaches to vocational psychology. Flexibility and active and reactive modes of adjustment, core concepts in the TWA (Dawis & Lofquist, 1984) become critical (Schein, 1990; Schneider, 1987). Savickas (1993) argued along similar lines for an emphasis on "enable" rather than on "fit" in career counseling, an issue first raised by Law (1991).

Interestingly, similar issues apply to selection. Researchers have addressed the problems of applying models that were developed for a comparatively stable work context to the current dynamic work situation (Hesketh & Allworth, 1994). Traditional selection approaches and some vocational theories are based on the assumption of stability of individuals and of work environments, an assumption that is increasingly in doubt. In future, employers will wish to select individuals who are capable of coping with change, learning new skills, and dealing with a range of different types of work. Clearly such individuals will need flexibility and well-developed active and reactive modes of adjustment (Dawis & Lofquist, 1984). In the selection context, Hesketh and Allworth (1994) argued that traditional matching approaches will remain valid and may be particularly important for short-term contract appointments, where immediate productivity will be required. However, new approaches to selection (and, one might add, to career counseling) are required when appointments are made for longer periods for which an individual's adaptability, flexibility, and capacity to cope with change become important. A matching approach, such as that typified by Holland (1985), although remaining useful, is not sufficient. What is needed is the extension of the matching approach to include a dynamic component capable of both explaining adaptation and providing a basis for psychologists to help individuals acquire the skills to adapt and cope with change. The systems component of the TWA does offer the potential of meeting this requirement.

DEVELOPING THEORIES THAT GENERALIZE

The issues raised in the preceding discussion become apparent when vocational psychology is treated as part of the broader area of work psychology (Europe) or industrial and organizational psychology (United States). The integration of vocational psychology with industrial and organizational psychology and retention of a cross-cultural perspective will help increase the relevance of vocational theory to the diversity of clients in the United States and to age groups other than those in college. Our first recommendation in theory building is for researchers to examine closely the developments in related fields and in mainstream psychology. We may find that we do not need specialist vocational theories but merely applications of more general theories.

If specific theories that are capable of generalization are to be developed, we recommend an idea drawn from the literature on the transfer of training and the generalizability of skills. As is evidenced in the training literature, psychologists have accepted that transfer is facilitated through the individual's understanding of general principles and that these general principles can be learned more easily from multiple examples (see Andrews, 1991; Gick & Holyoak, 1983; Hesketh & Bochner, 1993; Mrozek, 1992). Multiple examples facilitate the process of comparing and contrasting and fleshing out those components that are common and related to the general principle and those that are specific to the particular example. When the analogy is applied to vocational theory, it becomes apparent that there may be value in our developing theories through the ongoing process of comparing and contrasting different cultures. In this way, the universal aspects of the theory will be apparent, as will the need for specific components to deal with particular cultural contexts.

Our third set of suggestions is more general. By way of summary, we suggest that future vocational researchers (1) attempt to identify which components of the theory are universal and which may need to be understood within the relative context of culture and to state to which cultural and geographical domains the specific components apply; (2) provide more information about the national and cultural characteristics of samples used in research; (3) set out to test theories in cultures and systems other than those in which they were originally developed; (4) participate in multinational and multicultural research teams; (5) study literatures from other countries, continents, and disciplines; and (6) visit foreign countries and experience first hand differences that exist.

The inclusion of several chapters in the present handbook addressing cultural issues is evidence of the importance to vocational psychology of a cultural dimension. With this added perspective, the depth of research and theory in vocational psychology in the United States will provide a sound basis for research and practice in future years.

REFERENCES

Adamopoulos, J., & Lonner, W. J. (1994). Absolutism, relativism and universalism in the study of human behavior. In W. J. Lonner & R. Malpass (Eds.), *Psychology and culture* (pp. 129–134). Boston: Allyn & Bacon.

Andrews, S. (1991). Cognitive processes in skill acquisition: Implications for training. In B. Hesketh & A. Adams (Eds.), *Psychological perspectives on occupational health and rehabilitation* (pp. 219–241). Marrickville, Sydney: Harcourt Brace.

Athanasou, J. A. (1986). Vocational Interest Survey: Six experimental scales for the measurement of Holland's vocational types. In J. L. Lokan & K. F. Taylor (Eds.), *Holland in Australia* (pp. 139–148). Melbourne: Australian Council for Educational Research.

Bandura, A. (1977). Self-efficacy: Toward a unifying theory of behavioral change. *Psychological Review, 84*, 191–215.

Berry, J. W. (1979). A cultural ecology of social behavior. In L. Berkowitz (Ed.), *Advances in experimental social psychology* (Vol. 12, pp. 177–206). New York: Academic Press.

Berry, J. W., Poortinga, Y. H., Segall, M. H., & Dawen, P. R. (1992). *Cross-cultural psychology: Research and applications.* Cambridge, England: Cambridge University Press.

Betz, N. E., & Hackett, G. (1987). Concept of agency in educational and career development. *Journal of Counseling Psychology, 34*, 299–308.

Blau, G., Linnehan, F., Brooks, A., & Hoover, D. K. (1993). Vocational behavior 1990–1992: Personnel practices, organizational behavior, workplace justice and industrial/organizational measurement issues. *Journal of Vocational Behavior, 43*, 133–197.

Bochner, S., & Hesketh, B. (1994). Power distance, individualism/collectivism, and job related attitudes among employees in a culturally diverse work place: A test of Hofstede's theory. *Journal of Cross Cultural Psychology, 25*, 233–257.

Bond, M. H. (1991). *Beyond the Chinese face: Insights from psychology.* Hong Kong: Oxford University Press.

Bond, M. H. (1994). Continuing encounters with Hong Kong. In W. J. Lonner & R. Malpass (Eds.), *Psychology and culture* (pp. 41–46). Boston: Allyn & Bacon.

Bores–Rangel, E., Church, A. T., Szendre, D., & Reeves, C. (1990). Self-efficacy in relation to occupational consideration and academic performance in high school equivalency students. *Journal of Counseling Psychology, 37*, 407–418.

Borgen, F. H. (1986). New approaches to the assessment of interests. In W. B. Walsh & S. H. Osipow (Eds.), *Advances in vocational psychology: Vol. 1. The assessment of interests* (pp. 31–54). Hillsdale, NJ: Lawrence Erlbaum Associates.

Boyacigiller, N., & Adler, N. J. (1991). The parochial dinosaur: Organizational science in a global context. *Academy of Management Review, 16*, 262–290.

Cashmore, J. A., & Goodnow, J. J. (1986). Influences on Australian parents' values: Ethnicity versus socioeconomic status. *Journal of Cross Cultural Psychology, 17*, 441–454.

Chartrand, J. M., Dohm, T. E., Dawis, R. V., & Lofquist, L. H. (1987). Estimating occupational prestige. *Journal of Vocational Behavior, 31*, 14–25.

Church, A. T., Teresa, J. S., Rosebrook, R., & Szendre, D. (1992). Self-efficacy for careers and occupational consideration in minority high school equivalency students. *Journal of Counseling Psychology, 39*, 498–508.

Daniel, A. (1983). *Power, privilege and prestige: Occupations in Australia.* Melbourne, Australia: Longman Cheshire.

Dawis, R. V. (1991). Vocational interests, values, and preferences. In M. D. Dunnette & L. M. Hough (Eds.), *Handbook of industrial and organizational psychology* (2nd ed., Vol. 2, pp. 833–872). Palo Alto, CA: Consulting Psychologists Press.

Dawis, R. V. (1994). The theory of work adjustment as convergent theory. In M. L. Savickas & R. W. Lent (Eds.), *Convergence in career development theories: Implications for science and practice* (pp. 33–44). Palo Alto, CA: Consulting Psychologists Press.

Dawis, R. V., & Lofquist, L. H. (1984). *A psychological theory of work adjustment.* Minneapolis: University of Minnesota Press.

Dupont, J. B. (1979). *Inventaire personnel de J. L. Holland* [J. L. Holland's Personnel Inventory]. Issyles–Moulineaux, France: Editions Scientifiques et Psychologiques.

Erez, M. (1993). Toward a model of cross-cultural industrial and organizational psychology. In H. Triandis, M. D. Dunnette, & L. Hough (Eds.), *Handbook of industrial and organizational psychology* (Vol. 4, pp. 559–646). Palo Alto, CA: Consulting Psychologists Press.

Erez, M., & Earley, P. C. (1993). *Culture, self-identity, and work.* New York: Oxford University Press.

Fallers, L., & Fallers, M. (1976). Sex roles in Edremit. In J. Paristiany (Ed.), *Mediterranean family structure.* New York: Cambridge University Press.

Feather, N. T., & McKee, I. R. (1993). Global self-esteem and attitudes toward the high achiever for Australian and Japanese students. *Social Psychology Quarterly, 56,* 65–76.

Fitzgerald, L., & Rounds, J. (1989). Vocational behavior, 1988: A critical analysis. *Journal of Vocational Behavior, 35,* 105–165.

Fouad, N. A., Cudeck, R., & Hansen, J. (1984). Convergent validity of the Spanish and English forms of the Strong–Campbell Interest Inventory for bilingual Hispanic high school students. *Journal of Counseling Psychology, 31,* 339–348.

Fouad, N. A., & Dancer, L. S. (1992). Cross-cultural structure of interests: Mexico and the United States. *Journal of Vocational Behavior, 40,* 129–143.

Frese, M. (1982). Occupational socialization and psychological development: An underemphasized research perspective in industrial psychology. *Journal of Occupational Psychology, 55,* 209–224.

Frese, M., & Altmann, A. (1989). The treatment of errors in learning and training. In L. Bainbridge & S. A. R. Quintanilla (Eds.), *Developing skills with new technology* (pp. 65–86). Chichester, England: Wiley.

Frese, M., & Zapf, D. (1993). Action as the core of work psychology. In H. C. Triandis, M. D. Dunnette, & L. M. Hough (Eds.), *Handbook of industrial and organizational psychology* (Vol. 4, 2nd ed., pp. 271–340). Palo Alto, CA: Consulting Psychologists Press.

Gati, I. (1991). The structure of vocational interests. *Psychological Bulletin, 109,* 309–325.

Gergen, K. (1991). *The saturated self: Dilemmas of identity in contemporary life.* New York: Basic Books.

Gick, M. L., & Holyoak, K. J. (1983). Schema induction and analogical transfer. *Cognitive Psychology, 15,* 1–38.

Gottfredson, L. S. (1981). Circumscription and compromise: A developmental theory of occupational aspirations [Monograph]. *Journal of Counseling Psychology, 28,* 545–579.

Hackett, G., Betz, N. E., O'Halloran, M. W., & Romac, D. S. (1990). Effects of verbal and mathematics task performance on task and career self-efficacy and interests. *Journal of Counseling Psychology, 37,* 169–177.

Hansen, J. C. (1987). Cross-cultural research on vocational interests. *Measurement and Evaluation in Counseling and Development, 19,* 163–176.

Hansen, J. C. (1992). Does enough evidence exist to modify Holland's theory to accommodate the individual differences of diverse populations? *Journal of Vocational Behavior, 40,* 188–193.

Hansen, J. C., & Campbell, D. P. (1985). *Manual for the SVIB–SCII* (4th ed.). Palo Alto, CA: Consulting Psychologists Press.

Harrington, T. F. (1986). The construct validity of the Career Decision-Making System cross-culturally. *International Journal for the Advancement of Counseling, 9,* 331–339.

Harrington, T. F., & O'Shea, A. T. (1993). *The Harrington–O'Shea Career Decision-Making System revised manual.* Circle Pines, MN: American Guidance Service.

Herriot, P. (1992). Careers in recession? *British Journal of Guidance and Counselling, 20,* 231–238.

Hesketh, B., & Allworth, A. (1994, July). *Time-scale threats to traditional selection research.* Paper presented at the 23rd International Congress of Applied Psychology, Madrid.

Hesketh, B., & Bochner, S. (1993). Technological change in a multicultural context: Implications for training and career planning. In H. Triandis, M. Dunnette, & L. Hough (Eds.), *Handbook of industrial and organizational psychology* (Vol. 4, 2nd ed., pp. 191–240). Palo Alto, CA: Consulting Psychologists Press.

Hesketh, B., Elmslie, S., & Kaldor, W. (1990). Career compromise: An alternative account to Gottfredson's (1981) theory. *Journal of Counseling Psychology, 37*, 49–56.

Hesketh, B., Feiler, H., & Kanavaros, S. (1993). *Interests, work attitudes and the link between training and career development.* Report prepared for ICI. Sydney, Australia.

Hesketh, B., Feiler, H., & Kanavaros, S. (1994). The link between training and career development. *Training and Development in Australia, 21*(3), 6–10.

Hesketh, B., Gardner, D., & Lissner, D. (1992). Technical and managerial career paths: An unresolved dilemma. *International Journal of Career Management, 4*, 9–16.

Hesketh, B., & Kennedy, L. (1991). Changes and responsibilities: Policy challenges confronting careers guidance in New Zealand. *British Journal of Guidance and Counselling, 19*, 246–257.

Hesketh, B., & Westbrook, F. (1991). Creating a motivating environment. In B. Hesketh & A. Adams (Eds.), *Psychological perspectives on occupational health and rehabilitation* (pp. 112–142). Marrickville, Sydney: Harcourt Brace.

Hofstede, G. (1980). *Culture's consequences: International differences in work related values.* Beverly Hills, CA: Academic Press.

Hofstede, G. (1991). *Culture and organizations: Software of the mind.* London: McGraw–Hill.

Holland, J. (1985). *Making vocational choices: A theory of vocational personalities and work environments* (2nd ed.). Englewood Cliffs, NJ: Prentice Hall.

Holland, J. L., & Gottfredson, G. D. (1992). Studies of the hexagon model: An evaluation (or, the perils of stalking the perfect hexagon). *Journal of Vocational Behavior, 40*, 158–170.

James, D. (1992, September 4). Fred Emery: The man who reformed the workplace. *Business Review Weekly, 76*, 72–74.

Kagitcibasi, C., & Berry, J. W. (1989). Cross-cultural psychology: Current research and trends. *Annual Review of Psychology, 40*, 493–531.

Krumboltz, J. D. (1979). *Social learning theory and career decision-making.* New York: Carroll Press.

Krumboltz, J. D., Mitchell, A. M., & Jones, G. B. (1978). A social learning theory of career selection. In J. M. Whiteley & A. Resnikoff (Eds.), *Career counseling* (pp. 100–127). Monterey, CA: Brooks/Cole.

Lauver, P. J., & Jones, R. M. (1991). Factors associated with perceived career options in American Indian, White and Hispanic rural high school students. *Journal of Counseling Psychology, 38*, 159–166.

Law, W. (1991). *Careers work.* Cambridge, England: National Institute for Careers Education and Counselling.

Lent, R. W., & Hackett, G. (1987). Career self-efficacy: Empirical status and future directions [Monograph]. *Journal of Vocational Behavior, 30*, 347–382.

Leung, S. A., & Harmon, L. W. (1990). Individual and sex differences in the zone of acceptable alternatives. *Journal of Counseling Psychology, 37*, 153–159.

Levinson, D. J. (1978). *The seasons of a man's life.* New York: Knopf.

Levinson, D. J. (1986). A conception of adult development. *American Psychologist, 41*, 3–13.

Lonner, W. (1985). Issues in testing and assessing in cross-cultural counseling. *The Counseling Psychologist, 13*, 599–614.

Luzzo, D. A. (1993). Value of career-decision-making self-efficacy in predicting career-decision-making attitudes and skills. *Journal of Counseling Psychology, 40*, 194–199.

Marin, G. (1994). The experience of being a Hispanic in the United States. In W. J. Lonner & R. Malpass (Eds.), *Psychology and culture* (pp. 23–28). Boston: Allyn & Bacon.

Marsella, A. J., Tharp, R. G., & Ciborowski, T. J. (1979). *Perspectives on cross-cultural psychology.* New York: Academic Press.

Miller, G. A., Galanter, E., & Pribram, K. H. (1960). *Plans and the structure of behaviour.* London: Holt, Rinehart & Winston.

Morrow, P., Mullen, E., & McElroy, J. (1990). Vocational behavior 1989: The year in review. *Journal of Vocational Behavior, 37*, 121–195.

Mrozek, A. (1992). A new method for discovering rules from examples in expert systems. *International Journal of Man–Machine Studies, 25*, 411–438.

Murphy, K. R. (1993). Integrating research on work adjustment with research on job performance and behavior in organizations: Perspectives from industrial/organizational psychology. *Journal of Vocational Behavior, 43*, 98–104.

Nicholson, N., & West, M. (1988). *Managerial job change: Men and women in transition.* Cambridge, England: Cambridge University Press.

Offermann, L. R., & Gowing, M. K. (1990). Organizations of the future: Changes and challenges. *American Psychologist, 45*, 95–108.

Papanek, H. (1973). Pindah: Separate worlds and symbolic shelter. *Comparative Studies and Social History, 15*, 289–325.

Premack, D. (1965). Reinforcement theory. In D. Levine (Ed.), *Nebraska Symposium on Motivation Vol. 13* (pp. 123–180). Lincoln: University of Nebraska Press.

Pryor, R. (1991). Assessing people's interests, values and other preferences. In B. Hesketh & A. Adams (Eds.), *Psychological perspectives on occupational health and rehabilitation* (pp. 17–52). Marrickville, Sydney: Harcourt Brace.

Rachlin, H. (1980). Economic and behavioral psychology. In J. I. R. Shaddon (Ed.), *Limits to action* (pp. 205–236). New York: Academic Press.

Ronen, S., & Shenkar, O. (1985). Clustering countries on attitudinal dimensions: A review and synthesis. *Academy of Management Review, 10*, 435–454.

Rounds, J., & Hesketh, B. (1994). Theory of work adjustment: Unifying principles and concepts. In M. L. Savickas & R. W. Lent (Eds.), *Convergence in career development theories: Implications for science and practices* (pp. 177–186). Palo Alto, CA: Consulting Psychologists Press.

Rounds, J., & Tracey, T. J. (1994). *Cross-cultural structural equivalence of RIASEC models and measures.* Manuscript submitted for publication.

Rounds, J., Tracey, T. J., & Hubert, L. (1992). Methods for evaluating vocational interest structural hypotheses. *Journal of Vocational Behavior, 40*, 239–259.

Rousseau, D. M. (1990). New hire perceptions of their own and their employer's obligations: A study of psychological contracts. *Journal of Organizational Behavior, 11*, 389–400.

Savickas, M. L. (1993). Career counseling in the postmodern era. *Journal of Cognitive Psychotherapy: An International Quarterly, 7*, 205–215.

Schein, E. (1990). Organizational culture. *American Psychologist, 45*, 109–119.

Schneider, B. (1987). The people make the place. *Personnel Psychology, 40*, 437–453.

Schwartz, B. (1984). *Psychology of learning and behavior* (2nd ed.). New York: Norton.

Schwartz, S. H. (1992). Universals in the content and structure of values: Theoretical advances and empirical tests in 20 countries. In M. Zanna (Ed.), *Advances in experimental social psychology* (pp. 1–65). New York: Academic Press.

Schwartz, S. H., & Bilsky, W. (1987). Toward a psychological structure of human values. *Journal of Personality and Social Psychology, 53*, 550–562.

Shweder, R. A., & Sullivan, M. A. (1993). Cultural psychology: Who needs it? *Annual Review of Psychology, 44*, 497–523.

Super, D. E. (1957). *The psychology of careers.* New York: Harper & Row.

Super, D. E. (1990). A life-span life-space approach to career development. In D. Brown & L. Brooks (Eds.), *Career choice and development: Applying contemporary theories to practice* (2nd ed., pp. 197–261). San Francisco: Jossey-Bass.

Swanson, J. L. (1992). The structure of vocational interests for African-American college students. *Journal of Vocational Behavior, 40*, 129–143.

Tajfel, H. (1978). *Differentiation between social groups: Studies in social psychology of intergroup relations.* London: Academic Press.

Tetreau, B., & Trahan, M. (1986). *Test Visuel d'Interets* [Visual Interest Test]. Montreal, Quebec: Secorp.

Tetreau, B., & Trahan, M. (1989). *Teste Visual de Interesses Tetreau–Trahan, Manual para uso do Test* [Tetreau–Trahan Visual Interest Test, Manual for Use of the Test]. Montreal, Quebec: Secorp.

Tetreau, B., & Trahan, M. (1992). *Test Visual e Inventario Verbal deIntereses Profesionales (TVI–IVIP), Manual de Uso.* (edicion castellana). Montreal, Quebec: Secorp.

Tinsley, H. E. A. (1992). Introduction. *Journal of Vocational Behavior* [Special Issue], *40,* 109–110.

Tracey, T. J., & Rounds, J. (1993). Evaluating Holland's and Gati's vocational interest models: A structural meta-analysis. *Psychological Bulletin, 113,* 229–246.

Triandis, H. C. (1989). The self and social behavior in differing cultural contexts. *Psychological Review, 96,* 506–520.

Triandis, H. C. (1990). Cross cultural studies of individualism and collectivism. In J. Berman (Ed.), *Nebraska Symposium on Motivation: Vol. 37* (pp. 41–133). Lincoln: University of Nebraska Press.

Triandis, H. C. (1993). Cross-cultural industrial and organizational psychology. In H. C. Triandis, M. D. Dunnette, & L. M. Hough (Eds.), *Handbook of industrial and organizational psychology* (Vol. 4, 2nd ed., pp. 103–172). Palo Alto, CA: Consulting Psychologists Press.

Triandis, H. C., Bontempo, R., Vilareal, M. J., Masaaki, A., & Lucca, N. (1988). Individualism and collectivism: Cross-cultural perspectives on self-ingroup relationships. *Journal of Personality and Social Psychology, 54,* 328–338.

Vasil, L. (1992). Self-efficacy expectations and causal attributions for achievement among male and female university faculty. *Journal of Vocational Behavior, 41,* 259–269.

Zanc, N. W. S., Sue, S., Hu, L., & Kwon, J. H. (1991). Asian-American assertion: A social learning analysis of cultural differences. *Journal of Counseling Psychology, 38,* 63–70.

CHAPTER TWELVE

Current Professional Issues in Vocational Psychology

John D. Krumboltz
David W. Coon
Stanford University

At a time when employment and unemployment problems make front-page headlines around the world and the nature of the workplace is changing in fundamental ways, the opportunities for career counselors and vocational psychologists have never been brighter. Professionals in vocational psychology can make some major contributions to the solution of societal problems, but we professionals will need to put our own house in order at the same time.

In this chapter we identify and discuss some of the major issues facing the profession. We have organized them under four major headings: responding to a changing world, providing greater service to clients, training and nurturing career professionals, and evaluating outcomes.

RESPONDING TO A CHANGING WORLD

Vocational psychology came of age in response to the needs of the industrial revolution. Many specialized workers were needed to operate the machines and to staff the assembly lines. Workers within a given occupation needed to be quite similar to each other so that replacing any one would not be difficult. Turnover was expensive so finding workers who would be satisfied with their tasks was highly desired. Vocational psychologists rose to the occasion by developing classification systems and assessment devices that did a reasonably good job of matching persons to precisely defined occupations.

As the world moves into the information age, many of the old rules are crumbling. Rigid job descriptions are seen now as a hindrance to getting the work done. Multiple levels of supervisors appear redundant. Responsibilities are assigned to teams of diverse individuals rather than to a hierarchy. How are these and other changes going to affect vocational psychology? Issues that need to be addressed include the definition of the field itself, the ways in which professionals adapt to a changing workforce, and the rationale needed for professionals to respond appropriately.

Who Is a Professional in Vocational Psychology?

Professionals in vocational psychology hold a variety of positions and perform many different tasks. There are career counselors, counseling psychologists, labor department employees, economists, researchers, technicians, and authors, to name just a few. Defining today's career-development professional calls for a complex definition encompassing a number of parameters. Career-development professionals vary widely in their academic training and previous work experiences and are employed in a variety of settings with diverse responsibilities. These varied backgrounds create a rich and textured field with a healthy exchange of ideas and experiences shared in the literature, presented at professional conferences, and discussed in the workplace.

The National Career Development Association (NCDA) has identified 10 areas of competency for effective career counseling. These areas include knowledge and skills in individual and group counseling, individual and group assessment, program management and implementation, consultation, career planning information and resources, career-development theory, assisting special populations, effective supervision, ethical and legal issues, and research and evaluation (NCDA, 1992). NCDA (1988) has also published a resource guide describing six subspecialties of professional career counseling that are organized primarily by work environment. These specialties include private- and public-setting career counselors, career-development specialists in organizations, public-setting job-placement counselors, employment-search consultants offering job-search support, private employment agents who locate and secure jobs for a fee, and cooperative education instructors in school settings. Thus, from college career centers to corporate human resources departments, from counselors to educators to job-placement specialists to researchers, the umbrella of career-development and vocational psychology continues to expand.

The diversity of backgrounds and job titles appears confusing, and there is the temptation to impose some order on it. Some may argue that professionals need more prescribed training programs and supervised training hours for us to qualify as experts in vocational psychology. The world is changing so rapidly that efforts to constrain the field at this time may cause more harm than good.

How Do We Adapt Our Services to a Diverse Workforce?

Who are the clients of the 1990s, the year 2000, and beyond? What issues will they bring to career counseling professionals? The face of the U.S. labor force is changing. Like the general population, not only is it growing older, but it is also growing with rising numbers of racial and ethnic minorities and women, particularly working mothers (Hoyt, 1988; Johnston & Packer, 1987; Kutscher, 1987; Saveri, 1991). Legislation affecting the access to employment and the work-environment treatment of persons with disabilities and of gay men and lesbian women is bringing these workers "out of the closet" and into the workplace. These emerging faces carry with them concerns that challenge vocational psychologists to confront preconceived notions of career counseling, to learn new ways of thinking about career and personal issues, and to develop skills that meet the needs of a changing workforce.

In response to these changes, career counselors will need to view career development and identity development as parallel processes through which they encourage individuals to explore career and personal concerns together (Blustein, Devenis, & Kidney, 1989; Croteau & Hedstrom, 1993; Gottfredson, 1986; Herbert, 1990; Krumboltz, 1993; Pearson & Petitpas, 1990; Raskin, 1989). Effective career planning will best be accomplished by an understanding of the individual's perceptions of work and its importance in his or her life (Cook, 1991; Lucas & Epperson, 1990; Watson & Stead, 1990). Many clients will see work and other roles as firmly interrelated, and quality career counseling will involve helping them think through the intertwined issues.

A career can be conceptualized as providing a series of psychological costs and rewards, and individuals will vary in how they handle these reinforcements (Arthur, 1990; Gottfredson, 1986; Greenglass, Burke, & Ondrack, 1990; Nelson, Quick, Hitt, & Moesel, 1990). Uncertain economic times characterized by frequent layoffs and rising personal and family stress accentuate the interrelationship of career and personal issues (Frost & Clayson, 1991; Wegmann, 1991). Job loss, underemployment, and prolonged unemployment can produce various mental health problems (Herr, 1989). Effective career counselors today and in the future must understand the emotional consequence of job loss and underemployment.

Older Workers. Tomorrow's older worker with various family responsibilities will present different concerns than the younger workforce of decades past. Job security, health benefits, income, pension plans, and quality retirement programs will be priorities. Older workers who have been laid off or offered early retirement and who seek reentry will present new challenges to career-development professionals (Cytrynbaum & Crites, 1989; Fretz, Kluge, Ossana, Jones, & Merikangas, 1989; J. Myers, 1989).

Women. The growing number of U.S. society's working women will encourage career counselors and researchers to explore more closely how gender influences the roles, options, rewards, and costs for individuals (Cook, 1991; Crohan, Antonucci, Adelmann, & Coleman, 1989; Greenhaus, Parasuraman, Granrose, Rabinowitz, & Beutell, 1989; Long, 1989). Although Harmon (1989) described some changes in patterns of women's career choices, the effects of socialization and the parameters of personal and work contexts may still encourage women to make career choices that limit their goals and constrain their interests (Betz, Heesacker, & Shuttleworth, 1990; Stockard & McGee, 1990). In addition, models characterizing men's career development do not necessarily describe women's development (Fassinger, 1990; Ornstein & Isabella, 1990). Women seem to have different views of occupational achievement, interpersonal relationships, and the successful balance of work and family (Cook, 1993; Sullivan, 1992).

Therefore, counselors will need to explore more fully the meaning of work for female clients and recognize that multiple roles, friendships, dual-career relationships, and family are critical to many of them. The way women balance their priorities, however, may vary widely (Rosin & Korabik, 1990; Tomlinson–Keasey, 1990). Women perceive the having of both a family and a career as requiring certain costs for them, including a negative effect on career progression and salary. Many women find that the following work-related issues are major stressors in their lives: home conflicts, child-care responsibility, office politics, lack of career progress, sexism, discrimination, and sexual harassment (Anderson & Leslie, 1991; A. Gutek, Cohen, & Konrad, 1990; B. Gutek & Koss, 1993; Marshall & Jones, 1990; Nelson et al., 1990; Olson, Frieze, & Detlefsen, 1990; Stoltz–Loike, 1992).

Workers from Diverse Racial and Ethnic Backgrounds. Cultural factors associated with race and ethnicity can also affect the importance of work, career choice, and attainment and need to be examined in the context of people's life experiences. These concepts shape how a person views self, others, and the environment (Herbert, 1990; Watson & Stead, 1990). Many racial and ethnic groups face blatant cultural bias and employment discrimination, which are compounded by more subtle exclusion in the form of barriers to information sources and social networks (Greenhaus, Parasuraman, & Wormley, 1990; Martin & Ross–Gordon, 1990; Morrison & Von Glinow, 1990). These and other barriers, like poor education, poverty, and demanding care-giving roles, shape identity, modify career aspirations, and alter life goals.

New immigrants entering the labor force face many of these same problems as well as language barriers, culturally defined work ethics, and a lack of cultural knowledge concerning job-hunting techniques (Westwood & Ishiyama, 1991). The changing ethnic and racial composition of the workforce requires counselors to understand cultural differences and, at the same time, to appreciate that large individual differences exist among members of its various groups (Fukuyama, 1991; Leong, 1993). Clients will need counselor assistance in accessing key social and information networks critical for career development (Gottfredson, 1986; Latack, Josephs, Roach, & Levine, 1987).

Workers With Disabilities. Changing legislation will continue to affect persons with disabilities in the labor force. Many such persons, having struggled long and hard against discrimination, may have minimal early job experiences and may suffer from unemployment and negative self-concepts. From a career-development viewpoint, many career counselors have spent too long determining what careers are appropriate for persons with disabilities rather than involving them into the decision-making process (Curnow, 1989; Fohs, 1991; Hopkins–Best, 1987; Skinner & Schenck, 1992).

Gay Men and Lesbian Women. The vocational choices of lesbian women and gay men are also shaped by the realities of discrimination, harassment, and even violence in our society (Elliott, 1993; Hetherington & Orzek, 1989; Morgan & Brown, 1991). Most have grown up with negative stereotypes of themselves and of the careers available to them. Their role models have been limited or nonexistent (Hetherington, Hillerbrand, & Etringer, 1989). Throughout the life span, gay men and lesbian women face the issue of coming out in each social and professional arena where the choice to do so may have a real effect in limiting their options and their career progress (Shannon & Woods, 1991). Gay and lesbian clients may seek guidance in decision making about the coming out process, guidance in the effective integration of gay or lesbian identity and career identity (Croteau & Hedstrom, 1993), and information about lesbian- and gay-affirmative employers.

In their competencies, the NCDA avoids using the terms *sexual orientation, gay,* or *lesbian* when discussing special populations. They do, however, mention other special groups and "persons with the AIDS virus" (NCDA, 1992, p. 385). By omitting specific mention of gay men and lesbian women, NCDA unwittingly continues to encourage discrimination on the basis of sexual orientation in employment and in the field of career development.

How Does the Changing Nature of Work Affect Vocational Psychology?

In addition to the changing face of the labor force, the nature of work and employment is also changing. Intense global competition along with the acquisition and merger of domestic and worldwide corporations will continue to affect the labor force and the people vocational psychologists serve (Wegmann, Chapman, & Johnson, 1985; Saveri, 1991). Learning will be the key characteristic of all work and central to the experience of all workers. Skills will need to vary over time in virtually all positions. The individual's knowing how to learn will be of even more value to employers than job-specific knowledge.

These changes require constructive adaptation and demand that employees regularly learn new skills and attitudes and cope with new insecurities. The ability to adapt to a new technology and to new information will be critical in one's work and personal life. Those workers skilled in the effective management of information, including the ability to screen out unnecessary information and distraction, will be highly marketable. These changes alone will demand a greater tolerance for ambiguity, uncertainty, and constant change. The worker who survives will quickly sense the needs of consumers and will manager their careers accordingly (Bridges, 1993). Many workers will need to be change agents, implementing constructive change in their work environments while learning to market themselves and their ideas. Counselors and clients alike must come to view change as normal and healthy—staying motivated and committed in the face of change by demonstrating flexibility and adaptability (Savickas, 1993).

Effective communication, problem-solving, and analytical skills will be the basic skills necessary for access to the labor market. Individuals need to recognize that the pattern of behavior that produced a successful career 10 years ago may no longer be adequate or even relevant. The concept of a "job" defined by a narrow job description may become obsolete (Bridges, 1993). Stiff labor-market competition will demand the employee's efficient project completion and avoidance of "turf wars" created by rigid job descriptions.

Employees will need to demonstrate the ability to be both leaders and team players by learning when to take the initiative to lead or to collaborate and how to share responsibility for both success and failure. A major challenge for employers will be the development of new job functions that foster this horizontal team structure (Saveri, 1991) and that allow them to retain quality employees.

The changing nature of work and the workforce and the expanding parameters of our field fuel a variety of professional issues. They influence measurement outcomes, the components of effective career counseling, training and supervision, the structure of career education programs, ethics, and research. Fundamentally, our task is to understand how the work of the world is accomplished and how individuals can be helped to participate constructively in that work while creating satisfying lives for themselves.

PROVIDING GREATER SERVICE TO CLIENTS

How Can the Goal of Career Counseling Be Defined More Usefully?

The earliest definition of the field was provided by Parsons (1909), who suggested the matchmaker model. He proposed a three-step process: (1) know the individual, (2) know occupational requirements, and (3) exercise true reasoning to match the individual to an occupation. This trait-and-factor-matching model has served us well for decades, but we are now beginning to outgrow it as the world changes around us.

A more comprehensive definition of the mission of career counselors is to provide learning experiences that teach the skills of career problem solving and decision making (Fretz, 1981; Gelatt, 1962; Krumboltz & Baker, 1973; Peterson, Sampson, & Reardon, 1991; Spokane & Oliver, 1983). According to this definition, the individual's improved ability to make career decisions is the criterion for judging the success of career counseling.

However, career and personal issues are intimately intertwined. People's career concerns affect their families, work groups, and their larger communities. It is no longer sufficient to think of career counseling as just occupational matchmaking or as merely skill training.

Krumboltz (1994) has proposed a still broader mission for the profession in which counselors help their clients learn a variety of skills, interests, beliefs, values, work habits, and personal qualities so that they may create more satisfying lives for themselves in a constantly changing work environment.

How Can We Move Beyond Matchmaking to Promoting New Learning?

Much of today's theory, research, and practice rest on the traditional foundation of trait-and-factor theory and include the key concept of congruence, the idea that the degree of fit between an individual and the environment leads to beneficial career outcomes (Borgen, 1986; Holland, 1985; Spokane, 1985; Vondracek, Lerner, & Schulenberg, 1986; Zytowski & Borgen, 1983). Unfortunately, our emphasis on congruence fosters a job-matching process that implies there is one best job for the lifespan. It encourages the client to say, "Give me a test that tells me what I should do."

Counselors consistently face clients who are dissatisfied with traditional interventions and who value tests and computer-guidance systems above all other interventions. Although results of meta-analyses of the effectiveness of outcome studies demonstrate that no inventory offers particularly superior benefits to our students or clients (Oliver & Spokane, 1988; Spokane, 1985, 1991), individuals still barge through our doors with powerful expectations for such tools. Clients behave this way perhaps because inventories and guidance programs provide printed "answers" for clients to take with them or perhaps because these interventions require less personal responsibility and effort from clients who face real financial and time constraints in uncertain economic times. Client, employer, counselor, and agency expectations combined with each one's needs and constraints perpetuate the myth of the assessment answer and encourage the belief that these tools are both necessary and sufficient.

This job-match process and its tools encourage counselors to focus on diagnosis, not on client participation and action (Krumboltz, 1994). Once the answer is identified, the steps involved in implementing it can seem to be superfluous because implementation is not part of the trait-and-factor model. Yet implementation is often the toughest part of the career search because it involves a multitude of specific tasks and the almost certain experience of rejection. Accepting a job offer, any job offer, eliminates many client insecurities and diminishes *zeteophobia*, the fear associated with job searching (Krumboltz, 1993). The matching model, with its diagnostic endpoint, does not encourage individuals to look at how careers affect their lives and the lives of their significant others. Furthermore, the process does not empower clients to navigate for themselves. Counselors, in fact, do most of the work—choosing assessment instruments, interpreting results, amassing occupational information, diagnosing an optimal fit. If the job match is successful, counselors receive the credit, and clients learn very little to help themselves prepare for and adapt to the next set of changes. If the job match fails, counselors are blamed for providing an inaccurate forecasting service in which the client had no active role.

Our focus in career counseling has been narrowed not only by client expectations but also by employer beliefs in job-match success. Efficient and effective job matching was encouraged by the need of World War I commanders to determine quickly the best job for soldiers in their ranks. Today's employers also expect effective job matches to help them compete in the ups and downs of the warring marketplace. They hope to purchase needed skills, interests, and personal qualities from new ranks of employees. However, this hoped-for efficiency often overshadows the sound career decision making of all parties involved. Employers' immediate desires to fill vacant job slots seem more salient than planning for employee development.

On the one hand, employers limit their applicant pool with rigid job-description criteria, whereas, on the other, they request creative employees who will contribute in new ways to the team. When work organizations successively narrow the range of personalities inhabiting their environments, they jeopardize their ability to function creatively and lose the ability to respond to novel situations (Schneider, 1987). Congruence then may not always be beneficial either for workers or for their employers (Muchinsky & Monahan, 1987).

In contrast to the "one-best-fit" model, we are suggesting that an interactive learning process takes place between counselors, individuals, and the real world. Each component changes and adapts to each other over time and is influenced by historical, cultural, and social contexts (Vondracek et al., 1986). Career development proceeds both continuously and discontinuously through a series of choices, such as part-time work selection, and through critical choices at predictable transition points, such as high-school graduation (Osipow, 1983). Crisis points forced by the social environment, for example, unexpected unemployment or the need to provide elder care, also occur and can focus immediate attention on the process.

Change and uncertainty are becoming mainstays of career development and are shaking our field's best-fit trait-and-factor foundation. It is now clear that the changing natures of work, of the workplace, and of the individual shape one another, molding new occupations and reshaping old. Occupational choices then become reflections of how individuals see themselves and their possibilities in the world of work. Throughout the life span, adults question their current goals and evaluate ways to meet newly defined goals. The types of questions posed in this evaluation may change, but the questioning process continues (Riverin–Simard 1990; Williams & Savickas, 1990).

Students and employees may also find it wise to maintain open-mindedness and preparedness to handle the ambiguity of their fluctuating social contexts and to deal with changes in their interests, values, personalities, and life goals (Gelatt, 1989; Krumboltz, 1992b). Apparently people try to understand their interaction with their life situations and attempt to cope and learn from both change and uncertainty (Cabral & Salomone, 1990; Gottfredson, 1981; Krumboltz, 1994; Super, 1990). These learning experiences may either restrict or expand the range of personally acceptable career choices by affecting the current self-concept or future self image (Brooks, 1990; Hackett, Betz, O'Halloran, & Romac, 1990; Hesketh, Durant, & Pryor, 1990; Leung & Harmon, 1990; Taylor & Betz, 1983). Although individuals may seek out and attempt to create environments that allow them to express their preferred characteristics (Chartrand, 1991), they may also choose to expand the range of their own characteristics (Krumboltz, 1994). Thus, clients may benefit from seeing change and uncertainty as associated with their continuous learning and development (Riverin–Simard, 1990).

What Interventions Will Promote Diverse Learning Outcomes?

The educational interventions that are used in schools and counseling offices are equally applicable to the career counseling setting—cognitive rehearsal, positive self-talk, social-skills training, relaxation techniques, and guided imagery, to name just a few. Interventions should be tailored to help clients engage in learning ways to develop and implement personal qualities and strategies that enable them to integrate their career, personal, and leisure activities in satisfying ways.

Anticipating Changes in Goals and Values. As counselors, we do a disservice to clients if we do not demonstrate that many goals and values are subject to change. Helping clients challenge outmoded concepts about careers and work environments may help them see how better to adapt to changing conditions in their current and future workplaces. Counselors can utilize the process of informational interviewing as a forum for clients to investigate changes in the workplace and to challenge their preconceptions and beliefs. For example, individuals can learn from the experiences of others who have effectively managed successful career change while balancing the additional roles of primary caregiver and student. People are capable of learning to be receptive to alternative points of view and to their beliefs and goals changing with shifting personal and professional relationships and responsibilities.

Modifying Beliefs and Personality Characteristics. Cognitive rehearsal and restructuring, role playing and imagery work can be effective interventions for identifying and modifying unrealistic beliefs about the self that impede goal attainment. Career counselors often avoid efforts to help individuals modify aspects of their personality. However, consider the client who suffers in the job market because of poor interviewing performance stemming form inept social skills. After social-skills training the job seeker may practice relaxation skills and then try these new social abilities in casual informational interviews before using them in more critical job interviews. Counselors can develop viable referral networks and can work cooperatively with other professionals to help the individual whose personality characteristics and beliefs impede career development.

Overcoming Zeteophobia. Because a career decision affects the person's self-concept and relationships, it is crucial that the decision be made wisely. Lack of self-knowledge, lack of career decision-making abilities, and lack of information about the work world may contribute to the career problem, but they do not typically constitute its whole. Anxiety is highly associated with this decision. When the anxiety is so intense that the individual avoids activities associated with career exploration, it is termed *zeteophobia*, literally, a fear of searching out. Counselors need to name the fear, accept it as an understandable response to an overwhelming task, and then help clients confront the fear directly. The best way one can diminish any fear is to face gradually increasing exposure to the feared situations with support and encouragement. Nothing is gained by avoiding it.

Counselors need to encourage clients to think of their next choice as a temporary experiment—making the best decision realistically possible given what they currently know about themselves, the environment, and how they want to live. Career decisions affect life satisfaction. The line between career and personal counseling, if it exists at all, is permeable (Krumboltz, 1993).

Seeing Counselors as Learners Too. As counselors, we should use ethical interventions that encourage clients to learn activities that move them toward more satisfying lives. Counselors should not be encouraged to practice outside their competency or training, but most counselors are trained and competent in supporting clients to take active steps in exploring new experiences. We cannot ask people to make informed career decisions without looking at how they and those around them are affected by those decisions. A satisfying and healthy career identity affects and is affected by the healthy self. Career counselors are perfectly capable of using educational methods to help their clients, and they can learn new techniques at conferences, workshops, and professional training programs.

Counselors can match their practice preferences with current client goals, but counselors, too, should think of themselves as learners. The counselor's ability to deal successfully with an increasing variety of presenting problems may well become necessary for professional survival.

How Can We Better Integrate Career and Personal Counseling?

Changes and decisions do not occur in individualized vacuums. There is a strong interplay between personal, career, and societal concerns. Entering a new career or work setting means a profound shift in one's goals, values, and relationships. Such change often gives rise to stress, emotional problems, and the questioning of identity for both clients and their significant others. Career counseling is increasingly recognized as inevitably linked to a person's total functioning. Work influences how individuals spend the majority of their waking adulthood, determines interpersonal connections, maps out how and where they live, and shapes their dreams for the future. Career counselors, educators, and researchers must assess the structure and uniqueness of both individuals and their contexts over time in order to understand their interdependence and to assist people in understanding what work means to them in their current situations (Cook, 1991; Vondracek, 1990).

As counselors, we need to supplement the current theory and practice that is based solely on people's existing characteristics with models and strategies that incorporate clients' developing selves. The emphasis on job matching minimizes the importance of counselors' contributions. Research, training, supervision, and practice should be designed so that they promote healthy career development throughout the vicissitudes of life. If we continue to concentrate on merely matching individuals to potentially unstable occupations, we perform a disservice, even if we have taught decision-making and job-search skills. Moreover, we fall short of our goals as career educators and, subsequently, may erode trust in our profession.

Many counselors do more than just job matching, but they do so because they care, not because trait-and-factor theory or skill-training prescribes more (Krumboltz, 1994). These counselors perform needed follow-up work by coaching clients to work independently, encouraging students to try new behaviors and to seek out information, and helping individuals to understand the interrelationships of their multiple roles and current life goals.

We argue that the chief task of career counselors and educators is the promotion of the client's learning about skills, interests, beliefs, values, work habits, and personal qualities, which are all relevant to the creation of a satisfying life.

The counselor's goals are to help people learn to cope with internal and external changes, to motivate and inspire their constructive adaptation, and to help them bridge the various personal and professional contexts, all in order to help them meet goals and expectations for their lives as a whole. This means the constructing of an identity that incorporates career rather than the creating of a career identity completely distinct from the person as a whole. It means that the counselor must prepare individuals to manage change through an understanding of self and current life goals in a way that helps ease the times when job loss results from unexpected unemployment, from choice due to current dissatisfaction, or from planned retirement. Counselors must actively enlist and empower clients and students as full collaborators in the counseling and planning processes by providing learning experiences that encourage them to think about how they can create satisfying lives for themselves.

These learning activities must not only help clients identify current beliefs, interests, values, and personal qualities but also help them investigate anticipated change and potential development. Clients need to explore current life goals and careers that support goal development as well as brainstorm new visions of their future. We must help design learning experiences that increase individuals' awareness of their multiple roles and how interaction with their environments affects life satisfaction. And we must help clients generalize the notion that learning and changing are normal and even joyful parts of their career and personal lives.

This shift in focus raises a number of questions about current professional issues in the practice and research of career counseling and career education as well as issues in the training and supervision of career counselors.

TRAINING AND NURTURING CAREER PROFESSIONALS

How Do We Move Counselors Toward Valuing Open-Mindedness?

As counselors, we have had a fixation on decisiveness. Anyone who remained undecided about a career goal has been considered a problem in need of repair. We need to restructure our thinking. Instead of bemoaning a lack of decisiveness, we can celebrate the presence of open-mindedness.

Asking people to commit themselves to a life-long occupation has never made much sense, but in today's changing world it makes even less sense. Clients need courage to explore and experiment. We can encourage clients to try a new activity that may, or may not, move them closer to their presently conceived goals. In either case, we can coach clients to use what they learn for future decision making. When their goals are unformulated, we can encourage them to experiment with any one of the available alternatives just to begin finding out about the emotional and personal consequences.

The effect of change creates concurrent gains and losses that influence decision making. For example, a person may consider a move to a new state after the last company layoff to pursue a new job that promises more security and more income. The job, however, also is made up of less interesting work tasks, and the move clearly means the loss of a well-defined support network for family members. The counselor's charge is to promote learning that assists the client's consideration of the personal, social, and work realms, by serving as coaches, counselors, and educators, not merely as matchmakers. Career counseling should facilitate the learning of skills and work habits, the discovery of interests and beliefs, and the understanding of personal qualities, learning styles, and communication styles that in combination enable clients to create satisfying lives. We must recognize that these personal characteristics are all subject to change as the result of subsequent learning experiences. The changes of the individual, in turn, affect others at work and at home.

Our job is to help break down the massive task of "What shall I do with the rest of my life?" into "What would I like to try next that will help me learn something important toward building a satisfying life?" Together, the counselor and client must gain an understanding of the client's needs and must define goals for the counseling process. This process requires an investigation of both short-term and long-term goals, a clear understanding of the meaning and importance that the client attaches to work and leisure, and a serious commitment from the client to take some action consistent with these goals.

Counselors can promote successful accomplishment or adaptation in various goal arenas by helping clients take risks in learning. Every learning experience cannot be joyful, but even failures can teach something valuable. Client choices are influenced by the scarcity or abundance of learning opportunities in their social and work environments. We must actively enlist and empower clients and students as full collaborators in the counseling and planning processes by having them help generate, provide, and participate in learning experiences that encourage them to think about what constitutes satisfying lives for them. These learning activities can be built on current beliefs, interests, values, and personal qualities, but clients need to anticipate how they might want to change and develop these characteristics. Clients need to explore current life goals and careers that support goal development, as well as brainstorm new learning experiences to help envision future goals. We must help design learning experiences that increase individuals' awareness of their multiple roles and how interaction with their environments affects life satisfaction. Too, we must help clients explicitly focus on tentative decision making and on implementation activities with exploration and practice for future applications.

How Can Counselors Be Trained to Use Assessment Instruments to Promote New Learning?

The functions of assessment instruments and computer-guidance programs should be expanded (Krumboltz & Jackson, 1993). Counselors can use test results not only to summarize past learning but also to suggest new learning experiences. These tools can help the counselor to identify key themes, beliefs, and conflicts relevant to current career concerns and to create a framework of collaboration for identifying new skills to develop, new interests to explore, and old beliefs to challenge.

The majority of today's career assessments are based on the trait-and-factor model. Although counselors could use results from such assessments to encourage career exploration, the results are often used in ways that discourage exploration. Even when the assessments are used properly, counselors must counteract employer and client tendencies to hold up a test result as providing the right choice. Counselors must consistently reinforce the idea that test results are but one of many valuable pieces of information individuals can use to make informed decisions. Interest inventories, for example, are based on limited numbers of occupations and are built on samples from the very work groups the employers say desperately need different learning, thinking, communication, and personality styles. Furthermore, the current method of assessment and matching is based on people's previous knowledge about themselves and careers, and it gathers little or no information about their current situation, future dreams, or changing occupations. The intent of trait-and-factor theory and practice is the identification of the one best choice, and they are based on the assumptions that people, their occupations, and their environment remain stable—assumptions that are less accurate now than ever.

What Is the Nature of Needed Training Programs?

The realities of forthcoming changes in the nature of work and employment and the growing diversity of the workforce raise questions about training and supervision needs for trainees and professionals. In particular, how do graduate programs incorporate career counseling training that meets the changing needs of a multicultural workforce? If learning and change are the key characteristics of future work and employment, how can we best coach trainees in how to learn and adapt so they can help their clients and students do the same?

In our training programs we need to practice what we preach. If we advocate that clients take risks, then training programs should provide learning opportunities that require risk taking and that demonstrate trainees' capacity to change their skills, beliefs, attitudes, values, goals, and interests. If trainees learn to adjust to new demands in our own field, they will be better able to understand and empower their clients and students. Tomorrow's greatest risk of all lies, not in change, but in the unwillingness to risk change. We, as counselors, clients, researchers, and trainees, all need to concern ourselves not only with how the future affects us but also with how we can affect the future.

To this end, training programs must be developed so that they engender an understanding of the interrelationship between career counseling and multiculturalism. Effective career counseling will require both sensitivity to and competence in multicultural issues, from accurate assessment in multiple contexts to effective change-agentry skills.

Quality training will encourage trainees to explore the meaning of work in their personal, social, and cultural contexts and provide an opportunity for them to see how their work affects significant others. It will help trainees view career identity as part of personal-identity development and help them recognize career development and life planning as processes that can benefit from both short-term and long-term strategies. Ultimately, graduate programs can help trainees develop an array of counseling skills and a repertoire of learning tools that they can use to help individuals identify and implement the keys to more satisfying lives.

Training Program Philosophy

Our profession's training programs need a well-stated philosophy with goals and strategies that combine career counseling and multicultural training. The necessary elements of this combined training need to be clearly identified for trainees by an emphasis on the developmental nature of these processes and a delineation of the expectations for career counseling competence in multicultural contexts. These competency guidelines can be drawn from those developed by the National Career Development Association, by the American Counseling Association, and by the Division of Counseling Psychology of the American Psychological Association (D. W. Sue, Arrendondo, & McDavis, 1992; D. W. Sue et al., 1982; NCDA, 1992; Swanson, 1993).

To activate this philosophy, professionals can serve as change agents in our institutions by participating in the earnest recruitment of diverse students, staff, and faculty. Effective recruitment will not only provide more diverse professional work teams that are needed to effectively manage the multicultural labor force but also will create diverse and dynamic learning environments with opportunities for demonstrating models of healthy conflict resolution and cooperative learning. Faculty members can model commitment to scholarship in multicultural career issues in a number of ways. Actions would include this calling for faculty and student research support to study career development in multicultural contexts, giving professional presentations on research and effective career inventions within multiple contexts, serving as research mentors to students on related subjects or connecting students with appropriate mentors, actively participating in or developing workshops on multiculturalism and career issues, and providing advanced courses that bridge the processes.

Even with constricted budgets, training program personnel can still influence students, colleagues, the institution, and the local community. They can ask community leaders, practitioners, and researchers with expertise in career development and multicultural processes to serve as adjunct faculty or as supervisors. Faculty members can demonstrate to trainees effective in-service training, consultation, and referral skills by working in tandem with these local experts and, in turn, by providing similar services for staff at the local expert's work site. The changing nature of employment will encourage more part-time faculty and training staff who share and trade jobs. This situation can be turned to the trainee's advantage because the faculty and staff will necessarily demonstrate effective multicultural teamwork and the healthy balance between professional and personal contexts.

Current faculty and staff can positively affect the system by viewing the development of the training program in multicultural career issues as an inclusive process. The development of a supportive yet challenging learning environment is a responsibility of the whole department or agency and should not rest solely on the shoulders of underrepresented minorities. Once a safe and supportive training environment is established, people will share their personal histories and struggles, and tracking professionals must then be prepared to hear and learn from them (Buhrke & Douce, 1991). Beyond this, we must be prepared to help trainees do the same.

Training for Person and System Change. All counselors, students, and clients hold onto world views and behavior that reflect their gender, sexuality, socioeconomic status, religion, race, ethnicity, and culture. These perspectives, behaviors, and social contexts shape clients' experiences and mold crucial parts of career and personal identities (Blustein et al., 1989; Croteau & Hedstrom, 1993; Helms, 1990; Steenbarger, 1993). However, within this diversity there is a common thread. All human beings when evaluating choices must ask to various degrees, What is best for me, my significant others, and my cultural groups, now and in the future? (Christensen, 1989).

Unfortunately, client and student career concerns are usually decontextualized in career counseling. Typically, career and related distress is constructed by self and others as inherently client-based rather than as a consequence of influential contexts and significant others. In career counseling, we have emphasized insight rather than change, have labeled the individual as the problem, and have stressed testing, linear problem solving, and job match as the cure. Career concerns need to be explored in a broader context in which clients and counselors collaborate to assess how both the individuals and their contexts contribute to the problem (Katz, 1985; Steenbarger, 1993; Vondracek & Schulenberg, 1992). Through this collaboration, learning experiences can be created for person-change and context- (or system-) change strategies. Therefore, this model creates multiple change targets and potentially moves the counseling process beyond the client to family, school, peers, and institutions.

Quality career counseling in a diverse society must integrate brief and long-term interventions with person-change and system-change strategies. Counselor training must bring together brief counseling that identifies and challenges client beliefs with multicultural and contextual interventions that validate client world views (Helms, 1986; Pedersen, 1988; Steenbarger, 1993; D. W. Sue & D. Sue, 1990). Training efforts including course projects, practicum experiences, and internships can demonstrate and integrate these intervention strategies. Training in this larger perspective will inevitably result in challenging the present world views of trainees.

Steenbarger (1993) suggested a number of person-change and system-change strategies that can be expanded or adapted to career counseling. For example, brief system-change strategies may include media campaigns or outreach activities in established social structures, such as classes or community groups, that raise awareness of potential employment barriers or publicize agency programs and services. Short-term person-change strategies should focus on brief information and competency-building experiences. These may include career fairs, interviewing-skills workshops, and psychoeducational courses designed to help individuals function more effectively in their current contexts. Institutionalized beliefs and practices that disempower large numbers of individuals require collaborative efforts directed at long-term system change. These interventions may include efforts directed at policy changes, such as the expansion of health benefits for domestic partners, or at ecological interventions, such as the modification of the physical environment for persons with disabilities. Individuals who are routinely disempowered and discriminated against may require person-change strategies that afford the client time to build trust and the counselor time to identify appropriate learning activities and strategies. These strategies might include a combination of individual and group counseling and a series of skill-building workshops that allow for more client self-exploration and afford clients the opportunity to hear from others with similar views and experiences (Helms, 1990; Steenbarger, 1993; D. W. Sue & D. Sue, 1990).

An Integrated Training Model To develop competence in career counseling and multiculturalism, we encourage an integrated training model similar to that proposed by LaFromboise and Foster (1992). In their model, counseling, research, and teaching professionals serve as coaches to trainees and demonstrate skill, self-confidence, and a willingness to continue to learn and adapt to the changing needs of the multicultural work world. These coaches encourage student collaboration in the development of learning strategies and can be faculty, supervisors, and community role models actively involved in the program. The integrated model emphasizes a psychoeducational approach in which these coaches teach, facilitate, and model ways of thinking and development that challenge trainees' old beliefs and build new skills.

This integrated approach requires movement beyond models built on a single career course and a single multicultural counseling course. Trainees will need a solid understanding of career development and the cultural, historical, and social contexts of various underrepresented groups. Without a knowledge base provided through courses dedicated to career development and multicultural understanding, trainees will violate the goals and cultural values of the individuals they counsel. Trainees must understand that there may be culture-specific career development that influences the counseling process and the selection of appropriate assessments and interventions (Fassinger, 1990; Gainor & Forrest, 1991; Mael, 1991; McWhirter & Ryan, 1991; Morgan & Brown, 1991; Shannon & Woods, 1991; Yang, 1991). Training programs must have carefully embedded foundations courses early in the graduate-student experience so students can draw on their knowledge in subsequent classroom, practicum, and research experiences.

As S. Sue and Zane (1987) noted, a model based on a single multicultural course potentially magnifies minority differences, ignores heterogeneity within groups, and encourages trainees to use a cookbook approach in assessment and intervention. The one-semester career course can potentially create a cookbook approach of its own, one that highlights trait-and-factor assessment and subsequent job match. Because of its complexity, then, multicultural career counseling runs the risk of being built on limited exposure to the parallel processes of career-identity and personal-identity development, overgeneralization of sociocultural group differences, career development theories and assessment instruments with questionable multicultural sensitivity, and an emphasis on job match with limited consideration of multiple roles or contexts.

An integrated model not only incorporates these introductory courses but also incorporates career and multicultural material into relevant courses such as basic counseling skills and introduction to research methods. For example, role-play situations and research designs should include minority persons and relevant social contexts and developmental issues. Given the interrelationship of personal- and career-identity development and the association of career decision making with anxiety and depression, courses in human development, personality, and affective disorders could cover research and theory on work salience and adjustment for minority and majority persons. Even examples in statistics can include multicultural groups and career issues. This integration requires a concerted effort not only within the program but also across departments.

How do graduate programs encourage trainees to participate in and learn about constructive person-change strategies in an integrated model? As professionals, we need first to demonstrate our own capacity for open-mindedness and our preparation for change. We cannot assume that trainees arrive with similar understandings of self and the effects of sociocultural contexts on their lives, their career choice, and the counseling relationship (Ronnestad & Skovholt, 1993; Swanson, 1993). If we teach students not to make assumptions about clients based on their own group membership, then we as trainers must not do so. Increasing the diversity of students in a training program means that training goals must be flexible enough to address different levels of student readiness to learn new beliefs, activities, models, and skills (Swanson, 1993; Vondracek & Schulenberg, 1992). Training then includes the trainee's exploring the self and learning about her or his own multiple roles and contexts and their influences on decision making and behavior.

Swanson (1993) specified that effective career counseling requires both multicultural sensitivity and multicultural competence. Sensitivity implies a fundamental value shift that enables competence to be better learned and integrated. Learning opportunities that allow trainees to explore career development and multicultural sensitivity in a safe environment may require wise use of adjunct faculty so dual relationships that inhibit student learning can be avoided. A strong affective component is often a part of this learning, and, as a result, trainers will face personal and trainee resistance. Through their development of multicultural sensitivity, individuals examine preexisting beliefs about their personal and work worlds and explore necessary changes for more effective counseling. Students must first learn to recognize resistance, then explore how it affects career decision making, and finally consider how it blocks their helping behavior. A safe environment enables individuals to struggle with issues without fear of being attacked or labeled, by its focus on the influences that beliefs, biases, and institutional barriers have on people's perceptions of occupations and their appropriateness for themselves and others.

Even in a safe environment, individuals often get caught up in debating one form of discrimination versus another. Buhrke and Douce (1991) suggested that students can learn to see that debating one struggle against another, such as disabled persons' access to employment versus older workers' access to employment, only divides resources, draws attention away from societal barriers, and increases competition among disempowered groups. Training instead should raise students' sensitivity to individual struggles and increase their appreciation of the strength required to form positive career and personal identities in oppressive environments. Exploring world views, with myths and stereotypes repudiated by facts, can help trainees clarify their own professional limitations and, at the same time, encourage them to continue to learn how to work with the value struggles of multicultural workers (Buhrke & Douce, 1991). Both career development and multiculturalism are life-long learning processes that preclude a single-course experience.

Prepracticum Skill Development. Early in the training program, students should work with faculty, supervisors, and other students to assess their individual career and multicultural counseling competencies. Within an integrated learning model, the trainee will focus on developing a personal set of learning opportunities. Such opportunities can increase trainees' understanding of how individuals and their career choices are influenced by many different cultural factors at different times, including age, gender, sexual orientation, socioeconomic status, disability, race, and ethnicity (L. Myers et al., 1991; Pedersen, 1991; Steenbarger, 1993).

At specific points throughout the program, students should evaluate their career counseling and multicultural competencies with their mentors and supervisors. Evaluations could include the student's progress in developing a personal model of counseling that addresses the integration of career and multicultural development. These evaluations should help students recognize that their interests, beliefs, and skills may change with subsequent learning experiences. Faculty, staff, and supervisors should model for their students how they assess their competencies, how they continue to learn, and what tools they use to assist clients and students.

Learning experiences in training programs need to be didactic and experiential and encompass both brief and long-term person-change and system-change strategies. Because graduate training is self-selective, learning opportunities should be designed to broaden trainees' experience with educational, occupational, and social diversity. Both majority and minority persons employed in positions not traditionally associated with their group membership can be invited to speak about who and what influenced their decisions. It is important for faculty and staff to ask minority members to talk about their professional expertise in addition to their special competence in dealing with minority issues. In classes and supervision sessions, the leader can gather student reactions to taped counseling sessions or interviews, assign and discuss self-assessment and goal prioritization exercises, and use personal journals and cross-cultural interviews. Through these techniques trainees can explore the importance of work, leisure, and significant others in people's lives and overcome the simplistic notion that career counseling is just finding the one best job.

By collaborating on information interviews with older workers, trainees can increase their awareness of the scarcity or abundance of learning situations across social contexts, explore factors influencing identity development, and discover the different questions persons believe to be important in career decision making. Analysis of these interviews or relevant counseling sessions for examples of goal-setting and decision-making skills can reveal various degrees of individuals' successful adaptation in the face of changing work and social contexts. Sessions with older workers also help modify trainee preconceptions of these persons and the long-held beliefs that they contribute little or nothing to society (Schaie, 1993).

In counseling methods classes, role plays based on the triad model (Pedersen, 1981) and similar techniques can also demonstrate multicultural career intervention. More important, these role plays can show how minority membership influences different levels of career and life planning. For example, such role plays can reveal the differences between a situation in which a gay client contemplates coming out to his family and employer and another situation in which a 50-year-old man who happens to be gay expresses career dissatisfaction (Buhrke & Douce, 1991). These learning opportunities can raise trainees' awareness of the need to respect client desires or their own desires not to be open about various issues.

Exposure to career inventories and diagnostic instruments is necessary for competent career counseling and intervention strategies. However, thorough discussions of these tools need to increase student understanding of their limitations and raise questions about their appropriateness across cultural groups (Fouad, 1993). The interrelationship of career and personal issues also demands that career counselors have knowledge of the unique features in the diagnosis and treatment of anxiety, depression, and stress reactions experienced by oppressed persons and knowledge of the limitations of standard personality assessments (LaFromboise & Foster, 1992).

These learning opportunities can raise broader questions of the counselor's role in career development, demonstrating that some individuals will seek authority figures who provide information and job-seeking advice and that others will expect a facilitator who encourages reflection and personal exploration. Through this training process students will also need to face the question of whether or not career choice is primarily determined by the individual. Other factors such as family, religion, and military requirements may play important roles in the process (Bowman, 1993; Katz, 1985). Career counselors will need to expand the definition of career services, recognizing and incorporating legitimate cultural networks or natural support systems just as has been suggested for general mental health services (Brammer, 1985; LaFromboise & Foster, 1992; Padilla & DeSnyder, 1985).

Courses in group counseling and family systems present observation, role-play, and group-project opportunities that teach within- and between-group differences and similarities concerning various career issues such as work-role salience and family decision making (Bowman, 1993; D. W. Sue & D. Sue, 1990; Swanson, 1993). Group and family interventions with peer feedback can help challenge client views that career difficulties are solely individually based (Pyle, 1986). System and family contributions and distracters can be more easily identified in group processes and used by students to overcome career decision-making blocks (Hawks & Muha, 1991). For example, with group interventions used as long-term change strategies, the counselor may raise group members' educational aspirations and access with the intent of expanding their career options (Hotchkiss & Borow, 1990). Trainees need to learn that client heterogeneous-group versus homogeneous-group experiences should be carefully timed because effective learning and decision making is closely associated with positive identity development (Buhrke & Douce, 1991; Miranda & Storms, 1989; D. W. Sue & D. Sue, 1990). In fact, personal-identity development may affect individual-counseling strategies by the person's expressed preference for counselors or role models of same gender, orientation, race, or ethnicity (Helms, 1986; McDaniels & Gysbers, 1992; McDermott, Tyndall, & Lichtenberg, 1989).

Effective system-change strategies will also require training in curriculum design, consultation, and administration in order for the counselor to design workshops and classes, provide in-service training, mediate disputes, and manage programs and services that meet the needs of a multicultural clientele. In research methods courses, teachers can focus on persons and groups within their various contexts to encourage discussion of the generalizability of existing theories and interventions with a multicultural population. Research training can teach students to question the applicability of commonly used designs and clinical interventions for minorities, to explore a broader range of methods from critical incident observation to oral histories, and to generate methods of overcoming barriers to cross-cultural research. Research on multicultural career issues then can become an impetus for social action and policy development (LaFromboise & Foster, 1992; Stiles & Shapiro, 1989).

Practicum and Internship Training. Prior to practicum and internship placement, trainees must assess their career and multicultural counseling competencies and then examine the ability of internship agencies to provide the training and supervision they need. The training-program staff should evaluate training sites for staff diversity, supervisor career counseling competence, and supervisor multicultural sensitivity and competence. Program directors should monitor the quality of supervisors through site visits and supervisee feedback, paying specific attention to supervisor ability to manage diversity (Buhrke & Douce, 1991; LaFromboise & Foster, 1992; Swanson,

1993). Supervisors with experience in direct supervision of career counseling cases and with broad training in brief and long-term individual-, group-, and system-change strategies are recommended.

Practicum and internship experiences need to be varied and tied to the mentor model of skill building including modeling, observation, and coaching processes that ultimately give students an array of intervention tools and skills applicable to career counseling in multicultural society. Ideal training includes seminars and training modules, case studies, individual and group supervision, observation of supervisor counseling sessions, and exposure to a variety of issues from employee substance abuse and dual-career couples to job-readiness skills training and organizational change strategies.

The rising rates of unemployment and underemployment demand practicum and internship experiences that increase counselor trainee sensitivity to client work-role salience and social contexts and that develop trainees' key mental health skills to help clients cope with a range of emotional problems provoked by their situation (Cabral & Salomone, 1990; Cook, 1991; Serling & Betz, 1990; Vondracek, 1990; Vondracek, Hostetler, Schulenberg, & Shimizu, 1990). Supervisors can demonstrate positive person-change strategies by introducing emotion-focused and problem-focused coping that confronts system versus individual responsibility for unemployment. These strategies can also help the client to critically examine beliefs that encourage self-definition solely in career terms. Through these experiences, trainees not only sharpen assessment and counseling skills that help them differentiate client pathology from contextually driven developmental crises but also learn to question further the relevance of particular counseling theories and practices (Buhrke & Douce, 1991; LaFromboise & Foster, 1992).

Practicum and internship sites also have the potential to enhance the students' training in system-change strategies and to expand student experiences with multicultural team work. Career counseling training often concentrates on a remedial job-match model rather than on psychoeducational models of outreach, consultation, and advocacy. Little individual or system change occurs in educational or work settings through consciousness-raising strategies that do not also incorporate direct system-change strategies in schools, community, and government agencies and in local businesses (Corvin & Wiggins, 1989; Jackson & Holvino, 1988; D. W. Sue & D. Sue, 1990). Personnel at practicum and internship sites can demonstrate how to collaborate with community gatekeepers to improve service delivery, research, and interventions that modify barriers to employment and education.

Supervision

Unfortunately no body of literature exists that specifically addresses career counseling supervision. However, both instructional and therapeutic models that connect the theory and practice of multicultural and career counseling are needed for the training of today's counselors. We propose a learning model of supervision in which the supervisor–supervisee relationship changes over time. Trainees are coached from their roles as observers to fully participating counselors with growing competence and with the ability to generate rival hypotheses to their supervisor's assumptions (Triandis, 1993). Such supervision cultivates independence because the supervisor offers help with infrequently taught skills, mentors within cocounseling situations, uses the supervisory relationship itself to demonstrate counseling skills, and provides appropriate feedback (Ronnestad & Skovholt, 1993; Worthington, 1984). In career centers, this supervision model means a shift from trainees' watching workshops and counseling sessions with culturally similar clients to their observing live cross-cultural career interventions with immediate feedback.

Supervisors can model career assessment and behavior interpretation by demonstrating culturally appropriate direct service, outreach activities, or research training (LaFromboise & Foster, 1992). As coaches, supervisors help trainees anticipate clients' prejudicial remarks and behavior, discuss and role play the situation, and then debrief the experience. They can prepare students for client requests for personal information including questions about ethnicity and sexual orientation and explore client–counselor attraction regardless of participants' sexual orientation (Buhrke & Douce, 1991). Supervisors can help students see requests for a counselor with a particular cultural background as an important component of identity development rather than as personal rejection. They can then model competent referral practices (Buhrke & Douce, 1991).

Supervisors in a learning model seek professional development opportunities through workshops, conferences, and consultation, acknowledging that professional stagnation will likely engender stagnation in supervisees (Ronnestad & Skovholt, 1993) and knowing that the attitudes of both the supervisor and counselor potentially affect the client (Glenn & Russell, 1986; Lopez, 1989). Increasing the trainee's personal self-awareness and professional identity are notable processes in the supervision relationship. Yet, competent supervisors will work to circumscribe the relationship and consult with other supervisors to appropriately distinguish supervision from personal counseling.

Professional Development

Because career development and multiculturalism are defined as developmental processes, many of the experiential and didactic learning opportunities already mentioned can be incorporated in professional development activities of staff, faculty, and administrators. In addition, these experiences can foster individual professional development and organizational change. Career development and multicultural sensitivity and competence should not be reserved just for employees at the top of the organizational hierarchy. Even in times of tight budgets, the system should be designed so that all employees can participate in local, regional, and even national associations or activities that extend their competencies and further their own career development. As professionals, we need to remind ourselves that our front-line staff have frequent contact with students, clients, and community agencies and are often the last to have access to these learning opportunities.

Professional development begins at "home." It provides a structure that supports individual and organizational change and that rewards staff efforts to develop innovative multicultural career interventions, programs, services, and research. Some of this development can be accomplished by the professionals' designing in-house workshops, bringing in local experts for training seminars, effectively managing diversified work groups, modeling multicultural competence and sensitivity in research and supervision groups, and providing externally run career development or process groups for staff.

Administrative staff of programs and agencies need to perform periodic employee evaluations to identify barriers that impede workers' career development, learning opportunities, and constructive adaptation. Employers can show that they value employee input by developing programs that help eliminate these barriers. Mangers should form employee coaching and cross-training relationships that focus on skill development and the enhancement of both individuals and the system. Professional development activities should avoid exclusive one-to-one relationships, which only sponsor a limited number of individuals, create divisiveness, and maintain barriers to information and training for career advancement.

Faculty, staff, and administrators who act as system-change agents should be viewed as trailblazers who need support, encouragement, and guidance. Employees at all levels can be encouraged to serve on diversity councils, to join employee networks, to research and circulate relevant career and multicultural publications, and to facilitate career development and multicultural awareness programs in other departments. As professionals, we need to demonstrate to clients, employers, and students that in our own work environments we can increase respect for individuality and collaboration, enable employees to develop their potential, and manage the diversity of a multicultural work world in a way that enriches our agencies, organizations, and training programs.

EVALUATING OUTCOMES

Interventions that focus on the clients' learning require the identification and targeting of needed skills and knowledge, the design and monitoring of learning activities that assist the career development-process, and the assessment of change in people's behaviors, self-perceptions, and views of their environment.

How Do the Expanded Goals of Career Counseling Affect Standard Outcome Measures?

With learning and its applications resting at the center of our professional accountability, we can shift away from job match as our principal outcome. Outcomes can include any desired changes in skills, interests, beliefs, values, work habits, or personal qualities that our students or clients acquire through monitored learning activities (Krumboltz, 1994; Peterson et al., 1991). We can assess these changes psychometrically or anecdotally to determine the extent to which they help move individuals toward goal discovery or attainment, assist them in current and subsequent career and life adjustment, and increase their life satisfaction.

As Spokane (1991) suggested, career counselors and educators have nothing to fear. Our interventions work quite well on the whole, but we need to look at the underlying learning process to identify ways to strengthen their effects. This investigation raises complex issues related to how outcome is measured in our field. We often find it convenient to employ standard outcome measures with demonstrated validity and reliability (Spokane & Oliver, 1983) and to use multiple measures that cut across a common set of outcome domains (Fretz, 1981; R. Myers, 1986).

Standard measures, however, may not necessarily be measuring the most relevant outcomes. For example, as discussed previously, career indecision is often posited as an undesirable quality that needs to be overcome. A number of quite reliable and valid measures of career indecision exist. Should we use them just because they exist? If we conceive of career counseling as a learning process designed to open up new possibilities and to promote experimentation, then our striving for a permanent career decision could be counterproductive (Krumboltz, 1992b). Instead of striving to overcome indecision, we might learn to value and assess open-mindedness. Indecision is a problem in the trait-and-factor model because the third and final step is the matching decision. If the client cannot decide (despite intensive counselor efforts), then the three-step trait-and-factor model has not been consummated and both counselor and client feel frustrated. In contrast, under the learning model, the lack of a decision is a cue that the client remains open-minded and ready for additional learning experiences.

It is possible that job match and job placement as the principal outcomes in practice have limited the development of new outcome measures and have discouraged the use of existing measures from our own and related fields, such as, business, sociology, and developmental psychology. Consequently, many intervention outcomes will require the development of new instruments or the revision or adaptation of others.

What New Outcome Measures Are Needed?

Besides traditional job-placement and career-information outcomes, what outcomes are critical for changing individuals in a changing world? In general, we need to use learning processes that reduce client zeteophobia while promoting their exploration of social and work environments and how they interact. Given the amount of change people face in today's world, counselors and the individuals they see need to develop a greater acceptance of career indecision as a desirable byproduct of changing work roles and an uncertain future. They will also need to relate career activities to overall satisfaction and to see the important role that beliefs, self-perceptions, and self-efficacy play in decision making (Blustein, 1989; Gelatt, 1989; Krumboltz, 1991, 1992a; Stickel & Bonett, 1991; Taylor & Betz, 1983).

Peterson et al. (1991) placed importance on the understanding of how good decision makers operate, including the discovery of how they consider options and understand self, occupation, and environment. Peterson et al. suggested outcomes such as changes in individuals' negative self-talk, awareness of feelings, and consideration of self-interest versus effects on significant others. Counselors may need to measure a shift in clients' attitudes about themselves, career exploration, the learning process, and work or life planning. Researchers can then design studies to determine what interventions can best produce these changes.

The use of job-satisfaction and work-identity and career-identity measures could be supplemented with assessment of the role of work in one's life (e.g., Blau, 1988; Hackman & Oldham, 1975; Mirels & Garrett, 1971; Super & Nevill, 1986). Perhaps measures of life stressors, multiple roles and environments, and relevant self-efficacy (Stickel & Bonett, 1991) need to be implemented. The variety of issues facing clients with career concerns obviously leads to a plethora of potential outcome measures.

R. Myers (1986) recommended that vocational psychologists focus on outcomes relevant at the point where clients face a career decision. But we may have too narrow a conception of what constitutes a career decision. There are innumerable problems that face people as they cope with their education and work, for example, how to study more effectively, how to cope with sexual harassment in the classroom or workplace, how to deal with an obnoxious teacher or boss, how to deal with dual-career issues, or how to plan a satisfying retirement. Problems like these could be called career decisions because each problem affects one's career and requires a series of decisions about the best course of action. Perhaps we need to distinguish between *occupational direction decisions* and *career concerns.* An occupational direction decision is just one of many possible career concerns, which involve a complex array of interrelationships among individuals, their significant others, and their social and work environments.

Behavioral components also need to be incorporated in outcome and evaluation so that the underlying components of change can be determined. A career-planning scenario can be role played with participants asking how they handled the issues and what knowledge or activities contributed to their performance. Students, clients, instructors, counselors, peers, or significant others can record their reactions to how behavior has changed or improved and can evaluate their perception of what helped. The counselor can compare these perceptions and use them to refine interventions. Role plays and videotaped sessions of simulated job interviews can be rated by a counselor, employer, or student. Participants can replay tapes and write down their thoughts to uncover how they learned to handle the situation. In some settings, such as college career centers and employment agencies, it might be useful for job interviewees to give feedback anonymously to employers concerning their interviews. These rating sheets would provide both job seekers and employers an opportunity to examine interviews from a new perspective, one that could potentially increase their understanding of the underlying processes and their interviewing skills. In addition to many outcomes already discussed, feedback from videotaped counseling sessions or workshops could be used by clients to enhance their presentation skills.

As counselors, we need to learn from our own experience. For example, during informational interviewing and job-search activity, participants could be asked for feedback on effective and ineffective practices. We could thus accumulate evidence on job-acquisition rates and the length of time individuals remain on the job and then correlate these findings with alternative job-search strategies. All of this information could increase our understanding of career development and improve our services and programs.

How Can Research Studies Be Well Designed and Cost Effective?

The development and use of outcome measures and evaluation programs need to be considered within the mission, goals, and budget of the individual office or career services agency. Most programs and their staff are overextended already. The staff must compare the cost effectiveness of various programs and services to determine which ones meet the needs of clients at a manageable cost (Campbell, Walz, Miller, & Kriger, 1973; Oliver & Spokane, 1988; Spokane & Oliver, 1983). Many clients in uncertain economic times need immediate attention and require access to counselors with the training to manage complex mental health and career issues. In terms of amount of gain per hour, individual counseling has been found to be more valuable than other interventions (Oliver & Spokane, 1988), but if the service is not reimbursed, individual counseling wreaks havoc with an organization's staff time and budget. Individual career counseling also requires more homemade outcome measures tailored to the individual. Perhaps, creative agencies and counselors can design prototypical learning activities and outcome measures applicable to the individual that can be aggregated to shed light on underlying learning processes.

At the program level, Spokane (1991) raised the issue that, most of the time, group effectiveness is assessed according to precounseling–postcounseling changes in the individual participants, when randomly assigned control groups are needed for reliable comparison. The argument is without question a statistically sound one. Still, researchers should recognize that mean group differences can hide significant learning at the individual level. Perhaps in addition to expanding the number of groups evaluated, investigators should examine multiple single-case studies on key outcome variables. These multiple cases could help investigators determine where the learning occurs if well-designed cognitive and behavioral outcome measures are used. Researchers could assess outcome variables for group cohorts and their individual members over extended time periods to evaluate how the participants chose satisfying majors, internships, or jobs; changed beliefs that blocked effective decision making; or improved communication skills.

Self-studies by agencies and private practices and on-site visits by outside reviewers would provide counselors information for improving programs and services, for better understanding client and potential client expectations, and for establishing goals for staff training and continuing education.

In addition, there are issues that can confound the study of outcomes such as the therapeutic alliance; the personal characteristics of counselor, client, and the group; and client use of multiple programs and services. Often individuals are successful because they are "full-service" clients. On the other hand, some individuals who try everything seem unable to transfer learning to new situations or to make progress toward their goals. What are the blocks to their success? Efforts should be made to have clients, students, employers, and counselors identify which learning activities and personal characteristics were most helpful in meeting various goals and expectations. These characteristics should be presented to the less successful client and combined with identified learning activities.

Sampling problems can also cause outcome-interpretation difficulties. Counselors should try to collect information from as many participants in agency activities as possible. Self-section contributes to biased reporting, resulting in less effective change for agency and staff. Quality self-studies should also incorporate data from eligible parties who chose not to take advantage of the services. Such information can uncover unintentional ways counselors discourage participation and provide new ideas for needed programs and services.

Feedback gathered for the purpose of improving services is limited without follow-up data. Proper follow-up requires both money and time, and data should be gathered when possible at several time intervals after the service is terminated, for example, at 1-month, 6-month, and 1-year intervals. From a learning perspective, follow-up should capture how the programs and services fostered additional learning and skills that transferred to multiple situations and helped the individuals live more satisfying lives.

Any outcome study or evaluation takes some valuable staff time and budget dollars. If it is to be done well, it will require even more. Agencies can ease costs and staff time by recruiting local graduate students with necessary skills to assist in assessment, design, study implementation, and report writing. Paraprofessionals and volunteers can also help with basic data collection, telephone surveys, semistructured interviews, and less glamorous but very necessary time-intensive tasks. To advance our profession, we must continue to take evaluation seriously and to remind administrators and ourselves of its value. The study of outcomes and the evaluation of an organization requires planned attention and should be clearly stated as part of the goals and objectives.

Finally, not only interventions but also the theory behind those interventions need to be evaluated through research and everyday practice. It may be that outcome measures and program evaluation methods have not worked because the underlying theory was not relevant to the client's situation, to the learning that was taking place, or to the objectives of the program or service. We have discussed outcome and evaluation within a learning theory designed to improve career and life satisfaction. In part, we have done so because we believe both the interventions and the theory they represent can be researched and evaluated.

REFERENCES

Anderson, W. A., & Leslie, L. A. (1991). Coping with employment and family stress: Employment arrangement and gender differences. *Sex Roles, 24,* 223–237.

Arthur, N. (1990). The assessment of burnout: A review of three inventories useful for research and counseling. *Journal of Counseling and Development, 69,* 186–189.

Betz, N. E., Heesacker, R. S., & Shuttleworth, C. (1990). Moderators of the congruence and realism of major and occupational plans in college students: A replication and extension. *Journal of Counseling Psychology, 37,* 269–276.

Blau, G. J. (1988). Further exploring the meaning and measurement of career commitment. *Journal of Vocational Behavior, 32,* 284–297.

Blustein, D. L. (1989). The role of career exploration in the career decision-making of college students. *Journal of College Student Development, 30,* 111–117.

Blustein, D. L., Devenis, L. E., & Kidney, B. A. (1989). The development and validation of a two-dimensional model of the commitment to career choice process. *Journal of Vocational Behavior, 35,* 342–378.

Borgen, F. H. (1986). New approaches to the assessment of interests. In W. B. Walsh & S. H. Osipow (Eds.), *Advances in vocational psychology: Vol. 1. The assessment of interests* (pp. 83–125). Hillsdale, NJ: Lawrence Erlbaum Associates.

Bowman, S. L. (1993). Career intervention strategies for ethnic minorities. *The Career Development Quarterly, 42*, 14–25.

Brammer, L. (1985). Nonformal support in cross-cultural counseling and psychotherapy. In P. B. Pedersen (Ed.), *Handbook of cross-cultural counseling and therapy* (pp. 85–92). Westport, CT: Greenwood.

Bridges, W. (1993). Where have all the jobs gone? Unpublished manuscript.

Brooks, L. (1990). Recent developments in theory building. In D. Brown, L. Brooks, & Associates (Eds.), *Career choice and development* (pp. 364–394). San Francisco: Jossey–Bass.

Buhrke, R. A., & Douce, L. A. (1991). Training issues for counseling psychologists in working with lesbian women and gay men. *The Counseling Psychologist, 19*, 216–234.

Cabral, A. C., & Salomone, P. R. (1990). Chance and careers: Normative versus contextual development. *The Career Development Quarterly, 39*, 5–17.

Campbell, R., Walz, G., Miller, J., & Kriger, S. (1973). *Career guidance: A handbook of methods.* Columbus, OH: Merrill.

Chartrand, J. M. (1991). The evolution of trait-and-factor career counseling: A person X environment fit approach. *Journal of Counseling and Development, 69*, 518–524.

Christensen, C. P. (1989). Cross-cultural awareness development: A conceptual model. *Counselor Education and Supervision, 28*, 270–287.

Cook, E. P. (1991). Annual review: Practice and research in career counseling and development. *The Career Development Quarterly, 40*, 99–131.

Cook, E. P. (1993). The gendered context of life: Implications for women's and men's career-life plans. *The Career Development Quarterly, 41*, 227–237.

Corvin, S. A., & Wiggins, F. (1989). An antiracism training model for White professionals. *Journal of Multicultural Counseling and Development, 17*, 105–114.

Crohan, S. E., Antonucci, T. C., Adelmann, P. K., & Coleman, T. M. (1989). Job characteristics and well-being at midlife: Ethnic and gender comparisons. *Psychology of Women Quarterly, 13*, 223–233.

Croteau, J. M., & Hedstrom, S. M. (1993). Integrating commonality and difference: The key to career counseling with lesbian women and gay men. *The Career Development Quarterly, 41*, 201–209.

Curnow, T. C. (1989). Vocational development of persons with disability. *The Career Development Quarterly, 37*, 269–279.

Cytrynbaum, S., & Crites, J. O. (1989). The utility of adult development theory in understanding career adjustment process. In M. B. Arthur, D. T. Hall, & B. S. Lawrence (Eds.), *Handbook of career theory* (pp. 66–88). Cambridge, England: Cambridge University Press.

Elliott, J. E. (1993). Career development with lesbian and gay clients. *The Career Development Quarterly, 41*, 210–226.

Fassinger, R. E. (1990). Causal models of career choice in two samples of college women. *Journal of Vocational Behavior, 36*, 225–248.

Fohs, M. W. (1991). Family systems assessment: Intervention with individuals having a chronic disability. *The Career Development Quarterly, 39*, 304–311.

Fouad, N. A. (1993). Cross-cultural vocational assessment. *The Career Development Quarterly, 42*, 4–13.

Fretz, B. R. (1981). Evaluating the effectiveness of career interventions. *Journal of Counseling Psychology, 28*, 77–90.

Fretz, B. R., Kluge, N. A., Ossana, S. M., Jones, S. M., & Merikangas, M. W. (1989). Intervention targets for reducing preretirement anxiety and depression. *Journal of Counseling Psychology, 36*, 301–307.

Frost, T. F., & Clayson, D. E. (1991). The measurement of self-esteem, stress-related life events, and locus of control among unemployed and employed blue-collar workers. *Journal of Applied Social Psychology, 21*, 1402–1417.

Fukuyama, M. A. (1991). Response to the report of the second NCDA National Survey: Don't cut Asian Pacific Islanders short! *The Career Development Quarterly, 40*, 189–190.

Gainor, K. A., & Forrest, L. (1991). African American women's self-concept: Implications for career decision and career counseling. *The Career Development Quarterly, 39*, 261–272.

Gelatt, H. B. (1962). Decision making: A conceptual frame of reference for counseling. *Journal of Counseling Psychology, 9*, 240–245.

Gelatt, H. B. (1989). Positive uncertainty: A new decision-making framework for counseling. *Journal of Counseling Psychology, 36*, 252–256.

Glenn, A., & Russell, R. (1986). Heterosexual bias among counselor trainees. *Counselor Education and Supervision, 25*, 222–229.

Gottfredson, L. S. (1981). Circumscription and compromise: A developmental theory of occupational aspirations. *Journal of Counseling Psychology, 28*, 549–579.

Gottfredson, L. S. (1986). Special groups and the beneficial use of vocational interest inventories. In W. B. Walsh & S. H. Osipow (Eds.), *Advances in vocational assessment: Vol. 1. The assessment of interests* (pp. 127–198). Hillsdale, NJ: Lawrence Erlbaum Associates.

Greenglass, E. R., Burke, J., & Ondrack, M. (1990). A gender-role perspective of coping and burnout. *Applied Psychology: An International Review, 39*, 5–27.

Greenhaus, J. H., Parasuraman, S., Granrose, C. S., Rabinowitz, S., & Beutell, N. J. (1989). Sources of work–family conflict among two-career couples. *Journal of Vocational Behavior, 34*, 133–153.

Greenhaus, J. H., Parasuraman, S., & Wormley, W. M. (1990). Effects of race on organizational experiences, job performance evaluations, and career outcomes. *Academy of Management Journal, 33*, 64–86.

Gutek, A. A., Cohen, A. G., & Konrad, A. M. (1990). Predicting social-sexual behavior at work: A contact hypothesis. *Academy of Management Journal, 33*, 560–577.

Gutek, B. A., & Koss, M. P. (1993). Changed work and changed organizations: Consequences of coping with sexual harassment. *Journal of Vocational Behavior, 42*, 28–48.

Hackett, G., Betz, N. E., O'Halloran, M. S., & Romac, D. S. (1990). Effects of verbal and mathematics task performance on task and career self-efficacy and interest. *Journal of Counseling Psychology, 37*, 169–177.

Hackman, J., & Oldham, G. (1975). Development of the job diagnostic survey. *Journal of Applied Psychology, 60*, 159–170.

Harmon, L. W. (1989). Longitudinal changes in women's career aspirations: Developmental or historical? *Journal of Vocational Behavior, 35*, 46–63.

Hawks, B. K., & Muha, D. (1991). Facilitating the career development of minorities: Doing it differently this time. *The Career Development Quarterly, 39*, 251–260.

Helms, J. E. (1986). Expanding racial identity theory to cover counseling process. *Journal of Counseling Psychology, 33*, 62–64.

Helms, J. E. (1990). *Black and White racial identity: Theory, research and practice.* New York: Greenwood.

Herbert, J. I. (1990). Integrating race and adult psychosocial development. *Journal of Organizational Behavior, 11*, 433–446.

Herr, E. L. (1989). Career development and mental health. *Journal of Career Development, 16*, 5–18.

Hesketh, B., Durant, C., & Pryor, R. (1990). Career compromise: A test of Gottfredson's (1981) theory using a policy-capturing procedure. *Journal of Vocational Behavior, 36*, 97–108.

Hetherington, C., Hillerbrand, E., & Etringer, B. D. (1989). Career counseling with gay men: Issues and recommendations for research. *Journal of Counseling and Development, 67*, 452–454.

Hetherington, C., & Orzek, A. (1989). Career counseling and life planning with lesbian women. *Journal of Counseling and Development, 68*, 52–57.

Holland, J. L. (1985). *Making vocational choices* (2nd ed.). Englewood Cliffs, NJ: Prentice–Hall.

Hopkins–Best, M. (1987). The effect of students' sex and disability on counselor's agreement with postsecondary career goals. *School Counselor, 35*, 28–33.

Hotchkiss, L., & Borow, H. (1990). Sociological perspectives on work and career development. In D. Brown, L. Brooks, & Associates (Eds.), *Career choice and development* (pp. 262–307). San Francisco: Jossey–Bass.

Hoyt, K. (1988). The changing workforce: A review of projections 1986 to 2000. *The Career Development Quarterly, 37*, 31–39.

Jackson, B. W., & Holvino, E. (1988). Developing multicultural organizations. *Journal of Religion and the Applied Behavioral Sciences, 9*, 14–19.

Johnston, W., & Packer, A. (1987). *Workforce 2000: Work and workers for the twenty-first century.* Indianapolis, IN: Hudson Institute.

Katz, J. H. (1985). The sociopolitical nature of counseling. *The Counseling Psychologist, 13*, 615–624.

Krumboltz, J. D. (1991). *Manual for the Career Beliefs Inventory.* Palo Alto, CA: Consulting Psychologists Press.

Krumboltz, J. D. (1992a). Challenging troublesome career beliefs. (*CAPS Digest* EDO-CG-92-4). Ann Arbor, MI: ERIC Clearinghouse on Counseling and Personnel Services. (ERIC Document Reproduction Service No. ED 347481).

Krumboltz, J. D. (1992b). The wisdom of indecision. *Journal of Vocational Behavior, 41*, 239–244.

Krumboltz, J. D. (1993). Integrating career and personal counseling. *The Career Development Quarterly, 42*, 143–148.

Krumboltz, J. D. (1994, January). *A learning theory of career counseling.* Paper presented at meeting of the National Career Development Association, Albuquerque, NM.

Krumboltz, J. D., & Baker, R. D. (1973). Behavioral counseling for vocational decisions. In H. Borow (Ed.), *Career guidance for a new age* (pp. 235–284). Boston: Houghton Mifflin.

Krumboltz, J. D., & Jackson, M. A. (1993). Career assessment as a learning tool. *Journal of Career Assessment, 1*, 393–409.

Kutscher, R. (1987). Projections 2000: Overview and implications of the projections to 2000. *Monthly Labor Review, 110*, 3–7.

LaFromboise, T. D., & Foster, S. L. (1992). Cross-cultural training: Scientist-practitioner model and methods. *The Counseling Psychologist, 20*, 472–489.

Latack, J. C., Josephs, S. L., Roach, B. L., & Levine, M. D. (1987). Carpenter apprentices: Comparison of career transitions for men and women. *Journal of Applied Psychology, 72*, 393–400.

Leong, F. T. L. (1993). The career counseling process with racial–ethnic minorities: The case of Asian Americans. *The Career Development Quarterly, 42*, 26–40.

Leung, S. A., & Harmon, L. W. (1990). Individual and sex differences in the zone of acceptable alternatives. *Journal of Counseling Psychology, 37*, 153–159.

Long, B. C. (1989). Sex-role orientation, coping strategies, and self-efficacy of women in traditional and non-traditional occupations. *Psychology of Women Quarterly, 13*, 307–324.

Lopez, S. R. (1989). Patient variable bias in clinical judgment: Conceptual overview and methodological considerations. *Psychological Bulletin, 106*, 184–203.

Lucas, M. S., & Epperson, D. L. (1990). Types of vocational undecidedness: A replication and refinement. *Journal of Counseling Psychology, 37*, 382–388.

Mael, F. A. (1991). Career constraints of observant Jews. *The Career Development Quarterly, 39*, 341–349.

Marshall, M. R., & Jones, C. H. (1990). Childbearing sequence and the career development of women administrators in higher education. *Journal of College Student Development, 31*, 531–537.

Martin, L. G., & Ross–Gordon, J. M. (1990). Cultural diversity in the workplace: Managing a multicultural workforce. *New Directions for Adult and Continuing Education, 48*, 45–54.

McDaniels, C., & Gysbers, N. C. (1992). *Counseling for career development: Theories, resources, and practice.* San Francisco: Jossey-Bass.

McDermott, D., Tyndall, L., & Lichtenberg, J. W. (1989). Factors related to counselor preference among gays and lesbians. *Journal of Counseling and Development, 68,* 31–35.

McWhirter, J. J., & Ryan, C. A. (1991). Counseling the Navajo: Cultural understanding. *Journal of Multicultural Counseling and Development, 19,* 74–82.

Miranda, J., & Storms, M. (1989). Psychological adjustment of lesbians and gay men. *Journal of Counseling and Development, 68,* 41–45.

Mirels, H. L., & Garrett, J. P. (1971). The Protestant ethic as a personality variable. *Journal of Consulting and Clinical Psychology, 36,* 40–44.

Morgan, C. S., & Brown, L. S. (1991). Lesbian career development, work behavior and career counseling. *The Counseling Psychologist, 19,* 273–291.

Morrison, A. M., & Von Glinow, M. A. (1990). Women and minorities in management. *American Psychologist, 45,* 200–208.

Muchinsky, P. M., & Monahan, C. J. (1987). What is person–environment congruence? Supplementary versus complementary models of fit. *Journal of Vocational Behavior, 31,* 268–277.

Myers, J. E. (1989). *Infusing gerontological counseling into counselor preparation: Curriculum guide.* Alexandria, VA: American Association for Counseling and Development.

Myers, L. J., Speight, S. L., Highlen, P. S., Cox, C. I., Reynolds, A. L., Adams, E. M., & Hanley, C. P. (1991). Identity development and worldview: Toward an optimal conceptualization. *Journal of Counseling and Development, 70,* 54–63.

Myers, R. A. (1986). Research on educational and vocational counseling. In A. E. Bergin & S. L. Garfield (Eds.), *Handbook of psychotherapy and behavior change* (3rd ed., pp. 715–738). New York: Wiley.

National Career Development Association (1988). *The professional practice of career counseling and consultation: A resource document.* Alexandria, VA: American Counseling Association.

National Career Development Association (1992). NCDA reports: Career counseling competencies. *The Career Development Quarterly, 40,* 379–386.

Nelson, D. L., Quick, J. C., Hitt, M. A., & Moesel, D. (1990). Politics, lack of career progress, and work/home conflict: Stress and strain for working women. *Sex Roles, 23,* 169–185.

Oliver, L. W., & Spokane, A. R. (1988). Career counseling outcome: What contributes to client gain? *Journal of Counseling Psychology, 35,* 447–462.

Olson, J. E., Frieze, I. H., & Detlefsen, E. G. (1990). Having it all? Combining work and family in a male and female profession. *Sex Roles, 23,* 515–533.

Ornstein, S., & Isabella, L. A. (1990). Age vs. stage models of career attitudes of women: A partial replication and extension. *Journal of Vocational Behavior, 36,* 1–19.

Osipow, S. H. (1983). *Theories of career development* (3rd ed.). Englewood Cliffs, NJ: Prentice-Hall.

Padilla, A. N., & DeSnyder, N. S. (1985). Counseling Hispanics: Strategies for effective intervention. In P. B. Pedersen (Ed.), *Handbook of cross-cultural counseling and therapy* (pp. 157–164). Westport, CT: Greenwood.

Parsons, F. (1909). *Choosing a vocation.* Boston: Houghton Mifflin.

Pearson, R. E., & Petitpas, A. J. (1990). Transitions of athletes: Developmental and preventive perspectives. *Journal of Counseling and Development, 69,* 7–10.

Pedersen, P. (1981). Triad counseling. In R. J. Corsini (Ed.), *Handbook of innovative psychotherapies* (pp. 840–854). New York: Wiley.

Pedersen, P. (1988). *A handbook for developing multicultural awareness.* Alexandria, VA: American Association for Counseling and Development.

Pedersen, P. B. (1991). Multiculturalism as a generic approach to counseling. *Journal of Counseling and Development, 70,* 6–12.

Peterson, G. W., Sampson, J. P., Jr., & Reardon, R. C. (1991). *Career development and services: A cognitive approach.* Pacific Grove, CA: Brooks/Cole.

Pyle, K. R. (1986). *Group career counseling: Principles and practices.* Ann Arbor: University of Michigan, ERIC Counseling and Personnel Services Clearinghouse. (ERIC Document Reproduction Service No. ED 277937).

Raskin, P. M. (1989). Identity status research: Implications for career counseling. *Journal of Adolescence, 12,* 375–388.

Riverin–Simard, D. (1990). Adult vocational trajectory. *The Career Development Quarterly, 39,* 129–142.

Ronnestad, M. H., & Skovholt, T. M. (1993). Supervision of beginning and advanced graduate students of counseling and psychotherapy. *Journal of Counseling and Development, 71,* 396–405.

Rosin, H. M., & Korabik, K. (1990). Marital and family correlates of women managers' attrition from organizations. *Journal of Vocational Behavior, 37,* 104–120.

Saveri, A. (1991). The realignment of workers and work in the 1990s. In J. M. Kummerow, (Ed.), *New directions in career planning and the workplace: Practical strategies for counselors* (pp. 117–153). Palo Alto, CA: Consulting Psychologists Press.

Savickas, M. L. (1993). Career counseling in the postmodern era. *Journal of Cognitive Psychotherapy: An International Quarterly, 7,* 205–215.

Schaie, K. W. (1993). Ageist language in psychological research. *American Psychologist, 48,* 49–51.

Schneider, B. (1987). E = f (P, B): The road to a radical approach to person–environment fit. *Journal of Vocational Behavior, 31,* 353–361.

Serling, D. A., & Betz, N. E. (1990). Development and evaluation of a measure of fear of commitment. *Journal of Counseling Psychology, 37,* 91–97.

Shannon, J. W., & Woods, W. J. (1991). Affirmative psychotherapy for gay men. *The Counseling Psychologist, 19,* 192–215.

Skinner, M. E., & Schenck, S. J. (1992). Counseling the college-bound student with a learning disability. *School Counselor, 39,* 369–376.

Spokane, A. R. (1985). A review of research on person–environment congruence in Holland's theory of careers. *Journal of Vocational Behavior, 26,* 306–343.

Spokane, A. R. (1991). *Career intervention.* Englewood Cliffs, NJ: Prentice–Hall.

Spokane, A. R., & Oliver, L. W. (1983). The outcomes of vocational intervention. In W. B. Walsh & S. H. Osipow (Eds.), *Handbook of vocational psychology* (Vol. 2, pp. 99–136). Hillsdale, NJ: Lawrence Erlbaum Associates.

Steenbarger, B. N. (1993). A multicontextual model of counseling: Bridging brevity and diversity. *Journal of Counseling and Development, 72,* 8–15.

Stickel, S. A., & Bonett, R. M. (1991). Gender differences in career self-efficacy: Combining career with a home and family. *Journal of College Student Development, 32,* 297–301.

Stiles, W. B., & Shapiro, D. A. (1989). Abuse of the drug metaphor in psychotherapy process–outcome research. *Clinical Psychology Review, 9,* 521–543.

Stockard, J., & McGee, J. (1990). Children's occupational preferences: The influence of sex and perceptions of occupational characteristics. *Journal of Vocational Behavior, 36,* 287–303.

Stoltz–Loike, M. (1992). The working family: Helping women balance the roles of wife, mother and career women. *The Career Development Quarterly, 40,* 244–256.

Sue, D. W., Arrendondo, P., & McDavis, R. J. (1992). Multicultural counseling competencies and standards. *Journal of Multicultural Counseling and Development, 20,* 64–88.

Sue, D. W., Bernier, J. E., Durran, A., Feinberg, L., Pedersen, P., Smith, E., & Vasquez–Nuttal, E. (1982). Position paper: Cross-cultural counseling competencies. *The Counseling Psychologist, 10,* 45–52.

Sue, D. W., & Sue, D. (1990). *Counseling the culturally different: Theory & practice.* New York: Wiley.

Sue, S. & Zane, N. (1987). The role of culture and cultural techniques in psychotherapy: A critique and reformulation. *American Psychologist, 42,* 37–45.

Sullivan, S. E. (1992). Is there a time for everything? Attitudes related to women's sequencing of career and family. *The Career Development Quarterly, 40,* 234–243.

Super, D. E. (1990). A life-span, life-space approach to career development. In D. Brown, L. Brooks, & Associates (Eds.), *Career choice and development* (pp. 197–261). San Francisco: Jossey–Bass.

Super, D. E., & Nevill, D. D. (1986). *Salience inventory.* Palo Alto, CA: Consulting Psychologists Press.

Swanson, J. L. (1993). Integrating a multicultural perspective into training for career counseling: Programmatic and individual interventions. *The Career Development Quarterly, 42,* 41–49.

Taylor, K. M., & Betz, N. E. (1983). Applications of self-efficacy theory to understanding and treatment of career indecision. *Journal of Vocational Behavior, 22,* 63–81.

Tomlinson–Keasey, C. (1990). The working lives of Terman's gifted women. In H. Y. Grossman & N. L. Chester (Eds.), *The experience and meaning of work in women's lives* (pp. 213–240). Hillsdale, NJ: Lawrence Erlbaum Associates.

Triandis, H. C. (1993). Comments on "Multicultural Career Counseling." *The Career Development Quarterly, 42,* 50–52.

Vondracek, F. W. (1990). A developmental–contextual approach to career development research. In R. A. Young & W. A. Borgen (Eds.), *Methodological approaches to the study of career* (pp. 37–56). New York: Praeger.

Vondracek, F. W., Hostetler, M., Schulenberg, J. E., & Shimizu, K. (1990). Dimensions of career indecision. *Journal of Counseling Psychology, 37,* 98–106.

Vondracek, F. W., Lerner, R. M., & Schulenberg, J. E. (1986). *Career development: A life-span developmental approach.* Hillsdale, NJ: Lawrence Erlbaum Associates.

Vondracek, F. W., & Schulenberg, J. (1992). Counseling for normative and nonnormative influences on career development. *The Career Development Quarterly, 40,* 291–301.

Watson, M. B., & Stead, G. B. (1990). Work-role salience of South African adolescents. *Journal of Vocational Behavior, 36,* 249–257.

Wegmann, R. (1991). How long does unemployment last? *The Career Development Quarterly, 40,* 71–81.

Wegmann, R., Chapman, R., & Johnson, M. (1985). *Looking for work in the new economy.* Salt Lake City, UT: Olympus.

Westwood, M. J., & Ishiyama, F. I. (1991). Challenges in counseling immigrant clients: Understanding intercultural barriers to career adjustment. *Journal of Employment Counseling, 28,* 132–143.

Williams, C. P., & Savickas, M. L. (1990). Developmental tasks of career maintenance. *Journal of Vocational Behavior, 36,* 166–175.

Worthington, W. L. (1984). An empirical investigation of supervision of counselors as they gain experience. *Journal of Counseling Psychology, 31,* 63–75.

Yang, J. (1991). Career counseling for Chinese American women: Are they in limbo? *The Career Development Quarterly, 39,* 350–359.

Zytowski, D. B., & Borgen, F. H. (1983). Assessment. In W. B. Walsh & S. H. Osipow (Eds.), *Handbook of vocational psychology* (Vol. 2, pp. 5–40). Hillsdale, NJ: Lawrence Erlbaum Associates.

CHAPTER THIRTEEN

Leading Edges of Vocational Psychology: Diversity and Vitality

Fred. H. Borgen
Iowa State University

This concluding chapter highlights several features of the preceding chapters. I sketch some of my personal reactions to these chapters, most of which focus on a particular set of leading edges in the field of vocational psychology. The authors of the chapters in general had a mandate to cover developments in vocational psychology that have occurred since the first edition of this *Handbook* in 1983 (Walsh & Osipow). Many of the chapters have a sharp recency in their coverage, so it is appropriate that the theme of this chapter is "leading edges" in the field.

My goal is to comment on the preceding chapters in a way that will stimulate and encourage readers of them. I hope my comments will sharpen for readers the differences and similarities among the chapters. From my perspective, they are a diverse set, reflecting the healthy vigor and diversity that characterize current vocational psychology. The chapters are particularly diverse in the way they approach science, from the traditional to the postmodern. In similar ways, they are also diverse in their emphasis on quantitative versus qualitative ways of knowing.

Perhaps unfairly to him, in commenting on the preceding chapters, I focus most explicitly on the opening chapter by Savickas. I do this for a variety of reasons. First, the style of the Savickas chapter is the most remarkable of the *Handbook*. It has exceptional forcefulness and liveliness. Second, the substance Savickas presents is the widest and deepest of that in all the chapters. He vividly frames a set of epistemic issues he sees as critical for the future of the field. Third, Savickas sees the issues he presents as underlying much of this *Handbook*. They provide the metathemes underlying many of the other chapters. In short, the Savickas chapter is the one I find the most provocative and stimulating. My reactions to the Savickas chapter elicit in me an upbeat concluding view of this *Handbook*. I come to a somewhat more optimistic view about the accomplishments and current vitality of vocational psychology than does Savickas. The best current evidence for that, as I argue in the following sections, can be seen in the diversity and vitality of the preceding chapters in this *Handbook*.

SAVICKAS ON THEORETICAL ISSUES: CONVERGENCE, DIVERGENCE, AND SCHISM

In the leading chapter of this *Handbook*, Savickas starts off with a crescendo. Under his artful scholarship, the big issues in vocational psychology are deconstructed with vigor and clarity. The dynamism of his phrases depicts an intensity of theoretical jousting that only the strong or foolhardy would want to join.

Savickas perceives the field as facing two crucial issues, each a substantial intellectual problem to be resolved. First is *convergence*, that is, whether or not vocational psychologists should work to unify existing theories of career choice and development. Second is *divergence*, namely, the efforts by vocational psychologists to use postmodern thought to move beyond logical positivism as *the* philosophy of science for theory and research about vocational behavior. He sees these issues as causing vocational psychology's central *schisms*—splits in beliefs that separate theory from practice, vocational psychology from basic psychology disciplines, career counseling from psychotherapy, and vocational research agendas from each other.

Savickas is powerful and provocative in framing issues with vivid dichotomies. He wants to arouse the reader to think and to join the intellectual fray. He succeeds with me as a reader; I want to join the fray—and at points take issue with Savickas.

Savickas does a masterful job of sketching current discussions about the value of a convergence project in vocational psychology. He draws much from Savickas and Lent (1994), the central source on this topic. He effectively presents the pros and cons on whether or not it is productive or necessary for vocational psychologists to work toward unified theory.

I am not as comfortable with Savickas' treatment of what he terms *divergence*. This is his view of the field being at a crossroads where a new philosophy of science must be chosen. Savickas states that vocational psychologists now must choose between a philosophy of science based on logical positivism or one based on a postmodernist perspectivism. He says that the central issue under debate can be succinctly formed as a question:

"Which philosophy of science should structure vocational psychology in the twenty-first century? The issue begs for clarification before the field can progress beyond its current achievements." Savickas is an enthusiastic and colorful advocate for the postmodernist position. He writes that the concept of career has been besmirched by a postmodern discourse that has demythologized, delegitimated, and deconstructed it.

I applaud Savickas for the power with which he frames the issues, and for the new material he brings to our attention. His chapter must be the most forceful and cogent presentation of the postmodernist position in vocational psychology. Although admiring his achievements in the chapter, I must say I do not agree with some of what I understand as his descriptions of the state of affairs, what we must do about them, and what the consequences of our actions will be.

I do not agree that vocational psychology is dominated by a positivism, rigidly adhered to, that impedes its progress. I see many examples, such as an emphasis on agency and self-efficacy (Bandura, 1982; Betz & Hackett, 1987; Lent & Hackett, 1994), that reflect a field evolving and keeping up with new thinking. Moreover, working scientists do not pay much attention to the philosophy of science. If they do, they become philosophers of science rather than working scientists. Science is not a wholly logical enterprise.

A winner-take-all jousting between positivism and postmodern perspectivism is unnecessary. These terms become rhetorical red flags, but what they really mean for working scientists is often unclear. They overdraw the distinctions and create straw issues. A struggle between positivism and perspectivism can have didactic value, especially for promoting and explaining a postmodern view, but they are not choices we must inevitably make. We can have both—expanding our insights through perspectivism but also building on the empirical strengths of traditional research.

"IF YOU COME TO A FORK IN THE ROAD, TAKE IT"

Savickas' chapter can be read as saying that vocational psychologists have now reached a fork in the road, where they must make a choice between a traditional or a postmodern philosophy of science. My stance is, "Take both forks in the road." Indeed, I say the field has long done so, with little harm, other than to some perceived framing of logically incompatible alternatives. In the broad arena of counseling psychology, I have previously argued that these choices, despite their apparent logical necessity to some, do not have to be made. A field, especially one with such large practice implications, can thrive with methodological pluralism and even epistemological eclecticism (Borgen, 1984a, 1989, 1992).

Working scientists, and especially practicing career counselors, do not spend large amounts of time parsing logical inconsistencies in their paradigmatic assumptions. Nor is their success dependent on it. On the contrary, the ability to draw from a set of tools, attitudes, and assumptions that originally were seen as logically opposed, may be precisely what increases the utility of vocational psychology—both for theory and for practice. Tools derived from one paradigm can often be used quite synergistically in another paradigm. A prominent general example is the counseling relationship. The elements of an ideal counseling relationship were brought to us by Carl Rogers. In the early days there was raucous contention over Rogers' ideas. Today almost all therapists use at least some of the Rogerian relationship, yet they are more likely to label their brand of therapy as something else.

One of the most influential books in psychology—for theory and practice—is Bergin and Garfield's (1994a) *Handbook of Psychotherapy and Behavior Change*, now in its fourth edition. Beginning with the first edition in 1971, the editors have espoused empiricism within an eclectic position of theoretical openness. They even use a book title with room for opposing theoretical camps. Now in the 1994 edition, in their concluding chapter (Bergin & Garfield, 1994b), they reemphasize how important and productive this stance has been:

> This book gained its reputation and influence as a standard reference because it took an eclectic position of openness to diverse perspectives and insisted on an empirical appraisal of them. This view was not entirely popular at the time, though there were notable exceptions (Lazarus, 1967). Today this viewpoint appears to dominate the field. The empirical analysis and merging of behavioral and cognitive perspectives are the most notable examples.... Other examples are too numerous to mention. (p. 821)

Similarly, the current edition of Bergin and Garfield (1994a) reflects an increasing methodological openness, for example, with the chapter by Lambert and Hill (1994), who discuss single case and qualitative research. Even more remarkable is the distinctively postmodernist chapter on marital and family therapy by Alexander, Holtzworth–Munroe, and Jameson. Although reflecting the recognition of the value of new thinking and new paradigms, the Bergin and Garfield (1994a) handbook retains as its core a major compendium of research conducted within the received tradition. This influential body of scholarship has emerged despite the lack of consensus on core philosophical assumptions and epistemologies. My view is that vocational psychology of the past 25 years has also evolved within a similar zeitgeist, and that similar things can be said about it.

In reviewing expanding paradigms in counseling psychology, I have similarly taken the view that a field can thrive with apparently opposed paradigms and epistemologies (cf. Borgen, 1992). The progress of working scientists does not require that all the potential philosophic problems be fully resolved. For example, two of the most productive counseling psychologists of the last 15 years are Hill and Howard. Each, in different ways, has publicly struggled with paradigmatic and methodological issues about traditional research (e.g., Hill, 1982, 1984; Howard, 1984, 1986, 1989, 1991), yet each has produced prodigious and influential research within the received tradition. In the process they have also bumped the received tradition toward greater flexibility and openness. It is as if they have not needed to resolve all the potential logical and epistemic issues but, rather, have invested their energies in productive empirical programs, enlightened by their paradigmatic thoughtfulness.

IS VOCATIONAL PSYCHOLOGY ROBUST?

The Savickas chapter, plus parts of others in this *Handbook*, have given me pause to think that I might have been too optimistic in my prior evaluations of the epistemic base of vocational psychology. I previously remarked about the robustness of vocational psychology, its close linkage between its worlds of research and practice. Now there are signs of a wave of apparent disenchantment with the epistemic health of the field. Suddenly in the 1990s we see a new set of calls, by a new generation of vocational psychologists, who lament the state of the field and urge a rethinking of the way we "do" science in vocational psychology.

Just 4 years ago, I was writing optimistically about the vigor in vocational psychology (Borgen, 1991). In reviewing the previous 20 years of vocational psychology, I saw all sorts of signs of success by vocational psychologists doing normal science. I saw all sorts of reasons to celebrate both people and products, as the 20th anniversary of *The Journal of Vocational Psychology* was commemorated. Was I wrong in that assessment at that time? If not, has the field in the past 4 years taken a turn toward pessimism with the yield from traditional empirical work? Has a malaise about method set in within vocational psychology?

I wonder how out of touch I might have been for the past several years. Where have I been during the revolution? What is the basis for it? Am I too entrenched in the paradigms of my past that I cannot see the need for vocational psychology to reform itself for the next century? Perhaps I am in denial (or ignorance), but I am ready to reaffirm my optimistic assertion that vocational psychology is a healthy discipline, making progress on important problems with significant theoretical and practical implications. It is a field that has been expanding its paradigms, building on deep roots from the past, and adapting to cultural change.

Although there are now some signs of self-doubt in the discipline, there are also many signs of undiminished health. I covered these in some detail in my 1991 review (Borgen, 1991). Suffice it to mention some of the big books, reflecting the scholarly talents of a new generation of vocational psychologists. The series on vocational psychology, under the skillful and generative editorship of Walsh and Osipow, now includes several important volumes (Walsh & Osipow, 1986, 1988, 1990, 1994). The second edition of Brown and Lent's (1992) *Handbook of Counseling Psychology* indicates the central and established role of vocational behavior within counseling psychology. The Michigan State and Ohio State vocational psychology conferences have been successfully completed. The important book emerging from the first of these conferences (Savickas & Lent, 1994) reflects the vitality of the field and its intellectual excitement.

A HANDBOOK BRIMMING WITH DIVERSITY AND VITALITY

This *Handbook* stands as a testament to the current vitality and progress of vocational psychology. Each of the previous chapters reflects vitality in theory or research. The leading edges of the field are well displayed. It is a field characterized by diversity in paradigms, problems, and the people who are served.

Will the traditional logical positivists please stand up? I am not sure I can find exemplars in these chapters. There is little that is antiquated or out of touch with modern issues and counseling needs. Rather, we have a collection of chapters with fresh insights, vigorous research programs, integrations of research literatures, and new agendas for diverse applications of vocational psychology. As a group, the chapter authors represent the best and the brightest of a generation of vocational psychologists who are actively shaping the field.

Many of the most vigorous chapters represent the perspectivist view as much as they do the positivist view. For example, the authors are motivated to extend vocational psychology to more diverse coverage of gender and ethnicity. Closely attuned to the real issues of real clients, they bring the perspective of the person to the enterprise, be it theoretical or practice. Four of the chapters centrally address these issues with theory, research, or recommendations for practice, or all three. Vocational psychology has been a leading discipline in bringing new perspectives to gender and to race and ethnicity. The authors of these chapters represent the leaders in this scholarship. They have often framed the issues most cogently and also conducted the most influential research programs. These chapters are chapter 3 by Fitzgerald, Fassinger, and Betz; chapter 5 by Leong and Brown; chapter 8 by Subich and Billingsley; and chapter 10 by Fouad and Bingham.

The other chapters all reflect changing thinking and research progress, often about similar issues of diversity. Vocational psychology is a field responsive to new ideas and expanding paradigms. Generally, in reading these chapters I do not see their authors as preoccupied with the choice Savickas poses for us, that is, the choice between logical positivism and a postmodern perspectivism. Rather, my reading is that many of these authors are motivated as people and as practitioners to move the field to larger and more diverse perspectives. Without deep struggles over philosophy of science, they are simply moving to perform as vocational psychologists, often using traditional research methods. Often they warn us of the dangers of a narrow nomothetic model derived from research with traditional samples of White male participants. On the other hand, many of them are also actively working researchers within received traditions. They apparently have not found it necessary to adopt a postmodern, qualitative philosophy of science in order to make empirical progress with central issues. They do bring a perspectivism, a special insight into the phenomenology of the diverse people they study, but they also work with more traditional quantitative methods.

The feminist viewpoint has thus far had the greatest perspectivist influence in transforming and energizing vocational psychology. Notable, however, is how much this progress has been achieved through traditional research methods (Betz & Fitzgerald, 1987; Fitzgerald, Fassinger, & Betz, chapter 3 of this volume). Now we are seeing a similar transformation from the perspective of racial and ethnic minority experience of career life (Leong & Brown, chapter 5; Fouad & Bingham, chapter 10). Subich and Billingsley (chapter 8) also address numerous ways in which diversity perspectives could inform our assessment.

SOME QUESTIONS ABOUT VOCATIONAL PSYCHOLOGY

The process of writing this chapter has, like science itself, created for me more questions than answers. In Table 13.1 are some of the questions I have generated about the discipline of vocational psychology—its products, its people, and its processes. It would be nice if I could write a definitive paragraph addressing each of these questions. But doing so presupposes that there is a neat, definitive answer to every question and that I possess it. Neither is true. Rather, my intent with these questions is to stimulate dialogue and discussion. Many of them represent issues with which the discipline is wrestling, often implicitly and indirectly. No single individual will ultimately resolve these questions. They are issues that belong to the collective discipline and its shapers, and they will be collectively addressed by our future scholarship and research.

I also see these questions as the kinds of issues I want my graduate students to struggle with. These questions go beyond the direct facts of vocational psychology, and direct attention to context and embedded issues.

TABLE 13.1
Some Questions About Vocational Psychology—Some Possible Answers

Question	Answer
• How important is it that we have a single, comprehensive, and integrated theory of vocational psychology? For whom is it important? Is it equally important for scientists and practitioners?	Savickas and Lent (1994) Lent and Savickas (1994) Osipow (1990)
• Is eclecticism possible or desirable in vocational psychology?	Smith (1982) Borgen (1984a, 1984b, 1989, 1992)
• Is methodological pluralism desirable for vocational psychology? What are its advantages and disadvantages?	Bergin and Garfield (1994b) Gelso (1979, 1982, 1985) Howard (1983)
• What is the role of fads or of the zeitgeist in the development of vocational psychology?	
• What are the major competing paradigms or perspectives in vocational psychology? Which are waxing and which are waning?	Borgen (1991) Osipow (1983, 1990)
• What is the current relationship between science and practice in vocational psychology?	
• What are the essential things an effective career counselor should know?	Gelso and Fretz (1992) Spokane (1991)
• What have been the hottest research topics since 1980?	Walsh and Osipow (this volume)
• What is the most influential book in career counseling? (By influential I mean a book that affects the career planning and vocational self-understanding of the greatest number of American people.)	Bolles (1994)
• What are some of the enduring issues in vocational psychology?	
• How would one describe the discipline of vocational psychology?	Hesketh and Rounds (chapter 11, this volume)
• What should be the highest priorities for research and scholarship in vocational psychology?	
• Should vocational psychology shift to a postmodern epistemology?	Savickas (chapter 1, this volume) Subich and Billingsley (chapter 8, this volume)
• Should qualitative and narrative methods play a much larger role in vocational psychology?	Hoshmand (1989) Savickas (chapter 1, this volume) Polkinghorne (1983, 1984, 1988)
• How does vocational psychology currently overlap with other disciplines in psychology? Are there areas where greater overlap should occur?	
• What are the ingredients for a vigorous and robust discipline?	

So, I pose these questions to my students as they learn about the topic of vocational psychology. I encourage them to read the literature and to develop answers and judgments about these issues. These questions often yield lively class discussions that illustrate the cross-currents of a vigorous field.

In Table 13.1, I have indicated some sources that may help us to answer some of the questions. But because I do not know all the answers or all of the sources and because I want Table 13.1 to be a stimulus for others to fill in their own answers, I have shown potential sources for only some of the questions.

ANOTHER BIG BOOK IN VOCATIONAL PSYCHOLOGY

What is the most influential book in career counseling? By influential I mean here a book that affects the career planning and vocational self-understanding of the greatest number of American people. To my mind, the hands-down answer is Bolles' (1994) *What Color Is Your Parachute?* It certainly is read by many more adults than ever see a career counselor. It is so hugely successful that it is now revised every year. Our field would certainly be more useful as a formal discipline if we better understood the secrets of its success and the needs it meets in the real world. Moreover, Bolles' *Parachute* is just the leading exemplar for the dozens of similar books that populate the self-help sections of popular bookstores.

A quick perusal of Bolles' classic shows how many of its central themes fit the leading edges of vocational behavior. It bulges with the things people need in understanding and taking control of their career lives. It also shines in the arenas that are often touted as the new directions needed in a contemporary, empowering career counseling. Such concepts that are evident in *Parachute*, sometimes as metamessages are empowerment; agency; cognition; optimism, hopefulness; career as part of a whole life; respect for individuality; narration; qualitative understanding; action; self-assessment; self-understanding; and career exploration.

In current academic language, one could say that Bolles' message is that the career changer (or chooser) needs to conduct self-assessments, focusing on self-efficacy and agency. The person achieves a sense of empowerment by building a narrative about his or her assets, and this agentic mode is enhanced by the person's seeing the solutions as within her or his domain and then by acting to achieve these solutions. This language is the kind I have used in describing recent trends in vocational psychology (Borgen, 1991). Of course, Bolles presents the ideas in an engaging, lively workbook style that powerfully draws the person into these life-changing activities. Bolles' (1994) work is chock-full of exercises and checklists that help people think about, evaluate, and assess themselves. These active exercises engage people and make them responsible for the whole process, including its successes. From the perspective of big themes in academic psychology, Bolles illustrates the best in intervention that is client-centered, while also masterfully merging insight and action (Wachtel, 1987). Although employing these contemporary emphases, Bolles is also in touch with traditional career counseling insights. Especially is this true of the concepts of Holland (1985), who is routinely acknowledged by Bolles.

From the perspective of contemporary issues in vocational psychology, it is intriguing how much Bolles does to help people create and tell their own career stories. He artfully draws the person into sketching a picture of himself or herself and his or her ideal career. This narrative emphasis is evident in the subtitle, *How to Create a Picture of Your Ideal Job or Next Career* in his 1990 *The New Quick Job-Hunting Map*. He begins this booklet with the following passage:

> In order to hunt for your ideal job, or even something close to your ideal job, you must have a picture of it, in your head. The clearer the picture, the easier it will be to hunt for it. The purpose of this booklet is to guide you as you draw that picture. (p. 4)

NARRATIVE ASSESSMENT:
SKETCHING THE "MINDSCAPE"

Here, I would like to illustrate, by an example, that we are quite free to merge paradigms in ways that work in practice. We can be eclectic in our practical approaches and are not forced to make the difficult choices among what may appear as opposites. We can mix the quantitative and the qualitative; we can use our numbers to draw pictures.

One way that apparently opposite paradigms can be merged in vocational psychology is through what I propose as *narrative assessment*. By this I mean the explicit blending of quantitative and qualitative methods for the purpose of drawing a picture of the individual's psychic space. It can be seen as a blending of positivism and perspectivism, telling the individual's story. On reflection, I find that this is no different than what typically happens in sophisticated and client-centered applications of assessment. A set of scales or inventories are administered to a client; these scales often yield explicitly quantitative scores, at least for those scales, according to traditional psychometric principles, including appropriate norming. But then, in skillful application of assessment, these quantitative data are transformed, by counselor and client, into a rich narrative that captures the individuality of the client and highlights the most meaningful and salient themes. Together client and counselor build this personal tale as they weigh the test results and explore the deeply particular meaning of those results for the client. Beginning with testing tools with a sharply nomothetic base, client and counselor weave together a linguistic tapestry that tells a distinctly idiographic story of the client's psychological life. Illustrating the creative discovery that happens in the best counseling, client and counselor move from numbers to meaning to a narrative of the client's life.

Although recognizing that this blending of the quantitative and qualitative, of the nomothetic and idiographic, often occurs in the best practice of assessment for client empowerment and understanding, I wish to formally designate it as narrative assessment. By giving it a name, I hope also to honor and encourage the practice. I hope also to show how this blended viewpoint can take the best from several alternate perspectives and honor several different traditions within psychology.

In their definitive presentation of counseling psychology, Gelso and Fretz (1992) make clear the important role of assessment for helping clients understand themselves. They state that one assessment tradition unique to counseling psychology is

> using assessment to help clients gain new information and perspectives about themselves. Counseling psychologists, more than any other mental health professionals, give tests and test results to clients as a way of stimulating exploration of current concerns. Assessments provide clients with a psychological snapshot which they can use to reflect on and understand themselves. (p. 295)

Following Howard (1991), one might take this a step farther by saying that clients use this information to define themselves and to construct a narrative about themselves that shapes a future life story.

This approach is decidedly not "test 'em and tell 'em," as old-style directive counseling is sometimes caricatured. The approach represents a much more collaborative, egalitarian relationship between counselor and client. It is based on the assumption that although the counselor may know more about the tests, the client also knows more about the client. As collaborators, they bring together their expertise, and through a counseling dialogue, couched in all of the ideal conditions of an empathic and empowering counseling relationship, they sketch an idiographic narrative expressly for the client. The meaning of the test results for the client is crucial to this process. Some of the results are salient and sensitive for the client. Others have only passing interest, at least at this point. Here, as the tests results are examined, the client's phenomenology is crucial and is effectively encouraged and made salient by the counselor's empathic understanding. The stimulus value of test results, in the context of an ideal counseling relationship, can be tremendous. If the counselor facilitates the process, test results can stimulate the dialogue and the building of a client narrative in a way never envisioned in the nomothetic construction of the test.

The nomothetic principles and assumptions of test construction are not equivalent to the principles and assumptions of test interpretation. The technology engendering the tools does not dictate expressly how they must be used. The major issue, in practice, is how well the tools achieve the objectives for that particular counseling interaction.

Assessment, ideally conducted in a counseling context, becomes a dynamic process. It stimulates dialogue between client and counselor, through which are merged the expert perspectives each brings. Together they construct a narrative, but often one that is in process, tentative, and incomplete. In many career counseling settings, filling in the narrative requires external exploration by the client. Assessment raises issues that stimulate exploration by the client. Thus, for example, Randahl, Hansen, and Haverkamp (1993) conducted a well-designed study the results of which demonstrated that students, after completing the Strong Interest Inventory and receiving an interpretation, participated in more discussion and reading about careers than did those in a contrast group. This study illustrates the new emphasis on exploration validity for the use of an inventory within an assessment context, namely, the effect of an inventory in stimulating career exploration. This is a use that many assume is central in much career assessment, but the explicit demonstration of such effects by Randahl et al. is very important and useful to the field.

Like Bolles's *Parachute* (1994), this approach to narrative assessment is intended to actively engage clients in telling their own career stories. Similar metamessages are intended: empowerment; agency; cognition; optimism, hopefulness; career as part of a whole life; respect for individuality; narration; qualitative understanding; action; self-assessment; self-understanding; and career exploration. As currently sketched, this model of narrative assessment is not as effective as Bolles' method for stimulating clients to act on their own behalf. It needs more work in that regard.

CONCLUDING COMMENTS

The authors of each of the chapters in this *Handbook* in many ways recommend a new lens for viewing vocational psychology (Highlen & Hill, 1984). They raise our consciousness to new perspectives and new possibilities. The very diversity of issues and world views reflected in these chapters reflects the vitality in the field. It has a maturity and openness that permit diverse views to be heard, considered, and often incorporated.

Some see the field in the midst of a postmodern turn, perhaps markedly changing the shape of the future discipline. An alternative view is one that progress can occur with multiple world views and methods. I see that the field has prospered with the use of largely traditional research methods, vigorously pursued by scholars with distinctive perspectives. Progress can, and does, occur by evolution and an eclectic openness to new methods and insights. The many accomplishments and research agendas in this *Handbook* are testament to that.

REFERENCES

Alexander, J. F., Holtzworth-Munroe, A., & Jameson, P. (1994). The process and outcome of marital and family therapy: Research review and evaluation. In A. E. Bergin & S. L. Garfield (Eds.), *Handbook of psychotherapy and behavior change* (4th ed., pp. 595–630). New York: Wiley.

Bandura, A. (1982). Self-efficacy mechanism in human agency. *American Psychologist, 37,* 122–147.

Bergin, A. E., & Garfield, S. L. (Eds.). (1994a). *Handbook of psychotherapy and behavior change* (4th ed.). New York: Wiley.

Bergin, A. E., & Garfield, S. L. (1994b). Overview, trends, and future issues. In A. E. Bergin & S. L. Garfield (Eds.), *Handbook of psychotherapy and behavior change* (4th ed., pp. 821–830). New York: Wiley.

Betz, N. E., & Fitzgerald, L. F. (1987). *The career psychology of women.* Orlando, FL: Academic Press.

Betz, N. E., & Hackett, G. (1987). Concept of agency in educational and career development. *Journal of Counseling Psychology, 34,* 299–308.

Bolles, R. N. (1990). *The new quick job-hunting map: How to create a picture of your ideal job or next career.* Berkeley, CA: Ten Speed Press.

Bolles, R. N. (1994). *What color is your parachute? A practical manual for job-hunters and career changers.* Berkeley, CA: Ten Speed Press.

Borgen, F. H. (1984a). Are their necessary linkages between research practices and the philosophy of science? *Journal of Counseling Psychology, 31,* 457–460.

Borgen, F. H. (1984b). Counseling psychology. *Annual Review of Psychology, 35,* 579–604.

Borgen, F. H. (1989). Evolution of eclectic epistemology. *The Counseling Psychologist, 17,* 90–97.

Borgen, F. H. (1991). Megatrends and milestones in vocational behavior: A 20-year counseling psychology retrospective. *Journal of Vocational Behavior, 39,* 263–290.

Borgen, F. H. (1992). Expanding scientific paradigms in counseling psychology. In S. D. Brown & R. W. Lent (Eds.), *Handbook of counseling psychology* (2nd ed., pp. 111–139). New York: Wiley.

Brown, S. D., & Lent, R. W. (Eds.). (1992). *Handbook of counseling psychology* (2nd ed.). New York: Wiley.

Gelso, C. J. (1979). Research in counseling: Methodological and professional issues. *The Counseling Psychologist, 8,* 7–36.

Gelso, C. J. (1982). Editorial. *Journal of Counseling Psychology, 29,* 3–7.

Gelso, C. J. (1985). Rigor, relevance, and counseling research: On the need to maintain our course between Scylla and Charybdis. *Journal of Counseling and Development, 63,* 31–37.

Gelso, C. J., & Fretz, B. (1992). *Counseling psychology.* Fort Worth, TX: Harcourt Brace Javanovich.

Highlen, P. S., & Hill, C. E. (1984). Factors influencing client change in individual counseling: Current status and theoretical speculations. In S. D. Brown & R. W. Lent (Eds.), *Handbook of counseling psychology* (pp. 334–396). New York: Wiley.

Hill, C. E. (1982). Counseling process research: Philosophical and methodological dilemmas. *The Counseling Psychologist, 10,* 7–19.

Hill, C. E. (1984). A personal account of the process of becoming a counseling process researcher. *The Counseling Psychologist, 12,* 99–109.

Holland, J. L. (1985). *Making vocational choices: A theory of vocational personalities and work environments* (2nd ed.). Englewood Cliffs, NJ: Prentice–Hall.

Hoshmand, L. L. S. T. (1989). Alternate research paradigms: A review and teaching proposal. *The Counseling Psychologist, 17,* 3–79.

Howard, G. S. (1983). Toward methodological pluralism. *Journal of Counseling Psychology, 30,* 19–21.

Howard, G. S. (1984). A modest proposal for a revision of strategies in counseling research. *Journal of Counseling Psychology, 31,* 430–432.

Howard, G. S. (1986). *Dare we develop a human science?* Notre Dame, IN: Academic Publications.

Howard, G. S. (1989). *A tale of two stories: Issues in the narrative approach to psychology.* Notre Dame, IN: Academic Publications.

Howard, G. S. (1991). Culture tales: A narrative approach to thinking, cross-cultural psychology, and psychotherapy. *American Psychologist, 46,* 187–197.

Lambert, M. J., & Hill, C. E. (1994). Assessing psychotherapy outcomes and processes. In A. E. Bergin & S. L. Garfield (Eds.), *Handbook of psychotherapy and behavior change* (4th ed., pp. 72–113). New York: Wiley.

Lent, R. W., & Hackett, G. (1994). Sociocognitive mechanisms of personal agency in career development: Pantheoretical prospects. In M. L. Savickas & R. W. Lent (Eds.), *Convergence in career development theories* (pp. 77–101). Palo Alto, CA: Consulting Psychologists Press.

Lent, R. W., & Savickas, M. L. (1994). Postscript: Is convergence a viable agenda for career psychology? In M. L. Savickas & R. W. Lent (Eds.), *Convergence in career development theories* (pp. 259–271). Palo Alto, CA: Consulting Psychologists Press.

Osipow, S. H. (1983). *Theories of career development* (3rd ed.). Englewood Cliffs, NJ: Prentice–Hall.

Osipow, S. H. (1990). Convergence in theories of career choice and development: Review and prospect. *Journal of Vocational Behavior, 36,* 122–131.

Polkinghorne, D. (1983). *Methodology for the human sciences.* State University of New York Press.

Polkinghorne, D. E. (1984). Further extensions of methodological diversity for counseling psychology. *Journal of Counseling Psychology, 31,* 416–429.

Polkinghorne, D. E. (1988). *Narrative knowing and the human sciences.* State University of New York Press.

Randahl, G. J., Hansen, J. C., & Haverkamp, B. E. (1993). Instrumental behaviors following test administration and interpretation: Exploration validity of the Strong Interest Inventory. *Journal of Counseling and Development, 71,* 435–439.

Savickas, M. L., & Lent, R. W. (Eds.). (1994). *Convergence in career development theories.* Palo Alto, CA: Consulting Psychologists Press.

Smith, D. (1982). Trends in counseling and psychotherapy. *American Psychologist, 37,* 802–809.

Spokane, A. R. (1991). *Career intervention.* Englewood Cliffs, NJ: Prentice–Hall.

Wachtel, P. L. (1987). *Action and insight.* New York: Guilford.

Walsh, W. B., & Osipow, S. H. (Eds.). (1983). *Handbook of vocational psychology.* Hillsdale, NJ: Lawrence Erlbaum Associates.

Walsh, W. B., & Osipow, S. H. (Eds.). (1986). *Advances in vocational psychology: Vol. 1. The assessment of interests.* Hillsdale, NJ: Lawrence Erlbaum Associates.

Walsh, W. B., & Osipow, S. H. (Eds.). (1988). *Career decision making.* Hillsdale, NJ: Lawrence Erlbaum Associates.

Walsh, W. B., & Osipow, S. H. (Eds.). (1990). *Career counseling: Contemporary topics in vocational psychology.* Hillsdale, NJ: Lawrence Erlbaum Associates.

Walsh, W. B., & Osipow, S. H. (Eds.). (1994). *Career counseling for women.* Hillsdale, NJ: Lawrence Erlbaum Associates.

Author Index

Subject Index